THE INSIDERS' GUIDE® TO New HAMPSHIRE

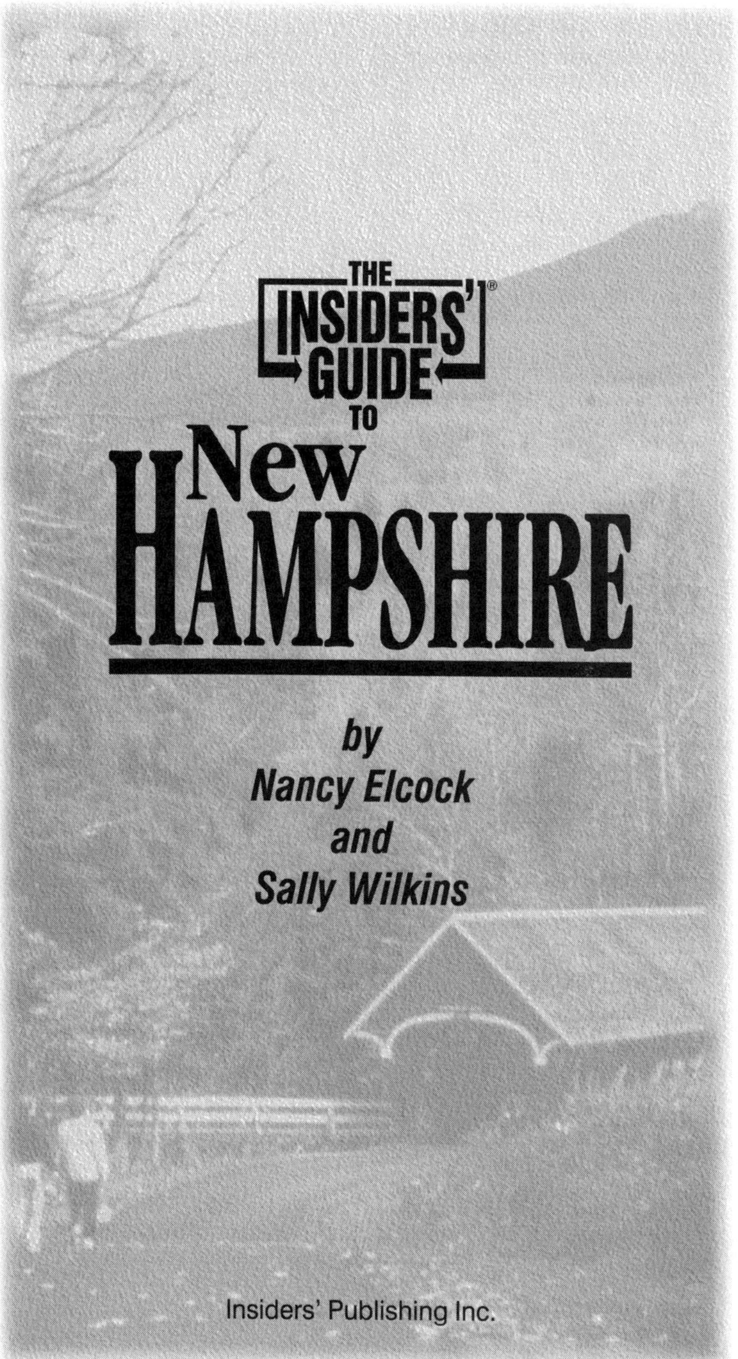

The Insiders' Guide® to New Hampshire

by
Nancy Elcock
and
Sally Wilkins

Insiders' Publishing Inc.

The Insiders' Guide®
An imprint of Falcon® Publishing Inc.
A Landmark Communications company
P.O. Box 1718
Helena, MT 59624
(800) 582-2665
www.insiders.com

Co-published and marketed by:
The Telegraph
17 Executive Drive
Hudson, NH 03051
(603) 882-2741

Sales and Marketing: Falcon Publishing, Inc.
P.O. Box 1718
Helena, MT 59624
(800) 582-2665
www.falconguide.com

Advertising: Sandy Russo and Kelley Steele
The Telegraph
17 Executive Drive
Hudson, NH 03051
(603) 882-2741

•

SECOND EDITION
1st printing

•

•

Printed in the United States
of America

•

Cover photos (clockwise from top left): A New Hampshire winter pastime; Glen Ellis Falls in Pinkham Notch (Dick Hamilton/White Mountain News Bureau); Swift River on the Kancamagus Highway (Dick Hamilton/White Mountain New Bureau). **Spine photo:** Mount Washington Cog Railway (The Mount Washington Cog Railway). **Facing page photo:** Covered bridge, Franconia Notch State Park (State of New Hampshire Tourism).

•

Publications from *The Insiders' Guide®* series are available at special discounts for bulk purchases for sales promotions, premiums or fundraisings. Special editions, including personalized covers, can be created in large quantities for special needs.
For more information, please contact Falcon Publishing.

ISBN 1-57380-094-5

Preface

Welcome to New Hampshire! You'll see that big blue sign as you cross the border into our corner of paradise. "Bienvenue!" it adds, in deference to our Canadian neighbors and their many cousins who live in the Granite State.

Welcome to a study in contrasts. New Hampshire isn't "Cow Hampsha" anymore — it's been a long time since we had more cows than people. Today our average citizen is far more likely to have a job in high technology than a barn full of critters. But we still look rural. People with vision have worked hard to preserve our open spaces and our rural character. Great stretches of land have been kept green. Roll along the highways and byways and you'll see plenty of cows, corn and forest.

This is not the forest primeval, but the forest resurgent. At the beginning of the 20th century, much of New Hampshire's forest had been decimated — stripped away by avaricious logging and the devastation of insects and fire that followed. You won't see any of the King's Pines that our Colonial forebears defied the Crown to cut. What you will see is evidence that people can work together and the earth can heal itself. We like to think other parts of the country could learn from our example. As this same 20th century draws to a close, vast expanses of mountain and valley are wooded again. Forestry is still an important industry here, but it's "forestry," not "logging" — a balanced approach that provides not just lumber and paper but wildlife habitat and scenery.

Such scenery! Whether you've come to visit or come here to stay, be sure you take time to explore. See the surf crashing on the rocks at Rye. Gaze in awe at the sparkling summits of the Presidential range. Wander through a forest glowing with the colors of autumn. We've given you lots of places to discover: chapters on water, open spaces, camping, fishing and hunting. And yet we've barely scraped the surface.

On the other hand, many visitors come here thinking there's nothing else to do but ski. We both know people whose spouses moved here under protest, believing they were leaving civilization behind. We think our Arts and Culture and Nightlife chapters should put that myth to rest. Within our borders we boast not one but three symphony orchestras, dozens of theaters, museums of art, history and science. We admit things can be pretty quiet here in winter, when people hunker down and work on staying warm, but a quick peek at our Annual Events chapter will show you we make up for that through the rest of the year.

"Welcome to New Hampshire — Now, Go Home!" So reads a bumper sticker common on New Hampshire highways. Maybe we're getting a little touchy about our sudden surge in popularity and population. After all, five New Hampshire communities have been showing up regularly on *Money* magazine's annual "Best Places to Live" list, with Nashua ranking first not once but twice (1987 and 1997) — the only city ever to repeat atop that list. Skim our Real Estate, Education and Retirement chapters and you'll begin to understand why. People come here for "quality of life." Some fear that a rapidly increasing population will change the characteristics that make this a great place to live.

New Hampshire people aren't anti-tourist, or anti-newcomer, either. We're just in love with our state, quirks and all, and afraid that someone will try to change it! If you've come to stay, take some time to get to know the place. Our roots are deep, and our traditions are strong. We've got that Yankee tendency to privacy, waiting until we're sure of someone before we make friends. That doesn't mean we're coldhearted. We're small enough to know each other, build communities and pull together. Many, many of our most involved citizens were once "flatlanders," born and bred somewhere else. Now they, too, call New Hampshire home.

We hope our book can help you feel at home here too. Use our descriptions to get started, then discover and explore. We're Insiders, but we don't know it all! What we bring to this project is a love of our home state and curiosity about its many opportunities. One of us has lived here since childhood, and knows no other home to compare to New Hampshire. One of us brings the insights of having lived in the South and in big cities. Between us, we hope we've given you a chance to get to know this wonderful place.

As you use the book, make comments in the margins. And when you're done, don't forget to tell us what you think. Tell us about your favorite places that we missed or about your great discoveries. We'd also like to know when a place doesn't live up to our description. So send your comments to us c/o Falcon Publishing Inc., P.O. Box 1718, Helena, MT 59624, or visit us on the Internet at www.insiders.com and make your comments there.

Welcome to New Hampshire!

About the Authors

Nancy Elcock

Nancy Elcock first stepped foot in New Hampshire in 1984 at a liquor store/rest area. That first exposure to "Live Free or Die" had a lasting impression, and in 1995 Nancy became a year-round resident of the Granite State. Before making New Hampshire her home, Nancy, a native Atlantan, lived in New York City for 13 years working in the publishing and entertainment industries.

Since moving to New Hampshire Nancy has enjoyed a more rural lifestyle. She's found out that snow-shoveling and yard work burn calories just as well as city workouts at the gym. She loves small-town living and the proximity of rivers, lakes and mountains.

An English major and experienced bookworm, Nancy likes living on the home turf of so many New Hampshire writers. Her enjoyment in reading the poems of Robert Frost deepens as her familiarity with his home state grows. His descriptions of the land and the people of New Hampshire make him one of her favorite and most accurate local guides.

In addition to reading and writing, Nancy enjoys canoeing and camping trips with family and friends and developing and maintaining her garden.

Nancy could never have undertaken this project without the support of her husband Tom McMillan and many new friends in New Hampshire. Natives and longtime residents have shared their knowledge and made the job of reporting inside information satisfying and a lot of fun. Southern hospitality is famous, but the residents of New Hampshire have taught Nancy a lot about a genuine welcome.

Sally Wilkins

Sally Wilkins isn't really a native of New Hampshire. She did spend childhood summers at her grandparents' homes in Chester and North Conway. She did get her first job in Intervale as a young teenager. And she finally moved to Hollis with her family at age 15. But as her husband, a descendent of one of the original settlers of Amherst, always reminds her, she's not a native and never will be. That says something about New Hampshire.

After college Sally and her husband returned to New Hampshire and built a home. They keep a small farm and he runs the family business, a sawmill that opened in 1808. They have five children who range in age from Little League to College Entrance Exams — natives, every one.

Despite her flatlander credentials, Sally has been active in her adopted community. She's particularly interested in the implications of suburbanizing New Hampshire, protecting the environment along with tourism and agriculture, and whether the Boston Red Sox will ever win the World Series. She has served on both the Planning Board and School Board in Amherst and is a Trustee of the Amherst Land Trust. She's been welcomed and supported by natives and transplants alike. That says something about New Hampshire too.

Sally writes for both children and adults. Her magazine credits range from *Expecting* to *Mature Years*, she has written two easy-to-read books for Pauline Press, and she writes columns for several New England periodicals. She is also an instructor at the RISE Institute at Rivier College in Nashua. Twice a cancer survivor, she encourages everyone to make the most of the opportunities life brings each day. She also observes that she could not have taken on or completed this project without the support of a very patient family, the aid of helpful friends and the grace of a loving God who is the source of all her strength.

Acknowledgments

Thanks to the entire state of New Hampshire. Every state employee cheerfully helped us with our quest, whether we were trying to pin down details on home-schooling requirements or find the covered-bridge expert. Voice mail messages were returned, and I never got "lost" in the system. Everyone who said they would mail something did so. New Hampshire business owners and workers not employed by the state were equally professional. Chefs discussed menus, administrators explained hospitals and skiers educated us on the finer snow points of the state.

Thanks to my friends who have had to put up with my obnoxious delight in throwing facts around. If someone mentions a mountain, I interject with elevation figures; let them bring up a town, and I'm likely to pipe in with details on the region, summer theater options and the name of a great little inn. Luckily, my friends have shared their own New Hampshire experiences and insights. Their thoughts gave body to the facts.

For me, the delightful bonus thank-you of this project continues to be my co-writer Sally Wilkins. She is a valued colleague and new friend whose professional attributes and personal strengths are equally admirable. Thanks to the fairy godmother who sent her my way. Sally's unfailing high spirits, well-trained mind and wicked sense of humor make her the ideal co-conspirator. Thanks to Becki Swinehart and John Harrington for pulling the second edition together and to John Armenio for his constant support.

—Nancy

The Apostle Paul, a busy man and a prolific writer, once commented "I can do all things through Him who strengthens me." Months of researching and writing this book certainly provided an opportunity to test that thesis! And indeed, the Lord proved faithful, providing help and strength all along the way.

Typically, of course, divine encouragement comes to us not via angels but through ordinary people. Many people went out of their way to make our project easier, more interesting, more fun. Everywhere we went people shared their experiences. Staffs at a dozen state offices, from Safety to Education to Fish and Game, were helpful and enthusiastic. I'm indebted to a host of librarians, town clerks, secretaries and webmasters who took the time to chase down a fact or come up with a name or an address. Chambers of Commerce are supposed to tell you about their members, and they did, but many chamber folks also shared insights about life in their communities, special events and traditions that we might never have heard about otherwise. Somersworth, Meredith and Hampton, your chambers are particular prizes!

Beth Fisher at the University Guest House in Durham is a one-woman tourism bureau. Thank you, Beth, for all the great tips! Thanks also to Sophia Lane in Winona, publisher of Summer World, for many years of chronicling life and the arts in New Hampshire and for sharing some of her knowledge with me.

One of the people I am most indebted to can't read my thank you here. Leslie Geleszinski lost her valiant battle with cancer just before the first edition went to press. She and I were fellow patients and shared hopes and miseries, and she invested time and knowledge when we were just starting on the monumental task of this book. Leslie, we miss you and are grateful for everything you gave to New Hampshire and to us.

I'm so glad to have worked on this book with Nancy. Her clear eye and cheerful outlook kept our focus sharp and preserved our perspective when I was ready to ride off in all directions at once.

Our Editors, Molly and Becki at Insiders and John and Erin at Falcon, have been helpful and patient. This was our only baby; they had many, all on different schedules. Good editing is a gift, and we thank them.

Thanks go also to my other editors, Sr. Kathryn at My Friend, Jennifer and Gwen at Twenty-third Publications, Cindy at *The Anvil* and Fr. Weinert at Liguorian, for their patience and flexibility as I juggled deadlines and tried to meet all my commitments.

I couldn't have done this project without the support of my family. They encouraged me to take on this project and put up with me while I worked on it. My husband, Tom, put in even more hours around the farm when I was out on the road or tied to the keyboard. My older kids, Becky, Aaron and Rachel, proved their independence and levelheadedness over and over, responding to frantic calls from Mom's cell phone with "everything's fine here" and "yes, well get dinner started." The younger ones, Kathy and Isaac, helped out by cooperating and compromising. They're getting used to my juggling deadlines and phone calls around their practices and lessons, and every time they see a new shop or restaurant they ask, "Is that in your book yet, Mom?"

My parents, Mac and Nancy Dunbar, drove carpools and stepped into breaches when my schedule fell apart. They went on vacation with us and entertained the kids while I wrote. No one will ever forget Grandpa on roller skates! Tom's parents, Barbara and Gerry Wilkins, helped keep things moving smoothly. Barbara, the mountain-climbing Gran, was a great source of information about hiking. We've always been grateful that we live close to all four of our parents; now we're even more so.

My friends at Community Bible Study and those in my writers group shared their favorite places and listened patiently to my frustrations. They researched my questions and prayed for my kids, my health and my computer.

Heartful thanks to Dr. Samuel Singer at the Dana Farber in Boston, who played a critical role in the second edition of this book, since without his gifts and skills I would not have been here to write it. Thanks also to the nurses and staff at Brigham and Women's hospital, who raised their eyebrows but didn't complain when I set up my laptop amid the IV poles at my bedside.

Thanks to all who had a hand in this project, and thanks to our Lord and Savior Jesus Christ, through whom this beautiful corner of the earth was created.

— Sally

Photo: David A. Leach Photography

Major General John Stark was the originator of the "Live Free or Die" motto.

Table of Contents

Directory of Maps

New Hampshire

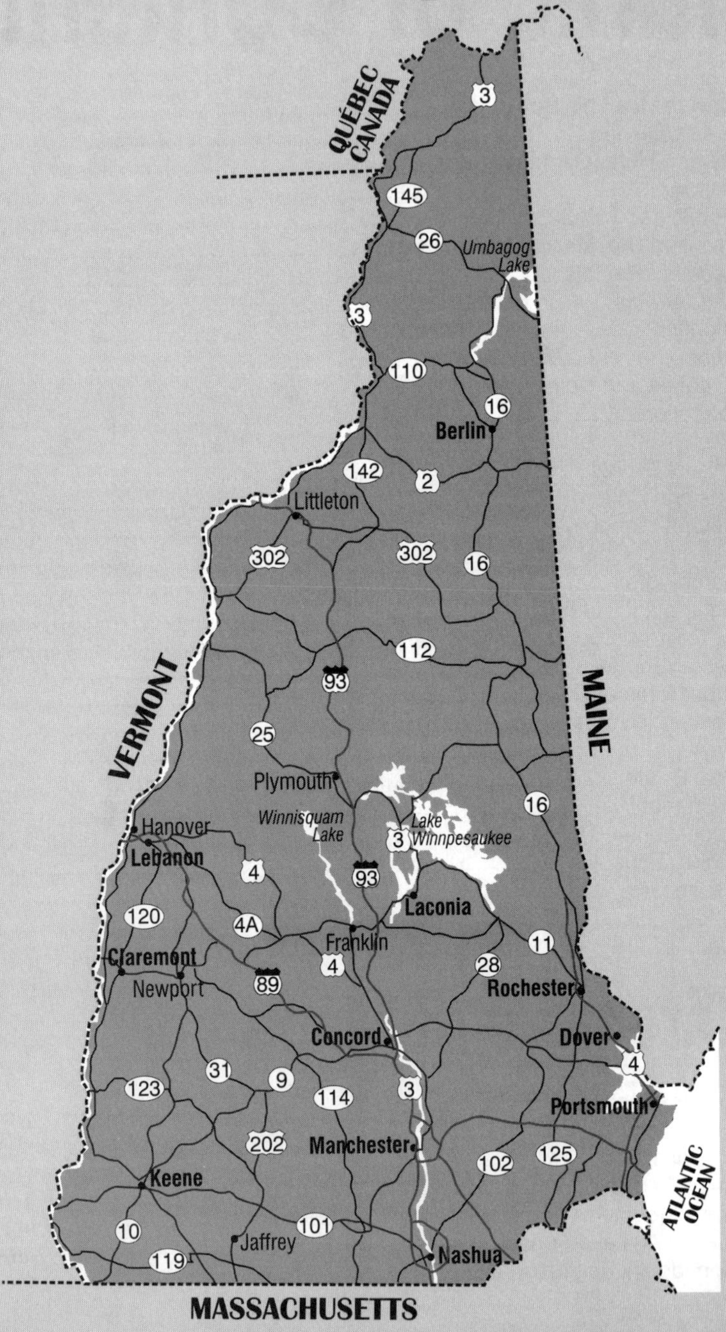

QUÉBEC
CANADA
3
145
26
Umbagog Lake
3
110
16
Berlin
142
2
Littleton
302
302
16
112
93
MAINE
VERMONT
25
Plymouth
Winnisquam Lake
Lake Winnipesaukee
3
16
Hanover
Lebanon
4
93
Laconia
120
4A
Franklin
11
Claremont
Newport
89
4
28
Rochester
Concord
Dover
4
31
9
123
114
3
Portsmouth
202
Manchester
125
102
ATLANTIC OCEAN
Keene
10
101
Jaffrey
119
Nashua
MASSACHUSETTS

Merrimack Valley Region

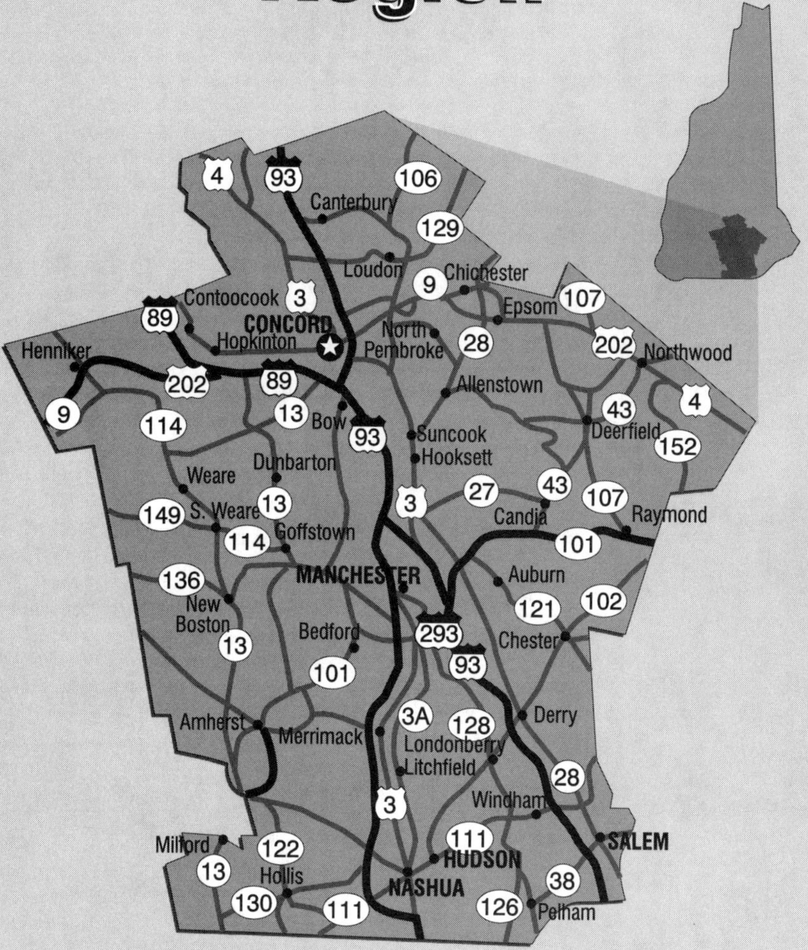

Seacoast Region

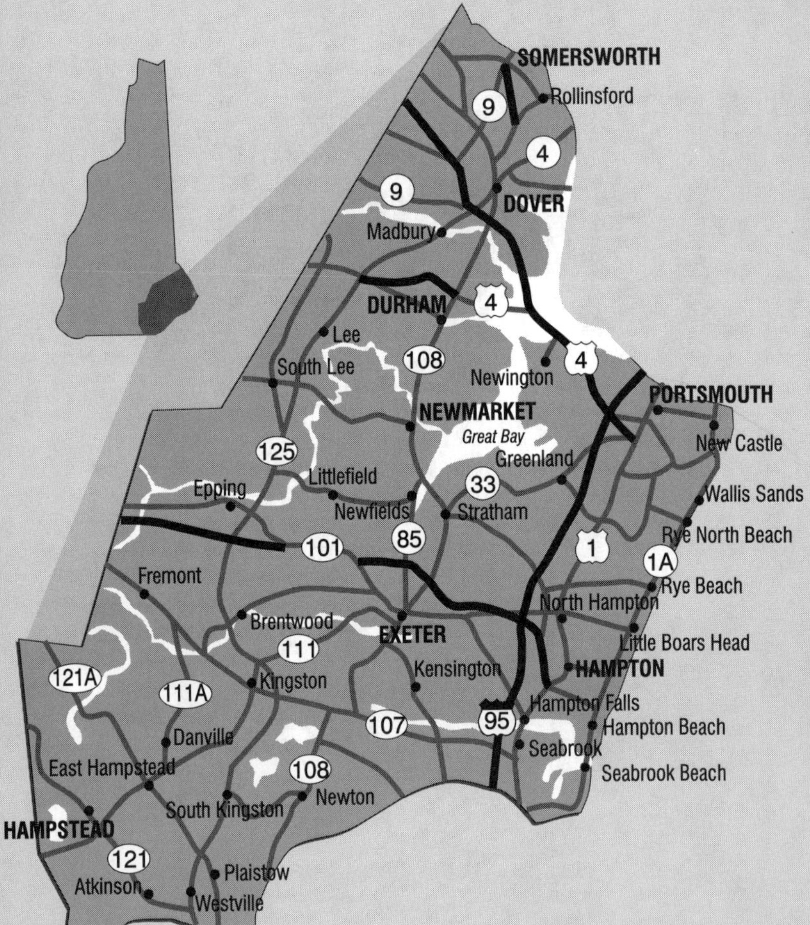
SOMERSWORTH
Rollinsford
9
4
9
DOVER
Madbury
DURHAM
4
Lee
108
South Lee
Newington
4
PORTSMOUTH
NEWMARKET
Great Bay
New Castle
125
Greenland
Littlefield
Epping
33
Wallis Sands
Newfields
Stratham
Rye North Beach
85
101
1
1A
Fremont
Rye Beach
North Hampton
Brentwood
EXETER
Little Boars Head
111
Kensington
HAMPTON
121A
111A
Kingston
Hampton Falls
107
95
Hampton Beach
Danville
Seabrook
East Hampstead
108
Seabrook Beach
Newton
South Kingston
HAMPSTEAD
121
Plaistow
Atkinson
Westville

The Lakes Region

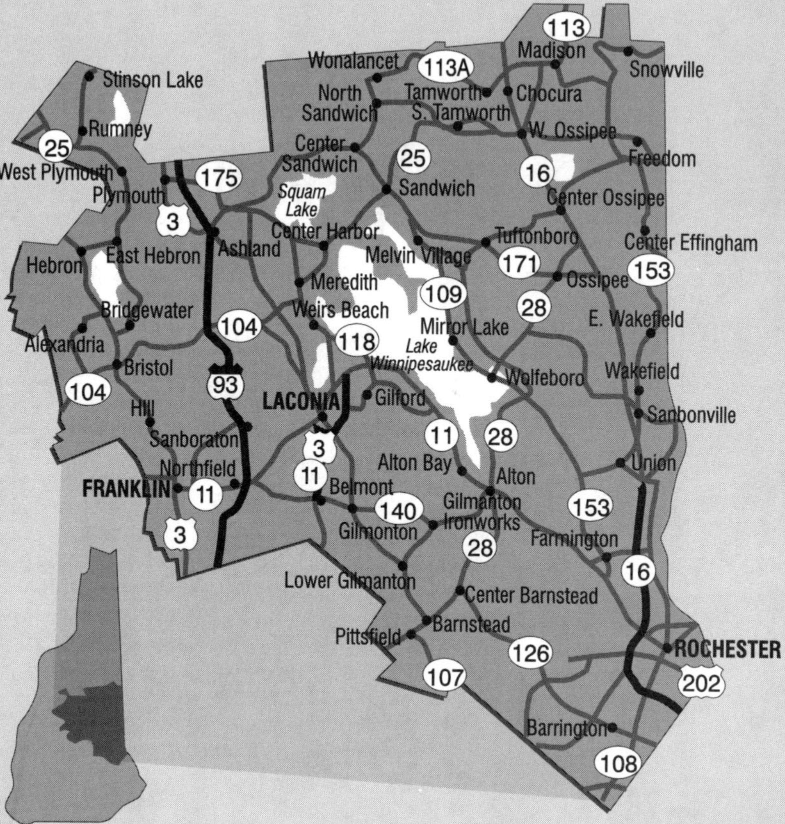

White Mountains and Great North Woods Regions

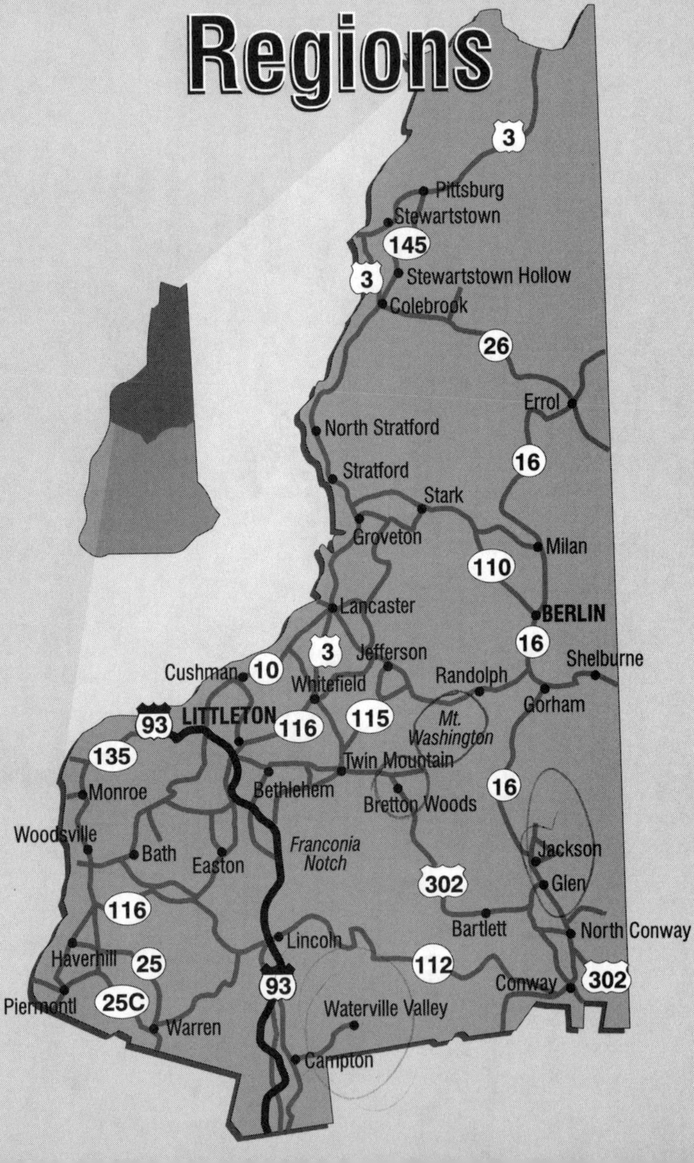

Dartmouth-Lake Sunapee Region

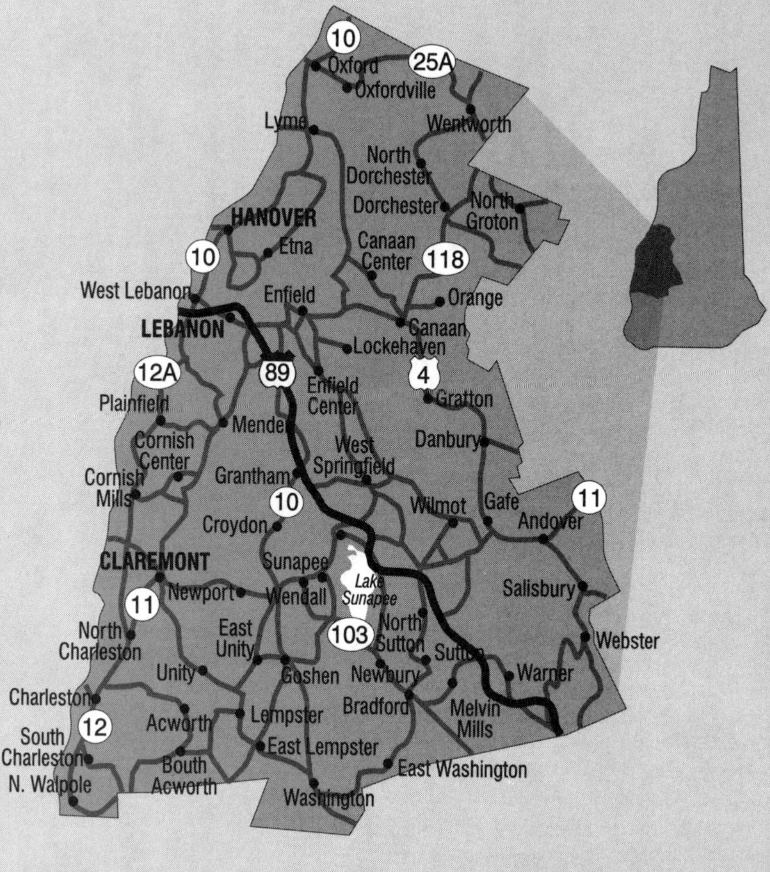

Monadnock Region

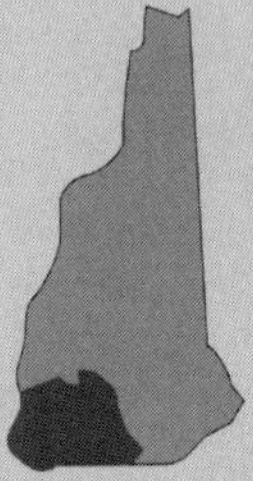

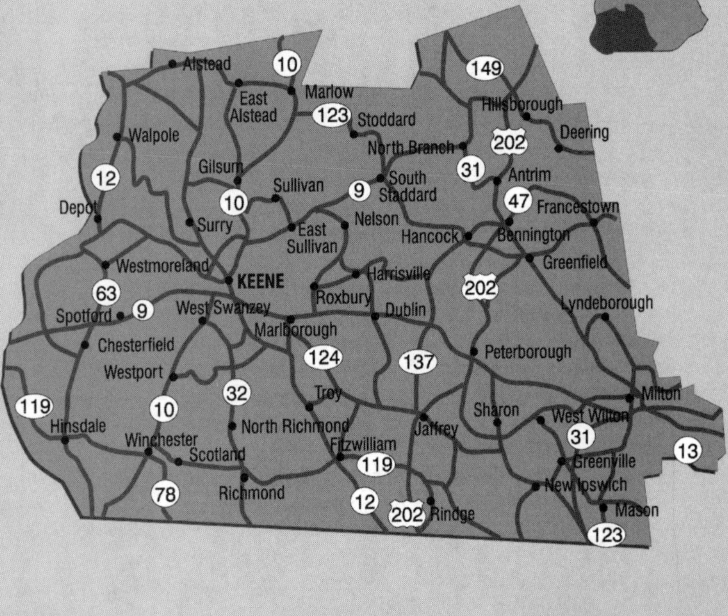

How to Use This Book

This book gives you a both an overview and Insider details on New Hampshire. We've included a lot of information about our wonderful state in chapters with descriptive names. You don't need to read the book in any order; flip to the chapters that interest you first or start with the Area Overview chapter to get a feel for the different regions. We've organized our book by subject matter — Restaurants, Shopping, Winter Sports, Camping, etc.

Within each chapter we've further divided the book by geographic region. The regions correspond to the regions defined by the New Hampshire Department of Tourism. The regions are Merrimack Valley, Seacoast, Lakes, White Mountains and Great North Woods, two regions we've combined in our listings, Dartmouth-Lake Sunapee and Monadnock. Look for the maps in the front of this book to see the geographical outline of each region.

Within each region, we've arranged our information alphabetically by town. If you're looking for a place to eat in Manchester, find Manchester on the regional map, turn to the "Merrimack Valley" heading in the Restaurants chapter and locate the write-ups for Manchester. Similarly if you are visiting a specific region (maybe you're an ocean lover and are planning on two weeks in the Seacoast region) or relocating to New Hampshire, you might start by reading the specific regional information in each chapter.

Newcomers may first turn to our Real Estate, Education or Healthcare chapters, but we think visitors will also be glad the information is there. Our experience indicates that visitors are often converted to newcomers. And regardless of your age, don't overlook our Retirement or Kidstuff chapters — it's never too soon (or too late) to study the alternatives.

Our information on places to stay is included in three chapters: Hotels and Motels, Bed and Breakfasts and Country Inns, and Vacation Rentals.

Because New Hampshire is a mecca of outdoor sports you'll find separate chapters on Winter Sports, Fishing and Hunting, Camping and Recreational Sports. We suggest you at least skim all the chapters for ideas of things to do. Our winter ski resorts are popular in the off-season with mountain bikers. (Mountain bikers, of course, would say that bike trails are popular in the off-season with skiers — it's all in your point of view.) And our Fishing and Hunting chapter contains information on wildlife areas that might be useful to a hiker or enthusiastic walker. It's a good idea for all outdoor enthusiasts to familiarize themselves with the general hunting seasons and understand that much of our land, unless otherwise posted, is open for hunting.

Book lovers will want to know that used and antiquarian bookstores are included in our Antiques and Collectibles chapter, and mainstream bookstores are written up in Shopping.

You'll be glad to know that in this world of changing area codes New Hampshire is delightfully consistent. The statewide area code is 603, so you don't need to dial the area code when calling from within the state.

Not quite so easy to explain are our addresses. Much of our state is rural, and location addresses often simply use a route number (no street number) and the name of the town. Furthermore, the location addresses are often not the mailing addresses. (Most mailing addresses are post office boxes or RFDs, which aren't helpful as you navigate into town.) We've given the location address, not the mailing address, unless the business does not have a physical address. Call for specific mailing addresses before sending for information or making reservations.

The best way to use the book is to carry it with you — in your backpack or in your car. Whether you're browsing for ideas or folding down the page corners to mark places you don't want to miss, the book is designed for anyone curious to learn more about New Hampshire.

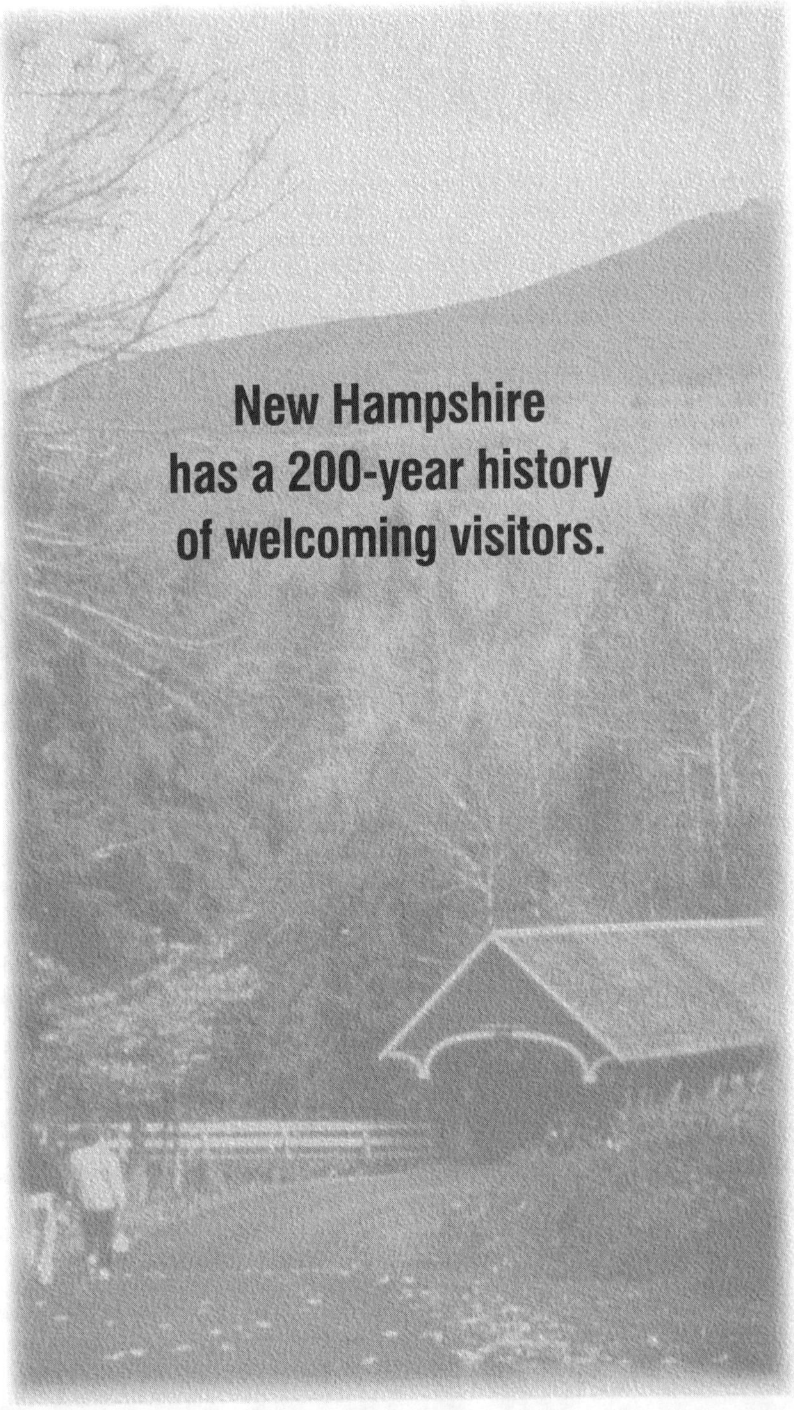
New Hampshire
has a 200-year history
of welcoming visitors.

Area Overviews

Welcome to New Hampshire, the Granite State. You are smack in the heart of New England both geographically and culturally. We're one of the original 13 colonies that formed the United States, and our state motto, Live Free or Die, was coined by Revolutionary War hero and New Hampshire native John Stark.

We've got about 240 towns, five cities and 42 state parks with more than 6,000 miles of trails. Mount Washington, with an elevation of 6,288 feet, is the highest mountain east of the Rockies and north of the Mason-Dixon line. It's the centerpiece of the 773,386-acre White Mountain National Forest, which is nearly a third of the land in the state. New Hampshire is 180 miles long. The width varies with a maximum distance of 93 miles and an average of about 50 miles. To the east are Maine and the Atlantic Ocean and to the west is the Connecticut River, which forms our boundary with Vermont. The tip-top of the state has northern and western borders with Quebec, Canada. Our entire southern border is shared with Massachusetts.

Residents of New Hampshire, both natives and newcomers, cherish their independence and privacy right along with the lack of state income or sales taxes. And if you're here for even a few days, you're bound to discover the biggest secret about New Hampshire. We have the friendliest citizens in the world.

The state of New Hampshire is divided into seven geographic regions. The Merrimack Valley Region runs right up the middle of the lower third of the state. Three of our five cities — Manchester, Nashua and Concord, the capital — are in this region. To the east is the Seacoast Region. We've got 18 miles of seacoast, and we're proud of every one of them. North and west of the Seacoast is the Lakes Region. Squam Lake was the location for filming the movie *On Golden Pond*. Lake Winnipesaukee and Newfound Lake are also in the region. The northern third of the state is divided into the Great North Woods and White Mountains regions. As the name implies, much of the Great North Woods Region is forested. You won't find too many mountains, but you will find a rugged landscape with rock ledges and river gorges. The White Mountains Region has lots of forest too, but you'll see that trails have been cleared for great downhill skiing and spectacular hiking. To the south and west of the White Mountains is the Dartmouth-Lake Sunapee Region. The region borders the Connecticut River and is named for Dartmouth College in Hanover and gorgeous Lake Sunapee in Newport. Also on the Connecticut River is the Monadnock Region, sometimes called the Quiet Corner. This region takes up the southwest corner of the state. The southern edge borders Massachusetts, and the eastern section runs up to the heavily populated Merrimack Valley.

What follows are brief descriptions of the seven geographic regions in New Hampshire. We hope they will help you plan your trip whether you're on vacation or scouting a possible new or second-home location. In our discussion of each region, we've highlighted the names of a few towns to help you get your bearings. (We can't highlight them all or we wouldn't have room to tell you about them.) Maybe you'll see that town you've been wanting to go to since you read about it in a great-aunt's travel diary. Or maybe it was your great-aunt's great-aunt that came here a century ago. New Hampshire has a 200-year history of welcoming visitors.

Merrimack Valley Region

The Merrimack Valley Region could aptly be named "The Rivers," for its character has been shaped not only by the Merrimack River but also by all its tributaries — the Nashua, the Nissitissit, the Souhegan, the Naticook and the Contoocook to the west, and to the east the Soucook, the Suncook, Beaver Brook and Cohas Brook. In the 1930s 24 electric generating plants and 61 industrial users combined to generate more than 110,000 horsepower from the Merrimack Drainage Basin.

Long before that, the rivers had been thoroughfares. First Native Americans, then white settlers traveled up and down the rivers, portaging canoes around the falls. Travel patterns were established, and when wagons and horses began to dominate, the roadways followed the rivers. Settlers forded streams, ran ferries and built covered bridges across the countryside. They built mill towns where there were falls, and farm villages where the floodplain made for fertile soil. Although most towns and villages throughout the region have become suburbanized, a distinction remains between the two: Towns are more likely to have a Main Street or a square lined with shops and restaurants, while villages remain spread out, their centers generally marked only by a green, a church and a community general store.

The big river has always been more of a barrier than a highway. **Hudson** and **Nashua**, **Litchfield** and **Merrimack**, separated by the Merrimack River, developed into separate and distinct communities, with characteristics that are different even today. And even today, you can see places across the river that it will take 30 minutes or more to drive to. Two bridges link Nashua and Hudson, and three span the river in Manchester, but there are no crossings in between.

Grantholders in London and Boston, who had never seen the land they owned, used the rivers as boundaries. Settlers in **Londonderry** once thought their 60-acre lots ran from West Running Brook all the way to the Merrimack — but when surveyors discovered how much land was really there, they created Derryfield (now Manchester) in between. **Amherst**, **Mont Vernon** and **Milford** were all defined in relation to the Souhegan. State boundary lines were not always clear: Nashua and **Hollis** were originally part of Dunstable, Massachusetts.

In cities like Manchester and mill towns like Milford you can still see the great brick buildings where farm girls and immigrant children spun cotton and stitched shoes on machines powered by the rivers. Today these buildings house restaurants, gyms and shops. Their legacy is the cultural diversity of this area. We remember when it was tough to ask directions on the west side of Manchester if you didn't speak French. Polish, Irish and Italian immigrants also made their marks in the Merrimack Valley, and if their descendants blend in with the Yankees, their place is taken by newcomers from Latin America and Southeast Asia.

The great Victorian houses where the mill owners lived in luxury are still here too. Some are apartment buildings now, while others have been restored to their former glory. In some cases a town will have two centers — one where the mill housing is clustered, another a hilltop gathering of fine homes. Today all the children go to school together, neighborhood distinctions blurring in a culture of T-ball and spelling bees.

Most of New Hampshire is a haven for tourists. The Merrimack Valley is a haven for business. In the boom years of the early 1980s, some economists called this "The Golden Triangle," for the wealth being generated by its high-tech companies and the escalating values of real estate in the area between Nashua, Salem and Manchester. The recession after the stock market's October 1987 fall and the real estate crash that followed put some tarnish on that shine. Today some Insiders might call it the Bronze Triangle, but both Manchester and Nashua appear regularly in the top ten of *Money* magazine's Best Places to Live, and in 1998 Salem ranked 150th.

Manchester's airport is big enough to be useful and small enough to be comfortable, and its traffic increases every month. Many residents still commute to Massachusetts, but more and more people are finding jobs in the high-tech firms along U.S. Route 3. It's not all work and no play here, though. Check out our theaters, especially the American Stage Festival in Milford and Nashua and the Palace in Manchester (see our Arts and Culture chapter). Or watch for minor league baseball, hot-air ballooning, country fairs and golf tournaments. There's always something happening in the Merrimack Valley.

Seacoast Region

New Hampshire's Seacoast is short, but it has a long history. Native Americans came here in spring to catch and smoke the year's supply of cod. The first explorers from Britain camped here on what's now called Odiorne Point in **Rye** before turning south to map Cape Ann and Cape Cod. Here, near **Durham**, there occurred the first bloody massacres of the long struggle between the native people and the newcomers. Here, from **Portsmouth**, the victorious Colonists shipped the wealth of their new land back to the markets of England: furs of animals the Europeans had never seen, timber from trees of a size long gone on the British isles.

Paul Revere rode to Portsmouth to warn that the British were coming four months before the ride made famous by Longfellow's poem. Come they did, only to discover that a band of patriots had reached Fort William and Mary, in **New Castle**, before them, overpowering the small contingent garrisoned there and carting away the arms and ammunition the British had been sent to secure! A year and a half later the people of **Exeter** turned out to cheer the newly signed Declaration of Independence. Independence is still dear to our hearts, attested by our controversial "Live Free or Die" license plates (which have nothing to do with taxes).

In the early 1800s, the allure of white sands and gentle surf brought hundreds of thousands here to "fun in the sun" at **Hampton**, to evenings of dining and dancing under enormous tents and later, wooden pavilions. Today our beaches attract visitors in all seasons, whether to work on the perfect tan, count migratory birds or bundle up against the wind and watch the winter surf.

Russian and Japanese diplomats came to Portsmouth in 1905 to sign the treaty ending their long war. Today Portsmouth is once again on the international map. With the economy improving across the country, industrial trade through the seaport has increased tremendously. Building materials, petroleum products, scrap metal and other heavy commodities ship through the deep harbor at Portsmouth, taking advantage of the same convenient waterway that attracted those earliest seamen to New Hampshire.

Hopes are high in the Seacoast that the Pease International Tradeport on the site of the decommissioned Pease Air Force base will expand the import/export business through the region even more. Plans are already underway for high-tech office space and industrial uses to take advantage of the airstrip. The area's economy, once heavily dependent on the military (hosting the Portsmouth Naval Shipyard as well as the Air Force base), is now a booming mix of high-tech firms, insurance companies, arts professionals and commuters, both traditional and telecommuters, attracted by the region's central location and glowing reputation.

Happily, the new industrialization is being conducted with more concern for the fragile seacoast environment than some previous development. The New Hampshire seacoast was a flash point in the conflict between environmentalists and industrialists for years during the decade-long battle over construction of the Seabrook Nuclear Power Plant. The environmentalists lost that battle and with Seabrook on line, New Hampshire's electric rates are among the highest in the country. (The legislature has instituted a deregulation/competition plan in hopes of relieving that burden on the economy.) Incidentally, our devoted eco-activists have not given up — in 1997 a 20th-reunion rally saw several protesters carted off to jail. Some had not been born when the Clamshell Alliance first proclaimed "Seabrook is for the birds!" Today the giant dome of the power plant dominates the coastline, but the awareness raised by the efforts of those who chained themselves to the gates at Seabrook has paid off. The power company even runs a science and nature center at Seabrook, teaching visitors about the delicately balanced ecosystem of the shoreline. (See our Attractions chapter for details.)

The estuary is part of a curious river structure that shapes the Seacoast Region — the ocean coming inland, as it were, so that the fishing boats sail right up to **Newmarket** and **Dover**. The saltwater/freshwater line is not at the beach but at the mouths of the rivers that empty into Great Bay. Twice a day the sea flows into the bay, mixing with the nutrient-rich freshwater brought down from the highlands by the Squamscott, Lamprey and Winnicut rivers. The salt marshes throughout the Great Bay teem with wildlife despite the severe impact of pollution on this fragile habitat. Stringent shoreline protection laws are now enabling the natural world to heal itself, and there is hope that birds and fish, shellfish and crabs, plants and seaweeds will once again thrive in the shallow water, constantly fed by the rivers and refreshed by the tides.

In addition to the many historic sites described in our Attractions chapter, most Seacoast communities have house museums, walking tours and historic monuments galore. Don't miss the opportunity to park the car and walk amid houses where Patriots and Tories debated the future of the land. Self-guided tours are available in Dover, Rochester and Portsmouth. Ask at the Town Hall or local chamber of commerce for maps and guides. The area also supports a thriving arts community, with music, theater, dance and the visual arts in abundance, not only in Portsmouth and around the University of New Hampshire at Durham but also in **Epping** and **Lee** and **Hampton Falls**. (See our chapter on Arts and Culture for details.)

Walk the sands or ride the sea, cruise the islands or explore the back roads. Whale-watcher or water-park fan, there's something for everyone on New Hampshire's Seacoast.

Lakes Region

In 1629 the Council for New England, under a charter from James I of England, granted a parcel of land between the Merrimack and Piscataqua rivers to John Mason and Ferdinando Gorges. Mason's grant was described as containing "divers lakes, extending back to a great lake and a river." (Captain Mason called the area New Hampshire, in honor of his home county.) Those "divers lakes" still define the area today — Winnipesaukee, Squam and Newfound being the largest of the 1,300 lakes scattered across the state.

John Wentworth, the last Colonial governor of New Hampshire, amassed a total of 6,000 acres beside the lake that now bears his name. There in **Wolfeboro** he built a manor house like those he had seen while a student in England. It was the first of the great "summer homes" of the Lakes Region. It would not be the last.

Before the Lakes Region became the great vacationland, however, it was the frontier. Settlers would travel up the rivers from the "built up" areas of Nutfield (now Derry), Pennycook (Concord) and Durham to find a place where a man could still buy land with the sweat of his own brow. In towns like **Sandwich** and **Tamworth** they cleared land, planted crops, ran trap-lines and shipped furs to Portsmouth. There was a wealth of fish in the lakes, and if the rivers weren't as powerful as the Merrimack, there was flow enough to drive gristmills and saw lumber. The settlers harvested the lakes themselves, too, cutting great blocks of ice to be packed in sawdust and sold, in the summer, for iceboxes in Nashua and Boston. Sheep from England adapted well to New Hampshire's harsh weather, and woolen mills dotted the landscape from **Boscawen** and **Franklin** north to **Ashland** and east to **Milton**. Still it was a hard living, and when the migration to the Midwest began, many New Hampshire families made the journey. The forest began to take back abandoned farmland across New Hampshire. The people of the Lakes Region discovered the most profitable thing they could do with their land was share it, and the tourism industry has reigned here ever since.

Wealthy travelers of the 19th century built elegant summer places on many of the old farms around the lakes. Then the railroad came through, opening the area to ordinary folks as well. Summer hotels and boarding houses sprang up in **Alton Bay**, **Weirs Beach** and **Meredith**, and the railroad companies ran steamboats on the lakes to transport summer people to the nearly 300 islands. Today the train rides are for scenery, and condos have replaced boarding houses, but crystal clear lakes against a backdrop of forests and mountains are still the center of attention in this magical place. It's no wonder eccentric millionaire Thomas Plant built Lucknow Castle in **Moultonborough**, (see our Attractions chapter for Castle in the Clouds) or that Massachusetts socialite Mrs. J. Randolf Coolidge worked to preserve the character of **Center Sandwich** (creating, in her efforts, a wonderful legacy: see our Shopping chapter for details about the League of New Hampshire Craftsmen). Here in New Hampshire they found (as you will too) beauty no amount of money could buy.

Convenient to the Merrimack Valley and Massachusetts and gateway to the White Mountains, New Hampshire's Lakes Region today is one big tourist attraction, especially in the summer. This means elegant homes on Squam Lake, marinas on Winnipesaukee and arts festivals on sculpted village greens. It also means motorcycle weekend in Laconia (picture thousands of Harley-Davidsons cruising a 5-mile stretch of roadway). In winter the Lakes region hosts ice-fishing derbies, winter marathons and the world championships of sled-dog racing (move over, Alaska!). In autumn the vision of mountain foliage against crystal sky and water is the perfect backdrop for country fairs or woodland hikes. In spring? Well, in spring the locals sweep the road sand off the street and get ready to welcome all the snowbirds back.

Whether you're canoeing across a silent inlet in **Holderness** or riding Molly the Trolley around Wolfeboro, we're sure you'll find a place in the Lakes Region that you'll want to return to again and again.

White Mountains and Great North Woods Regions

The Great North Woods and White Mountains regions encompass the northern third of the state. In the past the entire area was simply called the White Mountains region. Insiders had long divided the area using the expression "north of the notches" to refer to the less-mountainous upper part of the state, and we're happy to report that those in official control have finally fallen in step and made the Great North Woods our newest designated region.

You won't find a better place to get back

to nature than the Great North Woods Region. The region's boundaries are from the northern edge of the state south to **Berlin** in the east and **Whitefield** in the west. Berlin is the only city in the region. During the 20th century the timber industry was the dominant economic force in the city. Many immigrants came to Berlin to work for the logging companies. The city's international roots are now part of Berlin's growing tourist industry. The Northern Forest Heritage Park is currently adding exhibits demonstrating the life of the immigrant timber workers.

Much of the Great North Woods can be described as wilderness. Throughout the area you'll see miles of woods interrupted by lakes, rivers and ponds. The headwaters of the Connecticut River are near **Pittsburg**, and the Androscoggin River flows from Lake Umbagog (the middle syllable is emphasized and pronounced "bay") near **Errol**. If you can, take a canoe trip from the Androscoggin out into the lake. You'll see loons and ospreys and, with a little luck, the bald eagles that nest here.

The small towns of the Great North Woods are in the process of changing from an economy based on timber to one based on tourism. With lots of woods and miles of trails, the Great North Woods region has become a favorite destination for snowmobilers. It's also a mecca for those who prefer quieter moments of bird-watching or waiting for moose to appear at favorite waterside spots. A word of warning: Be careful driving in the Great North Woods as you may well encounter moose. Summer and fall are the peak moose periods, but you should always be alert since moose can be dangerous. If you hit one it can total your car in an instant. The average moose is more than 6 feet tall and weighs 1,000 pounds.

Heading west on N.H. 26 from Errol, you'll pass through **Dixville Notch**, always mentioned in presidential primaries and elections as the place where the first tallies are counted. It's the home of The Balsams Grand Resort Hotel (see our Hotels and Motels chapter). The hotel was built in 1866 with the lake in the foreground and the mountain as a backdrop. Even if you can't stop in for a week or two, the drive by is worth it.

Continue on to **Colebrook** and the beautiful rolling hills of the Connecticut River Valley. The very adventurous will head north to Pittsburg. This small town is an angler's paradise with the Connecticut Lakes and several beautiful streams. In winter the main activities are ice-fishing and snowmobiling. In summer it's fishing and moose-watching. In fact, Pittsburg is the home of the annual North Country Moose Festival (see our Annual Events chapter). Many local residents serve as hunting and fishing guides.

Whatever your outdoor tastes — camping, fishing, boating or just absorbing the bounty of Mother Nature — you'll be happy on the Great North Woods. The name says it all.

Just south of the Great North Woods region is the White Mountains region. The region is dominated by the White Mountain National Forest, a 780,000-acre national park established in 1911 by the Weeks Act. Before that time, there had been little to no land management and much of the area had been clear-cut by lumber companies. Nearly 100 years of land management has healed the scars. Forty-nine towns are within the White Mountain National Forest, and many attractions are part of the beautiful natural landscape. You can take the Cog Railway to the summit of Mount Washington or travel through the Mount Washington Valley on the Conway Scenic Railroad (see our Attractions chapter).

More than 6 million people visit the White Mountains region every year. Hikers will find easy and difficult climbs through the mountains of this region. Along the Saco River, there are boat rides for babies and whitewater that'll give you white hair. In Waterville Valley, you can shop for the hippest ski gear before join-

INSIDERS' TIP

Don't just watch out for moose. Watch out for moose-watchers — they are notoriously bad drivers. If you want to observe moose, pull off the road.

ing the crowds on the slopes or strap on your great-grandfather's wooden snowshoes and spend the day alone in fresh snow. If you choose the latter, just be sure and get the latest avalanche report first. No matter who you are or what time of year you visit the White Mountains Region, you can challenge yourself to do something you've never done before. We promise.

One of the most popular entry points to the White Mountains Region is the town of **Conway**. It was one of the first summer resort areas in the state. Conway and nearby **North Conway** are the heart of a year-round vacation industry. People come for skiing in winter, leaf-peeping in fall and hiking all year round. The towns are the area hubs for shopping (North Conway has more than 200 discount stores), eating out and lodging. (See our Restaurants, Hotels and Motels and Shopping chapters.) Many complain about the traffic, but no one denies that this is a vital spot for the New Hampshire tourism industry.

If you'd like a break from the busy North Conway area, travel west along the Kancamagus Highway (N.H. Route 112), which is a fine introduction to the White Mountains. This 34.5-mile road runs from Conway to the Pemigewasset River in **Lincoln**. The road climbs to nearly 3,000 feet, and many trails begin from points on the highway. The scenery is dazzling any time of year, from the new green in May to the snow in November through March. The Kancamagus Highway is the only federally designated Scenic Byway in New England. Mountains are everywhere — look for Mount Kancamagus and Loon Mountain to the south and Mount Cardigan and Mount Hancock in the north. You'll be traveling along the Swift River. Several campgrounds dot the banks of the river. Be sure to read our Camping chapter for details on reservations. The Loon Mountain Recreation Area is in Lincoln where the Kancamagus Highway ends. In winter you'll love skiing and in summer you'll enjoy the Papermill Theater productions.

You can head north to Cannon Mountain or southeast to **Waterville Valley**, both major ski areas. Waterville Valley is one of the towns along with **Thornton**, **West Thornton** and **Campton** that make up the Waterville Valley area. The area is surrounded by the White Mountain National Forest. Waterville Valley is a self-contained village that will make you want to change your name to Hans or Heidi as you ice-skate on the pond near Town Square or schuss down the slopes.

Another way to travel through the mountains from North Conway is via U.S. 302. Just north of North Conway on N.H. Route 16 is **Glen**, home of the Heritage-New Hampshire and Story Land attractions. Glen is in a small valley near the confluence of the Saco and Ellis rivers. Drive west on U.S. 302 along the winding Saco River and you'll see Attitash Bear Peak as you approach **Bartlett**. Continuing on U.S. 302 you'll pass over the Appalachian Trail in **Harts Location** and on through Crawford Notch State Park, 6,000 acres of mountain wilderness, trails and waterfalls.

Continue on through to the other side of the White Mountains via Crawford Notch. Legend has it that moose hunter and early surveyor Timothy Nash discovered this passage through the mountains in 1771. It's called Crawford Notch because Abel Crawford built a path making the notch accessible. It became the major throughway between the White Mountains and the Upper Connecticut River Valley, greatly influencing trade in the early 19th century.

Soon you'll arrive in historic **Bretton Woods**, famous as host for the 1944 conference that created the International Monetary Fund and home of the famous Mount Washington Hotel. The Cog Railway travels up Mount Washington from Bretton Woods. At a height of 6,288 feet, Mount Washington is the

INSIDERS' TIP

Our state capital, Concord, is pronounced with the accent on the first syllable, not like the supersonic plane. (Other unlikely pronunciations of Algonkian and British origin are too numerous to include here — listen carefully!)

highest peak in northeastern North America. Not surprisingly, the highest peak has some extreme weather. The highest (ever) recorded wind velocity is 231 mph, recorded at the Mount Washington Observatory in April 1934. At the summit is Mount Washington State Park (see our Parks and Open Spaces chapter).

From U.S. Route 302 you can turn south and drive on Interstate 93 through Franconia Notch State Park. Here you'll find Cannon Mountain and nature's granite masterpiece, The Old Man of the Mountain. If you're traveling in June, don't miss the beautiful lupines in Sugar Hill (see our Annual Events chapter) near **Franconia**.

The White Mountains Region is way too big and beautiful for us to give a complete overview. Take a skyride, take a hike, take as much time off work as you can to explore this awe-inspiring region.

Dartmouth-Lake Sunapee Region

This region is named for two local landmarks: Dartmouth College in Hanover and Lake Sunapee in Newbury, Sunapee and New London. Interstates 89 and 91 are the major highways into the area. (I-91 is in Vermont

The Primary: First in the Nation

Close-up

The joke (and it's an old one) goes like this: The ambitious young reporter, trying to find a new angle on the New Hampshire primary, goes out into the country to interview a "real Yankee." On the outskirts of a small town he finds a farmer in the barn, milking a cow. "Excuse me, sir," he says. "Could you tell me which candidate you'll be voting for this year?" The farmer stands up, pushes back his hat and ponders. "Dunno," he says, finally. "I haven't met them all, yet."

Things change. In the last election, between the two of us we met only three presidential candidates. But the fact that we met any at all explains part of why New Hampshire's first-in-the-nation primary has such an appeal and such a high "predictor" value.

New Hampshire has held a presidential primary in every election year since 1916. Since 1920, when Minnesota dropped its primary, New Hampshire's has been first in the nation. In 1952 the candidate's names were added to the ballot (before that only the delegates were listed). Since then, except for 1992, no one has ever won the White House without first winning the New Hampshire primary. (In 1992 our next-door neighbor and economic straight-shooter, the late Massachusetts Senator Paul Tsongas, won the Democratic primary. Bill Clinton was a close second.)

New Hampshire law dictates that the date of the New Hampshire primary shall be the first Tuesday in February of a presidential election year or one week before any similar election in another state. (Iowa's caucus, not being a popular election, doesn't count.)

As a consequence, every four years the circus comes to town. (Our first candidate-sighting of the 2000 Primary was an invitation to a lobster-bake with one Republican perennial — in August of 1998!) For months there's a candidate behind every bush — or at least in every diner and barbershop. As winter closes in, the national and international media arrive en masse, mobile broadcast booths and satellite dishes in tow. Small towns whose representatives never bother to visit them hold coffees where generals and ambassadors discuss the national debt with farmers and housewives. It's an economic boon and a traffic nightmare.

News anchors from New York and political operatives from Houston stomp around in the snow, interviewing each other because there are more of them than of us. School

— continued on next page

children ask questions of senators, and snowbanks bristle with signs. Obscure candidates run 30-minute mini-documentaries on television, and pollsters call at dinner time (sometimes two or three times a week).

In recent years there have been many objections raised to the influence that being first gives New Hampshire. We're not representative of the country, they say. We're a small media market. We're more homogeneous than much of the country. It gives a tiny number of voters a disproportionate amount of power.

To which New Hampshire retorts, "Damn straight." It's because we are small that retail politics are still the rule here. It is (relatively) inexpensive to run a campaign in New Hampshire. Anyone can run for President here (and sometimes it seems like everyone does). In 1992 (the last election without an incumbent in either major party), there were more than 40 names on the ballot. New Hampshire voters are sophisticated and politically savvy and still judge candidates more on the content of their messages than their style or their sound bites. So a relative unknown (like Jimmy "Who?" Carter) with a solid idea and the energy to get the message out has a chance to be heard in New Hampshire and to pick up momentum. And a big name with little behind it but money may be sent packing, faux fur hat in hand.

Photo: Don Hlmsel

Senator Robert Dole celebrates with his supporters in 1996.

No, we're not immune to the influences of modern political marketing. The changing media picture and our increasingly large population, including many transplants, is changing the political atmosphere even in New Hampshire. But we take our responsibility seriously. We listen to candidates. We examine their literature. We demand that they actually say something meaningful. And we don't talk to pollsters (or when we do, we hedge). So our vote on primary day rings loud and clear. It's our contribution to the process and our claim to fame. It's the First in the Nation. We love it.

and runs parallel to the Connecticut River.) The region's westerly border is the Connecticut River. The towns along the Connecticut River, in both New Hampshire and Vermont, are also called the Upper Valley. These river towns, even though in different states, have a shared history and a sort of large neighborhood bond.

The Indian name, Sunapee, is translated as Goose Lake, so named for the many flocks of wild geese that used to land here. A major recreation area, Lake Sunapee and Sunapee State Park with Mount Sunapee draw visitors for year-round sports fun. Look for specifics on Lake Sunapee in our Winter Sports and In, On and Around the Water chapters.

The region is dominated by three mountains. In addition to Mount Sunapee, there are Mount Kearsarge in the Warner-Wilmot area and Mount Cardigan in **Orange**. All three have clearly marked access routes and are excellent for hiking. (See our Parks and Open Spaces chapter.)

Dartmouth College in **Hanover** was founded in 1769 for "the education and instruction of youth of the Indian Tribes of this land … and also of English youth and any others." An Ivy League college, Dartmouth adds to the cultural richness of the region. In addition to year-round art exhibits and musical concerts, the college is a major draw for visiting artists and academics. Hanover is a

Photo: David A. Leach Photography

The State Capitol in Concord is the hub of New Hampshire government.

rich combination of New England history and college-town charm and energy. The best way to enjoy the town is to park in one of several clearly marked parking areas and set out on foot. If you've seen the Metropolitan Opera House in New York City, you may do a double-take when you first set eyes on the Hopkins Center for the Arts. Both buildings were designed by Wallace Harrison, with the Dartmouth building preceding the opera house by several years. (See our Arts and Culture chapter.)

Just south of Hanover lies **Lebanon**, the only city in the region. Located on I-89 just east of the Vermont border, **West Lebanon** is the major shopping area of the Upper Valley. (See Shopping for details.) If you can get past the modern shopping areas near the interstate, you'll find a charming town on a common. Park your car and walk to enjoy the small-town charm. The AVA Gallery and Arts Center on Bank Street features contemporary works by New Hampshire and Vermont artists.

The Dartmouth-Lake Sunapee Region has long been popular with painters and writers. A section of **Cornish** is called "Little New York" for the number of arty types who have frequented the region over the years. The home and gardens of sculptor Augustus Saint-Gaudens in Cornish are a National Historic Site. American writer Winston Churchill was a frequent visitor to the Saint-Gaudens estate along with artist Maxfield Parrish. (See our Attractions chapter.)

Strategically located on the Connecticut River, Cornish was originally called Mast Camp because it was the point where pine masts heading to England were shipped down the Connecticut River. Also in Cornish is the Cornish-Windsor (Vermont) bridge over the Connecticut River. It is the longest covered bridge in the United States. Another architectural delight is Blow-Me-Down Mill, designed by the famous (and infamous) New York architect Stanford White.

South of Cornish is **Claremont**. The Sugar River runs through Claremont, and the preserved mills speak to the manufacturing history of the town. Today the area is primarily residential with a strong summer population. This Upper Valley town is proud of its literary history and happy to include J.D. Salinger among its residents. It is also home to the first Roman Catholic church in New Hampshire, St. Mary's, built in 1823 in **West Claremont.** The Claremont Opera House on Tremont Square was built in 1897 and just celebrated its centennial with a second major overhaul.

Down the Connecticut River is the town of Charlestown, an important settlement during the French and Indian Wars. (See our Attractions chapter for Fort No. 4.) This is another New Hampshire town with an impressive Main Street. Built in 1763, the street is a mile long and 200 feet wide. The town has designed a wonderful walking tour with maps available in most local shops.

To the east is the town of **Newbury**, home of the south end of Lake Sunapee including Sunapee Harbor and all of Mount Sunapee. In addition to these natural abundances, the town is the location of The Fells Historic Site at the John Hay National Wildlife Refuge (see our Attractions chapter). Newbury is busiest in summer but never too crowded. Be sure to come to the League of New Hampshire Craftsmen's Fair in August at Lake Sunapee State Park.

The town of **New London** is near Lake Sunapee and is the cultural center of the Sunapee area. Colby-Sawyer College was founded here in 1837 and, as in Hanover, the college community is integral to the area's personality. Today New London has three distinct groups of residents in addition to the students. Elderly retirees spend the summer and early fall in town, early retirees (retired corporate executives who still work as consultants) live here year-round except for maybe three weeks in winter, and young professionals, who work as lawyers in nearby Concord or doctors at Mary Hitchcock Memorial Hospital in Lebanon, reside here with their families.

In addition to a portion of Lake Sunapee, New London is well-known for two other lakes in town — Pleasant Lake and Little Sunapee Lake. Both lakes provide excellent recreational opportunities including fishing. There's an annual Chocolate Festival in February at the New London Inn. And in summer be sure to make the curtain at the Barn Playhouse. Well-known throughout New England, the Barn Playhouse is a prominent summer-stock theater. From June through August, the Playhouse produces dramas and musicals as well as special productions for children. (See our Arts and Culture chapter.)

Don't be afraid to take unknown roads in this region. You'll find quiet country, old houses and no traffic. The natives are friendly and highly cultured (many are Dartmouth grads) in the Dartmouth-Lake Sunapee Region.

Monadnock Region

Welcome to New Hampshire's Monadnock Region. (The emphasis is on the second syllable, "nad.") Turn off the cruise control and enjoy our charming New England countryside. You won't have to look hard to find village greens, Colonial churches and town meeting houses. Chances are you'll see a historical marker or two near an elegant town building dating back to the latter half of the 18th or early 19th century.

There is no interstate highway running through this southwest corner of New Hampshire, so you don't have to worry about speeding past any quaint locales. In fact, this is a great region for taking an unplanned turn, following your instincts and exploring the unknown. In warm weather you'll find yard sales, fruit stands and evening music concerts. In winter gather at the wood stove or open fireplace in the local inn for a cup of hot chocolate or spiced tea. In autumn be prepared for the blazing tree-covered hillsides and out-of-

INSIDERS' TIP

Bring along binoculars and a good bird identification guide when touring New Hampshire. Even the most sophisticated city-slicker has been known to embrace the great outdoors once introductions are made.

this-world apples. And in spring be ready to tramp through a little mud on your way to a stack of pancakes dripping with fresh local maple syrup.

The region is named for Mount Monadnock in **Jaffrey**. The mountain is visible from many areas in the region and has long attracted artists, writers and summer residents to the area. Mount Monadnock is 3,165 feet high and one of the most-climbed mountains in the world. (Conventional local wisdom says that Mount Monadnock may have moved to No. 1 status since more and more people are choosing to drive up Mount Fuji in Japan, Mount Monadnock's longtime rival.)

The name Monadnock is the English rendition of the Algonkian Indian name for the mountain. It means "mountain that stands alone." In fact, during the 1700s geologists began using the term monadnock to describe any mountain with Mount Monadnock's specific geological attributes (technically, "a mass of residual, erosion-resistant bedrock rising from a surrounding plain"). Whether driving west on N.H. Route 101 coming off Temple Mountain or traveling the stretch of N.H. 124 between **Marlborough** and Jaffrey, you won't forget your first view of Monadnock. Read more about Mount Monadnock and Mount Monadnock State Park in our Parks and Open Spaces chapter.

Even if you don't climb Mount Monadnock, be sure to visit Jaffrey and **Jaffrey Center**, on the southern slope of the mountain. In 1749 there was a $500 bounty offered to those who settled in Jaffrey, and beginning in the 1840s tourists began coming here to climb the mountain. The influx of tourists resulted in the building of several resort hotels, one of which, The Monadnock Inn, still stands.

The part of town known as Jaffrey Center is where you'll find the charm and history. It's on N.H. Route 124, and the 1773 meeting house will be the signal that you've arrived. This is the town where Willa Cather spent her summers and wrote. She is buried in the old graveyard behind the meeting house. Also buried in the meeting house graveyard is Amos Fortune, a slave who bought his freedom, moved to Jaffrey and established a successful tannery. He left money for the town's school and church in his will, and this philanthropy is still recognized in the Amos Fortune Forum Series, held every summer since 1947.

Depending on who's counting, there are about 40 towns in the Monadnock Region. North of Jaffrey on N.H. 101 are two of the most well-known, **Dublin** and **Peterborough**. Dublin is home to *Yankee Magazine* and *The Farmer's Almanac*. It is also the third-highest community in the state. Peterborough may be the most sophisticated area in the region. Famous as the template for Grover's Corners in Thornton Wilder's *Our Town*, Peterborough is the home of the MacDowell Colony, the oldest arts retreat in the United States. Although many towns in the region were more active in the 19th century, Peterborough has remained a thriving center of culture and more than kept up with the 20th century.

From Dublin, you'll see signs pointing to **Harrisville**. Follow them. All of Harrisville is a historic district. The first settler was Abel Twitchell, who arrived in 1774. He was followed by at least six brothers and sisters who saw the manufacturing possibilities afforded by the plentiful and powerful water supply. The first factory was a sawmill, and by 1860 there were two competing woolen mills in town. The brick factory buildings are still standing, restored and maintained for historic documentation. The many lakes and ponds draw tourists and summer residents just as they attracted entrepreneurs more than two centuries ago.

If you can, take a spin through **Hancock**. Once a center of cotton manufacturing, the town is almost entirely residential today, with many summer residents. The most famous architectural landmark is the Congregational Church, built in 1820. It has a beautiful spire that houses a Paul Revere bell. Don't miss

INSIDERS' TIP

New Hampshire is a small state but not an easy one to cross. You'll be a happier traveler if you plan on an average speed of 40 mph and consider your transit as a sight-seeing trip.

the unusual semicircular carriage shed behind the church.

At the center of the village is the John Hancock Inn, which was built in 1789 and is the state's oldest inn. (See our Bed and Breakfasts and Country Inns chapter.) The Meeting House dates back to 1788 and is an excellent example of Colonial architecture. Hancock is also home to the Harris Center for Conservation Education. Formerly a private estate, the land is now a nonprofit land trust with 7 miles of trails and many educational family programs.

Just up the road on N.H. 123 is the Audubon Sanctuary at Willard Pond. If you are lucky enough to be passing by on a hot day, stop for a refreshing swim. The water is crystal clear (no motorboats allowed), and the lovely shoreline is set off by Bald Mountain. The entrance is in Hancock, although most of the sanctuary is in **Antrim**.

Just south and west of Jaffrey and not far from the Massachusetts border is **Fitzwilliam**. The town has a fenced common and an architectural gem in the 1817 town hall. Originally a Congregational church, the structure was rebuilt as a town hall after lightning struck the church. The foundation's granite blocks were pulled from the town quarry, and the bell was cast by Paul Revere's company. Fitzwilliam is a resort and retirement community today. It is also home to Rhododendron State Park, a National Natural Landmark with more than 16 acres of wild rhododendron (see our Parks and Open Spaces chapter).

The only city in the Monadnock region is **Keene**. Settled in 1736 and attacked and burned during the French and Indian War, Keene's population is now nearly 23,000. What the town calls the "widest Main Street in the world" leads straight to the beautiful United Church of Christ, which was built in 1787. This is Central Square, and besides being a historic treasure, it's everybody's focal point for directions. Keene is the shopping capital of the region with a delightful selection of small shops in the Colony Mill Marketplace as well as many national chains represented on the outskirts of town (see our Shopping chapter). Keene State College is here along with several historical buildings.

The Connecticut River forms the border between New Hampshire and Vermont (the river belongs to New Hampshire), and some of the state's best farmland is in the Connecticut River Valley. From **Hinsdale** near the Massachusetts border to the region's most northwesterly town of **Alstead** with its charming town centers and Historical Archives Building, the small towns close by the Connecticut River are some of the earliest New Hampshire settlements.

The other main rivers of the region are the Ashuelot and the Contoocook. The Ashuelot features a cluster of covered bridges in the **Swanzey** area, and the Contoocook is one of the few rivers in the United States that flows north. (The Contoocook flows north to Concord where it joins the Merrimack.) These rivers and the region's many lakes and streams have been a great influence in the development and history of the Monadnock region. Early in the settlement of the area, the water provided power for machines and factories. As small manufacturing and water-powered energy needs waned, these same bodies of water became mainstays, along with Mount Monadnock, of the vacation and tourist industries.

In addition to the state parks mentioned above, the Monadnock Region is home to the 13,000-acre Pisgah State Park, which spreads itself among Hinsdale, **Chesterfield** and **Winchester**. Miller State Park is in Peterborough and Greenfield State Park is in (you guessed it) **Greenfield**.

Without a doubt, the Monadnock region is a picnicker's paradise. So slow down and enjoy the views in this rolling countryside.

INSIDERS' TIP

Franco-American organizations like the Association Canado-Americaine are experiencing a resurgence, as descendants of immigrants try to recapture the language and culture their grandparents brought to New Hampshire.

For flying to New Hampshire we strongly recommend that you use a New Hampshire airport instead of Boston's Logan International.

Getting Here, Getting Around

You can get to New Hampshire by car, airplane or bus. We'll stretch that to include trains since Amtrak offers service to White River Junction, Vermont, which is just across the Connecticut River from Lebanon. Once you are here, the easiest way to get around is by car since public transportation does not serve the whole state. Buses run between Manchester, Concord and specific parts of the White Mountains Region and are a good alternative if you're planning a ski vacation.

Getting Here

By Car

If you're coming to New Hampshire from New York, Connecticut, western Massachusetts or Canada, you will likely travel on Interstate 91. It runs along the Connecticut River in Vermont parallel to the New Hampshire border. It is convenient to the Monadnock Region, Dartmouth-Lake Sunapee Region and the White Mountains Region.

If you're traveling from Maine into the White Mountains Region, you can enter New Hampshire on U.S. Route 2 or U.S. Route 302 traveling west. Entry to the Lakes Region is from Maine/N.H. Route 25. For the Seacoast Region, you'll find travel easiest on Interstate 95 if you're going to the ocean or U.S. Route 202 if you're heading inland.

To drive up from Boston, the easiest route into New Hampshire is Interstate 93. Manchester is 60 miles from Boston. Depending on traffic — especially on Mass. Route 128, Interstate 495 or I-93 — the trip can take anywhere from 1+ to 2+ hours. Barring a jackknifed tractor trailer, you can expect the shorter trip on Sunday mornings and the longer trip any weekday afternoon (coming out of Boston) or weekday morning (traveling into the city). If you are heading to the Seacoast, take I-95.

Beware: Boston is currently undergoing "The Big Dig," a massive reconstruction of all major arteries into and out of the city. It is the largest public works project ever undertaken in the United States and will be in progress until at least 2002. Once complete, Boston will be an even more beautiful city than it is today, but until then driving can be quite a hassle.

When traveling to New Hampshire from Boston's Logan International Airport, public transportation is the best option. If you insist on driving from Logan, avoid the 7 to 10 AM and 4 to 7 PM rush hours. To head to the Seacoast, follow signs to U.S. Route 1A. Head north on U.S. 1A until you can get on U.S. Route 1 going north. From U.S. 1 follow signs to I-95 N.

To enter New Hampshire via I-93, follow the signs from the airport exit to the Sumner Tunnel (you'll return to Logan via the Callahan Tunnel), and upon exiting follow signs to remain on I-93. The Sumner Tunnel currently charges a $1 toll. The Callahan Tunnel is free.

By Air

In the old days everyone assumed that you had to go to Boston in order to get to New Hampshire. That is no longer true. The Manchester airport (see write-up following) has become the hub of choice for Insiders as well as many residents of the northern Boston area. The airport has direct flights to Baltimore, Chicago, New York, Orlando, Philadelphia, Pittsburgh and Washington, D.C. More flights are being added. We like the airport because the parking lot is safe and reasonably priced, the check-in lines are shorter than Boston and the drive home can be two hours shorter than from Boston. We really love the fact that our luggage is always ready to be claimed within five minutes of landing.

The same convenience works for tourists. Manchester is in the Merrimack Valley and less than an hour from all regions excluding the White Mountains. Driving time from Manchester to Conway, a favorite destination in the White Mountains, is two hours. If you're heading to Pittsburg, in the Great North Woods, count on a four-hour drive.

The only other commercial (other than charter) flight airports in New Hampshire are the Lebanon Airport in the Dartmouth-Lake Sunapee Region and Dillant-Hopkins Airport in Keene in the Monadnock Region. You'll find details on the carriers serving these airports following this introduction.

If you prefer travel by private plane, you'll find 49 airports listed in the Airport Facilities Directory. You can get a copy from NOAA (National Oceanographic and Atmospheric Administration) by calling (800) 638-8972. This directory is updated every 56 days and gives detailed information on runways, lights, radio frequencies and airport services.

Manchester Airport

Brown Ave., Manchester
• (603) 624-6556

Manchester Airport is the largest airport in the state. This modern commercial facility opened in 1994 and offers big-city service with small-town convenience. The airport's success means we're hearing lots of talk about additional runways, flight patterns and noise pollution as well as wetlands preservation versus a new access road.

Fast food, a tavern with excellent food, smoking lounges, an observation deck and a vending machine with fresh flowers are some of the airport amenities. The well-supplied newsstand has a wide range of newspapers, magazines and books along with souvenirs, candy and travel supplies. Local taxis serve the airport, and shuttle services operate to and from Boston. These shuttle services will customize service whenever possible. Call ahead and ask about family rates and resort transportation. You can get door-to-door service whether you are staying in a hotel or with friends. Details on companies are in this chapter in our Limousine and Shuttle Bus section.

The following companies offer rental cars at the airport.

Avis, (800) 331-1212
Budget, (800) 527-0700
Hertz, (800) 654-3131
National, (800) CAR-RENT

Lebanon Airport

Exit 20 off I-89, West Lebanon
• (603) 298-8878

USAir Express operates a total of 10 flights a day to Boston, LaGuardia and Philadelphia. Rental cars are available from Avis, Hertz and National (look for these phone numbers under the Manchester Airport). The Tailwinds Restaurant at the airport is open Monday through Saturday. The airport is five to 10 minutes from Hanover and Dartmouth College and about 30 minutes from New London or Claremont. Look for transportation details under our Limousine and Shuttle Bus Service section in this chapter.

Dillant-Hopkins Airport

80 Airport Rd., Keene
• (603) 357-9835

This is an uncontrolled airport. One commercial carrier, Colgan Air, (603) 355-4883,

INSIDERS' TIP

Keep an eye out for deer and moose as you drive through the state and don't be surprised if you run up against a flock of wild turkeys.

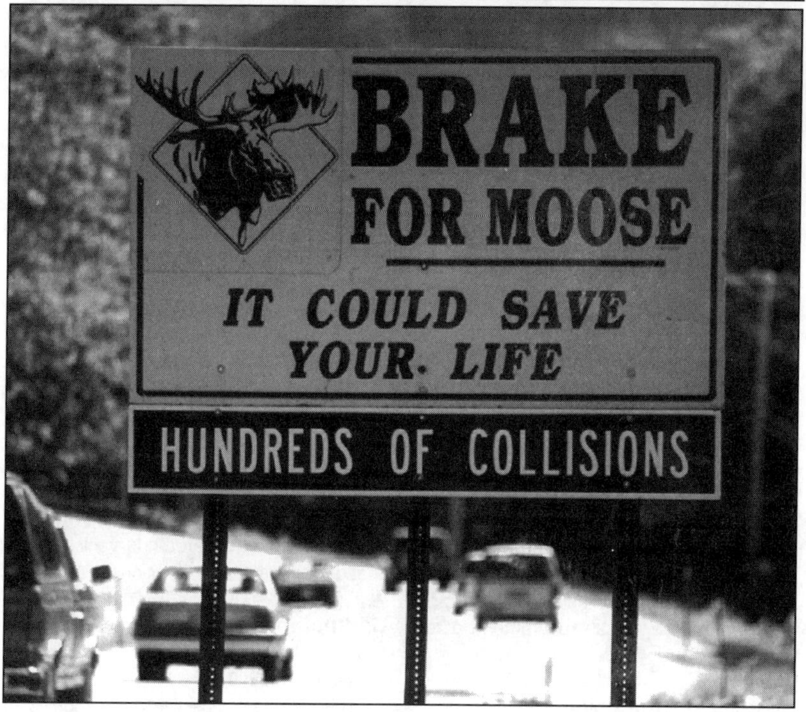

Photo: David A. Leach Photography

Always be alert for wildlife on the highways of New Hampshire.

serves the airport with flights to Rutland, Vermont, and Newark, New Jersey. You can rent a car from Avis, (800) 331-1212.

Logan International Airport
East Boston
• (800) 23-LOGAN

Logan International Airport is a great airport — if your travel plans are international. But for coming to New Hampshire we strongly recommend that you use a New Hampshire airport. If you do use Logan, here are a few details. Logan has five terminals named by letters A through E. Each terminal has its own parking lot, restaurants, newsstands and snack bars. A free shuttle service operates between terminals. Both automobile and air traffic in and out of Logan can be a problem. We recommend that you allow lots of extra travel time if you need to park, rent or return a car. If you want to get to New Hampshire from Logan and don't want to drive, look for choices in our Limousine and Shuttle Bus Service section in this chapter.

Rental car companies at Logan International Airport include:

Alamo, (800) 327-9633
Avis, (800) 331-1212

INSIDERS' TIP

New Hampshire's rest areas are wonderful. They are clean and often have picnic areas. A knowledgeable guide is usually on premises, and the vending machines always work. The north and southbound I-93 rest areas in Hookset (between Manchester and Concord) and the northbound I-95 rest area at Exit 1 in Seabrook are open 24 hours a day.

Budget, (800) 527-0700
Dollar, (800) 800-4000
Hertz, (800) 654-3131
National, (800) CAR-RENT

Limousine and Shuttle Bus Service

Whether you're looking for a ride to a local hotel or need to get the family and the skis to a White Mountains resort, the companies listed below can help. Most companies prefer to quote rates as prices vary depending on the size of the group and the destination. If you're traveling from Logan to Nashua, the cost is about $24 one way for one person and $50 one way for a family of five. We think it's best to always call ahead to get a price and make reservations. Be sure and ask about transportation when you arrange your overnight accommodations since many hotels, resorts and country inns have their own transportation service or can recommend a reliable local firm.

First Class Limousine

• (603) 883-4807, (800) 252-7754

This company can provide a private van for skiers and their equipment, a stretch limousine or an everyday shuttle ride for the single passenger. From Logan it serves more than 63 locations in New Hampshire including Manchester Airport. It's open all day, every day. Call ahead for rates and reservations. This company also operates The Airport Shuttle at the same telephone numbers.

Flight Line Inc.

• (603) 893-8254, (800) 245-2525

This company provides shuttle service between Logan and the Manchester Airport. It can be flexible about drop-off points from either airport as long as you give a call in advance. Call ahead for rates and reservations.

M & L Transportation Services Inc.

Logan Airport Shuttle

• (781) 938-8646, (800) 225-4846

This hourly shuttle travels between Logan and several major motels in Nashua as well as the Manchester Airport. They don't take advance reservations from Logan. You must call the local Massachusetts number after you are in the airport. You need to include the area code when you dial, but the cost is for a local call. The company will quote family and group rates. Reservations can be made daily from 8 AM to 11 PM, except Saturday. On Saturdays you can call from 8 AM to 10 PM.

McLaughlin Limousine Service

• (603) 886-9700, (800) 24-LOGAN

This company handles transportation needs between Logan and Nashua and surrounding areas. It offers everything from private limousines to shared-ride vehicles. Call ahead for rates and reservations.

Dartmouth Mini Coach

115 Etna Rd., Lebanon

• (603) 448-2800

This company has five daily shuttles to Boston's Logan airport. They drop off and pick up in Hanover and New London. Advance reservations are required. The company will arrange private drop-off and pickup service to the Manchester airport.

By Bus

Concord Trailways

• (800) 639-3317

There are 21 Concord Trailways stops in New Hampshire. Most of the stops are in the Merrimack Valley, Lakes and White Mountains regions. Buses run daily to connect Concord, Manchester, Londonderry, Littleton and Plymouth to Boston. There is service from Berlin south to Conway and continuing to Laconia with stops in between depending on the day

INSIDERS' TIP

We don't usually use the word "route" when giving directions. We refer to almost all roads by the number. For example, "Take 3 to exit 8 and get on 101."

and time. These routes connect with the Concord routes. It is best to call for schedule and price information.

Vermont Transit
- **(802) 864-6811**

Vermont Transit serves Hanover, New London, Concord, Manchester and Nashua with routes to Boston, Montreal and White River Junction and Burlington, Vermont. It also has service through Keene on the route from Montreal to New York City. This route also stops in Hartford, Connecticut. During the summer, Vermont Transit has service from the Manchester area to the Seacoast.

By Train

No train service runs directly to New Hampshire, but you can take Amtrak to White River Junction, Vermont, or to Boston's South Station and continue on to New Hampshire via rental car or bus service. Vermont Transit travels from White River Junction to New Hampshire, and Concord Trailways and Vermont Transit have service from a terminal within walking distance of South Station.

Amtrak, (800) 872-7245
Concord Trailways, (800) 639-3317
Vermont Transit, (802) 864-6811

Getting Around Once You're Here

Interstate and Limited-Access Roads

There are three interstate highways running through New Hampshire — Interstate 89, Interstate 93 and Interstate 95. Insiders always include a fourth, Interstate 91, in Vermont. There is a toll on I-95 near Portsmouth and a toll on I-93 in Hookset, south of Concord. Currently tolls are 75¢. There are no tolls on I-89 or I-91.

The short stretch of I-95 in New Hampshire serves the Seacoast Region. It runs north-south and connects New Hampshire to Massachusetts and Maine.

I-93 runs right up the middle of the state from north to south. It goes through Manchester, Concord and Littleton then crosses into Vermont just west of Littleton. Another way of thinking is that I-93 travels through the Merrimack Valley Region, the Lakes Region and the White Mountains Region.

Use I-89 to travel from east to west across the state from Concord to Lebanon. It is the main road of the Dartmouth-Lake Sunapee Region.

Manchester is the only city in New Hampshire with a perimeter interstate, Interstate 293. It circles Manchester, connecting N.H. Route 101, U.S. Route 3 and I-93.

U.S. 3 is known as the F. E. Everett Turnpike from the Massachusetts-New Hampshire border to Manchester. This portion of U.S. 3 is a south-to-north toll road, and the tolls are 75¢. It is a major route connecting the southwestern Merrimack Valley to I-93 in Massachusetts (via Route 128/I-95 or I-495) and on into Boston. It also connects with I-93 in Manchester via I-293.

Primary State Roads

With four names, U.S. Route 3 can be confusing. When it's a limited access road (see above), it's called the F.E. Everett Turnpike. When it's not limited access it's called U.S. Route 3, The Daniel Webster (or D.W.) Highway or N.H. Route 3A. In New Hampshire the addition of a letter to the highway number indicates the presence of a bypass road. For example, if you've got both U.S. 3 and N.H. Route 3A, U.S. 3 bypasses the center of town while N.H. Route 3A frequently doubles as Main Street.

U.S. Route 4 runs east-west from Ports-

INSIDERS' TIP

Get off the interstate and drive our back roads and main streets — but please observe local speed limits and passing zones.

mouth to Concord and continues west to Lebanon.

N.H. Route 9 runs east-west from Concord in the Merrimack Valley to Brattleboro, Vermont. N.H. 9 goes through Keene and continues west where N.H. Route 101 ends.

N.H. Route 16 is the main road for travel between the Seacoast Region and the White Mountains Region. The exit for N.H. 16 off I-95 in Portsmouth is clearly marked. N.H. 16 travels north through Rochester and West Ossipee in the Lakes Region and North Conway in the White Mountains Region. It continues into the Great North Woods through Gorham, Berlin and Errol.

N.H. 101 runs east-west from Hampton in the Seacoast Region to Keene in the Monadnock Region. N.H. 101A branches off in Amherst and runs from Milford to Nashua. N.H. 101A is a major thoroughfare with many restaurants, antiques stores and everyday and specialty shops. N.H. 101A and N.H. 3A (the D.W. Highway) are the commercial strips of the Merrimack Valley.

U.S. Route 202 is an east-west road from Rochester in the Lakes Region through Concord in the Merrimack Valley Region and Peterborough and Jaffrey in the Monadnock Region.

Public Transportation

The Seacoast Region has bus service that connects the towns of Portsmouth, Dover, Exeter, Stratham, Somersworth, Farmington, Durham and Newmarket. Prices range from 75¢ to $1.75 depending on the length of your trip. The majority of routes have regular weekday service. Some routes also have Saturday service. Call Coast (the managing company) at (603) 862-1931 for local schedules.

Greater Laconia Transit is the only public transportation company in the Lakes Region. Throughout the year they provide service between Laconia, Franklin and Plymouth. During the summer the company also offers double-decker bus service from Laconia to Weir's Beach and Meredith returning to Laconia. The cost varies depending on how far you travel, but most rides are $1 one-way. Call Laconia Transit at (603) 528-2496 for schedule information.

In the Merrimack Valley you can get around using public transportation in Concord, Manchester and Nashua. Concord has three bus routes connecting residential and industrial areas. Service is Monday through Friday, and fares are 75¢ except for seniors, who pay 50¢. Call Concord Area Transit at (603) 225-3295 for schedule information.

Manchester has 13 weekday routes and seven routes on Saturday. Riders pay 90¢ except seniors, who pay 45¢. Call the Manchester Transit Authority at (603) 623-8801 for schedule information. In Nashua six major bus routes serve the city. All originate downtown. The cost is $1 per ride except for seniors and students, who pay 50¢. For schedules call the Nashua Transit System at (603) 880-0100.

In the Dartmouth-Lake Sunapee region you'll find weekday bus service serving Hanover, Lebanon and White River Junction, Vermont. Fares are $1.25 with a free fare zone between the Hanover and Lebanon downtown areas. Some limited service is provided on Saturdays. Call Advanced Transportation in Wilder, Vermont, at (802) 295-1824 for schedules. Farther south in the region, weekday service between Claremont, Newport and

INSIDERS' TIP

Most Insiders put a shovel and bag of sand or cat litter in the trunk of the car for winter driving. The sand or cat litter can provide traction if you get stuck in snow. It's also helpful if you need to assist another driver.

Charlestown is provided by Community Transportation. Call (603) 542-0048 for details on fares and schedules.

Keene is the only area in the Monadnock region with public transportation. Six bus routes serve the city Monday through Friday. Fares are $1 a ride with a 10-ride pass available for $7. Call City Express for schedules.

Birchbark canoes, snowshoes, even toboggans that we rely on today were tools of survival developed by Native Americans.

History

The natural landscape is one of the most vital influences in the history of any location. Massive sheets of ice covered New Hampshire four times during the Ice Age, and as the ice melted it established our mountains, rivers, lakes and soil. The moving ice cut Franconia, Dixville, Crawford and Carter Notch and sculpted The Old Man in the Mountain. This melting ice also redeposited our ubiquitous granite — hence the nickname, The Granite State.

The last of the ice melted about 14,000 years ago. With the melting came plant and animal life. The great forests sprouted, fish filled the lakes, rivers and ocean, and large and small animals began to inhabit the land.

The first settlers are believed to have been Native Americans. Specific dates are difficult to pin down, but it is clear that Native Americans populated New Hampshire at least 5,000 years ago. Some sources place the first human habitation as long ago as 12,000 years ago. Archaeologists have found cultural remains in various parts of the state, with heavier concentrations near what is now Weirs Beach at Lake Winnipesaukee, Amoskeag Falls on the Merrimack River in Manchester and near the conjunction of the Ashuelot and Connecticut rivers in the Monadnock Region. The rich fishing grounds at all of these locations were fundamental in early settlement.

The Algonkian Indians were the first named inhabitants of the region. The many tribes making up the Algonkian people include the Abenaki and the Pennacook. You will notice many place names that acknowledge the Algonkian roots. Contoocook, Sunapee, Ammonoosuc, Piscataquog... you get the idea. These early inhabitants forged skills that early European settlers relied on for survival. Without learning from the Native Americans about how to grow, process and store corn, the early European settlers probably wouldn't have survived their first winters. Birchbark canoes, snowshoes, even toboggans that we rely on today were tools of survival developed by Native Americans. The Mount Kearsarge Indian Museum in Warner (see our Attractions chapter) is an excellent starting point for those interested in learning more about the first people of New Hampshire.

The Arrival of the Europeans

We know that Martin Pring, an English sea captain, explored part of coastal New Hampshire in June of 1603. His journey along the lower Piscataqua River preceded that of French explorer Samuel Champlain and the famous English sea captain, John Smith. Smith outlined the coast from Cape Cod to Maine, and it was his map that, when shown to the English royal family, inspired the appellation "New England."

The rich supply of fish led to temporary settlements by English fishermen on the Isles of Shoals, a group of islands about 10 miles off the mainland. There they dried their catch and took shelter before sailing back to England.

The first grant in what is now New Hampshire, given to Englishmen John Mason and Ferdinando Gorges in 1622, covered land from the Merrimack River to the Kennebec River. (Along with assuming control over land — "I claim these lands for the crown" — came the assumed power to give pieces of it away. These gifts of land were known as grants. Complicating the issue of grants was that very little of the land was accurately mapped. For example, early explorers believed the Merrimack River ran east to west, while the majority of its course is actually north to south.) Mason was given an additional 6,000 acres in 1629, covering land near present-day Portsmouth. Mason's home county was in Hampshire, England, hence the name New Hampshire. Both men died in England before traveling to the New World.

The first permanent white settlement was at Odiorne's Point, now the town of Rye, in 1623. Six thousand acres were granted by a council formed by the British king to David Thomson for the purpose of establishing a fishing village. By 1638 additional grants established settlements at Portsmouth (called Strawbery Banke), Dover, Exeter and Hampton. These were the only permanent settlements until 1673.

During these early years New Hampshire was under the administrative jurisdiction of Massachusetts. In January 1679 New Hampshire was once again declared a royal colony. A tug of war existed between England and Massachusetts for control over New Hampshire. For Massachusetts, New Hampshire represented more land and settlements for the spread of their religious beliefs. For England, control of the New Hampshire colony was a way to keep Massachusetts from becoming too powerful. The natural resources of the colony were in much demand in England.

Fur, Fish and Lumber

Three products were the core of early trade in the colony: fur, fish and lumber. The fur industry never lived up to expectations since over-trapping hurt supplies and beaver hats were out of fashion by 1700. The fishing industry was very important in New Hampshire, especially in Dover, which was largely made up of fishermen. Much of their trade was with Boston — Massachusetts had a huge fishing industry — as well as with Barbados and Virginia. The ancillary businesses of shipbuilding, sailmaking, netmaking, etc. thrived in the fishing environment.

Nothing was more important to New Hampshire industry than lumber. By the time New Hampshire was discovered, the great forests in England had been destroyed. England needed the wood from the colonies for new ships for its navy. New Hampshire supplied England with masts from 1634 to 1773. New Hampshire's huge white pines were so important that the crown branded trees for its exclusive use.

Lumber was also very important in trade with Barbados and other spirits-producing lands such as Madeira, which needed the wood for fuel to make whiskey and for the storage barrels. And the wild men of Portsmouth were happy to be able to trade directly for rum.

The Colonial Period

The most important family in the Colonial period (1680-1775) was the Wentworths of Portsmouth. The family first made money with a successful tavern in Portsmouth and parlayed its money through marriage and shrewd planning into shipbuilding and later political power. The family was smart, politically savvy and fond of rewarding friends and allies.

John Wentworth was lieutenant governor until his death in 1730. His son, Benning, became royal governor in 1741 and served until 1767, when his nephew, John Wentworth II, succeeded him. The second John Wentworth served until just before the outbreak of the American Revolution.

Nothing was more important in pre-Revolutionary New Hampshire politics than the rivalry between Massachusetts, England and New Hampshire. Massachusetts wanted the tax base of New Hampshire, and England wanted its masts. In addition, England was already concerned that the Massachusetts colony was too powerful. Through brilliant diplomacy the Wentworth clan and its representatives in England were able to establish a permanent border with Massachusetts in 1740. At the same time, they were able to enter into a relationship with Massachusetts

INSIDERS' TIP

Be sure to read the historical markers you see around the state. You'll find great historical detail about the immediate area. Typically a road sign will alert you to an upcoming marker, and often you'll find a place to pull off and park your car.

Waste not, want not: Yankee farmers used the rocks they pulled from fields to build stone walls. They lace the New Hampshire landscape to this day.

to fight as allies in the French and Indian War of 1754-63.

In addition to securing equality with Massachusetts, the Wentworths expanded their reign into present-day Vermont. The governing family extended the New Hampshire borders and increased the tax base for the colony, though these land grants were later the source of disputes solved by George Washington. Under Wentworth governance, a legal system and a system of taxation were established, and Dartmouth College was founded in 1769.

Revolutionary War

No Revolutionary War battles were fought in New Hampshire, but the state was quite active in supporting its fellow colonies. New Hampshire sent delegates to the first Continental Congress in Philadelphia in 1774. In the same year, 400 New Hampshire men attacked the British fort, Castle William and Mary at New Castle, stealing all of the fort's gunpowder. The next night they attacked again, stealing cannons and muskets. The bounty from these raids reduced the immediate gun power available to the British at the same time it provided the revolutionaries with weapons and ammunition for the newly formed militias. The last royal governor, John Wentworth II, knowing the jig was up, fled to Nova Scotia in June 1775, two months after the Battle of Lexington and Concord. That battle, on April 19, 1775, started the American Revolution.

As Wentworth fled the colony, John Stark, an experienced frontier fighter during the French and Indian War, emerged as New Hampshire's most important military leader. In 1775 Stark led more than 2,000 New Hampshire militiamen to Boston after the Battle of Lexington and Concord, and these men were a major force during the Battle of Bunker Hill.

In 1777 Stark was responsible for stopping the British at Bennington, Vermont, in one of the most important battles of the war. Stark's troops traveled by foot to Bennington and defeated the enemy, thus stopping the British attempt to cut New England from the other colonies. With this victory the Colonial troops gained confidence in their ability to defeat the better-armed British. Twenty years following the Battle of Bennington a celebratory reunion was held. Stark was unable to attend because of ill health, but he sent a toast, a portion of which — "Live Free Or Die" — is now the state motto.

In addition to leadership, the New Hampshire colony supplied the navy with at least 100 ships and 3,000 men. Many men were privateers using their own boats to intercept

Covered Bridges

Way before *The Bridges of Madison County* romanticized the covered bridge, New Hampshire appreciated its covered bridges as a unique bit of engineering history. Many of New Hampshire's original covered bridges have been repaired, restored or replaced. At one time at least 64 bridges were documented.

Close-up

The most frequently asked question about covered bridges is: Why were they covered? The hypotheses are more fun than the truth. One speculation is that bridges were covered to protect the wagon loads of hay, which, of course, makes no sense as the hay would have been exposed to the elements before and after crossing the bridge. This theory may have been inspired by the fact that the size of a bridge opening was based on the size of a wagon load of hay. Others like to think the bridges were covered to prevent horses from being spooked as they crossed the river.

The explanation closest to the truth is the bridges were covered to keep the snow off. Certainly the weight of the snow would have been a problem, and the roof protected the timbers from rotting. By reducing the exposure of the roadway to the weather, the bridge lasted longer.

Besides reducing the need for frequent repairs and replacements, New Hampshire's covered bridges had important social functions. They were a great place for advertisements — a sign discussing the virtues of the newest vitamin tonic or announcements of church socials and country fairs. And, of course, a covered bridge might have offered a couple a private place for a quick kiss.

The one pictured here is the Cornish-Windsor bridge over the Connecticut River in the Dartmouth-Lake Sunapee Region. At 460 feet, it's the longest wooden bridge in the country and the longest two-span covered bridge in the world. Like most covered bridges, it was originally a toll bridge. This bridge was heavily traveled at one time because Windsor, Vermont, was a temperance town and Cornish was not. Historical rumor has it that the toll to get into New Hampshire was less than the toll to get out. The state purchased the bridge in 1936, but the toll was not discontinued until 1943. The bridge was built in 1866 for $9,000.

Near the bridge you may see a sign for the "Bridge-Lady." The shop, which is inside a private home, is not open every day. If your timing is right and you catch it when it's open, you'll find postcards, T-shirts and bridge memorabilia. Chances are you'll be the only one on your block with such a unique souvenir.

You'll find covered bridges in every region. If you're interested in knowing more about the 51 surviving bridges (three additional

Photo: Tom McMillan

Covered bridges can be found along many of New Hampshire's roads.

bridges that were damaged by vandals are currently in various stages of reconstruction), you can order a copy of *New Hampshire's Covered Bridges: A Link With Our Past* from the New Hampshire Department of Transportation, P.O. Box 483, Concord, NH 03302, (603) 271-3344. The book is $15 plus shipping and handling charges.

British ships and create havoc in the supply lines. The warships included two built under the direction of John Paul Jones: the *Ranger* and the *America*.

In 1775-76 New Hampshire was the first state to write its own constitution to propose and adopt a government to replace that of the royal colony.

After the Revolution

New Hampshire was the ninth state to ratify the United States Constitution, in June 1788, thereby supplying the necessary two-thirds majority that put the document into effect. Before that, when the Revolutionary War ended in 1784, New Hampshire revised its own constitution to address problems facing the new state. One issue was finding a way to decentralize the political power that had been concentrated among the wealthy and those loyal to the royal governors. These concentrations of wealth and political power gave certain towns a great deal more authority than others. The early settlements of Portsmouth and Exeter, for example, had more sway in the assembly than the western towns along the Connecticut River.

Towns had been granted and settled by different factions. Some towns had developed relationships with Massachusetts because of shared religious convictions. Other towns were settled by former Massachusetts citizens eager to escape that Puritan-dominated colony. Towns along the Connecticut River resented the attempts of Portsmouth and Exeter to govern them. The revised constitution gave each town elected representation to the assembly, so the newest towns in the western part of the state now had a voice equal to that of Portsmouth or Exeter. To further appease the western towns, it was agreed that some legislative sessions would be held in Concord, a central location more convenient to most towns in the state. By 1808 the capital had been permanently established at Concord.

The state capitol was built from 1816-19, and it's the oldest capitol building in the United States in which a legislature meets. New Hampshire has the largest state legislature in the country, reminding us to this day that town government remains the key to New Hampshire government.

By the early 19th century, most of the land south of the White Mountains was under cultivation. The family farm was the strength of the economy, and the image of the self-sufficient, rock-wall building New Hampshire farmer was firmly established. The Seacoast Region had its heyday during the Colonial Era, but the Monadnock Region thrived in the early and mid-19th century. A number of churches and town halls were built during this time. Transportation was limited with few roads and bridges, and to some extent children stayed on the farm because there was nowhere else to go.

The railroad arrived about mid-century, opening up trade for farmers and manufacturers alike. Towns in the region flourished as the family farmer began to expand into small manufacturing. Glass factories were built in Keene and Stoddard. Some of the finest glass produced in the United States was made here from 1814-73. Sawmills and paper mills were built on many rivers. Small businesses specializing in cutlery and woodworking were prevalent throughout the region. As the railroad increased opportunities for commerce, it also increased the opportunity to leave home. Men began to go west where land was cheap. Women enjoyed the chance to earn money in the mills springing up along the major rivers. As much of the younger generation left the farms and pursued new opportunities, the local economies began to change.

A Brief Look at the Railroad

The first railroad was built in 1838 to connect Lowell, Massachusetts, and Nashua. In

1840 the state had 35 miles of railroad track. By 1870 it had increased to 900 miles. In 1874 at least 32 separate railroad lines were operating in the state. Each town had a small line that helped farmers get their goods to market. By 1890 the last of the independent lines was sold to the Boston and Maine Railroad. Known, with a bit of irony, as "the great corporation," the Boston and Maine succeeded in establishing a complete rail monopoly in the state by 1895. While the Boston and Maine Railroad was a dominant company, many said its "greatness" applied only to size, not deeds.

The Rise of Manufacturing

The rise in the importance of the mills changed the Merrimack Valley. The Amoskeag Mill opened in Manchester in 1830, and by 1850 it was one of the largest textile mills in the world. At its peak, the mill produced more than 500,000 yards of cloth per week. Along with the increased capacity came the need for more labor. Immigrants from Quebec and Europe settled here, bringing cultural diversity to the state as it changed from an agricultural and fishing economy to a manufacturing powerhouse. By 1919 the textile industry employed 439,000 people in New Hampshire. (For comparison, by 1954 the number employed was 172,000.)

New Hampshire was a strong supporter of the Union during the Civil War. Abraham Lincoln had visited the state several times before the 1860 elections (one of his sons attended St. Paul's School in Concord), and he easily won the state. New Hampshire sent more than 30,000 men to fight with the army. Equally important, the huge mills helped keep the northern forces supplied. Mills in Troy made the famous "New Hampshire" blankets that kept the Union horses warm in winter. In addition to clothing, the Amoskeag Mills retooled their foundries and supplied the Army with locomotives and rifles.

By the late 1800s New Hampshire was a major manufacturing state. The textile mills in Manchester employed more than two-thirds of the city's residents. The family farm was no longer the dominant lifestyle of the state. Manufactured goods were traded for food supplies, and self-sufficiency was no longer a practical ideal for most citizens. The railroad and the mills had changed the landscape.

The White Mountains and The North Country

Before the railroads, development in the northern part of the state was minimal. Darby Field was the first white man to climb Mount Washington in 1642, and it is assumed that he had Indian guides. Benning Wentworth gave land grants in the White Mountains to veterans of the French and Indian War, but the difficulty of the terrain as well as Indian inhabitants made settlements rare.

The Crawford family was one of the earliest arriving in 1791. Ethan Allen Crawford was born near Mount Washington in 1792. Later he and his father, Abel, built the first trail to the summit of Mount Washington. Ethan was the preeminent guide to Mount Washington. He led many scientists up the mountain so they could explore the unusual plant life. Along with the scientists came early tourists, eager to ascend the mountain.

By the mid-1850s completed railroad lines brought many tourists. Casual, boarding house accommodations gave way to grand European-style hotels. Mrs. Lincoln and two of her sons visited the White Mountains during the Civil War and took the new carriage road up Mount Washington. In 1876 the Appalachian Mountain Club (AMC) was begun,

INSIDERS' TIP

Cemeteries are interesting places to get a sociological view of an area. Look for dominant family names and notice life spans of the period. Follow up your graveside research with a visit to the local historical museum or public library.

and to this day its members are perhaps the most important caretakers and guides to the White Mountains.

Until 1867 more than 172,000 acres in the northern region had been owned by the state. In that year Governor Harriman sold this acreage to landowners and speculators for $25,000 (less than $7 an acre). Major railroads were built, and wholesale logging began. The timing was perfect since after the Civil War demand for timber was high. And in the 1880s a process for reducing wood to pulp was developed, greatly increasing the end-products for timber.

The town of Berlin, on the Androscoggin River, was a center for logging. The river provided water power as well as a means of transporting logs to a processing point. Between 1867 and 1904 virtually all woodland in the northern area was logged. The forests of the northern part of the state were ground zero for the logging and paper industries. Fortunes were made as the forests were cleared.

The 20th Century

By 1900 tourism was bringing about $700,000 a year to the state. At the same time the forests, which were part of the prime tourist area in the White Mountains, were being destroyed. The Society for the Protection of New Hampshire Forests formed in 1901 to organize and coordinate efforts to protect one of the state's greatest natural resources. The group remains active today. In 1997 they helped local homeowners in Milford stop development on land with historical significance.

Perhaps the most important federal legislation in New Hampshire history was the Weeks Act in 1911. This stroke of the pen created the White Mountain National Forest. Besides helping to conserve more than 700,000 acres for public use, the Weeks Act motivated local and state groups to set aside green places throughout the state. New Hampshire's state park system is a legacy of the work of early conservationists. The state economy is also a beneficiary of the Weeks Act: Tourism is a steady source of revenue for the state, and many small businesses depend on tourists for survival.

Manufacturing was the overwhelmingly dominant force of the economy early in the century. The Amoskeag Mill reigned until the 1920s when an extended strike began the decline that culminated in bankruptcy in 1936. Cheaper manufacturing facilities in the south as well as changes in fashion — shorter skirts and fewer petticoats — doomed much of the state's textile industry. The lumber industry was also hard hit in the '20s and '30s, and New Hampshire suffered with the rest of the nation during the Depression.

The United States' entry into World War II in December 1941 was the beginning of a resurgence of manufacturing in the state. The Portsmouth Naval Yard built ships to replace those destroyed at Pearl Harbor, and textile mills made everything from blankets to cloth for armed forces uniforms. The demand for paper was strong during the war years, which was good for the logging industry in the north country.

Tourism flourished in the 1950s. New Hampshire benefited from the postwar boom in automobile sales as lots of Americans bought cars, and the country began spending a lot of money on interstate highways. And it was in 1952 that New Hampshire began to gain national publicity by having the "first in the nation" presidential primary. Without question, the 45 years of national press coverage (every four years) is as important to tourism as our natural resources. Every four years the virtues, quirks, charms and independence of New Hampshire and its citizens are front-page and prime-time news.

The newest state industry is skiing. Along

INSIDERS' TIP

***New Hampshire, Crosscurrents in Its Development,* by Nancy Coffey Heffernan and Ann Page Stecker, is a great short history of the state. It is published by University Press of New England and available in local bookstores.**

The house of John Stark is located in Dunbarton, New Hampshire.

with fall foliage and New England charm, skiing forms the base of the important business of tourism. Tourism is particularly important because New Hampshire is the only state with neither an income tax nor a sales tax. Instead of broad-based taxes, this state depends on specific taxes such as restaurant and lodging taxes and taxes on liquor and cigarettes. As an additional revenue-raiser, the first state lottery was begun in 1964. The tax issues facing New Hampshire are among the biggest issues affecting our journey into the next century, and it's hard to spend a day here without hearing a debate on one of the various tax issues.

Looking Ahead

In 1996 New Hampshire elected its first woman governor, Jeanne Shaheen, a moderate Democrat in an overwhelmingly Republican state. Most of the questions facing her and the state revolve around taxes. In 1997 our system of school funding was declared unconstitutional by the New Hampshire Supreme Court. The current plan, in which local school funding comes from local property taxes, will have to be revamped. Our legislators and educational leaders are searching for creative answers, but for now the ideas are limited to funding schools through increased gambling revenues and an ever-rising cigarette tax. The new state-funded kindergarten program already depends on increases in the cigarette tax. In March of 1998 the un-heard of happened: by a 4-vote margin, the New Hampshire House passed an income tax. But the Senate couldn't agree, and the governor promised to veto it, so the search for a "no-broad-based tax" solution goes on. New Hampshire will certainly test the limits of user taxes in the coming century if its politicians continue to reject broad-based taxes as a source of revenue.

Another question facing the state is whether the town meeting will survive into the

21st century. Prior to 1997 most communities decided local issues at town meetings. Theoretically all residents would attend, issues (such as zoning and road maintenance) would be presented and discussed and then put to a vote. But beginning in 1997, towns began to have the option to choose ballot voting separate from the presentation-and-discussion meeting. You no longer had to attend the meeting in order to vote. Some towns retained the town meeting, and others have decided to try separating the vote from the meeting. Besides being a question about how we govern ourselves, the town meeting issue threatens to draw a line between newcomers and natives. The majority of residents are now believed to have been born outside the state. Although newcomers love the lack of taxes, they have not as a group shown much respect for the traditions of the state they call home. Many feel the annual town meeting is an old-fashioned, anachronistic way to decide town issues. On the other side, no tradition is more ingrained and more valuable, many think, than town meetings. How we vote and in what venue we vote is the key to life in New Hampshire in the next century.

The busiest season for lodging in New Hampshire is from the Fourth of July through mid- to late October.

Hotels and Motels

New Hampshire has been a tourist mecca since the early 19th century. An excursion to Mount Washington and the White Mountains was a formidable but popular vacation by the 1830s. The wealthier residents of Boston traveled to New Hampshire by horse-drawn carriage to escape the sweltering city heat. Trains extended the invitation to even more people, but it was the automobile that really opened the door. In addition to the White Mountains region, New Hampshire's Seacoast and Lakes regions were within easy driving distance of the country's largest metropolitan areas, and people came in droves. You'll find literally dozens of motels and cottages in all of our waterfront communities. If we covered all of the options, you would not be able to lift this book! Add the recent development of hotels catering to the corporate guest, and you can imagine how severely we have had to cull our list. So be aware that this is only a sampling of what New Hampshire has to offer.

If these places are filled, ask for recommendations of other, similar accommodations. New Hampshire's innkeepers are very happy to make referrals.

Because of the number and variety of overnight accommodations, we've devoted three chapters to the subject. This chapter features just a fraction of our many hotels and motels. Bed and Breakfasts and Country Inns are covered in our chapter by that name. For stays of a week or longer, be sure and check our Vacation Rentals chapter.

Most of our hotels are open year round, as are more and more of the motels. In the Lakes Region and Seacoast, some motels close for two to six months during the winter. If they're consistent, we've told you — but it's not uncommon for someone to decide "this year we were open, next year we're closing," or to take a month off one year and three the next. The "down time" in the White Mountains region is around November, when the leaves have fallen but the snow hasn't; and late April through mid-May, which marks the transition from snow-related adventures to summer fun. In the Great North Woods there are fewer accommodations but since they cater to outdoor sports enthusiasts their schedules follow the hunting and fishing seasons (see the Hunting and Fishing chapter for details).

The busiest season for lodging across New Hampshire is from the Fourth of July through mid- to late October. The Seacoast peak season begins in June and continues through early October. Other peaks include Christmas and New Year's and the school vacation weeks in February and April. And during winter, especially if there's lots of snow, the accommodations near the ski resorts are more likely to be full. Always make advance reservations to guarantee a room. The slower months are usually November and late April through mid-May, when instead of finding a motel with no vacancy, you're more likely to find a place closed for a week while the owners take a quick break in Florida. Again, call ahead to avoid problems. Many accommodations require a minimum stay during their busy times. This may be anything from two nights in a motel to a week in a cottage.

Price Code

In this chapter we've used the following guide for showing the cost of a one-night stay for two people during that location's high season. In addition to the room rate, you will pay an 8 percent New Hampshire Rooms and Meals tax. Some resorts may also add a flat rate to cover all gratuities.

$	**less than $75**
$$	**$75 to $150**
$$$	**$150 to $225**
$$$$	**more than $225**

You should always ask what is included in your room rate, such as meals and other food services or free access to athletic and fitness facilities. Often you will have a choice of plans or package deals with ski areas or attractions that we don't have room to detail.

Unless otherwise indicated, you should assume that pets are not allowed; smoking is allowed in at least some area, if not indoors then outside; and major credit cards are accepted. Note, too, that not all New Hampshire accommodations are handicapped-accessible, so be sure to ask about that if it's important to you. Remember that policies are always subject to change, so be sure you ask for details when calling for reservations. Nearly all hotels and motels have color TVs and cable in every room. We've noted exceptions, but if it's crucial to your trip, be sure and verify these entertainment options when you make your plans.

Merrimack Valley Region

Hill-Brook Motel

$ • 250 N.H. Rt. 101, Bedford
• (603) 472-3788

This simple, traditional motel offers a friendly welcome to travelers headed west from Manchester. The 18 air-conditioned rooms have one or two double beds, a desk and chair and optional kitchenettes, which may be rented by the week (there's a grocery store just down the street).

Sheraton Tara Wayfarer Inn

$$ • 121 S. River Rd., Bedford
• (603) 622-3766, (800) THE-TARA

If the distinctive covered bridge and waterfall at the Wayfarer look familiar, you've probably seen them behind dozens of TV reporters during the New Hampshire Presidential Primary. This hotel and convention center just outside of Manchester has housed more than its share of candidates. It's a much more suburban setting than the camera shots indicate, very convenient to both N.H. Route 101 and Interstate 93. The 194 rooms feature individual climate control and room service. The Wayfarer offers a health and fitness center along with indoor and outdoor pools. The Wayfarer Restaurant and Quackers Lounge will please almost every palate (see our Restaurants chapter).

Days Inn of Nashua-Hudson

$ • 90 Derry St., Hudson
• (603) 880-1700

This Days Inn is centrally located just across the bridge from downtown Nashua and only 10 minutes from the farmland of Litchfield. It offers free continental breakfast. Some efficiency units are available. Rooms have double beds, easy chairs and big TVs. Free HBO is available for guests.

Concord Comfort Inn

$$ • 71 Hall St., Concord
• (603) 226-4100, (800) 228-5150

Just off I-93, the new Comfort Inn in Concord offers basic hotel service and convenience. Guests enjoy complimentary continental breakfast and newspapers each morning. Indoor corridors connect all 100 rooms to the indoor pool, hot tub and sauna as well as the laundry facilities. The Comfort Inn also runs an airport shuttle for the convenience of its guests. Pets are welcome.

Center of New Hampshire-Holiday Inn

$$ • 700 Elm St., Manchester
• (603) 625-1000

This hotel and conference center in the heart of downtown Manchester has become a landmark, with its distinctive logo visible from the Granite Street bridge as you ap-

INSIDERS' TIP

Weirs Beach and Hampton Beach are distinctive for their resort atmosphere and densely packed vacation-oriented development. Neither one is a separate town, though merchants tend to use them as addresses for clarity. Legally, The Weirs is part of Laconia and Hampton Beach is part of Hampton.

proach the city. The hotel offers 250 executive and luxury guest rooms as well as a restaurant and lounge, a fitness center (including a whirlpool, sauna and indoor pool), and a huge banquet room that hosts every kind of gathering from presidential candidates' election-night bashes to the Farm and Forest Exhibition (see our Annual Events chapter). Perhaps as important as accommodating your body in this downtown location is accommodating your car. The hotel offers validated free parking in the attached parking garage.

Super 8 Motel

$ • 2301 Brown Ave., Manchester
• (603) 623-0883, (800) 800-8000

Sometimes you just want a clean place to stay, especially after you've been on too many airplanes. The Super 8 in Manchester is just four minutes from the airport. The 85 rooms are basic with cable TV, rental movies and phones. Most have two double beds and room for a cot or roll-away. The Executive King single rooms feature a recliner. Some suites have whirlpool baths. There is free continental breakfast and a coffee shop on-site.

The Highlander Inn at the Airport

$$ • 2 Highlander Way, Manchester
• (603) 625-6426, (800) 548-9248

This luxurious hotel and conference center is right at the airport, but you would never take it for an airport hotel. Set away from the main road on a beautifully landscaped site, the inn feels like it's out in the country. The comfortable elegance begins with the fireplace in the lobby and carries throughout the facility, with gracious furnishings in each of the 65 rooms, including desks with lots of work space and a large sitting area. Restful views and a full-service restaurant complete your afterwork or preflight stay.

Sheraton Four Points

$$ • 55 John E. Devine Dr., Manchester
• (603) 668-6110, (800) 325-3535

Purchased by Sheraton and renovated in 1997, this Four Points hotel is conveniently located just off N.H. 101 and S. Willow Road in the heart of Manchester's busiest commercial area. It's only 3 miles from the Manchester airport, to which the hotel offers complimentary transportation. Spacious rooms include a desk with room to work and a dataport for your computer. After work, an indoor pool and whirlpool will help you relax, or stretch your muscles at the workout club and wellness center. The restaurant and lounge feature New Hampshire-brewed Nutfield Ales.

The Fairfield Inn

$ • 4 Amherst Rd., Merrimack
• (603) 424-7500, (800) 228-2800

You're probably familiar with Marriott's

Fairfield Inns. The Merrimack hotel is just off the Everett Turnpike section of U.S. Route 3 at Exit 11, almost equidistant from Nashua and Manchester. All the guest rooms and suites have been decorated in a turn-of-the-century decor to give you a "welcome to New Hampshire" feeling. The rooms have cable TV, phone and dataports and a large work desk for business travelers. Children are welcome and stay for free, which along with free continental breakfast makes this a family bargain. An outdoor heated pool is a nice touch for business-weary travelers.

Merrimack Hotel & Conference Center

$$ • 4 Executive Park Dr., Merrimack • (603) 424-8000

Just off the Everett Turnpike at Exit 11, this full-service hotel offers 200 deluxe rooms and three parlor suites. Each can easily accommodate up to a family of five or a pair of business travelers. The hotel is conveniently located halfway between Nashua and Manchester. Eat in the restaurant, McGaw's Tavern, or take advantage of room service. The hotel offers an indoor pool and a health club with a whirlpool and steam room. Or step outside to enjoy the walking trails, horseshoes and other outside activities. The grand ballroom can be divided into three smaller banquet or meeting spaces, and the training center offers all the audiovisual equipment a corporate presentation could need. A pine grove and courtyard barbecue can also be reserved for functions.

Crowne Plaza

$$$ • 2 Somerset Pkwy., Nashua • (603) 886-1200, (800) 9-NASHUA

As you approach the Crowne Plaza from the highway, the first thing you'll notice is the birds. The palace motif is extended outdoors with a small pond/moat surrounded by grass, and the ducks just love it. Indoors it's elegant, too, with lovely sitting rooms downstairs and 213 large graciously furnished guest rooms upstairs. There are 12 suites on the concierge floor for even more luxurious treatment. The hotel has a full health club with indoor pool and sauna as well as a ballroom, amphitheater and every amenity a business traveler might need. Two restaurants, Speaker's Corner and The Chicago Steak Room, offer a variety of food and drink in casual and semi-formal settings (see our Restaurants chapter). There's a parking garage, which is nice in snow, but it's quite short — the 6-foot, 8-inch clearance wouldn't accommodate our van. Fortunately, there is open parking between the pond and the restaurant too. In the fall of 1998 the Crowne Plaza opened 20 extended-stay suites. Each has a kitchenette and two phone lines, and is designed to accommodate business travelers on two-to-three week stopovers, but with separate living rooms and bedrooms and two television sets each, these suites will be popular with families as well.

Howard Johnson Motor Lodge

$$ • 170 Main Dunstable Rd., Nashua • (603) 889-0173, (800) I-GO-HOJO

Just off U.S. Route 3 at Exit 5, this is Howard Johnson's the way it used to be. The 72 rooms on two floors offer basic comfort. Each can accommodate up to five guests (two double beds and a cot). There is free coffee service in the new lobby, and the lodge has an indoor pool. The restaurant and lounge are clean and popular with local people as well as guests.

Nashua Marriott

$$-$$$ • 2200 Southwood Dr., Nashua • (603) 880-9100, (800) 228-9290

You can see this hotel from U.S. 3, but once you get to it you won't feel close to the

INSIDERS' TIP

We are listing only street addresses for our accommodations. Mailing addresses are often different from street addresses, sometimes even in different towns. Please check with your host when you call for reservations.

highway. In fact, the builders managed to make the site feel secluded, although its location at Exit 8 puts it right next to one of the busiest commercial sections of the city. The newly renovated hotel has 241 guest rooms and three suites on the concierge level. The health club features basketball courts along with the indoor pool and whirlpool. A jogging or hiking trail through the woods takes advantage of the hotel's edge-of-town location. Pets are welcome. The restaurant serves three meals daily in a casual atmosphere at Allie's American Bar and Grille, and the facility offers more than 10,000 square feet of meeting space for functions and conferences.

Red Roof Inn

$-$$ • 77 Spit Brook Rd., Nashua
• (603) 888-1893

This hotel couldn't be more conveniently located, just off U.S. 3 when you cross the border from Massachusetts into New Hampshire and within a mile of the biggest shopping district in the state. Rooms offer extra-long full-size beds or king-size beds, free cable TV with Showtime, local phone calls and a newspaper. Business travelers are pleased to learn that fax and photocopy services are available and that each king room includes a large desk, speaker phone and a modem jack. Vacationers will be glad to know that small pets are welcome. The kids like the available video games. And everyone enjoys the complimentary morning coffee.

Red Roof Inn

$ • 15 Red Roof Ln., Salem
• (603) 898-6422, (800) THE ROOF

Just off I-93, the Red Roof offers basic accommodations for the family or business traveler. This hotel, built in 1987, offers 108 rooms, with a variety of accommodations. A business traveler choosing this spot for its proximity to the interstate might prefer a Business King room, equipped with a dataport, while families visiting nearby Canobie Lake Park and America's Stonehenge may request roll-aways and cribs. Pets are welcome.

INSIDERS' TIP

U.S. Rt. 1 and 1A run right along the ocean from the Massachusetts line to the mouth of the Piscataqua River. It is called Ocean Boulevard in all the coastal towns (Seabrook, Hampton and Rye) but the street numbers start over when you cross town lines. And while the numbers run north to south in Rye, they run south to north in the other towns.

Sheraton Tara

$$ • Tara Blvd., Nashua
• (603) 888-9970, (800) 325-3535

This is one of the Tara's Castle Hotels, and it's a very impressive sight as you come up U.S. 3 across the border from Massachusetts. Flags flutter from turrets on the hilltop castle, which sits above a reflective pond on a 16-acre landscaped site. Rooms are large enough to accommodate families or business travelers. Guests in the 330 rooms and deluxe suites may take advantage of a complete health club that offers aerobics classes and massage therapy. The Tara has both indoor and outdoor pools, tennis courts and a choice of an elegant restaurant, a casual pub, light dining in the lounge or room service.

Seacoast Region

Ashworth by the Sea

$$-$$$ • 295 Ocean Blvd., Hampton Beach
• (603) 926-6762, (800) 345-6736

Ashworth is an elegant hotel in the old-fashioned style, welcoming visitors back to a day when summers at the beach were relaxed and rewarding. This year-round resort is right in the heart of the Hampton Beach area, so the valet parking is a great amenity. Rooms are large and attractively furnished, each with queen- or king-size or two double beds, a sitting area with comfortable chairs for reading and spacious wardrobes. Cribs or cots are available to rent. All rooms have great ocean views. Sit on your private balcony and look out across the white sand to the crashing waves or enjoy a swim in the indoor or outdoor pool. The three restaurants will suit any dining mood, and there is nightly entertainment in the Breakers Lounge.

Jonathan's Motel

$$ • 415 Ocean Blvd., Hampton Beach
• (603) 926-6631, (800) 634-8243

Ocean Boulevard is the main drag in Hampton Beach, and Jonathan's is close enough to walk to all the attractions but far enough out that you don't have to listen to them all night! Each unit has double beds, a kitchenette and a balcony. Coffee and pastry are provided. There's on-site parking, a plus because of the beach crowds.

Comfort Inn at Yoken's

$$ • 1390 Lafayette Rd., Portsmouth
• (603) 433-3338, (800) 228-5150

Yoken's has been a landmark on U.S. Route 1 since the glory days before the interstate highways were built (see our Restaurants chapter). Now this full-service hotel makes it a place to stay as well. Just south of all of Portsmouth's historical and cultural sites, the Comfort Inn offers 121 rooms, an indoor pool and fitness center and complimentary extended continental breakfast with fresh fruit and toast.

Hampton House Hotel

$$$ • 333 Ocean Blvd., Hampton Beach • (603) 926-1033, (800) 458-7058

This hotel looks plain on the outside, but indoors you'll be treated to comfortable luxury. The rooms are spacious, with double or king-size beds, refrigerators and air conditioning. Suites have separate sitting areas. Each room has a private balcony with a view of the ocean. Vacationers and business travelers alike will appreciate the free coffee or hot chocolate and muffins in the morning and direct-dial phones. The game room appeals to kids, while the gift shop or meeting rooms may be of more interest to adult travelers. The hotel has its own parking area, which is monitored so you don't have to worry about your car. Hampton House is right in the middle of the Hampton Beach "strip," so all the great attractions are within easy walking distance of your room.

Atlantic Motel

$$-$$$ • 391 Ocean Blvd., Hampton Beach • (603) 929-1416

This motel, right on the strip at Hampton Beach, is one of the few facilities on the water that's open year round. If you're coming in the off-season, ask about their wonderful discounts and package deals. Rooms offer either two double beds or queen- or king-size beds, and each has a kitchenette, cable TV and air conditioning. Some have a private balcony, and there are oceanfront balconies on each floor for all guests to enjoy. The motel has private, off-street parking for guests and a heated outdoor pool if the ocean's too cold or the beach too crowded for you.

The Seascape Inn at Plaice Cove

$$ • 955 Ocean Blvd., Hampton • (603) 926-1750

This is one of the prettiest motels on the

INSIDERS' TIP

Schools in New England usually have one-week vacations in both February and April. Keep this in mind as you make your travel plans. Hotels and motels fill up early during these periods, as do airline seats and airport parking lots.

crowded beach road, with fresh white paint and flowers around the gazebo. The 19 recently renovated rooms, on two floors, are clean and comfortable. Each has a refrigerator so you can pack a picnic for the beach. Colorful linens bring the fresh summer sunshine indoors. Guests enjoy fresh coffee and baked goodies along with a complimentary newspaper in the morning, and beach privileges mean they can head for the sun and surf directly across the street. No smoking is allowed indoors. The Seascape is open mid-April to mid-October.

The Anchorage Inn

$$ • 417 Woodbury Ave., Portsmouth • (603) 431-8111, (800) 370-8111

Just off Interstate 95, this motel offers a choice of double rooms or suites, which have private whirlpools. Double rooms are plain but have a sitting area and room for a cot. Other rooms offer a king-size bed or an extra-long double bed. Suites are large, with a fully furnished living room and dining area in each (but no kitchen, only a wet bar). There's a pool, fitness center and sauna, and a complimentary continental breakfast is served from 7 to 10 AM. Pets are allowed in one section of the motel but must not be left unattended.

Howard Johnson Hotel

$$ • Interstate Traffic Cir., Portsmouth • (603) 436-7600, (800) I-GO-HOJO

Convenient and comfortable, this three-story hotel provides 135 rooms, a 24-hour restaurant with room service, a cocktail lounge and gift shop. There's also an indoor and an outdoor pool, exercise room and hot tub. Much of the hotel was renovated in 1997. Portsmouth and the Seacoast are just minutes away.

Meadowbrook Inn

$$ • Interstate Traffic Cir., Portsmouth • (603) 436-2700, (800) 370-2727

The newly renovated Meadowbrook looks like a motel on the outside but offers hotel-style services to guests in its 122 large rooms. Rooms are available with double beds or king-size beds and have plenty of room to spread out. Direct-dial phones and cable TV make your stay easier. It has an outdoor pool for use in-season, a fitness center, sports bar, lounge and valet laundry service. Kids younger than 12 can stay free with their parents and enjoy the complimentary breakfast.

Sheraton Harborside Portsmouth Hotel and Conference Center

$$ • 250 Market St., Portsmouth • (603) 431-2300 • (800) 325-3535

If you want to stay in a modern facility in the historic district, consider this full-service hotel. With 148 rooms and 20 condo-suites, the Sheraton can accommodate virtually anyone. Guests can enjoy the indoor pool and exercise room (if you're not exercised enough by walking all over old Portsmouth) and relax in the sauna. Two restaurants and two lounges featuring nightly entertainment round out the hotel's offering. (See our Restaurants chapter for details about the award-winning Harbor's Edge Restaurant.)

Susse Chalet

$-$$ • 650 Borthwick Ave. Ext., Portsmouth • (603) 436-6363, (800) 5-CHALET

Off the U.S. 1 Bypass, the Susse Chalet is a basic, comfortable accommodation with one or two double beds in each room. They offer free HBO and free local phone calls. Enjoy your free continental breakfast before you head out for the day and a dip in the outdoor pool when you return.

Anchorage Inn

$-$$ • N.H. Rt. 125, Rochester • (603) 332-3350

Halfway between the Seacoast and the Lakes, and immediately off the Spaulding Turnpike at Exit 12, the Anchorage Inn at

INSIDERS' TIP

A fully furnished kitchen doesn't do much good if there's no grocery store within 30 miles. Ask about the availability of supplies when you make your reservation.

Mount Washington Hotel

Close-up

New Hampshire native Joseph Stickney of Concord was the original owner as well as visionary who built the Mount Washington Hotel. Unfortunately, he died within a year of the 1902 opening, leaving ownership to his wife, Carolyn. She owned the hotel until her death in 1931. (The Princess Lounge, formerly Mrs. Stickney's private dining room, is so named because the widow married a French prince after her first husband's death.)

In the early days of the hotel, millionaires came for the summer. Mrs. Cornelius Vanderbilt stayed here, as did Thomas Edison and Babe Ruth. Bretton Woods, while not an incorporated town, has its own full-service U.S. Post Office. The resort even had a private train station, which is now Fabyan's Station Restaurant. The hotel was closed during World War II from the fall of 1942 until the summer of 1944. At that time it was chosen by President Franklin Roosevelt to house more than 700 delegates from 44 countries for the 21-day International Monetary Conference. The conference is now referred to as "Bretton Woods." Thanks to the conference, the hotel received a much-needed sprucing up — repainting, repairs of leaks and structural damage — as well as lots of international and national publicity. It was declared a National Historic Landmark in 1986.

Photo: Mount Washington Hotel and Resort

The Mount Washington Hotel and Resort is a luxury resort in the White Mountains region.

After the resort passed through a series of owners since the 1944 conference, the FDIC (owners after a savings and loan failure in 1989 resulted in foreclosure) sold the property to a local business group in 1991. So far, so good. Again the hotel has been painted and replumbed. Again families are discovering the convenience and ease of having everything in one place. It's not easy to run a luxury, high maintenance bit of history. But it's very easy to get used to staying at one. Think of it as your bit of historical re-enactment. For details about how the Mount Washington Hotel pampers guests today, see our write-up in this chapter under the White Mountains and Great North Woods Regions.

Rochester is a convenient stopover for people vacationing in the Granite State. The newly renovated motel has an outdoor pool and offers free continental breakfast to guests in the lobby/breakfast room. Efficiency units with kitchenettes are also available for longer-term rentals. Two double beds in most rooms and a sitting area that points the TV away from the beds make this a good family motel.

Best Western Seabrook Inn

$-$$ • corner of Strand Rd. and N.H. Rt. 107, Seabrook
• (603) 474-3078

This reasonably priced motel bills itself as a family resort, and they're not exaggerating. In addition to clean, comfortable rooms and a big complimentary breakfast, your kids will enjoy a seasonal petting farm with pony rides, a moonwalk, water slides and an outdoor heated pool and kiddie pool. They'll never want to leave, but with Hampton Beach and the seacoast just minutes away, you'll have to tell them they can drive the race cars when you get back.

Hampshire Inn and Conference Center

$$ • N.H. Rt. 107, Seabrook
• (603) 474-5700, (800) 932-8520

Every one of the 35 units in this facility is a luxury suite, decorated by the interior designer who was a former owner of the property. Suites feature queen-size beds and include microwave ovens, refrigerators and wet bars. Each room has a sitting area or separate sitting room, and some have private whirlpool baths. Corporate travelers appreciate the three conference rooms on site as well as the availability of fax service. Tourists and weekend-getaway guests like the convenient location and easy access to the beaches and attractions of the Seacoast. Everyone benefits from the fitness room, with its state-of-the-art workout equipment, indoor heated pool and welcoming spa. Continental breakfast is offered every day and includes fruit and cereal as well as muffins, pastries and bagels. Weekend-getaway packages in the off-season include meals at local restaurants.

Lakes Region

Sandy Point Beach Resort

$$ • N.H. Rt. 11, Alton Bay
• (603) 875-6000

Right at the point at the south end of Lake Winnipesaukee, Alton Bay sits at the junction of N.H. routes 28 and 11. At the north edge of the village, on a point of land curving out into the lake, the Sandy Point resort offers vacationers a range of accommodations for every kind of visit from May 1 until October 15. Guests enjoy the private beach, boating and fishing (dock rental at a nominal charge), basketball and horseshoes as well as a variety of indoor games. Motel rooms are all nonsmoking. Each motel room has two double or queen beds and cable TV. Some have air conditioning or refrigerators. (See our Vacation Rentals chapter for information on longer-term rentals.)

The Boulders Motel and Cottages

$-$$ • U.S. Rt. 3, Holderness
• (603) 968-3600, (800) 968-3601

The Boulders is the last motel left on Squam Lake. Virtually unchanged since the 1950s, it is now run by the second family to own it. When we visited, Paige Sandy (isn't that a great name for a lakefront innkeeper?) told us their guests always comment on the solid comfort of the original furnishings in the motel rooms and efficiency units. With 600 feet of shoreline, 100 feet of it a sandy beach, the Boulders is able to rent docks and moorings for guests' boats or rowboats and a canoe if you don't have your own craft. Units are not air conditioned, but the cross-ventilation and proximity of the lake make them pleasantly cool and comfortable. Guest rooms have televisions but no phones — you're supposed to be on vacation, remember? The motel is closed during the winter months. Actual opening and closing dates are flexible as the family lives here. (See our Vacation Rentals chapter for details about the cottages here.)

The Meadows Lakeside Lodging

$$ • N.H. Rt. 25, Center Harbor
• (603) 253-4347

With the "big lake" (Winnipesaukee) literally 15 steps from the door of this comfortable motel, a pool would be truly redundant. There is no cable TV, but the kids will love the

INSIDERS' TIP

Squam Lake is controlled by the Squam Lakes Association, which restricts development and enforces a 7.5 horsepower maximum on motorized craft. Squam and several other small lakes have no public access except for guests at those accommodations that have beachfront.

sandy beach and the nice town-operated playground right next door. Bring your boat and use the docks or moorings, or tour the Lakes Region and the White Mountains from this convenient location. Efficiency units with kitchenettes are especially family-friendly, and the owners welcome your pets for a small additional fee. The 39 rooms offer several combinations of double, twin and queen-sized beds. Some have patios or fireplaces. A few do not have phones. There's free coffee for guests in the morning.

Comfort Inn

$-$$ • West St., Ashland
• (603) 968-7668, (800) 228-5150

This hotel is conveniently located just off I-93 at the north end of the Lakes Region. Guests in the 41 rooms enjoy a free complimentary breakfast. The hotel has a game room, and there is an outdoor heated pool in season. Ashland is very close to both Plymouth (college town) and Holderness (boarding school), so be aware that special-events weekends may be surprisingly busy here. Rooms have one or two double beds and plenty of room for a family.

Misty Harbour Barefoot Beach Resort

$$-$$$ • N.H. Rt. 11B, Gilford
• (603) 293-4500, (800) 33MISTY

We first heard about this place from a friend whose father stayed here and raved about it. He described it as "just a little motel right on the street." It must have been dark when he checked in. There's a huge complex here, with luxurious suites and elegant motel units up the hill by the pool as well as the suites right on the beach. Lakeside suites also have private whirlpool baths, but everyone can enjoy the indoor and outdoor pools, sauna and whirlpool, game room, basketball court and lighted tennis court. A fleet of watercraft from canoes to Jet Skis is available to rent.

B. Mae's Resort Inn

$$ • 17 Harris Shore Rd., Gilford
• (603) 293-7526, (800) 458-3877

B. Mae's sits at the junction of N.H. 11 and 11B in a quiet corner of this busy region, but it has a lot to offer the traveler who finds it (and lots of signs to make it easier for you). In summer a two-night minimum stay is required for any of their variety of rooms and full-kitchen suites. The rooms are large and have two double or queen-size beds or one king-size bed. Every room has cable TV and a private deck. Suites add a sleeper sofa in the living room and a VCR. Swim in the indoor and outdoor pools or take advantage of the weight room and whirlpool. Walk to the beach and marina nearby. There's never a shortage of things to do in the Lakes Region. Children younger than 12 stay free with their families. Two great restaurants right next door make meals a breeze and offer live entertainment on weekends (see our Restaurants and Nightlife chapters for information on B. Mae's Eating and Drinking Establishments).

Landmark Inn of the Lake Region

$-$$ • 480 Main St., Laconia
• (603) 524-8000

The Landmark Inn recently purchased and renovated this old seven-story hotel in downtown Laconia. It's lovely inside, with a pleasant lobby/atrium where guests enjoy a complimentary continental breakfast. The rooms are attractive, each with two double or one king-size bed and a comfortable sitting area for reading or watching TV, and there are beautiful function rooms. The town of Laconia has been sprucing up recently and has an excellent shopping/dining area that's a five-minute walk from the Landmark Inn. In order to make the town as pedestrian-friendly as possible, officials created a one-way loop that is a bit tricky to negotiate. The easy entrance to the Landmark is from Rowe Court, which turns off U.S. Business Route 3 and runs behind Winnesquam Printing and Copying. If you miss it, go right through the shopping district, follow the loop around and it will bring you right back!

White Oak Motel and Lakefront Cottages

$-$$ • U.S. Rt. 3, Holderness
• (603) 968-3673

A variety of motel rooms, cottages (lakeview or poolside) and even a mobile home are available to rent at this friendly spot.

The McHughs serve free continental breakfast and have boats you can use if you don't bring your own. They have a large outdoor pool and an indoor whirlpool. Guests can use the phone in the office, and pets are welcome except during the busiest part of the summer (mid-July to mid-August). See our Vacation Rentals chapter for more about White Oak's cottages.

Christmas Island Resort

$-$$ • 630 Weirs Blvd., Laconia
• (603) 366-4378

The motel and efficiency apartments are comfortable, offering a choice of one king-size bed, two queen-size or doubles, or a double bed and a twin. Each efficiency unit has a kitchen and living room with separate bedrooms. What really sets this place apart is its location. It's right on the lake, with more than 1,000 feet of private frontage that encompasses two beaches and a boat dock and launch. Rowboats and paddleboats are available for guests who don't bring their own. In winter the Christmas Island caters to skiers and snowmobilers since it's just minutes from Gunstock and has direct access to two snowmobile corridors. The heated indoor pool, saunas and whirlpool are most welcome in winter too. The Christmas Island Steakhouse and North Pole Tavern are right next door (see our Restaurants chapter).

Lord Hampshire Motel and Cottages

$$ • 885 Laconia Rd., Winnisquam
• (603) 524-4331

We're not sure who Lord Hampshire is supposed to be, but since 1946 his top-hatted silhouette has welcomed people to this delightful combination of roadside motel and lakeside cottages. The motel rooms all have wonderful screened porches looking over the lake and optional kitchenettes (they're tucked behind a door which can be opened if you want to cook or left locked if you don't) which left us contemplating the joys of supper in the breeze. Motel rooms have air conditioning. If you want a phone the owners will hook one up at your bedside. There's more than 600 feet of lake frontage for swimming, boating and fishing. Rental boats are available, as is a limited amount of dock space for guests' boats. Children love the gently sloping private beach, giant sandbox and gymset. Lord Hampshire has cottages available for longer stays; see our Vacation Rentals chapter for details.

Barton's Motel

$$ • 1330 Union Ave., Laconia
• (603) 524-5674

Barton's is a family-friendly motel, operated by the same family since 1938! Two one-story buildings house motel rooms and efficiency units, each with two double beds, and several pretty two-bedroom housekeeping cottages (for a four-night minimum stay) surround a lovely outdoor heated pool. Guests can take advantage of 500 feet of private sandy beach on Lake Winnipesaukee, with a gentle slope perfect for small swimmers. Lawn chairs and picnic tables will tempt you to stay right here, but the attractions of the Lakes Region are close by, so you'll have to divide your time between activity and relaxation.

The Margate on Winnipesaukee

$$-$$$ • 76 Lake St., Laconia
• (603) 524-5210, (800) MARGATE

Our first reaction when we saw the Margate was, "Wow." This is a genuine resort complex, surprisingly located in the middle of little old Laconia. The four lodging buildings offer 146 rooms in a variety of styles, from simple motel units to two-bedroom family suites. Kids up to age 18 can stay free in their parents' hotel room and eat one free meal off the kids' menu for each adult meal purchased. There's a beach gazebo with a bar, indoor and outdoor pools, tennis courts, a health club with Nautilus circuit and other state-of-the-art equipment, sauna, tanning salon and certified massage therapist. The Blackstones restaurant and lounge treats guests to the very best in fine dining and entertainment (see our Restaurants and Nightlife chapters). Ask about package plans that include dinner and breakfast or ski packages offered in conjunction with Gunstock (see our Winter Sports chapter).

The Lake Motel

$$ • N.H. Rt. 28, Wolfeboro
• (603) 569-1100

The Bailey family has operated this motel and the famous Bailey's restaurant next door (see our Restaurants chapter) for half a century. They know Wolfeboro, and they know Lake Wentworth and Crescent Lake, on which they have 650 feet of pristine frontage for swimming, sunbathing or boating. (Your boat or theirs, and they do have a dock.) The motel has a tennis court and 16 acres of lawns and woodland to explore and enjoy. You're within easy walking distance of the beautiful town of Wolfeboro, Brewster Academy and an 18-hole PGA golf course at the Laconia Country Club (see our Other Recreation chapter). This is the oldest resort community in New Hampshire.

You can bring "quiet, well-behaved pets who leave nothing behind." The motel opens in mid-May every year and closes up for the season "sometime in October."

White Mountains and Great North Woods Regions

The Mount Washington Hotel

$$$-$$$$ • U.S. Rt. 302, Bretton Woods
• (603) 278-1000

This vintage treasure was built by railroad tycoon Joseph Stickney and opened in 1902. It is the largest and most complex hotel construction of the White Mountains region and took two years to complete. The style is Spanish Renaissance Revival — one of the late Victorian eclectic styles — known for both lavishness and orderliness. More than 250 master craftsmen were called in for the detailed plaster work, and Tiffany stained glass adorns the lobby. (Look for our Close-up on the hotel's history in this chapter.) The mile-long driveway leads to the hotel through some of the resort's 2,600 acres. Surrounding the resort are 18,000 acres of the White Mountains National Forest. On the grounds are a 27-hole PGA Championship golf course, 12 red-clay tennis courts and miles of individual scenic trails for horseback riding, jogging and mountain biking. The hotel is open from mid-May through mid-October.

The top of the line for these 197 rooms are the three Tower Suites, each with a fully renovated bedroom and sitting room and one and a half baths. The Victorian decor includes Queen Anne reproduction furniture. The views from the tower are 360 degrees, with Mount Washington and the Presidential range your home-away-from-home view. Families should ask about the Family Chamber, a series of two or three connected bedrooms with one or two bathrooms. The Renaissance rooms are larger than the Classic Rooms. At the turn-of-the-century, it was common for families to travel with nannies for the children. Think of the Classic Room as the nanny's room and the Renaissance Room as the parent's room.

The 900-foot wraparound veranda is a perfect spot for watching the leaves change color in fall or waiting for your traveling companion to return from golf or tennis or horseback riding. Meet there for a drink before heading into the elegant octagonal dining room for a four-course dinner. The menu changes every day. Most nights feature live music during dinner. Many guests take a spin around the dance floor between courses. (Our Restaurants chapter features complete information on all the dining choices in the resort.) The everyday activities at the hotel range from histori-

midweek $409-519 family chamber

INSIDERS' TIP

If you'd like to stay at The Mount Washington Hotel Resort but prefer to do your own cooking, rent a one- to five-bedroom condominium townhouse. Full kitchens are standard, and each townhouse has a private outdoor deck and living room/dining room combo with a fireplace. Rental prices include use of the resort sports club and free rides on the resort shuttle.

cal lectures to music recitals, morning walks to tennis clinics. Tours of the hotel are given several times a day, and two movies — classics and contemporary — are shown every night in the Mount Washington Room.

Activities at King of the Mountain Kids Kamp run from 9 AM to 4:30 PM and again in the evening from 6 to 9 PM. Special activities include many Grand Getaway packages and theme weekends. You might be part of a Big Band and Broadway Weekend or a Roaring '20s celebration with a Great Gatsby Antique Car parade. All rooms include breakfast and a four-course dinner. An 8 percent service gratuity is added to each bill.

Sky Valley Motel and Cottages

$ • U.S. Rt. 302, Bartlett
• (603) 374-2322, (800) 675-HOTEL

This is a family resort on 35 acres overlooking the Saco River. The entire facility has a 90-person capacity. Guests enjoy shuffleboard, badminton and volleyball. The outdoor pool is 100 feet by 50 feet, and the children's playground is visible from most units. The 10 motel units, two chalets, three cottages and four apartments all have color TV an Each motel room has an efficiency refrigerator, and other units have full kitchens. The largest apartment sleeps eight people in three bedrooms and a sleeping alcove and has two TVs. All have private baths. A few rooms have a tub or shower but not both. Sky Valley closes in winter. Families on a budget who prefer quiet to nightlife will be happy here. Story Land (see our Kidstuff chapter) is just 5 miles away, and the Mount Washington Auto Road and Cog Railway (see our Attractions chapter) are within a 20-minute drive.

The Bretton Woods Motor Inn ✱

$$ • U.S. Rt. 302, Bretton Woods
• (603) 278-1000

As part of the Mount Washington Hotel Resort, this motel offers lots of choices for guests. Every room has a view — you're overlooking the Presidential range and the grand Mount Washington Hotel — and a private balcony for enjoying it. For meals, choose from the full-service yet casual Darby's restaurant here or enjoy one of the restaurants at the hotel. Your room will most likely be decorated with a floral design, and you'll have one or two queen-size beds. All rooms have private baths. The hotel is closed during the winter while the motor inn is open year round. The Bretton Woods Ski Area is next door. Free shuttle service runs through the resort.

Colebrook House Motel and Restaurant

$ • 1 Main St., Colebrook
• (603) 237-5521

Hunters traveling to the Great North Woods may want to check out Colebrook House. Not only is it affordable, it also allows pets! New furniture complements the c. 1800 main building that houses seven of the 18 rooms here. The 10 motel rooms are modern but not fancy. The one cabin out back that sleeps six is ideal for groups. The restaurant is open for dinner Wednesday through Sunday and breakfast and lunch on Saturday and Sunday. The lounge is open everyday with entertainment on Thursday through Saturday nights. If you've come to the Great North Woods to snowmobile, you'll be glad to know you can hit the snowmobile trails from the parking lot.

Colebrook Country Club Motel

$ • N.H. Rt. 26, Colebrook
• (603) 237-5566

This 18-room Great North Woods motel is open year round. You can play golf on the nine-hole course when the weather's right, and in winter you'll enjoy the snowmobile and cross-country trails. Greens fees are waived for motel guests after 5 PM. (See our Other Recreation chapter for details.) The Colebrook Country Club Restaurant serves dinner Wednesday through Saturday. The lounge opens at noon Monday through Thursday and at 11 AM Friday through Sunday and features live music on Saturday nights.

Mittersill Alpine Resort

$$ • Mittersill Rd., Franconia
• (603) 823-5511

The original resort was built by Baron Hubert Van Pantz, an Austrian. It's now a year-round vacation-ownership property along with hotel rooms, suites with adjoining living and sleeping rooms, and Austrian-style chalets. The original buildings include the Alpine Lodge and riding stables (see our Other Recreation chapter). If you are skiing at Cannon Mountain, this is a great place to stay. You can read up on Cannon in our Winter Sports Chapter.

The Balsams Grand Resort Hotel

$$$-$$$$ • N.H. Rt. 26, Dixville Notch • (603) 255-3500, (800) 255-0600

A vacation at The Balsams Grand Resort Hotel takes place at an elegant, 15,000-acre private estate. An established resort since 1866, The Balsams was enlarged during the next 50 years until it reached the current capacity of 400 guests in 1918. The room price includes breakfast and dinner. Additionally, all of the resort activities are free to guests. For example, lift tickets are free, greens fees on the Donald Ross-designed golf course are part of the package, and guests don't pay extra for trail passes for cross-country skiing. The winter season at The Balsams runs from mid-December through March (read about skiing at The Balsams in our Winter Sports chapter). The summer season runs from late May through mid-October. The golf and tennis programs have full professional staffs who are happy to help you arrange anything from a tennis lesson to a golf tournament. Golf Digest rates the 18-hole course as No. 1 in New Hampshire.

The hotel's staff features a naturalist, and hotel programs include walks ranging from strolls to invigorating hikes. Rooms are in either the Dixville House (built in 1866) or in the Hampshire House addition of 1917. Family suites have connecting bedrooms, and parlor suites have a sitting room along with bedroom and full bath. The rooms might have flowered wallpaper or pastel-colored walls with white trim. Many bathrooms feature an oversize bath tub. The resort has 212 accommodations ranging from rooms with not much of a view to the Tower Suite, a romantic hideaway for couples. The reservations department is happy to give full details on each room.

All services and programs are geared and designed for guest satisfaction. The selection of free services for guests is wonderful for families. From golf and mountain biking in summer to ice-skating and snowshoeing in winter, the dilemma at The Balsams is what to choose. Special activities are organized for kids, and child care is available.

Breakfast choices range from low-fat cereal with skim milk to the grilled hash du jour with poached eggs. In between these extremes, you'll choose from a wide variety of muffins, bagels and breads as well as fresh fruit, jams and jellies. Dinners feature a delightful selection, with entrees ranging from a rack of veal with sliced potatoes baked in cream to shrimp scampi on fettuccine served with wilted spinach. Men are requested to wear a jacket at dinner, and appropriate clothing is expected of all guests at all times. Leave the tank tops at home, dust off your table manners and join the leisure class if only for a few days.

Errol Motel

$ • Main St., Errol • (603) 482-3256

If you don't plan on camping out in this part of the Great North Woods, this is your best bet for a place to stay in Errol. The motel has 12 rooms including three efficiency units that are usually rented to hunters and anglers. No food is available at the motel, but the efficiency units have coffee makers. The three restaurants in town all open at 6 AM. Dogs on leashes are OK, but you need to ask about other pets. You're just minutes from the Androscoggin River and Lake Umbagog, home of New Hampshire's only bald eagles.

Gorham Motor Inn

$ • 324 Upper Main St., Gorham • (603) 466-3381

Santa's Village, The Mount Washington Auto Road and Heritage New Hampshire are all an easy drive from the juncture of U.S. Route 2 and N.H. Route 16, where you'll find the Gorham Motor Inn. The one-story complex has 39 rooms with parking in front of each room. The outdoor pool is heated. There's no restaurant on premises, but you're right in town so you don't have far to go for meals. Two restaurants are a short walk away on Main Street. Snowmobile trails start right across the street.

Town and Country Motor Inn

$ • U.S. Rt. 2, Shelburne
• (603) 466-3315

If you'd have come here in 1956, you would have stayed in one of five cottages and shared a bathroom. Now you'll see 160 modern guest rooms with private baths. The Labnon family has owned and managed this success story since 1957. The motor inn is just east of Gorham on U.S. 2. You'll drive right through a large stand of white birch trees known as the Shelburne birches. (If you've got a volume of Robert Frost with you, this might be the time to reread "Birches.") The 200-seat restaurant serves three meals a day. If you don't ski or hike off the calories, you can try and slim down in the health club, which has an indoor pool, sauna and Jacuzzi. If you're a golfer, be sure and ask about golf packages. The Androscoggin Valley Country Club with an 18-hole golf course is just across U.S. 2 (see our Other Recreation chapter). Snowmobile trails are just out your door, and the Mount Washington Auto Road is just 8 miles away. If you need help planning your day, you can count on the expert guidance of the entire Labnon family.

Cabot Motor Inn

$ • 200 Portland St. (U.S. Rt. 2), Lancaster
• (603) 788-3346

The busy season here is June through Labor Day. This upscale Great North Woods motor inn was built in 1996. An indoor pool and sauna are part of the fitness center. All 54 rooms have a king- or queen-size bed, and three suites have kitchenettes. The dining room and lounge are open every day. Lancaster is the county seat of Coos County and home to the county fair every Labor Day weekend. Be sure and call ahead for reservations for this popular weekend.

Beacon Resort

$-$$ • U.S. Rt. 3, Lincoln
• (603) 745-8118

This 134-room former motel has accommodations ranging from cottages built in the 1950s to modern suites built in the 1990s. Hassle-free vacation amenities include indoor tennis courts, bocci courts and a full restaurant and lounge. Adventurers can explore along the nearby Kancamagus Highway — Lincoln is the western terminus — or spend a day at one of four swimming pools (two are indoor and open all year). This family resort is open all year.

Woodward's Motor Inn

$-$$ • U.S. Rt. 3, Lincoln
• (603) 745-8141

This Lincoln institution has been owned and managed by the Woodward family for more than 45 years. The 80 rooms include seven two-bedroom units as well as standard rooms with two double beds. Features include indoor and outdoor swimming pools, a sauna, Jacuzzi and racquetball courts. The restaurant is open for breakfast and dinner. This topnotch motor inn offers high standards of service.

Indian Head Resort

$$ • U.S. Rt. 3, Lincoln
• (603) 745-8000

The Indian Head Resort has more than 180 acres for lots of family fun in the White Mountains. The modern resort facilities include a lounge and restaurant and a full program of planned activities for kids ages 6 through 12. Kids of all ages will appreciate the trout-stocked lake and indoor and outdoor swimming pools. You'll find tennis courts too as well as a gift shop. The 90 rooms and 57 bungalows and cottages all have private baths. Some bungalows have galley-style kitchens. The Indian Head Resort is a favorite spot for family reunions. You can make your own plans or take advantage of the special group programs department. The lounge features frequent live entertainment, and the restaurant is open for three meals a day.

Drummer Boy Motor Inn

$$ • U.S. Rt. 3, Lincoln
• (603) 745-3661

The indoor and outdoor pools along with a sauna and Jacuzzi make this a relaxing spot for outdoor activists. Open all year, the Drum-

mer Boy is convenient for Loon Mountain visitors in and out of ski season. Many rooms include kitchen efficiencies. Adjoining rooms are available for families, and cots and cribs can be rented. Full cottages and a four-bedroom house round out the accommodations. The house and cottages are perfect for a group of skiers or a family with lots of cousins. Weekly rates are available.

Presidential Waterbed Motel

$$ • N.H. Rt. 16, North Conway
• (603) 356-9744

Calling itself the "Pocono" (Presidential of Conway North) of the White Mountains is one way to show off the special features of this classic motel. You can request a room with a heart-shaped tub or king-size waterbed. Honeymooners and couples looking to get away from it all can enjoy beautiful mountain views and whirlpool baths. The owners recommend Stonehurst Manor across the street for delicious dinners. No meals are served at the motel.

Kancamagus Motor Lodge

$ • N.H. Rt. 112, Lincoln
• (603) 745-3365, (800) 346-4205

A drive on the Kancamagus Highway (N.H. Route 112) is one of the most beautiful scenic tours we can recommend. If the traffic is heavy during fall foliage season, you'll be glad you've got one of the 34 rooms here reserved in your name. The motel is two stories, with parking convenient to each room. You'll get breakfast, featuring home-baked breads and pastries, from 7 to 11 AM. This is the only meal served. You'll find lots of lunch and dinner options in Lincoln (see our Restaurants chapter). All rooms have steambaths, and the outdoor pool is heated. The motor lodge is open year round.

Purity Springs Resort

$$ • N.H. Rt. 153, East Madison
• (603) 367-8896, (800) 373-3754

This longstanding resort has been at the heart of many a New Hampshire vacation. Opened in the late 1800s, the 1,400-acre prop-

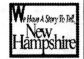

erty is nestled between the Lakes Region and the White Mountains Region. The winter (late December through March) and summer (early June through late October) seasons include lots of activities. Swimming, boating and fishing on Purity Lake are summer mainstays, and skiing at King Mountain dominates the winter. (Read about King Pine Ski Area and Purity Springs in our Winter Sports chapter.)

The resort is open on a bed-and-breakfast basis in between the main seasons. The main seasons feature vacation plans that include all-you-can-eat, family-style meals. Rooms vary from dormitory-style to new cabins with lots of amenities.

Tall Timber Lodge

$$ • Back Lake, Pittsburg
• (603) 538-6651, (800) 835-6343

A stay at Tall Timber provides the quintessential Great North Woods experience. It has been one of New England's premier sporting lodges for more than 50 years. One key to its success is its ambiance of understated luxury. You can hunt and fish all day — really rough it — with an expert guide, a delicious box lunch and beautiful unspoiled wilderness. Come back to "camp," whether it's a cozy guest room in the lodge or a private cabin, and relax before dinner. You'll have fun looking at the lodge's collection of trophy mounts and photographs commemorating years of successful hunting and fishing by guests. Most lodge rooms have private baths, and rooms with shared bath are great for families. Cabin size ranges from two to five bedrooms. All have private porches with rocking chairs and views of Back Lake. A new cabin with a fireplace and cathedral ceiling is called "Bess." The Bess accommodation is a private retreat with two bedrooms, two bathrooms, a sleep sofa in the living room, full kitchen with microwave and dishwasher, cable TV with VCR and a laundry room. The maximum number of guests for Bess is six, and it costs $995 per week. The dining room serves breakfast and dinner. Prices for lodge rooms include these meals and maid service. You can rent a cabin with or without these amenities. Tall Timber is open all year.

Best Western Red Jacket Mountain View

$$ • N.H. Rt. 16, North Conway
• (603) 356-5411, (800) R JACKET

The 164 rooms here include 12 two-bedroom townhouses. The remaining rooms are in the main building, and all include up-to-date amenities including refrigerators. The entire family will enjoy the indoor and outdoor Olympic pools, saunas, laundry facilities and game room. In summer and during other children's vacation periods, the hotel has a special complimentary kids program from 9 AM to noon. Tour the 40-acre grounds by horse-drawn carriage in summer and fall and by sleigh during the winter. The sledding hill is very popular in winter, and the hotel has sleds for guests. The dining room is open for three meals every day. The lounge is open for lunch during summer and fall and opens at 4 PM the remainder of the year. Most of the grounds and all dining areas are nonsmoking.

Mount Washington Valley Motor Inn

$-$$ • 1567 White Mountain Highway (N.H. Route 16), North Conway
• (800) 634-2383

If you're coming to North Conway to shop, this is a great place to stay. You're right in front of Settlers Green (see our Shopping chapter for outlet details) and within walking distance of lots of stores. The 60 rooms feature coffee makers and hair dryers as well as cable television. The pool is indoors and heated for year-round use, and in summer you have access to a beach on the Saco River. The restaurant serves breakfast every day and dinner on weekends. Ask about discount coupons for shopping and meals in the area.

Snowy Owl Inn

$$ • 407 Village Rd., Waterville Valley
• (603) 236-8383

Choose from 11 styles of rooms at this 80-room, modern-day country inn. The style is mountain-lodge traditional, with hardwood floors in the main lobby. All rooms have private baths. A standard room includes two double beds. The rustic flavor is updated with indoor and outdoor pools. Room prices include an extensive (French toast is included!) continental breakfast and a cheese and wine hour every day between 4:30 and 5:30 PM. No other meals are served. Skiing, mountain biking, swimming and hiking are just a few of the Waterville Valley activities. Look for details in our Winter Sports and Other Recreation chapters.

Dartmouth-Lake Sunapee Region

Claremont Motor Lodge

$ • Beauregard St., Claremont
• (603) 542-2540

This 19-room motel was renovated in 1997 and serves a free continental breakfast. Ten rooms have queen-size beds, while nine offer two double beds. All rooms include refrigerators. You're just a mile and a half from the center of Claremont and right next door to Dimick's, a casual restaurant with good food. Pets are welcome.

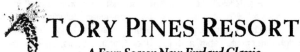

Shaker Bridge Motel

$ • S. Main St., Enfield
• (603) 632-4279

This is not a modern motel, but it's clean, charming and has beautiful views of Lake Mascoma just across the road. Free rowboats are available for fishing, and the motel has a small beach on the lake. No food is served on the premises, but each room has a small refrigerator, instant coffee and a hot-water kettle. The rooms have TV but not cable. The Shaker Bridge Motel is 8 miles from Lebanon, which is the closest town for dinner (see our Restaurants chapter).

Hanover Inn

$$$-$$$$ • S. Main St., On the Green, Hanover
• (603) 643-4300

You're in Hanover, so it's not unusual that Dartmouth College owns and manages the fanciest hotel in town. Sit on the front porch and watch the world go by. People have been meeting and eating and talking here since it opened as a tavern in 1780. The crowd today is used to the casual elegance that surrounds you here. We'd iron our clothes before meeting someone for tea — and we never iron. The 98 guest rooms are all delightful, and the larger suites are posh. Canopy beds and dressing tables complement the Colonial decor, while private baths, cable TV and air conditioning suit the modern traveler. Many of the inn's rooms are connected to the college's vast computing network. Dining choices include the upscale Daniel Webster Room, where you can plan your courses to satisfy all your fancy food cravings in one memorable meal, and the Ivy Grill, which specializes in American cuisine. You can also eat on the terrace just across from the Dartmouth Green. Read about all three in our Restaurants chapter. The inn is open all year. Many guests are Dartmouth alumni, so rooms go quickly at busy college events.

Chieftain Motor Inn

$$ • 84 Lyme Rd. (N.H. Rt. 10), Hanover
• (603) 643-2550

Ask for a room with a view of the Connecticut River. Cozy pine paneling and cable TV are in each of the 22 rooms. The peak season runs from June through October and during special events at Dartmouth. The motel doesn't have a restaurant, but complimentary fruit, cereal, pastries and coffee are available at the front desk every morning. Besides the convenience to Dartmouth College and Lebanon, the Chieftain is a great place to stay if you want to explore the Vermont side of the Upper Valley (see our Daytrips chapter).

Best Western Sunapee Lake Lodge

$$ • N.H. Rt. 103, Sunapee
• (603) 763-2010

You can't miss this modern (built in 1995) 55 room motel because it's right on the traffic circle as you come into town on N.H. Route 103. You're right across the street from the entrance to Mount Sunapee State Park for winter skiing and summer fun. The motel pool is indoor and open all year. A tanning booth and mini-gym are on premises for people who like their activities close by. All the rooms have hair dryers and several have full kitchenettes with microwave ovens and refrigerators. Murphy's Grill is next door serving breakfast on weekends and dinner every day.

Radisson Inn North Country

$$ • 25 Airport Rd., West Lebanon
• (603) 298-5906 (800) 333-3333

Friendly management, room service from the on-premises Garden Court restaurant and an indoor pool are just a few reasons to stay here when you visit the region. The 126-room motor inn is just off Interstate 89 at Exit 20 North. A wide variety of discounts — AARP, family, Bed and Breakfast — make it easy to find just the right package for your needs. Free shuttle service to the Lebanon Airport, which is less than five minutes away, makes the Radisson a favorite of business travelers.

Monadnock Region

The Econo Lodge

$ • 634 Francestown Rd., N.H. Rt. 47, Bennington
• (603) 588-6735, (800) 55-ECONO

The management hands out local maps and guide books to help visitors find the best place to swim or hike. Many of the 31 rooms

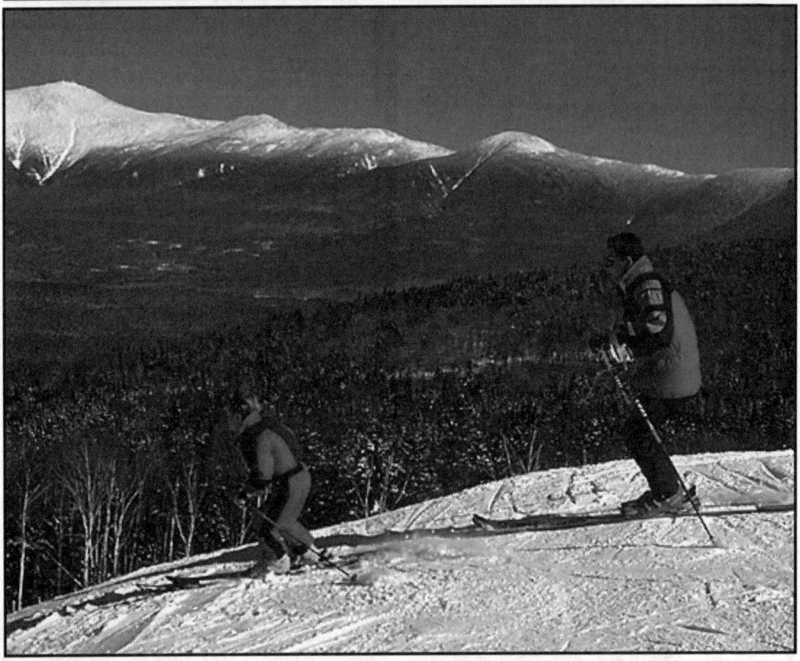

Ski resorts are popular near many of New Hampshire's hotels.

have balconies for seasonal viewing enjoyment. In winter you're just across the road from Crotched Mountain Ski Area. The Tory Pines Golf Resort is just a half-mile away in Francestown (look for details on Tory Pines in our Other Recreation chapter). A deluxe continental breakfast is included in the room rate. Each room has a coffee maker, and several also have microwave ovens and small refrigerators. Pets are allowed in four of the rooms for an additional $25. Be sure and make your pet's reservation when you make your own.

Best Western Sovereign Hotel

$$ • 401 Winchester St., Keene • (603) 357-3038

The only full-service hotel in Keene, the Best Western Sovereign features a restaurant and lounge along with free breakfast for adults (it costs $1.99 for kids) and an indoor pool. Each of the 131 rooms includes on-demand movie service and a coffee maker. Pets are welcome. Kids younger than 18 stay free with parents. This Best Western is popular with parents visiting their kids at Keene State College, so be sure and plan ahead in case your trip coincides with parents' weekend or graduation.

Days Inn

$$ • 175 Key Rd., Keene • (603) 352-7616

Pets are welcome at this 80-room motel. Complimentary continental breakfast is served in the lobby, and valet service is available in case you stick your sleeve in the jam. Several rooms feature VCRs and free videos from the Days Inn movie library. You can swim in the indoor pool and relax in the sauna. Remember that Halloween is a major event in Keene with the Pumpkin Festival and thousands of jack-o'-lanterns (see our Annual Events chapter). Call ahead for reservations.

Jack Daniels Motor Inn

$$ • Concord St., U.S. Rt. 202 N., Peterborough • (603) 924-7548

You're a 10-minute walk or a two-minute drive from the heart of downtown

Peterborough when you stay at The Jack Daniels Motor Inn. The 17 units offer privacy and freedom from breakfast chat for people who aren't the bed and breakfast type. Complimentary coffee and juice are available in the lobby in the morning. Other than that, you are on your own. Read our Restaurants chapter to learn about food options in Peterborough. The busiest months are September and October, but it's always best to reserve ahead at this popular spot.

Tory Pines Resort

$$ • 740 2nd N.H. Turnpike N., Francestown • (603) 588-2000

Tory Pines is a golf resort (see our Other Recreation chapter for a description of the golf facilities), but you don't have to be a golfer to enjoy the 780 acres of designated forest preserve and game sanctuary in the heart of the Monadnock Region. The 32 rooms have fireplaces and kitchenettes as well as color cable TV, air-conditioning and private baths. Suites include living rooms. Bright plaid fabrics highlight the comfortable, modern decor. Breakfast, lunch and dinner are served at the Gibson Tavern, built in 1799. The resort is best known for the Roland Stafford Golf School. Be sure and ask about "Play and Stay" packages and the "Golf Group Encounter." The pro shop offers a variety of lessons and sets up tournaments. Take N.H. Route 47 north from Francestown and follow the Tory Pines Resort sign at Schoolhouse Road (also known as the 2nd N.H. Turnpike North).

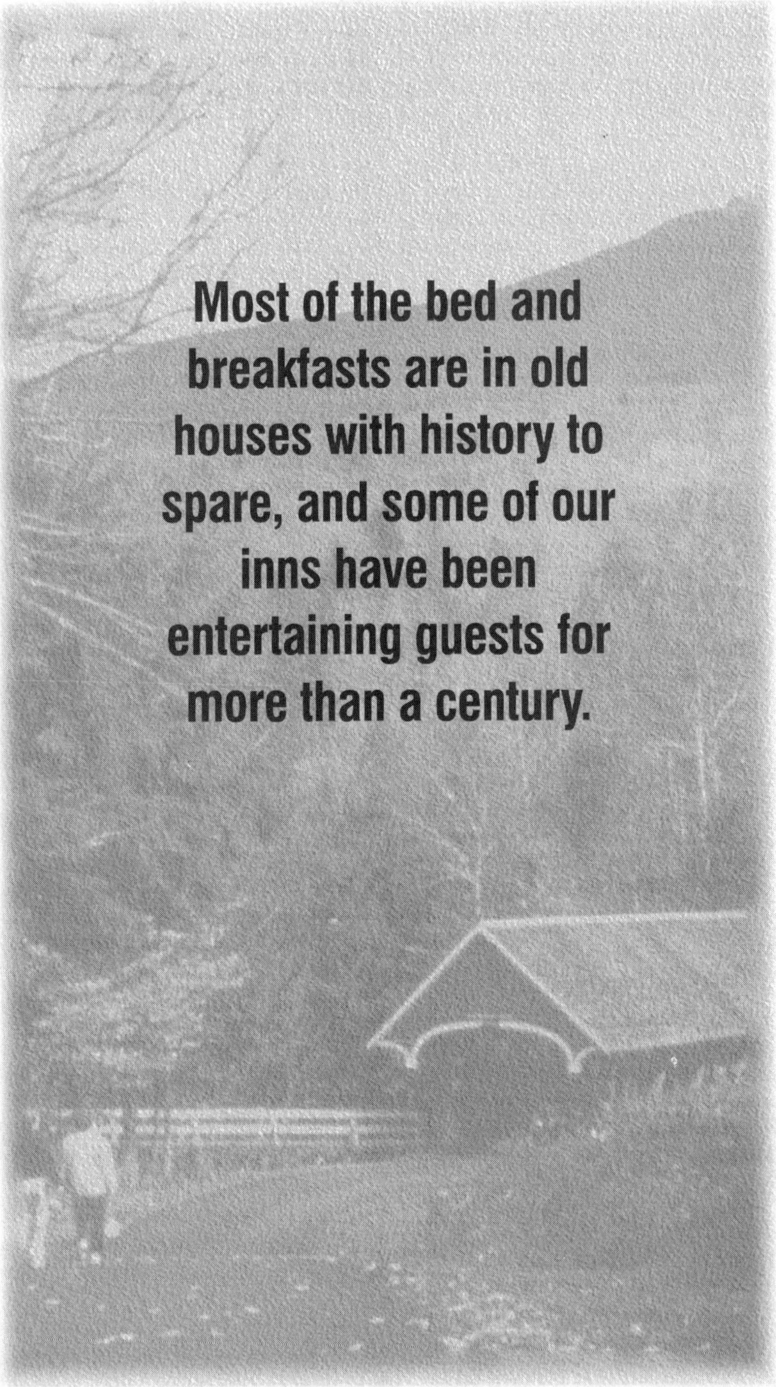

Most of the bed and breakfasts are in old houses with history to spare, and some of our inns have been entertaining guests for more than a century.

Bed and Breakfasts and Country Inns

For the kind of vacation where the room is part of the attraction, New Hampshire offers a wonderful assortment of bed and breakfasts and country inns. Most of the bed and breakfasts are in old houses with history to spare, and some of our inns have been entertaining guests for more than a century! You'll find things like antique furnishings, handmade quilts and fresh flowers in the rooms.

The owners of most of these establishments are emphatic about pets: They are not allowed! Although the larger inns generally accommodate children, many bed and breakfast inns will only accept children older than 10 or 12 years old (we'll tell you which ones). In part this is because of the breakage factor, but as one inn manager pointed out, there's generally "nothing" for them to do: no TV, no arcade, no pool. Instead you'll find parlors with books, jigsaw puzzles and pianos. However, some inns do have pools or tennis courts. Your host and hostess will be able to suggest local attractions, harvest festivals and church suppers only an Insider would know about.

The two types of inns — bed and breakfasts and country inns — offer different services. In general, country inns have full kitchens and dining rooms that serve two or three meals that are open to the public as well as guests. Meals are not usually included in the room price at country inns, although some offer coffee and pastry in the morning. Bed and breakfasts serve breakfast, and sometimes afternoon tea, to their guests only, and these are included in the price of the room. Please be aware that many establishments with the word "inn" in their names are licensed and operating as bed and breakfasts. If there is a full dining room, we have mentioned it.

Bed and breakfast facilities usually have a phone extension available for guests in the living room (use your credit card for long-distance calls), while inns may be able to provide a phone in each room. The TV is generally in the living room, as well, although a few inns provide TVs in guest rooms. Most bed and breakfast facilities ask you to smoke out of doors, while some inns provide a choice of smoking or nonsmoking rooms. If we don't mention smoking, it is not allowed.

High season throughout the state includes midsummer (July 4 through Labor Day) and foliage season (mid-September in the north to late October in the south). For many of our accommodations, other times are also very busy: weekends in May and June for inns that specialize in weddings, for example, or reunion and parents weekends in the towns with boarding schools. These you can really only discover by calling. Winter is high season in the ski areas, low in the rest of the state (many facilities just close down for the winter).

NACSAR Winston Cup auto race weekends in Loudon are so busy that inns and bed and breakfasts are booked years in advance! Reservations are always recommended on weekends and are absolutely essential throughout the summer.

Innkeepers in this state are helpful and more than willing to recommend other nearby inns (some even call other establishments to try and find you a room), but if you arrive without reservations on a summer weekend in the Lakes Region, the closest vacancy may be a hotel room back in Manchester.

Staying at an inn or bed and breakfast is like staying in someone's home. If you expect to come in after midnight and want an indoor pool and cable television in the room, consider the hotels or motels in our chapter by that name instead. If you need wheelchair access or a phone beside the bed, you'll probably be better off in a hotel-style facility too. Some inns do offer these amenities, though, so call ahead if they're important to you.

Many small towns have rural mail service from another town's post office, and we have given street addresses, not mailing addresses. Do check with your host before you mail a deposit into the great beyond!

Price Code

We've used the same price code here as in our Accommodations chapter. This code reflects the average cost of a one-night stay for two people during the high season. Some inns and bed and breakfasts include New Hampshire's 8 percent Rooms and Meals tax in their quoted price, but most do not. Ask when making reservations to avoid an unpleasant surprise at checkout. All establishments take major credit cards unless we warn you otherwise.

$	**less than $75**
$$	**$75 to $150**
$$$	**$150 to 225**
$$$$	**more than $225**

Resources

New Hampshire Bed and Breakfast Reservation Service

33 Red Gate Ln., Meredith • (603) 279-8348

With more than 150 members in the New England area, these helpful folks can assist you if all our recommended spots are already booked!

Merrimack Valley Region

Bed and Breakfasts

Fox Brook Farm

$$ • 17 Thornton's Ferry Rd. No. 1, Amherst • (603) 672-7161

This recently renovated 1876 farm offers beautifully decorated rooms with all the modern amenities (private baths, cable TV/VCR and in-room phones), views of rolling fields and a bird sanctuary next door. You can hike the trails on the 12-acre site, use the canoe to explore the brook or ride the mountain bikes to tour nearby Amherst Village, which is on the National Register of Historic Places. Select from four or five breakfast choices, from freshly baked muffins or coffeecake with fruit to a full eggs, waffles and sausage meal. Pick a time to eat, then sleep late if you like; your breakfast will be served whenever you want it. All the rooms are nonsmoking.

There is no unit designed for handicapped accessibility, but one is on the ground level. Children are welcome.

Stillmeadow Bed & Breakfast

$ • 545 Main St., Hampstead • (603) 329-8381

This 1850 farmhouse offers four comfortable guest rooms, each with a private bath and unique furnishings. An extended continental breakfast welcomes guests in the gracious dining room, and coffee and cookies are always available. Children are welcome here with prior approval — one of the rooms is designed to accommodate families with small children. There's a formal living room with a wood stove, and TV is available if you ask. (There's cable in the family suite). Smoking is allowed on the porch.

Breezy Hill Bed & Breakfast

$ • 119 Adams Rd., Londonderry • (603) 432-0122

Londonderry, once one of New Hampshire's most productive farm communities, still has some active farmland. Breezy Hill Bed and Breakfast offers you the chance to see New Hampshire agriculture in action. This 1850s farmhouse, surrounded by open fields, has a full-size garden, fresh eggs on the table and beautiful apple trees. Chickens and horses are part of the pastoral scene. Fresh-picked berries from across the street wind up at breakfast as homemade preserves. Your host will take you on a horse-drawn wagon tour of the farm if you'd like.

Inside the two guest rooms are decorated in antiques and reproductions, while the sitting room offers a TV/VCR and stereo for guests' use. The graffiti on the dining room table is a legacy of years in the library at a Lowell, Massachusetts, high school. Breezy Hill provides a private entrance for guests and will put a phone in your room if you need one, and you can plug in your modem. Smoking is allowed outdoors only. Well-behaved children are welcome, and you're welcome to enjoy the outdoor pool.

Zahn's Alpine Guest House

$ • N.H. Rt. 13 S., Mont Vernon
• (603) 673-2334, (888) 745-0051

This is a new building built and operated in the style of the guest houses owners Bud and Anne Zahn enjoyed during their many trips to the European Alps. It is very popular with visitors touring the many antiques shops of the Monadnock and western Merrimack Valley regions. Eight guest rooms are fitted out in European style with duvets and furnishings brought from Europe, to which the Zahns added American-style private baths and phones in each room.

Step out on to the perimeter balcony to watch the stars or breathe the morning air. Breakfast includes a variety of breads and muffins with coffee and juices. The common room, or Stube, is a comfortable sitting room, with microwave, refrigerator and dishware available for guests. At its heart is the Kachelofen, a tile oven built in exactly the style of those in the Alps — it keeps the whole room warm, but you can put your hand against it and not be burned. Smoking is allowed only on the balcony. Children are welcome.

Country Inns

Bedford Village Inn

$$$-$$$$ • 2 Old Bedford Rd., Bedford
• (603) 472-2001, (800) 852-1166

The farmhouse at the center of this elegant inn was built in 1810 by Josiah Gordon, a Revolutionary War veteran and son of the farm's original owner. The property was saved from commercial development by a committee of townspeople who worked for a zoning change to allow the inn to open in the mid-1980s. The farmhouse now houses a fine restaurant where pressed linens and fresh flowers accent the menu (see our Restaurants chapter for details.) The post-and-beam barn has been renovated to provide 12 sumptuous rooms (Italian marble whirlpool baths, king-size four-poster beds, balconies or fireplaces) and two apartments with full kitchens. Some areas are handicapped-accessible.

The inn is also able to offer function rooms in the barn for business meetings and wedding receptions in a stunning country setting. The parlors and other common areas are nonsmoking.

Centennial Inn

$$-$$$ • 96 Pleasant St., Concord
• (603) 225-7102

Concord's newest inn opened its doors in May 1997, though the handsome Victorian building was originally built in 1892. A massive renovation of the building by the Someplace Different hotel group preserved the unique woodwork and architectural details while providing the modern luxury accommodations. Enjoy the view from a private porch or through the 100-year-old glass. Guests can relax in the private whirlpool bath in their room or at the Hannah Dustin Lounge.

Each of the 32 guest rooms is unique, with the odd shapes and features typical of Victorian construction. Each also offers two phone jacks (so you can plug in your modem) and TV (two in some suites). The inn is within walking distance of downtown Concord, including the capitol and the Capital Center for the Arts, and it caters to business travelers with one suite that includes an office and others that include conference tables. The Franklin Pierce Dining Room promises elegant and unusual entrees for discerning palates (see our Restaurants chapter for details). Smoking is allowed in the lounge. Some handicapped-accessible units are available, and children are always welcome.

Colby Hill Inn

$$-$$$ • Western Ave., Henniker
• (603) 428-3281, (800) 531-0330

From the outside this 1795 farmhouse, with two New England barns, a sprawling carriage house and 5 acres of rolling hillside, looks much as it did 200 years ago. But inside you'll find modern convenience with old-fashioned hospitality. Each of the 16 guest rooms has a private bath, private phone and dataport and central air conditioning. Some have working fireplaces too. Summer guests enjoy the pool and volleyball. Winter guests chat by the fire in the parlor, while the "inn-dog," Delilah, keeps a watchful eye on the pastoral scene. Smoking is only allowed outdoors. Children older than 7 are welcome to accompany their families. The inn's gardenside dining room promises an enchanting experience for every meal (see our Restaurants chapter).

Seacoast Region

Bed and Breakfasts

The Silver Street Inn

$-$$ • 103 Silver St., Dover
• (603) 743-3000

For an elegant stay in a downtown location, the Silver Street Inn is a terrific choice. Enter through the side porch and you find yourself in a Victorian music room. The pressed-tin ceilings, Austrian crystal doorknobs and imported slate fireplace stones recall the wealth and pride of the original owners. The home was converted to a bed and breakfast in the late 1980s, and rooms offer period furnishings with modern amenities — private bath, TV, phone and air conditioning. A full breakfast is made to order (this is really a bed and breakfast, despite the name) but always features homemade muffins. Smoking is allowed only in a designated outdoor area. There is one handicapped-accessible room. Children are welcome (but we'd keep a close eye on the active ones: Indoors is full of antiques, and outdoors is close to the street).

The University Guest House

$ • 47 Mill Rd., Durham
• (603) 868-2728

You don't have to be visiting the University of New Hampshire to stay at this lovely four-bedroom bed and breakfast, but it is a favorite with visiting professors and parents alike. The rooms offer twin, double or queen-size beds, and there's a luxurious terry-cloth robe for each guest to wear down to the shared bath. The whole house is furnished with antiques and New Hampshire handcrafts, and your hostess, Beth, is a fountain of Insider information. Ask her for suggested activities, but be warned that you'll have to come back to try them all! Breakfast includes fresh-baked breads or muffins along with bagels, granola, yogurt and fresh fruit before you set out for your day in academia or to explore the back roads of the Seacoast.

The Inn by the Bandstand

$$ • 4 Front St., Exeter
• (603) 772-6352

This elegant Federalist home was marked for demolition in the 1970s. The protests that saved and restored it sparked a preservationist trend throughout the downtown area, over which the inn now presides like a grande dame.

Only converted for bed and breakfast use in 1993, the Inn by the Bandstand has nine rooms with cable TV, phone service, air conditioning and private baths. Several of the rooms include working (gas) fireplaces, and in 1998 a whirlpool was added to one room. In addition to the parlor breakfast of pastries, cereal and fruit, tea is available throughout the day, and sherry is available in the guest rooms. Two suites also include kitchen facilities.

Summer concerts in the Bandstand across from the Inn are an added attraction. There is parking out back (a big plus in Exeter). Smoking is not allowed.

Great Islander Bed and Breakfast

$$ • 62 Main St., New Castle
• (603) 436-8536

The only rooms available on the island of New Castle are the three at the Great Islander, right in the middle of the village. Typical for a Colonial home, the house is very close to the street and to its neighbors, although in the back there's room for a pool and a deck overlooking the river.

New Castle is an island to which you can

drive, over causeway and bridge, so the ocean is only about 3 blocks from the house. The Potts family has lived here since the 1950s, opening the bed and breakfast when the children left the nest. They serve an expanded continental breakfast to guests, who can also make use of the fully equipped kitchen and other common rooms. One room has a private bath and whirlpool, the other two share a bath.

The Inn at Christian Shore

$$ • 335 Maplewood Ave., Portsmouth • (603) 431-6770

This Federalist home, built around 1800, sits across from the Jackson House, the oldest house in Portsmouth (see our Attractions chapter). Many of Portsmouth's historic and cultural attractions are within walking distance of this lovely bed and breakfast. Each of the six rooms is furnished with antiques, although they all have TVs and air conditioning. Two of the rooms share a bath, the others have private baths. Two rooms have fireplaces.

A full New England breakfast is served in the beautiful dining room, and the wingback chairs welcome you to rest after walking the cobblestone streets. Children older than 12 are welcome.

The Inn at Strawbery Banke

$$ • 314 Court St., Portsmouth • (603) 436-7242, (800) 428-3933

This bed and breakfast is right in the middle of the oldest part of the city, although this house is a relative newcomer, as it only dates back to 1800. You can leave your car parked and have a full weekend of sightseeing on foot (and given the narrow 17th-century streets, that would be a good plan).

Each of the seven rooms has a private bath, and in 1998 the entire facility was air-conditioned. The house has cozy sitting rooms with books and TV for guests. Enjoy a hearty breakfast including New Hampshire maple syrup and seasonal fruits while you watch the birds at the feeders in the garden. Children older than 10 are welcome. Smoking is not allowed.

The Oracle House Inn

$$ • 38 Marcy St., Portsmouth • (603) 433-8827

You are not required to dress in 18th-century costume to stay here, but you will feel as though you ought to! The house was built in 1702 by an officer of the British Navy (New Hampshire was still part of Britain then). In the 1700s, the first daily newspaper in New Hampshire, *The Oracle of the Day*, was published here — hence the name given to this bed and breakfast. The house has been restored with original colors, antique and reproduction furniture and some modern amenities discreetly blended into the decor. Every room has a working fireplace. You'll enjoy an abundant continental breakfast, with fresh fruit, granola and yogurt as well as bagels and coffee. Right across the narrow street from Prescott Park and the harbor, you are only steps away from Strawbery Banke and the rest of the historic district. The owners will rent you a bicycle if you'd like to travel a bit farther without moving your car. The inn is able to accept small children with prior arrangements. Smoking is allowed on the patio.

Martin Hill Inn

$$ • 404 Islington St., Portsmouth • (603) 436-2287

Although the Martin family bought this land in 1710, the buildings that now make up the bed and breakfast were constructed in the first half of the 19th century. There are three guest rooms in the older main house and four in the guest house. Each room has a sitting area and private bath, and all the rooms are air conditioned. A flower-lined brick path joins the two houses.

Guests enjoy a full breakfast each morning in the elegant dining room. Martin Hill is not in the historic district per se (almost all of

INSIDERS' TIP

Country inns are always a popular dining choice for local residents as well as visitors. Guests at the inn need to reserve ahead the same as everyone else to be sure of getting a table.

Portsmouth looks historic); undoubtedly when the home was built, it was outside the city. Today the off-street parking is a valuable amenity. You are still within walking distance (about a mile) of the shops and historic sites along the waterfront. Children older than 16 are welcome guests.

Sise Inn

$$-$$$ • 40 Court St., Portsmouth
• (603) 433-1200, (800) 267-0525

This restored Queen Anne house in the heart of downtown Portsmouth is another of the Someplace Different company's elegant inns. Built in the 1880s as the home of successful merchant John Sise, the building's prime location encouraged its conversion to a series of commercial uses beginning in the 1930s. Now handsomely restored and with a matching addition off the back, the inn has 34 rooms, including several suites, and a variety of function rooms for meetings and elegant parties. A complimentary breakfast including croissants, yogurt and muffins is served the breakfast room. The guest rooms are furnished with antiques and reproductions but offer modern amenities: private baths, cable TV, phones and, in some rooms, whirlpools. Cassettes, videos and books are available for guests' enjoyment. Off-street parking makes this downtown location even more convenient. The inn offers smoking and nonsmoking rooms and has one room designed to be handicapped accessible. Children are welcome.

Rock Ledge Manor

$$ • 1413 Ocean Blvd., Rye
• (603) 431-1413

This bed and breakfast is open year round, and it's an impressive place to be during a winter squall, as the ocean is directly across the street! Sitting on the big porch and looking east to the Isles of Shoals, you could imagine yourself out at sea. The big mid-19th-century Victorian home has four guest rooms, an old fashioned sunroom full of plants and a formal breakfast room — all with sea views. Two of the guest rooms have private baths, and the other two share a full bath but have a private half-bath each.

A wonderful home-cooked hearty country breakfast at 8:30 every morning will set you up for a brisk walk or a swim off the sandy beach. Or head to Portsmouth, just a few miles up the coast, for museums and shopping. Children 11 and older are welcome. Smoking is not allowed anywhere on the property.

Country Inns

Three Chimneys Inn

$$$ • 17 Newmarket Rd.
• (603) 868-7800, (888) 399-9777

This elegant new inn in a restored 1649 homestead and carriage house is just a few blocks from the University of New Hampshire campus. The 24 guest rooms are furnished with Georgian mahogany and Edwardian drapes, beautiful tapestries, oriental rugs and working fireplaces or woodstoves. In a discreet nod to modern tastes they also offer private baths with whirlpools, two-line telephones and data ports, cable television and plenty of room for civilized conversation. A full breakfast and afternoon tea are included with your room, and you may also choose to have lunch or dinner in the casual ffrost Sawyer Tavern, the candlelit Maples dining room, or outdoors in the conservatory, under an old-fashioned grape arbor. Three Chimneys also has two suitably distinguished conference rooms for functions. The inn is handicapped-accessible, air-conditioned and completely non-smoking. Neither pets nor children younger than six can be accommodated.

The Inn of Exeter

$$-$$$ • 90 Front St., Exeter
• (603) 772-5901, (800) 782-8444

This Georgian brick mansion, once owned by Phillips Exeter Academy, is now one of the Someplace Different chain of inns in historic buildings. Originally built to accommodate dignitaries visiting their sons at school, the inn retains a character of quiet elegance. While walking through the door, you can imagine yourself as a member of the upper crust coming home, as a formal dining room and parlor appear before you see the registration desk. Rooms here are decorated with antiques but supply everything the modern traveler needs, including private baths, air conditioning, cable TV and telephones. The dining room and lounge serve three exquisite meals and are open to the public (see our Restaurants chapter). Facilities are also available for business conferences, wedding receptions or other meetings. Children are welcome here. There is a small charge for rollaway beds and cribs. Some rooms are wheelchair-accessible. In a nod to the "old-boy" tradition, smoking has always been allowed throughout this facility, but extensive renovations in 1998 included the creation of some nonsmoking guest rooms.

The Governor's Inn
$$ • 78 Wakefield St., Rochester
• (603) 332-0107

"Elegant but comfortable" is the Governor's very accurate self-description. The nine rooms in this 1920 Georgian Colonial vary in size and accommodations, but all have private baths, air conditioning, cable TV and telephones. A continental breakfast is served to overnight guests, while the restaurant is also open to the public for lunch and dinner (see our Restaurants chapter). Families or longer-term guests might ask about the Carriage House, which offers a three-, four- or five-room apartment with full kitchen. Many families rent the whole place for weddings, using the ballroom and garden for large gatherings or the gazebo for an intimate party, with the bridal couple and close friends or relatives housed right at the inn. There is no smoking allowed in the inn. Children are welcome.

Lakes Region

Bed and Breakfasts

The Glynn House Inn
$$ • 43 Highland St., Ashland
• (603) 968-3775, (800) 637-9599

Up the hill on a pretty side street in Ashland, the Glynn House is a classic Victorian home, complete with turrets, wraparound porch and gingerbread woodwork. Each of the nine bedrooms and suites is unique, with period furnishings and carved oak woodwork. All the rooms have private baths, seven have fireplaces and five have whirlpools. Enjoy a gourmet breakfast in the elegant dining room, then step out to the veranda and enjoy the birdsong while you plan your day. It's a comfortable drive to either the heart of the Lakes Region or the White Mountains, and Squam Lake is just a few miles away. Smoking is not allowed inside. Children older than 6 are welcome.

Pleasant View Bed and Breakfast

$ • Hemphill Rd., Bristol
• (603) 744-5547

This farmhouse, built in 1832 on some of the best farmland in the Lakes Region, has been housing travelers since the early 1900s. The present owners, the Appletons, renovated it and reopened it as a bed and breakfast in 1992. Each of the four guest rooms is decorated in a unique style. Two rooms have private baths; the other two share a bath. The Great Room, in a converted barn, offers a cozy chair next to the wood stove during winter months. The dining room, where you'll enjoy homemade and homegrown specialties at breakfast, still has the wide planks and corner posts of the original construction, as does the TV room. Open land runs right down to Newfound Lake, giving you a beautiful place to hike, leaf-peep or just sit and relax. Smoking is not allowed inside. Children older than 10 are welcome for a nominal extra charge. The inn can't accommodate pets.

Inn on Golden Pond

$$ • U.S. Rt. 3, Holderness
• (603) 968-7269

This 1879 country home is now a lovely bed and breakfast, with seven guest rooms and two extra-large suites. All the rooms are spacious and open, with comfortable, homey furnishings, private baths and plenty of room to spread out and relax. In addition, guests are welcome to enjoy a book or game in the sitting room, where a cozy fire brightens winter afternoons, or on the screened porch in the summer. There's cable TV in another room, so readers and viewers can avoid conflict. Breakfast brings freshly baked breads and muffins, homemade jams and delicious coffee as well as a variety of special treats in season. Children 12 and older are welcome, and they will enjoy hiking on the 50-acre wooded site or playing table tennis in the game room.

Pressed Petals Inn

$$ • Shepard Hill Rd., Holderness
• (603) 968-4417

Ellie Dewey has created a wonderful bed and breakfast. This restored Victorian home is charming and cozy with eight delightful little rooms, each with a private bath, and a comfortable living room where you'll enjoy fresh-baked breads with your morning coffee at a candlelit breakfast and delicious afternoon coffee and desserts. The porch looks out over a tree-shaded garden, and it's just a short walk to the lake. Although none of the rooms was built to be wheelchair accessible, those on the ground floor have tubs and are particularly favored by Ellie's older guests. She cannot accommodate children younger than 10. Smoking is allowed on the porch.

Lovejoy Farm

$$ • 268 Lovejoy Rd., Loudon
• (603) 783-4007, (888) 783-4007

On a quiet country road where you feel much farther than 8 miles from the bustle of Concord, you'll find this 1790s farmhouse that Art Monty has spent two decades converting into a comfortable bed and breakfast. The seven guest rooms in the farmhouse and carriage house all have private baths, ceiling fans and reading lights. Two larger suites have fireplaces, and guests gather around the wood stove in the informal family room, where the TV is, or the fireplace in the parlor to relax and enjoy the delicious snacks. There's a fireplace in the dining room, too, where guests savor full country breakfasts complete with fresh fruit, home-baked muffins and breads and pancakes or waffles with the farm's own maple syrup. Art is fluent in Spanish and French and can manage in German. He's an excellent

INSIDERS' TIP

We can't emphasize enough the difficulty of traveling with pets. Very few of our accommodations allow pets inside. (Some will recommend local kennels.) It's too hot in the summer and too cold in winter to leave animals in the car. They really will have a better time at home with a neighbor's kid to feed them.

cook and avid skier and cyclist. The inn can accommodate children and even pets.

The Atwood Inn

$$ • 71 Hill Rd., Franklin
• (603) 934-3666

This classic brick Colonial home is surrounded by lovely gardens where, weather permitting, you may enjoy your delicious country breakfast while you watch the birds. Breakfast may include French toast, pancakes or eggs along with ham, sausage or bacon and fresh fruit. At other times breakfast is shared in Maria Atwood's library. Restored with care to provide modern comforts while keeping the appeal of the original, the seven guest rooms are unique and elegant. Each room has a private bath, and four offer working fireplaces in winter. There is also a fireplace in the living room, where guests can gather for snacks in the afternoon. Smoking is not permitted. Children are welcome, and those younger than 12 may stay free with their parents.

Olde Orchard Inn

$$ • Lee Rd., Moultonborough
• (603) 476-5004, (800) 598-5845

The original owners of this farm, Batchelder and Abigail Brown, lived just across the lane from where the house stands today. Their youngest son made the main house's bricks by hand from clay in the pasture out back. He finished the house in 1812, and the farm remained in the Brown family right up to the mid-1990s. With 8 acres of apple trees and other fruit trees, this farm is awash in the scents and colors of blossoms in spring and fruits in summer and fall. A farm pond invites you to enjoy the paddleboat and canoe your hosts provide, unless you'd rather walk down to the lake. Or maybe lying in the hammock or reading in the screen house are more your style. In 1998 the inn added a sauna and spa for guests' enjoyment. You'll look forward to a comfortable night in one of the nine guest rooms, each air conditioned and with a private bath, and the full country breakfast in the morning. Children are welcome here, and the innkeepers will put you in adjoining rooms or slide a rollaway or crib into your room if you ask. The inn also has a one-bedroom summer cottage with a full kitchen if you prefer to cook for yourself.

Chebacco Ranch

$-$$ • N.H. Rt. 153, South Effingham
• (603) 522-3211

The "Best Little Dude Ranch in New Hampshire" is, as far as we know, the only dude ranch in New Hampshire. Just the same, it offers a nice bed-and-breakfast experience on a 200-plus-year-old farm. Their air-conditioned guest rooms are furnished in Western style and have private baths. Rooms are big enough to accommodate a couple of kids along with parents, although the older ones sometimes prefer to sleep in the hayloft. The Rutherfords have converted one old barn into an entertainment center, complete with satellite big-screen TV, more than 1,000 videotapes, musical instruments and the equipment to make and edit your own tapes and videos. The barn also offers a model train set, books and magazines, a pool table and games. The saloon serves no alcohol (this is a dry ranch), but it does offer Moxie and sarsaparilla for the brave of heart. And, oh yes, there are horses, more than 100 miles of trails and riding lessons for all abilities from raw beginner to accomplished equestrian (see our Attractions chapter). Relax those newly discovered muscles in the big hot tub, and you'll be ready for another terrific country-style meal.

Room rentals can include meals, riding and lessons in several combinations, or you can pay for only what you choose. Either way, children 3 to 12 years old stay for half-price, and those younger than 3 stay for free.s

Whispering Pines Bed and Breakfast

$$ • N.H. Rt. 113A and Hemenway Rd., Tamworth
• (603) 323-7337

"Just off the beaten path," is the way the Ericksons describe their cozy bed and breakfast, although it's actually right on one of the state tourism bureau's designated scenic routes. The four guest rooms are decorated according to themes: choose Springtime, Rosegarden, Memories or Woodlands. Guests relax in the comfortable sitting room with its soapstone stove and walk beneath the stars in this secluded woodland setting between the Lakes and the White Mountains regions. Foliage season here on the edge of the Hemenway Forest is simply an unforgettable experience. At breakfast, dine on freshly baked rolls and muffins in the paneled kitchen with its antique stove before you head out to explore the village or tour the Mount Washington Valley.

Smoking is allowed only in a designated outdoor area. Rooms are too small to accommodate extra people, but children older than 10 are welcome if you want to rent them their own room.

Black Swan Inn

$$-$$$ • 308 W. Main St., Tilton
• (603) 286-4524

On a former estate overlooking the Winnipesaukee River, this 19th-century Victorian home now invites guests to enjoy the majestic trees and bright flowers in the formal gardens or sit on one of the porches and enjoy the evening air. Seven guest rooms in the house are highlighted by the original oak, walnut and mahogany woodwork. Some have private baths. Share a quiet conversation in the living room, where the light filters through stained glass and lace curtains and a fireplace takes the chill off the air when needed. A full breakfast starts each morning off right, with pancakes, waffles or omelets, fresh fruit and home-baked breads. Just want a bowl of cereal? That's OK too. The Carriage House has also been converted and houses two suites with living rooms, private baths, telephone, TV and air conditioning. Children 12 and older are welcome.

Tuc'Me Inn Bed and Breakfast

$$ • 118 N. Main St., Wolfeboro
• (603) 569-5702

Once we saw this 1850 Colonial with the sunny screen porch, we couldn't resist going inside. It is truly a treasure. You can enjoy your home-baked breakfast on the porch when the weather is warm or in the elegant dining room when it's cool. The rooms are comfortable and homey, but the delicate carved wooden canopies and valances made by the hostess' husband and hand-crocheted canopies and quilts made by her mother are unlike anything in our homes! Each of the seven guest rooms in the house and converted barn is unique, with a variety of accommodations and decorative themes. Three have private baths, while the other four share baths (two rooms to one bath on the same hall). All guest rooms are air conditioned. The common areas include sitting rooms with TV and telephone and also a delightful music room where guests are welcome to play the piano and listen to the Victrola. Children are welcome, but parents should be aware that the house is filled with antiques, and the inn does not have high chairs or cribs.

Country Inns

Red Hill Inn

$$-$$$ • N.H. Rt. 25B and College Rd., Center Harbor
• (603) 279-7001, (800) 5-REDHIL

Walking around the Red Hill Inn reminded us of being at the Roosevelt "Cottage" at Campobello Island. This mansion was built in 1904 by the scion of the Tufts family (the father invented the soda fountain; the son was a golf course developer). Meticulously restored (there are fascinating before-and-after pictures in the lobby), the rooms are filled with the kinds of comfortable country furniture wealthy people escaped to on holiday in the early part of this century. Antique typewriters are the signature of the Red Hill Inn; we noticed at least one in each of the 26 guest rooms. The inn also has period phones, and they work! Most of the rooms in the inn have fireplaces, and some have balconies. Claw-

INSIDERS' TIP

Call ahead if you discover you'll be arriving late. Your hostess may be getting up at 5 AM to make muffins, and she'd probably rather leave the key under the mat than wait up for you!

foot bathtubs accent some private baths. Down the hill at the farmhouse there are more guest rooms, many with fireplaces and whirlpools, and more rooms in the guest cottages. In 1998 the inn added air conditioning throughout and built an outdoor hot tub and pool.

Gourmet meals in the dining room are enhanced by the harvest of the inn's herb gardens and local farm produce in season. You can choose to include breakfast or all three meals in the price of your room. (See our Restaurants chapter.) Smoking is permitted in some parts of the inn. Children are allowed but not recommended unless they're older than 10.

Gunstock Inn

$$ • 580 Cherry Valley Rd., Gilford • (603) 293-2021

This antique inn has 25 units, each with a private bath, shower and cable TV. Each room has a unique country decor, and all have beautiful views of the lake or mountains. Larger guest suites offer balconies, and everyone is welcome to sit on the deck and enjoy the peaceful setting. Not everything here is old-fashioned, though. The inn has a fitness center with an indoor pool, saunas and steam rooms. The family-style dining room serves dinner each evening and can accommodate weddings and other functions. For overnight guests, a "pantry breakfast" is included. You can enjoy freshly baked muffins or danish, bagels or toast with various toppings, a choice of cereals and fruits as well as several types of coffee, juices and teas. The newly remodeled building offers handicapped accessibility and air conditioning.

The Manor on Golden Pond

$$$-$$$$ • Shepard Hill Rd., Holderness • (603) 968-3348, (800) 545-2141

If you've ever imagined yourself living in an English country manor, this is the place for you. The house sits atop a hill overlooking Squam Lake, with an expansive lawn that stretches down to the shore. The boathouse grounds provide for swimming or fishing, and canoes are available to guests. Enjoy the tennis courts, swimming pool, croquet and other lawn games. Then stroll back up to the manor, where each of the 17 guest rooms is decorated in a unique style, from Empire to Colonial to hunting-lodge. Every room has a view, most have working fireplaces and all have private baths, some with whirlpools. Rooms are air conditioned. The parlors are fabulously appointed, and there's a genuine English pub, The Three Cocks, in the manor. Elegant breakfasts, afternoon tea and dinner are included with your room, and the ever-changing gourmet menu in the dining room will have you wishing you could stay forever. In 1998 the old guest cottages down by the water were replaced with four new luxury cottages, each with a king-size bed, fireplace, Jacuzzi and entertainment center. Continental breakfast for two is included with your stay at the cottage. Children younger than 12 are not allowed at the manor (except at the Carriage House — see our Vacation Rentals chapter). There is no smoking anywhere at the inn.

The Inns at Mills Falls

$$-$$$ • U.S. Rt. 3, Meredith • (603) 279-7006, (800) 622-MILL

Here's something new under the sun — actually, three somethings. These are new inns in the tradition of the great inns of the past but with all the amenities of a modern resort. The Inn at Mill Falls was created 15 years ago in the renovation of an old mill building. The waterfall that powered the mill and gave the inn its name still runs under the building. The inn is connected by a covered bridge to the Mill Falls Marketplace (see our Shopping chapter). Until three years ago the Inn at Bay Point was a bank, but now instead of safety-deposit boxes it features stunning lake views from every room and lake access from its private dock and beach. And in 1998 Chase House at Mill Falls was built on the site of the old Chase's Country Town House restaurant. The inns offer a total of 101 rooms with something for everyone, including some rooms with whirlpools and some with balconies. Chase House has 23 luxury rooms right on the lake with fireplaces and balconies. All the rooms at Bay Point and Chase House are handicapped-accessible, and some are specially designed to be wheelchair friendly. The inns are mostly nonsmoking with a few smoking areas. Children are welcome, and those younger than 12 stay free with their parents.

The inns also have meeting rooms and several outstanding restaurants. Giuseppe's Showtime is an Italian-style bistro, Swasey's Back Porch features fabulous breakfasts and coffees, Mame's is the New England traditional dining room, and the Boathouse Grille features a contemporary menu and a display kitchen. See our Restaurants chapter for more details.

White Mountains and Great North Woods Regions

Bed and Breakfasts

The Country Inn At Bartlett

$$ • U.S. Rt. 302, Bartlett
• (603) 374-2353, (800) 292-2353

You can choose classic bed and breakfast ambiance in one of six guest rooms in the main house built in 1885, or you can stay in one of three cottage buildings housing a total of 10 guest rooms. The cottage buildings offer modern private baths and TV, while the inn rooms share baths. One inn room has a private half-bath. Many, but not all, rooms in both the main house and the cottages have fireplaces. The front porch has rockers waiting for returning hikers. Innkeeper Mark Dindorf welcomes outdoor adventurers. He's been taking care of guests here for 14 years and can arrange anything, but his specialties are outdoor excursions. He loves to talk with guests about their plans and can advise and guide a family on the perfect hiking, skiing or mountain-biking itinerary. You can cross-country ski from your door or downhill ski at Attitash Bear Peak, which is just 2 miles away.

Breakfast certainly takes into account the caloric needs of the athlete. Start with juice and muffins and work up to an any-style omelet. French toast and blueberry pancakes are usually on the menu too. The inn has menus from all the nearby restaurants to help you plan lunch and dinners. And a family-style meal for groups of six or more at the inn is possible with advance notice. Kids are welcome. Discounts are available for children who stay in the same room as parents. Check when you make your reservations. Pets can stay in the cottage, but should not be left unattended if you leave the property. Smoking is only allowed outside.

Jackson House Bed & Breakfast

$$ • N.H. Rt. 16, Jackson
• (603) 383-4226, (800) 338-1268

This lovely country home was built in 1868, and innkeeper Susan English-Maloney arrived in 1986. The atmosphere is casual, befitting the typical outdoor enthusiasts. You're close to Wildcat, Attitash and Cranmore for skiing and not far from the base of Mount Washington for viewing, climbing and driving. Eight of the 12 guest rooms have private baths. Four rooms have gas fireplaces, and the guest living room has a wood-burning fireplace. Most of the rooms have double beds with single beds available in the shared-bath accommodations. Families are welcome although very small children are discouraged since the house is not baby-proof.

Breakfast is straightforward with a choice of blueberry pancakes (the blueberries are from the garden in summer), French toast made from home-baked bread or a cheese omelet. Breakfast is served every day from 7:30 to 8:30 AM. During warm weather, you can relax on the canopied front porch or enjoy the view from one of the Adirondack chairs on the lawn. You can take a nap in the hammock or use the Jacuzzi in the solarium. A two-night minimum is required during fall foliage season and school vacation weeks. Reservations are strongly suggested.

Inn At Jackson

$$-$$$ • Thorn Hill Rd., Jackson
• (603) 383-4321, (800) 289-8600

The grand lobby entrance and stairway are a hint that this 1902 house was custom built. The design was by well-known New York City architect Stanford White, and the client was the Baldwin family (of Baldwin piano fame). The house was converted to an inn in the 1920s. The 14 spacious guest rooms each has a private bath. Five rooms on the third floor also have cable TV and air conditioning. Five guest rooms have fireplaces. In addition to large guest rooms, there is a bar area (no alcohol is served here, but guests can bring their own) with ice and soda machines.

The outdoor hot tub with Jacuzzi is very popular with skiers and hikers, and everybody likes the fireplace in the living room. You can sit quietly and put your feet up while you plan the next day's outing with the help of innkeeper Ginger Stieber. She is a great source for ideas on what to do. She will help design a personal package weekend if you'd like to surprise your traveling companion. Ginger is also the breakfast chef and an excellent baker. You can expect treats such as cinnamon-currant coffee cake or pumpkin-walnut bread to accompany your choice of eggs or breakfast specials such as pancakes and waffles. In winter the grapefruit comes straight from Florida. A two-night stay is required for winter weekends and during fall foliage season. Smoking is allowed in a few guest rooms but not in the common areas.

The Jefferson Inn

$$ • U.S. Rt. 2, Jefferson
• (603) 586-7998

Marla Mason and her husband, Donald Garretson, bought The Jefferson Inn in 1994. The Victorian house was built in 1896 and converted to a bed and breakfast inn in 1983. Guests rave about the hospitality and the breakfasts. Marla is the breakfast chef and prides herself on offering a variety of main courses to compliment the fresh fruit and beverages that are served each morning. You might get to try her Dutch Babies, an individual raised-dough cradle filled with blueberries and raspberries. Sign up the night before for one of three breakfast seatings.

Thirteen rooms include nine rooms with private baths and two two-bedroom suites. Each suite has one bathroom and can sleep as many as six people. The rooms are de-

Photo: David A. Leach Photography

Cooling off in the crisp waters of the Swift River just off the Kancamagus Highway.

lightful, but guests here thrive on the outdoor life. Along with your reservation confirmation, you'll receive a guide prepared by the owners on what to do in the area. The inn offers ski packages with Bretton Woods and golf packages with Waumbek Golf Course just across U.S. Route 2. From Thanksgiving until Christmas, weekend accommodations include "Take Home a Piece of New Hampshire" activities. Guests are invited to a nearby Christmas tree farm to pick out a complimentary holiday wreath and Christmas tree and to take an old-fashioned sleigh ride. The Jefferson Inn is open all year, although the owners may close for a couple of weeks in November and April. The Fourth of July through mid-October is the busiest season, but reservations are necessary all year. There's no smoking indoors, but if you must, you can puff on the porch.

Applebrook Bed and Breakfast

$ • N.H. Rt. 115A, Jefferson
• (603) 586-7713, (800) 545-6504

Kids are welcome at this rambling Victorian farmhouse. The atmosphere is very informal and casual, and kids running through the house won't cause alarm. Room choices include bedrooms with private baths, bedrooms with shared baths and one multi-bed, dormitory-style room. The living room is for everyone. Enjoy the fire in the wood-burning stove, and talk to other guests about what they did that day or get some advice from Martin Kelly and Sandra Conley about where to eat dinner. And if you're alert enough after dinner, take a few minutes to enjoy the outdoor hot tub. You'll be ready to undertake any of the many nearby activities after sampling the soup-to-nuts breakfast choices. Start your day with fresh fruit and cereal and move on to eggs, pancakes or French toast. Once you've fueled up, take off for Six Gun City and Santa's Village right in Jefferson or in winter hit the slopes at Wildcat, Cannon or Bretton Woods. You're a 30- to 40-minute drive from any one of these year-round adventure centers. Applebrook Bed and Breakfast prefers to maintain a nonsmoking environment. It is open year round. Well-behaved dogs are welcome, and the innkeepers will consider other pets. Be sure and reserve in advance.

The Buttonwood Inn

$$ • Mount Surprise Rd., North Conway
• (603) 356-2625

Claudia and Peter Needham have run the Buttonwood Inn since 1995. Their hard work was rewarded in 1998 when the inn was named one of the top 25 small inns in the United States. They describe the ongoing renovation as taking the rambling 1820s cape from early Victorian attic to sophisticated Shaker. The renovated bedrooms include design details such as full-wall murals and Shaker-style furniture built to the inn's specifications. Several rooms have white pine floors that have been painted or stenciled. All 10 guest rooms have private baths. Two family-style suites accommodate four and five guests each. The inn is happy to accommodate entire families and has had extended families take over the entire inn during Thanksgiving. Well-behaved children are welcome, although it's fair to say the inn specializes in couples.

Breakfast always includes eggs, cereal and fresh-baked muffins and breads. A breakfast special, such as French toast, is featured every day. The dining room has private tables in case you're not the type to talk to strangers first thing in the day. The owners pride themselves on their concierge services. They'll help you plan your itinerary, find the perfect dinner and pack a breakfast to go if you have to leave at 5 AM for the airport. Backpacks, water bottles and polar fleece blankets (great for outdoor picnics) are just a few of the amenities on hand for guests. The 17 acres of grounds are at the end of a dead-end road just 2 miles from N.H. Route 16 in North Conway. An indoor pool and extensive gardens are part of the serene package. The downstairs parlor has a TV and VCR. The extensive common space guarantees lots of room for everyone. Smoking is permitted on the outdoor porch.

Cranmore Inn

$-$$ • Kearsarge Rd., North Conway
• (603) 356-5502

Now open as a bed and breakfast, the Cranmore Inn has offered guest rooms for more than 130 years. Since the early 1980s success belongs to Chris and Virginia Kanzler. Their warm hospitality makes relaxing on the front porch seem as important as bagging that next peak. Kearsarge Road is a quiet residential street one block from North Conway's Main Street. You can walk to dinner in less than five minutes. Fourteen of the 18 rooms have private baths with the remaining two-room suites joined by a shared bath. The inn is cozy with a communal TV room and a separate parlor with a piano (guests are welcome to tickle the ivories) and fireplace. Picnic tables surround the outdoor pool. You can order a full breakfast off the menu from 8 to 9 AM. Work off the calories at the Cranmore Sports Club, which is about a quarter-mile away. Guest privileges are included with your room. No smoking is allowed in guest rooms or in the dining room.

Country Inns

Wayside Inn

$ • U.S. Rt. 302 at Pierce Bridge, Bethlehem
• (603) 869-3364, (800) 448-9557

"I am owner and chef. My wife is owner and everything else," is how Victor Hofmann describes the division of labor at this combination inn and motel. The Hofmanns have owned, managed and loved the Wayside for more than 12 years. The inn was built in 1825, and the motel rooms were added about 20 years ago. All of the rooms in the inn were renovated in 1998. Each room has a private bath, and all rooms have either a queen- or king-size bed. You'll find rocking chairs and patchwork quilts in the bedrooms and pedestal sinks and claw-foot tubs in most of the bathrooms. (The bathrooms also have the modern convenience of wall-mounted hair dryers.) The motel accommodations include air conditioning and cable TV; the inn rooms do not.

Victor Hofmann's culinary skills are one of the reasons to stay here. Read about the Riverview Restaurant in our Restaurants chapter. Meal plans are available. The Ammonoosuc River and two nearby golf courses highlight the summer season, while skiing at Bretton Woods is less than 15 miles away. The inn is closed for April and November. During December the Wayside Inn is open on weekends to coincide with the pre-Christmas activities in Bethlehem. The inn is a family affair with lots of guests returning for the quiet charm and excellent food.

Bretton Arms Inn

$$$ • U.S. Rt. 302, Bretton Woods
• (603) 278-1000

The Bretton Arms Inn was built in 1896 and is part of the extended Mount Washington Resort property. The All 34 rooms and three suites are appointed with comfy stuffed chairs and sofas covered in floral fabrics. Each room has a private bath, and most rooms have queen-size beds. The Bretton Arms Inn is a National Historic Landmark. The strong Victorian flavor takes you back a century. The cross-country ski center is adjacent to the inn. Other locations within the resort are easily reched via the free shuttle.

Breakfast and dinner are served in the dining room. Be sure and ask about packages when you call for reservations.

Darby Field Inn

$$ • Bald Hill Rd., Conway
• (603) 447-2181, (800) 426-4147

The original farmhouse was built in 1826 and converted to an inn in the 1940s. Part of the magic here is that you're just 3 miles from the center of Conway, but feel a million miles from the traffic. The casual atmosphere means no one is going to faint if you put your feet up, and slacks and sweaters are the usual dining attire. Fourteen of the 16 rooms have private baths. Breakfast is primarily for guests of the

INSIDERS' TIP

Innkeepers tend to be fonts of information. Looking for a romantic little park or wondering when the historical society is open? Want to buy a local cookbook, rent a bicycle or have someone make you an heirloom quilt? Just ask.

inn, but dinner is served to guests and outsiders alike. Marc Donaldson has owned and managed the Darby Field Inn since 1981.

Guests can enjoy the outdoor swimming pool in the summer and the cross-country ski trails during the winter. Those ski trails become great walking or mountain bike paths once the snow melts and the sun dries up the mud. The inn is closed for April, although exceptions have been made for family reunions and weddings. Peak season is foliage season in September and early October. During this time, the inn prefers for guests to stay under the Modified American Plan (MAP), which includes breakfast and dinner in the room price.

Ellis River House

$$-$$$ • N.H. Rt. 16, Jackson
• (603) 383-9339, (800) 233-8309

This inn caters to couples looking for a romantic interlude. Innkeepers Barbara and Barry Lubao love to help plan special packages for couples. From very private weddings to an anniversary surprise, you can count on thoughtful details, such as monogrammed champagne glasses. The 20 guest rooms have private baths, and most have working fireplaces. The furniture is antique, but you won't feel constrained by the decor. The inn is comfortable and relaxed, with cable TV in every room as well as central air conditioning. The outdoor pool is heated, and there's a full-service pub on the premises. You can fly fish for trout in the Ellis River on the inn's 380 feet of riverfront or try your luck on the nearby Wildcat and Saco rivers. Special packages are available throughout the year. Try the Dine Around Plan, which includes meals at five area restaurants. A two-night minimum applies on weekends, and a three-night minimum is in effect for holiday weekends such as President's Day. No smoking is allowed on the premises.

Sunset Hill House

$$$ • Sunset Hill Rd., Sugar Hill
• (603) 823-5522, (800) 786-4455

Stay on a ridge 1,700 feet high, and watch the sun set in Vermont's Green Mountains and rise over New Hampshire's Presidential Mountain range. These views are one reason this spot was developed during the "Grand Hotel" era of the region. Before skiing and water slides, people traveled to the White Mountains region for the spectacular views. The inn was built in 1882. That luxurious standard of the original period is maintained today. Each of the 30 guest rooms is delightful. All rooms have private baths, and some include a Jacuzzi. If your furnishings aren't antique, you'll appreciate the quality of the reproductions. You can find lots of entertainment here, but participation is not required. The inn has its own cross-country trails and golf course. Weekend activities at the inn might include fly fishing instruction or gourmet cooking.

Special prices are available for Romantic Getaways and Alpine Ski and Stay packages. Sunset has winter specials for Loon, Cannon and Bretton Woods (see our Winter Sports chapter). But if you'd like to spend the day in the hammock or by the fire, no one will mind. The goal here is to help you get away from it all. The inn is open year round and offers bed and breakfast plans as well as those including both breakfast and dinner. Two-night stays are required for some packages and during foliage season. The entire property is nonsmoking.

Dartmouth-Lake Sunapee

Bed and Breakfasts

The Inn on Canaan St.

$$ • Canaan St., Canaan
• (603) 523-7310

Canaan Center is one of the oldest communities in the region, with many of the main street houses built in the 18th century. The main street is Canaan Street, and the inn here was built in the early 1800s with many additions over the years. The inn is next door to Cardigan Mountain School (see our Education chapter), and Cardigan Mountain is visible from the front door. The five bedrooms include three with private baths and a two-bedroom suite with a large shared bath between. All the rooms are comfortably upscale with antique beds and dressers. Oriental rugs, properly worn, are spread throughout the house.

Lee and Louise Kremzner have owned the inn since 1983. Louise says that any talk of remodeling makes returning guests shudder. They count on the understated elegance that makes this inn an easy place to relax and enjoy the surrounding beauty. The 14-acre property is on both sides of the road, and guests can walk through the trees to Canaan Street Lake. The beach has a lifeguard during the summer. All of Canaan Street is on a ridge, and you'll see Killington in Vermont as you look west. You'll have your own table in the dining room for the breakfast buffet. An egg dish and meat dish are always included with the healthful options of fruit, granola and yogurt. Louise bakes delicious fruit scones, and in fall you're sure to see baked apples on the sideboard. Louise is flexible in meeting guests' special food requests. Just be sure and ask ahead when you make reservations. The inn is open all year, and the environment is nonsmoking.

The Chase House

$$ • N.H. Rt. 12A, Cornish
• (603) 675-5391

Even when the house is full (18 guest maximum), you'll feel as though you're the privileged friend of wealthy landowners. This Federal-style historic landmark is the birthplace of Salmon Chase, President Lincoln's Secretary of the Treasury and subsequently the Chase of Chase Manhattan Bank. We think the best thing about The Chase House is the welcoming warmth of Barbara Lewis. (More than 50 percent of the guests are repeats.) She and her late husband bought the house in 1991. The eight bedrooms include six with private baths. Two queen suites include a single bed in addition to the canopied queen-size bed. Children are not encouraged, although those older than 12 are eligible as guests. Since 1995, Barbara has had the assistance of Ted Doyle in day-to-day operations, although she continues to be the exclusive breakfast chef. You can expect a full country meal with treats such as Amish pancakes or cheese strata. All guests eat in the dining room at one sitting. The Chase House is popular for festive events including weddings. The 1,200-square-foot function room dates back to 1810 and was reassembled on the premises after being found by Barbara in Vermont.

The New Year's Eve Party is an annual favorite and includes dinner and dancing. Reservations are required throughout the year, and New Year's reservations must be made by September 30. Throughout the year the minimum stay on weekends is two nights. From mid-September to mid-October the two-night minimum applies all week. Pets can't stay here, but excellent accommodations for them exist nearby. Details can be given when reservations are made. No smoking is allowed on the premises.

Loch Lyme Lodge

$-$$ • 70 Orford Rd. (N.H. Rt.10), Lyme
• (603) 795-2141, (800) 423-2141

The main lodge is the farmhouse built in 1784. It is open for guests year round. From May to September, an additional 25 cabins are available to rent (see our Vacation Rentals Chapter). Three rooms are open year round in the Main Lodge. They share a bath along with another bath downstairs. A full breakfast is served on the sun porch. It really is family-style as you'll be joined by the Barker family: Paul, Judy and their two sons.

The surrounding 100 acres are open for exploration. Bring your cross-country skis in winter and your hiking boots for spring, summer and fall. If you want to get away from the city and vacation like your great-grandmother, give a call to Loch Lyme and hope they've got room for you.

White Goose Inn

$$-$$$ • N.H. Rt. 10, Orford
• (603) 353-4812, (800) 358-4267

Their motto of "we give 120 percent" is one reason the White Goose Inn is often booked up to a year in advance. The speaker is Karin Wolf, who with her husband, Manfred, has owned the White Goose Inn since 1983. The 15 guest rooms are in two houses. One was built in 1770, the other in 1988. Most rooms have private baths, but some in the older house share a bath. The newer rooms include one two-bedroom suite with one-and-a-half baths. The houses are set on 8 acres in the heart of the Upper Valley within a quarter-mile of the Connecticut River. The natural setting includes two ponds for swimming and a deck overlooking a circular flower garden and pergola. The maple trees are more than 200 years old. Breakfast is served from 8 to 9:30 AM every day. Specialties include Karin's home-baked fruit muffins and Dutch baby pancakes, individual ramekins filled with pastry and fruit. After breakfast you can explore nearby Hanover, canoe on the Connecticut or just relax at "home." The bird-watching is wonderful, including a great blue heron that spends its days here.

Reservations are a must. Parents of Dartmouth students and summer campers keep the rooms full. Many guests come from Europe, and it is not unusual for one family to engage all the rooms. The minimum stay is two nights. Smoking is allowed outdoors.

Country Inns

Alden Country Inn

$$ • 1 Market St., Village Common, Lyme • (603) 795-2222

Insiders still call this the Lyme Inn. The 1993 update by new owners Mickey and Tami Dowd hasn't altered the outward appearance of this 1809 landmark, but inside you'll find lots of changes. The 14 guest rooms now have private baths, phones and air conditioning. You can eat in the dining room or the small bar area. Stay here if you'd like something more formal than a tent and sleeping bag after a day hiking the nearby Appalachian Trail. For winter sports enthusiasts, you're just 3 miles from the Dartmouth Skiway.

New London Inn

$$ • 140 Main St., New London • (603) 526-2791, (800)526-2791

Every time we drive into New London, we slow down, take a deep breath and decide we're ready to retire. While we look for our retirement farmhouse or modern condo, we would be happy to spend a few days at this classic New England country inn. The inn, overlooking the Town Green, was built in 1792. The 29 rooms have private baths, and several rooms are large enough to include a cozy sitting area. Your room will have a view of the perennial garden, the Town Green or Main Street. You can book a single, double, queen or king room — the bed size is consistent with the name. Chintz fabrics with designs by Ralph Lauren complement the English and American antique furniture. Downstairs the library and sitting room are designed for your comfort.

Cozy up to the sitting room fireplace in winter. And enjoy great food nearly all year round. (The inn is closed during parts of November and April.) The dining room features a continental breakfast buffet (included in your room rate), and dinner is served Tuesday through Saturday. Brunch is served on Sunday. Call well ahead of your visit: The inn suggests making reservations five to six months in advance. The inn is a two-minute stroll from Colby-Sawyer College so graduation weekend and parents' weekend may require very early reservations.

Monadnock Region

Bed and Breakfasts

Apple Gate B & B

$ • 199 Upland Farm Rd., N.H. Rt. 123 S., Peterborough • (603) 924-6543

Ken and Diane Legenhausen have owned Apple Gate since 1990. The Colonial house was built in 1832 and modernized (indoor plumbing and heating) in 1945. Each of the four rooms has a private bath. The living room has a fireplace, and breakfast is served in the candlelit dining room. Breakfast might include oven-baked pancakes, eggs and home-baked muffins. In late summer and early fall, guests can pick their own fruit in the apple orchard next door. The Sharon Arts Center is 3 miles down the road. Temple Mountain and Miller State Park are within a five-minute drive.

The Loafer Inn

$ • 27 Main St., West Swanzey • (603) 357-6624

The Monadnock region has been called the quiet corner of New Hampshire. Insiders know it's one of the best spots in the state for lazy days and screened porches. At the Loafer Inn guests are encouraged to take the lazy name to heart. Put your feet up, read a book, listen to the backyard waterfall (a recent innovation) and let small town life revive you.

The 16-room house was built around 1792. Two of the six bedrooms have private baths. All of the rooms have charm. You'll find rocking chairs and floral wallpaper, lace curtains and clocks that sound the time. The loving restoration has been done by innkeepers Richard and Cheryl Munson. The Loafer Inn opened in 1997 and has already become a big hit with business people. You might find traveling surveyors spreading their maps on the dining room table when they come in from working the region or parents resting after a visit with their kids at Keene State College. (Keene is just about 10 minutes from the Loafer Inn; see our Education chapter.)

Cheryl's Blueberry French Toast Casserole is a breakfast specialty. You'll always have a hot dish as well as fresh fruits and homemade breads. And in case you're not the type to loaf all day, the Munsons can help you find just the right recreational activity, whether it's boating or searching out the beautiful covered bridges in the immediate area.

The Loafer Inn is not for kids younger than 12, and the only pets allowed are the dog and cat already in residence.

The Greenfield Bed and Breakfast Inn

$-$$ • junction of N.H. Rt. 31 N. and N.H. Rt. 136, Greenfield
• (603) 547-6327

Get away from it all at The Greenfield Bed and Breakfast Inn. You can't miss the only Victorian mansion on the road. Vic and Barbara Mangini own this charming getaway and are proud that they've helped put tiny Greenfield on the map. They cater to harried career couples in need of a rocking chair and a front porch. Most of the 12 rooms have private baths, and one two-room suite with a shared bath is good for families. The rooms have names like Delilah and Sampson (a king-size bed and mountain view) and Casanova, which shares a bath with Heidi. All rooms have TV, and several rooms have fax machines and modems. Vic and Barbara can help you plan just the right walk or drive for your day's pleasure. Greenfield State Park, with Otter Lake and a sandy beach, is a two-minute drive from the inn. And you won't be in a hurry for lunch after eating Barbara's delicious breakfast. Home-baked muffins, eggs and breakfast meats are right alongside the specially mixed Glorious Granola. Advance reservations are always suggested, but between November 1 and April 1 you can get last-minute discounts on available rooms.

Peterborough Manor Bed and Breakfast

$ • 50 Summer St., Peterborough
• (603) 924-9832

Word of mouth among outdoor enthusiasts keeps the rooms full at this very reasonably priced establishment. Australia native Peter Harrison and his wife, Ann, preside over the informal ambiance at this delightfully renovated Victorian. The six main guest rooms have private baths. Bunk accommodations are also available. The continental breakfast is simple in keeping with the casual attitude of the hosts. You can expect coffee, tea, muffins, toast and pastries. A guest kitchen gives you a chance to prepare and store your own supplies.

Stepping Stones Bed and Breakfast

$, no credit cards
• 6 Bennington Battle Tr., Wilton Center
• (603) 654-9048

Gardeners and garden lovers should make a beeline to Ann Carlsmith's delightful house and grounds. When we visited, the apple blossoms and an early rhododendron were blooming, and two orioles were feeding on the deck. The natural landscape continues inside where an enclosed porch and

INSIDERS' TIP

Bed and breakfast licensing does not allow hosts to serve meals to non-guests.

Photo: David A. Leach Photography

Jane Fonda and Katharine Hepburn held a mother-daughter talk on this gazebo in the film *On Golden Pond*.

kitchen are filled with flowering plants and herbs. Chances are you'll be greeted by the two friendly German shepherds (two cats are also in residence) as you park your car near the old barn. From the front door you'll pass through the weaving room on the way up the stairs to one of three guest rooms. Each room has a private bath, and all feature throws woven downstairs. Breakfast shows off another of Ann's skills. Unless you ask, you won't find calorie counting part of the breakfast plan. She'll whip up asparagus with hollandaise sauce to go with poached eggs and perhaps add a side of hash-browned potatoes. And cream is always available to go with the fresh fruit. Stepping Stones is open all year. Reservations are strongly suggested. More than three-quarters of guests have stayed here before.

Country Inns

Fitzwilliam Inn

$ • N.H. Rt. 119, On The Common, Fitzwilliam
• (603) 585-9000

This double-porched Greek Revival house is in the middle of another classic Monadnock New England village. The Fitzwilliam Inn has music concerts on Sunday afternoons during the winter, and innkeeper-soprano Barbara Wallace is an expert baker specializing in desserts. Read about the inn's food in our Restaurants chapter. The inn has 28 guest rooms, the majority of which have private baths. The rooms are not fancy, but the matching curtains and wallpapers might remind you of a great-aunt's guest room. Kids are welcome here, and you can make arrangements to include a crib in your room. Older kids will have fun walking around town and finding the 1779 fire engine at the Blake House, a small historical museum with flexible hours. Pinnacle Mountain is just down the street from the inn, and Rhododendron State Park, with its outstanding flowers, is a five-minute drive.

Red Brick Inn

$ • 4 High St., Greenville
• (603) 878-4028

This c. 1856 inn has 12 guest rooms, 10 with private baths. The building was remodeled and restored in 1995. Breakfast is included in the price of your room and is available from 5:30 AM to noon during the week and from 7 AM to noon on weekends. Dinner is served nightly. The rooms are decorated with much of the original 19th-century furniture. The refurbished iron bed frames and wooden dressers were made in Greenville and are evidence of the mid-19th-century local factory bustle that took place throughout New Hampshire.

The Hancock Inn

$$ • 33 Main St., Hancock
• (603) 525-3318

If we had to pick one town to exemplify the New England postcard image of village green, town meeting house and village inn, it would be Hancock. Built in 1789, the inn has 11 guest rooms with private baths. One room features murals by Rufus Porter (also at the Birchwood Inn, described later). All rooms have some original decorative details from the 1830s. The hooked rugs and hand-stitched quilts are modern-day versions of period crafts. Guests will appreciate the tea cozy-coverings on the televisions warning that removal will result in a fast return to the 20th century. Great care and ingenuity are evident throughout the inn. One room features a claw-foot bathtub in the actual room, as the bathroom was too small for the addition of this amenity. And the smallest room in the inn has a grandly spacious bathroom. The dining room has a fireplace and serves classic American food such as country roast chicken. Dinner is served every night.

The Wright Mansion

$-$$ • 695 Court St., Keene
• (603) 355-2288

The host here is Bill Hermann, who's quickly made a name for himself and his beautiful, understated, elegant inn. The Wright here is the same as the silver-polish conglomerate; the house was built in 1936 for the grandson of the founder. It's a Georgian Revival and has a formal dining room, wood-paneled study and lovely formal gardens on the 2-acre grounds. You can choose from six rooms. Four rooms have separate baths, and two rooms share a bath. The room most frequently requested is the Master Bedroom. It has a queen-size canopy bed, tiled fireplace and four large windows overlooking the gardens. The bathroom has a tiled shower, two sinks and a large, old-fashioned tub. The Webster room features a bed and blanket chest from Daniel Webster's homestead. (He might not have slept at The Wright Mansion, but Daniel Webster certainly slept in the bed.) The framed samplers are authentic and will make even the most modern of us think about learning to cross-stitch. The food is wonderful — the word chef is not used indiscriminately. Look for details in our Restaurants chapter. Reservations are a must.

The Birchwood Inn

$$ • N.H. Rt. 45, Temple
• (603) 878-3285

Even if you can't stay here, you should try and get by for breakfast or dinner to see the beautiful murals in the dining room. The murals were done in 1825 by itinerant painter Rufus Porter. One of the oldest inns in New Hampshire, the Birchwood is smack in the middle of this quaint New England village. Five guest rooms have private baths, and two bedrooms share a bath. Breakfast is served Tuesday through Sunday except from November to April when breakfast is only available on weekends. Breakfast is included in the cost of a night's stay. Special morning treats are Judy Wolfe's homemade jams and Bill Wolfe's homemade sausage. The Wolfes have owned the Birchwood since 1980. He takes care of the outdoor plantings and main course cooking, and Judy bakes desserts. Dinner reservations are required.

Some of the best properties are hidden treasures you'll discover from a hand-painted sign at the end of a dirt road or a 3-by-5 card tacked up at the country store.

Vacation Rentals

If you fall in love with New Hampshire, you may decide you want to come back and stay longer. You'll be looking for a nice place where you can cook your own meals and maybe throw in a load of wash, a place where the kids can go to bed and the adults can sit up and read or play cards. A place like home — but not too much like home. You'll be in the market for a longer-term rental.

New Hampshire has a long history of vacation homes, beginning with the Pemaquid and other native peoples who lived in the inland forests through most of the year but migrated to the seacoast in the spring to catch a year's supply of fish and get away from the black flies. They slept on the sand under the stars. This practice is no longer allowed under local ordinances, so you'll need to find some shelter.

Many of the agents listed in our Real Estate chapter also handle some vacation rentals. Some agencies specialize in this area, and we've given you a few names here. Agencies typically list private homes and cottages that the owners use for a couple of weeks and rent out for the rest of the summer. In some cases the agent also handles upkeep and cleans in between guests, occasionally even providing linen services. In others the guests are expected to provide their own linens and leave the house as clean as they found it. Be sure to ask what the expectations are when you talk with the agent.

We've also described some of the many cottages and condos that rent directly to the public. Some cottages are associated with motels and are like little villages with cottages of various sizes. Often motel cottages are available for shorter-term rentals as well and make a nice option for families traveling with little ones. Condominiums are frequently rented through time-share associations. Many of our condominium facilities are affiliated with timeshare programs, so if you own a week somewhere else, an exchange can be an excellent, affordable way to vacation in New Hampshire. The largest timeshare company operating in New Hampshire is RCI (Resort Condominiums International). You can get in touch with them at (800) 338-7777. Another tried and true way to locate a rental property is to keep your eyes open and a notepad at hand as you're sightseeing. Some of the best properties are hidden treasures you'll discover from a hand-painted sign at the end of a dirt road or a 3-by-5 card tacked up at the country store. These private rentals can be wonderful, but if they're awful you have no recourse to a commercial agent, so be sure all the expectations are explicitly understood by both sides before you sign a lease.

Always note and report any breakage or other damage you find in a property (commercial or privately rented) when you arrive so that everyone knows you weren't responsible for it. Of course, if your six-year-old *does*

INSIDERS' TIP

A "camp" is typically a very rustic cabin in the woods, often without electricity or with a diesel generator and frequently only accessible by off-road vehicle, horseback or boat.

break a lamp, be sure to replace it or make arrangements to pay for it. (Security deposits are typically included with agency rentals.)

Vacation rentals are common in the Seacoast, White Mountains and Lakes regions, available in the Monadnock, Dartmouth and Great North regions, and virtually nonexistent in the Merrimack Valley. You can expect to pay from $550 to $750 per week for a two-bedroom cottage within walking distance of the waterfront. (There are almost no cottages or homes actually on the ocean. The seawall and the road provide some protection to Seacoast homes during our winter storms. In the Lakes Region there are many properties that run right down to the water's edge.) A complete house or condo with all appliances, several bedrooms and more than one bath can run as high as $3,000 per week. You may be able to negotiate a lower price if you rent for a month or the whole summer, and in the off-season these properties are much less costly (although many have no heat and are closed up in winter).

Photo: Courtesy of the Hampton Beach Chamber of Commerce

Hampton Beach is a popular spot for long-term rentals

Merrimack Valley

Condos, Cottages and Cabins

Residence Inn by Marriott
246 Daniel Webster Hwy., Merrimack
• (603) 424-8100

You can rent here by the night or weekend, but the specialty is long-term rentals. Each unit is an apartment, and they range in size from studios to two-bedroom units. Full kitchens (including dishes), personal voice mail, mail delivery and the on-site laundry enable guests to make themselves at home. At the same time, there's hotel-style daily housekeeping, complimentary continental breakfast with newspapers, complimentary light supper on weekday evenings, an on-site exercise facility and a complimentary grocery-shopping service. Sporting equipment and games are also available for guests' use. We were ready to move in! Kids and pets are both welcome.

Seacoast Region

Condos, Cottages and Cabins

Seaside Village
1 Ocean Blvd., North Hampton
• (603) 964-8204

Part old-style motel, part modern townhouse, this summer hideaway has the look and feel of 60 years of family relaxation and enjoyment. You literally step out the door of your room and onto the beach. Thirteen of the units have full kitchens and no daily maid service (bring your own linens), and six are

INSIDERS' TIP

When you book your vacation rental, ask how far away the grocery store is. You may want to shop before you check-in.

motel rooms. Some of the units are air conditioned, but the sea breeze in the evening is usually adequate and much more pleasant.

Wren's Nest Village Inn

3548 Lafayette Rd., Portsmouth

• (603) 436-2481

This inviting complex is just far enough out of town to be relaxing but close enough that all the attractions are only minutes away. Nine buildings are grouped on the 4-acre site, offering a total of 35 rooms with a variety of accommodations from motel rooms to suites to cottages (the most expensive are the suites with whirlpools). One- and two- bedroom country-style cottages and deluxe suites have full kitchens and separate living room areas. Porches, decks and attractive landscaping invite guests to sit out and enjoy the quiet. A lovely continental breakfast is served in the lobby each day.

Crown Colony Cottages

1381 Ocean Blvd., Rye

• (603) 436-8923

With pretty white cottages and a small motel overlooking a green front lawn to the ocean and the Isles of Shoals, Crown Colony is a peaceful spot to spend a night or a week. Sandy Wallis Sands beach is just a few steps from the door of your unit, and you can be in Portsmouth, Hampton Beach or even Maine in 15 minutes by car. Units vary, ranging from one or two double beds to two-room units with twin beds for the kids. Each cottage has a kitchenette and cable TV. If you rent by the week, you must provide your own towels as well as daily upkeep. The motel rooms have mini-fridges and daily housekeeping services. The units have a nice outside sitting area with beach umbrellas and deck chairs where you can enjoy the fresh sea breezes.

Hoyt's Lodges

891 Ocean Blvd., Rye

• (603) 436-5350

This is one of those rare places on the east side of the road, so that the lawn runs down to the rocky shore. Ten units, each with one or two bedrooms, offer a variety of accommodations, from a studio suitable for a single guest or couple (with a sweeping view of the ocean) to units that will allow a family to spread out and feel at home. Every unit has a barbecue and umbrella-table on an old-fashioned porch, as well as a full kitchen. Units have cable television but no phones. Linens are provided. Pets are not allowed. Hoyt's is open from mid-May to mid-October.

Wallis Sands Place

1035 Ocean Blvd., Rye

• (603) 436-5882

These large cottages are directly across the road from pristine Wallis Sands Beach. Some of the ten cottages are contemporary style, some are more traditional or rustic. Half are one-bedroom units and the others have two or three bedrooms each (the maximum number of guests in a three-bedroom unit is seven). Each cottage has a full kitchen (with stove top and microwave oven), an indoor dining area and a nice porch or deck. Picnic tables and grills on the grassy grounds provide another option for dinner! Blankets and pillows are provided, but you bring your own sheets and towels. There are television sets in the cottages but not phones (you can use the payphone in the office). On Sundays in summer the hosts serve a complimentary breakfast on the deck. You may use a check for your deposit but payment on arrival must be made in cash or travelers check: they do not accept credit cards. Pets are not allowed. The cottages are available from the beginning of May to the end of September.

Agents

Preston Real Estate

186 Ocean Blvd., Seabrook

• (603) 474-3453, (800) 424-3453

63 Ocean Blvd., Hampton

• (603) 926-2604

Whether you need a long- or short-term rental, during summer vacation or winter's quiet, Preston's is a good place to start your search. The company handles everything from the professional looking for a two-year rental for the whole family to the vacationer who wants a seaside cottage for a week.

Lakes Region

Condos, Cottages and Cabins

Sandy Point Beach Resort

N.H. Rt. 11, Alton Bay
• (603) 875-6000

Sandy Point has kitchenette cottages and one-bedroom apartments for rent on a daily and weekly basis (weekly only in summer). These units, which vary in size and sleep from two to six people, are rented with no services — guests bring their own linens and pick up after themselves. Guests have access to a private beach and boating facilities (including dock rental) as well as indoor and outdoor games.

The Boulders Motel and Cottages

U.S. Rt. 3, Holderness
• (603) 968-3600, (800) 968-3601

In addition to the motel described in our Hotels and Motels chapter, the Boulders has a variety of two- and three-room efficiency units and three housekeeping cottages to rent for periods from two nights to a week or more. These must be booked and paid for well in advance, as they are filled throughout the summer. The accommodations range from one room with a king-size bed and a kitchen area to two-bedroom units with additional sleep sofas and a kitchen/dining area. The Boulders has a long sandy beach and extensive shoreline on Squam Lake, and the owners have rowboats and canoes to rent if you don't bring your own boat to tie at their dock or mooring.

The Manor on Golden Pond

Shepard Hill Rd., Holderness
• (603) 968-3348, (800) 545-2141

Children younger than 12 are not allowed at the Manor (read the description in our Country Inns section and you'll understand why), but families can still enjoy this stunningly beautiful location overlooking Squam Lake and use the tennis courts, pool, boats and lawn games. Two family suites at the Carriage House are available by the week in summer. Each has one bedroom with twin beds and one with a king-size bed, fireplace, TV, phone and a full kitchen. Pets and smoking are not allowed.

White Oak Motel and Lakefront Cottages

U.S. Rt. 3, Holderness
• (603) 968-3673

A variety of lakeside cottages and a mobile home are available for rent by the week at this friendly spot. The cottages have tiny but usable kitchens, and some have wonderful screened porches. The McHughs serve free continental breakfast and have boats you can use if you don't bring your own. They have an outdoor pool and an indoor whirlpool. Guests can use the phone in the office, and pets are welcome except during the busiest part of summer (mid-July to mid-August).

Summit Resort

White Oaks Rd., Laconia
• (603) 366-4896

The Summit is a timeshare resort, but it also rents condominiums by the night or the week to nonmembers. Each two-bedroom, two-bath unit has luxury appointments for as many as six people, including fireplace and air conditioning, dishwasher, phone and whirlpool bath. Guests also have full use of the health club, indoor and outdoor pools (with water slides), tennis, racquetball, spa and sauna. This resort is open year-round.

The Anchorage on Lake Winnisquam

725 Laconia Rd., Tilton
• (603) 524-3248

Thirty cottages, an apartment and two

INSIDERS' TIP

Not all renters accept credit cards: we've told you if we know, but be sure to ask. If you need all your cash to pay for your room you won't be able to buy souvenirs!

Our lovely Lakes Region is a great place to spend a week — or more.

houses share a mile of lake frontage on the shore of Lake Winnisquam. All the units are fully equipped with linens and dishes (though not with phones or air conditioning). Four private sandy beaches with rafts tethered offshore allow for swimming, diving and sunbathing. A variety of boats is available, or you can dock your own here. More than 30 acres of woods and lawn invite guests to picnic or walk in the woods and pick wild berries. A playground for children and games for young and old are part of the attraction. The Anchorage is open from May through October. In July and August the Anchorage tradition includes campfires, arts and crafts and an end-of-the-week barbecue for all guests.

Lord Hampshire Motel and Cottages

885 Laconia Rd., Winnisquam
• (603) 524-4331

Step back to a simpler time at this delightful combination of roadside motel and lakeside cottages. As we noted in our Hotels and Motels chapter, the motel rooms here all have screened porches looking over the lake and optional kitchenettes (they're in a closet that's unlocked if you rent "with" kitchenette). Down by the water the studio cottages also have screened porches, while the larger ones have awning-type windows for a similar effect. More than 600 feet of lake frontage and a deck built over the water encourage swimming, boating and fishing. Non-motorized boats are available to rent as is a limited amount of dock space for guests' boats. Children love the gently sloping private beach, giant sandbox and gym set. Lord Hampshire is open from May into November.

Agents

Century Lakes Management

130 Lake St., Bristol
• (603) 744-5411, (800) 342-9767

This agency handles rentals in the Newfound Lake area, the western (and less-commercialized) section of the Lakes Region. The agency offers everything from little cottages to luxury townhouses, with something for virtually every price range.

Preferred Properties

N.H. Rt. 25, Center Harbor
• (603) 253-4345, (800) 639-4022

This independent firm is the largest broker of vacation properties in the Lakes Region. It lists private houses, cottages and camps for people who don't use their places through the whole summer as well as some that are exclusively rentals. In addition, Preferred Properties lists boat-related properties such as dock rights, dry racks and other accommodations that are in great demand at this time. Many people return to the same cottage or camp year after year and book next year's week before they go home, so call early if you want to find a place on the water during the summer!

Strictly Rentals

N.H. Rt. 25, Center Harbor
• (603) 253-9800, (800) 782-9575

As the name proclaims, this agency specializes in vacation rentals. It has an extensive listing, with everything from full-sized lakefront homes to condos to small summer cottages. You can ask for fireplaces or screened porches, lakefront properties and places with beach access (which tend to cost less than places right on the water). Rentals begin in January, but don't despair if you've waited until the last minute, because sometimes a cancellation will open up even for the following week. The agency also has some year-round properties, so you can book that snowmobiling or skiing vacation or the week of the big ice-fishing derby.

White Mountains and Great North Woods Regions

Condos, Cottages and Cabins

Mittersill Alpine Resort

193 Mittersill Rd., Franconia
• (603) 823-5511

The original resort opened in 1945. Beginning in 1978, the resort became a vacation-ownership property. You own a vacation week rental, and you can buy a week in any season. The company is managed by a non-profit homeowners association. You can own anything (for a week) from an Austrian-style chalet to an efficiency apartment. Enjoy the indoor and outdoor pools, health club and tennis courts.

The Golden Eagle Lodge

6 Snows Brook Rd., Waterville Valley
• (603) 236-4551

As soon as you see the Golden Eagle Lodge, you'll be glad it's where you're staying. Even before you walk into the two-story lobby, you'll know you are in a luxurious spot. The lodge was built in the late 20th century, and the design pays homage to the hotels built in the late 19th century. This delightfully modern version of a grand hotel includes the convenience of condominium living combined with the service of a fine hotel. It's right on the pond across from Town Square. Shopping and restaurants are just out the front door. Each of the 140 one- and two-bedroom condominium units here is equipped with a full kitchen and living room. Substitute the word suite for condominium, and you'll begin to get an accurate image of the accommodations here. After a day of skiing or biking, you'll be glad to relax in the indoor pool, whirlpools and sauna.

Windsor Hill Condominium

Jennings Peak Rd., Waterville Valley
• (603) 236-8321

Rent a fully furnished one- to three-bedroom condominium any time of year and enjoy the modern village of Waterville Valley. The minimum stay is two days, and if you stay for a week, the seventh night is free. Included in the price is use of the White Mountain Athletic Club, which features swimming pools, whirlpools and saunas, tennis courts, a nine-hole golf course, and canoes and paddleboats. The 10-acre grounds include barbecue grills and picnic tables. In winter take the free shuttle bus to either the downhill or cross-country ski centers. Check out our Winter Sports chapter for Waterville Valley skiing information.

Dartmouth-Lake Sunapee Region

Condos, Cottages and Cabins

Eastman

N.H. Rt. 10 (Exit 13 from I-89), Grantham
• (603) 863-4444

This private resort community is just 10 minutes from Lebanon. The recreational sports include golf, tennis and boating (see our Other Recreation chapter). You can also relax on one of seven beaches on Eastman Lake. Two- to four-bedroom condominiums are available for a minimum stay of two nights. In July and August the minimum stay is one week. Ask about renting an entire house if that best suits your needs. Very few units allow pets so if Fido must come, be sure and call well in advance. A new golf course clubhouse opened in April 1997. It features the Grill Room, which is open for lunch and dinner every day during the summer.

Loch Lyme Lodge

70 Orford Rd., Lyme
• (603) 795-2141, (800) 423-2141

Beginning in 1919 Loch Lyme Lodge has offered family vacations in the heart of the Connecticut River Valley. The Barker family continues the tradition of hospitality and timeless, low-tech recreation. You can fish, play tennis, swim and lounge the summer away while staying in one of 14 cabins available for weekly rentals. Cabins have one or two bedrooms, living room, bathroom, kitchen and porch. In addition to the cabin rental, the housekeeping fee includes the use of all Loch Lyme facilities, daily firewood delivery, trash collection and fresh linens twice a week. Food plans vary. Full meal service begins in late June and continues through Labor Day. Currently reservations are being accepted through 2001.

Monadnock Region

Agents

Hampsey and Grenier Associates

371 Main St., Jaffrey
• (603) 532-4336

If you're ready for a vacation in the Monadnock region, this is the company to call. Whether you're looking for a cabin or a mansion, want to stay for a week or a year, Hampsey and Grenier is happy to help. They manage rental property throughout southern New Hampshire and can find just the right place for you.

INSIDERS' TIP

Be sure you understand the mechanics of heating your rental unit. If it's a wood stove and you haven't built a fire since Boy Scouts, ask! If it's propane, do you know where the shut-offs are? (If it's kerosene you should know that kerosene heaters are not legal for indoor heating in New Hampshire.)

Restaurants

This may be our favorite chapter because we have such a wonderful variety of restaurants in New Hampshire. It was certainly the most fun to "work" on. We've tried to help you find the place to fulfill your food fantasies, whether they're about classic New England seafood, Yankee pot roast or fresh-from-the-orchard apple pie.

We've stayed away from national chains — we figure you know them — but we've included a section covering a few statewide chains. Don't forget to check here as well as in the region you're visiting. We can't help but be proud of local success. And if you should one day see a Foodee's Pizza in Wichita, remember you heard about it here first.

Speaking of local success, you may be surprised by the quality of pizza in New Hampshire. You can find everything from elegant thin-crust pizza with a light layer of tomato to thicker, rustic crusts capable of holding a mountain of Italian sausage. Another surprise may be the overall quality of the fresh vegetables. Our ground isn't covered with snow all the time, and many restaurants and inns grow their own vegetables and herbs. You'll also find vegetarian choices at many restaurants. In fact, one trend we've noticed is that restaurants are offering more vegetarian choices than they did a few years ago.

It's best to assume all restaurants on our list are nonsmoking. Even those that have smoking areas now may not in the future. Be sure to call ahead and ask about smoking if it's important to you.

Price Code

Our price code reflects the cost of entrees for two, not including appetizers, alcohol, dessert, tax or tip. Some of the fancier restaurants only serve complete meals, so be sure and read the details that follow the dollar signs. We have tried to include restaurants in a variety of price ranges, and the highest priced category will frequently include four courses. The New Hampshire meals tax is 8 percent, and many restaurants add a 15 percent gratuity to groups of six or more. Unless we tell you otherwise, you can pay with a major credit card.

$	$15 and less
$$	$16 to $30
$$$	$31 to $49
$$$$	$50 and more

Statewide Favorites

Blake's Ice Cream Restaurant

$ • 53 Daniel Webster Hwy., Manchester • (603) 627- 1110
353 S. Main St., Manchester • (603) 669-0220
Mall of New Hampshire, 1500 S. Willow St., Manchester • (603) 668-6554
222 Elm St., Milford • (603) 673-6300
Fox Run Mall, Fox Run Rd., Newington • (603) 431-7460

This local chain is an Insider tradition. Once the retail side of a big dairy farm, Blake's is known for wonderful ice cream and special seasonal flavors. It also serves big country breakfasts; a nice variety of sandwiches, salads and burgers; and dinner entrees from stir-fry to surf and turf to fried liver and onions. Each location serves three meals every day.

Foodee's Pizza

$ • 2 S. Main St., Concord • (603) 225-3834
66 Third St., Dover • (603) 742-5055
45 Lyme Rd., Hanover • (603) 643-8852
Loon Mtn. Base Lodge, Lincoln • (603) 745-6281
167 Union Sq. (called the Oval), Milford • (603) 672-5333
165 Deer St., Portsmouth • (603) 431-2100

A local pizza success story, Foodee's

opened in 1985 in Hillsboro and was soon winning "best pizza" awards from as far away as Boston. All the stores are known for natural, healthy pizzas and a variety of freshly made crusts including sourdough and whole wheat. You can also order a deep-dish Chicago-style pizza. The menu features international choices, with refried beans and guacamole on the Mexican pizza and olives and feta cheese on the Greek. Vegetarian choices include spinach with green and red peppers. All locations are open every day for lunch and dinner.

Newick's

$$ • 431 Dover Point Rd., Dover
• (603) 742-3205
696 Daniel Webster Hwy., Merrimack
• (603) 429-0262
845 Lafayette Rd., Hampton
• (603) 926-7646

Newick's opened in 1948 and has since expanded into a chain with four locations (the other one is in Maine.) Newick's draws crowds of Insiders with a variety of seafood dishes including enormous seafood platters mounded with sea scallops, clams, shrimp and haddock. (They do offer a smaller version or allow you to split one.) Combo plates, pasta dishes and a dozen lobster dishes fill out the menu, with a couple of burgers and a chicken sandwich in case you have a non-seafood eater in your party. Newick's has a full bar to complete the meal. The fish market allows you to have the freshest fish at home too. It's open every day, year round. The Merrimack location has 500 seats and still has a waiting line, which is a pretty solid endorsement.

The Ninety-Nine Restaurant & Pub

$-$$ • 1308 Hooksett Rd., Hooksett
• (603) 641-2999
1685 S. Willow St., Manchester
• (603) 641-5999
10 St. Laurent St., Nashua
• (603) 883-9998
N.H. Rt. 28, Salem • (603) 893-5596
831 Lafayette Rd., Seabrook
• (603) 474-5999

This New England chain now has five New Hampshire locations with new sites under construction. For a quick, tasty lunch or dinner, the selection here is excellent: salad plates, chicken dishes, a variety of pastas and great steaks and ribs. Friendly service includes crackers and cheese or popcorn while you wait — not that the wait is long. A wide selection of beers and ales is available in the pub or with dinner, including one ale brewed especially for the Ninety-Nine.

Shorty's Mexican Roadhouse

$-$$ • N.H. Rt. 101, Bedford
• (603) 472-3656
N.H. Rt. 3-A, Litchfield
• (603) 424-0010
1050 Bicentennial Dr., Manchester
• (603) 625-1730
328 Nashua Mall, Nashua
• (603) 882-4070
Fox Run Mall Fox Run Rd., Newington
• (603) 430-2825
N.H. Rt. 12 A, West Lebanon
• (603) 298-7200

All the locations of this popular eatery are busy every weekend and most weekday evenings. Customers come for a variety of Mexican and Southwestern dishes, including some unusual combinations (ravioli with black beans, for example, or a quesadilla filled with smoked salmon and goat cheese). Some American-style meals are offered for the faint of palate. Although many items on the menu are only mildly hot, the option to add more spice is available at the customer's request. Shorty's is open daily for lunch and dinner.

Weathervane Seafood Restaurant

$-$$ • N.H. Rt. 101, Bedford
• (603) 472-2749
U.S. Rt. 4, Chichester
• (603) 225-4044
2 Dover Point Rd., Dover
• (603) 749-2341
Daniel Webster Hwy., Nashua
• (603) 891-1776
N.H. Rt. 28, Salem
• (603) 893-6269
N.H. Rt. 12-A., West Lebanon
• (603) 298-7805

This chain started on the coast of Maine and today continues the tradition of serving fresh seafood at reasonable prices across

New England. The Weathervane is known for fresh seafood — grilled, fried, broiled and boiled to perfection. The menu offers unusual niceties. Most meals come in a standard size (large) and a smaller size (what you'd probably eat at home), and most combo-plates allow you to choose what you'd like to combine — fish and shrimp, chicken and calamari, oysters and smelts, whatever you prefer. The Weathervane is open for lunch and dinner every day.

Merrimack Valley Region

Greenhouse Cafe

$$-$$$ • N.H. Rt. 101-A at Craftsman Ln., Amherst • (603) 889-8022

When Insiders are looking for a present for someone special, a gift certificate to the Greenhouse is almost always on the short list. This airy restaurant, specializing in Swiss cuisine, has been recommended in *The New York Times* and catered banquets for many of New Hampshire's rich and powerful. The veal dishes are exquisite, but there are plenty of other choices too. On Sunday the Greenhouse serves a champagne brunch, and Tuesday is Romance Night, with wine and piano music to enhance your meal. The Greenhouse serves lunch and dinner every day except Monday and brunch on Sunday. We recommend making reservations on weekends.

Bedford Village Inn

$$$ • 2 Village Inn Ln., Bedford • (603) 472-2001, (800) 852-1166

Serving three meals daily and Sunday brunch with a fanatical attention to detail has made the Bedford Village Inn a legend in New England. The menu changes seasonally, using the freshest ingredients. Have something you'll never find anywhere else. How about smoked Scottish salmon for breakfast or a pizza made with field greens for lunch? Even the lighter fare in the Tap Room has a certain something that lets you know the chef cares about your meal. As for dinner? Well, the Inn offers lobster as an appetizer, but we'd recommend something smaller so you'll be able to finish your roast pork with barley and blueberry sauce or veal chop with forest mushroom vinaigrette. Try not to drool on the menu; this is a classy place. The dining room is open every day except Christmas.

C.R. Sparks

$$ • 18 Kilton Rd., Bedford
• (603) 64-SPARK

The casual atmosphere at C.R. Sparks belies the artfully prepared dishes you'll enjoy. The open-hearth kitchen features a wood-fired oven and open-flame grill that give all their fish and steak dishes an intriguing twist. Rotisserie-cooked meats are another specialty here. Our vegetarian had no trouble selecting from the pasta and salad selections, and you could make a meal on the appetizers (in fact, one of our party did just that). We were there at lunchtime, but plan to return at dinner some evening to explore the beer and wine list more fully. C.R. Sparks is open seven days a week.

The Grist Mill Restaurant

$$ • 520 South St., Bow
• (603) 226-1922

A rustic restaurant on the banks of the Turkey River, The Grist Mill offers a variety of baked seafood dishes and grilled steak and chicken. The shrimp and scallops are fresh and tasty, but Insiders really recommend this restaurant for its appetizers — some people just order a selection of their favorite appetizers and call it a meal. Previous uses of the site included several different water-powered mills. The grist (or grain) mill that gave the restaurant its name was the scene of an ill-fated courtship and the tragic death of the miller's only daughter. Locals still refer to the water above the dam as Polly's Pond.

Luisa's

$ • 19 S. River Rd., Bedford
• (603) 668-0581
788 S. Willow St., Manchester
• (603) 627-0006
671 Hooksett Rd., Manchester
• (603) 625-1331

This is our favorite place to eat when we take those extended shopping trips to Manchester. All the Italian specialties are terrific (chicken pesto with ziti is the biggest seller), but the calzones are absolutely wonderful. Luisa's even has Italian beer to go with your meal. It's open daily for lunch and dinner.

The Wayfarer Restaurant

$$$ • 121 S. River Rd., Bedford
• (603) 622-3766

The Wayfarer offers a choice selection of dinner entrees (meat, fish and fowl), prepared according to your instructions and accompanied by seasonal fresh vegetables and gourmet condiments. Or enjoy one of the chef's specialties — smoked chicken, perhaps, or penne pasta with smoked Gouda sauce. Every item on the menu is a treat, but beware the dessert cart if you're dieting! Breakfast and lunch are also served here daily, and Quackers Lounge is open for a drink and, sometimes, live music. See our Hotels and Motels chapter for more about the Sheraton Tara Wayfarer Inn.

The Creamery Restaurant

$$$$ • Shaker Village, Canterbury
• (603) 783-9511

Enjoy a family-style meal (all guests sit together at long trestle tables) with cooking unlike anything we get in our families! The four-course candlelight dinner offers you a choice of a pork, seafood, chicken, lamb or beef main dish, prepared according to Shaker tradition with simple, fresh ingredients, which

INSIDERS' TIP

The letters P.A. on a menu mean "priced accordingly," which means the price varies daily depending on wholesale costs. "Market Price" is also used to indicate a fluctuating price. It's quite common to see these notations next to lobster and clams. Be sure and ask your server to explain how the price is calculated.

are generally from local farms. Dinner is served only on Friday and Saturday evenings, but lunch is available at mid-day every day. See our Attractions chapter for details about Canterbury Shaker Village.

Capital City Diner

$, no credit cards • S. Main St., Concord • (603) 228-3463

Everyone who works in Concord recommends the Capital City Diner! This authentic 1950s diner at the south end of Main Street is now a part of the Common Man family, with the same terrific menu as the Tilt'n Diner up in the Lakes Region. Try shepherd's pie, country fried chicken, a great sandwich or a burger. Drop a quarter in the jukebox, flip through the copies of *Life* magazine from the 1950s and 1960s and try the diner's own root beer. Capital City Diner serves three squares a day, seven days a week.

Cat'n Fiddle

$$ • 118 Manchester St., Concord • (603) 228-8911

This is a Concord institution, run with a personal touch by a family that came from Greece a quarter-century ago. Insiders like it as a place to bring out-of-town guests or clients. You'll enjoy roast beef or turkey, teriyaki chicken and beef, seafood and a salad bar. Cat'n Fiddle is open for lunch and dinner, seven days a week.

Egg Shell Restaurant

$, no credit cards • 30 Manchester St., Concord • (603) 225-0011

Brookside Mall, 563 North N.H. Rt. 106, Loudon • (603) 783-4060

Neither of these restaurants would catch your eye, but Insiders rave about them. (The original Loudon store is in a strip mall near the racetrack, and the Concord location shares a shopping center with an auto parts store.) The Egg Shell serves breakfast and lunch every day. Omelets are the stars here, with 13 variations on the menu and more ingredients you can ask for to customize your choice. Sandwiches and burgers fill out the menu, along with fish or chicken 'n' chips (except on Saturday).

The Franklin Pierce Dining Room at the Centennial Inn

$$$ • 96 Pleasant St., Concord • (603) 225-7102

The chef at this new yet traditional inn varies the menu with the seasons to take advantage of the best fresh ingredients available. For example, the summer dinner menu recently offered herbed goat-cheese strudel made with eggplant and phyllo, a grilled sea bass on red pepper polenta and a grilled ostrich appetizer. The restaurant also serves more traditional seafood, poultry and meat dishes for those who prefer the familiar. Breakfast and lunch are also served in the dining room, with a similar variety on the menu, and recently the inn has added a Sunday brunch buffet. See our Bed and Breakfasts and Country Inns chapter for more details about the Centennial Inn.

Colby Hill Inn

$$$$ • The Oaks, Western Ave., Henniker • (603) 428-3281

Breakfast here is just for guests of the inn, but at dinner the inn welcomes any guest (older than 7) looking for a special meal with a wonderful view. The menu changes often, using the best fresh produce and Chef Michael's inspiration. Colby Hill chicken, stuffed with lobster, leeks and boursin cheese, is the inn's signature dish and should give you a hint of what you'll find here. Delightful and unusual sauces complemented the lamb, swordfish, scallops and duck dishes we found, served with freshly baked bread. Loyal diners can be placed on the mailing list to receive updates as the menu changes.

Stevie P's Yacht Club

$$ • 49 Lowell Rd., Hudson • (603) 886-5191

This charming seafood house serves a great variety of fresh fish and shellfish along with a good selection of non-seafood choices, all at very reasonable prices. Many of the guests are on a first-name basis with the staff, sharing anecdotes and pictures — in other words, people come back often! The platters are piled high, and the service is prompt and friendly (although you may wait a while for a seat). Sunday through Thursday the menu features five different all-you-can-eat choices. Whether you choose baked stuffed haddock or chicken pot pie, we think you'll be coming back too. Stevie P's is open for lunch and dinner every day.

The Homestead

$$ • Mammoth Rd., Londonderry
• (603) 437-2022

The Homestead is a restored Colonial home on one of the busiest intersections in southern New Hampshire. The crowd in the parking lot is a good indication of the food inside, and the Homestead has a very loyal following. The menu offers more than 30 different meat, seafood, pasta and poultry dishes, each with a nice twist such as a special sauce, stuffing or topping to dress it up. The Homestead serves lunch and dinner daily and Sunday brunch. The original Homestead, in Laconia, shares this delightful menu!

Basil's at the Highlander Inn

$$ • 2 Highlander Way, Manchester
• (603) 625-6426

Basil's is essentially at the airport, but you don't feel like you're in an airport restaurant when you're here. The quiet setting and lovely decor make both Basil's and the Highlander Inn attractive for weddings and parties as well as business travelers. (See our Hotels and Motels chapter for the Highlander.) Choose from artfully prepared fresh seafood, steak or pasta. Basil's serves breakfast, lunch and dinner daily.

Clam King

$ • 791 Second St., Manchester
• (603) 669-2868

The Clam King is one of those places you have to learn about from an Insider. You might never stop in based on its plain, 1950s exterior or cafeteria-style dining room. You might not even drive this far down Second Street, where it sits among auto-repair shops and fast-food restaurants. But Clam King is a locals' favorite. Everything is absolutely fresh, from the crunchy salads to the heaping seafood platters. The homemade onion rings are an experience. There are barbecued ribs and burgers if you're not a seafood fan, and you'll need a doggie bag to bring home what you can't finish. It's open for lunch and dinner every day.

Fratello's Ristorante Italiano

$$ • 155 Dow St., Manchester
• (603) 624-2022

We were thrilled to try this beautiful restaurant in one of Manchester's renovated mills. Opened in August of 1997, this is the newest location of the local family- owned business that includes the Homesteads in Bristol and Londonderry and the original Fratello's in Lakeport. The atmosphere is casually elegant and the food is exquisite, combining large helpings and a very attractive presentation. Seafood or pasta, beef or veal or chicken, every item shows attention to detail that makes eating here a very special experience. The pizzas are cooked over an open flame and can be as plain or as gourmet as you like: how about hot cherry peppers with artichoke hearts and feta?

Nutfield Ale & Steak House

$$ • 55 John Devine Dr., Manchester
• (603) 666-3030

This restaurant was added when the Sheraton Four Points chain took over the hotel in 1997. You can enter from the street or through the hotel. The pub features microbrewed beers and ales from Nutfield Brewery over in Derry and melt-in-your-mouth steaks fixed in a variety of tempting ways: Portobello mushrooms and garlic-and-onion chutney are just two of the tempting add-ons. You'll also find lamb chops, chicken, crab cakes and salmon on the menu as well as a good assortment of salads and sandwiches. The restaurant serves a full breakfast, lunch and dinner every day.

The Puritan-Back Room

$-$$ • 245 Daniel Webster Hwy. N., Manchester
• (603) 623-3182

Ask Manchester Insiders where they eat out, and the Back Room is generally the first or second place mentioned. At the front of the restaurant are the function rooms and a take-out window that serves three meals a day, seven days a week, along with lots and lots of Puritan's own ice cream, for which the place is duly famous. Drive around back and enter there for the restaurant (hence "Back Room"). You will find a great selection, including lamb, beef, chicken and seafood, and at least five daily specials. In most cases meals are available in two sizes, which is nice for those with less-than-giant appetites. The restaurant also has a children's menu. The Back Room is open for lunch and dinner every day.

Stark Mill Brewery & Restaurant

$$ • 500 Commercial St., Manchester • (603) 622-0000

Right by the river in a remodeled mill building, the Stark Mill folks produce a nice variety of beers and serve some terrific food to go with it. They serve lunch and dinner every day. Specialty pizzas, such as eggplant and feta, burritos and tacos, tabbouleh and hummus vie for your attention with steaks, ribs and daily specials. Close your eyes and point, if you must, they're all good. And though the wine list is lovely, lovers of good beer will find plenty to try out. Take notes, because Stark Mill ales are now available in local grocery stores. See our Nightlife chapter for observations about the live music at the "SMB" (as they call it).

The Yard

$$ • Junction of Mammoth Rd. and S. Willow St., Manchester • (603) 623-3545

This popular restaurant and lounge on the outskirts of town attracts a loyal following with fresh pasta dishes, seafood and terrific beef — prime rib, filet mignon, sirloin kabobs and teriyaki are notable. Save room for dessert because their mud pie is famous. The Yard is open Monday through Saturday for lunch and dinner, and serves brunch and dinner on Sundays. See our Nightlife chapter for information on The Yard's busy lounge.

Beacon's of Boston

$$ • 4 Continental Blvd., Merrimack • (603) 424-1211

From the parking lot you can see that you're on one of the busiest intersections in New Hampshire, but step inside and you'll feel like you've walked into a friendly English pub. Choose from a dozen prime beef cuts, fresh fish or succulent chicken for your lunch or dinner. Sit back, relax and enjoy the free entertainment until it's time for your business meeting or to get back on the highway. Beacon's is closed on Sundays except for special functions.

Country Gourmet

$$$ • 438 Daniel Webster Hwy., Merrimack • (603) 424-2755

Although we can't prove that he ever ate here, this inn was in business when Daniel Webster was making the trip back and forth from Boston to Concord along this road. We do know that Andrew Jackson stayed here before the Civil War. The ancient building was rescued and renovated in 1978, preserving the pumpkin pine wainscoting. Since then it has developed a reputation for excellence in dining. Cajun cooking is a specialty here, and we don't know of another New Hampshire restaurant serving 'gator tail. You'll have to choose between grilled, blackened or sautéed seafood, unless of course you select roast duckling, veal scaloppine, lamb Santarini or another delicately prepared delight. The full bar offers local beers as well as V.S.O.P. cognacs. (See our Nightlife chapter for Stormy

INSIDERS' TIP

The Old Country Store and Museum in Moultonborough has been in continuous operation since 1781. (But the oldest general store in the United States is down the lake in Tuftonborough Center.) One of the original Concord Coaches is on display at the Museum.

Mondays, the lounge.) Dinner is served here every night. We're guessing you'll be planning a return visit before you're done.

Hannah Jack Tavern

$$ • Daniel Webster Hwy., Merrimack • (603) 424-4171

Don't let the "tavern" in the name fool you — this is a very nice restaurant. The restored 18th-century home offers intimate dining, as there are only a few tables in each room. Steak, chicken and seafood dishes, home-baked breads and a crowd-pleasing salad bar win kudos from Insiders, who frequently mention Hannah Jack as a place to bring out-of-town guests. If it's hard to decide, the menu provides for mix-and-match combos. The Hannah Jack serves dinner every night and lunch Monday through Friday.

The Lobster Boat Restaurant

$$ • 453 Daniel Webster Hwy., Merrimack • (603) 424-5221

We'd be remiss if we didn't tell you about this local favorite. Great lobster dinners and other giant seafood platters keep people coming back here year after year. Even if the parking lot is full, the food is worth the wait. The Lobster Boat serves lunch and dinner Monday through Friday and dinner all day on weekends. Look for the lobster boat gone aground on the roof!

Silver Maple Restaurant

$$ • 356 Daniel Webster Hwy., Merrimack • (603) 429-1688

For a casual lunch or an elegant graduation dinner, lovers of real Chinese cuisine will enjoy the Silver Maple. Neptune's Blessing combines lobster, scallops and shrimp, but if you're dieting you can feel just as blessed with the spicy orange chicken with water chestnuts and broccoli. Our vegetarian appreciates finding a variety of options on the menu here. Silver Maple is open for lunch and dinner every day.

The Mile Away

$$$ • 52 Federal Hill Rd., Milford • (603) 673-3904

Relax in the c.1810 barn and admire the wide pine floors and hand-hewn beams. Come in cold weather, and you'll enjoy the two large working fireplaces. In 1995 two of Milford's most talented teachers (each had been honored as New Hampshire Teacher of the Year) reopened one of the region's old favorite restaurants. Take all the time you want to enjoy several courses of delicious continental favorites. Veal Piccata Milanaise is just one of four veal choices, and seafood regulars include seafood Newburg and baked, stuffed Maine lobster. Maple custard and peach Melba are dessert options, and the pastry tray has lots of beautiful temptations. The restaurant serves dinner every day except Monday, and opens at 2:30 PM on Sunday.

Tortilla Flat

$ • 595 Daniel Webster Hwy., Merrimack • (603) 424-4479

Tortilla Flat has been selling authentic Mexican food in Merrimack since before the Southwestern craze began. Now you can barely get a seat in the place on Saturday night. Choose your dining room based on whether you prefer big-screen TV sports or Mexican folk music. Then decide on your meal. Will it be a chimichanga, quesadilla, burrito or enchilada? Do you prefer beef, chicken, cheese or vegetarian filling? Would you like rice, refried beans or black beans? If you're not clear on the distinctions, they'll be happy to explain. Or you can just have a burger or steak. Tortilla Flat is open every day for lunch and dinner.

INSIDERS' TIP

Parking for Nashua's downtown restaurants can be a challenge. Look for the big blue "P" signs directing you to several municipal parking lots on the side streets. In the evening, try bank parking lots, which are available after hours.

Giorgio's Italian Eatery

$• Edgewood Shopping Plaza, Nashua St., Milford
• (603) 673-3939

This looks like an unlikely spot for a real Italian restaurant, and in truth many people just come here for take-out pizza. The pizza is fabulous. But there's genuine Italian cooking going on here too, and the pasta dishes, Parmesans and pastries will knock your socks off. (Our absolute favorite is linguini with clams and white sauce.) Everything is freshly homemade except the pasta, which is imported from Italy. Giorgio's is open for lunch and dinner every day.

Kelly's Seafood and Sirloin

$$ • 251 Elm St., Milford • (603) 672-6422

New England specializes in good fried seafood, and Kelly's is no exception. The fried shrimp is our favorite, but friends rave about the scallops and oysters too. All seafood (except clams) is available baked or broiled as well. You're sure to see a summer special of steamers (bite-size clams steamed open and served with clam broth and melted butter) and lobster. Whatever the season, you can always get a bowl of delicious chowder. Our favorite is the fish, but others swear by the lobster stew. The barbecue ribs are popular, and we've noticed that a lot of people go for the foot-long hot dog. New menu additions include lobster Alfredo and shrimp scampi. Kids are welcome at this casual spot. Hamburgers and grilled cheese sandwiches are sure to suit if seafood doesn't. Kelly's is open for lunch and dinner every day and adds breakfast on weekends.

LuCille's Dinette

$, no credit cards • On the Milford Oval, Milford
• (603) 673-8599

The rejuvenated Milford Oval boasts a wealth of terrific little eateries — we wish we had room to list them all. LuCille's is a relative newcomer that has built a fiercely loyal clientele. LuCille's tends to overflow at lunchtime, but fortunately, if the weather is nice, you can take your sandwich and sit on the green. Come in at breakfast for wondrous homemade muffins, and then come back at lunch for a sandwich, a turkey dinner or a bison burger! LuCille's is open for breakfast (at 5 AM) and lunch every day.

Allie's American Grille

$$ • 2200 Southwood Rd., Nashua
• (603) 880-9100

This is the restaurant in the Marriott Hotel (see our Hotels and Motels chapter). It serves a variety of cuisines, a little Italian, a little Southwestern, some New American and some old favorites too. The menu includes suggested wines with each entree, so you can order like a connoisseur even if you haven't got a clue.

Allie's is open for breakfast, lunch and dinner every day and serves brunch on Sundays.

Anthony's North End

$$ • 28 Railroad Sq., Nashua
• (603) 889-5797

This doesn't look like a place where you'd find fine Italian food, but Anthony's has a loyal following among Nashua Insiders, many of whom had mothers who learned to cook in the Old Country. Sicilian-style foods are a specialty, but you'll find all your favorite pasta dishes from farther north too. The restaurant, in an old downtown hotel building at the north end of Main Street, is open seven days a week for lunch and dinner.

Charman's Restaurant & Lounge

$$ • 537 Amherst St., Nashua
• (603) 883-4052

When we were very young, Charman's was halfway to Grandma's house and a good place to stop for supper. The mysterious (to us) Greek, Italian and American dishes and the fresh seafood made it hard to decide then, and they still do! The restaurant moved across the street a few years back, and it's no longer out in the middle of nowhere, as the city has spread down the N.H. 101-A corridor. The food is just as good as we remember. The restaurant is open every day for breakfast and serves lunch and dinner Monday through Saturday.

Country Tavern

$$ • 452 Amherst St., Nashua
• (603) 889-5871

Mom used to say, "That's the prettiest house on the road, too bad it's so close to the street." Then the shopping areas spread, and we were afraid this 1741 farmhouse would be torn down. Instead, the lovely home was converted into this terrific restaurant. A great selection of steak dishes, wonderful seafood and creative chicken and pasta means there's something for every taste here. They are proud of their ghost, Elizabeth, but we have to say the food is worth stopping for even if you didn't see her *Hard Copy* segment. The Country Tavern serves lunch and dinner daily and Sunday brunch.

Martha's Exchange

$$ • 185 Main St., Nashua
• (603) 883-8781

This brew pub is one of Nashua's hottest restaurants, and without a reservation you can easily wait two hours for a seat on Friday evening. The menu includes roast lamb and pork as well as Parmesans, stir fries and steaks. Insiders insist that the Tornados Surf & Turf au Poivre is the best dinner entree, but we haven't tried every meal on the menu yet, so who knows? The beer is wonderful. The pub rotates the selection, depending on what's brewing, but generally has a pale ale, a brown ale, a stout and a seasonal brew as well as a home-brew root beer (nonalcoholic). The Downtown Brown is our favorite. Martha's serves lunch and dinner every day and breakfast on weekends. There's sports on the TV over the bar and occasional live music.

Coyote Cafe

$$ • 207 Main St., Nashua
• (603) 883-1610

Right in the heart of downtown, Coyote's Southwestern decor and Mexican food have earned it a great reputation in a city with many great restaurants. Even the pasta and seafood dishes here have a Southwestern flair. How about grilled scallops with pumpkinseed pesto, roasted garlic, cream and roasted red peppers? Or maybe chicken sauteed in salsa picante on angel hair pasta? Of course the cafe has enchiladas, tacos and fajitas too, and an award-winning chili. Tequila is the favored drink from the full bar. Coyote serves daily lunch and dinner and Sunday brunch.

Crowne Plaza Hotel

$$-$$$$ • 2 Somerset Pkwy., Nashua
• (603) 595-4155

These two restaurants at the Crowne Plaza Hotel (see our Hotels and Motels chapter) can accommodate a variety of tastes. Speakers Corner Pub ($$) is open for breakfast, lunch and dinner and offers sandwiches, steaks, seafood and pasta dishes for a range of prices and appetites. The Chicago Steak Room ($$$$), hidden away at the back of Speakers, is designed to have the feel of an old-fashioned club or dining car. Dinner is brought to your table on a "presentation cart" so you can select precisely what you want. Choose from the finest aged beef, fresh swordfish and shrimp, fresh vegetables and fine wines. Finish with cordials, cappuccino and one of the elegant dessert creations.

La Hacienda del Rio

$$ • Daniel Webster Hwy. S., Nashua • (603) 888-3353

Insiders say this is one of the best places to eat Mexican food in the state, and the busy parking lot seems to bear that out. In addition to fajitas, enchiladas and chimichangas, you'll find unusual entrees such as calabacitas lancha, which is a baked stuffed zucchini, or estofa camarones, shrimp stuffed with crab meat served with a cilantro dressing. They also have a full American menu — steak, chicken, sandwiches and burgers — to accommodate all tastes for lunch or dinner every day.

Lilac Blossom

$$ • 650 Amherst St., Nashua • (603) 886-8420

Not your typical Chinese restaurant, the Lilac Blossom offers a delightful, airy ambience with china, linen and waiters in tuxedos. The food is delicate and delicious. You'll find traditional Szechuan, Hunan and Cantonese cuisine as well as some unique specialties of the house. Whether you try the Lilac Scallop, Chicken Amazing or Tangerine Beef, or just split a PuPu Platter, you're in for a treat. It's open for lunch and dinner every day — we especially like to come for lunch, when the moderately priced specials provide enough for another meal at home!

Michael Timothy's Urban Bistro

$$$ • 212 Main St., Nashua • (603) 595-9334

Tucked into a couple of storefronts in Nashua's revitalized downtown, you'll find this intimate dining room. Fine china, nice linens, cool jazz (see our Nightlife chapter) and gourmet meals make this a very special spot for lunch or dinner. You won't be surprised by the line on the sidewalk if we tell you Michael Timothy's won the *Telegraph's* 1998 Reader's Choice awards for the best new restaurant, best jazz club, best creative cuisine, best wine list and best brunch in greater Nashua. Whether you select roast duck, braised salmon and clams, wood-grilled pork medallions or any of the other elegantly served delights, we're sure you will be glad you came.

The Modern Restaurant

$ • 116 W. Pearl St., Nashua • (603) 883-8422

It probably was modern when it opened in 1935, but today this downtown Nashua icon is a classic. Multiple generations of Insiders have family traditions of dinner at the Modern every week (there are different dinner specials each evening), and multiple generations of the Quebecoise founder's family have run the place. There aren't many restaurants left where you can choose meat loaf on Tuesday or chicken livers and bacon on Saturday. But not to worry if those sound too plain, the menu includes steak, chicken and prime rib and seafood every night in addition to the three to six daily dinners. Families are always welcome here. The Modern is open for lunch and dinner every day.

Nashua Buffet Restaurant

$, no credit cards • 25 Canal St., Nashua • (603) 889-3370

Since 1921 this unpretentious restaurant has been serving Nashua residents three square meals a day. Broiled or fried seafood, steaks and roast meats or poultry are served homestyle — no fancy sauces, just meat and potatoes with a vegetable. Every meal is simple and tasty, and the breakfast omelets are a special treat.

Osaka Tea Garden

$$ • Lamplighter Sq., 295 Daniel Webster Hwy., Nashua
• (603) 888-9090

This restaurant is a delightful surprise. Its location at the end of a shopping center across from the Pheasant Lane Mall doesn't seem like the place to find an authentic Japanese restaurant, but when you walk through the door you'll think you're in Kyoto. The sushi bar invites you to sit down and select your favorites, which are safely under glass and on ice but right where you can see everything. Take off your shoes to dine in the Ta-Ta-Mi room. If you don't want to be quite that authentic, eat in the regular dining room. Either way, the paper-and-wood panels and blond wooden furniture set the stage. And then comes the food! The menu features sushi and sashimi, tempura and teriyaki of all kinds, all served with misoshiru (soup) and salad. There's even a children's menu with chicken, shrimp or beef and rice. The Tea Garden is open daily for lunch and dinner.

Skyview Cafe and Brewery

$$ • 385 East Dunstable Rd., Nashua • (603) 897-0005

We have a weakness for brew pubs, but even if we were teetotalers we'd love the Skyview. This new restaurant is on the very south end of Nashua (almost in Massachusetts) but well worth the drive — although with beers ranging from a 5 percent India pale ale to an 11.2 percent barley wine, the highest alcohol content of any beer in New Hampshire, you should designate a driver before a night out here. We particularly like the Trappist-style Abbey Triple and the strong ale. The atmosphere here is airy rather than traditional pub-dark: brightly colored tile, big windows and plenty of room to move around. The food isn't traditional, either. Fabulous chicken dishes and wonderful seafoods and steaks come forth from the wood oven, complemented by fresh fruits and truly unique salads and sandwiches. The Skyview serves lunch and dinner every day. See our Nightlife chapter for more about live entertainment in the star-lit lounge.

Villa Banca

$$ • 194 Main St., Nashua • (603) 598-0500

This restaurant on the corner of Main and E. Pearl streets is housed in the old Indian Head Bank building, and the bank motif has been preserved throughout the dining room. The food here is all Italian, with specialties from every part of that cuisine-rich peninsula. You'll have to choose from delicacies such as chicken cannelloni, veal and lobster, chicken sausage ravioli and gnocchi with gorgonzola cream sauce, all served with pasta that's made fresh every day and complemented with wine from the vault. Villa Banca's hours are better than a bank's: It's open every day but Sunday (it's a bank, remember?) for lunch and dinner. Come when the weather's nice and dine al fresco.

Ya Mamma's

$$-$$$ • 42 Canal St., Nashua • (603) 883-2264

When you see the factory-neighborhood location, you won't believe you've found an acclaimed restaurant, but once you try the food you'll be convinced. The absolutely fresh and individually prepared Italian specialties will have you wishing for a larger appetite, especially when you see the desserts! One thing we particularly like is that most of the dinners are available with a choice of meats, so if the Carcioffo sounds wonderful but you don't like eggplant, you can have it with chicken instead. Or if the Marguerita veal is appealing but you feel like seafood, you can have it with shrimp or calamari. Ya Mamma's serves lunch on Thursdays and Fridays and dinner every day.

Good Neighbors Cafe and Bakery

$, no credit cards • Mill St., New Boston • (603) 487-2260

This rustic cafe, right in the center of the village of New Boston, grew out of a bakery and is still best known for wonderful breads and rolls. Now it serves breakfast and lunch, including the baked goods, of course, with the addition of fresh eggs, deli choices, veggies and lovely pasta dishes. We especially like the seats outside over the river, but when it's chilly outside you can sit by the windows, and it's almost as pretty.

Molly Stark Tavern

$$$ • N.H. Rt. 13, New Boston • (603) 487-2733

This old-fashioned tavern is housed in a historic building just south of the village. The restaurant is named for the cannon that was named for the famous wife of Gen. John Stark. The four-pound gun was given to the New Boston Artillery Company of the Ninth New Hampshire Regiment some time after it was captured in the Battle of Bennington (see our History chapter). A mix of dinner choices includes prime rib or seafood, chicken or shrimp jambalaya, homemade quiche and roast rack of lamb. Occasionally live music completes the scene. Although it is rather a long ride, the Molly Stark is one of the restaurants most often recommended by Insiders from the Souhegan Valley. Just consider the scenic drive part of the entertainment! The tavern also offers nature trails down to the river and lovely gardens for guests to explore. The Molly Stark serves dinner every evening with a pub lunch on Saturday and Sunday brunch. Only a few Insiders remember that back in the 1950s this farmhouse was the headquarters of the Gravity Research Foundation, established by Roger Babson with the goal of developing an "anti-gravity insulator."

The Common Man

$$ • 88 Range Rd., Windham • (603) 898-0088

This member of the Common Man family was an instant hit when it opened in Windham in 1996. The menu includes rotisserie chicken and duckling, maple-barbecue pork spareribs and a vegetable strudel, just to give you a sampling. The downtown restaurant serves dinner every evening and a Sunday brunch that features lobster croissant along with eggs Benedict.

Seacoast Region

Three Chimneys Inn

$$-$$$$ • 17 Newmarket Rd., Durham • (603) 868-7800, (888) 399- 9777

Three Chimneys is a stately, Old World-style inn convenient to the University of New Hampshire or the interstate. There are two dining choices here. The ffrost Sawyer Tavern ($$) offers an eclectic menu ranging from batter-dipped frog legs to keilbasa and pastrami. Each appetizer, salad and entree has something unexpected: beef tips with asparagus and a Portobello sandwich with truffle mayonnaise were two that caught our eye. For an even more elegant dinner, try The Maples ($$$$) where you'll find fish, beef and fowl in exquisite sauces to please the most jaded palate.

The Terrace Restaurant at the Inn at Exeter

$$$ • 90 Front St., Exeter • (603) 772-5901, (800) 782-8444

The dining here is as elegant as the lodging (see our Bed and Breakfasts and Country Inns chapter). Whether it's Belgian waffles at breakfast, a simple sandwich at lunch or the sesame-crusted salmon or vegetable ragout at dinner, every dish is prepared with the freshest ingredients and a sharp eye for detail. And it tastes as wonderful as it looks.

The Galley Hatch Restaurant

$$ • 317 Lafayette Rd., Hampton • (603) 926-6152

For a quarter-century The Galley Hatch has been serving residents and tourists on the Seacoast with fresh seafood, artfully prepared veal dishes and deliciously different chicken and beef choices. The Galley Hatch's terrific bakery provides fresh bread and intoxicating desserts (which you can buy to bring home if you're stuffed). Ask about their dinner-and-movie package with the Hampton Cinema Six, right next door. The Galley Hatch serves lunch and dinner seven days a week.

Little Jack's Seafood Restaurant

$-$$$ • 539 Ocean Blvd., Hampton Beach • (603) 926- 8053

You won't believe the selection of fresh seafood at Little Jack's. In addition to lobster, clams, mussels and haddock you may find mahimahi, tilapia or catfish — whatever is fresh and tasty off the boat the day you dine. The restaurant has landlubbers dinners too, but who could choose baked chicken or even prime rib over lobster Newburg or fresh swordfish? Oh, all right, we have a seafood-hater in our family tree too (but we try to hide her). Little Jack's is open for lunch and dinner seven days a week from April through September.

Ron's Landing at Rocky Bend

$$$ • 379 Ocean Blvd., Hampton Beach • (603) 929-2122

For fresh seafood, succulent veal, steak or chicken with a distinctive flair, Ron's Landing offers a wide selection of Mediterranean and American-style entrees. How about wild mushroom and lobster linguine? Or maybe a pappardelle made with scallops, shrimp and littleneck clams? All the seafood is guaranteed to be fresh, as are the pastas, vegetables and sauces. The view from the lounge is beautiful, but you'll probably want to sit out on the deck by the water. Ron's serves lunch and dinner daily and brunch on Sunday and offers a full bar and wine list.

Asia Chinese and Polynesian Restaurant

$ • 42-46 Third St., Dover • (603) 742-0040
$ • 99 River Rd., Newington • (603) 431-3121
$ • 2466 Lafayette Rd., Portsmouth • (603) 436-3343

The restaurant Seacoast Insiders are most likely to mention when asked about Chinese food is this local chain with the Polynesian decor. Whether you like your dinner hot and spicy or mild, you'll find a favorite on the extensive menu. Especially nice are dishes combining local seafood in traditional dishes: Asia Splendor offers fresh lobster, shrimp, chicken and beef stir-fried with mushrooms, water chestnuts and greens, and scallops with snow peas puts a new flavor in an old favorite. Of course the restaurant has beef and snow peas too. Asia serves lunch and dinner daily and a big Sunday buffet that's an Insider tradition.

Barnstormers Restaurant

$$$ • 27 International Dr., Portsmouth • (603) 433-6700

Self-described as "The Business Address," Barnstormers is becoming the premier place to entertain clients on the Seacoast. The French-trained Chef Desi has created a menu offering classic American steaks and pork chops alongside Thai chicken, seafood pasta dishes and blackened salmon. The piano lounge and sports bar offer a choice of romantic or casual entertainment for before or after dinner. Barnstormers is also open for lunch.

The Blue Mermaid

$$ • The Hill, Portsmouth • (603) 427-2583

With the only wood-grill on the Seacoast, the Blue Mermaid offers grilled seafood, grilled chicken, grilled steaks, even grilled pizza! Or try an unexpected twist, like a lobster quesadilla. Every ingredient is as fresh as the sea air on the patio, where you can enjoy an award-winning Margarita along with your dinner and live music on the weekends. The Blue Mermaid is open for lunch and dinner every day.

Maple Syrup

Close-up

Maple trees grow all over North America, but sugaring is limited to the areas of the northeastern United States and southeastern Canada that have the slow run-up to spring we have perfected here in New Hampshire. During warm, sunny days in late February and March, the sweet sap rises in the trunks of the trees. At night, as the temperature falls back below freezing, the sap falls, only to rise again the next warm day.

Native Americans taught the early settlers to tap the trees by opening a small hole through the bark and into the wood to allow some of the sap to drip out as it ran up the trunk. A reed or curl of bark kept the hole from sealing up immediately and directed the flowing sap into birchbark buckets. The sap was boiled down to make a slightly sweet drink. It could also be boiled longer to produce a sweet, flavorful syrup, or even longer until nothing remained but the sugar.

The process hasn't changed much in 400 years. Wooden pails and tin buckets replaced birchbark cups and hollow logs. Carved wooden spiles replaced hollow reeds. Metal taps took their place and are still in use by many farm operations today. And commercial maple producers have moved to plastic. Their sap runs through miles of plastic tubing to large collecting tanks. No more snowshoeing through the woods with heavy pails of sap!

Photo: Tom Wilkins

How sweet it is! Traditional tin pails adorning maple trees are a sure sign that spring is on the way.

With no containers for cooking over the fire, the native people boiled the sap by heating rocks in the fire and dropping them into the liquid. It must have taken a very long time to make a year's supply of syrup with this method. Between 30 and 40 gallons of sap must be boiled down to yield a gallon of syrup (the amount varies because the amount of sugar in the sap varies). For sugar you must reduce it even further. Eight gallons of syrup will produce about a pound of maple sugar. Since the Native Americans' diet was about 12 percent maple sugar, they must have spent hundreds of hours heating and reheating rocks.

Iron pots for boiling made the process easier. It still took many hours and a hot fire, and the sap had to be tended to be sure it didn't burn. The traditions of sugaring turned all this work into a

— continued on next page

party, as families gathered to share the chores of collecting sap, chopping firewood, stoking the fire and boiling the sap. The fire burned all day and into the night. Meals were cooked and eaten at the sugarbush, and children slept bundled under straw in the wagon as the sap boiled on. Sugaring-off, a sort of winter picnic at the close of the season, was a time to visit with friends and celebrate the harvesting of the year's first crop.

If you decide to tap your backyard maples, the local hardware store will have metal taps for sale in late winter. These are shaped rather like a funnel, about the size of your thumb and have a hook for hanging whatever you're collecting in. You can buy special maple pails with covers and holes for hanging, or buy some empty plastic buckets from a bakery and cut a notch in the lid. Some people use one-gallon plastic milk jugs, but an average tree will put out three to four gallons of sap on a sunny day, so unless you're prepared to collect the sap every couple of hours, bigger is better.

The traditional day for tapping is George Washington's birthday, (that's February 22, not the Monday holiday), or sometime in the end of February — later north of Concord. Warm days and cold nights are the key. With a hand drill and a 7/16- or 1/2-inch bit, drill a hole in a maple tree about 2 inches deep. Hammer the metal tap into the hole and hang your pail. Any kind of maple tree will do, although sugar and rock maples are most productive.

In the old days, people would hang buckets all around the tree, but a combination of air pollution, acid rain and non-native insect pests is stressing the maple trees now. The New Hampshire Department of Agriculture recommends that no tree less than 12 inches in diameter (chest height) be tapped. From 12 to 16 inches, one tap is okay, and for larger trees, you can set an additional tap for each 6 inches in diameter up to a maximum of four taps without harming the tree. (Diameter is roughly one- third the circumference, so you can measure your tree with a string.)

Now comes the process of boiling off most of the water, concentrating the sugar in the remainder to make syrup. Don't make the mistake of trying to boil sap on the stove! The scent gives the kitchen a pleasant warmth, as gallons of sticky steam waft through the house, settling on carpets and furniture, loosening wallpaper, condensing and dripping from the ceiling. If you don't want to boil your sap over an outside fire, try this tip from a transplanted Insider family: They make two or three gallons every spring in a big roasting pan on the gas grill.

Boil sap slowly and use a candy thermometer to monitor the process. As the sap boils down, gradually add fresh sap. The syrup will turn light brown as it thickens. It burns very easily, especially as it approaches the finishing point, so watch it carefully.

Syrup is ready when it boils at a temperature seven degrees above the boiling point of water. Check your thermometer in boiling water each time you use it, because the boiling point varies depending on the weather.

Filter the syrup through a special syrup filter, multiple layers of cheesecloth or a couple of coffee filters as you funnel it into canning jars. Leave a half-inch of headspace and process the jars, and the syrup will keep for years on the shelf (if you don't eat it all!) If you don't process the jars, keep the syrup in the refrigerator.

The New Hampshire Department of Agriculture, (603) 271-2505, has detailed information available about back yard maple production, as does County Extension (check under U.S. Government in your phone book for the local Extension office).

Dinnerhorn Oyster Bar and Bratskellar Pub

$$ • 980 Portsmouth St., Portsmouth • (603) 436- 0717

Seafood is the specialty here, so whether it's the raw oysters and cherrystones on the bar or the swordfish, shellfish or shrimp, you can be sure all the ingredients are fresh and carefully prepared. The Dinnerhorn offers an extensive non-seafood menu too, with veal, beef and lamb choices, pasta and even sandwiches. The frozen drinks here are a treat, and the wine list complements your meal nicely. On the other hand if you just want a quick meal and a beer, the Bratskellar serves terrific sandwiches, nachos and pizza. Both rooms serve lunch and dinner every day.

The Dolphin Striker

$$$ • 15 Bow St., Portsmouth
• (603) 431-5222

The Dolphin Striker offers the most modern American cuisine in a historic setting. How about sautéed lobster with sun-dried tomatoes, pine nuts and ravioli in Marsala cream sauce? Or if you're not a seafood fan, perhaps a grilled veal porterhouse with plum tomato coulis and basil-sunflower pesto is more your style. The restaurant also offers vegetarian entrees as well as salads and sandwiches, and, of course, you can have your lobster plain if you insist. The Dolphin Striker is open daily for lunch and dinner. A stunning assortment of elegant desserts completes your dining experience. See our Nightlife chapter for the Spring Hill Tavern, the adjoining pub.

Dunfey's Aboard the John Wanamaker

$$$ • 1 Harbour Pl., Portsmouth
• (603) 433-3111

For a truly unusual dining experience, find your way down to the pier in Portsmouth and cross the gangplank to this refurbished tugboat! Gleaming brass fixtures, shining crystal and crisp linens complement a menu that changes with the seasons. Duck or tuna, steak or chicken, you're sure to find your meal enhanced by the sights and sounds of the river. Dunfey's serves dinner Wednesday through Sunday evenings.

Harbor's Edge

$$ • Sheraton Portsmouth, 250 Market St., Portsmouth
• (603) 431-2300

For elegant surroundings and a wonderful meal, this restaurant at one of Portsmouth's newer hotels (see our Accommodations chapter) is a terrific choice. The harbor is indeed just outside your windows as you dine on grilled seafood and new American cuisine in an atmosphere that's casual and friendly but still very nice. Harbor's Edge is open for lunch and dinner every day and serves Sunday brunch.

The Oar House

$$$ • 55 Ceres St., Portsmouth
• (603) 436-4025

When you think there can't possibly be another way to serve seafood, check out this fine restaurant in the historic Merchant's Row on the waterfront in old Portsmouth. Seafood Alfredo, Bouillabaisse made with lobster, littlenecks, mussels and shrimp, and salmon en papillote (wrapped in parchment) are just a few of the unusual choices at the Oar House. You'll also find chicken, pork and lamb prepared to order, fresh salads and a raw seafood bar. The Oar House is open seven days a week for lunch and dinner as well as brunch on Sundays.

The Old Ferry Landing

$$ • 10 Ceres St., Portsmouth
• (603) 431-5510

This restaurant really is on the site where the ferries used to load for the crossing of the Piscataqua River. Since 1973 it has served the freshest seafood platters and lobster feasts as well as salads and sandwiches. Frozen drinks and local beers are cool on a hot summer day. The Old Ferry Landing serves lunch and dinner every day from April until fall.

Phoenix Rising

$ • 3510 Lafayette Rd., Portsmouth
• (603) 431-6995

This is an old favorite with a new name — until 1998 this was the Seacoast location of the Insider-beloved Tortilla Flat Restaurant in Merrimack. It's still operated by the same family, and you can still choose from a variety of Mexican specialties here, some with a New England twist (crab meat enchiladas). If you have dining companions who don't do Mexican, they can order burgers, chicken or steak.

Cafe Mirabelle

$$$-$$$$ • 64 Bridge St., Portsmouth
• (603) 430-9301

Classic French cuisine with a light touch is the hallmark of this casually elegant restaurant. All types of meat and seafood appear here at their best, delicately seasoned and accompanied by gourmet cheese and wine sauces. Cafe Mirabelle serves dinner Wednesday through Sunday. Or come at lunch time, Wednesday through Saturday, for fluffy crepes with fillings like lobster, artichoke hearts, eggplant or wild mushrooms. Sunday brunch is a great chance to taste a variety of creative dishes. It's closed Monday and Tuesday.

Pier II

$$ • State St., Portsmouth
• (603) 436-0669

Don't be put off by the un-gentrified exterior of this building. The restaurant inside is terrific. Great menu choices, fresh seafood and a huge salad bar make this a favorite stop in Portsmouth. From most seats you have an exciting view of the river (our kids love to watch the drawbridge being raised). Our favorite time to come is for the all-you-can eat Sunday Brunch, but if you are here at a busier time of day, you'll be glad to know the public parking garage is just a few steps away.

Porto Bello Ristorante Italiano

$$$-$$$$ • 67 Bow St., Portsmouth
• (603) 431-2989

Wondering if there are any restaurants on the Seacoast that don't specialize in seafood? Look no further! It helps if you speak Italian when you order here, but the servers will be happy to translate for you if you can't. Antipasto, pasta and meat courses are made with the freshest ingredients and a variety of specialty cheeses, delicately seasoned and often simmered in wine. Save room for dessert — the selections are Italian wonders too. Porto Bello is open for dinner Tuesday through Saturday and serves lunch Friday, Saturday and Sunday.

The Portsmouth Brewery

$$ • 56 Market St., Portsmouth
• (603) 431-1115

Squeezed in among the shops on Market Street, you'll find this classic brew pub. The food here is tasty and freshly prepared, with terrific nachos and club sandwiches, fajitas and burritos and grilled pizza (red or white) as specialties. But the real news is the beer. Portsmouth Brewery's hand-brewed ales and lagers are available in New Hampshire grocery stores under the Smuttynose label (smutty is an old word for sooty, and a smuttynose was a type of sailing ship), but there's a much larger selection on tap here than the brewery bottles for distribution. There's also a full bar if you're not a beer-drinker, and live music on weekends. You can eat outside in the courtyard, but it hasn't any view, so we recommend the dining room where a glass wall allows you to watch the brewing process. It's open for lunch and dinner every day.

Portsmouth Gaslight Co.

$-$$ • 64 Market St., Portsmouth
• (603) 430-9122

A favorite with the college and career crowd, the Gaslight Co. offers a choice of dining outside on the deck, upstairs in the lounge or downstairs where the brick pizza oven glows. Anywhere you choose, you'll enjoy pasta, seafood, chicken and truly unique pizzas, all made with fresh vegetables and delightful sauces. See our Nightlife chapter for more about the Gaslight Co. It's open for lunch and dinner every day.

Sakura

$$-$$$$ • 40 Pleasant St., Portsmouth
• (603) 431-2721

If you manage to tire of our wonderful New England shore food, Sakura offers a full sushi bar and traditional Japanese food in a remodeled downtown restaurant with a sunken dining area. The selection includes tuna and shrimp along with such unusual delicacies as eel and octopus. Lunch and dinner are served daily in summer and Tuesday through Sunday from September through May.

Yoken's Thar She Blows Restaurant

$$ • 1390 Portsmouth Rd., Portsmouth
• (603) 436- 8224

Long ago, when U.S. Route 1 was the only way up the Seacoast, we used to watch for Yoken's spouting whale sign on our way to great-grandmother's. When we saw it, we knew we were almost to Maine. Today Yoken's is part of the Comfort Inn complex, but the

Famous for its maple syrup, Parker's Maple Barn in Mason produces the sweet stuff in a large evaporator.

delightful restaurant with its gift shop (supposedly New England's largest, see our Shopping chapter) full of maritime souvenirs remains a favorite of Insiders old and new. The seafood is still outstanding, the chicken and beef dishes delicious, and the ice cream and strawberry shortcake are worth stopping for even if you're not on your way to grandma's. Yoken's serves lunch and dinner daily.

The Stockpot
$$ • 53 Bow St., Portsmouth
• (603) 431-1851

What could be more appetizing than dinner on the deck overlooking the ocean? Maybe lunch in the dining room, out of the heat of the sun but still with a full view of the waves. As you can guess from the name, the specialty here is homemade soup, with a salad or sandwich if you like. But the menu is not limited to light fare: try the Swiss artichoke pie with Mornay sauce or Portuguese chicken if you're really hungry. Seafood and burgers (including a veggie burger) round out the menu.

Saunders at Rye Harbor
$$$ • 175 Harbor Rd., Rye
• (603) 964-6466

Whether it's a sunset dinner on the deck in summer or a cozy lunch by the fireplace in winter, the meals at Saunders have been pleasing local palates for more than 75 years. You can choose from lobster, fixed any way you like, or a dinner menu with two dozen options. Prime rib and fresh salmon or swordfish share the headlines with seafood mixed grill and jambalaya, New England style. Who says New England cooking is dull? The restaurant is open every day.

Lakes Region

The William Tell Inn
$$ • N.H. Rt. 11, West Alton
• (603) 293-8803

A surprise on the shore, this restaurant looks plain, but the food is special. Specialties here include fondue, weiner schnitzel and sauerbraten. The restaurant also offers several other veal dishes and several entrees with a provençal style. It's open every day for lunch and dinner and for Sunday brunch in early afternoon.

The Common Man
$$ • Main St., Ashland
• (603) 968-7030

This is the oldest member of the Common Man family, Insider favorites for more than 25 years. Whether you choose seafood (check out the shellfish stew), steak, chicken or duck, you're in for an uncommon treat. The staff ages its own beef, receives its fish fresh every day and makes incredible desserts (they're known for their white chocolate). The Ashland location serves dinner every night and lunch every day but Sunday. (Other Common Man locations include Lincoln in the White Mountains and Windham in the Merrimack Valley as well as several other "family members" with other names and menus.)

Double Decker Restaurant

$-$$ • 680 State St., Belmont
• (603) 524-4644

This unpretentious restaurant offers a full-service dining room and take-out window for lunch and dinner every day. It offers a wide variety of seafood and chicken choices along with sandwiches and burgers.

Hickory Stick Farm

$$-$$$ • 60 Bean Hill Rd., Belmont
• (603) 524-3333

This lovely c. 1800 farmhouse houses a delightful restaurant, one beloved by summer visitors since 1950. The specialty of the house is roast duckling with an orange sherry sauce, but the restaurant offers a variety of chicken, steak, lamb and seafood temptations as well. Many of the recipes prepared in the kitchen are family favorites passed down through generations. We think they'll be among your favorites too. Reservations are definitely required. Hickory Stick is open for dinner every evening except Monday from Memorial Day until Columbus Day and Sundays for a buffet brunch. In the winter the restaurant serves dinner Friday and Saturday evening and brunch on Sunday.

Pasquaney Restaurant and Wild Hare Tavern

$$ • 1030 Mayhew Tnpk., Bridgewater
• (603) 744- 9111, (800) 745-7990

This is the restaurant at the Inn on Newfound Lake, a Lakes Region fixture since 1840. For exquisite dining in a pristine country setting, either the dining room or the veranda will provide a perfect backdrop. Every dish, whether fish, fowl or meat, is prepared with the finest ingredients and attention to detail. Vegetarian meals, although not on the menu, can be requested, as each dish is individually prepared. Prime rib with Yorkshire pudding is served in addition to the regular menu on Friday and Saturday evenings. The Wild Hare Tavern is an intimate, English-style pub where you can enjoy a cocktail or specialty coffee. The Pasquaney Restaurant is open for dinner every day and brunch on Sunday year round. Ask about Murder Mystery Dinners, comic evenings that are booked months in advance.

The Homestead

$$ • N.H. Rt. 104, Bristol
• (603) 744-2022

Good food at good prices make this Homestead a popular spot for lunch or dinner. The house was built in 1788, and the rooms in the original house are cozy, with low ceilings and fireplaces. A recent addition allows guests to eat in the greenhouse room, if you prefer a more open setting. The Homestead is open for dinner daily. Sunday brunch here is an Insider favorite. Like the Londonderry Homestead, the menu here is extensive — you'll need to come back often to sample the seafood, prime rib and other delightful entrees.

Chequers Harbour

$$ • N.H. Rt. 25, Center Harbor
• (603) 253-8613

This is a popular spot, as the crowded parking lot will demonstrate (and some of the patrons' "vehicles" are tied up over at the town dock!). The decor has been compared to that of the old-style camps scattered across the Lakes and White Mountains regions, which is to say rustic, eclectic and comfortable. Pasta is the house specialty, with a variety of sauces and unique fillings, but Chequers' salmon and mussels dishes are favorites. The menu is all new in 1998 and features fresh and unusual seafood, beef and veal dishes as well as amazing and unique pizzas and some intriguing salads. Chequers is open for lunch and dinner every day. Check out the pizza buffet on weekdays at lunchtime. Stella's Tavern opens at 4 PM with a lighter menu and great frozen drinks on the patio. (The patio was screened in 1998 for an even nicer experience.)

The Red Hill Inn

$$$ • N.H. Rt. 25 B, Center Harbor
• (603) 279-7001, (800) 5 RED HILL

You're going to have to hunt a bit to find this beautifully restored inn and farm (see our Bed and Breakfasts and Country Inns chapter), but it will be worth it. Take U.S. Route 3 north out of Meredith to the junction with N.H. Route 25 B. Go right and continue about a quarter-mile. You'll see a sign for The Red Hill Inn. Follow the sign, and go to the top of a long driveway. The menu offers seafood, steak, veal and pork, all prepared with fresh ingredients, (herbs are grown just outside the door) and served with homemade breads and fresh vegetables. Wine suggestions are included with each dish on the menu. This is the only place we know where you can order roast pheasant or rabbit, which adds to the feeling that you've stepped into a time warp. In summer lunch and dinner are served daily at the Red Hill, except on Sunday when there is brunch instead of lunch. Thursday through Sunday evenings you'll enjoy live piano music with your dinner. Save room for one of the scrumptious desserts — they're famous in their own right. (From Columbus Day to Mother's Day the inn doesn't serve lunch.)

Corner House Inn

$$$ • Main St., Center Sandwich
• (603) 284-6219

For more than 100 years locals have dined at the Corner House. Choose from peach duckling, veal Oscar, steak, pork, pasta or the catch of the day. The menu always includes a mix of the traditional and familiar with more unusual foods or uncommon presentations. Dinner at the Corner House is a special evening out. The walls of this Colonial farmhouse are an extension of the display from Surroundings at Red Gate (See our Arts and Culture chapter), so the decor is part of the attraction. Breakfast is for overnight guests only, but lunch and dinner are open to all. Come in early on Thursday evening for the Dinner and Storytelling special.

Stafford's in the Field

$$$$ • off N.H. Rt. 113, Chocorua
• (603) 323-7766, (800) 833-9509

Everything about Stafford's is picture-perfect, from the wildflowers in the field to the antiques in the dining room. The food is perfect too, with a prix fixe menu likely to include mock turtle soup, filet mignon with cognac and cream, and homemade cakes too rich to pass up, even when you are full. Stafford's Rosemary Pork Chops recipe was featured in *Bon Appetit* magazine! Dinner is served here nightly. This isn't a stuffy place, but it is very nice. Reservations are required.

B. Mae's Eating & Drinking Establishment

$-$$ • N.H. Rt. 11, Gilford
• (603) 293-4351

The restaurants at B. Mae's offer something for everyone. You can enjoy a light meal of chowder, chili or chicken in the casual atmosphere at O'Sullivan's Pub ($), a rotisserie meal at the new Patrick's Pub & Eatery ($) or a deluxe feast at Wade & Molloy's Steak House ($$), where in addition to steak the menu includes lamb and veal, chicken, duck and seafood. There is also a daily pasta special. Fine wines, imported and domestic beers and microbrews complement your meal. All three restaurants are open daily for lunch and dinner. See our Hotels and Motels chapter for more about B. Mae's.

Victorian House

$$-$$$$ • 2645 Lakeshore Rd., Gilford
• (603) 293- 8155

Enjoy an elegant meal in this 19th-cen-

INSIDERS' TIP

Lakeport and the Weirs or Weirs Beach are all called "Laconia" in the phone book, as are parts of Belmont and Gilford. Insiders only use Laconia to mean the center of town (where N.H. routes 11-A, 106 and 107 and U.S. Route 3 intersect).

tury inn where hospitality has been the tradition for 175 years. Whether you select angel hair primavera prepared with fresh herbs, beef Wellington with pâté de foie gras or one of the other gourmet offerings, this will be a meal to remember. The chef (who was on staff at the Ritz Carlton in New York before escaping to the relative peace of the Lakes Region) recommends you plan at least two hours to enjoy your meal. The Victorian House serves dinner every evening, and reservations are strongly recommended.

StoneCoast Brewery

$ • 546 N. Main St., Laconia
• (603) 528-4188

If you're wondering why a brewpub in downtown Laconia is called StoneCoast, it's because the original StoneCoast is in Maine. The beer is terrific (designate a driver; it's potent stuff), and the soups, chowders and chilis will warm your heart. Burgers, sandwiches and downhome entrees (pot roast, lasagna or black beans and rice) round out the menu, which is available from early afternoon on. StoneCoast offers live entertainment Wednesday through Saturday evenings.

The Manor on Golden Pond

$$$$ • U.S. Rt. 3, Holderness
• (603) 968-3348, (800) 545-2141

The two four-star dining rooms at the Manor offer a choice of prix fixe three- or five-course meals every evening. Meals are open to the public, and reservations are required. Guests choose between two options for each course, and the menu changes nightly. When we visited the staff was preparing herb-crusted rabbit, potato-leek soup, stuffed chicken and grilled pork. The chocolate sampler for dessert made us gain weight just by looking at it! Dinner guests are welcome to have a drink in the Three Cocks English-style pub before dinner. See our Bed and Breakfasts and Country Inns chapter for more on this luxurious inn.

Blackstone's at the Margate

$$$ • 76 Lake St., Laconia
• (603) 524-7060

Whether your taste runs to steak, seafood or new American cuisine, you'll find something to love at Blackstone's. It serves breakfast and dinner but no lunches, and it's closed on Sunday evenings. See our Hotels and Motels chapter for more about the Margate Resort.

Christmas Island Steakhouse

$$ • U.S. Rt. 3, Laconia
• (603) 366-4664

It doesn't look like much on the outside, but the lunches and dinners here are anything but plain! You'll find entrees like hazelnut chicken, filet mignon and stuffed shrimp, and the house specialty is prime rib, roasted to perfection and cut to your order. The menu also includes a variety of Italian dishes and terrific appetizers. Downstairs the North Pole Tavern offers a variety of sandwiches, burgers and appetizers in a pub atmosphere with music, darts and sometimes live entertainment.

Las Piñatas Mexican Restaurant

$$ • 9 Veterans Sq., Laconia
• (603) 528-1405

This restaurant in Laconia's old railroad station was opened in 1991 by a family from Mexico City whose son and daughters had come to Laconia as exchange students. They offer meals in a setting that's all New Hampshire but with food that's genuine Mexico. Drawing on abuela's (Grandma's) recipes, Las Piñatas offers traditional Mexican dishes and a new special every weekend. Meals are prepared to order, so you can choose how hot or mild you'd like your seasoning. Las Piñatas is open every day for lunch and dinner. The restaurant is smoke-free. See our Nightlife chapter for Amando's Cantina at Las Piñatas.

Oriental Gardens

$$ • 89 Lake St., Laconia
• (603) 524-0008

Great Chinese food prepared without MSG, an all-you-can-eat buffet with more than 100 choices and local delivery — it's no wonder Oriental Gardens is an Insider favorite. Szechuan- and Yu Hsiang-style dishes complement the traditional Cantonese menu, and the staff warns you if a dish is very spicy. There are a few unexpected tidbits on the menu (onion rings?!), but the old standbys are here too. Dragon and Phoenix is a delicious saute of chicken and lobster. Oriental

Gardens is open 365 days a year, serving lunch and dinner daily.

Road Kill Cafe

$ • U.S. Rt. 3, Laconia
• (603) 524-4700

This is the original of a chain that now stretches from the Maine wilderness to Cape Cod. If you tend to be queasy you may want to pass on this, but if you have kids in your party, they'll insist on stopping here. The ambience is recycled automotive (read junk yard), and the menu lists such choices as "Pail o' Nightcrawlers" (french fries), "Blasting Zone Burrito" and "Brake and Scrape Sandwiches" with names like "The Chicken That Didn't Make It Across the Road." Get the atmosphere? If you really love it, you can buy a T-shirt, coffee mug or poster to remember it by.

Fratello's Ristorante Italiano

$$ • 799 Union Ave., Lakeport
• (603) 528-2022

Fratello's is run by the same people who operate the Homestead restaurants, although if you try them both (and we think you should) you'll find the only thing they have in common is excellent, creatively prepared food. Fratello's offers authentic Italian cuisine that world-traveling Insiders compare favorably to what they've eaten on the Italian Peninsula. Choose from pesca (fish), pollo (chicken) or any of the other wonderful dinners, add one of the many antipasti (salads) and zuppe (soups), and you'll think you're dining in Italy, especially when you hear the Italian music from the piano. Fratello's is open for lunch and dinner daily.

The Boathouse Grille

$$$ • U.S. Rt. 3 and N.H. Rt. 25, Meredith
• (603) 279-2253

The Boathouse Grille is the main restaurant in the Inn at Bay Point/Mills Falls complex (see our Bed and Breakfasts and Country Inns chapter). It is also a member of the Common Man family of restaurants, which are mainstays in New Hampshire. The Boathouse features light and airy dining overlooking the lake, with lots of glass and plants to make you feel almost like you're outside. (If you come by boat, you can tie up at the dock.) The menu changes weekly, offering rack of lamb and rotisserie duckling or chicken along with steaks and some seafood. One unusual vegetarian dish is the Raclette Tarte, made with seasonal vegetables (so it's always a bit different) in a basil cream with a walnut crust. The Boathouse serves lunch and dinner daily.

Cafe Lafayette Dinner Train

$$$$ (price includes train fare) • Hobo Rail Station, N.H. Rt. 12, Lincoln
Meredith Station, Mill St., Meredith
• (603) 745-3500, (800) 699-3501

The Indian Waters, a restored 1924 Pullman coach, leaves Meredith Station Wednesday through Sunday evenings for a lovely two-hour trip along the shore of Lake Winnipesaukee. While you watch the sailboats and travel through the Weirs to Paugus Bay, you'll enjoy a five-course dinner served in the style of European trains of bygone days (think Orient Express). One evening's menu offered a choice of chicken cordon bleu, shrimp in a maple-mustard cream sauce or pork tenderloin medallions in brown Madeira, but since the food is prepared to order on board, using the freshest local ingredients, the menu will vary. Children eat for about half-price, or consider the family-style dining on the Lakeside Train on Wednesday and Saturday nights. Less elegant and more kid-friendly, the Lakeside offers a turkey dinner with all the fixings that parents will enjoy too. In 1998 Cafe Lafayette added a dinner run from Lincoln aboard a newly rebuilt DOME Pullman, the Granite Eagle. See our Attractions chapter for more about the Hobo Train and Winnipesaukee Scenic Railroad.

INSIDERS' TIP

If you can eat dinner early (before 6 PM), you'll find restaurants less crowded and service a bit quicker. Many restaurants even offer early-bird discounts on the dinner menu.

Camp

$$ • 298 Daniel Webster Hwy., Meredith • (603) 279-7006

In 1998 Chase's Country Towne House, a family restaurant beloved by Insiders, made way for Chase House, the newest of the Inns at Mill Falls complex. The folks at the Inns know a good thing when they eat there, so they turned to the Common Man family to create a new restaurant. Taking a cue from the successful and popular Boathouse Grille, Camp provides a casual atmosphere with an excellent mix of food styles sure to please both the picky and adventurous eater. For starters you can try fried smelts or a wild mushroom tart. Too unusual for your party? Then we suggest the Stack O' Rings (fried onion rings) served with homemade ketchup. Salad choices include both fresh greens tossed with cheese and garlic and a chunky lobster salad. You want a sandwich? Try grilled swordfish or a veggie burger. At dinner you'll have several seafood choices such as pan-fried trout or grilled striped bass. Chicken pot pie and venison were the dinner specials last time we were in town. Camp's very special s'more dessert features chocolate, marshmallow and graham cracker. If that's not for you, try the fresh berries with Creme Anglais.

The Woodshed

$$$ • Lee's Mill Rd., Moultonborough • (603) 476-2311

The Woodshed is renowned in the Lakes Region for terrific food that's elegantly prepared and served. Whether you eat by the fireplace or out on the year-round porch, you'll know you've chosen well. The prime rib with lobster is indulgent but wonderful, but it's hard to choose when the lamb and chicken dishes sound so tempting. The Woodshed has a full liquor license and offers sumptuous appetizers in the lounge, so plan to come for cocktails if you can. On the other hand, the children's menu prevents the "I don't want any of these fancy things" crisis. The Woodshed serves dinner only, Tuesday through Sunday.

George's Diner

$ • 10 Plymouth St., Meredith • (603) 279-8723

At George's Diner, home-cooked old-fashioned suppers are waiting every evening: New England boiled dinner or pot roast on Thursday, roast beef or turkey on Tuesday, ham and beans on Sunday. Four nights a week supper is all you can eat. But it's breakfast that makes George's an Insider favorite. The diner starts serving early, and the breakfast menu is good right through lunch (great lunch choices too!). Starting that early has its price, though — supper's over by 8 PM.

Giuseppe's Show Time Pizzeria & Ristorante

$$ • Mills Falls Marketplace, Meredith • (603) 279-3313

This restaurant is celebrating 10 years as part of the Inn at Mills Falls/Bay Point complex (see our Bed and Breakfasts and Country Inns chapter). The atmosphere is casual and festive, with a variety of Italian specialties on the menu, including many vegetarian options (baked ziti with eggplant and broccoli is delicious). The restaurant also serves gourmet pizzas, seafood and sandwiches for both lunch and dinner every day. See our Nightlife chapter for more on Guiseppe's.

Hart's Turkey Farm Restaurant

$-$$ • Junc. of N.H. Rt. 104 and U.S. Rt. 3, Meredith • (603) 279-6212

Once there were several "turkey farm restaurants" in New Hampshire (when we used to have more turkey farms). Although the farm was sold, Hart's remains, continuing the tradition of home-style dining in its comfortable dining rooms. The restaurant serves ample portions of roast turkey, of course, with all the fixings, prime rib, seafood, steaks and sand-

INSIDERS' TIP

When we say "clams" in New England, we mean whole clams. If you don't like the bellies, ask for clam strips.

wiches. A nice touch at Hart's is a "less than Harty" menu for those with appetites smaller than the gargantuan "Harty" portions but bigger than the children's menu size. Finish your meal with a piece of homemade pie. It's like Sunday dinner at grandma's without getting your cheeks pinched. Hart's is open for lunch and dinner every day except Thanksgiving, when they close early (4 PM) so their staff can eat turkey at home!

Mame's

$$ • 8 Plymouth St., Meredith
• (603) 279-4631

Small, cozy rooms with a Colonial decor make for an intimate dining experience in this 1825 brick house near the Mill Falls Marketplace. Beef and seafood dishes are a specialty here, with homemade breads and desserts to complement your meal. If you have a small appetite, you'll be glad to know the lunch menu is available all evening. Mame's is open for lunch and dinner each day as well as brunch on Sunday. It offers early-bird specials and a dinner theater program in association with the Lakes Region Theater (see our Arts and Culture chapter).

Jorue Chinese and Thai Restaurant

$-$$ • 41 Park St., Northfield
• (603) 286-7888

Jorue is a favorite in the Lakes Region and northern Merrimack Valley for both Chinese and Thai food. Try the Gulf of Siam (mixed seafood in coconut milk-curry sauce) or choose from five Thai duck dishes. On the Chinese side of the menu you'll find orange-flavored scallops or a hot coral shrimp sauté along with the traditional stir-fry favorites. Jorue serves lunch and dinner every day, 365 days a year.

The Italian Farmhouse

$$ • U.S. Rt. 3, Plymouth
• (603) 536-4536

This is the Italian in-law of the Common Man family of restaurants, and boy can she cook! The menu is not extensive, but there is plenty to choose from, all of it fresh and prepared to order. Farfalla, fettucine and lasagna made with veal, sausage, seafood and vegetables will have you singing opera by dolci (dessert). The Farmhouse serves dinner Tuesday through Sunday, along with a Sunday brunch buffet.

The Governor's Inn

$$$ • 78 Wakefield St., Rochester
• (603) 332-0107

Breakfast at The Governor's Inn is only for overnight guests (see our Bed and Breakfasts and Country Inns chapter). But at lunch and dinner, anyone can enjoy fine dining in this former colonial governor's home. Menus are an eclectic mix of the gourmet and the familiar. You can enjoy steak or scallops, salmon or rack of lamb or a homey pot roast with potatoes and carrots. At lunch the inn offers jambalaya, fettuccine and meat loaf. Check out the new courtyard, and dine al fresco if the weather is fine. Lunch is served Monday through Friday, and dinner is served Tuesday through Saturday evenings, with live music on Fridays.

Tilt'n Diner

$ • U.S. Rt. 3, Tilton
• (603) 286-2204

Insiders recommend the Tilt'n Diner, and when you've enjoyed the classic diner cooking, you'll know why. Where else will you find chicken and biscuits, chop suey or meat loaf? The diner has seafood, burgers and sand-

INSIDERS' TIP

Casual, family restaurants usually don't accept reservations. Call ahead if you're worried about waiting, and ask about peak hours and less busy times. It's best to make a reservation at smaller restaurants and inns, especially those that specialize in gourmet dinners. It never hurts to call ahead, as details might have changed since our last visit.

wiches too, and you can get breakfast all day. Save room for the ice cream! Tilt'n is part of the Common Man restaurant group. They brought the diner in from Massachusetts and restored it in 1992, complete with a jukebox and neon lights. Monday nights are Cruise Nights, when collectors of vintage cars gather to show off their prize vehicles.

M/S Mount Washington Dinner Cruises

$$$$, price includes tickets • on the pier, Weirs Beach
• (603) 366-BOAT

Each summer the *Mount Washington* hosts more than 70 dinner/dance cruises on Lake Winnipesaukee. Beginning in 1998 the chef on board has been the beloved former owner of Chase's Country Towne House. Choose Italian, seafood, beef or chicken from the new and evolving menu. Or call about the theme cruises with dinners to match. Families will be pleased to learn that children younger than 12 receive $10 discounts Monday evenings and Wednesday through Friday evenings and sail for free on Tuesday evenings. Singles tickets are discounted on Thursdays. See our Attractions chapter for more details about the *Mount Washington*.

Bailey's

$-$$ • S. Main St., Wolfeboro
• (603) 569-3662

Since 1938, summer in Wolfeboro has meant ice cream at Bailey's by the lake. Operated by the same family as the Lake Motel (see our Hotels and Motels chapter), Bailey's serves lunch and dinner every day from mid-May through October. Whether you choose ham, steak, seafood, salad or one of the nightly dinner specials, you'll know why Bailey's has been a Lakes Region favorite for three generations.

Loves' Quay

$$$ • 51 Mill St., Wolfeboro
• (603) 569-3303

A quay, if you're wondering, is a landing area for a boat, and your chef's name at this new lakeside restaurant is Mike Love. "Lovingly" prepared seafood is a specialty of the house, but there are delightful beef, chicken and pork dishes if you're not a fish-lover. Loves' Quay serves dinner only, Wednesday through Sunday, and Sunday brunch.

The Wolfeboro Inn

$-$$$ • 90 N. Main St., Wolfeboro
• (603) 569-3016, (800) 451-2389

This country inn offers a choice of dining experiences. Wolfe's Tavern ($-$$) serves three meals daily in a casual setting, and its extensive menu is complemented by a great selection of beers. At dinner time the 1812 Dining Room ($$-$$$) offers a slightly more formal option. You can choose prime rib or steak, seafood or pasta dishes in a cozy country atmosphere and sit by the fireplace in winter. The 1812 is open Thursday through Saturday from November 1 to mid-May and every day May through October. The tavern is open year round.

White Mountains and Great North Woods Regions

Riverview Restaurant Wayside Inn

$$ • U.S. Rt. 302 at Pierce Bridge, Bethlehem
• (603) 869-3364, (800) 448-9557

Victor Hoffmann is the chef at the Riverview. He's also co-owner of the Wayside Inn along with his wife, Kathe. You'll find Swiss specialties, such as fondue, along with pork loin roasted with shallots accompanied by perfectly roasted potatoes. The Saturday night menu always includes roast beef. This is what home cooking is all about when the cook at home is a trained chef. The sauces are simple and sublime. Dinner is served Tuesday through Sunday from 6-9 PM. Reservations are recommended.

Tim-Bir Alley

$$$, no credit cards • Guider La., Bethlehem
• (603) 444-6142

This 36-seat gem is in the Adair Country Inn. The menu changes frequently, but we'll give you a few recent choices to give you an idea of the culinary delights you'll find. For a starter you might try the ginger-soy shrimp on noodle-peanut pudding or the butternut squash ravioli. Main course choices include salmon with sunflower seed crust, lamb chops with wild mushrooms and rosemary-balsamic glaze and linguine with smoked chicken and sun-dried tomatoes. For dessert try the espresso cheesecake with warm hazelnut sauce or the white chocolate glazed pear tart. Dinner is served all year from Wednesday through Sunday. Reservations are a must. Pay by cash or personal check.

The Mount Washington Hotel

$$-$$$$ • U.S. Rt. 302, Bretton Woods • (603) 278-3457

This grand hotel was designed for the socialites of the early 20th century. Be sure to read about the Mount Washington Hotel in our Hotels and Motels chapter. There are five restaurants within the resort complex.

Main Dining Room ($$$$). This elegant room, with Tiffany stained glass and huge picture windows with views of Mount Washington and the Presidential Mountain Range, seats up to 500 people. The octagonal shape of the room was designed to avoid seating someone in a corner. The Main Dining Room is open for breakfast and dinner during the hotel's summer season, which runs from mid-May to mid-October. The country breakfasts include everything from fresh fruit, pancakes and eggs to bacon, sausage and potatoes. But the real fun begins at dinner. The executive chef and his staff offer 10 different dinner menus, which are rotated daily. The cuisine concentrates on American and European favorites. Entrees include braised veal with spinach, prosciutto and sun-dried tomatoes and baked salmon with mussel and scallion sauce. Herbivores might choose the wild mushroom stroganoff with grilled polenta. Appetizers, such as smoked mussels and shrimp and fresh fruit with cheese, are included in the four-course dinner. The pastry chef offers a freshly baked selection of pastries as well as ice cream and sherbet every day.

Stickney's Restaurant and Lounge ($$). This casual restaurant is a favorite spot for golfers and tennis players. You can eat out on the patio or inside in what used to be the hotel's billiard room. You can always get a cup of clam chowder to start with and move on to hot and cold luncheon choices. Cold dishes include a tropical fruit and yogurt salad plate as well as a traditional chef's salad. If you want something a little heartier, try the baby back rib sandwich or the Fairway burger. And for a real New England lunch, follow that chowder with a lobster roll and cole slaw. Desserts include cheesecake, pie and ice cream. Stickney's is open for lunch every day from mid-May until mid-October.

Bretton Arms Country Inn ($$$). In case you're visiting New Hampshire when the Mount Washington Hotel is closed, you'll be glad to know the restaurant in the Bretton Arms Country Inn is open year-round for breakfast and dinner. Breakfasts are hearty with fruits, French toast and pancakes along with eggs, bacon and sausage. The dinner menu leads with smoked Atlantic salmon or cheddar ravioli with smoked duck breast for appetizers. Following those delights are entrees such as New England seafood on lobster fettucine, roast rack of lamb and pan-seared medallions of pork with pecans. Dessert selections are up to the pastry chef, but you can expect a delicious choice of freshly baked pastries as well as traditional flavors of ice cream.

Darby's Restaurant and Hearthside Lounge ($$). You'll find Darby's in the Bretton Woods Motor Inn. It's open year-round for breakfast and dinner. Breakfast choices are traditional country favorites with fresh fruit, pancakes, eggs, potatoes and various breakfast meats. Many of the dinner entrees are "home-cooked" favorites such as chicken pot pie and roast turkey with cranberry relish. The vegetable stir-fry includes cashews, and the

INSIDERS' TIP

You'll see clam and lobster "rolls" on lots of seafood menus. Always ask, but it usually means a top-split hot dog roll filled with either fried clams or lobster salad.

chef always prepares a pasta special. Try the New England apple crisp for dessert.

Fabyan's Station Restaurant and Lounge ($$). The Mount Washington Hotel used to have its own railroad station. That station has been restored and converted to Fabyan's, a popular spot for lunch and dinner during the peak winter and summer seasons. Skiers will be happy to see the hearty entrees. Try the hot bacon turkey melt or grilled Reuben. Or maybe you'd like baked lasagna or spaghetti and meatballs before heading back to the slopes. The clam chowder comes by the cup or bowl, and the appetizer servings of nachos or beef chili with melted cheese will help take the edge off your hunger while you decide on an entree. If you've got room for dessert, try the pie à la mode or freshly baked cakes and pastries. Fabyan's is open from late December until early April and from mid-June through mid-October.

Red Parka Pub

$$ • U.S. Rt. 302, Glen
• (603) 383-4344

You don't have to be a skier to have fun here, but this has been an apres ski favorite for more than 25 years. You'll have fun whether you eat in the cozy pub or upstairs in the dining room. Steak and ribs are the featured items here. The ribs are pork, and the sauce makes you think you're in North Carolina not northern New Hampshire. As at all great steakhouses, there's seafood on the menu too. Kids will love their own special menu, which features chicken fingers and burgers. The salad bar is loaded with goodies, but be sure to save room for the made-on-premises mud pie. The crust is made with Oreo cookies and filled with coffee ice cream. The restaurant is open every day for dinner. Reservations are not accepted.

Olde Timbermill Restaurant and Pub

$$ • Millfront Marketplace, Main St., Lincoln
• (603) 745-3603

If you've got a group that can't decide what to eat, this is the place to come. The dinner menu includes everything from grilled steaks to vegetarian stir-fries. Seafood lovers can choose from nine entrees including blackened swordfish and seafood pie. Those who favor pasta might try the spinach and roasted garlic ravioli or pan-seared pork tips tossed with bow tie pasta. The pub menu has burgers and sandwiches as well as an excellent beer selection. The restaurant is open every day beginning at 11:30 AM. Dinner is served from 5 PM.

William Tell Restaurant

$$-$$$ • N.H. Rt. 49, Campton
• (603) 726-3618

Families are welcome at this upscale but friendly restaurant. The dining room seats 125. Reservations are a good idea, especially on weekends. Seafood entrees might include fresh salmon with capers or grilled swordfish. A mouth-watering meat specialty is sautéed venison medallions served with a mushroom and sun-dried blueberry sauce. The kids' menu features all-time favorites, such as hamburgers. The restaurant is open every night for dinner and serves brunch on Sunday.

Italian Oasis and Brewery

$$ • 127 Main St., Littleton
• 444-6995

Four brewed-on-premises beers are always on tap, including a seasonal special. In spring the special was Sap Beer in honor of the maple syrup season. Pasta specials include ravioli and manicotti, but the restaurant also has a great selection of chicken, beef and seafood. A dinner special is Paella Valenciana with mussels, shrimp, chicken and saffron-flavored rice. In warm weather, eat outside on the patio that overlooks the White Mountains. The greenhouse dining room is beautiful all year round, but it provides an especially welcome bit of nature during winter. The pub overlooks Main Street, and the horseshoe-shape bar is a great place to get to know some locals. The restaurant is open for lunch and dinner every day.

Stonehurst Manor

$$$ • N.H. Rt. 16, North Conway
• (603) 356-3113

If a day at the discount malls in North Conway has you wondering just what quality is, we advise that you check out the delicious and carefully prepared food at Stonehurst Manor. At dinner, start with Juniper Gravlax, fresh Atlantic salmon cured on the premises. Or you can try the portobella mushroom stuffed with lobster, scallops and shrimp. Entrees include wood-fired roast chicken, roast venison and a rack of lamb for two. Pasta picks include capellini tossed with lobster, artichoke hearts and chopped tomatoes and farfalle (bow ties) with wild mushrooms and snow peas. You can also order pizzas with a difference. The Hawaiian includes fresh pineapple, and another comes covered with maple sausage. Dessert choices include chocolate fondue with fresh fruit and fresh-baked apple pie. Dinner is served every night.

Sunset Hill House

$$-$$$ • Sunset Hill Rd., Sugar Hill
• (603) 823-5522, (800) 786-4455

Dinner is served in both the tavern and the main dining room. Rose McGee's Tavern is a bistro-style restaurant with a light seasonal menu. It features a stir-fry of the day along with burgers, burritos and individual pizzas. The tavern is a popular place among guests of the nearby bed and breakfasts. The main dining room is more formal. "Country club casual" is the way one employee described the dress code. Four-course a la carte dinners are served. The menu changes with the season, but typical appetizers are grilled cod cakes or steamed mussels. Main course choices include a beef entree such as grilled tenderloin with broiled tomatoes or poached salmon and asparagus. For desserts try the warm apple strudel à la mode or a chocolate ice cream torte. Both restaurants include vegetarian selections and are open for dinner seven days a week during summer and through foliage season. The rest of the year dinner is available Thursday through Sunday.

Chile Peppers

$$ • Town Sq., Waterville Valley
• (603) 236-4646

Everybody loves Chile Peppers. And Chile Peppers loves families. It's one of Waterville Valley's most popular spots and sure to please everyone in your group. The Mexican favorites include sizzling fajitas. Fresh vegetables are sautéed with your choice of meat, chicken, shrimp or more vegetables. The Colorado Chicken is grilled with Southwestern herbs and topped with salsa fresco, a spicy mix of fresh melon. Standard dinners include New York sirloin and baby-back ribs. The children's menu has a taco choice as well as those perennial kid's favorites, hot dogs and grilled cheese sandwiches. The famous dessert is key lime pie, but they also serve a chocolate mousse and Spanish flan. The restaurant is open for lunch and dinner during ski season and the summer. The rest of the year only dinner is served.

Woodstock Inn

$$-$$$ • 135 Main St., Woodstock • (603) 745-3951

You've got three dining choices in this Woodstock favorite. Newcomers and longtime patrons enjoy the brewpub. It features seven made-on-premises beers as well as homemade root beer. You've got a 148-item menu to pick just the right food to go with your draft. Try the nachos for a snack or the hearty "brewchetta" pasta with lots of savory tomatoes. If you want a little less noise, you might want to eat in the casual dining room. The menu is the same as in the bar, but the scene is quieter. Finally, for diners who like a fancy lunch or dinner, there's the Clement room. This fine-dining option includes rack of lamb and duck flambé. Other favorites include a traditional Caesar salad prepared at your table and a tender filet mignon. You'll enjoy the special touches, which include a sorbet before your entree and an edible chocolate cup containing a touch of peppermint schnapps served after dinner. The restaurant is open every day for lunch and dinner.

Dartmouth-Lake Sunapee Region

The Charlestown Heritage Restaurant and Diner

$ • 122 Main St., Charlestown • (603) 826-3110

If you're taking the kids to the Fort at No. 4, you might want to stop here for breakfast or lunch. Both meals have a kids' menu with choices such as one pancake with one sausage for breakfast and chicken fingers for lunch. The regular breakfast menu includes three-egg omelets and homemade biscuits with gravy. Lunch choices include turkey, roast beef and tuna sandwiches on fresh baked bread. Grilled tuna melts and Reuben sandwiches along with hot dogs and burgers are a few hot lunch choices. The diner is open from 6 AM to 2 PM every day. Breakfast is available all day.

Indian Shutters Restaurant

$$ • N.H. Rt. 12, Charlestown • (603) 826-4366

You'll get a history lesson along with your meal here. The name comes from the special window shutters designed to close and bolt from the inside in case of an Indian attack. This restaurant has a large, airy dining room in addition to smaller cozy rooms with fireplaces. The restaurant specializes in Italian favorites such as the baked stuffed manicotti, spaghetti with meatballs and veal Parmesan served with spaghetti. Seafood choices include baked stuffed haddock as well as fried or broiled fish, shrimp and scallops. Steaks and prime rib dinners are available in 12- or 16-ounce servings. The restaurant serves lunch and dinner. It is closed on Monday.

Everything But Anchovies

$ • 5 Allen St., Hanover • (603) 643-6137

As you might expect, pizza is the featured item here — and yes, you *can* get anchovies. More than 26 toppings are available, and pizza size ranges from the 8-inch individual to the 24-inch giant. Quesadillas, burritos and subs are available as well as burgers and melts. All-you-can-eat spaghetti is just one of the pasta dishes. Daily dinner specials always include at least one homemade pasta. The kids' menu features dinosaur-shaped chicken nuggets along with peanut butter and jelly, grilled cheese or plain spaghetti. You get free refills on fountain soft drinks. Breakfast, lunch and dinner are served every day in addition to a Sunday champagne brunch.

The Hanover Inn

$$-$$$$ • Main St., Hanover • (603) 643-4300

You can choose from two dining rooms at this Dartmouth College-owned inn. The more formal choice is The Daniel Webster Room, which is always included in discussions about the best food in New Hampshire. Entree choices include classics such as aged sirloin with scalloped potatoes, leeks and morels, and the unusual, such as sauerkraut-stuffed duck with wild rice and a Spring Bock beer sauce. You might choose baked oysters with tarragon and hazelnuts to start or maybe

Photo: David A. Leach Photography

This signpost in Berlin tells you exactly where you stand.

snails with orzo and sun-dried tomatoes. The wine list is extensive. If you'd like something a bit more casual with a modern international influence, you might prefer The Ivy Grill. Appetizers include steamed dim sum and a hot wild mushroom tart. Main dishes range from grilled calf's liver to lobster and crab ravioli. And, in case you travel with a picky eater, you can always get a burger. The restaurants have separate but equal space on the terrace overlooking the Dartmouth green. Both restaurants serve lunch and dinner every day. You can also eat breakfast in the Daniel Webster Room. If you enjoy food and like to see how an institution remains true to it history while incorporating modern food ideas and flavors, either of these restaurants is sure to please.

Molly's Balloon

$$ • 43 S. Main St., Hanover
• (603) 643-2570

Everyone is sure to find something to their liking here. Mexican choices include nachos, quesadillas and a taco salad. If Italian fare is your favorite, you can choose from more than 10 pasta dishes including a grilled veggie pasta or a peppered chicken linguine. You can pick a soup and sandwich combo or choose one of the main course salads. Besides a wide choice of burger toppings, you can actually choose whether you'd like a beef, chicken or veggie patty. The homemade dessert tray is full of tempting tarts and cakes, and you can always get a simple dish of ice cream or order the Cookie Jar, three homemade cookies served with a glass of milk.

Patrick Henry's

$$ • 39 S. Main St., Hanover
• (603) 643-2345

Walk down a few steps just off Main Street and enter a dark paneled tavern that serves delicious food from lunch into the late night. In warm weather, you can sit at one of the outdoor tables on a narrow deck. Whatever the season you'll enjoy the wide variety of sandwiches — from turkey boursin to a double-decker club — salads, soups and stews. You can always get nachos, and the soups include New England fish chowder as well as a daily special. For dinner go for the traditional shepherd's pie or chili served over cornbread with cheese and black olives. Carrot cake tops the dessert list, and there's a hot-fudge brownie sundae for chocolate lovers.

Panda House and Bamboo Garden

$$ • 3 Lebanon St., Hanover
• (603) 643-1290

Panda House specializes in Chinese food, and Bamboo Garden is the place to go to satisfy cravings for sushi and sashimi. The two restaurants share dining space and a menu, and you're welcome to order a bit from each cuisine. Bamboo Garden selections include California rolls with crab meat, avocado, cucumber and fish eggs as well as miso soup and seaweed salad. Chinese choices are extensive with such standards as Dragon and Phoenix, which combines lobster with chicken, and crispy sesame beef. Hunan, Cantonese and Peking specialties are all represented on the menu. Additionally you can choose simple steamed entrees served with mixed vegetables. Both restaurants serve lunch and dinner.

Sweet Tomatoes Trattoria

$$ • 1 Court St., Lebanon
• (603) 448-1711

Insiders know that "Sweet Tomatoes" is the place for authentic Italian food. If that's your kind of place, drive around the Lebanon green and look for bright red awnings. Park in the rear and head in for a great dinner. The atmosphere is cheery and casual with everyone enjoying delicious pasta or pizza. The menu offers delightful dilemmas. Should you start with a fresh green salad or the antipasto platter? Do you want the Ravioli Ripieni (a three-cheese ravioli with tomato, basil and garlic sauce) or Gamberetti E Cavatappi, which translates as sautéed shrimp, zucchini and plum tomatoes served over linguine? If pizza cooked in a wood-fired stone hearth oven turns on your taste buds, you can choose one featuring artichoke hearts and garlic or roasted sausage with tomato and mozzarella. Just in case you want more, the restaurant serves a variety of Italian desserts including tiramisu and cannoli. The restaurant is open every day for lunch and dinner.

The Flying Goose Brew Pub and Four Corners Grille

$$ • intersection of N.H. Rts. 11 and 114, New London
• (603) 526-6899

If you're not driving, this is the place to relax with a pint of Wiegelman's Wildflower Honey Ale while you enjoy the mountain views from the screened deck just off The Flying Goose Brew Pub. The honey comes from a local beekeeper, and the beer is brewed right here. You can also get golden ales, pale ales and wheat ales. Try the porter or Hedgehog dark ale and whatever else might be on tap. Hungry? Then walk five steps to enter the Four Corners Grill. We love the baked artichoke hearts stuffed with crabmeat dressing to start with (they're called Goose Hearts on the menu). Popular main courses include Boston haddock with a cracker crumb and chive crust and Crocketts Corner Chicken, a boneless breast stuffed with shrimp, basil and roasted red pepper. Lunch and dinner are served every day with sandwiches available until 4 PM.

Inn at Pleasant Lake

$$$$ • 125 Pleasant St., New London
• (603) 526-6271, (800) 626-4907

Originally a farm that took boarders, the

Inn at Pleasant Lake was recently purchased by Linda and Brian MacKenzie, who reopened the dining room and now serve dinner every night except Tuesday. Brian graduated from the Culinary Institute of America and serves a five-course, prix fixe dinner. The dinner includes soup, salad, entree and dessert as well as a mid-meal palate refresher that might be a sorbet or a compote of dried fruit. The menu changes daily. Summer favorites include essence of asparagus soup and baby salad greens with a citrus vinaigrette. Look for straightforward presentation with glamorous sauces. You might be served a butter-rich beurre blanc sauce one night and a fresh red pepper coulis the next. Dessert selections might include an apple tart, chocolate mousse and napoleons. The restaurant is part of the12-room inn.

MacKenna's Restaurant

$ • New London Shopping Ctr., Main St.,
• (603) 526-9511

George Washington never slept here, but Barbara Bush had New England clam chowder and a sliced chicken sandwich for lunch during the 1992 presidential campaign. John MacKenna has been cooking in New London since moving here in 1965. Sandwiches and burgers are always available, but you can also try the deep-dish chicken pie, which features John's homemade crust, or tender Yankee Pot Roast. Light eaters will appreciate the mini-meal menu featuring smaller portions (and prices) of the roast beef dinner, broiled or fried haddock and other favorites. The restaurant is open for breakfast, lunch and dinner every day.

Peter Christian's Tavern

$$ • 186 Main St., New London
• (603) 526-4042

We love the casual atmosphere and the great food in this New London institution. It opens every day at 11 AM and serves great food straight through the late-dinner hours. The menu offers the same selection throughout the day, so you can get a hearty bowl of beef stew at lunch or a half-sandwich at dinner. The sandwiches are not your run-of-the-mill sliced meat and pale tomato on bread. Instead look forward to "Peter's father's favorite," a scrumptious combination of roast beef, sliced onion, tomatoes and spinach wlth a tantalizing cream cheese and horseradish blend instead of common mayo. And you have a choice of at least six varieties of bread. Sandwiches are popular, but the last time we were there, the shepherd's pie was the favorite at our table. The cheese tortellini with sun-dried tomatoes and the white pesto lasagna are two outstanding pasta choices too. A list of daily specials is placed on the table so you don't have to memorize a server's litany. We never have room for dessert, but the sundaes and cakes are huge with lots of whipped cream. The tea and coffee selections include decaf and herbal varieties.

The Millstone

$$ • Newport Rd., New London
• (603) 526-4201

This is a favorite spot for dinner before catching the evening performance at the Barn Dinner Theater. Favorite appetizers include herb-stuffed mushrooms, Maine crab cakes and seafood sausage. Linguine with seafood, roast duckling and portobello paella are a few sample entrees. The lobster, Caesar and chef's salads are popular main course items. The Millstone is open every day for lunch and dinner. It's a good idea to make dinner reservations, especially if you're planning to eat before the play.

Lui Lui

$-$$ • Powerhouse Mall, N.H. Rt. 12-A, West Lebanon
• (603) 298-7070

Tell the shoppers in your group that you'll

INSIDERS' TIP

New England is known for wonderful ice cream, and New Hampshire has lots of local producers who will show you why. Take advantage of the roadside stands and storefront shops advertising local ice creams and enjoy!

check out this bustling Italian restaurant while they enjoy the mall. While you wait, have an order of the bruschetta, fresh Tuscan bread toasted and topped with your choice of tomatoes, cheese, pesto or roasted sausage. Or maybe you should entertain yourself with a bit of pasta — you can choose from 20 dishes including homemade lasagna. Or try one of the wood-fired pizzas. You can "build" your own from more than 30 toppings (you pick, they assemble) or try one of their commended combinations. If time is short once the shoppers arrive, suggest one of the express pizza or pasta lunches. Lunch and dinner are served every day.

The Seven Barrel Brewery Pub

$$ • N.H. Rt. 12-A (exit 20 off I-89), West Lebanon
• (603)298-5566

Authentic pub fare such as Toad-in-the-Hole (sausage enclosed in pastry) and Cock'a'Leekie Pie (chicken, leek and vegetable pot pie) are the perfect accompaniment to the many brewed-on-premises beers and ales. In case you prefer American bar food to English pub food, don't worry. You have a choice of burgers and sandwiches for lunch, and after 5 PM you can order sirloin steak or broiled scrod. For a light touch, try the corn fritters or Buffalo chicken wings. Lunch and dinner are served every day.

Monadnock Region

Griffings' Riverside

$$ • N.H. Rt.13, Brookline
• (603) 673-4698

A crowded parking lot is the best way to tell you you've found the restaurant. It's right on N.H. Route 13, 5 miles north of the Massachusetts state line. Most of the diners are repeat customers. (We know because we see them.) It's a favorite for family food that we can't, won't or don't have time to cook. We like the Surf City special, which offers a combo of ribs, chicken or New York sirloin with fried or baked shrimp, scallops or fish. And it's nice to know you can get a turkey club if you're not up to pigging out. The special senior citizens menu allows for reduced portions at reduced prices (with certain restrictions during dinner on weekends). The restaurant is open for lunch and dinner every day and breakfast on Sunday.

Audrey's Cafe

$ • N.H. Rt. 101, Dublin
• (603) 876-3316

Just 5 minutes from Friendly Farm (see our Kidstuff chapter), Audrey's is a smart stop for all ages. Breakfast includes wonderful waffles — plain or with lots of fruit and whipped cream — lots of omelets and a regional favorite, baked beans with toast and coffee. You can even get Southern country sausage gravy served over biscuits. Lunch favorites include hot and cold sandwiches, burgers and salads. Daily specials include a homemade soup and might feature a veggie roll-up or a baked ham platter. The kids menu offers hot dogs, grilled cheese or peanut butter sandwiches. Breakfast and lunch are served every day, and dinner is served on Friday and Saturday.

Del Rossi's Trattoria

$$ • N.H. Rt. 137, Dublin
• (603) 563-7195

Need to replace those calories after climbing Mount Monadnock? Come on over and pick a pasta to suit your tastes. Our favorites include the Fettucine Med, which means the homemade pasta is tossed with black olives, diced tomatoes, capers and feta cheese. A special lasagna is offered everyday, and you can get a side order of homemade pork sausage seasoned with fennel, garlic and pepper. The restaurant buys local produce, eggs and milk. Several dishes are vegetarian, and the restaurant will always do its best to alter a dish to suit your tastes. The restaurant is open for dinner nightly. Look for details on the extensive musical entertainment in our Nightlife chapter.

Fitzwilliam Inn

$$$ • N.H. Rt. 119, Fitzwilliam
• (603) 585-9000

We usually order a complete dinner here, which includes everything from soup du jour to dessert and coffee or tea. Roast duck stuffed with apples is a favorite, as is the pan-roasted salmon. Traditional dishes include a

Caesar salad and baked onion soup, while a contemporary influence can be sampled with the vegetable spring roll with orange plum sauce. Two pasta dishes are on the current menu, including the roasted garlic and spinach ravioli. The inn serves three meals a day.

Hancock Inn

$$ • 33 Main St., Hancock
• (603) 525-3318

Waitresses and waiters wear period clothing to match the history of this inn, which was built in 1789. The only thing here that's not steeped in history is the menu. Start with lobster ragout, which features a tarragon beurre blanc sauce, or try the Nantucket Seafood Chowder with fish, scallops and shrimp. The most popular main course is the Shaker cranberry pot roast with garlic mashed potatoes. If you'd like something from the sea, you can opt for corn-crusted rainbow trout or salmon served with roasted pepper vinaigrette. The main dining room features a fireplace and a lovely view of the garden, while a smaller room is perfect for a private dinner. The inn is open to the public for dinner only.

Brewbakers Cafe

$ • 97 Main St., Keene
• (603) 355-4844

You can curl up on the couch and read one of several newspapers or perch in a window seat and watch the action on Main Street while you enjoy a cinnamon roll or contemplate the effects of another espresso. Besides a wide choice of coffees, this cozy cafe has excellent sandwiches and delicious soups. Sandwiches are made to order — go ahead and try a little horseradish with the roast beef — and soups change daily. Pastries are available all day (if they don't sell out) and you can get soup and sandwiches for lunch or supper. Brewbakers is closed on Sunday.

Tory Pines Resort

$$$ • just off N.H. Rt. 47, Francestown
• (603) 588-2000

You'll enjoy dining in the Gibson Tavern that was built in 1799.Try the traditional Caesar salad and an appetizer of pan-fried crab cakes with mustard sauce. Or start with Crostini Formaggio, which is grilled flat bread topped with pesto sauce, provolone cheese and plum tomatoes. Follow that with the 10-ounce grilled New York sirloin. Pasta dishes include penne Primevera with vegetables and fettucine Alfredo, to which you can add chicken and broccoli. If you're trying to keep your belt at the same setting, try the grilled salmon served on a bed of lemon-seasoned noodles and julienne vegetables. Desserts change frequently, but you can expect seasonal fresh fruit with raspberry or lemon sherbet as well as double chocolate fudge cake.

Michael's Jaffrey Manor

$$ • 13 Stratton Rd., Jaffrey
• (603) 532-8555

Besides being home to Mount Monadnock, Jaffrey is home to one of our favorite spots for lobster. You'll find lobster specials here all year round. You can have surf and turf featuring one or two lobsters, a New England clambake with steamers and lobster or pasta with fresh lobster sauce. We've noticed other people really love the fried shrimp and prime rib, but we swear by the lobster. Besides the food, you'll enjoy the wonderful photographs of Mount Monadnock. The restaurant is a short walk from the stoplight in the middle of town.

Elm City Brewing Company

$$ • Colony Mill Marketplace, 222 West St., Keene
• (603) 355-3335

This restaurant is a mainstay in the wonderful Colony Mill Marketplace (see our Shopping chapter for more on this former mill complex originally constructed in 1838). You'll have a choice of five brewed-on-premises beers as well as a menu featuring a wide-variety of sandwiches and American-style pub food. We love the spicy chili served over rice and the cheeseburger served with thick-cut French fried potatoes. If you'd like something a little fancier, try the chicken piccata served with the season's fresh vegetables or the pan-fried cajun catfish. Ask for the "half pints" menu for kids younger than 12. It features such favorites as peanut butter and jelly and grilled cheese sandwiches. Elm City Brewing Company is open everyday for lunch and dinner, but it closes at 6 PM on Sunday.

The Wright Mansion

$$$$ • 695 Court St., Keene
• (603) 355-1155

This is the place to celebrate a college graduation or treat your significant other to a bit of luxury. The menu changes with the season. In winter try grilled Italian sausage served with polenta or a boneless breast of duck with brandy currant sauce. Summer treats include a braised vegetable plate along with lamb chops and grilled or poached salmon. Sauces are made from homemade stocks, and the herbs are grown in the garden. Homemade ice cream, strawberry shortcake and a heavenly devil's food cake with fudge icing are typical dessert choices. Reservations are required. The food is cooked toreador, and all ingredients are the freshest of the day. All dinners are prix fixe and include soup, appetizer, entree, salad and dessert.

Parker's Maple Barn and Sugar House

$$ • 1316 Brookline Rd., Mason
• (603) 878-2308, (800) 832-2308

Do you ever get a craving for pancakes with whipped butter and real maple syrup? If so, bring those taste buds to Parker's Maple Barn. You won't find a wider variety of pancakes — buckwheat, blueberry, whole wheat and raspberry to name a few — and luckily breakfast is served all day. You can get bacon, sausage and ham with your pancakes or choose the homemade ham hash instead. If you're a coffee drinker, you'll appreciate the insulated carafe of freshly brewed Java that's left with your first cup. The delicious maple syrup gives Parker's its name and much of its fame. The sugaring season starts here around the first of March and runs for six weeks. Saturday and Sunday feature tours of the sugar house and horse-drawn carriage rides to entertain the kids while you wait for your table. Insiders know that a wait of three hours is possible on a beautiful Sunday morning in March, which is peak season. Besides the great breakfasts, Parker's Maple Barn serves lunch every day and dinner Thursday through Sunday. Fried chicken, maple ribs and burgers are featured at lunch, and dinner choices include barbecue chicken, grilled salmon and maple-baked ham and beans. Parker's opens at 7 AM on weekends and 8 AM during the week. The restaurant is closed from mid-December to mid-February.

Pickity Place

$$-$$$ • Nutting Hill Rd., Mason
• (603) 878-1151

Relax in the 1768 cottage and enjoy a five-course lunch, which is served every day. Reservations are usually necessary, as the three lunch seatings fill up fast. The menu changes seasonally but count on fresh-baked breads, exotic salads, homemade soups and delicious entrees.

Grovers Corners

$$ • Northgate Plaza, U.S. Rt. 202, Peterborough
• (603) 924-9296

Grovers Corners is a consistently reliable casual meeting place. The choices span a broad range. Start with Ultimate Nachos, move on to the veggie Stir-fry Salad and finish off with a steak and cheese submarine sandwich. If you prefer seafood, try salmon tortellini with a garlic wine sauce. The full children's menu includes hot dogs and peanut butter and jelly. The restaurant serves lunch and dinner every day and breakfast on weekends.

The Peterborough Diner

$ • 10 Depot St., Peterborough
• (603) 924-6202

You'll feel like a native as you eavesdrop on local business talk at lunch. Fast service and a wide-ranging menu are two reasons why this diner has been open for more than 50 years. Try the kielbasa and egg special if you're really hungry, or the blueberry pancakes or Belgian waffles. Lunch includes hot

INSIDERS' TIP

Most restaurants offer smoking and nonsmoking sections. If you don't care, you'll generally be seated more quickly in the smoking section.

and cold sandwiches including six different club sandwich combos. Pasta, seafood and chicken highlight the dinner options. The children's menu features spaghetti and meatballs along with burgers, grilled cheese and peanut butter and jelly sandwiches. The diner is open for three meals every day, and breakfast is available all day long.

Nick's Seafood and Steaks

$$ • N.H. Rt. 10, West Swanzey • (603) 352-6664

At this restaurant just 4 miles south of Keene, the name says it all. The food is straightforward — charbroiled steaks and fried, broiled or baked seafood, with pork chops thrown in for the hard-to-please. The ambiance is friendly and professional. You'd be comfortable bringing a date here, whether it's your mate or your mom. Kids are welcome as long as they bring adult appetites. The restaurant is open for dinner every day and lunch on Sunday.

The Melting Pot

$, no credit cards • Main Street, Wilton • (603) 654-5150

This restaurant opened in 1998 and has transformed the "downtown scene" in this charming town. It's open Tuesday through Friday from 6 AM to 2 PM and weekends from 6 AM until noon. You can get eggs anyway you want, but our breakfast favorite is the cheese omelet with delicious home-fries and toast. Pancakes are always on the menu and you'll want to check out any specials. Lunch is soups and sandwiches with wonderful sides such as homemade potato salad or French fries. It's bright, cheery and cash only.

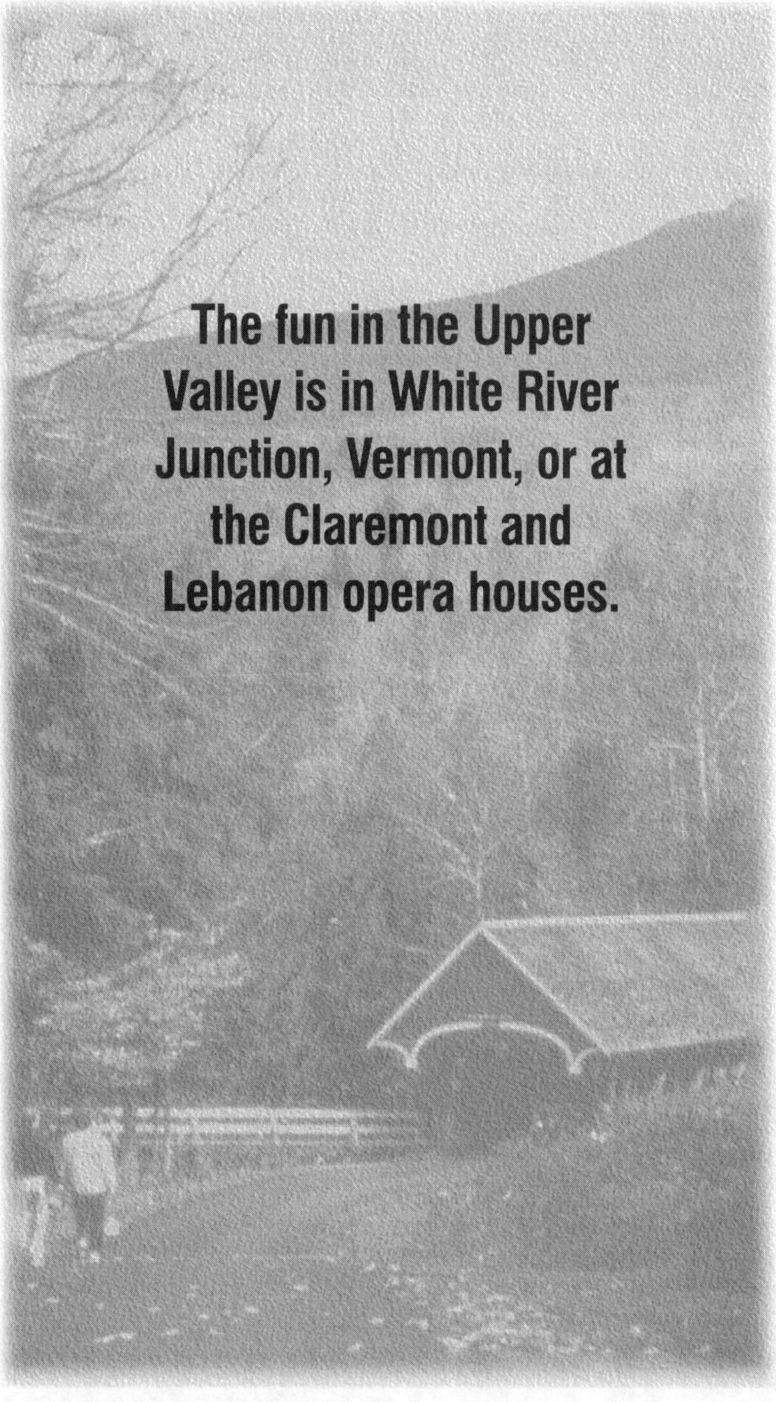
The fun in the Upper Valley is in White River Junction, Vermont, or at the Claremont and Lebanon opera houses.

Nightlife

Most of our nightlife is local — contradancing at the town hall, church suppers and bingo down at the lodge. We're not kidding. The roads here are not lined with neon and nightclubs. We do have lots of summer theater, so look for nightlife ideas in our Arts and Culture chapter. That's also the place to find information on local venues so you can see what might be happening during your visit. For example, visitors to the Dartmouth-Lake Sunapee Region should see what's on at the Hopkins Center before making evening plans. You might find a concert or dance performance that interests you.

Also, 20-something Insiders know that the fun in the Upper Valley is in White River Junction, Vermont, or at the Claremont and Lebanon opera houses. In the Monadnock region, always check the Colonial Theatre in Keene and the happenings on the Keene State College campus.

And don't overlook the local papers and their weekly entertainment listings along with *The Boston Sunday Globe* New England edition, which includes a "New Hampshire Weekly" section. Also look for *Jam Music Magazine* at music shops and venues throughout the state. It carries extensive statewide listings of who's playing where as well as reviews, ads and articles of interest to professionals in the music scene.

When you do find some late-night fun here, please remember that you must be 21 to drink and that alcohol and driving don't mix. Our roads can be hard to drive in the best of conditions, so please don't jeopardize your life or ours by drinking and driving. Make sure your group always includes a designated driver.

Merrimack Valley Region

The Olde Road II
390 Daniel Webster Hwy., Bedford
• (603) 668-7263

The Olde Road now has several different options for your entertainment. Mr. C's Showplace Lounge offers country-western dancing, including instructions Thursdays from 7 to 11 PM and Fridays from 7 PM to midnight, with a $5 cover. The Time Out Lounge features DJ music on Saturday nights from 8:30 PM to 1 AM. Meanwhile, in Mr. C's Sports Bar & Deli the pool tables are open, there are table games going and darts competitions rage. Saturdays when Baby Jake's Band plays there's a $3 cover.

Chantilly's Entertainment Complex
89 Fort Eddy Rd., Concord
• (603) 225-7709, (800) 290-7709

Chantilly's complexes have billiards and music, contests and games every night. Here in Concord the bar is called the Speedway Lounge and the racetrack theme predominates. Sunday and Wednesday there is karaoke with cash prizes (and Wednesday there's always a Wet T-shirt contest). You can dance to DJs from Sunday to Thursday, then come back Friday and Saturday for live music. Some weeks the bands are tribute groups for such rock legends as Aerosmith and the Grateful Dead. Other nights local favorites play, and a couple of times a month the club will host a nationally-known band. Recently Southside Johnny, Eve 6 and Saxon have entertained here. Call for a schedule of upcoming events, and to reserve tickets for the national bands.

Hermanos Cocina Mexicana
11 Hills Ave., Concord
• (603) 224-5669

Hermanos' terrific Mexican cuisine and authentic south-of-the-border decor complements the live music in the lounge Sunday through Wednesday nights from 6:30 to 10 PM. Most often the musicians are jazz instrumentalists, though jazz vocals and folk artists are sometimes booked. All the musicians are professionals who play across the Northeast. There's never a cover charge.

Nutfield Ale House

22 Manchester Rd., Derry
• (603) 434-9678

Nutfield has been brewing up a storm in New Hampshire for years now, and now guests can stop at the brewery itself for a pint and a snack. No entertainment (unless you want a tour of the brewery), just good beer and good conversation in a pleasant, relaxing atmosphere. The Ale House is open Thursdays 5 PM to 8 PM, Fridays from 5 PM to 10 PM, Saturdays from noon to 10 PM and Sundays from noon to 6 PM. (Still hungry? See our Restaurants chapter for the Nutfield Steak House and our Annual Events chapter for Brewed and Baked in the Granite State.)

Circle 9 Ranch Country Dance Hall

Windymere Dr., off N.H. Rt. 28, Epsom
• (603) 736-8443

This huge dance hall is part of the Circle 9 Campground complex (see our Camping chapter for more about Circle 9). The red and white tile dance floor is 40 feet square and there's still plenty of room for tables and chairs where you can catch your breath. The southwestern decor is carried over into the patrons' dress, which runs to jeans and cowboy hats. The Circle 9 hosts live country-western bands for dancing from 8 PM to midnight every Friday and Saturday night and offers lessons on Tuesdays. The crowd is a mix of die-hard country fans and people just out to try the latest line-dance, and the casual atmosphere invites kids and adults alike to relax and have fun. The hall is climate-controlled, which makes it even more attractive on a steamy July evening. Circle 9 has twice been named New Hampshire Club of the Year by the Country Music Association.

Whippersnappers

N.H. Rt. 102, Londonderry
• (603) 434-2660

Whippersnappers offers live music Thursday through Saturday nights from 8:30 PM to 12:30 AM. The style varies: sometimes Big Band, sometimes light jazz. There is no cover charge, and the full menu is always available. Whippersnappers attracts an upscale crowd to its intimate, tasteful setting.

antics Grill and Games

6 Huse Rd., Manchester
• (603) 626-8427

In addition to the popular video arcade and virtual reality games, on Friday and Saturday evenings antics hosts Antics After Dark!, an 18+ dance club on the "roof" of the restaurant (but still inside the building). The fun begins at 8 PM and runs until 1 AM. These evenings have become very popular with local singles. Dance to a D.J. and polish up your karaoke, or, if you're not in a musical mood, drinks from the full bar can be taken to the game floor below (see our Kidstuff chapter for more about antics). On Wednesday nights, in conjunction with WGIR (see our Media chapter) antics offers Office Lazer Wars — a great way to get rid of those cubical blues!

Billy's Sports Bar and Grill

34 Tarrytown Rd., Manchester
• (603) 625-6294

Here's the place to watch Holyfield's next fight or the NCAA finals. Satellite receivers and 23 TVs mean there's something for every sports fan at Billy's, and there's never a cover charge. A very informal, have-a-beer-and-watch-the-game spot in a working-class neighborhood.

Chantilly's Entertainment Complex

Maple Tree Mall, 545 Daniel Webster Hwy. N., Manchester
• (603) 624-9336

For an evening of billiards, various contests with big cash prizes, and a stage so close to the dance floor that you can chat with the musicians, head over to Chantilly's. Monday is Ladies night, Thursday and Friday are karaoke nights, there's dancing to DJs on Sunday and Tuesday. Wednesday is College night and Fun night is Thursday. Friday and Saturday nights enjoy live music from great local Top-40 cover bands and nationally-known groups (you'll find many of the same groups here as at Chantilly's in Concord). Chantilly's is noisy-casual and draws a young crowd ready for a good time.

Club Dancesport at the YMCA

30 Mechanic St., Manchester
• (603) 627-2417

For those who love ballroom dancing and those who've never tried it but would like to, Friday evenings the Y is the place to be. From 7 PM to 10 PM the dance floor hosts dancers of all ages and ability levels. Both singles and couples are welcome, and the $5 fee includes comforting explanations for those whose education in this area has been neglected.

Club Merri-mac

201 Merrimack St., Manchester
• (603) 623-9362

This downtown nightclub welcomes gay and lesbian patrons every day but Wednesday. They open in the late afternoon (call for specific hours, which vary) and close around 11 PM Sunday through Tuesday and at 1:30 AM Thursday through Saturday. Dance to DJs on Friday and Saturday nights. This is a members-only club (a year's membership is $10), but new members are always welcome.

The Colosseum

865 Second St., Manchester
• (603) 624-2876

This huge club caters to a young, often raucous crowd. Three dance floors offer dancing to live bands with classic rock, alternative rock or Top-40 music. Friday and Saturday nights there's also stand-up comedy, and on Sunday there's karaoke with big cash prizes.

Crystal's Lounge at the Center of New Hampshire/Holiday Inn

700 Elm St., Manchester
• (603) 625-1000

Crystal's is a gracefully appointed hotel lounge in the heart of downtown Manchester. Bright city lights shine through multi-story glass to mingle with the sparkle of stemware and conversation inside. On Thursday nights DATEline New England runs singles dances at Crystal's. On Fridays, Crystal's often has a live band, and Saturday is comedy night. The cover charge varies depending on the act. See our Accommodations chapter for more about this Holiday Inn.

Front Runner

22 Fir St., Manchester
• (603) 623-6477

Front Runner is a members-and-guests-only nightclub primarily for gays, lesbians and bisexuals, but everyone is welcome for music, trivia, games and parties. Annual membership is $20, and you must apply and show identification to join. The club is open from 3 PM to 1:30 AM every day. Monday means line dancing and two-steppin' from 7 to 11 PM (they'll teach you). There's a buffet on Sunday afternoon and live music on Sunday evenings. The rest of the week the club has DJs and games. Members pay no cover charge except for special events. Front Runner also sponsors picnics and HIV testing and publishes a quarterly newsletter.

Jillian's

50 Phillippe Cote St., Manchester
• (603) 626-7636

Jillian's fills most of the ground floor of one of Manchester's old mill buildings with what they call a "food and entertainment universe." The space is dominated by TVs: big, bigger and biggest, they hang in every corner and several walls are completely covered with them. Most of the time they're tuned to a variety of sporting events, although movies and popular series also get airtime here (mostly without sound, since the stereo fills the room, but if you ask, they'll turn on the closed-captioning). The bar is well-stocked

INSIDERS' TIP

It's not unusual during the summer for towns to sponsor a weekly music concert on the town green, square or oval. Sometimes it's a local barbershop quartet or a high school choral group. You might also hear a visiting chamber music group or band.

and the food ($) is more restaurant- than bar-quality. If the weather is fine you can eat out on the patio. Jillian's also offers an expansive billiards room, with 16 tournament-quality tables for which you can pay by the hour (at $3-4 per hour) or play all day on a $6 pass. A side room is filled with the latest in video arcade and simulator games, or you can try your hand at Ping-Pong or darts. There is also shuffleboard and foosball by the windows overlooking the Merrimack River. Kids can play here during the day but after 8 PM they must be accompanied by an adult. Two cigar lounges and a gourmet cigar menu complete the picture. Jillian's calendar is filled with promo nights sponsored by the big beer companies. Wednesday nights *South Park* fills the screens, and Monday is Ladies night.

The Riverside Room at Stark Mill Brewery & Restaurant

500 Commercial St., Manchester
• (603) 622-0000

The "SMB," as they call it, offers a variety of live entertainment both downstairs in the pub and upstairs in the club (neither is particularly formal). Some nights feature stand-up comedy; others offer blues or jazz. Often there's a full band, but sometimes an individual artist will play. Thursday night is always an open-mike jam, an opportunity for professional musicians and serious amateurs to be heard and get feedback from an appreciative and knowledgeable audience. See our Restaurants chapter for information on the Stark Mill's great food and microbrews.

Socialite Singles

35 W. Brook St., Manchester
• (603) 429-3941

The Socialite Singles group holds a dance with a DJ, 7:30 to 11:30 PM every Friday night at the American Legion Hall. In 1998 this group of singles aged 40 to 90 celebrated 25 years of ballroom dancing (with some county-western or line dancing mixed in for variety). Regulars bring a snack to eat at the coffee break, but the coffee is included in your $6 ticket, and the Legion's bartender will be happy to provide you with something more sustaining if you need it! Get dressed up and bring a friend — or meet a new one.

The Yard

Junction of Mammoth Rd. and S. Willow St., Manchester
• (603) 623-3545

Every Friday and Saturday night the Yard's regulars enjoy lively dancing to rock music from The Yard's house band, Powerplay. "Casual but nice" clothes are appropriate at this attractive lounge (see our Restaurants chapter for more on the Yard's famous Sunday brunch buffet). A state-of-the-art light and sound system keeps the music pounding. See our Restaurants chapter for menu details.

Silo's Steakhouse

641 Daniel Webster Hwy., Merrimack
• (603) 429-2210

Silo's entertains guests with live jazz by local guest artists every Wednesday night in the loft and solo piano on Friday and Saturday evenings. Dark wood, barn beams and big potted plants contribute to the rustic atmosphere, but the music is very cool and the listeners know and appreciate good food and good music.

Stormy Monday Cafe

438 Daniel Webster Hwy., Merrimack
• (603) 424-2755

Known for terrific blues, Stormy Monday (at the back of the Country Gourmet Restaurant) attracts top musicians and a knowledgeable clientele. The cafe menu offers complete meals (seafood, pasta, chicken or steak) or terrific munchies to accompany the extensive beer list (all our local brews as well as imports and the American standards are available). A full bar is also available, and the specials include offerings from the Country Gourmet (gator tail, anyone?). See our Restaurants chapter for more on that very nice restaurant and this historic building.

Michael Timothy's

Urban Bistro/Wine & Jazz Bar
212 Main St., Nashua
• (603) 595-9334

Michael Timothy's offers elegant food and elegant jazz in a downtown setting. They have live jazz, mostly instrumental, Thursday through Saturday from 9 PM to 1 AM and Sundays from 6 to 10 PM as well as a Jazz

Microbreweries and Home Brewing

Close-up

Maybe it's our crystal spring water, drawn sparkling and cold from the granite bedrock. Maybe it's the independent "live free or die" spirit. Whatever the reason, New Hampshire has been at the forefront of the microbrew movement since well before much of the country had even heard of beers with regional and varietal distinctions. Today we have several established brewers, a number of start-ups and dozens of people brewing for themselves and their friends who are being told "you should sell this!"

Communications Ink

Most of our established microbreweries have pubs, and you will find them listed in our Restaurants and Nightlife chapters. Many distinctive brews are available at local grocery stores. Both breweries do tours, where you can learn the difference between a lager and an ale, smell the hops and malt and enjoy a taste of New Hampshire with a head.

Should you be inspired to try your hand at this ancient art, you'll find supplies, support and advice at brew-supply stores and home-brewers clubs across the state.

Buffet Brunch on Sundays from 10 AM to 2 PM. There is no cover charge. Recently the crowds here have spilled out into the street, adding to the faintly Parisian atmosphere of the place. See our Restaurants chapter for details on the international cuisine. Michael Timothy's is closed on Monday.

Contradancing

Milford Town Hall Auditorium, Union St., Milford
• (603) 672-8252

On the second and fourth Fridays of every month from 8 to 11 PM, the Milford Parks and Recreation Commission sponsors traditional New England contradance, square dancing and line dancing, with a few old-fashioned country waltzes sprinkled into the mix. All levels and ages of dancers and musicians are welcome to join in the fun. Admission is $5, with no charge for children younger than 12. This is an alcohol- and smoke-free event. Please bring clean shoes to protect the floor.

Nick's Sports Bar and Grille

4 W. Hollis St., Nashua
• (603) 886-1334

Nick's invites adults (21 and over) to shows beginning at 9 PM every evening. Tuesday, Wednesday, Friday and Sunday are karaoke nights (and Wednesday is Ladies Night), Thursday is a dance mix, sometimes with open mike, and on Saturday night Nick's brings in live rock and roll. The downtown setting attracts a lively singles crowd. There is never a cover charge.

Sharky's Entertainment Complex

Globe Plaza, 300 S. Main St., Nashua
• (603) 882-7726

Sharky's has carved out a niche with a concentration on "tribute" shows — groups specializing in the works of others artists, such as Motley Crue, Pearl Jam and Alanis Morissette, play nearly every weekend. They have DJ dance jams on Thursday nights, karaoke for cash on Wednesday and game nights on Monday and Tuesday. Billiards, darts and drinks round out the evening. Casual but proper dress is required, and you must be 18 to enter. The cover charge depends on who's playing.

Skyview Cafe and Brewery

385 E. Dunstable Rd., Nashua

• (603) 897-0005

Nashua's newest brewpub rates a place in our Restaurant chapter for its stunning food, but you'll want to stop in on a Friday or Saturday evening to enjoy the live entertainment and sample the old-world style beers. Most often the music is Top-40 and classic rock, but the brewpub is beginning to bring in some jazz and softer acts as well. There is never a cover charge, and the beers come in smaller sizes for smaller appetites (or those who want to try several kinds) as well as hefty British pint glasses.

Together of New Hampshire

6 Trafalgar Sq. (at Exit 8), Nashua

• (603) 882-8732, (800) 688-5644

Together (a singles club) holds DJ dances on Friday and Saturday nights, usually at either the Crowne Plaza or the Sheraton Tara (see our Accommodations chapter for more on these hotels). The crowd averages 300 to 400 people and includes all ages of singles. Dances run from 8 PM to 1 AM and cost $8 if you arrive before 9 PM and $10 after. The price includes hors d'oeuvres, door prizes and free parking. Neat casual dress is required — no jeans, please.

Seacoast Region

Hampton Beach Casino Ballroom

169 Ocean Blvd., Hampton

• (603) 929-4100 box office, (603) 929-4201 concert listing

There was a time in the history of the Hampton Beach tourist scene that ballroom dancing under the stars was the high point of an elegant summer season. Today the Ballroom, more commonly called "Club Casino," hosts music, comedy and variety shows throughout the summer. Ticket prices (general admission and reserved) are $15 to $40, depending on the act, and they get some big-name talent: Willie Nelson, Sinead O'Connor, Pat Benetar, Jethro Tull and Tower of Power are among recent performers.

The Sea Shell Stage

Hampton Beach

• (603) 926-8717

In summer Hampton Beach hosts live music seven nights a week on the Sea Shell. On any given evening you may see a show band, rock 'n' roll group, blues musicians or even a polka band. Sometimes they have a variety show, talent show or karaoke. And every Wednesday night the show ends with a fireworks display at 9:30 PM. For information, visit the Chamber of Commerce visitors center next door at 180 Ocean Boulevard, or call the number above. See Hampton Beach in our Attractions chapter, and while you're there check out the Portsmouth Harbor cruises for a different look at the fireworks.

The Stone Church

5 Granite St., Newmarket

• (603) 659-6321

Friday and Saturday nights the doors open at 8:30 PM, and great local musicians begin to play at 9:30 PM. Jazz, blues and alternative music makes this a popular spot for listeners and musicians alike. The story of the Stone Church is inspiring in itself: first built by the Methodist congregation back in 1836, the building later became a Catholic Church. After the Catholics expanded the space and then outgrew it again they converted it to a function hall. After the war it passed into private hands and was at various times a roller-skating rink and a factory. A glue fire nearly destroyed the second floor and the building was closed and went unused until 1969. At the height of the folk music era several local music-lovers purchased the building and opened it as a music club. From the beginning the emphasis has been on the music and the musicians: the current owners call it "a music club where alcohol is served, not a bar with music." Local groups who came through here and went on to become big names include Aztec 2 Step and Phish. Extensive renovations in the 1990s enabled the Stone Church to expand beyond just acoustic/small group performances, but even with the dance floor in front of the stage and a new sound system the tone is still intimate.

Daniels Hall

U.S. Rt. 4, Nottingham
• (603) 942-8525

Daniels brings in a DJ for singles dances on Friday nights and oldies dances for singles or couples on Saturday nights. Both evenings are BYOB; set-ups, tonic and coffee are provided. Burgers and pizza are available. Proper dress is required. Tickets cost $7, but ladies who arrive before 8 PM on Friday get in for $5. The music begins at 8:30 PM. Oldies dances feature a twist contest with a $100 prize. Do you remember when?

Cataqua Public House at The Redhook Ale Brewery

35 Corporate Dr., Portsmouth
• (603) 430-8600

"Cataqua" is derived from the name of the river, "Piscataqua." Redhook claims it means "Divine Waters" and is therefore an appropriate reference to their microbrews. You be the judge! The Public House is open every day but Monday. Hours and scheduled entertainment varies, but there's always live music Saturday from 9 to 11 PM. All shows are free.

Club 1 North

948 U.S. Rte 1 Bypass, Portsmouth
• (603) 431-5400

This private club for members ($20/year) and guests caters only to the gay/lesbian/transgendered community on the Seacoast. The club is not fancy, but there's dancing, karaoke, games, food and drink from 8 PM to 1:15 AM Wednesday through Sunday. Wednesday night the entertainment is male videos, but the other evenings focus on music, with a different style each night. As we write the schedule is Retro on Sundays, Top-40 on Fridays and Euro hot and Techno on Saturdays, but call to be sure.

The Elvis Room

142 Congress St., Portsmouth
• (603) 436-9189

Very hip, very cool, working hard at being different, the Elvis Room is hard to categorize. Some nights it has hard-core alternative acts, some nights there's folk music and poetry readings, and some nights it's just a great place to gather. Cover charges vary so it's best to call ahead. The music starts at 9 PM (call for a calendar). It's open until 2 AM every day. Monday nights are for the 21 and older crowd only; the rest of the week anyone 17 or older is welcome.

Krewe Orleans at the Sheraton Portsmouth Hotel

250 Market St., Portsmouth
• (603) 431-2300

Here's a little bit of Bourbon Street on the New Hampshire seacoast. There's dancing here every night, sometimes with live music in the early evening, featuring DJs and karaoke from 8 PM to closing at midnight (1 AM on Friday and Saturday). Look for ladies night, men's night and other non-cover options. See our Hotels and Motels chapter for more about this unusual Sheraton Hotel in Portsmouth.

Meadowbrook Inn

Portsmouth Traffic Cir., Portsmouth
• (603) 436-2700

If you remember hanging streamers in the gym for prom night and bands in suits and ties, you'll feel right at home in this casual, comfortable dance hall. Friday evenings DJ Johnny William's theme is Dance Club and Saturdays it's a Sock Hop. Either night you'll be transported back to a simpler time. It's always "remember when" oldies music. Twist the night away and snack off the buffet from 8 PM to 1 AM. Cover is $5 for couples and $3 for singles, and on the first Friday of each month the ladies dance for free.

Muddy River Smokehouse

21 Congress St., Portsmouth
• (603) 430-9582

Muddy River is known for great blues and great barbecue. Friday, Saturday and Sunday the doors open at 7:30 PM, and shows begin at 9, with a variety of groups ranging from local talent to big national stars. Ticket prices vary from free to $20 for acts such as Maria Muldar or Peter Wolf. Thursdays are dedicated to alternative music with the same hours. There are 26 beers on tap, and the food, which includes a variety of salads, grilled fish, steaks and, of course, ribs of all kinds, is fresh and prepared on site.

Spring Hill Tavern at The Dolphin Striker

15 Bow St., Portsmouth
• (603) 431-5222

Local artists entertain patrons Tuesday through Saturday evenings in the Spring Hill Tavern. The music starts when the dinner hours start to fade, generally about 7 PM on Sunday, between 8 and 9 PM on Friday and Saturday, and sometime in between during the week. There is no cover charge.

The Portsmouth Ball Room

41 Vaughn Mall, Portsmouth
• (603) 433-2009

Friday night dance parties from 8 PM to midnight may feature bands or country dancing, always in a chemical-free environment. This is the place to salsa! Admission is generally $6, rising to $15 when there is a live band. The hall still has a certain air of grandeur, but while proper dress is encouraged you certainly don't need to come in formal attire!

Portsmouth Gaslight Co.

64 Market St., Portsmouth
• (603) 430-9122

Eat on the deck, in the lounge or in the downstairs dining room where you can watch your pizza bake in the brick oven. Stay for the live music on the deck almost every night in summer and in the lounge in winter, and you'll know what makes this a favorite with the college and career crowds.

The Press Room

77 Daniel St., Portsmouth
• (603) 431-5186

For music you can listen to in an atmosphere conducive to conversation and camaraderie, The Press Room offers live music seven nights a week. It also has piano lunches on Friday and Saturday, a Jazz Grill on Sunday and Monday nights and a full menu of nightly dinner specials with shows Thursday through Sunday. The music ranges from elegant pop to rock to jazz, with an emphasis on showcasing local talent. Friday and Sunday evening there's a $5 cover charge, and Saturdays it's $6.

Lakes Region

Contradancing

Academy Building, Gilmanton
• (603) 267-7227

From 8 to 11 PM on the second Saturday of each month (and occasionally other Saturdays too), the town office building reels with traditional New England square, line and circle dances and country waltzes. All dances are easy to learn — just follow the caller's instructions. There's no need to bring a partner, but do bring clean shoes to protect the floor. Admission is just $5 each, $10 for a family, for a fun evening in a smoke- and alcohol-free environment.

Amando's Cantina at Las Piñatas Mexican Restaurant

9 Veterans Sq., Laconia
• (603) 528-1405

Genuine Mexican food and drinks are enhanced with genuine Mexican music most of the week and live entertainment on Friday and Saturday evenings. From 8:30 PM to midnight, listen to cool folk and instrumental art-

INSIDERS' TIP

Coffeehouses, poetry slams and special benefit concerts abound in church basements and school auditoriums across the state. Keep an eye out for posters, and you can attend something different every weekend.

ists while you munch on hot specialties of the casa.

Forever Young Restaurant and Lounge

Downtown Laconia Mall, Laconia
• (603) 524-9317, (800) 255-9317

Whether you're looking for dancing and drinks or darts and pool tables, Forever Young has something fun for you. There's live rock 'n' roll on weekends and free pool on Wednesday night. A full menu is always available. The casual pub atmosphere draws a young crowd, although during the height of summer their are plenty of greying rock fans exercising the promise of the lounge's name!

Galaxy at the Oriental Gardens

89 Lake St., Laconia
• (603) 524-0008

Thursday through Saturday nights, rock 'n' roll at the Club Galaxy. Some nights there's a DJ, other times a live band. A spectacular light show adds to the fun. Thursday evenings there's no cover charge for ladies. The starry-decor and theme are part of the fun, but don't expect to see the blue soloist from Star Wars (fortunately, no one has ever been caught in crossfire between Darth Vader's Stormtroopers and Jedi rebels here, either).

StoneCoast Brewery

546 N. Main St., Laconia
• (603) 528-4188

If you're wondering why a brewpub in downtown Laconia is called "StoneCoast," it's because the original StoneCoast is in Maine. The beer is terrific (designate a driver; it's potent stuff). StoneCoast offers live entertainment Wednesday through Saturday evenings.

Giuseppe's Showtime Pizzeria & Ristorante

Mill Falls Marketplace, Meredith
• (603) 279-3313

The Pizzeria is part of the Inn at Mill Falls complex (see our Bed and Breakfasts and Country Inns chapter). Along with terrific gourmet pizzas, Giuseppe's has live music every night. Happy hour is Monday through Friday from 4 to 7 PM, and Giuseppe's hosts Open Stage on Sundays from 8 to 11 PM. If you're tired of shouting to be heard, the acoustic guitar and piano artists here will be a welcome change.

M/S Mount Washington

Weirs Beach
• (603) 366-5531, (888) 843-6686

What could be more romantic than dancing on deck under the stars? In addition to wonderful dinner cruises and daytime trips, the *Mount Washington* runs a dance cruise for those 21 and older each Wednesday evening at 9 PM. Tickets are $17. Reservations are strongly recommended, and boarding is no later than 15 minutes before departure. (See our Attractions and Restaurants chapters for more about the *Mount Washington*.)

Bull & Bier Haus Grill

53 S. Main St., Plymouth
• (603) 536-2260

This spot is popular with the college crowd for live music Wednesday through Saturday (beginning at 10 PM — this is a young crowd!), Foosball, darts and an all-you-can-eat salad bar. Thursday is Mexican night. It's open 11:30 AM to 1 AM, although the kitchen closes at 11:30 PM. The Bavarian theme is carried out

INSIDERS' TIP

Contradances are not square dances. Contra means you're across from your partner. A line of men will line up across from a line of women. Dances usually include a walk-through so everyone has an idea of what to do. Some dances have a lesson that starts about a half-hour before the dance. Ask when you call the number listed in the paper. Casual clothes are fine. Women usually wear skirts — not because it's required, but because it's more fun to dance in one.

in the dark beams and white walls, but the setting is good-old-American college town.

Safe & Sound

41 Hanson Rd., Rochester
• (603) 330-0068

In just two short years, this chem-free club has developed such a terrific reputation that it's booking bands from all over the country. It tends to attract high school students for the hard-core and straightedge bands and an older crowd when the act plays softer music. Air hockey, pool and billiards and an extensive list of nonalcoholic beverages and coffees complete the scene. The club is open Wednesday and Thursday from 4 to 9 PM, Friday and Saturday from 4 PM to midnight and Sundays noon to 6 PM.

Contradancing and Square Dancing

Tamworth Town House, Tamworth
• (603) 323-8687

A variety of callers and musicians visit here on Saturday evenings to lead the dancing. Traditional square and contradancing may be the focus one evening, while another week everyone will try their hand (or is that foot?) at early-American or European folk dancing. Call to find out what's coming up. The dances run from 8 PM to 11PM, and beginners are welcome. Everyone brings snacks to share, and the admission is $5 ($1 for those younger than 8). Please bring clean, soft-soled shoes.

Peter's Pub at Shalimar Resort

U.S. Rt. 3, Winnisquam
• (603) 524-1984

If you think of pubs as dark and low-ceilinged you'll be surprised at Peter's. Think of it as your local pub gone on summer vacation: it's bright and airy and looks uncannily like a cafeteria or one of those beach-front fish-and-chips spots. It's a great place to enjoy a friendly pint, watch some sports on the big-screen TV and play a little competitive darts. Friday and Saturday evenings Peter's brings in live entertainment, mostly local bands. Peter's opens Monday through Saturday at 4 PM and on Sunday at 1 PM, and while most of the guests are staying at the Shalimar the pub is open to all.

Square Dancing

On the Boardwalk, Weirs Beach
• (603) 366-4770

Thursday evenings in July and August you can do-si-do and swing your partner under the stars. Winnipesaukee Squares hosts this free evening of Western-style square dancing from 7 PM to 9 PM. Whether you and your partner dance every week or you'll need to find a partner at the beach, this is a fun way to spend a summer evening. It's even fun to watch.

White Mountains and Great North Woods Regions

Colebrook Country Club Motel

N.H. Rt. 26, Colebrook
• (603) 237-5566

At Colebrook, you can hear live music every Saturday night. It's usually country or country-rock. The music starts at 9 PM and goes until 1 AM. There's no cover charge.

Red Parka Pub

U.S. Rt. 302, Glen
• (603) 383-4344

This popular ski pub has live music on Friday and Saturday nights all year long. The genre is described as contemporary rock 'n' roll. Music begins at 9 PM and goes to about 12:30 AM. There's never a cover charge.

Legends

1291 Town Sq., Waterville Valley
• (603) 236-4678

At Legends you'll get a DJ playing your requests every night during the winter and summer seasons. The ski season also features a folk guitar concert on Sunday afternoons. In summer the music is live on Friday and Saturday nights. The age range of customers is 21 to 70, and music varies according to the crowd. Rhythm and blues and country rock are likely to be heard. Cover charges are rare, but check when you call to ask about the band. Music starts about 9 PM.

The Red Fox Tavern at The Valley Inn

Tecumseh Rd., Waterville Valley
• (603) 236-8336

You can catch blues and a little rock here on Saturday nights from about 8:30 until 11 PM. Sometimes there's music on Fridays too, but it's best to call ahead. You'll never pay a cover charge.

Woodstock Inn

135 Main St., Woodstock
• (603) 745-3951

Live music rocks the Woodstock Inn on Friday and Saturday nights all year. Classic rock and Top-40 are the mainstays. On Thursday and Sunday a DJ plays requests. In summer, starting around July 4, you'll hear light rock on the patio just about every day. During ski season you might catch live music during the week. Call ahead to check on cover charges as they vary with the season and the group.

Dartmouth-Lake Sunapee Region

The Seven Barrel Brewery Pub

N.H. Rt. 12-A (Exit 20 off I-89), West Lebanon
• (603) 298-5566

Enjoy a nice variety of beers and great brew-pub fare while you listen to live music on Friday and Saturday nights. It's usually a three- or four-piece band specializing in the blues. There's no cover charge.

Monadnock Region

Rynborn Restaurant and Blues Club

Main St., (U.S. Rt. 202 and N.H. Rt. 31), Antrim
• (603) 588-6162

Blues, blues, blues is the only way to describe the music here. Live music is played Thursday through Sunday with a cover charge on Friday and Saturday. The cover is $5 for local bands and $10 for big-city groups. The lounge is closed on Monday and Tuesday.

DelRossi's Trattoria

N.H. Rt. 137, .25 mile north of N.H. Rt. 101, Dublin
• (603) 563-7195

Music is featured all weekend at this fun Italian restaurant. But don't expect opera. Instead you'll be treated to mostly folk and bluegrass with occasional forays into a bit of rock 'n' roll. The cover charge varies with the group. The music begins around 8:30 PM on Friday and Saturday nights and at 7 PM on Sunday.

Copperfield's Lounge at the Best Western Sovereign Hotel

401 Winchester St., Keene
• (603) 357-3038

Friday and Saturday nights feature live music with bands concentrating on Top-40 dance music. The dance floor rocks during the week too, as the DJ spins classic rock and Top-40 tunes. On Wednesday and Thursday the DJ plays country music. Occasionally live music is available during the week. There's no cover charge, and the music begins at 8:30 PM.

Elm City Brewing Company

Colonial Mill Marketplace, Keene
• (603) 355-3335

This restaurant and brewpub is becoming a hot spot for evening entertainment too. Thursday nights always feature live music; no set style — you might get blues, you might get rock, you might get country. Friday and Saturday nights are more likely to be theme nights. A Gilligan's Island night featured free admission with an appropriate costume (can you tell this is a college town?). The cover is never more than $5 and usually $2 or free. Call for details.

The Town Hall Theatre and The Screening Room

Main St., in the Town Hall, Wilton
• (603) 654-FILM

The marquee at this theater frequently announces that one of the movies showing is a "New Hampshire Premiere." The Wilton

Town Hall Theatre is most famous for hosting the Star Wars premiere in 1977, but Insiders know it's one of the few movie theaters around that shows "art" movies. In New Hampshire that includes mostly foreign and independent films. The popcorn is popped right before your eyes, and the sound system is Dolby. The owner will ask whether the audience prefers fresh air or air conditioning. A correct answer to the movie quiz (for example, name Jimmy Stewart's female co-star in *Mr. Smith Goes to Washington*) will win you a reduced price for future shows.

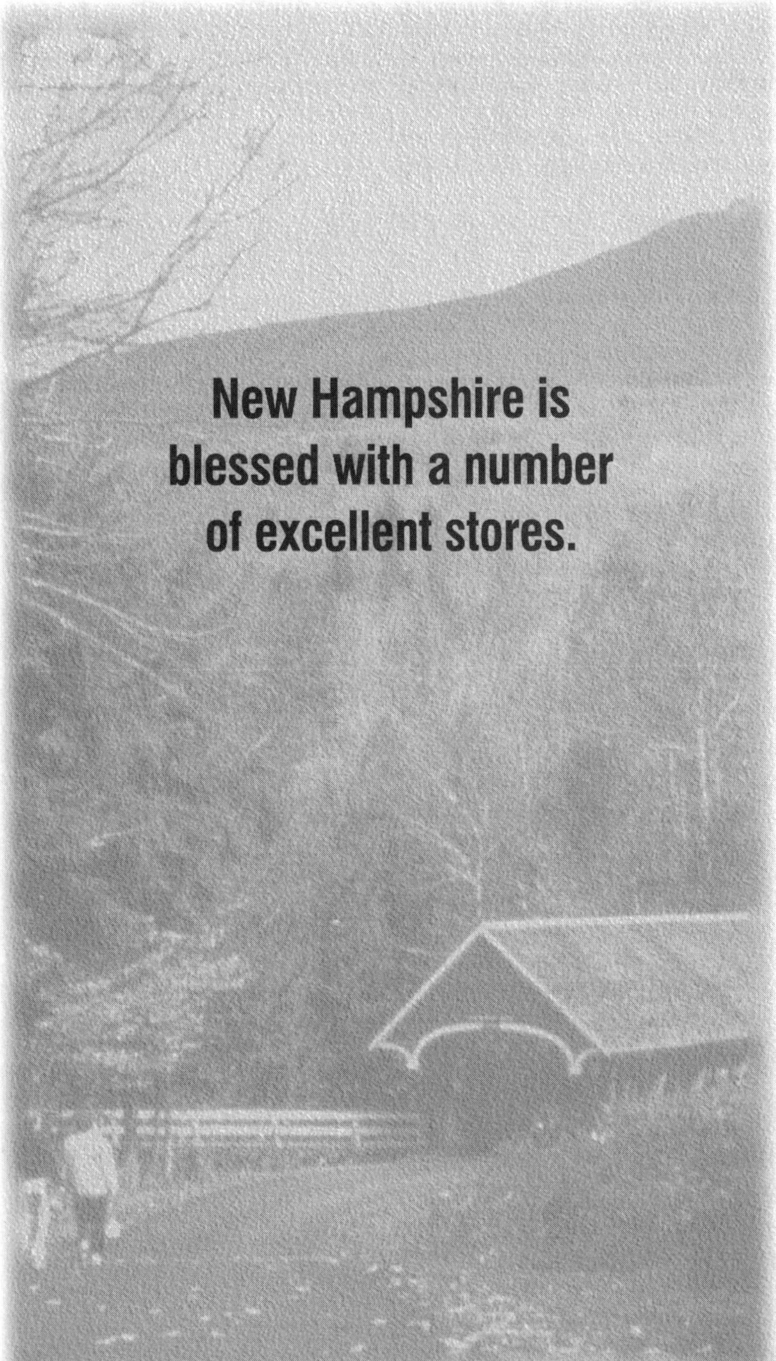

New Hampshire is blessed with a number of excellent stores.

Shopping

We always thought the primary recreational activities in New Hampshire took place out of doors in parks and forests and on rivers, mountains and streams. After putting this chapter together, we think shopping should be one of the state's recreational wonders.

We've been delighted (and exhausted) by the variety of stores in the state. We haven't concentrated on national chain stores, but it's safe to assume that an area near each of the malls we talk about includes fast food, gas stations and Istores such as Wal-Mart.

Our Main Street shopping sections are ways of letting you know about a few towns where you can park and walk the downtown shopping area. It's a fun way to see a town, and it's a great way to get to know an area. Our bookstore section speaks for itself. As writers, we've loved bookstores throughout our lives. They nourish, entertain and delight us. Looking for bargains on used books? Look in our Antiques chapter where we include used books and our many antiquarian bookstores.

New Hampshire is blessed with a number of excellent stores. We've done our best to give you a good sampling, but we're sure there are still many great ones to discover. "Discover" is the appropriate verb for shopping. Most of us stumble upon the shops that become our favorites. We've tried to share our favorites and discover a few new ones for you. For more shopping opportunities, see our Antiques chapter.

Merrimack Valley Region

Malls

Bedford Mall
S. River Rd. Bedford
• (603) 668-0670

This nice older mall has suffered since the advent of its giant competitor down the highway in Manchester. Nevertheless, it continues to be clean, well-lit and home to a variety of lovely stores. Marshalls and MVP Sports and Bobs are the big stores here. The movie theater is still here, and you'll also find gift shops, linens and some great kiosks offering the work of local craftspeople. If you join Strides, their indoor walking program, you won't feel so badly about enjoying candies, nuts, ice cream or pizza from the shops along the way!

Fort Eddy Road
Concord • no central phone

Just off I-93 at the north end of Concord you will see a whole development of shops with bright green roofs. This collection of plazas is part upscale outlet and part down-home shopping center. It houses a variety of stores including an L.L. Bean Factory Store, Poore Simons and Casual Male, but you'll find Bookland and Bradlees here too. Have a snack at Pizzeria Uno and then check out the gift shop at the Christa McAuliffe Planetarium, which is way out at the end of the road (see our Attractions chapter).

Steeplegate Mall
270 Loudon Rd., Concord
• (603) 224-1523

Sears, JCPenny and Steinbach department stores anchor this mall in the northeast corner of Concord. Specialty shops inside include Victoria's Secret and Two Moon Traders for clothes, World of Science for the kids and 60 others for gifts, jewelry, housewares and electronics. Applebee's is the only restaurant in the mall itself, but virtually every chain restaurant seems to be represented on Loudon Road.

Mall of New Hampshire
1500 S. Willow St., Manchester
• (603) 669-0433

This is the mall that began the never-ending competition to be the BIGGEST MALL in New England. Currently they're renovating and expanding *again* and have proclaimed themselves "All the mall you'll ever need." They just may be right. The anchor stores here, Best Buy, Filene's and Sears, cover a pretty broad assortment of wares. They also have a Disney Store, a food court and World of Science, a really nice science-oriented toy store where the staff actually understand and will explain what they sell. You'll also find the usual collection of clothing, electronics and jewelry stores. Just in case you can't find exactly what you need, the whole of S. Willow Street is one enormous shopping strip, with several miles of superstores from Home Depot and Barnes & Noble to Service Merchandise, Circuit City and Petco.

Nashua Mall

off Broad St. (U.S. 3 Exit 6), Nashua
• (603) 883-3348

This was the first enclosed shopping mall in New Hampshire when it opened in 1969. Today it is dwarfed by mega-malls in Nashua and Manchester, but it still has a loyal Insider following. There are the Strutters, an indoor walking club sponsored by St. Joseph's Hospital. Members receive discounts from stores in the mall, and prizes when they achieve mileage goals. This is also a favorite place for young moms with strollers to stretch their legs and treat the kids to a snack. Bradlees and Burlington Coat Factory anchor the mall, while smaller stores inside include Balsams, a card and gift shop (where we used to buy cards for our high-school sweethearts); Designer Gifts, a shop with a selection of art reproductions, elegant bath and body products, candles, tapestries and linens; and Rainbow Crafts, which carries Yankee Candles, Salmon Falls Pottery and Annalee Dolls along with many other locally handcrafted gifts.

Pheasant Lane Mall

310 Daniel Webster Hwy., Nashua
• (603) 888-2331

This mega-mall actually straddles the state line, but although you may park in Massachusetts, all the stores are in tax-free New Hampshire. The anchor stores, Filene's, Sears, JCPenney and Macy's, are two stories tall (this is where our kids learned to ride an escalator), with two levels of smaller shops around an airy center that's open ground to roof with lots of plants and sunshine. Winner of the *Nashua Telegraph*'s 1998 Reader's Choice Award for Best Mall, this is a "come and spend the day" spot for many families (ask for complimentary wheelchairs and strollers, and child-find ID bracelets at customer service). You'll find Disney Store, Victoria's Secret, Eddie Bauer and a CVS drug store, along with 140 other stores, pushcarts and kiosks and an extensive food court. One small shop merits special mention: in addition to a wide selection of lovely lingerie and bathing suits, Lady Grace offers fitting and customizing prostheses and clothing for women who have had mastectomy—they can even process the insurance paperwork. Beyond the mall, the Daniel Webster Highway is a solid 2-plus miles of shopping centers and warehouse stores, with major chains offering books, computers, clothes, Oriental rugs and just about anything else you can imagine.

The Mall at Rockingham Park

99 Rockingham Park Blvd., Salem
• (603) 894-4411

This beautiful new mall across from Rockingham Park racetrack has more than 130 stores and an ample food court. You'll get your exercise too, walking the length of this two-story mall with its multilevel concourses. JCPenney, Filene's, Macy's and Sears are the anchor stores here. Specialty shops include Learning Express and Gap Kids for the younger set; Abercrombie & Fitch and Cambridge Sound Works for adults; and Brookstone and Radio Shack for the whole family. The "strip" in Salem is along Broadway, or N.H. Route 28, which is on the other side of the interstate from this mall (the road goes under the highway). There you'll find the older Rockingham Mall, home to the truly amazing discount store known as the Christmas Tree Shop, a host of big chain superstores such as Staples and Wal-Mart and the highest number of computer and electronics stores per mile in the state.

Downtowns and Main Streets

Concord

• (603) 226-2150

Downtown Concord incorporates Main Street and the first three or four blocks of a number of cross-streets, including Pleasant Street and Warren Street. Several squares and plazas front Main Street and host outdoor events and sidewalk sales. Look for sophisticated women's clothing at April and Friends at 54 N. Main Street and clothes for professional men and women at McQuade's, 45 N. Main Street. Step over to StarBellies Children's Clothing at 26 Pleasant Street if you're dressing the kids. You'll find wonderful furnishings for your home among the hardwood pieces as Pompanoosuc Mills on Main Street, Heart and Soul at 34 Pleasant Street and David Levine Oriental Rugs at 34 Warren Street. For your walls you can stop at McGowan Fine Art, 10 Hill Avenue, New Hampshire Clocks, 74 N. Main Street, or Rowland Studio at 23 N. Main Street. Be sure to check out the handcrafted gifts by local artists at the League of New Hampshire Craftsmen at 36 N. Main Street and some from far away at Gondwana Imports, which is at 86 N. Main Street. Unusual gifts can also be found at Capitol Craftsman, 16 N. Main Street. Caardvark, at 47 N. Main Street, is loaded with funny cards, rubber stamps, calligraphy implements and assorted art and artifacts. The museum store at the Museum of New Hampshire History in Eagle Square is another source for unique gifts and souvenirs.

Manchester

• (603) 645-6285

Manchester's main street is Elm Street (Main Street having been on the wrong side of the river). The downtown shopping and business district encompasses an area 10 blocks long and eight blocks wide — from the restored mill buildings along the Merrimack River that house University of New Hampshire–Manchester on the west to Beech Street on the east, and from the Granite Street Bridge on the south to the Notre Dame Bridge on the north. Within this area you'll find City Hall and the library, the chamber of commerce and several institutions described in our Arts and Culture chapter. And of course there are some great stores outside this part of the map too.

There is a lot of on-street parking in

Manchester so finding a space isn't generally a problem. The busy street has angled and parallel parking, and check out the three parking garages (Victory Street, Canal Street and at the Center of New Hampshire on Granite Street). Many downtown retailers display "Shoppers Park Free." Ask for details about receiving free parking validation along with your purchase. There's also a public parking lot just west of Elm Street. Or park at the old Zayre's plaza on the corner of Elm Street and Lake Avenue, where Staples is. The parking lot is enormous and never full.

Among the stores you'll find in downtown Manchester are two classic clothing stores. George's Apparel at 675 Elm Street is the old-fashioned, full-service men's store where they really do help you select a suit and then tailor it for a perfect fit. McQuade's, 844 Elm Street, is an old New Hampshire shop with another store in Concord. Inside the Manchester store, along with a great selection of business and casual wear for men and women, you'll find two unique gift shops: With Heart & Hand and Foxgloves. For shoes, your choices range from Mickey Finn, where you'll find Doc Marten's and steel-toed logging boots, to Ye Olde Cobbler Shop at 1279 Elm Street, with a great selection of Western boots and an actual cobbler who can fix your beloved leather boots, build orthotics and orthopedic lifts and even repair modern, all-synthetic hiking boots. Oh, you wanted shoes? Try Bee Bee Shoe Store on the corner of Granite Street and Canal Street or Mortt's at 52 Dow Street. Benton Shoes at 814 Elm Street offers high-fashion and funky shoes for women at bargain prices. But for ballet slippers, you'll want to stop at Martin's at 817 Elm Street. They have all the name brands for dancing shoes and leotards and stockings for dancers and skaters.

Speaking of art, you'll find works of modern and traditional fine art, much of it by regional artists, at Art 3 Gallery and Framers, 44 W. Brook Street. Hatfield Gallery, 34 Hanover Street, specializes in restoring and framing oils and prints and carries paintings and crafts by local artists. Music is represented here, too, with Belisle Music at 657 Elm Street selling all kinds of instruments and the Manchester Community Music School providing instrumental instructions and voice lessons at 83 Hanover Street.

Looking for wearable art? Fran Cook, Goldsmith, makes custom-designed jewelry in the Hampshire Plaza Mall and enclosed office complex at 1000 Elm Street. Pearson's at 926 Elm Street stocks luxury watches and elegant diamonds and estate jewelry, as does Desjardins at 1069 Elm Street. Insiders recommend Bellman Jewelers, 1650 Elm Street, for appraisals and repairs of your jewelry. Lemay Brothers is Manchester's oldest jeweler. It's been in business since 1884. You'll find its collection, which includes crystal and fine china as well as watches, rings and pearls, at 1225 Elm Street.

If all this shopping makes you hungry, restaurants and coffee shops along the sidewalks will tempt you. If you like fine European pastries, try Lala's Hungarian Pastry Shop in the 800 block, or if that's too decadent, how about a nutritious bowl of soup or a salad at Dena's Natural Way in the Hampshire Plaza Mall at 1000 Elm Street. (You'll find other fine downtown eateries in our Restaurants chapter.) In summer, look for the Farmer's Market on Thursdays across from Victory Park on Concord Street.

Downtown Manchester houses offices, restaurants and banks as well as retail space. It seems every year another old mill space is renovated or an old office building gets a facelift. It's not picture-postcard material, but it is a thriving urban center and worth walking through.

Milford

• (603) 672-4567

Milford's Union Square, which Insiders call "The Oval," is a recently renovated downtown highlighted by an antique bandstand, brick walkways, flower boxes and tiny parks beside the Souhegan River. The Milford Town Hall, the old Eagle Hall and the Latchis Theater building are landmarks on three sides of the square. Park your car in the lot behind the Town Hall and explore. Harvey's Music on Union Square sells and repairs musical instruments of all kinds and Simple Additions on Middle Street (behind the Town Hall) can outfit your home. At Lorinda's Thrift Shop, 16

Nashua Street (beside Town Hall), you can save by dressing yourself or your kids in consignment clothes. The Fish Bowl in the old Eagle Hall on Union Square sells not only tropical fish but also exotic pets and birds. Flowers on the Oval, across Union Square, offers cut flowers and makes the most realistic-looking silk arrangements we've ever seen. Across the square Insider kids (old and young) frequent the Army-Navy Store, while their mothers prefer Hick's Jewelers, the old-fashioned, unintimidating jewelry store next door. Three antiques shops, six restaurants, the library and a barber shop and all add to the lively atmosphere on The Oval.

Nashua

• (603) 594-3360

If you've read our Restaurants chapter, you already know downtown Nashua is a dining hot spot. There are some wonderful shops sprinkled among those restaurants too, so park in one of the municipal lots a block back from Main Street and come for a stroll. The main shopping district starts at the bridge over the Nashua River and runs south to Hollis Street and even beyond, south of the hospital (SNHMC). It also includes about the first three blocks of W. Hollis, W. Pearl and High streets. There's a full-service music store, Darrell's Music Hall, at 75 Main Street; a real old-fashioned cobbler shop, Downtown Cobbler, 83 W. Pearl Street; and an old-fashioned drugstore, Wingate's Pharmacy at 131 Main Street. Look for fine jewelry at Cardin Jewelers, 125 Main Street, and Burque Jewelers, Nashua's oldest jeweler, still at 89 W. Pearl Street. The old New Hampshire Jewelry Institute building at 231 Main Street was renovated in 1998 and has been reopened as Mike's Jewelry. Check out deMontigny and Scontsas, a jewelry, card and gift shop, and Habitat on Main Street, offering an eclectic assortment of antiques, topiary, furnishings and art for home and garden. They're all in the block from 169 to 173 Main Street. Fortin-Gage Ltd. sells lovely gifts, including Waterford crystal, along with fresh flowers at 86 W. Pearl Street. City Traditions opened at 98 Main Street in January of 1999 and carries a variety of unusual gifts.

R.B. Croteau, at 92 W. Pearl Street, can

help you with another kind of treasure: photos of your children or your ancestors (restoration of old photographs is a specialty here). Back on Main Street, DesignWares, at 206 Main Street, offers art and accessories for your home and yourself, and just down the street at 221 Main Street, ArcLight's experts will help you see your home in a new light. Nearby you'll find a new-fashioned tobacconist, Castros's Back Room, purveying fine domestic and imported cigars, tobaccos, humidors and political discussion at 178 Main Street. Some members of your party may prefer to move on to Enchanted Lace, at 144 Main Street, for luxury linens and toiletries, or The Golden Halo at 86 Main Street for a wealth of Catholic and non-denominational inspirational gifts. You can find more Christian gifts, music and literature over at the Harvest Bookstore at 17 Factory Street. Linger in any of the coffee shops, snack bars and other stores you'll find downtown, and enjoy the Nashua experience.

Bookstores

Booksmith

Bedford Mall, S. River Rd., Bedford
• (603) 669-7583
Nashua Mall, Broad St., Nashua
• (603) 889-9202

These mall bookstores offer a variety of paperback and hardcover books for adults and children along with some magazines, maps, travel guides and study aides.

Cornerstone Book Center

25 S. River Rd., Bedford
• (603) 624-6867, (800) 924-6867

This is a Christian bookstore with a wide selection of books, tapes and gift items for all ages. It also has a great collection of videos to rent.

Bookland

30 N. Main St., Concord • (603) 224-7277
Ft. Eddy Plaza, Concord
• (603) 225-5555
Granite State Marketplace, Hooksett
• (603) 626-0788

Bookland has a large selection of hardcover and paperback books, including bestsellers and old favorites. It also stocks posters, music and books-on-tape as well as a variety of magazines and newspapers.

Gibson's Book Store

29 S. Main St., Concord • (603) 224-0562

This is Concord's only independent bookstore with a complete line of hardcover and paperback books for children and adults. It has the United States Geological Survey Maps for New Hampshire in stock and keeps a good selection of cards and stationery on hand as well. If you still don't find what you're looking for, the staff will order it for you.

Lauriat's Books

Steeplegate Mall, Concord
• (603) 226-2004
Mall at Rockingham Park, Salem
• (603) 893-1266

The Lauriat's chain claims to be New England's largest bookseller, and after more than 120 years in business, it is surely one of the oldest. In New Hampshire Lauriat stores are in malls. You'll find a broad selection of popular titles in stock.

Book Corner

Hood Commons, Crystal Ave., Derry
• (603) 434-0811

Book Corner offers a good selection of books at discounted prices along with Hallmark cards and gifts. A Lauriat's affiliate, this store can bring the buying power of that big chain to this small-town setting.

Good News Book Store

N.H. Rt. 28, Londonderry
• (603) 432-7961, (800) 458-3724

This Christian bookstore stocks a variety of books, videos and music along with curriculum materials and church supplies. It is well-known around New England and frequently fills special orders.

B. Dalton Bookseller

Mall of New Hampshire, Manchester
• (603) 622-6441
Fox Run Mall, Newington
• (603) 436-0483

B. Dalton offers a large selection of

bestsellers, genre fiction and children's books. Frequent buyers can join a discount club. If you're a bookaholic, the annual membership will be recovered in just one trip!

Cambridge Bookstop

43 Hamel Dr. (Northside Plaza), Manchester • (603) 623-8850

This is one of our favorite bookstores (and we never met a bookstore we didn't like). It has a great selection of books and is particularly strong in children's books, New England titles and local authors. In addition, it runs children's story hours, brings in authors to speak and sign books, and encourages reading with lots of fun activities.

The Toadstool Bookshop

614 Nashua St., Lorden Plaza, Milford • (603) 673-1734

This branch of the store based in Peterborough is a favorite with local writers, artists and book-lovers. The selection is huge (in fact, the store recently expanded), and if what you want isn't on the shelf, the staff will order it for you at no charge, regardless of who the publisher is.

Barnes & Noble

1609 S. Willow St., Manchester • (603) 627-5766
Webster Square at Daniel Webster Hwy. and Spit Brook Rd., Nashua • (603) 888-0533
125 S. Broadway, Salem • (603) 898-1930

Barnes & Noble bookstores are known nationwide for their great selection, relaxed atmosphere, overstuffed chairs and discount prices. The stores also offer children's story times, author visits and a good selection of regional titles in each store.

New Hampshire's newest Barnes & Nobles have become instant hits with Nashua and Salem bibliophiles. In addition to the huge selection you expect from this national giant, these two Barnes & Nobles have lovely cafes, with coffee, tea and croissants to accompany your new book.

Annie's Book Stop

493 Amherst St., Nashua • (603) 882-9178
254 Daniel Webster Hwy., Nashua • (603) 888-6699

These stores are exceptional examples of the pre-read paperback chain. In addition to a huge selection of paperback novels in every genre (neatly arranged to make them easy to peruse) the stores also offer a wonderful assortment of new and used children's books, cookbooks, regional titles, computer books and self-help materials. All the used books are in great condition, and even the new books are at discounted prices.

Borders Books and Music

76 Ft. Eddy Rd., Concord • (603) 224-1255
281 Daniel Webster Hwy., Nashua • (603) 888-9300

These new branches of the mega-bookstore and cafe opened in 1998 with nearly 200,000 books and 50,000 music titles in stock. The knowledgeable staff is more than willing to help shoppers overwhelmed by the sheer volume available, and a cup of coffee will restore you if you're exhausted or accompany you if you can't wait until you get home to enjoy your new book. Borders also hosts a variety of events each year, including book discussion groups, children's story times and appearances by authors and musicians.

Waldenbooks

Pheasant Lane Mall, Nashua • (603) 888-2938
Lilac Mall, Rochester • (603) 332-8622

This national chain carries hardcover and

INSIDERS' TIP

Look for "PYO," Pick Your Own farms and orchards. Bring your own containers and go home with the freshest fruit, berries and vegetables money can buy. The Department of Agriculture prints a county-by-county listing of farms with PYO operations. Call 271-3552 for a copy.

paperback books for adults and children along with music, videos and other gift items. Waldenbooks has a nice selection of regional titles. Ask about their discount card — if you're a book-lover, the savings can add up!

De Colores Bookstore
471 S. Broadway, Salem
• (603) 893-9342

De Colores is a Christian bookshop with a broad selection of titles. It offers books for children and adults, music and videotapes and gift items in all price ranges. It also has a large stock of Bibles and other books in Spanish.

Mystery Lovers Ink
8 Stiles Rd., Salem • (603) 898-8060

A pen dripping ink (or is it blood?) is the symbol of this shop, which sponsors author visits and discussion groups for those who love this addicting genre.

Specialty Shops and Stores We Love

The Basket Barn
212 N.H. Rt. 101, Amherst
• (603) 673-2716

This shop has been an Amherst fixture for nearly 40 years. The long red barn on the road to Manchester is filled not only with baskets but also with wicker furniture and furnishings of every description, gourmet foods, gifts and silk flowers. Whether you want to a set of wicker place mats for a wedding gift or a wooden birdcage for your porch, there will be something here to suit your taste and price range.

The Bird House
276 N.H. Rt. 101, Amherst
• (603) 672-6377

The Bird House is an unusual shop, selling all kinds of birdhouses, bird feeders, nesting boxes and assorted accessories such as squirrel baffles and garden decorations. Many of the birdhouses are handcrafted by New Hampshire woodworkers. On the same property, Earth and Tree, (603) 673-8707, has wonderful doll houses and miniatures of all kinds. Somehow one expects to see the dolls having tea with the sparrows while exchanging interior decorating tips.

The Casual Cat Picture Framing
112 N.H. Rt. 101-A, Amherst
• (603) 882-1443

Don't skip the Casual Cat just because you're not looking for a frame. It has an extensive selection and does very professional framing, but the store is a treasure trove of art and collectibles from engraved stone to carved wood and blown glass. (And yes, there is a cat, but she's not for sale.) There is something here for every taste and price range, but be warned: you're not likely to leave empty-handed.

Consignment Gallery
74 N.H. Rt. 101-A, Amherst
• (603) 673-4114

In the 10 years it's been open, this shop has become an Insider favorite, and in 1998 it won a *Nashua Telegraph* Reader's Choice award. Taking in quality furniture and jewelry on consignment, displaying it in attractive, homelike arrangements and providing knowledgeable advice to sellers and buyers alike are the secrets of success here. Whether you need a unique wedding gift or a complete bedroom or dining room set, chances are you'll find it here or in their Bedford shop at 273 S. River Road. Or come back in next week, because new consignments are always arriving.

Earthward
42 N.H. Rt. 101-A, Amherst
• (603) 673-4322

Earthward has been providing organic fruits, grains, juices and other foods and natural herbal and homeopathic remedies to Souhegan Valley residents since the days when only wild-eyed hippies worried about toxins in food. Many of their foods are produced on local farms.

Frederick's Pastries
109 N.H. Rt. 101-A, Amherst
• (603) 882-7725

People from other parts of the state are

jealous when they find out we live close enough to Frederick's to pick up cakes on impulse. They drive long distances for these to-die-for tortes and pastries. Frederick's wedding cakes are also known statewide.

Salzburg Square

N.H. Rt. 101, Amherst

• (603) no central phone

This shopping center, designed to look like a Tyrolean village, has brick walkways, benches and flower boxes to brighten your shopping experience. Each of the dozen shops here is unique, and the products are topnotch, from the toys at Gepettos to the hat boxes and linens at Enchanted Lace. Lovely gifts come from Rachel's Curios & Collectibles, and special clothes for special children are on sale at Little Kids Duds. The chocolates and gourmet jelly beans at Once Upon a Time are Insider favorites. Don't miss The Amherst Shoppe for unique handmade items with a New Hampshire theme as well as many fine collectibles and gifts from around the world.

Craftings

25 S. River Rd., Bedford

• (603) 623-4108

This shop, which used to be on Elm Street in Manchester, has a great selection of regional handicrafts on display. You'll be enchanted by the blown glass, traditional woodworking and metalwork, and unusual jewelry and china. We saw wooden toys and puppets for less than $10 and whimsical sculptures for nearly $1,000 — truly something for everyone.

Heritage Herbs & Baskets

1 Hannah Dustin Rd., Canterbury

• (603) 753-9005

You'll breathe deeply as you wander through the acre of herb gardens here and be inspired to bring something home, either a finished basket or wreath or a book and the makings of your own dried arrangement.

Shaker Pine

418 Shaker Rd., Canterbury

• (603) 783-4403

The Shaker brothers and sisters may be

gone, but their spirit lives on in the work of local woodworker David Emerson. His traditional toys, boxes and furniture reproductions can bring the spirit of simplicity into your home.

Covered Bridge Frame Shop
Fountain Sq., Contoocook
• (603) 746-4996

This shop and its art gallery overlooking (and over) the Contoocook River offer framing services, original works of art and art advice to visitors year round. It's closed Sunday and Wednesday (although if someone is in when you phone, it'll open by appointment.) See our Arts and Culture chapter for more about the galleries.

Joanna's Specialty Gift Shoppe
17 Libby St., Goffstown
• (603) 647-8090

Joanna's specialty is handpainted china. She will design something wonderful for your grandchild's christening, best friend's wedding or any other occasion. Or choose something from the beautiful selection here.

The Fiber Studio
9 Foster Hill Rd., Henniker
• (603) 428-7830

New Hampshire's leading supplier for fiber arts, the Fiber Studio sells all kinds of yarns, including hand-dyed silks and mohairs and native wools. It has looms and knitting machines, which the store not only sells but the staff also can teach you to use, running classes in the 200-year-old barn that houses the shop. Craft supplies, especially for jewelry-making and an assortment of handcrafted jewelry, are also on display. Finally, the Fiber Studio has what may be New Hampshire's largest selection of buttons, in materials from wood and bone to pewter.

The Golden Pineapple Gift Shop
49 Old Concord Rd., Henniker
• (603) 428-7982

In Colonial times, a pineapple was a symbol of hospitality. You'll have no trouble finding a hostess gift in this large shop filled with handcrafts. Handcrafted pottery (including unusual Blueberry Pottery from Maine), fine linens, toys and collectibles are among the gifts available here.

Brookdale Fruit Farm
41 Broad St., Hollis • (603) 465-2240

This wonderful year-round farm stand is the retail arm of a farm that has been raising fruits and vegetables in Hollis for more than 100 years. Insiders from all over southern New Hampshire make the pilgrimage to Hollis for fresh produce, pies and jams, baked goods and maple products. The attached gift shop overflows with wind chimes and silk flowers, cards and Christmas ornaments. Brookdale also sells bedding plants, trees and shrubs in season and offers pick-your-own blueberries, strawberries and apples.

Oblate Retreat House Gift Shop
200 Lowell Rd., Hudson
• (603) 882-8141

This retreat center has an extensive ministry in recovery and codependency as well as traditional Catholic spirituality. The books on the shelves in this shop reflect those interests. In addition, it has a good selection of children's books and a nice assortment of gift items including jewelry, figurines and home accessories.

Sara's Southwest Connection
121 Lowell Rd., Hudson
• (603) 880-7635

Whether you're looking for clothing, pottery, kachinas or cowboy boots, if your taste runs to Southwestern decor, you'll be delighted with this store. Beginning in the big barn at the back, the collection runs through every room in this old New England farmhouse. There is a wonderful variety of pottery and ceramic items, barbed-wire sculpture, rugs, lamps and Navajo jewelry. Suede, leather and woolen clothing all feature distinctive Southwestern designs. One room offers gourmet foods and cookbooks.

Mack's Apples
230 Mammoth Rd., Londonderry
• (603) 434-7619

Londonderry used to have more apple trees than people. It's grown a lot since then, but we're grateful Mack's has survived. The farm store offers jams and jellies, apples, pumpkins and seasonal vegetables, cider and maple syrup. Choose decorations from nature, like Indian corn and dried flower wreaths, or select a gift basket for a friend. Pick-your-own fields at Mack's are accessed by a ride in the hay wagon (seasonal), adding to the fun.

Cathedral Church Goods

316 Granite St., Manchester • (603) 669-0011, (800) 257-3014

This store is crammed with books, gifts and religious items for Catholics. Whether you're looking for an anniversary card, an uplifting tape or a helpful book, chances are you'll find it here. Need a medal for an obscure saint, a hand-carved crucifix or an inexpensive gift for a neighbor's First Communion? They'll have it.

Zyla's

Daniel Webster Hwy., Merrimack • (603) 424-4373

People drive from all over to shop at Zyla's. This large store is crammed full of overruns, salvage and other bargains. If you need tools or fishing tackle, household items or a child's birthday present, consider checking at Zyla's, but be prepared to hunt for what you want. The staff here is virtually invisible, and the merchandise is piled high and deep. Consider it an adventure.

Emerald City Arts

In the Granite Town Plaza, Elm St., Milford • (603) 672-8686

Without a doubt the most eclectic store we know is Emerald City Arts, featuring an assortment of crafts, toys, clothes and collectibles, many created by local craftspeople. The founder was a true citizen of Oz, author of a book based on the Frank Baum originals, *The Winged Monkeys of Oz*. In 1998 he had to sell the shop, but the new owners are committed to keeping the funky, over-the-rainbow atmosphere intact. Look for the Tin Man out front, then you'll know you're not in Kansas anymore.

Expressions Gallery

172 South St., Milford • (603) 673-2136

Expressions offers a wonderful selection of gifts, including stained glass, cast bronze, wind chimes, posters and fine-art originals and prints. It also does custom framing. In addition, Expressions sells fine custom furniture and cabinetry.

Impressions Wildflower Pottery

123 South St., Milford • (603) 673-5167

Impressions is only open Thursday, Friday and Saturday, but if you love pottery, it is definitely worth tweaking your schedule to stop in. Freshly picked New Hampshire wildflowers leave their "impression" on the wet clay, creating unique and beautiful tiles, clocks, dishes and other fine gifts.

Toyland

321 Nashua St., Milford • (603) 672-1537

You won't find much here that's based on the latest cartoon craze, but for a great selection of nice toys in a variety of price ranges, you can't beat Toyland. Insiders know the worst part of this store is getting your kids out of it, especially if they've started to play with the wooden train set in the back. Toyland offers a small supply of hobby materials, rocketry needs and craft supplies along with educational toys and games.

Woodworkers Gallery

469 Nashua St., Milford • (603) 673-7977

This unique store offers a selection of handcrafted original furniture designed and made by a local craftsman. Unique accessories, accent pieces and gifts made by other local people are also on sale here.

A.L. David & Company

505 W. Hollis St., Nashua • (603) 595-1997

This is a jeweler's jewelry store. Not only does it offer handcrafted pieces custom-designed and made by a master craftsman, it also offers repair, restoration and reproductions of antique jewelry. This is the place many retail jewelers send their repairs out to, but Insiders know you can go directly there yourself.

Barmakian Jewelers

300 Daniel Webster Hwy., Nashua • (603) 888-7800

Even if you're not in the market for a diamond brooch, you should stop in at this store just north of the Pheasant Lane Mall for the sheer experience of it. Oriental rugs, chandeliers, ornate antique furniture and perfect lighting set off the fine jewelry, and, of course, you will be treated with the utmost courtesy as you consider your purchase.

Building 19 1/15

420 Amherst St., Nashua • (603) 880-0119

Okay, it's embarrassing to admit that this is on our favorites list, but in case you're not familiar with the Building 19 chain, we thought we should warn you. Inside you'll find a bizarre assortment of toys and books, computers and telephones, furniture, rugs, clothes, sports equipment and anything else it can offer under the store's slogan of "Good Stuff, Cheap." Not all of it is particularly good, but there are genuine bargains here amid the odd lots, salvage and overruns. It's also a terrific place to bring a child who desperately wants to buy *something*.

Covered Bridge Arts and Crafts Center

449 Amherst St., Nashua • (603) 889-2179

This old favorite among Insider crafters is a bridge to creative inspiration. In addition to supplies for needlework, macrame and stamping, the shops in the Covered Bridge offer classes in all these and stenciling, tole painting, quilting and lampshade piercing besides.

INSIDERS' TIP

In New England, a "Spa" is a small store, the place on the corner where you buy cigarettes or candy, beer or milk and the daily paper along with your lottery ticket.

The Apple Barn Inc.
N.H. Rt. 13, New Boston
• (603) 487-3460, (800) 482-3460

This flower and garden center in the middle of New Boston village positively overflows with bedding plants, flowering shrubs, fruit trees and gardening supplies. Just looking at it makes you want to go home and plant something!

Seacoast Region

Malls and Outlet Malls

Fox Run Mall
Fox Run Rd., Newington • (603) 431-5911

The Fox Run Mall is anchored by Sears, JCPenney, Filene's and Macy's. More than 100 stores and many push carts provide for a complete shopping trip. The Disney Store is here, as is the Gap, but you'll also find Eastern Mountain Sports, Northern Reflections and Wicks'n'Sticks. Portsmouth's wonderful toy store, G. Willikers!, has a branch here.

North Hampton Factory Outlet Center
Lafayette Rd., North Hampton
• (603) 964-9050

Clothes, shoes and housewares predominate at this outlet center, where 20 stores offer bargain prices every day. You'll find Bass shoes, American Tourister luggage, Bed & Bath linens and shops with factory-direct prices on coats, kitchen gadgets and every kind of clothing. Take time to browse in the Seacoast Art Association gallery while you're here.

Downtowns and Main Streets

Dover

Dover has a Main Street, but the main street in Dover is Central Avenue between Upper Square (by the fire station) and Lower Square, where you'll find access to three public parking lots. An Insider favorite is Downtown Dover Crafts, 464 Central Avenue, a shop featuring the work of more than 250 local craftspeople. Items here are both beautiful and affordable. Across the street is Rivers Camera Shop, 454 Central Avenue. It's been in business since 1930, and in addition to excellent camera service, they also make telescopes. If you're looking for fine jewelry, check out A.E. Alie & Sons at 460 Central Avenue, or for custom-made pieces, Jewelry Creations at 388 Central Avenue. For another kind of gift, try Just the Thing! handcrafts or Featherfew Herb Shoppe, both at 453 Central Avenue. Check out Farnham's Department Store, at 432 Central Avenue, for an old-fashioned clothing store where someone can actually help you find clothes that fit.

Walk another block and Harvey's Bakery, 376 Central Avenue, will tempt you with the smell of fresh-baked bread, pies, cakes and cookies. Nicole's Hallmark, at 386 Central Avenue, stocks a good selection of collectibles along with the cards and gifts. If you walk just a bit beyond Lower Square you'll find Photosmith at 263 Central Avenue, a complete film-developing lab, and Ubiquitous Antiques at 284 Central Avenue, which offers not only antiques but also a variety of other quality used items. And at the other end, you'll find Puddlejumpers, 629 Central Avenue, a shop full of classic children's clothing and toys, Emporium Framing, 652 Central Avenue, with original art works by regional and national artists, and Garrison Hill Florists, 835 Central Avenue, who've been in the flower business in Dover for more than 110 years.

Durham

At first glance, Main Street in Durham appears to be entirely occupied by the University of New Hampshire. Insiders recommended looking a bit deeper to find The Out Back, an art supply shop with lots of fun and inexpensive gifts and toys as well as paints and brushes, at 44 Main Street. In the same building our sources suggest The Licker Store, a coffee shop and local gathering place where you can play a game of chess or read a book while sipping your espresso. Houghton's True Value Hardware, at the corner of Main Street and Jenkins Court, wins Insider praises for being "a real hardware store, where they can help you find, cut, fit or order what you really need." We were told the Durham Marketplace, across Main Street on Mill Road, was a traditional grocery store (the kind with counters and cases) offering local vegetables, seafood and beer — a good place to pack a picnic.

Exeter

Downtown Exeter hugs the Squamscott River, so it's not surprising that the main street here is Water Street. These antique buildings house shops for all ages. Serendipity, at 24 Water Street, is an Insider favorite, with imported gifts and brass items. The Chocolatier at 27 Water Street tempts shoppers with fine chocolates and candies, or for something more substantial, have a little something in the courtyard at Masseno's Riverside Cafe, 33 Water Street. Whirlygigs, 85-B Water Street, has a wonderful assortment of unusual and interesting toys on display, while Time of Wonder Children's Bookstore, 131 Water Street, stretches the imagination. You'll also want to check out trends gift gallery at 37 Water Street for unusual gifts, popular collectibles and a huge selection of Pooh stuff.

If you're shopping for someone a little older, Exeter's League of New Hampshire Craftsmen is at 61 Water Street, and Exeter boasts not one but two terrific bookstores, Water Street Books at 125 Water Street and Exeter Bookstore at 13 Spring Street (right at the corner of Water Street).

Portsmouth

Portsmouth's Waterfront area includes some wonderful shopping experiences, but the driving will drive you crazy. Leave the car at the High Street parking garage or one of the lots on State Street or Maplewood Avenue. The shops are concentrated in the old section of the city between U.S. Route 1 and the Piscataqua River, an area less than a mile across at its widest point. The streets loop and crisscross, and the shops are tucked in everywhere, along with wonderful restaurants, coffee shops and historic landmarks. Take your time and explore. Use the free downtown map or get on the Portsmouth Harbour Trail to zero in on a particular spot (see our Attractions chapter close-up on Walking Trails).

If you're looking for artwork, you've come to the right place. Check out the New Hampshire Art Association at 136 State Street (see our Arts and Culture chapter for details), Gallery 33 at 111 Market Street or the Pierce Gallery of Fine Art and Framing at 105 Market Street.

The Maritime Gallery, at 110 State Street, specializes in art with a seafaring theme, including great scrimshaw pieces. Fine handcrafts are also available at Tulips, 19 Market Street, salamandra glass studio, 7 Commercial Alley, and Bow Street Candle & Mug, 8 Bow Street. And don't miss Not Just Mud at 57 Bow Street for an astounding collection of glass art.

Other great gifts can be had at Tugboat Alley, 2 Ceres Street, for gifts with nautical themes and New Hampshire souvenirs. A Compleat Mystery Bookshop, at 7 Commercial Alley, is a favorite of Seacoast armchair sleuths. Pet-lovers will like It's Raining Cats and Dogs, 13 Commercial Alley, which offers "gifts for pets and their people," and The Cat House, 10 Ladd Street, with every conceivable cat-related gift. Little Timber, 5 Congress Street, sells intriguing items with a nature theme, while The Christian Marketplace Bookstore at 110 Congress Street offers books, music and gifts for all ages.

If there are children in your group (or on your gift list), Portsmouth has some terrific toy stores. Treehouse Toys, 143 Market Street, and G. Willikers!, 13 Market Street, both offer PBS favorites, imports and classic dolls, trains and books. Another great place for toys is the Macro block between Market and Ceres streets. Wholly Macro, Macroscopic and Macro offer toys, clothes, gifts and imports you really have to see to comprehend. New in 1998, Macrosonic specializes in world beat instruments and discs.

If you're looking for something romantic, try Wisteria Tree Jewelers at 9 Commercial Alley, or Anne's for lingerie and fragrances at 100 Ladd Street. Or find something heavenly at Angels'n'Things, 140 Congress Street.

Shopping for yourself? Try WaterMonkey Funky Outfitters at 33 Vaughn Mall (between Congress and Hanover Streets) or Footnotes, 64 Bow Street. Eagle Photo and Video Supply, 6 Congress Street, can not only supply you with everything you need for your camera, but also provide expert advice on its wide selection of binoculars and telescopes. Gardeners Cottage on State Street has great garden tools and books. While you're shopping in downtown Portsmouth, don't overlook the Dunaway Store at Strawbery Banke (see our Attractions chapter). It has a great assortment of authentic crafts and historic pieces, New England and New Hampshire collectibles, books, gourmet foods and trinkets for the kids.

Somersworth

High Street is the center of shopping for Somersworth. Insiders recommend Timeless Bouquets at 59 High Street for gifts and the Good News Bookstore at 58 High Street, which has a selection of non-religious books as well as Christian books, tapes and posters. You can find some bargains and some nice antiques at Round-Robin New & Used Furniture, 69 High Street. An old-fashioned hardware store with knowledgeable salespeople, Dumont's Hardware, is at 77 High Street.

Bookstores

Little Professor Book Center

403 Congress St., Portsmouth
• (603) 436-1777

Little Professor shops are quirky and independent. Both of these have a large section of New England books as well as children's and adult titles in all subjects. The staff does special orders and mailing, so you can find the book you wanted for Cousin Nigel and have it shipped directly to him in London.

Stroudwater Books

898 Central Ave., Dover • (603) 742-6743
775 Lafayette Rd., Portsmouth
• (603) 433-7168

This wonderful bookstore offers new and used books, magazines and cards, and educational games. It rents books on tape, special orders happily and the Portsmouth location has a cafe in the store. What more could we ask for? How about children's story times and author readings? Stroudwater does those too.

Exeter Bookstore

13 Spring St., Exeter
• (603) 772-5181, (800) 743-5181

This is the bookstore of Phillips Exeter Academy (see our Education chapter), so it stocks lots of textbooks, school memorabilia and related supplies. It also offers a fairly extensive selection of non-scholastic books, with a particular bias toward subjects of interest to high school students.

Water Street Bookstore

125 Water St., Exeter • (603) 778-9731

Insiders rave about this bookstore, with its broad selection of books and terrific newsstand. The staff is knowledgeable and willing to help you find a book whose title you don't recall or an author like the one your daughter loves but has exhausted. Or you can curl up in the window seat and peruse on your own.

Specialty Shops and Stores We Love

The Christmas Dove

Junction of N.H. Rts. 9 and 125, Barrington
• (603) 664-7712, (800) 550-DOVE

We'll confess to being pushovers for anything Christmasy, but this store is truly extraordinary. It's a big barn filled to the rafters with the scents, sounds and sights of Christmas. From inexpensive trinkets for trees or stockings to Christmas collectibles from around the world (one brand per room!) to one-of-a-kind handcrafted decorations, there is something here to put the spirit of Christmas into the most recalcitrant Scrooge. The Christmas Dove also has shops in Ogunquit, Boston and New York. We can't speak for New York, but of the three in New England, we like ours the best.

Calef's Country Store

Junction of N.H. Rts. 9 and 125, Barrington
• (603) 664-2231, (800) 462-2118

There was a time when every small town had a general store. Calef's captures the spirit of those old stores with penny candy, a cheese wheel, molasses barrel and a large variety of New England gifts. Stop in for a snack or just sit a spell on the big front porch.

Red's Shoe Barn

35 Broadway, Dover
• (603) 742-1893
N.H. Rt. 125, Plaistow • (603) 382-7688

The largest shoe store in New Hampshire draws shoppers from all over the state to its two locations, especially when it's time for the dreaded back-to-school shoe-buying session. The selection and prices enables Red's to compete successfully with the outlet stores.

Tuttle's Red Barn

151 Dover Point Rd., Dover
• (603) 742-4313

Insiders told us this is the oldest family farm in America. It's still a family farm, with a terrific year-round stand that offers bread and cookies from its bakery along with fresh local produce and nursery, bedding and greenhouse plants for your garden.

Salmon Falls Stoneware

Oak Street Engine House, Dover
• (603) 749-1467

This shop makes and sells authentic salt-glazed stoneware such as our Colonial ancestors used. The pottery is a distinctive gray with blue designs and is rugged enough for everyday use. Stop by the shop and watch the pottery being made before you choose your own unique piece to take home.

Emery Farm

U.S. Rt. 4, Durham
• (603) 742-8495, (800) 480-8495

This farm has been in operation since the mid-1600s! Today the farm stand attracts visitors with fresh-baked goods, local maple syrup and honey and craft gifts made by local artisans as well as fresh produce in season. The farm sells bedding plants and herbs in spring and Christmas trees in December. (After the holidays they close until spring.) Emery also has pick-your-own berries and a pet-the-animals area for the kids.

Harlow's Bread and Cracker Company

8 Exeter Rd., Epping
• (603) 679-8883

If you brake for bakeries, as we do, you'll want to stop here. Fresh breads draw you in with their aroma, and cookies seal your fate: more diets! Maybe just a few freshly baked crackers with some cheese wouldn't hurt. But how to choose when there are so many kinds? Try one of each? Or come back tomorrow.

Exeter Handkerchief Company

48 Lincoln St., Exeter
• (603) 778-8564

This is no longer the fabric company our grandmothers made daytrips to before sewing our back-to-school clothes. They've always specialized in home-decorating supplies, but now they also have upholstery fabrics, curtains and bedding. But the selection and the service (including doing the job for you if you're not up to it) have preserved Exeter's place in the hearts of sewing Insiders.

A Bit of Sara

594 Main St., Hampstead
• (603) 329-5618

This shop, in a restored Meeting House, offers a wonderful selection of gift items in country and Victorian styles. Pottery and garden items, wind chimes and wall hangings appeal to your eyes and ears, while candles and cosmetics tickle your nose and teddy

INSIDERS' TIP

From the first warm days of spring until well after the first frost, New Hampshire suburbs sprout yard sales every weekend. (Sometimes barn or garage sales, but never "tag" sales.) One family's castoffs become another family's great finds, and the possibility of finding a real collectible or antique brings the dealers out too. Follow the signs or check the local paper and enjoy the hunt — it's part of the fun.

bears beg to be patted. It's a feast for your senses.

Cactus City Boot Company

826 Lafayette Rd., Hampton
• (603) 929-0027

If you've got a hankerin' for something Western, look for the big green cactus on U.S. Route 1. You'll find hundreds of Western-style boots, hats, belts, clothing and gift items that will have you singing "Home on the Range."

Sanborn's Fine Candies

293 Lafayette Rd., Hampton
• (603) 926-5061, (800) 926-5061

Who can resist homemade chocolates, fudge and saltwater taffy? Not us! Sanborn's has a huge selection of sweets and lots of other New Hampshire gifts that won't put on the pounds.

Misty Meadows Herb Shoppe

185 Wednesday Hill Rd., Lee
• (603) 659-7211

This shop starts with herbs and moves out through concentric circles of related products and services — from herbal foods, remedies and garden plants to garden ornaments, candles, music and incense and finally to tarot card readings, wellness consultations and tools and books for the practice of "magick."

Country Curtains Retail Shop

2299 Woodbury Ave., Newington
• (603) 431-2315

You're probably familiar with the Country Curtains catalog, with its simple line drawings and tempting descriptions. The shop is even more inspiring than the book. Every home decorating problem has an answer in this collection, all with a distinctive New England country flair.

Flora Ventures, Inc.

165 Main St., Newmarket
• (603) 659-2751

Insiders recommend this florist for flowers and plants for gifts or to brighten your home. It has silk and dried flowers, plants from the greenhouse and fresh flowers from around the world. Bonsai trees and orchids are among the more unusual plants you'll find here.

The Great American Country Gift Shop

Seacoast Village Mall, U.S. Rt. 1, North Hampton
• (603) 964-9330

This gift shop stocks lots of collectibles, including Harbour Lights and Precious Moments. It also offers more than 30 pieces representing local spots for you to add to your porcelain village scene.

Portsmouth Fabric Company

112 Penhallow St., Portsmouth
• (603) 436-6343

Insiders rave about this place, even if they don't sew! The assortment of natural fiber cloth and designer fabrics available here will amaze and inspire you. Handpainted cottons and wonderful quilting fabrics just beg to be taken home and made into something beautiful. You'll also find a great variety of unique buttons.

The Whale at Yoken's

Lafayette Rd., Portsmouth
• (603) 431-8188

This gift shop goes on forever! You can buy any kind of New Hampshire or Seacoast souvenir here, from original art to cast crystal and pewter figurines to plastic back scratchers and candy.

Great Bay Pottery

U.S. Rt. 1, Rye
• (603) 964-1118

This studio and showroom offers a delightful assortment of stoneware objects, from votives and lamps to plates and jars, all with the traditional cobalt blue or unusual teal accents. Everything is hand-thrown and decorated.

Westwinds

402 High St., Somersworth
• (603) 692-3577, (800) 437-3581

Westwinds has flowers and gifts for all occasions. Insiders recommend the selections of fruit baskets, dried arrangements and unusual gifts. Westwinds also sells greenhouses, if you're inclined to try your green thumb at home.

Lakes Region

Malls and Outlet Malls

Lilac Mall

N.H. Rts. 16 and 125, Rochester
• (603) 332-9234

A Sears and a JCPenney anchor this small mall, which also offers a supermarket, Waldenbooks, gift shops and a cinema. Several discount stores are an attraction here, including Fashion Bug and Woodworkers Warehouse. And don't miss the treats at Goodie's Gift and Gourmet!

Lakes Region Factory Stores

120 Laconia Rd., Tilton
• (603) 286-7880

Conveniently grouped around a spacious parking lot, and with a playground for the kids, this is the outlet center that most appeals to us. It's relatively small, with only 50 stores, but that's still more than we can cover in one day. Our favorite is the Book Warehouse, but most people come for the clothes: Bugle Boy and Levi's Outlet by Designs, London Fog and Eddie Bauer.

The OshKosh B'Gosh and Carter's Childrenswear stores are pilgrimage sites for expectant mothers and those with young children. You'll also find bargains on shoes and luggage, housewares and accessories. Shop on!

Downtowns and Main Streets

Laconia

Laconia's downtown has been beautifully restored to create a shopping district you can walk through, with the Belknap Mill and Rotary Heritage Park as its centerpiece. To get to the free parking, take the right before you start down the one-way section of Main Street. Don't worry that you'll be miles away — from the parking lot you walk into the middle of the district. Among the delightful shops you'll find here are the Sundial Shop with a selection of gifts and collectibles, and the Maharaja's Royalty for bargain clothes and accessories with an Indian flair. Native Americans own and run Trading Bear, a gift shop filled with authentic crafts and gifts. The young and young-at-heart love the Toy Box and Rails & Crafts. The Bending Birch craft shop, the Soda Shoppe restaurant and Cherry & Webb invite visitors into the downtown building now called the Laconia Mall, which opens on to both Beacon and Belknap Streets but is accessible on foot from the Main Street shopping area. Also on Main Street you'll find the Tree of Life Christian Book Store and the StoneCoast brew pub right in the middle (see our Restaurants chapter). A block away at Veteran's Square in the Old Railroad Station you'll find las Piñatas (see our Restaurants chapter), alongside Kramer & Hall Goldsmiths, makers of fine one-of-a-kind jewelry, and The Black Cat, where you can indulge in gourmet coffee or premium cigars or just have a drink and sit outside to watch the people. Of course, not everything in Laconia is new. Just down Church Street from the Black Cat, Happy Jack's Cigar and Pipe Shop has been in business for 65 years.

Meredith

Meredith's downtown is a success story, transformed over the course of 10 years from a decaying highway intersection to a thriving center of commerce. The excitement began with the restoration of an old mill building, now part of the Mill Falls Marketplace at the junction of U.S. Route 3 and N.H. Route 25. In the restored mill you'll find Giuseppe's Cafe (see our Restaurants chapter), Lee's Candy Kitchen (a branch of the shop in Wolfeboro), The Country Carriage for gifts and collectibles and, at the top of the whimsically decorated stairs, Upcountry Pastimes, with gifts, sportswear and accessories for every taste, from golfers and fishermen to gardeners and children. Also in the Marketplace are Oglethorpe ... Fine Arts & Crafts, offering wonderful handmade gifts, and House of Iris, where you'll find works of art, gift baskets, crafts and gift items all paying tribute to that distinctive flower. Voila is an upscale beauty shop for men and women, and after they've finished perming and pampering you, the Creative Clothing Co. and Adornments can outfit you in unique and creative style. Widdershins is a Lakes Region icon after 15 years of providing an eclectic shopping experience best described as "Flower Children go shopping." The store is full of wind chimes and T-shirts, incense and candles, jewelry and clothing and bizarre and beautiful artifacts from India, Africa and the South Seas. Follow Main Street around the corner, and you'll find the Alexandria Lamp Shop, filled with both new and antique beauties. Cam's Country Emporium offers furniture, books, gifts and decorations with a country flavor. Before you climb back into your car, check out Fermentation Station with everything for the home brewer and a full line of tobacco and cigar products, and Hunters' Yarns & Needlework for your crafts.

Wolfeboro

Wolfeboro's downtown is squeezed in between Lake Winnipesaukee and Back Bay, with the result that everything is tightly clustered and perfect for a walk-about shopping trip. The on-street parking on Main Street is adequate (try Mill Street if it's crowded).

For gifts and souvenirs, check out Black's Gift Shop and The Paper Store. Don't miss the stairs to the second floor in the back; that's where some of the nicest gifts are displayed. Sky's the Limit offers flags, windsocks and a variety of collectibles. Take a tour at Hampshire Pewter, the company that decorates New Hampshire's tree at the White House every year. Reproductions of the store's ornaments and other wonderful pewter items are avail-

INSIDERS' TIP

Mall-walking programs offer encouragement and companionship as you log miles in a climate-controlled, no-cars-or-dogs environment. Ask at customer service or information booths for schedules and club information.

able in their Table Top Shop. The Art Place offers framing for whatever you bring in but specializes in needlework pieces. Check for your favorite scenes among the paintings by local artists on display here (see our Arts and Culture chapter).

You'll find clothing from elegant to silly at Jessamine's, Wolfeboro Casuals and MountainTops Custom T-shirts, all on North Main Street, Julie's Ladies Apparel, in Railroad Square or a few steps up the road at Milligan's Pendleton. While you're up the hill, look in at Country Corner Creations and Cornish Hill Pottery for crafts and gifts. Check out the fun toys at Uncle Jimmy's Whiz Bangs, or refresh your spirit across the street at the Marian Center, a shop with gifts, books and music in the Catholic tradition. Other Insider favorites in Wolfeboro are Bread and Roses Bakery, the Yum Yum Shop and Lee's Fine Confections, where the scent of chocolates being made will carry you directly to the counter. There's a branch of Piche's Ski and Sports just a block off Main Street at 107 Lehner Street too.

Wolfeboro Falls is just a quarter-mile across the bridge out of Wolfeboro's downtown, so if you've got a shady parking space you may want to walk over to Kokopelli, where you'll find jewelry and fetishes handmade by Southwestern artists and Native American craftspeople, and the League of New Hampshire Craftsmen shop, both on Center Street in Wolfeboro Falls.

Bookstores

Book Corner
U.S. Rt. 3 (Belknap Mall), Belmont
• (603) 524-9222

Here's another local bookshop with ties to a big chain. This store is affiliated with the Lauriat chain. You'll find a complete selection of children's and adult titles and all the bestsellers.

Bayswater Book Co.
Main St., Center Harbor
• (603) 253-8858

From the bestseller list to the required reading list, Bayswater offers books of all kinds for readers of all ages. It arranges author visits, offers story hours for children and specializes in finding just the right book, tape or toy for the bored child (or teen or spouse) threatening to spoil your vacation.

Innisfree Bookshop
Mill Falls Marketplace, Meredith
• (603) 279-3905

This is the Lakes Region version of the popular store in Lincoln. It has an exciting selection of regional titles along with a full line of books for every interest. The children's section ranges from books for babies to thrillers for young adults and also includes educational toys, games and puzzles.

Camelot Book & Gift Shop
16 N. Main St., Wolfeboro
• (603) 569-1771

Camelot has much more in stock than just books, but what a selection of books they have! A great regional section includes just about every hiking guide ever written, the arts and crafts section has instructional books for skills we've never heard of, and the children's section made us feel the wonder of our first library card all over again. Now add wine and cheese parties, gourmet snacks, author's readings and signings, and children's story hours, and you'll have an idea of what's in store.

The Country Bookseller
Railroad Ave., Wolfeboro
• (603) 569-6030

This nice bookshop has a good selection of both hardcover and paperback books. It brings in authors for a book-signings series throughout the summer months.

Specialty Shops and Stores We Love

Vintage Fret Shop
20 Riverside Dr., Ashland • (603) 968-3346

This fascinating store occupies the building that once housed the local blacksmith. Now it shelters an amazing assortment of stringed instruments, including some celeb-

Photo: David A. Leach Photography

America's oldest general store is located in Tuftonborough Center.

rity pieces and many fine new and used guitars and banjos, autoharps and mandolins. It also offers lessons and can handle repairs. Maybe it's time to dig out that old fiddle and try it again?

Senter's Marketplace
N.H. Rt. 25B, Center Harbor

Originally, this town was called Senter's Harbor, not for its location but for the family who settled here. Which explains why this shopping center is called Senter's Marketplace. Here you will find Keepsake Quilting, (603) 253-4026, the largest quilting shop in America and an Insider favorite with more than 6,000 bolts of cotton fabric in stock. Senter's is also home to Keepsake Yarnworks, (603) 253-4725, a great source for knitting supplies, and Pen Feathers, (603) 253-4331, for cards, rubber stamps, journals and calendars.

The Designery
43 Maple St., Center Sandwich
• (603) 284-6915
375 Dan'l Webster Hwy., Meredith

This is a shop and studio entirely dedicated to handweaving. It prepares and dyes a variety of yarns (mohair, alpaca and silk as well as wool) that you can use to create shawls and pillows, place mats and jackets. The shop also sells handcrafted toys, pottery, lampshades and other items, so you're sure to find something that strikes your fancy. The shop in Meredith, new in 1999, offers the same intriguing assortment of crafts and houses the Designery's 12-foot-wide loom. Stop in and watch it in action.

Sandwich Home Industries/League of New Hampshire Craftsmen
Main Street, Center Sandwich
• (603) 284-6831

Center Sandwich is where it all started, and this cottage shop on the village green stands not only as a wonderful gift shop but also as a tribute to the vision that brought neighbors together to form the league in 1932 (see our Arts and Culture chapter for more on the league). Like all the other league shops, it's impossible to describe what you'll find here because the wares are ever-changing. You can be sure that there will be fine examples of pottery and metal work, jewelry and fabric crafts, woodwork and weaving for gifts or to brighten your own home. This store is only open from May through October.

Surroundings Fine Arts Gallery at Red Gate
Holderness Rd., Center Sandwich
• (603) 284-6888

Local scenes painted on barrel staves and

original book-cover art, wood carvings and watercolors — you'll find all these and more at Surroundings. See our Arts and Culture chapter for more details, and see the shop itself for the painted stairs, the view from the hill and the art!

Brock Roberts Art & Floral Gallery

140 Court St., Laconia
• (603) 528-1829

Expert framing of art and needlework is just the beginning at this shop. The art on display includes watercolors by local people and prints and posters by world-renowned artists. You'll also find mirrors, wreathes and other accessories for your home.

Loran Percy Art & Crystal Gallery

N.H. Rt. 11-A, Gilford • (603) 524-4855

This intriguing shop features the work of two local artists, a father and daughter. He paints in oils, and the walls of the shop feature an extensive collection of scenes from around the region. She is a crystal cutter, trained in Austria, with a collection that includes pendants, trays, etched windows and Christmas ornaments. This is a don't-miss stop, even if you don't buy anything.

The Moccasin Shop

N.H. Rt. 11, Gilford • (603) 524-5555

This kind of store was once fairly common in New England, but there aren't many left. You'll find a variety of leather items here, not only wonderful moccasins and slippers but also belts, gloves and vests. Add Native-American style silver-and-turquoise jewelry, maple sugar candy, pottery, T-shirts and assorted New Hampshire souvenirs, and you'll get the picture.

Pepi Herrman Crystal Inc.

3 Waterford Pl., Gilford
• (603) 528-1020, (800) HANDCUT

This is a place Insiders bring their houseguests to watch master craftspeople create timeless beauty. Handcut crystal jewelry, dishes and chandeliers come to life before your eyes. Pepi Herrmann's experts can also repair old crystal and cut glass and make reproductions of antique pieces. Visitors are welcome to tour the studio and museum as well as the shop. There's even a "cafehaus" where you can get a light snack.

Piche's Ski and Sports Shop

318 Gilford Ave., Gilford
• (603) 524-2068

Here and at their downtown Wolfeboro location, the people at Piche's go out of their way to provide for the outdoor enjoyment of their customers. They rent, sell and service skis, snowboards, toboggans and skates in winter, switching to bicycles, water skis, in-line skates and camping equipment in summer. While-you-wait skate sharpening and free cross-country lessons with rentals are examples of the kind of service that has made Piche's an Insider favorite.

Brick House Antique Reproductions

Junction of N.H. Rts. 140 and 107, Gilmanton • (603) 267-1190

In a meticulously restored early 19th-century farmhouse, you will find an outstanding collection of antique reproductions. These are new pieces made by traditional methods, using the same tools and techniques the original craftspeople would have used. Wood and clay, fabric and paper appear in perfect beauty and proportion. We suspect the original owners never had it so good!

Laconia Pottery

45 Court St., Laconia • (603) 528-4997

Stop in at this working studio to watch potters creating their unique pieces of stoneware and pottery. You might get a chance to spin the wheel and mold a piece yourself —

INSIDERS' TIP

The *New Hampshire/Maine Factory Outlet and Off-Price Handbook* is a free catalog available at tourist information centers in both states. Inside you'll find up-to-date listings, handy maps and even money-saving coupons for your favorite shops.

or sign up for a class. Or you might just choose to browse through the gallery and select a mug, pot or decoration to take home.

Annalee Doll Museum and Gift Shop

Reservoir Rd., Meredith
• (603) 279-6542

People all over the world collect these delightful dolls. Stop at the museum to learn their history, then wander through the gift shop to add to your own collection — or start one! See our Attractions chapter for more on Annalee.

Old Burlwood Country Store

U.S. Rt. 3, Meredith
• (603) 279-3021

This is a spot Insiders bring their guests to show them "a real country store," which is kind of funny because it's only been here for a few years! The owners have re-created an authentic country store feeling, though. They have penny candy, cheese under a glass dome, pickles in a barrel and maple sugar candy. They also stock garden accessories, wooden lawn furniture, lamps, pottery, linens and — well, we think you get the idea.

Christmas Loft

U.S. Rt. 3, Meredith
• (603) 279-5711

Come in for a walk through a winter wonderland, any time of year. The Christmas Loft has three locations in New Hampshire: The other two are in the White Mountains, in North Conway and North Woodstock. You'll find whole rooms filled to overflowing with Byer's Choice, Department 56 and other favorite collectibles. Twinkling lights reflect off sparkling crystals. If you're just looking for a few inexpensive gifts, you'll find them here. Sign up for their newsletter, so you'll know when they're having special sales or contests!

League of New Hampshire Craftsmen

279 Daniel Webster Hwy., Meredith
• (603) 279-7920

The work of artisans from around the state is displayed in this bright airy shop. Precisely what you'll find on any visit we can't say, but we know it will be beautiful.

The Old Print Barn

Winona Rd., Meredith
• (603) 279-6479

This 19th-century barn houses a remarkable collection of original prints, antique and contemporary, and other paper works of art. See our Arts and Culture chapter for more details.

Towle Hill House

N.H. Rt. 25 E., Meredith
• (603) 279-6260

Look here for shower gifts: both bridal and baby. This beautiful old farm is now a very nice gift shop — actually two gift shops in one, since it has a complete "Baby Boutique" in addition to beautiful pewter, dinnerware and bakeware, lamps and other accessories.

Winnepesaukee Forge

31 Foundry Ave., Meredith
• (603) 279-5492

If you think blacksmithing died with the Colonial era, think again. The craftspeople at Winnepesaukee Forge make furniture, gifts and accessories from iron, glass and granite. One of their candelabra and several other pieces were used by Steve Martin and Goldie Hawn in the movie *Housesitters*. More recently, the Disney Company commissioned Winnepesaukee Forge to create a suitable mirror for a new gift shop dedicated to classic Disney villains at the Orlando theme park. You will be astounded at the variety of objects on display, and perhaps inspired to have something made especially for someone you love.

Spinnit Farm & Fibers

322 Gov. Wentworth Hwy., Mirror Lake
• (603) 544-3240

If you're a knitter or spinner, be sure to take the scenic route along the east side of Winnipesauke. This shop is worth hunting for. Spinning wheels, native fibers and a great selection of yarns for hand-knitting are what you'll find, along with all sorts of knitting accessories, advice and inspiration.

Carriage House Crafters

Marvin Rd., Moultonborough
• (603) 253-9724

This pretty little carriage house with the bright-colored flags flying out front is a collective shop representing almost 100 craftspeople from around New England. All sorts of decorative items, from painted slates to stained glass, are on display, along with leather goods, wood crafts and stitchery of all kinds. The flags are made by the proprietor, Mary LaVasseur, who will be happy to create one especially for you.

Chick-A-Dee Station

N.H. Rt. 25, Moultonborough
• (603) 253-4571

This cute little shop has everything the dedicated bird-lover needs to attract birds to the yard. Feeders and birdhouses, seeds and suets, even birdbaths are for sale. It also has a collection of bird-related gift items.

The Old Country Store

Junction of N.H. Rts. 25 and 109, Moultonborough • (603) 476-5750

This general store has been in operation since 1781. At one time it included a tavern, and for many years it housed the post office. For several years the upper floor of the building served as the town's Meeting Room. Today there's a fascinating little museum up there, and a Concord coach is parked in the shed. The rest of the store is very much in

INSIDERS' TIP

Start a collection of linen dish towels for a friend, relative or yourself. It's an inexpensive way to share or remember your vacations, and they don't take up too much room in your luggage.

business, with penny candy and pickles and cheese, New Hampshire souvenirs and a wealth of gift ideas. There's also a good supply of old-fashioned kitchen utensils out back and some wonderful New Hampshire books, maps and posters. This place is so popular they've had to expand the parking out back and put in a porta-potty in the summer, but it still has the traditional feel of the country store and some real bargains to boot.

Wm. H. Powers Woodworking Inc.

N.H. Rt. 171, Moultonborough
• (603) 476-2466

For custom furniture, accessories and cabinetry, the William Powers workshop is worth driving out of the way for. (From the Old Country Store, take N.H. Route 109-E east to N.H. Route 171.) Every piece of cherry, maple, birch or pine is lovingly shaped, polished and stained or waxed by hand. Powers specializes in Shaker and Early American styles and will work from your description or idea to design a new heirloom.

Tower Gallery Spirited Gifts

28 Summer St., Northfield
• (603) 286-9999

This gallery in a historic Northfield home offers a mix of works by local artisans, including etchings and watercolors, silk screens and stained glass, along with instruments, kaleidoscopes and assorted trinkets and odd bits. A great selection of cards and CDs are part of the mix, and 5 percent of your purchase cost goes to your choice of charitable causes. See our Arts and Culture chapter for more about Tower Gallery.

Green Mountain Furniture

N.H. Rt. 16, Ossipee
• (603) 539-2236

This huge building has a wealth of wonderful furniture beautifully displayed. You can walk through and see how everything fits together rather than looking at a sea of couches or a forest of chairs. Green Mountain Furniture also has a basement collection of leftovers and odd bits at discounted prices. A Christmas shop full of ornaments and collectibles and a nice assortment of cards and small gift items complete this great browsing or buying experience.

Plymouth Ski & Sports

103 Main St., Plymouth
• (603) 536-2338

As you might expect in a college town at the edge of both the mountains and the lakes, this sports shop has an extensive selection of equipment for a huge variety of sports. Tennis rackets and in-line skates share space with backpacks, crampons and ice axes. The store has a large assortment of camping gear as well.

Calico Cupboard

Main St., Rumney
• (603) 786-9567

If you're a sewing person, this is the kind of store you walk through saying, "I could make that!" The nice thing is, at Calico Cupboard, you can buy the directions and materials or a pre-made kit, so you *can* make it yourself. Or, if you're not likely to get around to it, just buy the finished product to bring home and enjoy.

Shanware Pottery

1819 N.H. Rt. 25, Rumney
• (603) 786-9835

Richard Wetterer produces one-of-a-kind pieces in stoneware and porcelain. You can watch him at work in his rustic studio, choose one of the fine pieces of pottery on display or describe your dream and have him design a piece especially for you.

Woodland Books & Toys

N.H. Rt 25, Tamworth
• (603) 323-7118

Finding this toy shop on the road to Tamworth was a bit like discovering an enchanted place in a children's story book. Wonderful toys, imported games and puzzles and a nice selection of children's books entice child and parent alike. And since the policy here is "sure, you can play with it," the visit is peaceful and pleasant for everyone. (They even have a porta-potty out back — can you tell this shop was designed and run by a couple of moms?)

Country Braid House

462 Main St., Tilton
• (603) 286-4511

This barn, built in the 1800s, houses a workshop where you can watch rugs being made and see displays of the finished products. Kits and advice are available if you're inspired to give it a try, or you can choose from hundreds of handmade rugs in all shapes and sizes and 250 color combinations.

Winnisquam Gifts and Lakeview Crafts

754 Laconia Rd., Tilton
• (603) 528-4457

This gift shop is the home business of the Bouley family. In addition to their own delightful wooden silhouettes for your lawn or garden (dogs, man leaning against fence, etc.), they sell the work of many other local craftspeople. From picnic tables to whirly-gigs, maple sugar candy and other souvenirs and a wonderful assortment of teddy bears and dolls in handmade clothes, you'll find something here for every taste and budget.

Spider Web Gardens

N.H. Rt 109-A, Tuftonboro
• (603) 569-5056

An abundance of flowers, bedding plants and garden accessories greet you as you discover this beautiful spot. If you're trying to brighten your backyard, fill a window box at your campsite or bring a gift to your hostess, this is a great place to look.

Basket World

U.S. Rt. 3, Weirs Beach
• (603) 366-5585, (800) 528-3304

If you think wicker is just for porches and baskets are just for picnics, you haven't been to Basket World. Whether you're redecorating your guest room or hunting for a wedding gift, you'll find something wicker or woven here that will suit the bill. Basket World is north of the boardwalk section of the Weirs, on the way to Meredith. On a summer weekend you might want to go to Meredith first and come south to Basket World.

Handy Landing

1184 Weirs Blvd., Weirs Beach
• (603) 366-2232

Here's a store with parking spaces on one side and boat slips on the other. The business has been here for more than 50 years, having just recently been sold by the original owners. Over the years they had a number of sidelines, including rental cabins and a boat launch. Today the general store offers convenient food, camping supplies and fishing gear and boat fuel for the many travelers on both land and lake.

Tramway Artisans

Junction of N.H. Rts 16 and 25, West Ossipee • (603) 539-5700

This collective shop displays more than 70,000 craft and gift items by local artists. You'll find jewelry, handcrafts, antique reproductions, candles, cards and more as you explore the two floors of gifts in stock. They also have souvenirs and inexpensive gifts, so don't be afraid to bring the kids.

White Mountains and Great North Woods Regions

Malls and Outlet Malls

Millfront Marketplace

8 Lincoln Center North, Lincoln
• (603) 745-6261

Part of the Mill at Loon Mountain complex, the Millfront Marketplace includes about 20 shops in three renovated mill buildings. The four-screen movie complex is the largest

INSIDERS' TIP

Don't forget museum gift shops when you're looking for special purchases. The same goes for many of our attractions. Sometimes the best tourist shopping is right there at a tourist center.

tenant, and Innisfree Bookshop (see our description under Bookstores in this chapter) adds to the cultural scene. Sun Dancer specializes in Southwestern designs, and Original Designs Company (known as OD) features silk screen and embroidered T-shirts, sweat shirts and hats. Treasures is a multipurpose gift store, and The Country Carriage specializes in collectibles, soaps and toiletries and candles.

Mountain Valley Mall

N.H.Rt. 16, North Conway • (603) 356-5843

This one-story enclosed mall has JCPenney and Kmart as anchor stores and includes a Waldenbooks, House of Fabric and Fashion Bug. If you're camping or setting up housekeeping during your vacation, you'll be glad to know the mall includes a Shop 'N' Save grocery store.

Settlers' Green Outlet Village Plus

N.H. Rt. 16, North Conway
• (603) 356-7031

You don't have to be an Insider to take advantage of the money-saving opportunities at Settlers' Green. Visitors from Maine and Massachusetts love the double savings of outlet prices and no sales tax. The outlet mall has an Orvis Factory Store for the outdoor sports enthusiast, Famous Footwear and Nine West for Imelda Marcos shoe-ins, Carter's Childrenswear and a Rugged Bear Outlet for kids' clothes, and a Banana Republic Outlet and J.Crew Factory Store for fashionable grown-ups. You can shop for everything from sunglasses and watches to underwear and accessories. Hunt for your bargains in more than 30 stores. The mall is open every day.

Tanger Factory Outlet Centers

N.H. Rt. 16, North Conway
• (800) 4-TANGER

Three Tanger centers dot N.H. 16. They are within a mile of each other, but since you might be carrying lots of bags, you may want to drive. If you're only interested in one particular store, you should call in advance to make sure the store is still open. The retail business is always changing (that's why we love to shop), and it's best to double check. Going north on N.H. 16 you'll see the L.L. Bean Outlet Center on your right about a half-mile after U.S. 302 feeds into N.H. Rt. 16. We think this is the most upscale of all the North Conway discount malls. Besides the L.L. Bean anchor store, you'll enjoy the discounts available at Anne Klein, Joan and David, Geoffrey Beene and Oneida Silver. Across N.H. 16 you'll see Clover. That's the name of the mall with anchor stores of Liz Claiborne and Calvin Klein. You'll also enjoy Coloratura, which specializes in ladies clothing and casual as well as boardroom jewelry. This is also the place for Polo/Ralph Lauren. The third Tanger mall in North Conway is The Red Barn Factory Stores. The anchor stores are OshKosh B'Gosh, Casual Corner and Corning Revere. We think you'll enjoy the Rocky Mountain Chocolate Factory too.

Bookstores

Wonderland Book Store

14 Exchange St., Gorham
• (603) 466-2123

One of the charms of this bookstore is the "I read this" knowledge of the owner and her bookworm staff. The store specializes in books by New England authors as well as books about New England. And, not surprisingly, you'll find a great selection of books focused on New Hampshire's outdoor adventures. Trail guides for hikers and bikers as well as field guides of wildlife and wildflowers are the perfect choice for outdoorsy types. You can find all the current titles from the New York Times Bestseller List, but we suggest you check out the shelf space devoted to self-published books. The store is open Monday through Saturday and Sunday by chance.

Innisfree Bookshop

Millfront Marketplace, Lincoln
• (603) 745-6107

This 5,000-square-foot general interest bookstore opened in Lincoln in 1985. A mainstay of the Millfront Marketplace, Innisfree has a great selection of regional books. The selection of local guidebooks for recreational sports — hiking, canoeing and climbing — is very complete. The area for children's books includes games, toys and plush toy tie-ins. You'll be glad to see the wide selection of audio books. The tape and CD collection includes lots of children's favorites. The store is open every day.

Village Book Store

81 Main St., Littleton
• (603) 444-5263, (800) 640-9673

Bring the whole family to this 9,000-square-foot book emporium. You'll find more than 50,000 books including 25,000 children's books. Although we don't think you need a lure to get a young reader in the bookstore habit, your kids might be interested in the toy department adjacent to the children's books. And in case your crowd likes to listen to books, you'll like the full audio department. In addition to books on tape, you can affect a change of aural scenery with a visit to the music department. The only thing you won't find here is a cup of coffee. The store is open every day.

White Birch Books

2568 Main St., North Conway Village
• (603) 356-3200, (800) 597-1176

When asked to describe her bookstore's strength, owner Donna Urey said it was the store "recommends" — books she and her staff recommend as a result of their own reading. They also have a very strong northern New England regional section of fiction and nonfiction as well as topographical maps that are popular with hikers. The card selection is one of the best in the valley. You'll enjoy the renovated Victorian-style building. The store is open every day.

Bye The Book

Main St., North Conway Village
• (603) 356-2665, (800) 491-2665

Although we don't wish you any rainy days during your visit to the White Mountains region, if you happen to get a bit of weather that keeps you off the mountains, Bye the Books is a stop you'll be glad you had to make. The staff loves to help you find just the right book, whether you're shopping for yourself or for your children. The children's books are hand-selected by the staff. So are the books for young adults. You'll find the Newbery Award winners as well as some staff favorites. The Eastern philosophy section is more complete than many and is quite popular.

Specialty Shops and Stores We Love

Middle Earth

91-95 Main St., Berlin
• (603) 752-7400, (800) 469-7401

This Great North Woods gift shop specializes in antique sterling silver and turquoise jewelry. It's from the Southwestern part of the United States, and the collection includes rings, bracelets and necklaces. You'll also enjoy the selection of leather belts, pocketbooks and wallets.

League of New Hampshire Craftsmen

2526 Main St., North Conway
• (603) 356-2441

The League of New Hampshire Craftsmen represents more than 800 craftspeople. You'll find league stores in each region except the Monadnock region. The content of each store is different, but you can expect to see examples of both contemporary and traditional craft. You'll find furniture, weavings, pottery, jewelry and needlework. Don't worry if you don't plan on buying, browsers are welcome.

INSIDERS' TIP

Thirsty? New Hampshire's 70 state liquor stores sell all alcoholic beverages with an alcohol content of more than 6 percent by volume, and New Hampshire Wine Outlet shops stock more than a half-million bottles at a time. Beer and wine are available in grocery stores (beer is available virtually everywhere except liquor stores).

Flea markets are a New Hampshire tradition.

The Hand Crafters Barn
N.H. Rt. 16, North Conway
• (603) 356-8996

Three floors of American-made crafts are housed in this delightful 18th-century barn. More than 35 booths show off the work of mostly New England artists. Textile designs and pottery lead the way with wood designs and crafts close behind. This multifaceted shop is open all year.

Dartmouth-Lake Sunapee Region

Malls and Outlet Malls

Powerhouse Mall
N.H. Rt. 12A, West Lebanon
• (603) 298-5236

Eastern Mountain Sports (look for a full description in the Specialty Shop section of the Monadnock region) is the anchor store here. You'll also find the Anichini Outlet, a delightful selection of elegant linens at a discount from their normally very expensive retail prices. Check out Best Sellers for books (see our description under Bookstores) and save a few minutes for the great women's clothing stores. You'll find Doc Martens, funky socks and unusual stockings along with great clothes at Ellistar. Next door, you'll find a lovely lingerie shop called Jessica's. We like this mall a lot. It's not too big, and it's packed with goodies.

Bookstores

The Corner Book Shop
1 Pleasant St., Claremont
• (603) 543-3011

With nearly 13,000 titles, this delightful independent bookstore manages to keep the natives from getting restless. You'll find all the bestsellers as well as a great selection of children's books. The religion section is very strong and includes gifts as well as books. In case you want to communicate with someone back home, you can pick up a card or a box of stationery. The bookstore is open every day.

The Dartmouth Bookstore
33 S. Main St., Hanover
• (603) 643-3616

Not surprisingly this is one of the most wonderful bookstores we've ever gotten lost in. With more than 150,000 titles, it is also one of the largest bookstores in New England.

You'll find a floor of children's books, rows of scholarly texts and more fiction than anyone could read in a lifetime. You'll also find great school supplies, music and videos. But trust us, books are the star here, and if you're a bookworm you may never leave. The store is open every day but Sunday.

Best Sellers
Powerhouse Mall, N.H. Rt. 12A, West Lebanon • (603) 298-7980

While the rest of the family shops for linens or sports equipment in the mall, you can have a delightful time browsing through this independent bookstore. Don't let the name fool you. This store has a wonderful selection of books that may never make a bestseller list. The cooking and gardening sections are particularly strong, and there's a varied selection of children's books.

Morgan Hill Bookstore
170 Main St., New London • (603) 526-5850

This 2,000-square-foot, independent bookstore specializes in quality paperbacks and hardcover books. Fine fiction, travel and history are particularly strong, as are children's books. Tourists and townies alike enjoy the selection of regional books, including guides as well as works by New England authors. Morgan Hill rents and sells audio books. The bookstore is open every day.

Specialty Shops and Stores We Love

Dorr Mill Store
Guild Rd., Guild • (603) 863-1197

Crafters alert! If you love wool, don't miss the Dorr Mill Store. This 6,500-square-foot store specializes in wool for hooking, braiding and quilting. You might compare rug hooking techniques with a shopper from Canada. The wool clothing is also superb, featuring sportswear from Pendleton and sweaters designed by Susan Bristol. Men's clothing is included as well with dress shirts and sports jackets as well as sweaters. But the real attraction here is the wool. Dorr Mill Store has evolved from a shop using leftover cloth from the local mill to a major supplier of wool for artists and crafters throughout the United States and Canada. The store has a full mail-order business too.

League of New Hampshire Craftsmen
13 Lebanon St., Hanover • (603) 643-5050

There are eight of these shops in regions throughout the state (except the Monadnock Region). The League of New Hampshire Craftsmen represents more than 800 craftspeople. You'll find furniture, weavings, pottery, jewelry and needlework.

Artisan's Workshop
186 Main St., New London • (603) 526-4227

This is the place to look for prints featuring Lake Sunapee trout. You'll see hand-knit scarves and gloves, jewelry and paintings featuring local scenes. You can walk through the store to Peter Christian's Tavern, which we rave about in our Restaurants chapter.

Jewelry and Design Center
41 Glen Rd., West Lebanon • (603) 298-8833, (800) 371-4996

Jewelry connoisseurs will want to visit this varied collection of beautiful adornments. Contemporary — many made on the premises — and antique jewelry pieces are on display and for sale along with jewelry boxes, clocks and special decorative accents for your home. Glen Road is just past the main entrance to Powerhouse Mall. The center is open every day but Sunday.

The New England Soap and Herb Company
120 S. Main St., West Lebanon • (603) 298-8588, (888) 934-HERB

It's hard to pick a favorite item here. The tiny store is full of heavenly smells, and the extensive inventory includes products for the mind, body and spirit. We had a cup of herbal tea and continued a day of research with renewed energy. Whether it's tea or bath oil or dried flowers for your own crafts, you'll be glad you stopped by.

Monadnock Region

Malls

Colony Mill Marketplace
222 West St., Keene
• (603) 357-1240

These buildings were constructed in 1838 as the Faulkner and Colony Woolen Mill. The mill closed in 1953 but was restored in 1983 as a wonderful shopping mall. The stores are not part of national chains. Instead you'll find a variety of shops, with a range of items sure to suit an entire family. Ye Goodie Shoppe is a personal favorite. The chocolates are handmade on the premises and are delicious. The Toadstool Bookstore (see our description under bookstores) is a favorite shopping spot along with Perfecta Camera, which is a great place to pick up more film, add a lens and get your Mount Monadnock hiking pictures developed. Trendy females will love True Necessities. The clothes are great, but the accessories are fab. Eat at the Brickyard Steakhouse or the Brew Pub (see our Restaurants chapter). The food court features both a deli and bakery with a glassed-in eating area. The marketplace is open every day.

Downtowns and Main Streets

Peterborough

Main Street, School St., Depot Square and Grove Street make a wonderful shopping stroll through downtown Peterborough. Depot Square is the place to park. It's off School St., which runs between Main and Grove Streets. Begin at the Toadstool Bookshop, 12 Depot Square (see our description below under Bookstores). In the same building you'll enjoy The Thirsty Ear music store, which specializes in jazz and classical and has an excellent folk collection. It carries sheet music too. Around the corner (still at 12 Depot Square) is Peterborough Craft Supplies with dollhouses and appropriate accessories as well as patterns, flosses and beads.

Across the parking lot, you'll see 12 Pine, our favorite place to buy an eat-in or take-out home-cooked meal. Besides food, you can buy fresh flowers, fresh bread and gourmet food products. Walk through 12 Pine and exit into a parking lot edged by several fun shops. At Spokes and Slopes you'll find a full line of bicycles including mountain bikes and exercise bikes as well as skis and accessories. To the right of Spokes and Slopes is Haskell and Russell Antiques and to the left is Sharon Arts Downtown, the retail arm of the Sharon Arts Center (see our Arts and Culture chapter for more on the Sharon Arts Center).

Continuing around the Depot Square you'll find Red Chair Antiques and Casual Comforts. The casual comforts range from soft quilts to broken-in rocking chairs. We also recommend you stop in Paper and Roses. This small store specializes in greeting cards and stationery. Last time we were in we bought a beautiful handmade greeting card with a painted wooden poppy on the front.

When you've finished touring the stores in Depot Square, head back to School St. Up the slight incline is Grove Street. The Field Mouse, 95 Grove Street is great if you need to buy a hostess gift. The Winged Pig, 26 Grove Street is a great clothes stores for women of all ages. At Wit's End, 8 Grove Street, specializes in gift baskets and unusual jewelry. Take a right on Main Street and stop in Steele's, 40 Main Street, for lots of great paper products. Steele's has a wide variety of stationery, cards and gift wrap as well as a full line of office supplies.

Just down the street Ginger and Pickles, 32 Main Street, has elegant accessories for

INSIDERS' TIP

Although most stores are open on Sunday afternoons, it's best to call ahead and make sure.

the home. Morgan's Way, 28 Main Street, has an eclectic selection of women's clothes including great hats and beautiful fabric totes and bags. If you're invited to a soiree and have no idea what to wear, you'll find both guidance and an outfit here. We're sorry to report that Joseph's Coat, 26 Main Street, was destroyed in a 1999 New Year's fire. We hope it's back in business soon.

Bookstores

The Toadstool Bookshop

Colony Mill Marketplace, Keene
• (603) 352-8815
12 Depot Sq., Peterborough
• (603) 924-3543

Roam through lots of well-organized categories or cozy up on the couch and read to your heart's content. One of the many charms of all the Toadstool Bookshops is the relaxed atmosphere that's conducive to browsing. Combine that with a very well-read knowledgeable staff, and you've got great bookstores. The staff whizzes through computer information and finds just the book on just the subject you're looking for. They special order with a smile and call as soon as your book arrives. Index cards with brief reviews by staff and customers dot the shelves. The stores are open every day.

The Peterborough store also has a great spot to eat called Aesop's Tables. The bookstore is open every day, but Aesop's Tables takes a rest on Sunday.

Parnassus Book Center

North Meadow Plaza, Walpole
• (603) 756-9254

This small independent bookstore can certainly satisfy your everyday book fix, whether it's contemporary fiction and nonfiction or another great book for your children. What sets it apart is the owner's particular concentration on medical books, particularly the field of complimentary medicine. You'll find an unusually strong selection of books on herbal remedies, aromatherapy, acupuncture and other alternative healing arts. Another strength is the periodical section. You won't find the same magazines you see in most grocery stores, but rather political periodicals and fine art publications.

Specialty Shops and Stores We Love

Hall Manufacturing

N.H. Rt. 130 at the intersection with N.H. Rt. 13, Brookline
• (603) 673-4841

Hall's has saved us more than once as we contemplated birthday and holiday gifts for the hard to please. This factory retail outlet specializes in durable, practical carryalls. You'll find a great selection of tote bags, backpacks, toiletry kits and duffel bags. The log carriers are always a favorite with New Englanders. Everything you see is made on the premises. You can watch the skilled workers cut, sew and embroider these handy items.

Harvest Thyme Herbs

Dooe Rd., Dublin
• (603) 563-7032

You'll find the usual herbal wreaths and dried lavender at Harvest Thyme Herbs, but the specialties of the house include original gift baskets and nine different dry mixes to combine with sour cream for wonderful dips. The baskets have themes, such as Hot and Spicy, featuring four hot dip mixes, Mexican popcorn and a string of dried chili peppers. The Bird Watcher's Basket includes birdseed as well as tea for the hours you sit by the window watching. Some baskets have coordinating handmade potholders and others feature New Hampshire-made candles. The shop is open Wednesday through Sunday from May through December. Follow the signs from N.H. 101 at the intersection with N.H. 137 in Dublin.

Hedge House

N.H. Rt. 101, Dublin
• (603) 563-8833

You'll find a large collection of old and new Fenton Art Glass at this unusual shop in Dublin. You'll see handpainted glass, cranberry glass and large Victorian-style glass lamps. Limited-edition Patchell-Olson prints of rustic New England scenes are printed on canvas and resemble oil paintings. The store has a number of Christmas items including nativity scenes made of glass and Christmas tree music boxes.

Keene Mill End Store
55 Ralston St., Keene • (603) 352-8683

You can find buy fabric, trim, even a sewing machine at this full-service fabric and notions store. You'll find everything for all your sewing or home-decorating projects. The store has complete upholstery department. You can also choose from lots of styles of custom blinds and pick up accent rugs and pillows. Dress fabrics include knits, wool and flannels as well as challis, dotted swiss and quilted fabric. If you're planning a wedding, you should check out the bridal department. The complete sewing center is open Monday through Saturday.

Pickity Place
Nutting Hill Rd., Mason
• (603) 878-1151

Gardener's alert! More than 5 acres of lovely herb and perennial gardens are tucked away off the dirt road access. The greenhouse and garden shop will enable you to attempt your own recreation at home. Tools and plants are for sale with a wide selection of heaths and heathers. Beside the garden shop is a gift shop with beeswax candles and other handcrafted treats. Read about eating at Pickity Place in our Restaurants chapter.

Granite Lake Pottery
Franklin Pierce Rd., Munsonville
• (603) 847-9908

You'll find nearly 150 different pieces of handmade, hand-decorated stoneware in the 1820s farmhouse that's home to Granite Lake Pottery. The original pieces include a wheel-thrown bathroom sink. Dinnerware, lamps and planters come in several designs including Blue Lupine, Country Floral and Victorian. The Victorian design features cranberries and blue forget-me-nots. All of the dinnerware is safe to use in the dishwasher, microwave and oven. The store is open every day but Sunday. To get here take N.H. 9 east out of Keene and follow the signs for Granite Lake.

Eastern Mountain Sports
1 Vose Farm Rd., Peterborough
• (603) 924-7231

If you're inspired to try camping (or skiing or hiking or climbing) while in the region and don't have appropriate clothes and equipment, don't worry. You'll find everything you need at EMS (Insiders use only the initials when referring to this favorite store). Socks, jackets, long underwear, tents, sleeping bags, trail guides, trail food, skis, snowshoes — you name it, it's here. In winter you can rent skis and snowshoes. EMS sponsors clinics in climbing and cross-country skiing. The staff is very knowledgeable and always happy to help you set up a tent or demonstrate a gadget. Most of the malls have branches of EMS, but this is the mother store.

North Gallery at Tewksbury's
Intersection of N.H. Rts. 101 and 123 S., Peterborough • (603) 924-3224

If you're coming off Temple Mountain into Peterborough on N.H. Route 101, take a left at the blinking light marking N.H. Route 123. If you're driving east, take a right. Immediately on your right you'll see a three-story post-and-beam barn attached to a white Colonial house. The barn is the North Gallery. The store specializes in fine American crafts, but the inventory is varied enough to please all shoppers. The crafts are accompanied by gifts ranging in cost from $1 to $100. A large inventory of cookbooks and a huge selection of contemporary toys are two specialties. Starting in August and lasting through the holidays, you'll be treated to an outstanding selection of Christmas ornaments and decorations. The store is open every day throughout the year.

Bursey's Farm Stand
438 Gibbons Hwy. (N.H. Rt. 101), Wilton
• (603) 654-6572

The Farm Stand is just a part of this wonderful food and flower market. Open year round, it specializes in fresh greens, vegetables, fruits and flowers. The wide selection

of organic produce and natural and health food products is tempting to even the most ardent consumer of potato chips. Gourmet food products include salad dressing, pastas and wonderful chocolate. Apples, mums and pumpkins line the entrance in fall, pansies herald spring and overflowing hanging baskets of petunias are the look of summer. You can always buy house plants and cut flowers. In late spring and early summer you'll see annuals and perennials. If you're planning a picnic, don't miss the fresh-baked bread from local bakeries. Bursey's is open every day.

Frye's Measure Mill

Frye Mill Rd., Wilton Center
• (603) 654-6581

After touring the region and getting a good dose of Colonial ambiance, come to Frye's and find just the right bit of history to take home. The beautiful Colonial and Shaker box reproductions are made right here. The water-powered woodworking shop is 138 years old. The gift shop includes folk art pieces including beautiful handmade quilts. Lovely pottery and pewter pieces are also featured. The easiest way to find the mill is to take N.H. 31 N. out of Wilton on Forest Street. Drive 2 miles and turn left at the sign for Frye's Measure Mill.

Putnam's Clothing

41 Main St., Wilton
• (603) 654-6564

We think of Putnam's for a lot more than clothes. You'll find magazines, pottery, stationery, penny candy and local news. This is the place to rent a tux, ship a package, drop-off dry cleaning and get your hunting and fishing licenses. The clothes are great too. Look for sweaters, long underwear, overalls (the real ones) and lots and lots of charm.

Whether your passion is Colonial silver or piggy banks or daguerreotypes, a dealer probably can lead you to a source.

Antiques and Collectibles

Whether you are an old pro at digging out bargains at estate sales or just getting started in your search for items that had a life before you met them, you will have a wonderful time exploring the many and varied antiques and collectibles shops in New Hampshire.

It is not unusual to see corner cupboards from the 1700s priced near $20,000. Nor is it rare to find funky pilsner glasses for less than $10 each. It isn't necessary to have a lot of money to spend in order to have fun. If you're just starting to collect, you'll have a wonderful time exploring our shops and educating yourself about what's out there.

It seems to us that the trend is toward group shops. In this chapter, we tell you about lots of the group shops because we think they're fun to browse through, and they offer a lot to see at one stop. Dealers can share rent and space and take turns minding the store. It's hard for dealers to keep the cupboards full if they're always watching the store. Don't forget that dealers are an excellent resource as you search for something. They know the territory better than anyone else. Be sure and ask owners about where you might find a particular item. Whether your passion is Colonial silver or piggy banks or daguerreotypes, a dealer probably can lead you to a source.

One of the best sources for information is the Directory of New Hampshire Antiques Dealers. The guide contains a full listing for member dealers including a description of each dealer's specialties. To receive a copy of the directory, send a self-addressed stamped envelope (they suggest two 33¢ stamps for postage) to New Hampshire Antiques Dealers Association, P.O. Box 2033, Hampton, NH 03843. Their annual show is held every August in Manchester (see our Annual Events chapter). The show is a great place to meet a lot of dealers at once and see everyone's best offerings.

Another good source for information is the trade publication *Unravel the Gavel.* You'll find articles and timely information on auctions and antiques shows. A recent issue discussed details of Victorian jewelry with tips on what to look for in order to establish authenticity. *Unravel the Gavel* is issued 11 times a year — you won't get a January issue — and subscription information can be obtained by writing or calling *Unravel the Gavel,* 9 Hurricane Road No. 1, Belmont, NH 03220, (603) 524-4281. *New Hampshire Antiques Monthly,* a free newspaper chock-full of advertisements and articles aimed primarily at dealers, can be picked up in most antiques shops around the state.

A word to the wise in buying antiques and collectibles: Buyer beware! We can't guarantee that items sold in the shops we mention are what they say they are. We certainly hope you don't run into any unscrupulous dealers, but it is possible that the items you buy may not be exactly what they are claimed to be. Remember that shop owners can be fooled too. We suggest that you make certain you understand the return policy. While you might not expect your money back on a $10 item that turned out to be made in China instead of America, you should ask about cash refunds on items that cost more than a few hundred dollars. If the written cash-back offer is not part of the conditions, then make sure you love your purchase for what you see and not what you think it is.

In this chapter we have also listed a sampling of bookstores where you'll find antiquarian and used books. These stores will have you crossing your fingers for a rainy day. If it's too wet to climb a mountain or too cold to swim in the lake, pay a visit to any of the booksellers mentioned here and have a grand day looking for a copy of that old favorite book you lost track of, or the one your mother threw out by mistake.

These stores are also great places to pursue hobbies and passions. One store specializes in radio broadcasting, another has a great collection of theological books. We have limited the book shops we discuss to stores that are open with regular hours. Many additional and excellent dealers are available by appointment only. If you'd like a copy of the membership listing of the New Hampshire Antiquarian Booksellers Association, send your request to Homestead Bookshop, P.O. Box 90, Marlborough, NH 03455. If you're in New Hampshire in mid-September, be sure to visit the Annual Antiquarian Book Fair in Concord (see our Annual Events chapter). It's the second-oldest book fair in the country and features dealers from more than 10 states.

Remember, this book is a guide, not a directory. We couldn't possibly list all of the antiques stores in our state, but we've recommended a good sampling to get you started.

Merrimack Valley Region

Shops

Antiques Trail

N.H. Rt. 101-A from Nashua to Wilton

Most of the shops have been here for a long time, but the concept of the Trail is relatively recent. Group shops predominate, as they do in most parts of the state now. The first shop on the Trail, House of Josephs in Nashua, (603) 882-4118, is actually at 523 Broad Street, just off Amherst Street (which is what Route 101-A is called in Nashua). This is a 30-dealer shop offering a wide variety of items large and small. At the other end of the Trail you'll find Here Today on Main Street in Wilton, (603) 654-5295, a delightfully eclectic collection of "old stuff."

The New Hampshire Antique Co-op on Elm Street in Milford, (603) 673-8499, may deceive you with its plain exterior, but inside you'll find a very good example of a multi-dealer shop, with items displayed by category. You'll find art and furniture, ephemera and rugs nicely displayed.

In the middle of the Trail you'll find Antiques at Mayfair, housed in two big old chicken barns in Amherst, (603) 595-7531 and (603) 598-9250. The buildings (nicely cleaned) offer a terrific setting for the many dealers who display furniture and accessories, clothing, collectibles, books and glassware in a wide range of ages and prices. Several other group shops are on the Amherst stretch. Look for The Golf Guy and His & Her Antiques, (603) 881-7722, where items are divided with the clothing, dolls and jewelry on the one side and sports memorabilia on the other.

There are several nice shops right on the Milford Oval (Union Square), which is where the Trail bends around the Souhegan River. The collection at Milford Antiques, (603) 672-2311, includes lots of intriguing religious items as well as furniture and china. Sandi's Antiques, (603) 672-5448 has a nice assortment of collectibles, while the Alphabet Soup Company, (603) 673-1033, features a combination of antiques and reproduction furniture and accessories for the home and garden.

Bell Hill Antiques

155 N.H. Rt. 101, Bedford
• (603) 472-5580

This shop looks small on the outside, but the selection inside the New England cape is delightful. It's a multi-dealer shop specializing in American country artifacts, which are displayed in room settings so you can imagine them at home. The store is open daily year-round.

Big Kids Collectables

14 East Broadway, Derry
• (603) 437-1952

This downtown Derry shop specializes in antique and collectible toys and games (and has some new stuff too). It has a great selection of Lionel trains, antique jukeboxes and pinball machines and shelves full of things that will have you saying, "I had one of those!" It's open Tuesday through Saturday year round.

Log Cabin Antiques and Collectibles

182 Rockingham Rd., Londonderry • (603) 434-7068

This group shop has a great selection of household items, collectible ephemera, jewelry, comic books and dolls. It's open every day except Monday and Wednesday year round. The shop has 25 dealers and most items are pre-1950's 20th century. You'll find pottery, depression glass and cookie jars as well as larger pieces such as sideboards.

Used and Antiquarian Books

Mori Books

141 N.H. Rte. 101-A, Amherst • (603) 882-BOOK

This wonderful shop is crammed with a huge selection of antique books and ephemera as well as inexpensive paperbacks. Everything is in good order and easy to find, and owner Richard Mori remembers what you're collecting and keeps an eye out for special "finds" for you. This store has one of the best selections of children's series books we've seen. Other specialties are Boy Scout memorabilia and Tasha Tudor books.

Seacoast Region

Shops

Antiques Alley

U.S. Rt. 4 from Dover to Chichester

This is the granddaddy of the antiques zones in New Hampshire, and at this point it's a self-perpetuating ethos: Every time a building on U.S. 4 is for sale, everyone's first thought is "What a great place for an antiques shop!" Not all of the antiques shops along the road are technically part of the Antiques Alley group, whose 14 members commit to staying open year round. There are probably 40 shops along this 25-mile stretch of U.S. 4. You'll find all manner of stores here, from The Barn in Epsom, (603) 435-8744, a delightfully casual collective shop with tables spread with ephemera and auto parts as well as genuine antiques, to the very nice Sleigh Bell Antiques in Northwood, (603) 942-9988, with its select assortment of fine furniture and accessories. Most of the shops along the Alley are group shops, which makes for an interesting assortment of items but can be distracting if things are grouped by the dealer rather than by type. You'll find that every shop has it's own system for organization. It's always a good idea to ask if you've got a specific wish list.

We especially like Willow Hollow Antiques in Northwood, (603) 942-5739, because the display is orderly: All the kitchenware is together, games and toys are grouped in cabinets and counters, etc. The various dealers have coded tags which keeps the bookkeeping straight. Special treats at Willow Hollow are old postcards of New Hampshire, filed by town, and a huge case of antique marbles. Coveway Corner Antiques in Northwood, (603) 942-7500, has an intriguing assortment of household goods and toys, including items from the 1950s and '60s as well as plenty from the 1800s.

Antiques Avenue

N.H. Rt. 125 from Plaistow to Lee

This miniature of Antiques Alley intersects with that mother lode of antiques at the Lee traffic circle. Red Bell Antiques Co-op in Kingston, (603) 642-5641, is particularly strong on collectible glassware and china. Carriage Towne Antiques and Uniques in Kingston, (603) 642-7085, is a new group shop committed to keeping the quality of goods high and prohibiting reproductions. Kingston's Antiques and Collectibles in Kingston, (603) 642-8535, has a large variety of all kinds of antiques and a truly amazing assortment of collectibles: Elvis and Disney as well as Hummel. Brentwood Antiques, (603) 679-1500, in the Castle at Brentwood shopping center features "Dealer Day" the second Thursday of each

month — a chance to talk with the specialists about their offerings. Plaistow Commons in Plaistow, (603) 382-3621, has a section specializing in furniture to complement the extensive display of its 200-dealer shop.

Ubiquitous Antiques

284-286 Central Ave., Dover
• (603) 749-9093

It's hard to believe that one store holds all the assortment of furniture, accessories, ephemera and collectibles that you'll find here. Turnover stores is high, so check frequently if you're looking for something specific. The store is open Tuesday through Saturday.

Antiques on Lincoln Street

50 Lincoln St., Exeter
• (603) 772-0040

This group shop offers a nice selection of country and Victorian furniture, glassware, artwork and accessories. The two-story shop has a general line of antiques. Much of the furniture has been refinished so it's a good place to look if you aren't in the mood for a project. It's open every day except Sunday.

Antiques at 161 Court Street

161 Court St., Portsmouth
• (603) 431-5599

This shop specializes in high-quality antiques, and it's nicely arranged to display the beautiful furniture, accessories and china, mostly from estates around the Seacoast area. On Thursdays the shop owners will appraise items you bring into the shop. The store is open Tuesday through Saturday year round.

Antiques at Rye Center

655 Wallis Rd., Rye
• (603) 964-8999

This is a high-quality shop where the antiques are handled and displayed with great care. Detailed labels on the antiques help novices understand what something is or why it's worth that price and sometimes give you a sense of the history of the particular piece of furniture, household object, toy or decorative craft. The store is open every day.

The Wingate Collection

94 Portsmouth Ave., Stratham
• (603) 778-4849

This shop in an antique Colonial home offers a great selection of furniture — chests and trunks, benches and washstands, tables and cupboards along with lovely accessories. It specializes in French Canadian antiques, but the collection is not limited to those. It's open every day year round.

Used and Antiquarian Books

Northwood Old Books

U.S. Rt. 4, Northwood
• (603) 942-8107

This is a very well-organized shop with a great selection. They have a nice assortment of children's books and an extensive collection of gardening and cookbooks. Most interesting to us was one of the larger assortments of New Hampshire town histories we've seen.

Bob's Books

150 Congress St., Portsmouth
• (603) 427-1323

This antiquarian book dealer specializes in religion and history, but most of his 40,000 volumes cover the whole spectrum of used and antique books. He does appraisals and searches, so if you can't find what you need to complete your collection, leave your name, and he'll try to find it.

INSIDERS' TIP

Antique stores are great places to find furnishings for small rooms or hard-to-fit nooks and crannies around the house. People were not as large 150 years ago, and everything from desks to beds were made on a smaller scale than much of the furniture built today.

Portsmouth Bookshop
1 Islington St., Portsmouth
• (603) 433-4406

This historic mansion (built in 1720) makes a great setting for this enormous collection of books. Specialties here are children's books and art books, but you're sure to find something you like no matter what your interests.

Lakes Region

While the Seacoast and the Merrimack Valley have their alleys and avenues, there is no strip of antique shops in the Lakes Region, where the roads wind and thread their way across narrows and down points. Instead there is a nice brochure known simply as "The Yellow Map" that points out various shops. It's available at visitors centers. There is also a nice cluster of antique shops in downtown Meredith, around the Mill Falls Marketplace.

Remember When
52 Summer St., Bristol • (603) 744-2191

This shop has a broad assortment of ephemera, books, jewelry and other small pieces (salt and pepper shakers, teapots, etc.). Beads and buttons are a particular specialty here. The owners are experts at restringing beaded jewelry. In winter (November through April), the store is only open on Friday and Saturday The rest of the year it's open every day but Wednesday.

Almost All Antiques
100 New Salem St., Laconia
• (603) 527-0043

Whether you find the name intriguing or cautionary, you'll find the selection in this group shop worthwhile. There is a nice variety of furniture, including some primitives, lots of art pieces, some art deco and plenty of accessories. Despite the name, their policy is "no reproductions." The store is open every day year round.

Country Tyme Antiques and Collectibles
U.S. Rt. 3, Laconia
• (603) 524-2686

More than 150 dealers display their wares here in this two-level shop. You'll be pleased to find memorabilia and ephemera nicely displayed along with toys, books and postcards. Glassware, lamps and furniture are all included in this huge shop. The store is open daily year round. It also has a gift shop for used (but not antique) items and reproductions.

Burlwood Antiques Center
U.S. Rt. 3, Meredith
• (603) 279-6387

Insiders never fail to mention this as a great place. It's housed in a 19th-century barn, and the three floors contain what many antiquers believe is the largest selection of antiques in the Lakes Region. The selection is varied, as you would expect with 170 dealers, but you can count on finding glassware and paintings, advertising items and paper goods. One whole floor is set aside for furniture. It's open daily May through October. The rest of the year it's closed.

Lakewood Station
N.H. Rt. 16, Ossipee
• (603) 539-7414

Ossipee is developing an antiques zone of its own, and this multi-dealer shop is a big piece of the picture. The shop, which is open every day, features general antiques including furniture, glass and china. They also have some collectibles.

Treasure Hunt Antiques
465 N.H. Rt. 16, Ossipee
• (603) 539-7877

This is a big multi-dealer shop with something for every taste. It has a variety of collectibles, furniture, old books and ephemera, and the dealers keep their booths up with frequent changes of stock. The shop is open daily year round.

Elkin's Trash & Treasures
26-28 N. Main St., Rochester
• (603) 332-1848

Here's a shop for a day when you want to poke around with the thrilling anticipation of what you'll find. Elkin's has a nice mix of the ordinary and the unusual, both antiques and collectibles, and a variety of furniture styles.

The owner specializes in art deco items. The shop is open Thursday through Monday year round.

Dow's Corner Shop

N.H. Rt. 171, Tuftonboro Corner
• (603) 539-4790

Hands-down, this is the most-frequently mentioned antiques shop in the Lakes Region — possibly in the whole state. The big old barn is stuffed with antiques of every description. One room features china and glass, and the owners are cabinetmakers with an eye for fine details in furniture. They love to explain antiques and swap stories. Dow's Corner Shop is open every day from May through October and will open for you in winter if you call them.

Used and Antiquarian Books

Mary Robertson-Books

U.S. Rt. 3, South, Meredith
• (603) 279-8750

This shop has a delightful selection of both old and new books. It specializes in children's books and craft books but also has a good general selection and a large section of New England titles.

White Mountains and Great North Woods Regions

Shops

Carousel Antiques

Berkley St., Bethlehem
• (603) 869-5755

Once you've figured out the outside paint scheme of your new Victorian home, take a trip to Bethlehem for antique furnishings. You'll find bedroom, dining room and living room furniture. Wash stands and dressers complement the bedsteads, and buffets and china closets match the dining room table and chairs. All the furniture is hand-carved. The shop features just about everything you might have found in a Victorian home including lamps, desks and bookcases. Call ahead for directions and to make sure someone is minding the store.

Checkered Past Antiques

154 Guider Rd., Bethlehem
• (603) 444-6628

This 100-year-old barn is stocked with a variety of goods. Checkered Past is a small multi-dealer shop. You'll find antique furniture as well as quality reproductions.

If you can't afford an authentic Colonial table, you might want to ask about the custom-built reproduction furniture that is built here. The furniture is made from tiger maple. The glass and china are the real thing and another strength of the shop. Guider Road is just before the junction of U.S. Route 302 and Interstate 93. The shop is open every day all year except for Wednesdays from October to July.

Chris Curran Antiques and Collectibles

E. Main St., near the Maplewood Country Club, Bethlehem
• (603) 869-2089

You'll find a interesting general line of goods here, not so much antiques as collectibles and knickknacks. You'll enjoy the glass and china that might remind you of your grandmother's house. You'll find some furniture here too. It's not easy to be specific because turnover is high. The shop is open every day in summer and foliage season. Call ahead during late fall, winter and spring.

Tara

60 Glen Rd., Gorham
• (603) 466-2624

This shop specializes in antique prints and maps. The maps focus on the White Mountains, with much of the material from around 1850. Some older state and county maps are also available. Prints include lithographs such as those by Currier and Ives. The shop is open all year, but it's always a good idea to call ahead.

North Conway Antiques and Collectibles

White Mountain Hwy., North Conway
• (603) 356-6661

This is one of the largest group shops in Northern New England with displays from more than 75 dealers. You might find some genuine antiques, and you'll definitely find a wide selection of collectibles. Whether your desire is soft drink memorabilia or Depression glass, you're likely to find it here. The shop is open every day all year.

Potato Barn Antiques Center

U.S. Rt. 3, Northumberland
• (603) 636-2611

This is an eclectic collection of goods representing several dealers. It's a good spot to find old tools and vintage clothing. You'll find fun costume jewelry, which, if it's not too expensive, is always a good idea for the grandchildren's dress-up trunk. The Potato Barn has 6,500 square feet of space and new merchandise coming in every day. The center is open Thursday through Monday from April through December. From January through March you can shop Friday through Sunday.

Used and Antiquarian Books

Titles and Tales

73 Main St., Littleton
• (603) 444-1345

Book lovers beware! You could get in serious trouble here. The two floors and 4,000 square feet of space hold more than 60,000 volumes. Prices range from $1.50 to $1,000 per book. You'll find a great selection of general interest books as well as special categories such as New Hampshire and White Mountains literature, militaria and an excellent theology selection. The store is open every day year round.

Dartmouth-Lake Sunapee Region

Shops

Colonial Farm Antiques

N.H. Rt. 11, New London
• (603) 526-6121

At Colonial Farm, 12 dealers offer a variety of items. You'll find 19th-century furniture, Oriental rugs and American quilts. Given that New London has three nearby lakes, this is a great place for decoys as well as prints featuring trout and other fish. The shop is open every day from Memorial Day Weekend through the end of October. The store is 2 miles east of Exit 11 off I-89.

Priscilla Drake Antiques

33 Main St., New London
• (603) 526-6514

Be sure and make this Main Street stop part of your New London tour. Even if you're not in the market for buying, you'll have a great time browsing through the high-quality mix of items from four dealers. A few individual consignments are always on hand too. Furniture might include slant-front desks and chests of drawers. Other items include silver, quilts and daguerreotypes. Specialties also include china and glassware. The shop is open every day from Memorial Day through mid-October.

INSIDERS' TIP

Learn what's involved in collecting by starting small. If you like china, see how difficult it would be to collect a full set of a particular period pattern. You don't have to buy it, but do take notes and keep track of where it turns up. In observing and learning the availability and price variations, you will begin to acquire the skills required for collecting.

Colonial Antiques Market

Colonial Plaza, N.H. Rt. 12A, West Lebanon • (603) 298-8132

This is both an antique center and a flea market. Most of the action is on Sunday, when you'll find more than 60 dealers buying, selling and trading their wares in the outdoor area. The rest of the week you'll have fun looking at the indoor booths, which specialize in everything from militaria to prints and paintings. Additionally, you'll find a good collection of 20th-century furniture and household items indoors. The market is open all year and is at Exit 20 off I-89.

Kearsarge Lodge Antiques

Kearsarge Valley Rd., Wilmot • (603) 927-4594

The specialty here is Americana, including folk art, painted items and architectural garden pieces. You'll find tramp art, Adirondack specialties and early toys. Boat and ship models are another specialty as well as antique fishing gear and lots of beautiful decoys. The country furniture selection is very strong with lots of pine tables and cupboards. To round out the wide selection, expect to see oil paintings and lots of china and glassware. The Kearsarge Lodge is open every day except in winter, when it might be closed Monday and Tuesday.

Used and Antiquarian Books

Books By The Lake

N.H. Rt. 114, Bradford • (603) 938-2315

You'll find more than 45,000 volumes of both general interest and scholarly books in this delightful store overlooking Lake Massasecum. You can find a used paperback here that's perfect for a lakeside read or a special volume or two on Irish studies. Cookbooks and children's books are another specialty. The shop is open on Wednesday through Sunday year round. Monday and Tuesday hours are by chance, with chance being on your side more often in the summer than in the winter.

Monadnock Region

Shops

The Fitzwilliam and Richmond Antiques Shop Guide lists 14 antiques stores that are within just a few miles of each other on or nearby N.H. Route 119, the scenic main road connecting the towns. Send a self-addressed, stamped envelope to Carol Hayward, 122 Fitzwilliam Road, Richmond, NH 03470, to receive a free brochure with details about each shop, including addresses, phone numbers and areas of special interest. The antiques shops in Richmond and Fitzwilliam make a fine centerpiece for a day in the country. As we head toward the 21st century, it's nice to take a ride back to the 19th. See our Annual Events chapter for information on the Fitzwilliam Antiques Fair.

The Alstead Group

N.H. Rt. 123, Alstead • (603) 835-7810

You won't find too many collectibles here, but you will see period antiques specializing in historic Americana. Look for country furniture, militaria and toys. Other than American products, the shop specializes in Oriental porcelain. The shop is always closed on Wednesdays, and from January to April it is also closed on Thursdays.

Bloomin' Antiques

N.H. Rt. 12, 3 miles south of N.H. Rt. 119, Fitzwilliam • (603) 585-6688

Goods from about 35 dealers are represented here with items from both the 18th and 19th centuries. This is a good place to look if you like Orientalia. As with all multi-dealer shops, you can find a wide variety of goods depending on the day you look. Chances are you'll always see a good selection of lamps, clocks and toys. Bloomin' Antiques is open every day throughout the year, but you should call ahead on Tuesdays to make sure someone will be in.

Fitzwilliam Antique Center

Junction of N.H. Rts. 12 and 119, Fitzwilliam
• (603) 585-9092

More than 40 dealers show off their 19th-century treasures in the heart of the Monadnock region. You'll find everything from rugs and furniture to glass and china. If you're looking for just the right touch for your mountain cabin or hunting lodge, you'll enjoy the wide selection of country accessories. The center is open every day all year.

The Barn of Hancock Village

4 Main St., Hancock
• (603) 525-3529

This shop is just across the street from the beautiful Hancock Inn (see our Bed and Breakfasts and Country Inns chapter) and is a fun stop to keep you in the mood of the 19th century. The shop specializes in furniture, but you'll also find china, silver and glassware. And in case you're wondering what kind of artwork will look just right with your period purchases, you'll enjoy the gallery of contemporary art featuring the work of local artists. The shop is open from mid-May through the end of October. It is closed on Mondays.

Antiques at Colony Mill

222 West St., Keene
• (603) 358-6343

More than 200 dealers have booths in this refurbished old mill complex. You'll find everything from period and country furniture to silver, art pottery and prints. Antique toys, dolls and quilts are next to prints and paintings. This is the ultimate place to browse and see a wide variety of antiques and collectibles. This multi-dealer market is open every day all year

Noah's Ark Antiques Center

N.H. Rt. 101, Wilton
• (603) 654-2595

You'll find items from 234 dealers in this packed-to-the-gills shop. The parking lot is always full, and we understand that lots of dealers shop here. We like to Christmas shop here, which should tell you that you can find a good supply of affordable collectibles. China, silver, glassware and jewelry are here in abundance. In fact, there's just about everything except large pieces of furniture. You might find a child's chair, but this isn't the place to look for a sofa. This group shop is open every day all year.

Used and Antiquarian Books

Rainy Day Books

N.H. Rt. 119, Fitzwilliam
• (603) 585-3448

You'll find many wonderful books here, with prices beginning at $1 and continuing upward. Two categories are particularly strong. Rainy Day Books has the one of the most extensive collections on radio and radio broadcasting in the country. You'll find technical as well as historical books on this subject.

The other real strength is books on European monarchy; the store is a leading dealer nationwide in this subject. Cookbooks, books on polar expeditions and mountaineering and books on textile arts are other strong collections. And if you find yourself captivated by the towns of the region and want to look for books on a particular town's history, this is the spot. The store is open every day but Wednesday from mid-April through mid-November.

INSIDERS' TIP

"Ephemera" is a collective term for all those wonderful old magazines and advertising trinkets, postcards, souvenirs and other assorted "stuff" most of our grandparents threw out long before we were born.

Eagle Books

19 West St., Keene

• (603) 357-8721

New Hampshire town histories are well represented in this general antiquarian shop. You aren't likely to find used paperback mysteries, but you might well find a lovely hardback edition of *Jane Eyre* for less than the price of a modern paperback edition. New stock comes in nearly every day. You'll find lots of American history too, with a strong selection of books written in the 1930s for the Writers Project of the WPA (Works Progress Administration). The shop is open every day but Sunday all year.

Homestead Bookshop

N.H. Rt. 101, just east of the village, Marlborough

• (603) 876-4213

Homestead Bookshop is a landmark in the region. It has been in business for more than 28 years and has more than 45,000 volumes to explore. You'll find paperbacks priced at eight for $1 on the porch. Inside prices increase, with books ranging from $1 to several hundred dollars. A fun trip down memory lane is the juvenile series books. Robert Kinney, 1997 President of the New Hampshire Antiquarian Booksellers Association, is the proprietor.

Beyond Words

N.H. Rt. 101, Wilton

• (603) 654-6404

Be sure and stop by Beyond Words as you drive along N.H. Route 101 in Wilton. You'll see the store just before the southbound turnoff for N.H. Route 31. You'll find more than 50,000 books on just about any subject you can think of, but owner Deborah Robinson says the shop's particular strengths are regional books, children's books and books on religion. We know someone who found a copy of an old Seahunt adventure book based on the Lloyd Bridges television series. You'll find everything from used books that cost a dollar to first editions and out-of-print editions costing hundreds. The store is open every day.

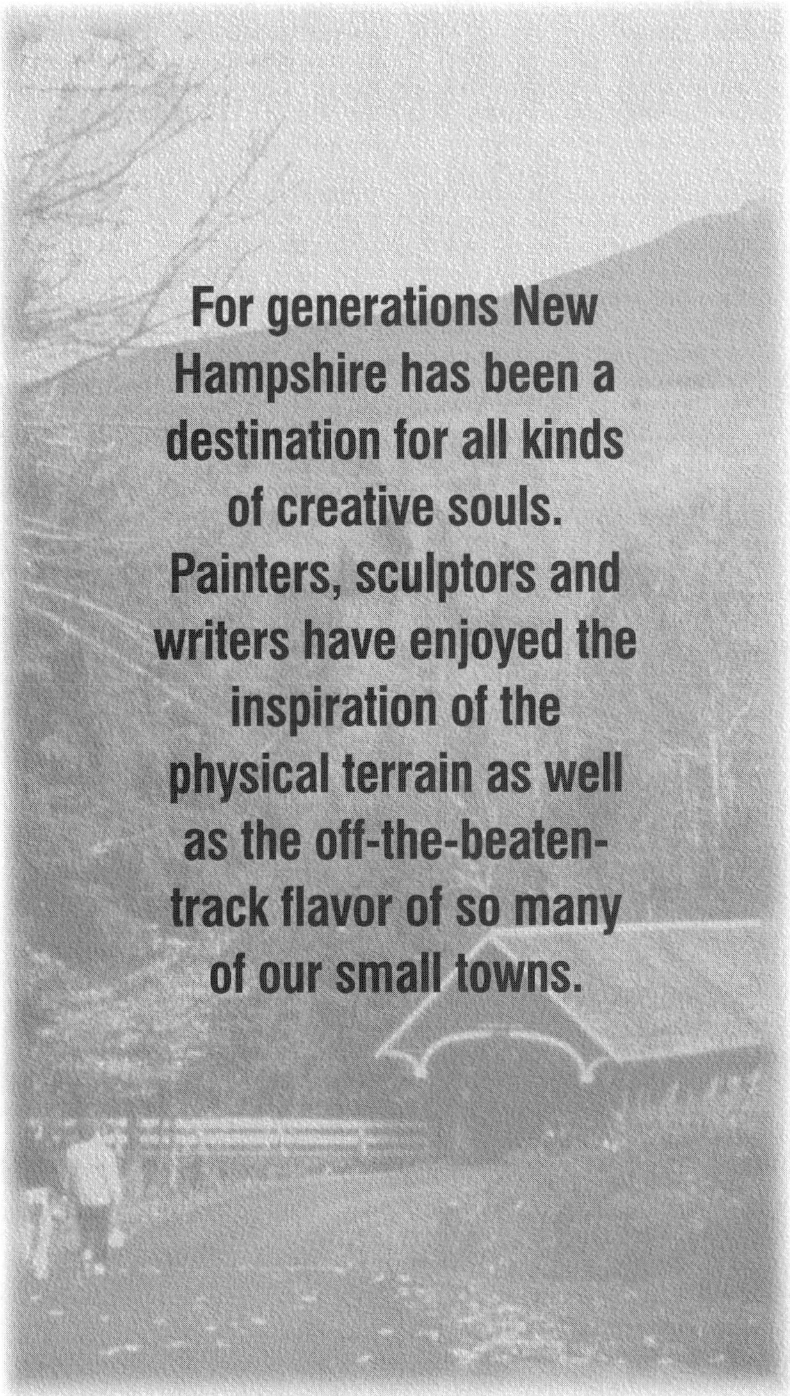

For generations New Hampshire has been a destination for all kinds of creative souls. Painters, sculptors and writers have enjoyed the inspiration of the physical terrain as well as the off-the-beaten-track flavor of so many of our small towns.

Attractions

New Hampshire has been attracting visitors for nearly 200 years. The first path to the summit of Mount Washington, the star attraction of the White Mountains region with an elevation of 6,288 feet, was cleared in 1819. Mount Monadnock in that eponymous region was an early destination for residents of nearby Massachusetts. Besides the clean mountain air, they enjoyed both the cool water and abundant fish in the lakes and ponds in the region. You'll see that in many cases our wonderful attractions continue to take advantage of our natural resources. We also have a rich history, and many of our landmarks have been preserved or re-created for today's tourist.

For generations New Hampshire has been a destination for all kinds of creative souls. Painters, sculptors and writers have enjoyed the inspiration of the physical terrain as well as the off-the-beaten-path flavor of so many of our small towns. But we appreciate that small-town fun might need a little enhancement to fully serve modern families, so you'll find lots of planned entertainment and specific tourist considerations throughout the state. Whether it's water slides, historic homes or mountain vistas atop your list, each region in our state offers something for everyone.

It's important to note that most attractions are seasonal. The season varies slightly by region and attraction, but in general, the "yes, we are open" season begins in mid-May with weekend hours and expands to daily operation after Memorial Day. Some attractions go back to weekend-only operation after Labor Day and close down as the last leaves fall from the trees. The high tourist season in New Hampshire is from July 4 through the end of the foliage season in October. If a particular attraction is tops on your list, and you plan to visit during May or October, we suggest you call in advance to make sure of the hours during those months.

Merrimack Valley Region

Canterbury Shaker Village

Exit 18 off I-93, Canterbury
• (603) 783-9511

The Shakers were a religious community that thrived throughout the eastern United States during the late 18th and 19th centuries. Although their numbers have dwindled (there are a few Shakers still living in Maine), they left a legacy of simple living, simple pleasures and simple joy, which are reflected in the architecture, furniture, recipes and music we still value today. The Canterbury Village, once home to as many as 300 people, is now open to visitors. The last Shaker to live here, Sister Ethel Hudson, died in 1992. Experts on Shaker heritage explain the community lifestyle and demonstrate traditional crafts. Light lunches are available from the Summer Kitchen. (See our Restaurants chapter for fine dining at The Creamery.) The village is open weekends only in April, November and December, and daily from 10 AM to 5 PM May through October. Admission, including the guided 90-minute tour, costs $9 for adults, $4 for kids ages 6 to 15 and is free for children younger than 6. A family ticket costs $22.

Christa McAuliffe Planetarium

3 Institute Dr., Concord
• (603) 271-7827

This state-of-the art planetarium is dedicated to the memory of New Hampshire teacher Christa McAuliffe, who died in the explosion of the space shuttle *Challenger* in 1986. Hands-on exhibits about the history of space exploration are informative and pass the time while you wait to "board" a spaceship for your show. The shows involve the audience through interactive technology — everyone votes at crucial points in the narrative, and the outcome determines what planets or solar systems the spaceship will visit next. The story lines are a bit farfetched, but kids enjoy the game. (There are different shows recommended for different ages; see our Kidstuff chapter for details.) The photography, including shots from the Hubble telescope, is truly exceptional. Walk-ins are usually seated without trouble, but reservations are accepted and a good idea if your group is large. The planetarium also sponsors free Skywatch events and celebrations of astronomical events. Open year round, it is closed Mondays, major holidays and the last two weeks in September. Admission is $6 for adults and $3 for seniors and youngsters. To get there, take Exit 15E off I-93, then Exit 1 off I-393.

Museum of New Hampshire History

Eagle Sq., Concord • (603) 226-3189

The museum moved into this renovated factory/warehouse in 1995, preserving the historic building and providing for display of the many artifacts in the society's collection. Gather around the campfire and hear an Abenaki tale, see an ancient dugout canoe and a historic Concord Coach, and climb the replica fire tower for an eagle's-eye view of Concord. The museum is open year round, Tuesday through Saturday 9:30 AM until 5 PM, Sunday 12 to 5 PM and Thursday and Friday evenings until 8:30 PM. It closes on holidays. The museum is open on Mondays during the summer. Admission is $5 for adults, $2.50 for 6 to 18 year olds. Family admission is $15. It's always free for children younger than 6 and for everyone on Thursday and Friday after 5PM. Parking is free; have your ticket validated at the desk. (This museum is one stop on the Coach and Eagle Trail walking tour. See our Close-up in this chapter.)

New Hampshire State House

107 N. Main St., Concord
• (603) 271-2154

New Hampshire's State House is the oldest state capitol in which a legislature (the country's largest) still meets in its original chambers. Monuments and statues on the grounds honor New Hampshire natives, notably Daniel Webster, John Parker Hale (the first person ever elected to the U.S. Senate as an abolitionist), Franklin Pierce and John Stark. A self-guided tour shows you 150 portraits of major political figures, the Hall of Flags, murals and documents. The visitors center is open weekdays 8 AM to 4:30 PM and closes on major holidays. Admission is free.

The Pierce Manse

14 Penacook St., Concord
• (603) 225-2068, (603) 224-7668

The Pierce Manse is the home of the only New Hampshire citizen ever elected President (although Daniel Webster tried). Although he is little known today, Franklin Pierce was a hero of the war with Mexico and at the time was the youngest President elected. He and his wife had three sons; one died at three days old, one died in this house at age 2 and the oldest was killed in a railroad accident two months before his father's inauguration. The manse, which houses period furnishings and family memorabilia, is open June 15 through Labor Day, Monday through Friday 11 AM to 3 PM. Admission is $3 for adults; $1 for students age 12 to 18 and $.50 for children younger than 12.

Taylor Up and Down Sawmill

Island Pond Rd., Derry • (603) 271-3556

Although this 19th-century sawmill has been completely restored and is functional, it is presently not running due to state budget cuts. You can picnic on the grounds. The Division of Forests and Lands hopes to raise funds to operate the mill for visitors again in the future. The mill is a wonderful peek at the history of an industry that is still a critical part of the New Hampshire economy.

Robert Frost Farm

NH Rt. 28, Derry • (603) 432-3091

This is the place where Robert Frost proved he was a much better poet than farmer! The farmhouse, typical of New Hampshire buildings of the late 1800s, is open for visitors. Some of the furnishings belonged to the Frost family; others are authentic to the turn of the century, when he lived here. Nature trails on the site enable visitors to enjoy the same natural wonders that inspired Frost's poetry. Guided tours and a video are available. The buildings are open Thursday through Monday from 10 AM to 5 PM in summer (mid-June through Labor Day). From mid-May to mid-June and Labor Day to Columbus Day they're open for the same hours on Saturday and Sunday only. Admission is $2.50 for adults and free for anyone younger than 18. The grounds are open without charge year round.

Stonyfield Farm Yogurt

10 Burton Dr., Londonderry
• (603) 437-4040

From cow to incubator to cooler, learn how yogurt is made. Try a sample and take home some "moo"chandise (attention, cow fans). The factory is open Tuesday through Friday from 9:30 AM to 5:00 PM, and from 9:30 AM to 4:00 PM on Saturdays. Tours begin every hour from 10 AM until 4 PM except Saturdays when the last tour begins at 3 PM.

Amoskeag Fishways/Fish Ladder

Fletcher St., Exit 6 off I-293, Manchester
• (603) 626-FISH

Because the Amoskeag dam prevented fish from swimming upriver to spawn, Public Service Company constructed a fish ladder here — really a series of "water elevators" that carry the migrating fish up and over the dam. An underwater window allows visitors to watch as hundreds of fish, mostly alewife, swim past. Keep an eye out for the occasional Atlantic salmon (pictures painted on the wall will help you identify species). An audiovisual show and guided tours explain both the historic significance of the site, where native Americans came to fish each spring, and the waterpower generating plant still operating today. In recent years the Fishways people have joined forces with New Hampshire Audubon to run workshops on watershed protection and wildlife restoration, including monitoring the peregrine falcon now wintering in Manchester. Call for schedule.

Admission is free. The fishways are open Monday through Saturday from 9:30 AM to 5 PM except when the fish are running (May 5 to June 14); then they're open daily 9 AM to 6 PM.

Lawrence L. Lee Scouting Museum

Bodwell Rd., Exit 5 off I-93 at Camp Carpenter, Manchester
• (603) 669-8919

This museum houses scouting memorabilia from 1900 to the present, including uniforms, collectibles from international scouting organizations, commemorative buckles, stamps and periodicals. New Hampshire's Boy Scout/astronaut Alan Shepard donated the flag he carried to the moon and back. Picnic areas and nature trails on the grounds make this a great family stop. The museum is open Saturdays only from September to June and daily from 10 AM to 4 PM in July and August. Admission is free, but donations are accepted.

Anheuser-Busch Brewery Tours, Clydesdale Hamlet

Exit 10 off Everett Tpke., Merrimack
• (603) 595-1202

One-hour tours of the brewery end with the opportunity to sample the best-selling beer in America (soft drinks are also available). The Bavarian-style hamlet is home to the famous eight-horse hitch, and the Clydesdales welcome visitors. These truly impressive animals are worth the visit. Tours are free. It's open all year, Memorial Day through Labor Day daily from 9:30 AM to 5 PM, May 1 through May 23 and September 2 through October 31 daily from 10 AM to 4 PM, and November 1 through April 30 Thursday through Monday 10 AM to 4 PM. It's closed major holidays.

America's Stonehenge

Off NH Rt. 111-E, North Salem
• (603) 893-8300

You'll be amazed by these stone-age monuments: walls and roofs constructed from slabs of stone weighing 4 to 11 tons and a calendar circle of standing monoliths, all built without tools by an unknown culture thousands of years before any known European descendants of "the other Stonehenge" builders arrived on the scene. Take a self-guided tour, watch the informational video and visit the museum. It's open special hours on astronomical dates such as equinoxes and solstices.

This site is open 9 AM to 7 PM every day from the summer solstice (around June 21) to Labor Day. From April 1 to the solstice and Labor Day to November 30, it's open daily from 10 AM to 5 PM. They also open for celestial events during winter: winter solstice in December and spring equinox in March. Call for details of those observances. Admission is $7 for adults, $5.50 for seniors (older than 62), $5 for teens ages 13 to 18 and $3 for children ages 6 to 12. Children younger than six are admitted free.

Canobie Lake Park

Exit 2 off I-93, Salem • (603) 893-3506

First opened in 1902, Canobie still features an antique carousel, a 1936 (but more recently rebuilt) roller coaster, and a paddlewheel boat ride. But there's plenty of zoom for today's thrill-seekers too, with four roller coasters and more than 75 games and attractions. The Corkscrew is 73 feet high, and Insider kids report it's awesome! A scaled-down section of the park enables younger visitors to enjoy themselves without scaring their parents to death. Fireworks in July and August, clowns and other acts, swimming and food galore round out the fun.

The park is open weekends mid-April to Memorial Day and Labor Day to late September and daily from Memorial Day to Labor Day, noon to 10 PM. It closes Sundays at 6 PM. Adult tickets are $19, children less than 48 inches tall get in for $12, and there's no charge for children younger than 2. Enter the park after 5 PM for just $12. Discount coupons are frequently available in local businesses.

Seacoast Region

Woodman Institute

182-190 Central Ave., Dover • (603) 742-1038

This complex includes the Damm Garrison House, built around 1675, and two houses from the early 19th century, including the home of John Hale, abolitionist senator from New Hampshire. The Damm Garrison house, a hand-hewn log cabin with portholes to allow for defense in Indian raids, houses a collection of early American household tools and farm implements. The Woodman house shelters an eclectic collection that includes specimens of most of the region's native mammals, rocks and butterflies. Penacook artifacts are displayed in another room, and President Lincoln's saddle highlights the Civil War collection. The third building, Hale House, is filled with antique furniture from the time of Senator Hale's residency and many historical items. The Institute is open 12:30 to 4:30 PM Wednesday through Sunday from April through January. It only opens Saturday afternoons from January to April. No admission is charged, but donations are encouraged.

American Independence Museum

One Governors Ln., Exeter • (603) 772-2622

On a beautiful 2-acre site in the heart of Exeter's historic downtown, the museum is housed in the National Historic Register's Ladd-Gilman House. Exeter was the first capital of New Hampshire, and the museum focuses on the Colonial period and the time of the American Revolution. The extensive collection includes two draft copies of the U.S. Constitution with editorial notes. The museum is open May 1 to October 31, Wednesday through Sunday from noon to 5 PM. Admission to the park is free. The museum tour is $4 for adults, $3 for seniors, $2 for ages 6 to 18 and free for children younger than 6. Group discounts are also available. Folsom Tavern, saved from demolition and moved to its present location on Spring Street in 1929, is managed by the museum. Tours of the tavern may be arranged.

The third weekend in July the museum hosts a festival celebrating the signing of the Declaration of Independence (the official copy, which took two weeks to arrive in Exeter by horse from Philadelphia, is housed in the museum.) See our Annual Events chapter for details.

Casino Cascade Water Slide

D St., Hampton Beach • (603) 926-4541

Speed slides, slaloms and a splash pool — here's a fun place to cool off with a swish down one of four water slides. The Casino is open 9 AM to 9 PM daily from Memorial Day to Labor Day. Prices are $1 for one ride, $4 for five rides or $16 for an all-day pass. From 9 to 11 AM you can slide as much as you like for $6, and from 6 to 9 PM you can ride for $7.

Hampton Beach

Ocean Blvd., Hampton
• (603) 926-8718, (800) 438-2826

Hampton Beach is both a community and an attraction. Hampton Beach is, in the words of our youth, a "happening." There's an old-fashioned boardwalk, with arcade games from your grandparent's childhood as well as your child's. The indoor amusement centers are open year round, but Hampton Beach really comes alive in the summer. Hear free concerts on the beach every night, and see the fireworks on Wednesdays and holidays. Try kite-flying and parasailing and dancing under the stars. There's a playground for the kids and nightclubs for the grown-ups (see our Nightlife chapter). And, oh yes, there's a beach! Two miles of white sand and gentle surf — but remember, the Atlantic is *c-c-cold* up here!

Tuck Memorial Museum

40 Park Ave., Hampton • (603) 929-0781

The museum's collection includes early furniture, farm equipment and pictures. Children will be interested in the re-created 1850s school room and firefighting museum. The museum is open from 6 to 8 PM on Wednesday and 1 to 4 PM Thursday, Friday and Sunday from July 1 through Labor Day. During June it's only open on Sunday afternoons. There is no charge for admission.

Flag Hill Winery

NH Rte. 155, Lee • (603) 659-2949

You've heard that proverb about "when life hands you lemons?" Well when life handed Frank Reinhold a huge crop of lemons, he didn't make lemonade: he made wine. The New Hampshire Winery went out of business just as his first commercial-sized harvest of grapes ripened, so Frank pressed, bottled and aged them himself. The result was not just a delightful selection of red and white wines but a whole new attraction for the Seacoast: a winery. In a 1796 post-and-beam barn on the 250-year-old farm, the Reinholds opened a visitors center: tasting area, gift shop and function space. A Harvest Festival each September welcomes local people to assist with the picking, stomp barefoot in the barrels of grapes and enjoy a free meal. Tours of the winery are not limited to the harvest season, however: visitors are welcome Wednesday through Sunday from 10 AM to 5 PM year round. There is no charge for tours or tasting, children are welcome and the trails through the vineyard are handicapped—accessible.

Fort Constitution

NH Rt. 1B at U.S. Coast Guard Station, New Castle • No phone

First built in the 1600s and called Fort William and Mary, this fortification was built to defend Portsmouth Harbor. It was captured on December 14, 1774, by New Hampshire Patriots who had been warned by Paul Revere that — you guessed it — the British were coming. Armament taken from the Fort that night was used four months later against the British at the Battle of Bunker Hill in Boston. Interpretive panels guide you through this fascinating glimpse into Colonial America. The fort is open from 10 AM through 5 PM daily year round. Admission is free.

Fort Stark

Wild Rose Ln., New Castle • No phone

This fort, originally constructed in 1746, was rebuilt and updated continually throughout the nation's history. Fort Stark was actively fortified in every war from the American Revolution to World War II, when it was a submarine spotting site. Evidence of construction from various eras makes this a favorite with military buffs, while the spectacular views of Portsmouth Harbor attract more pacifist tourists. The fort is open 8:30 AM to 4:30 PM on weekends in spring and fall and daily from Memorial Day to Labor Day. Admission costs $2.50 for adults and is free for those younger than 18.

Albacore Park

600 Market St., Exit 7 off I-95, Portsmouth • (603) 436-3680

The USS Albacore was a prototype submarine built at the Portsmouth Naval Shipyard and commissioned in 1953. At the time she was the fastest submarine ever designed. Now she sits in the center of this lovely park, within view of Portsmouth Harbor. Visitors are amazed to see how 55 men lived in a 205- by 27-foot teardrop and are moved to remember those who served and died in the Submarine Service through the years. The park, visitors center and Memorial Garden are free and open 9:30 AM to 5:30 PM from May 1 to Columbus Day. Admission to the submarine is $4 for adults, $3 for seniors, $2 for ages 7 to 17 and free for those younger than 7. A family ticket is $10.

Isle of Shoals Steamship Company

Barker Wharf, 315 Market St., Portsmouth
• (603) 431-5500, (800) 441-4620

Narrated cruises of historic Portsmouth Harbor give visitors the opportunity to see the coast and islands as Capt. John Smith did in 1614. Stories and myths abound in this harbor, and the tour guides have secrets to share. Isle of Shoals also offers a lighthouse tour, whale watches, a fall foliage trip to Great Bay Wilderness and many other specialty tours. Added in 1997 was a 45-minute Portsmouth Harbor cruise geared especially for families. Another favorite is the Lobster Clambake Cruise. All trips offer a full galley (seagoing snack bar) and bar service. Reservations are recommended. Tours are scheduled from May 1 to Labor Day. Ticket prices vary by length of cruise: Adults prices range from $15 to $25, children's (ages 3 to 11) prices range from $8 to $16. Senior tickets are $1 off except for dinner cruises. It's free for people younger than 3 and older than 79.

Jackson House

Northwest St., Portsmouth
• (603) 436-3205

This is the oldest house in New Hampshire (built about 1664) and an early example of plank frame (as opposed to log) construction. Step inside and you'll feel you've walked into the 17th century. The apple orchards, filled with old-fashioned cultivars, are a lasting tribute to the agricultural heritage of the earliest colonies.

Jackson House, which is managed by the Society for the Protection of New England Antiquities, is open from 11 AM to 5 PM on Saturday and Sunday from June 1 to October 15. Tours begin every hour on the hour. Admission is $5, $4.50 for senior citizens and $2 for children younger than 12. Town residents and SPNEA members are admitted free.

John Paul Jones House

Middle and State Sts., Portsmouth
• (603) 436-8420

The great sea warrior Jones didn't own this house, but he roomed here. The house was built in 1758. It's now a museum of 18th- and 19th-century artifacts. The house is open to visitors June 1 to mid-October, Monday through Friday 10 AM to 4 PM and Sunday noon to 4 PM. Admission is $5 for adults and $2.50 for children.

John Langdon House

143 Pleasant St., Portsmouth
• (603) 436-3205

Built in 1782, this was the home of John Langdon, one of the leaders of the Patriot raid on Fort William and Mary. Langdon was later governor of New Hampshire. You can still see why George Washington called this "the finest house in Portsmouth." Don't miss the ornate woodwork or the enclosed rose garden. The house is open June 1 to October 15, Wednesday through Sunday from 11 AM to 5 PM. Admission is $5.

Moffatt-Ladd House

154 Market St., Portsmouth
• (603) 436-1118

This house was built in 1763 by a wealthy merchant and later lived in by William Whipple,

INSIDERS' TIP

New Hampshire is a photographer's paradise. Take a few extra minutes and pack those special lenses and filters. If you're an amateur, we suggest picking up one of the simpler cameras that shoot panoramic pictures.

a signer of the Declaration of Independence. The home is ornately paneled and furnished and surrounded by formal gardens graced by a chestnut tree planted in 1776. The house is open from 10 AM to 4 PM Monday through Saturday and 2 to 5 PM Sunday from June 15 to October 15. Admission is $5 for adults and $2 for ages 7 to 12. Children younger than 7 get in free.

Portsmouth Harbor Cruises

Ceres St. Dock, One Harbour Pl., Portsmouth
• (603) 436-8084, (800) 776-0915

The *Heritage* has been cruising Portsmouth Harbor and the inland rivers for 14 years. Take a peaceful sunset cruise along the coast, a jaunt across the open sea to the islands or an exploration of the inland rivers. The cruises last an hour or two. A full bar and galley are available on every trip. (The Heritage can also be chartered for private functions). Prices range from $8.50 to $16 for adults, $7.50 to $15 for seniors and $6 to $9 for children. Children younger than 2 ride for free. Family discounts are available for the morning Harbor cruise. Cruises run May through October. Reservations are strongly recommended, and the schedule varies so call ahead.

Portsmouth Livery Company

Market Sq., Portsmouth
• (603) 427-0044

Take a tour of historic Portsmouth, ride along the waterfront or just enjoy a quick spin around the downtown area in a horse-drawn carriage, complete with handsomely attired driver. Tours range from 5 to 40 minutes and from $10 to $35 per group. Or, for $25 per family, try the "Ride To, Walk Back" tour, which includes admission to the Children's Museum of Portsmouth (see our Kidstuff chapter). Reservations are not required for tours, although the carriages may be booked for special occasions.

Red Hook Ale Brewery

35 Corporate Dr., Portsmouth
• (603) 430-8600

Red Hook started as a microbrewery in 1981 in Seattle, where they established a reputation for producing small batches of distinctive (some would say quirky) ales and porters. In 1996 Red Hook opened an East Coast brewery at the old Pease Air Force base to make its beer available to the growing number of microbrew aficionados in New England. Now partially owned by Anheuser-Busch, Red Hook offers tours of its Bavarian-looking brewery. Watch the brewing and bottling process and, of course, sample the results! Admission is just $1. Call for times.

Rundlet-May House

364 Middle St., Portsmouth
• (603) 436-3205

Here's a sumptuous merchant's mansion, built in 1807. It still has its original landscaping and outbuildings, which is unusual, especially in a city home. The house is open June 1 to October 15, Wednesday through Sunday from noon to 5 PM. Admission costs $5 for adults, $4.50 for seniors and $2 for children ages 6 to 12.

Strawbery Banke Museum

Marcy St., opposite Prescott Park, Portsmouth • (603) 433-1100

When the first Colonists settled in what's now Portsmouth, they found wild strawberries growing on the banks of the Piscataqua River and called their settlement Strawbery Banke. The town received its "new" name of Portsmouth in 1653. The Puddledock subdivision, now site of Strawbery Banke, was developed in 1690. Fifteen buildings in the museum complex have been restored to different historic periods, so a tour of Strawbery Banke takes the visitor on a walk through time from 1690 to 1955. Costumed interpreters stay in character as they describe their daily lives, while other guides introduce the houses and shops, explain the ongoing restoration process and demonstrate methods of boat-building, coopering and other activities. Be sure to step down to the water and sit on the recreated Gundalow and learn about these unique boats which were designed specifically to ride the tides on the Piscataqua River. The museum is open every day from 10 AM to 5 PM. Tickets, which are good for two consecutive days, are $12 for adults, $8 for children ages 7 to 17 and free for children 6 and younger. A

Photo: Mt. Washington Cog Railway

The Cog Railway winds to the top of Mount Washington.

family pass costs $28. Other historic houses in Portsmouth are within easy walking distance of Strawbery Banke but are not included in this admission.

Warner House

150 Daniel St., Portsmouth • (603) 436-5909

This Georgian-style mansion was built in 1716. Its most unusual features are the period wall murals, believed to be the oldest in the United States. You can see them for yourself June through October, Monday through Saturday from 10 AM to 4 PM and Sunday 1 to 4 PM. Admission is $4 for adults and $2.50 for children.

Water Country

Exit 5 off I-95, U.S. Rt. 1, Portsmouth • (603) 436-3556

New England's largest water park features tubing, giant water slides, a huge wave pool and a kiddie lagoon. There are totally crazed, thrill-a-minute rides (one is aptly named the Screamer) for the teens and fountains and waterfalls for the little ones. Life vests are free and required for children between 42 and 48 inches tall who venture onto the wilder rides. Tube rental is not included in the admission, and although they are not absolutely necessary your kids will definitely want them. Although there is plenty for younger children to do, parents of little ones often mention the crowds at the park as a drawback. Teens, on the other hand, adore the place. Water Country is open weekends only from Memorial Day to mid-June, then every day mid-June to Labor Day. Hours are 10:30 AM to 6:30 PM until July 1 and 9:30 AM to 7:30 PM July 1 to Labor Day. The park also hosts concerts and shows in the evenings. Anyone taller than 4 feet pays $25.95. Those shorter than 4 feet pay $17.95. Look for discount coupons at area businesses.

Wentworth-Coolidge Mansion

Off NH Rt. 1A, Little Harbor Rd., Portsmouth • (603) 436-6607

What did 18th-century political power buy? Forty-two rooms of rambling comfort. This mansion was home to Benning Wentworth, Colonial governor from 1741-47, although the oldest part of the building is believed to date back to 1695. The provincial government met in the council chambers here during the run-up to the Revolution. The mansion is open 10 AM to 3 PM Tuesday, Thursday and Saturday and 12 to 5 PM on Sunday from Memorial Day to Labor Day. Admission is $2.50 for adults and free for anyone older than 65 or younger than 13.

NH Seacoast Cruises

NH Rt. 1A, Ocean Blvd., Rye

• (603) 964-5545, (800) 964-5545

The Granite State is a sizable craft, licensed for up to 150 passengers on two decks. The naturalists on board are students in zoology and biology, and the observations made on whale watches are used in cetacean (whale) research. Their whale-sighting rate is so high (99 percent) that they give rain checks to passengers if no whales are sighted. In addition to lengthy whale-watch expeditions, NH Seacoast Cruises offers evening Isles of Shoals tours, complete with seafaring tales and stops to see the Hampton Beach fireworks from off Boars Head.

Whale-watch expeditions run weekends mid-May to Memorial Day, Wednesdays and weekends June 1 to June 21 and September 2 to October 12, and daily from June 21 to September 1. Tickets are $20 for adults, $18 for seniors and $15 for children. Note that these trips are about four hours long. This company runs Evening Isles cruises every Wednesday from the last week of June through the end of August and on Memorial Day, Independence Day and Labor Day. Watch the fireworks from the deck!

Seacoast Science Center at Odiorne Point State Park

Ocean Blvd., Rye

• (603) 436-8043

Whether you come inside to get out of the July sun or to escape the chill of a March sea breeze, you'll be glad you took the time at this combination nature center/art gallery/historical site in the middle of the state park. The building is the last of the homes and buildings which stood on this point when the federal government purchased and fortified the entire area to protect the Portsmouth Naval Shipyard during World War II. In the late 1950s, what was then Fort Dearborn was sold to the State of New Hampshire (over the protests of descendants of those displaced by the Navy, including the Odiornes who had settled in the 1600s). In the park you can climb the earth embankments, batteries and bunkers, play in tidepools and see a sunken forest. Also on display is EDALHAB, an underwater habitat built at the University of New Hampshire in 1968 and designed to allow as many as four divers to live and work under water for two to four days. The 12'x8' tank was fitted out with two bunks, a desk, chairs and cabinet space. Show this to your kids and dare them to complain about sharing a room! Inside the Science Center children enjoy the tide-pool touch tank and the creatures in the thousand-gallon Gulf of Main deep harbor display. Adults find the historical artifacts and the stunning views of the shore equally intriguing. Pick up a schedule of upcoming tours, presentations and workshops: you may want to come back for a guided tour of the marsh or to dine on seaweed and other wild tidbits. The park is open daily from 8 AM to dusk, and costs $2.50 for those 12 and older (free for children younger than 12). There is an additional $1 fee for the Science Center, which is free to children younger than 5 and open from 10 AM to 5 PM every day except Christmas, Thanksgiving and New Year's Day.

Old Sandown Meeting House

Fremont Rd., Sandown

• (603) 887-3946

This 1773 meeting house gives visitors a taste of 18th-century class structure: Will you sit in the family box pews, the completely enclosed slave pews or the narrow, uncomfortable front-row benches reserved for paupers and penitents? It's open by appointment March through November. Admission is free, but donations are welcome.

Old Sandown Railroad Depot

Sandown Center, NH Rt. 121A

• (603) 887-4520, (603) 887-3259

Once the busiest freight depot in the country, this 1873 building houses railroad memo-

INSIDERS' TIP

Travel with comfortable shoes and clothing. You'll have an opportunity to be active at many of our attractions and won't want to slow yourself down by wearing city clothes.

rabilia, telegraph equipment, World War II and Civil War periodicals, tools and household artifacts. It's open Memorial Day to Labor Day, Sundays only from 1 to 5 PM. Admission is free.

Science and Nature Center at Seabrook Station

NH Rt. 1, Seabrook
• (603) 474-9521, (800) 338-7482

This center, run by the Seabrook Nuclear Power Plant, includes hands-on museum exhibits, a salt marsh nature trail and picnic areas. Films in the visitors center theater include a video tour of the nuclear power plant, and visitors can also explore the operator training center with its simulated control room. Bus tours of the site allow a closer look, although visitors are not allowed inside the plant. The center is open year round, Monday through Friday 10 AM to 4 PM. Admission is free.

Lakes Region

Whipple House Museum and Pauline Glidden Toy Museum

Pleasant St., Ashland
• (603) 968-7716

Originally built as a two-family house, the Whipple House provides a fascinating glimpse of family life in the mid-1800s. Furnishings in the parlor, kitchen and upstairs bedrooms make the visitor feel as though Dr. and Mrs. Whipple and their children may return at any moment. A few steps through the garden takes you to the neighboring home, one of the oldest residences in Ashland, which is now overflowing with toys. Every shelf in every room will bring cries of "Oh look!" and "I had one of those!" as the collection ranges from 1850s nesting blocks to 1960s board games and beach pails. From July through Labor Day, both houses are open Wednesday and Saturday 1 to 4 PM. The Toy Museum is also open the same hours on Thursday and Friday. Whipple House is free, and the Toy Museum asks for a $1 donation.

Daniel Webster Birthplace

North Rd., off NH Rt. 127, Franklin
• (603) 934-5057

Daniel Webster was not the man who wrote the dictionary. That was Noah. Daniel Webster was a politician and statesman, born here in 1782. He was known in his day as a mighty orator, a reputation preserved in the Stephen Vincent Benet story *The Devil and Daniel Webster,* in which he beats the original attorney, Lucifer, in a contract case over a man's soul.

The original home, built around 1773, was restored in 1913. It's open weekends mid-May to mid-June and Labor Day to Columbus Day, and daily from mid-June to Labor Day. Hours are 10 AM to 6 PM in all seasons. Admission is $2.50 for adults. Anyone younger than 18 is admitted free.

Golden Pond Tour

Squam Boats Dock, U.S. Rt. 3, Holderness
• (603) 279-4405

Captain Pierre Havre and his canine first mate, Bogie, have built their tour around the locations from the Katherine Hepburn/Henry Fonda movie On Golden Pond. You'll recognize the "Thayer" cottage and Church Island. The tour season runs from Memorial Day through the foliage season (about mid-October). Havre sails daily at 10:30 AM and 1:30 and 3:30 PM. People older than 11 pay $10, children 12 and under, $5.

Science Center of New Hampshire

NH Rt. 113, Holderness • (603) 968-7194

The Science Center, slated to be renamed the Squam Lakes Natural Science Center on January 1, 2000, is a wildlife feast for children of all ages. The 200-acre sanctuary features a .75-mile-long exhibit trail. Visit native black bear, whitetail deer, otters, foxes and birds of

INSIDERS' TIP

On rainy days, rain hats are a lot easier to carry and keep track of than umbrellas. They weigh less and take up almost no room in a daypack.

prey, including a bald eagle. The animals, most of which have been injured or orphaned and could not survive in the wild, are housed in open pens or cages replicating their natural habitat. The center also has educational displays on loons and other animals that would not do well in captivity. A second trail leads visitors through four major New Hampshire ecosystems — forest, pond, marsh and field — while a third (for the ambitious) climbs to the summit of Mount Fayal for a stunning view of Squam Lake. Ask at the desk about the scheduled naturalist talks throughout the day, or take potluck as you encounter the staff caring for the animals along the trails.

The animals are here year round, but the center is only open May 1 to November 1 from 9:30 AM to 4:30 PM (last admission is at 3:30 PM). Pets are not allowed. From May to June and September to October, admission is $6 for adults and $3 for ages 5 to 15. In July and August, when there are more demonstrations, adults pay $8 and kids 5 to 15 pay $4. Children younger than 4 always get in free.

Squam Lake Tours

U.S. Rt. 3, Holderness • (603) 968-7577

This two-hour pontoon boat tour includes the locations for the movie On Golden Pond, including Church Island with its outdoor chapel and organ. Tours depart daily at 10 AM, 2 PM and 4 PM from May through October. The cost for adults is $10, and children's tickets are half-price. Reservations are strongly recommended.

Belknap Mill

Mill Plaza, Beacon St. E., Laconia • (603) 524-8813

When the Industrial Revolution came to New Hampshire, textile mills sprang up along every river. The Belknap Mill, built in 1823, is the oldest unaltered brick knitting mill in America. It has been reborn as a cultural center for the Lakes Region. It houses exhibits in arts, crafts, history and the sciences and hosts classes and workshops. The Mill is open all year, Monday through Friday from 9 AM to 5 PM. Admission varies, depending on what's happening inside.

Annalee's Doll Museum

Hemlock Dr. off NH Rt. 104, Reservoir Rd. off U.S. Rt. 3, Meredith • (603) 279-3333, (800) 433-6557

Even if you're not a collector of the whimsical Annalee dolls with the elfin faces, you'll find this a fascinating stop. The museum features dolls dating back more than 50 years, and the period clothes and poses of dolls from the '50s, '60s and '70s will bring a smile to your face. A picnic area and playground will keep the kids occupied if mom wants to check out the gift shop in peace. Both the museum and shop are open 9 AM to 5 PM daily year round, and there's no admission charge (but just see if you can get away without buying a cute little something!).

Winnipesaukee Scenic Railroad

Meredith Station, off U.S. Rt. 3 N., Meredith • (603) 279-5253 (July/August), (603) 745-2135 (year round)

The trains are classic antiques, the scenery is the beauty of the Lakes region, the snacks are delightful, and the conductors are talkative. This two-hour tour leaves every two hours from 10:30 AM to 4:30 PM. Picnic lunches are available (not included in the price), or you can bring your own snacks. (Insider's hint: Even if you feed them immediately before boarding, kids probably will want to eat on the train. The lunches are just sandwiches and chips, but the novelty of eating on the train whets young riders' appetites.) This train is operated by the same folks who do the Hobo Train out of Lincoln, and in fall they run special foliage trips from Meredith north into the Pemigiwasset. Dinner trips and holiday specials sometimes leave from Laconia, Tilton and Northfield stations; call for details.

You can also ride the Scenic Railroad from Weirs Beach Station (hourly departures 11 AM to 5 PM), but Insiders know there's more parking in Meredith — and you can get off the train at Weirs, play the arcades and ride back later.

Tickets are $8.50 for adults and $6.50 for children ages 4 to 11 for the two-hour trip or $7.50 and $5.50 for the one-hour ride. Children younger than 4 ride free.

Walking Trails

One of the best ways to get to know a place is to explore it slowly, on foot. A number of towns in New Hampshire have put together maps or booklets outlining walking tours of their communities. Here's a sample of what they're like. Ask at town hall, the chamber of commerce or the local library to see if a walking tour has been created in your community.

Close-up

The Coach and Eagle Trail

The capital city's historic walking tour begins at Eagle Square on N. Main Street in Concord. An illustrated brochure, available at most tourist information centers, describes each of the 17 buildings on the tour, all within easy walking distance. (All but two are within a five-block square.) Highlights of the tour include the New Hampshire State House, America's oldest state legislative building still used for its original purpose, and the Christian Science Church, of which Mary Baker Eddy personally directed the building here in 1901. A second, less well-known Concord tour of the Historic District on North Main and Penacook Streets has been developed by the group Heritage Concord. Most of these buildings are still in private hands, although the Kimball-Jenkins Estate and the Franklin Pierce Manse are open to the public (see the write-ups in this chapter).

Portsmouth Harbour Trail

Portsmouth's Harbour Trail connects a number of historic houses and other sites, many of which are described in this chapter. A 32-page souvenir guidebook for the trail is available from the Market Square Visitors Kiosk in summer or the Chamber of Commerce Tourist Center any time. From the noise of the docks to the serenity of Prescott Park, the Harbour Trail gives an overview of this remarkable city. You can walk it in an hour if you don't stop anywhere — but we're betting you will! On weekends in summer "trail rangers" are available to lead you on the tour.

Photo: Sally Wilkins

Manchester's section of the Heritage Trail leads walkers through the old manufacturing district by the river where The Mill Girl looks back at one of the city's historic textile mills.

Tilton and Northfield Historical Walking Trail

The historic centers of these two towns are really a single village, divided by the Winnipesaukee River that once powered the grist mill at the center of the 18th-century village. This new walking trail highlights this unity, leading visitors past 38 points of interest, 24 on the Tilton side of the river, 13 on the Northfield side and one on an island in the middle!

Beginning with the set of statues representing the continents, the legacy of the eccentric Charles Tilton is apparent everywhere. Both towns are wonderful examples of early Victorian architecture,

— continued on next page

and 19 of the structures and monuments on this trail are on the National Register of Historic Places. A brochure with a map and detailed description of the trail can be found at most tourist information centers in the Lakes Region or obtained from Inherit New Hampshire (another nonprofit historic preservation group) at P.O. Box 268, Concord, NH 03302.

The Heritage Trail

In 1988 the State Legislature authorized the building of the New Hampshire "Heritage Trail," a walking trail that will someday stretch 230 miles from the Canadian border to the Massachusetts line. The trail runs roughly along the Merrimack River to the Pemigiwasset, up Franconia Notch and then along the Connecticut River to Canada. You'll see brown and white signs for the Heritage Trail in many towns along the Merrimack River where the work has already been started. At present only bits and pieces have been built, and corridor protection is an ongoing effort.

Each town is planning, developing and funding its own link, so each section will be different. In some places, it's an open park or wooded trail. In others, it winds through historic neighborhoods, highlighting mills or railroads or architecture. Some sections are strictly for walking, others are open to off-road vehicles.

In Merrimack the trail leads past 83 feet of waterfall, in Bedford it features an ancient apple tree and a bald eagle roost. Concord has chosen the Capitol, of course, but also the Planetarium. Plymouth remembers Daniel Webster, while in Franklin the history recalled is the relocation of the town of Hill, moved to make room for the Frankllin Falls Dam. Other towns along the route are still plotting and planning, and the next century will be well underway before anyone can actually walk from Massachusetts to Canada on the Heritage Trail.

For information about the Heritage Trail, call the New Hampshire Division of Parks and Land, (603) 271-3556.

New Hampshire Farm Museum

Exit 18 off Spaulding Tpke., NH Rt. 125, Milton

• (603) 652-7840

Built to preserve and celebrate New Hampshire's rural past, the Farm Museum is both a collection and a teaching facility. Guided tours of the farm house and self-guided tours of the barn bring the 19th century to life. The Plummer Homestead, part of the complex, is a working farm that demonstrates animal husbandry, gardening and heritage arts and crafts. There is also a working blacksmith shop, a cobbler shop, a country store and an extensive collection of antique tools and farm implements. The 50-acre site also includes nature trails and picnic areas. Special events (spring planting, sheep shearing, spinning and weaving, etc.) are held throughout the season. The museum is open 10 AM to 4 PM on weekends mid-May to mid-June and Labor Day to mid-October. The same hours apply Wednesday through Sunday early- to mid-June until Labor Day. Admission is $5 for adults and $1.50 for children 12 and under, with no charge for kids younger than 3. A family membership costs $30 and includes admission to all events for one year.

Castle Springs

NH Rt. 171, Moultonborough

• (603) 476-2352

The Castle in the Clouds, as it's known, was built by an eccentric millionaire named Thomas Plant. The grounds are beautiful, the views are spectacular, and the castle looks like it was dropped here by accident on its way to Europe. Waters from the springs that give the site its name are bottled and sold in stores throughout the area. Recently a microbrewery has been added, taking advantage of the purity of the water. Tours of the bottling facility and brewery are included in the price of admission to the park. Admission is $4 and free for children 10 and younger. For a tour of the castle you'll need to purchase combination tickets instead: Adults $10, seniors $9, children 11 to 18 $7. Horseback riding ($25 for a one-hour ride) allows you to explore more of the 5,200-acre park, or you can hike the wooded trails, picnic in the garden and feed the trout at your leisure. The park is open weekends mid-May to mid-June and daily June 17 to Labor Day from 9 AM to 5 PM. From September 4 to October 22, hours are 9 AM to 4 PM every day. Brewery tours can be arranged in the off-season.

Longneck Llama Ranch
321 Shaker Rd., Northfield
• (603) 286-7948

New Hampshire's largest llama farm offers tours, treks and mini-hikes. The trek is a six-hour excursion over wooded trails; you walk while the llama carries your gear. At noontime there is a break for casual exploration and a gourmet picnic lunch. The mini-hike, about half as long, is open to anyone older than 3 who can climb a short, steep grade. A snack is included. Both hikes include a tour of the farm, or you can just have the one-hour tour, including information about llama history and photo opportunities with adorable baby llamas. Picnicking on the grounds is encouraged, but the owners suggest that you pack some carrots or apples to share with the llamas! A gourmet trek costs $45 per person, and mini-hikes are $25 per person. Both hikes require a minimum of four people, and reservations are required. Tours are $15 per group of up to 15 people and $1 per each additional child. The farm is open from 10 AM to 4:30 PM Friday, Saturday and Sunday from May through October (or by appointment year round). Hikes are scheduled from May 15 to October 29. The gourmet trek runs 9 AM to 3 PM, and mini-hikes can be scheduled for either morning or afternoon.

Mary Baker Eddy House
Hall's Brook Rd., North Groton
• (603) 786-9943

Mary Baker Patterson (later Eddy) was the founder of Christian Science. The Longyear Foundation, based in Massachusetts, maintains a number of houses associated with Mrs. Eddy, three of them in New Hampshire (North Groton and Concord are open only by appointment). Mrs. Patterson, who later remarried, lived in this cottage during one of the most difficult periods of her life from 1855 to 1860. The mysterious illness and loneliness she suffered here led her to study the Bible, which eventually developed into the teachings of Christian Science. The houses are open from May 1 through October 31, Tuesday through Saturday 10 AM to 5 PM and Sunday 2 to 5 PM. Admission is $3 for adults, $1.50 for seniors and students, and free for children younger than 12. Admission includes the Mary Baker Eddy house in Rumney. Go to Rumney first and arrange there for admission here (see the subsequent listing for the Rumney house.)

Recycling and Environmental Visitors Center
90 Rochester Neck Rd., Exit 12 off I-95, Rochester
• (603) 330-0217, (800) 847-5303

Tour a recycling center? Really, it's a fascinating process. Turnkey Recycling will demonstrate composting, landfill, gas-to-energy, materials recovery and recycling, and state-of-the-art trash technology. The Isinglass River Canoe Launch and Picnic Area are right next door. Free tours of the recycling operation require an appointment.

Mary Baker Eddy House
Stinson Lake Rd., Rumney
• (603) 786-9943

Mary Baker Patterson (later Eddy) lived in this house in Rumney for two years, writing poetry and studying the Bible. This was the beginning of what became Christian Science. In 1862, at the height of the Civil War, she left in search of a cure for her lingering illness. The house is open May 1 to October 31, Tuesday through Saturday from 10 AM to 5 PM and Sunday 2 to 5 PM. Admission is $3 for adults, $1.50 for seniors and students, and free for children younger than 12. Admission covers the North Groton house too.

Polar Caves
Exit 26 off I-93, Tenney Mountain Hwy./N.H. Rt. 25, Rumney
• (603) 536-1888, (800) 273-1886

The Polar Caves were formed when the

side of a mountain crumbled and fell in the wake of a retreating glacier. The resulting jumble of boulders is laced with caves and passages, through which paths have been laid and connected by sturdy wooden staircases and walkways. The brochure for the self-guided tour is detailed and instructive. The wooded site also offers a nature walk, a maple-sugaring display, a very tame herd of fallow deer, exotic birds and picnic grounds. A tip: When it's 90 degrees in the shade and so humid you can't move, it's about 65 in the caves. Now you know why they call them "polar" (the only bears are on the sign). The caves and park are open daily from mid-May to mid-October, 9 AM to 5 PM. Admission is $9.50 for adults and teens, $4.75 for children ages 6 to 12 and free for children younger than 5.

Remick Country Doctor Museum

Main St., Tamworth • (603) 323-7581

This museum was established in 1996 with a generous bequest from the country doctor himself. Like his father before him, Dr. Edwin Crafts Remick made house calls and gave aid and comfort to generations of farmers in this rural area. Now their 400-acre farm, homestead and offices are open to the public, offering a glimpse of life in a simpler time. The furnishings in the examining rooms are not all that different from the family's living area, very unlike the high-tech equipment we've come to expect in a doctor's office. The Hillsdale Farm complex, on the same grounds, continues to operate as a working farm, and visitors can learn about the care of horses, cows and chickens as well as traditional games and skills from the turn of the century. The museum is open in July and August only. Hours are from 6 to 8 PM on Wednesday through Saturday evenings and from 1 to 4 PM on Saturday and Sunday afternoons. They're also planning many special events; call for a schedule. Admission to the museum is free.

The Museum of Childhood

Off NH Rt. 16, Wakefield • (603) 522-8073

Have you ever known someone whose collection was so huge they said, "We'll have to buy another house to hold it?" That's how The Museum of Childhood began. This collection-gone-wild, with dolls and puppets, trains and teddy bears, miniatures and music boxes, is described as "a place where everyone can have a second childhood and feel good about it." Re-creations include a Victorian child's bedroom, an 1890s one-room school and a blacksmith's shop. The museum is open Monday and Wednesday through Saturday 11 AM to 4 PM and Sunday 1 to 4 PM from Memorial Day weekend through Labor Day weekend. Admission is $3, $1.25 for children younger than 9.

Funspot

NH Rt. 3, Weirs Beach • (603) 366-4377

Looking for something to do on a cold, rainy day? Or maybe everyone's had too much sun already? Funspot offers more than 500 games inside a three-level entertainment building. Bowling (your choice of tenpins or traditional New England-style candlepins), bumper cars and arcade games, pinball and bingo are just a few of the possibilities. Outside in summer there's miniature golf and a driving range. Funspot holds charity fund-raisers, arts and crafts shows, holiday parties and occasional fireworks displays too. It's open daily year round. There's no general admission charge, but you pay to play each game.

M/S Mount Washington

Weirs Beach
• (603) 366-5531, (888) THE MOUNT

Spend a leisurely day or evening cruising Lake Winnipesaukee on this 230-foot ship. Breakfast, lunch and cocktails enhance your daytrip, while evening cruises include a dinner buffet, live entertainment and dancing. The water is crystal clear, the mountains ring the lake in splendor, and the crew is attentive. For a shorter cruise, you can book portage with the mail on the M/V *Sophie C,* which does one- and two-hour cruises out of Weirs Beach daily, or the M/V *Doris E,* with one- or two-hour runs leaving hourly from 10:30 AM to 2:30 PM and another at 7 PM (a half-hour earlier from Meredith). On the *Mount Washington,* daytime cruises lasting three hours cost $15 for adults and teens, $7 for ages 4 to 12. The two-hour cruises are $13 and $6. Dinner cruises cost $20 to $40 for adults, depending on food and entertainment, and $10 less for children younger than 12. Tickets on the *Sophie C* are $12 for adults and teens, and $6 for 4- to 12-year-olds. A one-hour trip on the *Doris E* is $8 for adults and $4 for 4- to 12-year-olds. The two-hour trip is $12 for adults and $6 for kids age 4 to 12. Kids younger than 4 go free on all trips except dinner cruises.

NH Antique and Classic Boat Museum

NH Rt. 11-B at Weirs Bridge, Weirs Beach • (603) 524-8989

If your interests include history and watersports, you'll find this brand-new museum a fascinating stop. More than 500 artifacts bring memories to visitors young and old, and the comment "we had one of those" is often repeated. Twenty classic watercraft demonstrate the history and evolution of boating technology and the impact of those changes on the culture of the Lakes Region. The museum is open from Memorial Day to Columbus Day. Hours are 10 AM to 6 PM Monday through Saturday and 10 AM to 4 PM on Sunday. Admission is $4 for ages 12 to 64, $2 for children and seniors.

Surf Coaster

NH Rt. 11B, Weirs Beach • (603) 366-4991

SurfCoaster features a half-acre wave pool and the quieter Barefoot Lagoon, gentle Kiddies' Slides (for anyone who doesn't relish the thrillers) and Twin Boomerangs (for those who do). There's a tubing river ride with cascades and a Spray Ground where you can experiment with water's fascinating phenomena. Pay one fee and play all day. The park is open 10 AM to 8 PM daily from the end of June to the second weekend of August. Mid- to late June and mid- to late August, it closes at 7 PM and from September 1 on, it closes at 4 PM. Admission is $18.99 for adults and $13.99 for those shorter than 48 inches tall.

Weirs Beach Water Slide

U.S. Rt. 3, Weirs Beach • (603) 366-5161

Get a great view of Lake Winnipesaukee from the top of the longest water slide in New Hampshire (if you can keep your eyes open). Both twisters and speed-slides are hits with the kids. Weirs Beach Water Slide has the advantage of selling individual and multi-ride tickets, two-hour unlimited passes and all-day admissions, so if the kids are dying to slide and the thought of a day in a water park is killing you, this is the place to compromise. The slide is open from mid-June to Labor Day, 10 AM to 5 PM. Tickets are $6.99 for seven rides, $9.99 for 14 rides or $12.99 for an all-day pass. For $10.99 you can slide as much as you want for two hours. Children shorter than 48 inches tall can ride the Tunnel Twister or Super Slide with an adult, using a Toddler Ticket, which costs $5.99 and covers five adult-and-child rides.

Winnipesaukee Scenic Railroad

Weirs Beach Station., U.S. Rt. 3 S. • (603) 279-5253 in July/August

Enjoy scenery, snacks and a real old-fashioned train ride. See the railroad's listing under Meredith for more details. Hourly departures from Weirs Beach leave between 11 AM and 5 PM. Tickets from Weirs are $8.50 for adults and teens, and $6.50 for children ages 4 to 11 for the two-hour trip, or $7.50 and $5.50 respectively for the one-hour ride. Children younger than 4 ride free.

Blue Ghost

Lakes Region Sports, 11 S. Main, Wolfeboro • (603) 569-1114

The *Blue Ghost* is primarily the U.S. Mail Boat for Lake Winnipesaukee. If there's room (make reservations at Lakes Region Sports), you can go along for the ride as the boat does a 60-mile loop, making more than 30 stops at camps and islands on the eastern end of the lake. The boat leaves at 10 AM every day except Sunday (in summer). Cost is $20 for adults and $10 for children, and the boat can only take 10 passengers.

Molly the Trolley The Wolfeboro Trolley Company

60 N. Main St., Wolfeboro • (603) 569-5257, (800) 339-5257

Molly the Trolley began taking visitors on tours of the "oldest resort town in America" back in 1978. Since then the cheerful red trolley car and her informative drivers have become local favorites. An All-Day Pass allows riders to hop on and off at any of the Trolley's fourteen stops, as often as desired. All of Wolfeboro's favorite sites are close to the Trolley stops, and what an improvement over trying to park and repark the car during tourist season! A pass costs $3 for an adult, $1 for children 4 through 12 and is free for children younger than 4. Ask about package deals with the Barnstormers and Lakes Region Summer Theatre (see our Arts chapter) and three local restaurants: The Woodshed, Mame's and Patrick's (see our Restaurants chapter).

The Millie B
The Wolfeboro Trolley Company
60 N. Main St., Wolfeboro
• (603) 569-5257 (800) 339-5257

In 1998, for her tenth birthday celebration, Molly the Trolley received a sister: the *Millie B,* an antique mahogany speedboat. On board the *Millie B* guests can explore Lake Winnipesaukee just like their grandparents did back in the Roaring Twenties. Cruise among the islands, fill your eyes with the stunning views of the mountains, and listen to the skipper's tales of the glamour days of wooden speedcraft. Tours on the *Millie B* leave the Wolfeboro Town Docks every half-hour from 10 AM until 8 PM, seven days a week. Fare is $9 for adults and $5 for children ages 4 through 12, while those younger than 4 ride for free. And yes, you can ride Molly to meet Millie at the Town Docks.

Wright Museum of American Enterprise
77 Center St., Wolfeboro
• (603) 569-1212

The Home Front comes alive in this World War II museum, which features a large collection of military vehicles, authentic uniforms and memorabilia of daily life from 1939 to 1945. Videos help set the scene, while the opportunity to visit an actual 1940s kitchen and living room, soda fountain and dentist's office recollect the past with vivid clarity. It's an eye-opener for kids and an eye-mister for those who remember the war.

The museum is wheelchair accessible. From April 1 through October 31, the museum is open daily from 10 AM to 4 PM. In November, February and March, the museum is only open on weekends from 10 AM to 4 PM. The museum is usually closed in December and January. Admission is $5 for adults, $4 for those older than 55 and $3 for kids ages 9 through 17 and veterans. Children younger than 9 get in free.

M/V Winnipesaukee Belle
90 N. Main St., Wolfeboro
• (603) 569-3016

Take a 90-minute narrated tour of Lake Winnipesaukee on board the *Winnipesaukee Belle.* This newly renovated 200-passenger boat, with its paddle wheels and upper deck awning, offers a leisurely cruise on the lake showing off Winnipesaukee's many beautiful islands. The ship makes three 90-minute cruises a day, leaving at 10:30 AM, 12:30 PM and 2:30 PM. The ship is owned and operated by the Wolfeboro Inn, but you don't have to be a guest to book passage. Tickets are $10 for adults, $5 for kids 4-12, and $3 for kids under 4. Guests at the Inn ride free.

White Mountains and Great North Woods Regions

Attitash Bear Peak
Alpine Slide and Waterslides
U.S. Rt. 302, Bartlett
• (603) 374-2368, (800) 223-7669

There is a mountain of fun here beginning with the Alpine Slide, a .75-mile descent on a self-controlled sled. If you can still breathe, move on to the waterslides, which now include Buddy Bear's Playpool for kids ages 2 to 7. You can also take the chairlift to the White Mountain Observation Tower for a 360-degree view of northern New England. The summit elevation is 2,350 feet, and you'll climb an additional six stories to make it to the top of the tower. After your climb, refuel at the base lodge cafeteria, which is open from 10 AM until 3 PM. Attitash Bear Peak opens at 10 AM and closes at 5 PM. An all-day ticket is $19, or single-ride tickets are $8. Kids younger than 4 get in free with a paying adult.

Mount Washington Cog Railway
U.S. Rt. 302, Bretton Woods
• (603) 278-5404, (800) 922-8825

Go back in time on the world's first mountain-climbing railway. You'll travel 6,288 feet to the top of the highest summit in the Northeast on a coal-fired steam train. The three-hour round-trip ride begins at Marshfield Base Station and travels 2.75 miles up Mount Washington. It's sometimes called "The Railway to the Moon." The grade gets as extreme as 37 percent on the Jacob's Ladder trestle, making it one of the steepest tracks in the world. The train makes the trip rain or shine from early May to late October.

Old Peppersass was the first train to reach the summit on July 3, 1869. The inspiration for the story of *The Little Engine that Could,* this original locomotive is on display at the Marshfield Base Station. A museum, gift shop and restaurant are also in the base station.

This is one of the most popular attractions in New England so it's smart to make reservations at least a week in advance. This is especially true if you plan on being here after July 4. Tickets are $39 for adults and teens, $35 for seniors and $26 for children 6 through 12. Children younger than 6 ride free as long as they sit in an adult's lap. If they need a seat, the $26 price is charged.

Flume Gorge
Franconia Notch Pkwy., Franconia
• (603) 745-8391

View the free 15-minute introductory film at the visitors center and then follow the 2-mile walking trail through this natural gorge. The walk is moderately easy. The trail is mostly packed gravel with sections of boardwalk across the gorge. Sixty well-graded steps are interspersed along the path. You can take a shuttle bus for the first .5 miles of the walk to avoid the steepest downhill section. You'll find plenty of spots to rest along the way. The gorge extends 800 feet at the base of Mount Liberty. The granite walls are 12 to 20 feet apart and rise up from 70 to 90 feet. You'll see rare mountain flowers, waterfalls and mountain vistas as you travel through this Ice Age wonder on the moderate walk. The cost is $7 for adults and teens and $4 for children 6 to 12. There is no charge for children younger than 6 if they are traveling with an adult.

Cannon Aerial Tramway
Franconia Notch Pkwy., Franconia Notch
• (603) 823-5563

This is another great way to enjoy the glory of the White Mountains. When it opened in 1938, the aerial tramway was the first in the United States. The current 80-passenger tram was installed in 1980 and travels all the way up to the 4,200-foot summit of Cannon Mountain. Once there, you can spend the day at the top enjoying the walking trails, observation deck and souvenir shop. The tramway runs daily from the middle of May through October with departures every 15 minutes. The round-trip cost is $9 for adults and teens and $5 for children 6 to 12.

New England Ski Museum
Next to the Cannon Mountain Aerial Tramway Base Station, Franconia Notch
• (603) 823-7177

This nonprofit museum is a must for anyone interested in the history of skiing in America. The two-room exhibit space includes a large-screen video projection area. There you'll see exciting videos such as *Legends of American Skiing,* which includes vintage skiing footage and interviews with the legends. Time permitting, the staff is happy to preview the many videos that are for sale. The museum changes its main exhibit annually at Memorial Day. From Memorial Day to Columbus Day, the museum is open every day from noon to 5 PM. From December 1 through March 31, the museum is open Friday to Tuesday from noon until 5 PM. Admission is free. The museum is closed during the spring and late fall.

Old Man of the Mountain
Franconia Notch Pkwy. (U.S. Rt. 3), Franconia Notch

This granite "profile" is one of the most famous natural landmarks in the state. The Old Man's head measures 40 feet from chin to forehead and is made up of five ledges. Remember, this is no man-made monument like Mount Rushmore. Nature carved this pro-

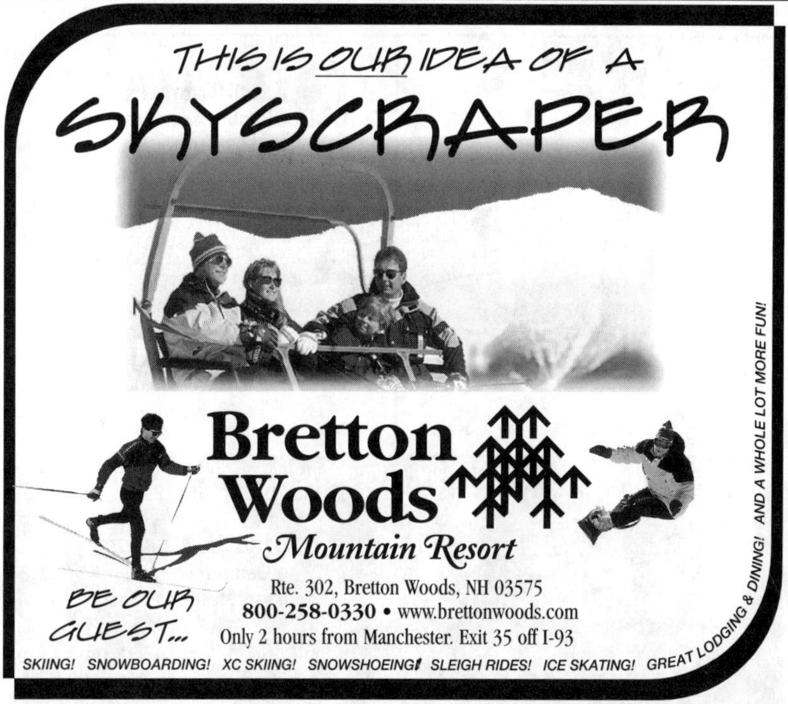
THIS IS OUR IDEA OF A
SKYSCRAPER
Bretton
Woods
Mountain Resort
Rte. 302, Bretton Woods, NH 03575
800-258-0330 • www.brettonwoods.com
Only 2 hours from Manchester. Exit 35 off I-93
BE OUR
GUEST...
SKIING! SNOWBOARDING! XC SKIING! SNOWSHOEING! SLEIGH RIDES! ICE SKATING! GREAT LODGING & DINING! AND A WHOLE LOT MORE FUN!

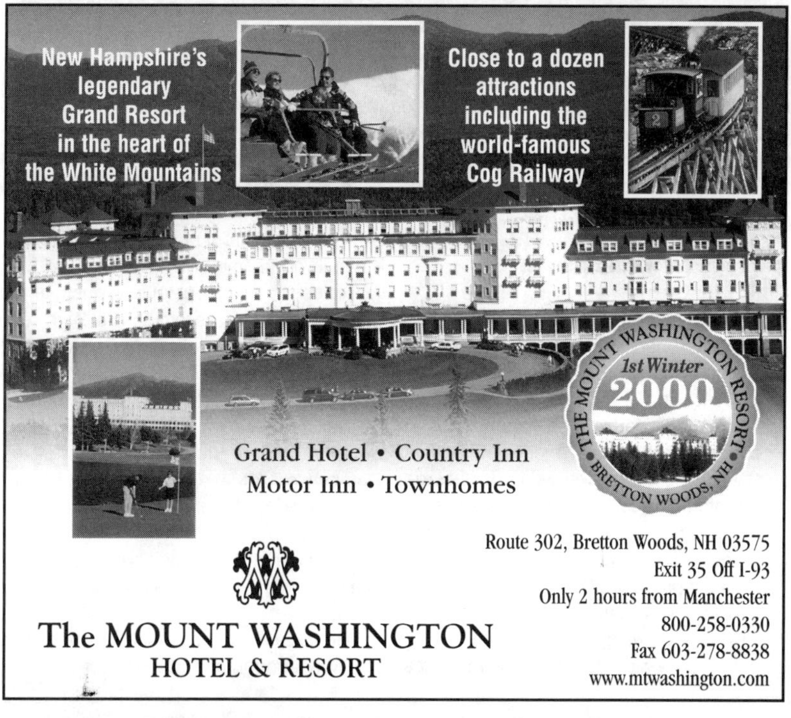
New Hampshire's
legendary
Grand Resort
in the heart of
the White Mountains
Close to a dozen
attractions
including the
world-famous
Cog Railway
THE MOUNT WASHINGTON RESORT
1st Winter
2000
BRETTON WOODS, NH
Grand Hotel • Country Inn
Motor Inn • Townhomes
Route 302, Bretton Woods, NH 03575
Exit 35 Off I-93
Only 2 hours from Manchester
800-258-0330
Fax 603-278-8838
www.mtwashington.com
The MOUNT WASHINGTON
HOTEL & RESORT

file thousands of years ago. The natural sculpture is 1,200 feet above Echo Lake. After your visit, you may notice that the New Hampshire highway signs all are marked by this distinctive face. You will see signs for viewing areas as you drive along the parkway.

Heritage-New Hampshire

NH Rt. 16, Glen
• (603) 383-9776

Travel through time and visit 300 years of history beginning in 1634. This exhibition hall showcases all of New Hampshire's history under one roof. You will "sail" from England across the Atlantic Ocean, meet early settlers and hear a speech that was written by George Washington. You can visit the Amoskeag Mills on the Merrimack River and get a hint of autumn beauty on the simulated train ride through a reproduced Crawford Notch.

Heritage-New Hampshire opened on July 1, 1976. (It is owned and operated by the Morrell family, which also owns and manages Story Land next door; see our next entry.) More than 80,000 people visit Heritage-New Hampshire every year. Outside a 16-foot-high by 120-foot-long mural depicts New Hampshire history through 1930. Inside are life-size re-creations of many of the mural subjects.

In a change from past years, visitors now travel through time with their own trail map (as opposed to group tours). Much of the exhibit is interactive, so you can talk with and question historical characters. You can also take part in events such as tapping a maple tree and delivering a land grant to a settler.

Besides being a great place to learn more about our wonderful state, Heritage-New Hampshire is known to Insiders as one of the best rainy-day destinations. All the exhibits are indoors and completely wheelchair-accessible. Take note: No snack bar or restaurant is on the premises, but North Conway Village is just 10 minutes away.

Heritage-New Hampshire is open from mid-May through mid-October from 9 AM to

Photo: David A. Leach Photography

America's Stonehenge in North Salem is constructed of slabs of stone weighing from 4 to 11 tons.

5 PM. From mid-June until September 1, the closing is at 6 PM. Admission is $10 for adults and teens and $4.50 for children 6 through 12. Admission is free for children younger than 6.

Story Land

NH Rt. 16, Glen • (603) 383-4186

Forget about action figures. Fairy tales have come to life here for more than 40 years! You and your kids will meet Cinderella, Heidi's grandfather and the old woman who lives in a shoe. There are stories from all over — even outer space. Seventeen rides, a snack bar and a picnic area are on the premises. The admission price includes unlimited rides and parking. As you plan your vacation, it's good to know that Story Land is next door to Heritage-New Hampshire. See our Kidstuff chapter for more on Story Land.

Moose Tours

Gorham Information Center, Main St., Gorham
• (603) 466-3103, (800) 992-7480

Take a two-hour tour through prime moose-sighting country in northern New Hampshire. The success rate for spotting a moose is 97 percent. They aren't hard to see since a typical adult moose weighs about 1,000 pounds and is about 6 feet tall at the shoulder. Moose like salt and are therefore attracted to moist, roadside areas in spring and summer. The salt in these areas was used to melt ice and snow on roads during the winter. The 24-passenger air-conditioned bus departs once a day from the information booth in Gorham, across from the Berlin City Bank. The bus leaves every evening (exact time depends on sunset) from late May until mid-October. The ride begins with a 30-minute video on the logging and papermaking history of the Berlin area. Reservations are a good idea. The cost of the tour is $15 for adults and $10 for children younger than 12. Please bring a car seat for children under 4.

Mount Washington Auto Road

NH Rt. 16, Pinkham Notch, Gorham
• (603) 466-3988

You don't have to spend much time in New Hampshire to notice the many cars with bumper stickers proclaiming "This car climbed Mount Washington." First opened in 1861, this 8-mile road to the 6,288-foot summit of Mount Washington is a favorite of Insiders and visitors alike. You can drive your own car or relax (and save automobile wear and tear) with a guided tour in a modern van. If you choose to drive yourself, pick up a free audio cassette with information and stories about the history, geography, climate and wildlife of the area.

If you plan on driving your own car, make sure the cooling system and brakes are in good shape. Allow between 35 and 45 minutes for each leg of the trip as the maximum speed (in both directions) is 20 miles per hour. If you take the guided tour it's 30 minutes each way.

The original transportation to the summit on this road was horse-drawn carriages. Then, like today, one could choose between riding in a special carriage behind a professional team or trying one's luck with your own team and wagon. Once on top, take your time and enjoy the views. You are now in the 52-acre Mount Washington State Park. The visitors center includes a post office, snack bar and gift shop. See our Parks and Open Spaces chapter for details.

The auto road is open from mid-May through late October, weather permitting. The toll is $15 per car and driver with an additional $6 charge per adult or teen and $4 for each child age 5 through 12. The guided tour is $20 per adult or teen and $10 for children 5 through 12. The guided tours are usually in the morning, so call ahead if that's your plan. Ask about the special tours for sunrise and sunset views.

Hartmann Model Railway and Toy Museum

Town Hall Rd. at NH Rt. 16 and U.S. Rt. 302, Intervale
• (603) 356-9922

If you're a model train buff, you're sure to love the collection assembled by Roger and Nelly Hartmann. The collection includes American favorites such as Lionel and American Flyers as well as models from Germany and Switzerland. Each of the 14 operating layouts is exquisitely detailed. One features fire brigade engines, while another depicts the train that ran through Crawford Notch, New Hampshire, in the 1950s. If you've traveled up Mount Washington on the Cog Railroad or taken a ride on the Conway Scenic Railroad (both described in this chapter), you might be particularly vulnerable to the goodies in the Brass Caboose Hobby Shop. You'll find books and magazines about trains as well as an extensive selection of trains and accessories. The museum is open all year, and the entrance fee is $5 for adults and $3 for kids between ages 6 and 13. Children younger than 13 must be accompanied by an adult.

Santa's Village

U.S. Rt. 2, Jefferson
• (603) 586-4445

Experience Christmas from Father's Day to Columbus Day at Santa's Village. Rides for kids of all ages include the Yule Log Flume and the Skyway Sleigh. The admission price includes all the rides you want as well as entry to shows such as *Elfis* and *Jingle Jamboree,* where everyone sings Christmas carols. And, of course, the village has several gift shops and dining choices to keep everyone happy. See our Kidstuff chapter for more on Santa's Village.

Six Gun City

U.S. Rt. 2, Jefferson
• (603) 586-4592

You might not think "Wild West" when you think New Hampshire, but you will after a visit to Six Gun City. Have a look at the different wagons the pioneers used to travel West, including an authentic Concord Coach from 1846. Then mosey on over to the ranch and take a look at the miniature burros. Watch out for bank robbers and don't be surprised if the kids are deputized. Thoroughly modern kids will enjoy the water slides and minigolf. The price of admission includes unlimited rides. See our Kidstuff chapter for details.

Clark's Trading Post

U.S. Rt. 3, Lincoln
• (603) 745-8913

Clark's Trading Post is another New Hampshire attraction with a long history. When it opened in the 1920s, it featured trained dogs as part of the entertainment. Today the performing animals are North American Black Bears. You might see the bears play "Bearsketball" by dunking a ball through a hoop, or weigh themselves after a milk and honey treat. Bear demonstrations begin when the park opens in spring, but the full shows don't usually begin until July 1. Once begun, the bear shows continue throughout the season.

Take time to enjoy the relaxing ride along the Pemigewasset River on the White Mountain Central Railway. The more active members of your group might want to try the bumper boats. And if you like to step back in time, be sure to see the mysterious Tuttle House, where pool balls run uphill, Avery's Garage and the 1884 Fire Station. Get your picture taken at Kilburn's Photo Parlor and sample ice cream at the nearby old-fashioned ice cream store.

Clark's Trading Post is open on weekends beginning in late-May and daily beginning mid to late-June. Daily operation continues through Labor Day when the schedule goes back to weekends only. The Trading Post closes in mid-October. Several 30-minute shows are held each day, and admission to the show arena is included in the general admission. Hours are 10 AM through 6 PM, and admission tickets are $7 for those 6 and older and $2 for children 3 to 5. Children younger than 3 get in free.

Loon Mountain Park

Exit 32 off I-93, Kancamagus Hwy., Lin coln • (603) 745-8111

Here's another skyride to show off the dazzling beauty of the White Mountains. One of New Hampshire's most popular ski areas, Loon Mountain is also a warm-weather favorite. The ride to the summit is in an enclosed gondola. At the top are lumberjack shows, glacial caves and a playground for the kids. Shops, restaurants, nature shows, hiking trails and an observatory can also be found at the top. The one-way ride to the summit takes 10 minutes. An all-day skyride ticket costs $9.50 for adults, $8 for seniors older than 64 and $5.50 for children 6 through 16. Kids younger than 6 travel for free as long as they are with an adult.

Whale's Tale Water Park

Exit 33 off I-93, U.S. Rt. 3, Lincoln • (603) 745-8810

For the water lovers in your group, Whale's Tale Water Park has a 17,500 square foot pool with eight different waves. Slides, pools, rivers and a special pool for the very young provide fun for everyone. Lifeguards are always on duty. Free tubes are part of the package, and you can rent life vests for a reasonable fee. See Kidstuff for details.

Conway Scenic Railroad

NH Rt. 16 at Norcross Cir., North Conway • (603) 356-5251, (800) 232-5251

The Conway Scenic Railroad is a must-see for train buffs and nature lovers. You have a choice of two trains and three great trips. The Valley Train stays in the Mount Washington Valley for the 55-minute round-trip to Conway or the 105-minute round-trip to Bartlett. Both Valley Trains run two or three times a day, and each offers at least one train a day with dining service. The trains have coach bench seating in most cars as well as limited first-class seats in the refurbished turn-of-the-century Pullman car. The first-class car includes individual wicker chairs — a reminder of bygone days of elegant train travel.

In addition to the Valley Train, there's the Notch Train, which travels through Crawford Notch. The 5-hour trip is a nonstop explosion of breathtaking beauty. No one questions the claim that the Notch Train travels through the finest natural scenery in the Northeast. And take it from an Insider, you'd rather have someone else doing the driving while you're trying to absorb the awe-inspiring sights. The Notch Train has regular coach seating as well as first-class accommodations, although the first-class seats are more like first-class airline seats than the restored Pullman Parlor Car of the Valley Trains.

Both trains offer live narration complete with the history of the area. Snack bars are on all trains in addition to the dining car on the designated Valley Trains. Both trains have air conditioning in first class.

Prices vary depending on the train, class of service and age of passenger. Basic prices range from $42 per adult or teen for first-class travel on the Notch Train to $6 for children 4 through 12 on the coach-class trip to Conway. Children younger than 4 ride free as long as they are able to sit in a companion's lap. Reservations are accepted and strongly recommended for travel during foliage season in September and October. The season opens with the Easter Bunny Express on the Valley Trains, with regular weekend service beginning in mid-April. The Notch Train opens about mid-June. Both trains continue service through mid-October, weather permitting. As with all seasonal schedules, it is best to call ahead to make sure you can travel on the train of your choice.

Lost River

NH Rt. 112, Kinsman Notch, North Woodstock
• (603) 745-8031

Lost River Gorge is another New Hampshire glacial gift. The area's glacier activity formed this natural wonder thousands of years ago. A self-guided tour over wooden stairs and walkways help you through the granite crevasses, caverns and waterfalls. The tour lasts about an hour, and the Lost River comes in and out of view along the way. A great place for botanists, the Lost River Gorge has more than 300 varieties of flowers, ferns and shrubs.

It's a good idea to wear appropriate shoes and have a jacket handy for shady spots and cloudy days. There is a gift shop and snack bar and free parking. The cost is $8 for adults and teens and $4.50 for children 6 through 12. The hours are 9 AM through 5 PM except for July and August when the park stays open until 6 PM. The last tickets are sold one hour before closing.

Dartmouth-Lake Sunapee Region

The Fort at Number 4

Exit 7 off I-91, NH Rt. 11, Charlestown
• (603) 826-5700

The original stockade was built here in 1744. This replica is a soup-to-nuts education in Colonial dress, language and crafts. In addition to the stockade are barns, nine outbuildings and a watchtower. This settlement was vital during the French and Indian War. At that time, Charlestown and The Fort at Number 4 were the most northerly New England settlements on the Connecticut River. In addition to the fort, there are 63 buildings on Charlestown's Main Street listed on the National Register of Historic Buildings.

The Fort at Number 4 is open every day from 10 AM to 4 PM from May through October. The cost is $6 for adults and $4 for children ages 6 to 11. Children younger than 6 get in free.

Saint-Gaudens National Historic Site

Off NH Rt. 12A, Cornish
• (603) 675-2175

The Irish-born American sculptor Augustus Saint-Gaudens lived and worked here from 1885 until his death at age 59 in 1907. The sculptor's work in bronze was part of an American Renaissance taking place in this small village on the Connecticut River. The site features full-size copies of his pieces including the well-known bust of Abraham Lincoln. In addition to the original house and furnishings, you can tour the artist's studio, gallery and gardens. During the life of Saint-Gaudens, frequent visitors included artist Maxfield Parrish and American novelist Winston Churchill, both of whom had summer houses in the region.

The house is open from Memorial Day through Halloween from 9 AM to 4:30 PM, and admission costs $4 for adults. Those younger than 17 are admitted for free. The grounds are open every day from dawn to dusk.

Ruggles Mine

U.S. Rt. 4, Grafton • (603) 523-4275

Last mined commercially in 1959, this 190-year-old, open-pit mine and caves on Isinglass Mountain is the place for mineral exploration. Giant rooms and tunnels for exploration make Ruggles Mine a favorite with kids (see our Kidstuff chapter).

Ruggles Mine operates on a seasonal schedule of weekends from mid-May to mid-June and every day from mid-June through mid-October. The hours are 9 AM to 5 PM except in July and August when the park is open until 6 PM. Admission is $15 for those 12 and older, $5 for children 4 through 11 and free for children younger than 4.

Aerial Ride up Mount Sunapee

Mount Sunapee State Park, NH Rt. 103, 3 miles west of Newbury • (603) 763-2356

You don't have to be a skier to enjoy a skyride into the wild blue yonder. During warm-weather months, the Mount Sunapee ski-lift operates as an aerial ride up the 2,743-foot mountain. The entire trip takes just less than an hour. The ride itself is 22 minutes up and 22 minutes down. In between you get to enjoy the view of this 2,893-acre, year-round recreation area.

The Aerial Ride is open every day from mid-June through Labor Day. From Memorial Day to the mid-June opening and from Labor Day through Columbus Day, the ride operates on a weekend-only schedule. New management has announced that ticket prices will increase for the 1999 season. In 1998 the cost was $5.50 for adults and $2.50 for kids.

M/V Mount Sunapee

Sunapee Harbor • (603) 763-4030

Enjoy a lively hour-and-a-half-hour tour of Lake Sunapee on this 150-seat tour boat. You'll enjoy Captain Dave Hargbol's live narration throughout the cruise as he tells you about the lake's history. You'll learn about early steamships as well as the first lakeside Native American settlements. Kids always enjoy the attention given them by the Captain. He might ask them up to the helm and takes time to answer all their questions. You can sit in one of 55 seats on the upper deck or enjoy the cruise from the shaded lower deck. Soft drinks and snacks are sold on board. The ship leaves port daily at 10 AM and 2:30 PM from mid-June through Labor Day. From mid-May to mid-June and from Labor Day through mid-October the ship sails only on weekends at 2:30 PM. The cost is $10 for adults and $6 for children younger than 12.

M/V Kearsarge

Sunapee Harbor
• (603) 763-5477

This genuine re-creation of a 19th-century steamer cruises the lake for one hour and 45 minutes. Enjoy dinner as you listen to the captain explain the history of the Lake Sunapee steamer. The vessel seats 70 in bentwood cane chairs at mahogany tables. The white linen tablecloths and napkins add to the Victorian charm of the boat. A dinner buffet is included in the ticket price. You might sail during the Hawaiian Luau dinner or perhaps the Italian buffet. And don't miss Sweet Street, a dessert line with lots of fresh baked pies and cakes. The M/V *Kearsarge* sets sail every day from mid-June through Labor Day. Cruises are at 5:30 PM and 7:45 PM on Tuesday through Sunday and 5:30 PM on Monday. The cost is $22 for adults and $11 for children younger than 12. Kids younger than 5 sail free.

The Fells Historic Site at the John Hay National Wildlife Refuge

NH Rt. 103A, Newbury
• (603) 763-2452

This was the Lake Sunapee summer home of John M. Hay, statesman, author and private secretary to President Lincoln. The house is not furnished, but the extensive grounds are beautiful with nature trails, formal gardens and delightful views of Lake Sunapee. Guided tours are offered on weekends from late May through October. The grounds are open all year from dawn to dusk. Admission is free. There's a half-mile mile walk from the parking lot to the estate, with handicapped parking available.

Mount Kearsarge Indian Museum

Kearsarge Mountain Rd., Warner
• (603) 456-2600

We think this treasure trove of Native American artifacts is a must-see in the region. Besides seeing such local cultural artifacts as

INSIDERS' TIP

There's lots of parking in Hampton Beach if you look a block away from the ocean. You'll find a municipal lot and several commercial lots off Ashworth Avenue.

a birch canoe and sweet-grass baskets, you will also find artifacts of the Anasazi Indians of New Mexico. To get there take Exit 8 off I-89 N. or Exit 9 from I-89 S.

Knowledgeable tour guides lead you through exhibits featuring hundreds of artifacts representing 15,000 years of the history of native peoples. The tours leave every hour on the hour, and you must be part of a tour. If you arrive early, enjoy the 2-acre outdoor display that includes a tepee as well as plants used by Native Americans for food, medicine and dyes. Craft demonstrations, lectures and films are featured throughout the season. Call ahead to see what's planned during your stay in the region. The Dreamcatcher gift shop has books, music, jewelry and crafts. The museum is open every day from May 1 through October. From November 1 until the weekend before Christmas the museum is just open on weekends. The hours are 10 AM to 5 PM Monday through Saturday and 12 to 5 PM on Sunday. The last tour begins at 4 PM. The admission is $6 for adults and $4 for children 6 to 12.

Monadnock Region

Friendly Farm

NH Rt. 101, Dublin
• (603) 563-8444

The Friendly Farm has more than 7 acres filled with barnyard animals. You can feed and pat the animals as well as learn a lot about pigs, cows, horses — even bees! The farm is open from late April through Labor Day. You'll find more details in our Kidstuff chapter.

Franklin Pierce Homestead

junction of NH Rt. 9 and NH Rt. 31, Hillsborough
• (603) 478-3165

New Hampshire's only President may have been born in the hinterlands, but he was no stranger to the life of the upper class even before he was elected to power. His boyhood home, built in 1804, reflects his family's affluence in its impressive construction, elegant furnishings and hand-stenciled walls. There's even a ballroom upstairs that's as long as the house! The house is a National Historic Landmark and is managed as a state park. The house is open Memorial Day through Columbus Day from 10 AM to 4 PM Monday through Saturday and 1 to 4 PM on Sunday. Admission for adults is $2.50, while children younger than 18 get in free.

Mount Monadnock

Mount Monadnock State Park, NH Rt. 124, 4 miles west of Jaffrey
• (603) 532-8862

Even if you don't climb Mount Monadnock, you'll be glad if you just get close to it. Forty miles of trails wind up the mountain, and most go to the top. If it's a clear day, you'll see all of New England from the summit. The park and visitors center are open all year. You'll find maps of all the trails in the visitors center. See our chapter on Parks and Open Spaces for details.

Silver Ranch Airpark

Jaffrey Airport, NH Rt. 124, Jaffrey
• (603) 532-8870

Harvey Sawyer is the man to talk to if you'd like a scenic ride over the Monadnock area. Silver Ranch Airpark is open every day, weather permitting. The airpark has several planes including an antique 1946 Piper Cub (one passenger in addition to pilot), a Cessna Sky Hawk for three passengers and a twin-engine Piper Aztec for five passengers.

You can arrange just about any length tour of the area, with most rides in the 10 to 40 minute range. Prices start at $12 per person. Sawyer has a wealth of knowledge about the Monadnock Region and is one of the best local tour guides. It's best to call ahead for reservations.

Historical Society of Cheshire County

246 Main St., Keene
• (603) 352-1895

This vibrant historical collection is an extensive archive for genealogical research. The permanent exhibit includes fine specimens of early glass and pottery from the Monadnock region. There are also three to four changing local history exhibits. The museum is open year round Monday through Friday from 9 AM until 4 PM except Wednesday when the museum is open from 9 AM to 9 PM. The collection is also open on Sunday from 9 AM to noon. There is no charge for admission.

Wyman Tavern

339 Main St., Keene • (603) 352-1895

This historic attraction is home to period furnishings from 1770 to 1820. This is where the first Dartmouth College trustees met, establishing the school in 1770. It was also the meeting place for the New Hampshire minutemen in 1775 on their way to the Battle of Concord. The museum is open June 1 through Labor Day, Thursday through Saturday from 11 AM to 4 PM. The admission price is $2.

Barrett House and Forest Hall

Main St., New Ipswich • (617) 227-3956

This stately three-story Federal-style residence was the set for the Merchant-Ivory film of the Henry James novel *The Europeans.* The grounds are extensive and include the original carriage house. A ballroom as well as period rooms with furnishings befitting a museum are features of the interior. The estate is open Saturday and Sunday from June 1 through October 15, with a $4 admission charge.

Cathedral Of the Pines

Off NH Rt. 119, Cathedral Rd., Rindge • (603) 899-3300

This outdoor place of worship is a magnificent natural glory. The cathedral was partially formed by the hurricane of 1938, which cleared the view. It has been enhanced by the love and national pride of a family remembering their son and all citizens who died serving their country.

Originally, these nearly 300 acres were the property of the Sloane family. They enjoyed their summer home in the Monadnock area, and their son, Sanderson Sloane, made plans for his own home within the grounds. He was killed during World War II when his plane was shot down over Germany. Subsequently the entire property was dedicated as a national memorial. It is an emotional expression of gratitude that the world was spared as well as a specific remembrance for all the lives given toward this goal.

The cathedral ceiling is formed by pine trees. Behind the simple stone altar is Mount Monadnock. The Memorial Bell Tower has four bronze bas-reliefs designed by Norman Rockwell. The bell tower is specifically dedicated to women — military and civilian — who died serving their country. Flower gardens and a collection of military memorabilia are also on the grounds.

The Cathedral Of the Pines is an ecumenical, nondenominational house of worship. The cathedral holds an Easter celebration, although regular services do not begin until Memorial Day. Civic organizations such as the Masons and the Lions Club often use the facilities. In addition, it is available for weddings and other appropriate private functions. This is not a tourist attraction; it is a memorial. The grounds are open May 1 through October 31. The hours are 9 AM to 5 PM.

New Hampshire is classic camp country. Children can spend the heart of the summer exploring nature and learning about themselves.

Kidstuff

Our kids think we should start with the bad news and get it over with: There is no super-size, extra-colossal theme park with roller coasters and monorails in New Hampshire (although several of our larger attractions have added rides to please the amusement-park crowd). We have no complexes so large that you must ride a bus from the parking lot to the front gate, and the Great Mouse only comes here on vacation.

On the other hand, we have a wealth of wonderful activities for families with kids. Some we've already told you about in our Attractions chapter so we'll just remind you of them here. Other logical places to look for fun things to do are our Recreation, Beaches and Watersports, and Annual Events chapters. Here in Kidstuff we've concentrated on places you probably wouldn't try unless you have kids to entertain — not that you won't enjoy them too.

Both Hampton Beach and Weirs Beach boast the kinds of old-fashioned amusements kids can spend a whole day at: bumper cars and pinball games, skeeball and whack-a-mole, as well as the new video and virtual reality games. You can demonstrate the nickel baseball games you played as a kid, and your kids can explain the intricacies of the latest video mayhem. Park the car and spend the day: between the sand and the water on the one side and the games and junk food on the other, these beaches make for classic family summer memories.

Local parks and recreation departments provide a wide range of activities for kids (and sometimes for adults too). Swimming lessons and teams of all kinds, arts in the park and reading contests, film festivals, environmental camps and traveling excursions are all on the list of recreation department activities in New Hampshire. If you're relocating or renting for the whole summer, call the local town hall and library to find out what's available. Our larger cities also have parks, where you'll find crafts, games and sports programs in summer, and YMCAs with extensive programming for kids — everything from gymnastics and swimming lessons to rock climbing and ropes courses. In the smaller communities, school playgrounds are generally open throughout the summer months. Health clubs have begun offering summer day camp programs too. Often these serve as a day-care option for working parents, but the activities are also available for kids who just register for a week or two.

Another place to look for fun is at our art museums and theaters. Almost all of them offer workshops and production experiences for kids. Day camps in summer provide opportunities for children to work with professionals and get in-depth training in a variety of arts and sports, but we don't have room to include them all here. We have included a section on overnight camps, but it only describes a few of the many camps operating in New Hampshire. The New Hampshire Camp Directors' Association directory is more than 50 pages long! You can obtain one by calling (800) 549-CAMP, or look for it in tourist information centers.

In winter, ski areas have special programs for children, and many communities flood fields to provide for ice-skating (see our Winter Sports chapter). Insider kids keep busy with dance and music lessons and sports all year round. Basketball is our premier indoor sport, even for children as young as second grade. Gymnastics and karate keep hundreds of youngsters fit through the winter, and many schools offer free trial lessons or mini-classes. Check the Yellow Pages under specific sports or call health clubs and inquire — often pools and kids' activities are open to nonmembers for a fee. Local recreation departments also offer a variety of activities. Call your town or city hall to inquire.

Parenting New England, a free monthly newspaper published in Nashua, has an extensive calendar section listing family activities. Look for it at area libraries, doctors' offices and stores, or call (603) 888-1872.

Fun Things To Do

Merrimack Valley Region

Bedford Golfland Inc.
549 Donald Rd., Bedford
• (603) 624-0503

This is classic minigolf, with cartoon characters and a shipwreck decorating the 18-hole course. They've also added batting cages and a driving range, and there's an ice-cream stand for after the game. They open at 7 AM and stay open until 10 PM, so you can avoid playing in the heat of the day. Your first game is $3.50 per person, the second is $2.50, and the third round is free.

Charmingfare Farm
774 High St., Candia
• (603) 483-5623

This Barnyard Petting Farm has been introducing kids to animals for a decade. You'll find all the animals you'd expect (cows, goats, sheep), some you wouldn't (check out their wolves) and a few you may not even recognize (do you know what an alpaca is?). The petting zoo is open from the first weekend in May to the beginning of October, Thursday through Sunday from 10:30 AM to 3:30 PM. Admission is $5 per person for everyone older than 6 months. You can add a pony ride or horse-drawn hayride for $2. Charmingfare also does seasonally themed hay wagon and sleigh rides, some with an optional barbecue.

Christa McAuliffe Planetarium
3 Institute Dr., Concord
• (603) 271-STAR

Kids love the interactive shows at the Planetarium. Add some time with the hands-on activities in the exhibit area and watch and read about the tragic 1986 Challenger mission, and you'll have filled an afternoon with fun and education. Call to find out which show is at what time — the little kids' show is called Wonderful Sky, but they all like Pathfinders and Skybound, too. In 1998 the Planetarium added Through the Eyes of the Hubble, bringing photos from that super-telescope to stargazers of all ages. And in 1999 another new show opened: Destination Mars! uses information from the recent Mars landing and 3-D computer graphics for a "you-are-there" experience. The Planetarium also has special programs when there's something special in the sky — eclipses, comets and solstices all are cause for an educational celebration. See our Attractions chapter for details about the schedule and admission prices. During school vacation weeks reservations are advisable.

Discovery Room at Fish & Game Headquarters
2 Hazen Dr., Concord
• (603) 271-3211

Fish & Game would like everyone to understand how important it is to manage our resources, and the Discovery Room is a good place to learn about this. You'll discover wild New Hampshire with hands-on exhibits and displays. The Discovery Room is open without charge, Monday through Friday from 8 AM to 4:30 PM. They also run a variety of special events exploring the birds, beasts and fish of New Hampshire. Call to find out what's coming up.

Point of View Farm
160 South Rd., Deerfield
• (603) 463-7974

This farm offers hour-long hay rides and sleigh rides with themed decorations at Halloween and Christmas. Wagons stop by a campfire to roast marshmallows or hot dogs halfway through the ride, and guests can use the meeting room for a picnic or birthday party afterward. Rides leave every hour, but you must have a reservation. Monday through Friday from 10 AM to 4 PM, one wagon costs $35 and holds up to 20 people. (They don't mix groups so if there are four of you it's $35 for four.) Friday evenings from 5 to 9 PM and all day Saturday and Sunday the charge is $6 for adults and $4 for children with a $35 minimum.

Legends Golf and Family Recreation

18 Legends Dr., Hooksett • (603) 627-0099

Legends offers a challenging miniature golf course, driving range and putting green, batting cages with varying pitching speed and an arcade with pinball and video games. Lights for night play and covered cages and ball dryers extend the playing time here. Summer hours are 8 AM to 10 PM and 8 AM to 9 PM on school nights. It closes earlier in spring and fall when it's cold. Cost varies with the activity, ranging from $4 for minigolf for kids younger than 12 ($2.50 for replays) to $7.50 for a bucket of balls off the grass tees. The snack bar sells ice cream, hot dogs and drinks.

Space Center

51 Zapora Dr., Hooksett • (603) 621-5150

Insider kids like this arcade because you get more games for your money than at some of the national chains. There are games for all ages, from preschoolers to teens, including laser tag. A playground, bumper cars and a train and carousel (all space-themed) keep the little ones occupied. Older kids who prefer the arcade games like being able to exchange their tickets for a receipt, which they're less likely to lose while saving up for a big prize. There is no charge for admission, just to play.

TeeOff/Mel's Family Entertainment Center

454 Charles Bancroft Hwy. (N.H. Rt. 3A), Litchfield • (603) 424-5360

You can't miss TeeOff, as its enormous net looms over the flat Litchfield countryside. The two 18-hole miniature golf courses are complemented by waterfalls, a driving range and various-speed batting cages ($1 for 16 pitches). A particular favorite with kids is the replica of Fenway Park's Green Monster. If you're up for more than just entertainment, take a lesson. Finish off with ice cream and a few rounds at the arcade to cool off. It's open 10 AM to 9 PM every day. Go-cart rides are $5, and minigolf is $4 per person, with discounts if you buy multiple rides or games.

The Children's Metamorphosis

217 Rockingham Rd., Londonderry • (603) 425-2560

This children's museum is specifically geared to the ages of 1 to 8! Almost 20 different learning centers invite children to explore things such as stickiness, colors and the natural and physical sciences. Role-playing rooms include a post office, grocery store, emergency room and construction site. There are touchable live animals in the nature center and bubbles in the water-play room. Kids can make a souvenir to bring home, put on a puppet show and dig for dinosaur pieces. Bring your lunch; there's a picnic area in the back yard. Admission cost is $3.75 per person (no charge for babies younger than 1), with a family rate of $7. Such a bargain! The Met is open 9:30 AM to 5 PM Tuesday through Sunday, 1 to 5 PM on Sunday and from 5 to 8 PM on Friday evenings. It's open Monday from 9:30 AM to 5 PM during school vacations.

Amoskeag Fishways Learning Center

Fletcher St., Manchester • (603) 626-FISH

Programs at the Fishways are organized by the Audubon Society, New Hampshire Fish and Game, U.S. Fish and Wildlife and Public Service Company, which owns the Amoskeag dam. Subjects are different every month. Most are of interest to kids. Watch the peregrine falcons over Manchester, experience the life of an Atlantic salmon or build a bat-box. See our Attractions chapter for more about the Amoskeag Fishways.

Majestic Youth Company

Hevey Theatre, 281 Cartier St., Manchester • (603) 669-7469

In 1999 the non-profit Majestic Theatre Trust began this workshop-based program for aspiring actors ages 7 to 15. Majestic has always been committed to bringing live theater to as many people as possible and this program continues that process. The emphasis in the summer program will be on exploring all aspects of theater and developing performing skills. Auditions are held in early June and the workshop culminates in the performance of a complete production in late August. Cost for the summer is just $50, but young people are asked to commit to keeping up attendance throughout the summer. See our Arts and Culture chapter for more about the Majestic Theatre Trust.

Pine Island 4-H Environmental Education Center

2849 Brown Ave., Manchester
• (603) 627-5635

The Center runs monthly outings designed to get families to appreciate nature together. Seasonal activities (maple-sugaring, snowshoeing, spring-searching) and wildlife observations (beavers, whales, eagles) take place at a variety of sites in southern New Hampshire. Most activities run about three hours and are suitable for all but the youngest children. The schedule varies so call for details.

Science Enrichment Encounters

200 Bedford St., Manchester
• (603) 669-0400

This is kid-sized science museum has recently moved to this newer, much larger home. Nearly 100 exhibits now include a dinosaur exhibit called Science for Early Explorers and a Chemistry Lab. Everything is designed for hands on, and in, to experience electricity, light, magnetism, mirrors, gravity and lots of other fun phenomena. The whole thing is the brain-child of a local inventor and entrepreneur, and what a great gift to the children of New Hampshire he has made! The staff members are young and enthusiastic, and parents can turn older kids loose while they help younger ones experiment. SEE, as it is universally known, is open weekends from noon to 5 PM and weekdays from 10 AM to 3 PM. The price for admission is $4.

antics Grill & Games

76 Huse Rd., Manchester
• (603) 626-8427

This indoor arcade and grill has managed to develop two distinct followings: the junior birthday-party set and a lively teen and singles crowd (see our Nightlife chapter). One side of the bright new building (which is just down the hill from the Mall of New Hampshire) is dominated by a huge indoor playground of the tubes, nets and slides variety, called "Soft-Play." Unlike most such structures, this one is not restricted to little kids, and older ones enjoy clambering up and sliding down. (Also unlike many such play areas, however, there is a charge to play here. One free ticket to Soft-Play is included with each lunch purchased at the Grill.) There are kid-friendly arcade games in this area as well. On the other side of the central restaurant (which features pizza and other casual foods) is an extensive assortment of video games, electronic simulators and a laser tag room, along with the pieces antics is best known for among Insider teens: several "virtual reality" games. All games including laser tag and the playground are played for tokens, which are 4 for $1 (if you'll be there a while, your best deal is 112 tokens for $20). The grill serves lunch, supper and beverages every day, and the arcade opens at 11 AM Monday through Friday and at 10 AM on weekends. Sunday through Thursday the doors close at 9 PM, but you can play until 1 AM on Friday and Saturday.

Good Times Family Fun Center

746 Daniel Webster Hwy. N., Merrimack
• (603) 429-0513

This is a roller-skating arena where families are comfortable and competitive skaters hone their skills. Roller- and in-line skates are available for rent ($3), or you may use your own if they have never been worn outside and have heel or toe stops that are not black. Another favorite here, especially for older kids, is laser tag. Sundays in July and August there's a flea market here too (indoors if it rains). The center is open Tuesday, Thursday and Friday from 4 to 6 PM at an admission cost of $2.50. Friday nights there's an early skating session from 7 to 10 PM for $5.50 and a late session from 10 to 11:30 PM for $3.00. Saturday sessions are 10 AM to noon, $3.00; 2 to 4:30 PM, $4.50; 5:30 to 7:30 PM with Christian music, $3.00; and 8 PM to 11 PM, $5.50. Sunday afternoon it's open from 2 to 4:30 PM for $4.50, and Sunday night is artistic skating night, when skaters dance and do figures (like figure-skating) to organ music from 6:30 to 9 PM for $4.

Kids Kove Playground

Twin Bridge Park, Daniel Webster Hwy., Merrimack • No phone

This wonderful playground draws families and school groups from all over the Merrimack Valley. Kids conquer castles and cross bridges, climb parapets and steer ships, all on one amazing wooden structure. Even older kids love to clamber around on this one. There are swings and slides, too, and plenty of parking. It's open from 7 AM to dusk, and it's free!

Classes/Peacock Players American Stage Festival

14 Court St., Nashua • (603) 886-7000

Over the years the Stage Festival has encouraged many area young people in their theatrical ambitions. Today young actors and actresses from around the region perform at a nearly professional level after months of intensive work with the Peacock Players. A recent production of Little Women sold out almost every show, and with more than proud parents and siblings in the seats. The Stage Festival also offers classes for all ages, beginning with "Two by Two Theatre" for toddlers and parents and continuing through the school years and up to a new series of classes for adults. Prices range from $40 for a six-week preschool program to $200 for a 12-week Shakespeare class for teens. Peacock Players holds auditions for three shows each year: call (603) 889-2330 for more information.

FunWorld

200 Daniel Webster Hwy., Nashua • (603) 888-1940

This is an arcade dressed up to look like a castle. Indoors there are kiddie rides, bowling alleys, minigolf and zillions of games ("more games than Disney," their sign proclaimed the day we were there). The indoor playground includes a 101-foot-long slide that's three stories high! They also have a room for small children and a nifty bracelet-style admission system that will trigger an alarm if a child leaves the building — very reassuring for parents with more than one to watch. There are outdoor go-carts for older children. Cost for the playground is $4.99, and adults are admitted free of charge. Some games require purchased tokens.

Canobie Lake Park

North Policy Rd., Salem • (603) 893-3507

Whether they long for roller coasters or are happy on the merry-go-round, kids want rides, and in southern New Hampshire that means Canobie Lake. Plenty of snacks, games and shows complete the picture. The minimum required height for many of the rides is 48 inches. See our Attractions chapter for more details or call and ask for the schedule of special events.

Granite Skate

51 Pelham Rd., Salem • (603) 898-3430

Granite Skate offers roller skating with Top-40 music, skate rentals (quads only, although you can use in-line skates if you have them) and a snack bar. It's open Wednesday from 4 to 6 PM and 7 to 9 PM, Thursday 10 AM to 12 noon, Saturday morning from 10 AM to 12 noon and Sunday evening 6 to 8:30 PM. It costs $3, including skate rental. Thursday evening is Family Night — from 6:30 to 9 PM a group of up to seven can skate for $10 including skates. The Saturday afternoon session is from 1 to 4 PM and costs $3, with a $1 charge for skate rental. Friday and Saturday evenings from 7:30 to 11 PM the cost is $5, and there is a $1 charge to rent skates.

INSIDERS' TIP

Don't let our cool mountain air make you forget sun block! Be sure your kids have the appropriate lotion as well as hats, shirts and long pants. And don't forget to cover the feet. Bug repellent is a good idea too. Our beautiful summers attract black flies, mosquitoes and deer flies.

Little Nature Museum
59 Boyle Rd., Weare
• (603) 529-7180

The Little Nature Museum has been introducing children to rocks and reptiles and the rest of New Hampshire's wild world for years. In addition to an eclectic collection of samples and educational exhibits, there is a nature trail on the site. The museum offers natural science workshops on a variety of subjects geared to different age groups (bears, bugs and butterflies, terrarium-building and the life of a field are one summer's offerings). It's open by appointment, at a cost of $3 for adults and $2 for children, or call for a schedule of events, which generally include admission.

Seacoast Region

Hampton Beach Casino
169 Ocean Blvd., Hampton
• (603) 926-4541 (800 GET-A-TAN)

When you need to get the kids out of the sun, the Casino offers a plethora of activities. Older kids love the arcades; younger ones enjoy sand art, ball pits and toddler rides. The Casino also has a waterslide.

The Children's Museum of Portsmouth
280 Marcy St., Portsmouth
• (603) 436-3853

If your kids would like to build a sculpture from "found" materials, explore the heavens and sail the seven seas, this children's museum in an old house in Portsmouth will enthrall them. Hands-on exhibits invite kids to learn about themselves and their world. The museum is open Tuesday through Saturday from 10 AM to 5 PM, Sundays from 1 to 5 PM and Mondays from 10 AM to 5 PM during school vacations (including summer). Admission is free for children younger than 2, $4 for children and adults and $3 for seniors. Children younger than 12 must come with an adult, and, frankly, there isn't much here for teens. Portsmouth Livery offers a package with the Children's Museum called "Ride to . . .Walk Back." For $25 the family can enjoy a carriage ride and tour of historic Portsmouth either to or from the Children's Museum. Then on the way back, you can take your time and explore the narrow streets. This package is available whenever the museum is open and the weather permits.

Joker's Family Fun 'N' Games
2460 Lafayette Rd., Portsmouth
• (603) 431-7770

Whether it's raining or cold or you've had too much sun already, sometimes an indoor activity sounds good. Joker's offers more than 150 arcade and video games, indoor mini go-carts, laser tag, and an indoor train, playhouse and Ferris wheel. But it's best known and loved by kids for the three-story jungle gym. The newest excitement here is Space Ball, a volleyball game played on a trampoline. It's open Monday through Thursday 11 AM to 9 PM, Friday 11 AM to 11 PM, Saturday 10 AM to 11 PM and Sunday 10 AM to 8 PM. Admission is free, and you pay to play. No one older than 12 is allowed in the playhouse, but there's plenty more for them to do.

NH Theater Project Theatre Classes for All Ages
738 Islington St., Suite 3-A, Portsmouth
• (603) 431-6644

In small weekly classes (no more than ten students each) children, teens and adults explore acting techniques, vocal delivery, movement, direction and characterization. Skills are developed through scene work and monologues, theatre games and story. There are classes for children as young as 6, and each of the children's classes includes no more than a three-year age spread to facilitate a developmentally-appropriate program. The teen classes are for ages 13 through 16, while older teens move into the adult classes.

INSIDERS' TIP

Pyrotechnic lovers? You can see fireworks all summer at Weirs Beach on Sunday nights at 10 PM. and Hampton Beach on Wednesdays and holidays at 9:30.

Classes are taught by accomplished actors with teaching experience. Fees are $80 to $90 for a 10-week session.

Water Country

U.S. Rt. 1, Portsmouth
• (603) 436-3556

Every Insider child knows the advertising jingle for this huge water park by heart. They start singing it about March, and by the time the gates open at Memorial Day, they can't wait to get wet. There are different rides for different sizes, including a kiddie pool with miniature water slides for the very young. The Lazer Runner tag game is popular with teens, but it's not included in the admission to the park. Tube rental isn't included either, and believe us, they'll want tubes. Weather permitting, the park is open Memorial Day weekend and the first two weekends in June then daily until Labor Day. See our Attractions chapter for hours and prices.

Hilltop Fun Center

N.H. Rt. 108, Somersworth
• (603) 742-8068

Hilltop offers miniature golf, go-carts, a batting range, golf driving range and a family game room. Children must be at least 10 years old and 54 inches tall for the go-carts, but there are junior carts for 4 to 9 year olds or older kids who are too short for the big cars. Go-cart rides cost $3.50, and junior carts cost $2.50. Minigolf is $4.25 or $3.75 for children younger than 11. It's open Monday through Thursday from 10 AM to 10 PM and Friday and Saturday from 10 AM to 11 PM.

Lakes Region

Science Center of New Hampshire

N.H. Rt. 113, Holderness
• (603) 968-7194

Children love the close encounters with the animals here, and the animal-life playhouse (climb a spider web, crawl through a rabbit warren, etc.) will keep them occupied for an hour. Different ages will appreciate different activities here, and you can send the older ones off on their own while you stay with the younger set. No pets, please. The name will change on January 1, 2000, to the Squam Lakes Natural Science Center. See our Attractions chapter for more details, hours and prices.

Pirate's Cove

U.S. Rt. 3, Meredith
• (603) 366-5058

This is a New Hampshire version of the minigolf chain. Sparkling waterfalls and rugged granite provide the backdrop for the 18-hole course. It costs $5.50 for an adult to play one round and $4.50 for kids younger than 12. It's open from 9 AM to 11 PM all summer.

ZEEUM, Children's Museum and Shop

28 Lang St., Meredith
• (603) 279-1007

Here's an interactive museum where kids can play for hours and learn at the same time. Bubbles, magnets and pendulums teach physics, and the fire truck, playhouse, grocery store and dress-up clothes encourage role-playing. The music room is a special treat, as are the computer games. Other activities explore weather, maps and trains. Everyone loves to watch the balls climb to the ceiling and roll along the winding track in the energy room, and there are lots of neat things in all price ranges at the shop, so you can keep the fun going when you leave. The ZEEUM is open Wednesday through Saturday from 9:30 AM to 5 PM and Sundays from noon to 5 PM. Admission is $5 for kids older than 2; free for the younger ones (the museum is set up for children as old as grades 3 and 4).

Winnipesaukee Scenic Railroad

Meredith Station, off Rt. 3 N., Meredith
• (603) 279-5253 (July/August) or (603) 745-2135 (year round)

Most kids are nuts about trains, and the people who operate this train are nuts about kids. The two-hour ride begins every two hours from 10:30 AM to 4:30 PM. See our Attractions chapter for prices and more details.

New Hampshire Farm Museum

Exit 18 off Spaulding Tnpk., Rt. 125, Milton
• (603) 652-7840

If your kids insist on rides and arcades

they'll think this is boring, but our American Girl doll fans love the chance to imagine themselves in the 19th century. Nature trails and picnic areas make this a good family stop. See our Attractions chapter for more details, schedule and prices.

White's Miniature Horse Petting Farm

280 Dowboro Rd., off S. Pittsfield Rd., Pittsfield • (603) 435-8258

Children love coming face to face with the miniature horses, donkeys and goats at this peaceful farm. All the animals are gentle (even the full-sized ones, like llamas), and guests can go right in the pasture with them. Bring your camera and extra film. See our Attractions chapter for more details, prices and schedule.

Polar Caves

N.H. Rt. 25, 4 miles west of Plymouth • (603) 536-1888

Kids discovered the Polar Caves near the turn of the century. The reason for the name is that the temperature in one of the caves averages 55 degrees even in the heat of summer. A three-quarter mile self-guided tour includes six caves as well as a nature trail and old-fashioned sugar house. It takes just more than an hour to see it all. See our Attractions chapter for details and prices.

Daytona Fun Park

N.H. Rt. 11 B, Weirs Beach • (603) 366-5461

As you might guess from the name, the primary attraction here is go-cart racing. Kids love to drive these hot rods around the track, and with the two-seater version, a parent can take a little driver out for a spin too. Minigolf, batting cages (10 pitches for $1.25), a bungee-cord/trampoline combination and a giant ride-in gyroscope complement the go-cart rides. In 1999 they added a climbing wall to those options. The park is open daily, weather permitting, from 10 AM to 11 PM. Go-cart rides cost $3.25 for one, $9 for 3 or $29 for 10 rides. Children shorter than 4 feet tall can ride with a parent or 16-year-old sibling for $1. Minigolf costs $4 for adults and $3 for children younger than 12.

Funspot

U.S. Rt. 3, Weirs Beach • (603) 366-4377

Funspot offers more than 500 games for kids of all ages: most of them of the video arcade variety. It has bumper cars even preschoolers can drive, bowling (candlepin and ten-pin), miniature golf for the kids and a driving range for the grownups. Funspot is one of the few Weirs Beach attractions that is open all year. It's warm in winter, cool in summer and has free parking and free admission (pay to play). Tokens cost $20 for 125 and they will disappear! See our Attractions chapter for more information.

Surf Coaster

N.H. Rt. 11B, Weirs Beach • (603) 366-4991

What child can resist the urge to get wet? Surf Coaster offers plenty of wet and plenty of wild for the whole family. The Barefoot Action kiddie lagoon is especially nice for those with small children, and the Spray Ground actually encourages siblings to have fun together. See our Attractions chapter for schedules and prices.

Weirs Beach Water Slide

U.S. Rt. 3, Weirs Beach • (603) 366-5161

If the kids just want to slide, this is the place for your family. The assortment includes the longest slide in New England along with some with astonishing speed and remarkable twists and turns. There are slides for all levels of ability and bravery here, and you can purchase tickets for a specific number of rides or amount of time if you don't want to stay all day. See our Attractions chapter for schedule and ticket prices.

Pirate's Cove Adventure Golf

U.S. Rt. 3, Winnisquam • (603) 528-6434

Despite the rowdy-looking mascot, Pirate's Cove offers miniature golf on a creatively landscaped course without the usual assortment of cute buildings and cartoon people. The two 18-hole courses traverse waterfalls, streams, boardwalks and grassy slopes. If Blackbeard were here, he'd want to know who

Photo: David Brownell/State of NH Tourism

A family enjoys a sunny day at New Castle Beach.

wasted his treasure on gardeners! Bumper cars and bank-shot basketball are further attractions, and there's a small arcade if the kids haven't had enough. It's open from 9 AM to 11 PM every day. Minigolf is $5.50 for adults and $4.50 for children, bumper boats are $3.50 per ride and basketball is $2.00 per game. A package deal for one of each is just $8 per person; $10 to play both golf courses.

White Mountains Region

Attitash Bear Peak Alpine Slide and Waterslides

U.S. Rt. 302, Bartlett • (603) 374-2368

Kids and adults enjoy the water slides as well as the ski lift ride to the top of Attitash Bear Peak. This warm weather adventure is open on weekends from late-May through early October and all day from late June through Labor Day. Look for price information in our Attractions chapter.

Story Land

N.H. Rt. 16, Glen • (603) 383-4186

Story Land is a 30-acre amusement park with a 40-year history of providing family entertainment. Some of the characters you'll meet while walking through the park are Peter Rabbit and the Three Little Pigs. The kids can visit the Three Bears' house and see the hut where Heidi's grandfather lives. All of the 17 rides have themes — from the fairy-tale inspired Cinderella's Pumpkin Coach to the modern-day Voyage To the Moon. Rides range from a quiet boat cruise to the fun Polar Coaster. Don't worry, the rides here are not daredevil but instead emphasize fun. Kids can drive an antique car or take a spin in a teacup. The shows include "Farm Follies," an animated variety show starring a scarecrow, and "Tales of Wonder," which features genies and dragons. Story Land is open every day from early June through the beginning of September. It is open on a weekends-only basis from Labor Day through Columbus Day. The hours are 9 AM to 6 PM. The admission price is $17 and includes "all rides, all shows, all day." The last ticket is sold 45 minutes before closing, and tickets purchased after 3 PM may be used for another full day in the same year. Children younger than 4 are admitted free. Reduced rates are in effect during early June. A limited number of strollers are available on a first-come, first-served basis. Pet kennels are also available. Story Land is next door to Heritage-New Hampshire, which you can read about in our Attractions chapter.

Moose Tours

Gorham Information Center, Main St., Gorham • (603) 466-3103

The whole family will enjoy seeing and learning about these north country inhabitants on this two-hour bus tour. See our Attractions chapter for more information.

Hartmann Model Railway and Toy Museum

Town Hall Rd. at N.H. Rt. 16 and U.S. Rt. 302, Intervale • (603) 356-9922

Some adults enjoy the 14 working layouts of model trains just as much as kids, so you'll find details on this working museum in our Attractions chapter.

Santa's Village

U.S. Rt. 2, Jefferson • (603) 586-4445

Experience Christmas all summer long at Santa's Village. Kids of all ages will love the fun rides such as the Yule Log Flume and the Skyway Sleigh. And shows like "Jingle Jamboree," where everyone sings Christmas carols, and "Almodarr's Illusion Magic Show," with birds appearing from thin air, will entertain the whole family. Everybody loves elves, are the inspiration behind the new "Elfabet" game where kids hunt for 26 elves throughout the village. Prizes are given to successful searchers. You can eat at Seasonings, the full-service restaurant, or Nick's Pizza Emporium. For sweets, decorate your own gingerbread man at the bake shop or stop by the Candy Cane Store for homemade fudge. Tickets are $15 and include all rides and shows. Children younger than 4 are admitted for free. The park is open every day from Father's Day weekend through Labor Day. It's also open weekends only from Labor Day through Columbus Day. The summer hours are 9:30 AM to 6:30 PM. On fall weekends, Santa's Village closes at 5 PM.

Six Gun City

U.S. Rt. 2, Jefferson • (603) 586-4592

Just when you think the White Mountains can't possibly offer another surprise, there's Six Gun City with fun for the whole family. It's an Old West town complete with cowboys, bank robbers and posses. The Concord Coach on display was manufactured in New Hampshire in November 1846 and is the oldest in existence. The 100 other horse-drawn vehicles give authenticity to thoughts of pioneer travel. Be sure and bring your bathing suits and towels to enjoy the Tomahawk Run Waterslide and Cheyenne Falls children's waterslide. Changing rooms are provided. You don't need to change for the new Prospector's Plunge Water Coaster, but you might get a little damp as you bobsled down the course in an inflatable sled. Nature and animal lovers will have fun seeing the rare Jacob Sheep, and everybody is enchanted by the Miniature Diamond B Ranch with miniature goats, burros and horses. If you've never seen a horse less than 30 inches tall, this is the chance. The sheriff is always busy catching outlaws — be especially alert around the bank — and he needs all the help he can get. Kids can become deputies and join in the fun of keeping law and order at Six Gun City. You can get snacks, soft drinks and ice cream while you check out the town. You are welcome to

INSIDERS' TIP

Be sure and bring a big bag if you're planning on a day at a water park. You'll need it to carry bathing suits, towels, shoes and sun block.

bring your own food and use one of the several picnic tables on the premises. Admission is $12.45 with unlimited rides. The park is open every day from 9 AM to 6 PM from mid-June through Labor Day. You can visit on weekends beginning Memorial Day.

Hobo Railroad
Hobo Junction, east of I-93, Lincoln
• (603) 745-2135

While kids will certainly enjoy getting their bandanna and authentic Bindle Stick, lots of the fun here will appeal to adults too. Special five-course dinner trains (a turkey special for Mother's Day), a Fourth of July fireworks bonanza and fall foliage rides are all part of the fun.

Whale's Tale Water Park
Exit 33 off I-93, U.S. Rt. 3, Lincoln
• (603) 745-8810

Bring your bathing suits, sun block and towels to enjoy a great day at this beach in the mountains. Willie's Wild Waves is a pool with waves the size of ocean breakers, and Moby Dip is a speed slide you won't forget. You can take a tube down a 360-foot, figure-eight-shape slide at Beluga Boggin into the slower paced Jonah's Escape, which features a gentle float through a White Mountains canyon. Little kids will love Whale Harbor with its smaller-scale slides and fountains. EMT and Red Cross trained lifeguards are always on duty. Just in case you get a little waterlogged, take a break in the arcade, which has a pool table and video games. You can also enjoy tetherball, volleyball and horseshoes. Little ones will have fun in the sand box and on the swings. The park is open every day from 10 AM to 6 PM from mid-June through Labor Day, weather permitting. Admission is $17.00 except for "squirts," (children younger than 4) and "Fountains of Youth" (seniors older than 65), who get in for free. After 3 PM the price drops to $11. The admission ticket includes tubes and all-day fun in the wave pool, water slides and Jonah's Escape. Life vests are available for rent. Important: Pants with rivets (like cut-off jeans) or belt buckles, footwear and eyeglasses are not allowed on slides. No food or beverages can be brought inside the park, but a picnic area is next to the parking lot. A snack bar is inside the park with food and soft drinks. Dressing rooms with showers, umbrellas and lounge chairs are all available.

Dartmouth-Lake Sunapee Region

The Fort at Number 4
N.H. Rt. 11, Charlestown
• (603) 826-5700

This is where John Stark assembled the New Hampshire militiamen to fight the British at Bennington, Vermont. Kids will learn about Colonial dress, language and crafts, and there are barns, outbuildings and a watchtower to explore. Adults enjoy the history here as much as kids so look for details in our Attractions chapter.

Ruggles Mine
U.S. Rt. 4, Grafton
• (603) 523-4275

Kids have a great time exploring the mountain caves here formed by the mining production that began in 1803. The winding tunnels lead to huge rooms with walls glittering with traces of minerals. The most common minerals mined were mica and feldspar, and the commercial mining business continued until 1959. Not everything here is underground. You'll get great views of Cardigan, Kearsarge and Ragged Mountains. Ruggles Mine operates on a seasonal schedule of weekends from mid-May to mid-June and every day from mid-June through mid-October. The hours are 9 AM to 5 PM except in July and August when the park is open until 6 PM. Admission is $12 for adults, $5 for children ages 4 to 11 and free for children younger than 4.

Mount Kearsarge Indian Museum
Kearsarge Mountain Rd., Warner
• (603) 456-2600

Kids will love listening to the trained guides explain how Native Americans lived on the land before European settlers disrupted their way of life. Medicine Woods is 2 acres of plants and trees that were used for medicine, food, dyes and everyday items such as rope. Adults love this museum, too, so we've included our full write-up in the Attractions chapter.

Monadnock Region

Friendly Farm
N.H. Rt. 101, Dublin • (603) 563-8444

Little kids have been learning about animals here since 1963. The Friendly Farm has more than 7 acres filled with barnyard animals. Your little one can feed a baby goat and cuddle a soft lamb. You'll see all the farm animals- horses, cows, pigs, goats, sheep, ducks, geese and more. You can watch eggs hatch in the incubator and pick up a new chick if you are very careful. City kids of all ages will have a great time here. It's just big enough to entertain the older kids without being too big for the toddlers. The farm is open every day from late April through Labor Day and on weekends through mid-October. Admission prices are $3.75 for children 1 through 12 and $4.75 for everyone else. Bring an outdoor snack and take advantage of the shady picnic tables. You can purchase feed for a quarter and feed the animals before or after your own meal.

Greenville Wildlife Park
18 Blanch Farm Rd., Greenville • (603) 878-2255

We can't think of a better use for a defunct condominium development than a zoo! Glen and Kathy Eldridge have been rescuing and raising exotic animals for many years, and their Furry Friends Petting Zoo has been a feature at festivals and carnivals around the state. Now they can welcome guests to the animals' home. Lions and tigers and bears line the pathways between the derelict condos, which are gradually being refurbished to house creatures who don't live happily outdoors in New Hampshire. Inside you can have close-up meetings with huge tortoises, alligators, cavies and snakes. Over time the Eldridges will be creating more natural habitat spaces for the animals, keeping the cages for rehabilitation space. Many animals born here in Greenville are sold to the large parks in the southern United States, so you might meet a baby hyena or leopard here who'll be famous someday! The park is open every day from 10 AM to 5 PM from April through November, and weekends the rest of the year. Admission to is just $3 for children and adults.

Andy's Summer Playhouse
582 Isaac Frye Hwy., Wilton • (603) 654-2613

Andy's is "Theater by children for people of all ages." We're writing it up in Kidstuff to make sure you don't miss this opportunity for your stage-struck child between the age of 8 and 18. The budding thespian can audition for the mainstage theater and touring show company. Five plays are performed each summer, and the schedule involves four weeks of rehearsal and two weeks of performances. Recent productions were Brenda Starr: Reporter and Alice in Wonderland. The cost is $250 per child for the season. Other summer opportunities for talented kids include a playwrighting lab, young directors lab and an apprentice program for behind the scenes work such as set and costume design. One-week workshops specialize in movement, comedy and storytelling. Prices on labs and workshops vary. For information write Andy's Summer Playhouse, Post Office Box 601, Wilton, NH 03086.

Summer Camps

New Hampshire is classic camp country. Think lakes, canoes, woodworking and archery. Add to those soccer, gymnastics and aquatic ecology. Think rock-climbing and ropes courses and art and chamber music. Your children can spend the heart of the summer exploring nature and learning about themselves. If you would like to learn more about the camps in New Hampshire, write to the New Hampshire Camp Directors' Association, P.O. Box 427R, Londonderry, NH 03053 and request the association's directory. We've included a few sleepover camps here to give you an idea of the wide variety of summer experiences available at camps in New Hampshire. The camp season is approximately mid-to-late-June to mid-to-late-August. Day camp choices are too many and varied to include here. Read the local paper, call the town recreation department and ask fellow parents about what's available in your area. Many art museums offer summer classes, theater companies have summer performance experiences, and lots of town pools have classes in swimming, diving and lifesaving. Call the local County Extension office for information on 4-H camps. Many schools have summer programs for kids, too, especially private schools.

Merrimack Valley

Bear Hill 4-H Camp

159 Deerfield Rd., Allenstown
• (603) 485-9889
Winter address: Moiles House,
180 Main St., Durham 03824

A variety of camps are run at this facility in the middle of Bear Brook State Park. There are one- and two-week sessions for boys or girls ages 8 to 15 as well as some coed programs and half-week junior camps for children ages 6 to 8. Campers can register for a traditional camp program or a specialty camp in areas such as fishing, shooting sports, mountain biking and swimming or non-sports specialties like cooking, sewing, photography or rocketry. Bear Hill also runs Pioneer Camp, where kids sleep in tents instead of cabins and cook their own meals over campfires instead of eating in the dining hall with everyone else. The season here runs from the last week in June to the middle of August, and most programs are either one or two weeks long. Average cost is $260 per week.

Camp Young Judea

9 Camp Rd., Amherst • (603) 673-3710
Winter address: 29 Hunnewell St., Wellesley, Mass. 02181

This coed camp for Jewish children ages 8 to 15 offers a program of watersports (including wind surfing), traditional camp sports, tennis, drama and arts and crafts. The camp provides kosher food and Jewish cultural activities including music and dance in an environment that encourages children to be proud of their Jewish heritage. The camp season runs from mid-June to mid-August. Tuition is $1,850 for a four-week session or $3,350 for the whole eight-week summer.

Camp Merrimac

329 Camp Merrimac Rd., Contoocook
• (603) 746-3195
Winter address: 14 Joyce Ln., Woodbury, NY 11797

Camp Merrimac offers a traditional camp experience for boys and girls ages 6 to 16 with individualized instruction in watersports on the lake, team and individual sports such as basketball, golf, volleyball, gymnastics and racquetball and an intensive program of tennis instruction. They even have an ice arena for hockey and figure-skating! Creative arts activities, rocketry and computers are also included. The camp is open from the end of June to the third week in August, with four two-week sessions. The cost is $1,150 for one session and runs up to $4,200 for the whole summer.

Camp Carpenter

300 Blondin Rd., Manchester
• (603) 623-5962
Winter address: 571 Holt Ave., Manchester, N.H. 03109

New Hampshire's Boy Scouts of America, the Daniel Webster Council, operate this traditional camp on the edge of New Hampshire's largest city for boys entering 2nd through 5th grade. The camp offers watersports, archery, nature activities, crafts and games. Many Scout troops arrange to come as a group and bring their own leaders, but individual campers, called "pioneers," are also welcome. The camp is open from the end of June to the third week in August, at a cost of $165 per person per one-week session (less for troops with leaders). They also offer a multi-week discount.

New Boston Livestock Camp

N.H. Rt. 13, New Boston • (603) 487-3837
Winter address: 468 Rt. 13 S., Milford 03055

This 4-H camp is operated by the U.N.H. Cooperative Extension service on the New Boston fairgrounds. Most campers, ages 8 to 15, bring their own animals to camp, except during the popular Barnyard week, when children who don't own farm animals get to try their hand at milking, currying, shearing and other farm tasks. Other traditional camp sports

www.insiders.com
See this and
many other
Insiders' Guide®
destinations online.
Visit us today!

and activities round out the day, except there is no waterfront here. There are just three one-week sessions each July. Horse week costs $190, Sheep/Goat/Cow week and Barnyard week are $150 each.

Lakes Region

Camp Brookwoods (Boys) and Camp Deer Run (Girls)

Chestnut Cove Rd., Alton
• (603) 875-3600

This pair of Christian camps is beginning to see third-generation campers among the boys and girls who attend each summer, and more than 70 percent of the campers each year are returnees. Campers ages 8 to 12 attend either the boys or girls camp programs, while there is a coed option for the 12- to 18-year-olds. The two camps enjoy 1,800 feet of frontage on Lake Winnipesaukee, so watersports are a big part of the program. Older campers are also offered the opportunity to go on more than 100 extended camping, climbing and canoeing trips on the mountains and rivers of northern New England. This is traditional backpacking (carry your own stuff), but not all the trips are arduous. The season runs from the third week in June to mid-August, with four two-week sessions. Cost is $975 for a two-week session, $1635 for four weeks, $2545 for six weeks or $3,375 for the whole summer.

Camp Berea Inc.

RFD No. 1, Box 452, Bristol
• (603) 744-6344

Berea is operated by a coalition of evangelical churches from across the Northeast. They offer boys camps, girls camps and coed camps for kids in grades 1 to 12. More than 70 percent of their campers each season are returnees, which says a lot for the program. Activities include watersports (the camp has 1,000 feet of frontage on Newfound Lake), mountain climbing, island campouts and a challenge course. Riflery, archery and swimming are taught by certified instructors. Cabins are modern, and each has its own bathroom and shower. Spiritual growth activities are a part of every program. The camp season runs from the third week in June to the end of August. Tuition is $275 for a one-week junior session, $475 for a two week regular session. Some activities carry extra charges.

Camp Wicosuta

RFD No. 1, Box 453, Bristol
• (603) 744-3301
Winter address: 216 Country Club Rd., Newton, Mass. 02159

"Wico" specializes in making camp a positive experience for every girl, even the first-timers. They utilize a "Big sister" program to create a real family atmosphere for their campers, girls ages 6 to 16, who come from as far away as California. A special effort is made to bunk campers together with others who share the same interests and even personality traits in order to make everyone more comfortable. Campers also choose from among the 30-plus activities available, including dance, drama and horseback riding as well as water sports on Newfound Lake to build a "custom" camp experience. The seven-week season runs from mid-June to mid-August. A three-week season is $3,300; the full seven weeks cost $5,400.

Camp Tohkomeupog

N.H. Rt. 153, East Madison
• (603) 367-8362, (800) 414-2267

In addition to a traditional sports program and waterfront activities, "Tohko" offers boys ages 6 to 16 a mountain or canoe trip each week, with enough varied locations that a camper could, over the course of several years, become a member of the Appalachian Mountain Club's 4,000-footer club by climbing all 48 4,000-foot peaks in New Hampshire. Back at camp there are ropes courses and a climbing wall. The emphasis here is on building self-esteem and an appreciation of nature while having a terrific time. Sportsmanship is more important than competition, and the challenge courses and rock-climbing encourage teamwork and communication. From the third week in June to mid-August the camp offers two-week sessions for grades 2 through 4 at a cost of $1,145 per session, or for any age group four weeks for $2,290 or $3,990 for the whole summer.

Camp Cody for Boys

Ossipee Lake Rd., Freedom
• (603) 539-4997, (800) 493-CODY
Winter address: 18 Black Rock Tnpk., Redding, Conn. 06896

This is a traditional camp program with a twist — it's structured so that the older a camper is, the more elective his activities become. In addition to extensive assortment of waterfront and sports activities, campers ages 7 to 16 can explore model rocketry, photography, woodworking and automechanics, just to name a few. Younger campers try some of everything, older ones can specialize. An extensive trip program offers the options of hiking in the Presidential Mountain Range, whale-watching off the coast of New Hampshire, white-water rafting in Maine, kayaking, biking and canoeing trips at sites as far away as Canada and Acadia National Park. The camp season runs from the end of June to the third week in August and costs $2,650 for the first four-week session, $3,000 for the second session or $5,000 for the full summer. Some trips have additional cost.

White Mountains and Great North Woods Regions

Barry Conservation Camp

Berlin Fish Hatchery, York Pond Rd., Berlin • (603) 449-2591
Winter address: UNH Cooperative Extension, Moiles House, 180 Main St., Durham, NH 03824

Kids between ages 10 and 15 can spend a week in the White Mountains learning about conservation. The camp is jointly run by the New Hampshire Department of Fish and Game and the University of New Hampshire Cooperative Extension. Kids study everything from Aquatic Ecology to Firearm Safety, and they'll learn about wildlife management as well as fishing. The camp opens in late June and runs through mid-August. The cost is approximately $220 per week.

Camp Walt Whitman

On Lake Armington, Piermont
• (603) 764-5521
Winter address: CWW, P.O. Box 558, Armonk, NY 10504

Camp Walt Whitman celebrated its 50th anniversary in 1998. Every summer, nearly 350 boys and girls spend a month or eight weeks on more than 300 acres in the White Mountains. Campers are between the ages of 7 and 15. The emphasis here is sports but you don't have to be a jock to have fun. Coaching in gymnastics, street hockey and rollerblading are offered in addition to traditional camp activities such as hiking, camping and woodworking. The 11 tennis courts are clay, and the camp has a heated swimming pool in addition to a spring-fed lake. Camp opens in late June and runs through mid-August. The cost is approximately $2,800 per month.

Dartmouth-Lake Sunapee Region

Camp Moosilauke

Upper Baker Pond, Orford
• (603) 353-4545
Winter address: P.O. Box E,
Orford, NH 03777

Boys from ages 7 to 16 have enjoyed Camp Moosilauke since 1904. Campers spend three and a half or seven weeks in the White Mountains, concentrating on team and individual achievement. The land sports include tennis, baseball, soccer, archery, lacrosse and football. Boys can swim, windsurf, kayak, sail and water-ski on the camp's mile-long lake. And, of course, the summer plans include lots of outdoor trips, which concentrate on canoeing, backpacking, rafting and hiking. The camp costs about $1,800 for two and a half weeks, $3,400 for four and a half weeks and $4,600 for seven weeks. The season runs from late June until mid-August.

Monadnock Region

Boston University Sargent Camp

36 Sargent Camp Rd., Hancock
• (603) 525-3311

Boys and girls ages 10 to 16 can spend one or two weeks developing self-confidence and leadership skills as they learn self-reliance in a community environment. Campers explore outdoor life through rock climbing, mountain biking and ropes courses. Safety and fun are emphasized. A noncompetitive community atmosphere is the goal of each session. The cost is about $250 per week. Older campers may stay two weeks. The camp is open for three weeks from mid-July through early August.

Camp Glen Brook

35 Glen Brook Rd., Marlborough
• (603) 876-3342 LW

The Monadnock region has several schools dedicated to the Waldorf Educational model so it's not surprising that they have a camp here. Classic camp activities for boys and girls ages 8 to 13 include swimming, horseback riding, hiking, archery, canoeing and camping along with music, arts and crafts, drama and folk dancing. Campers also care for the gardens, forest, buildings and farm animals. The cost is $1,975 for three weeks and $3,400 for six weeks. Camp begins in late June and runs through mid-August.

Camp Takodah

55 Fitzwilliam Rd., Richmond
• (603) 239-4781
Winter address: Cheshire County YMCA,
P.O. Box 647, Keene 03431

Kids from 7 to 16 can enjoy 2 or 4 weeks in the heart of the Monadnock region. For the most part, July sessions are for boys and August is for girls. One week of coed camping for kids 7 to 10 is available. In addition to the traditional camp experiences of swimming, boating, archery and crafts, the camp offers a concentrated soccer camp for boys ages 11 to 13 and adventure camp for 13 to 16-year-old boys and girls. All campers enjoy the high ropes course and wind surfing program. The end of the summer is celebrated with a special family camp. The camp opens in the latter part of June and runs through late August. The cost is about $620 for two weeks, with Cheshire County residents getting a price break of about $100.

Fleur de Lis Camp

Howeville Rd., Fitzwilliam
• (603) 585-7751
Winter address: Box 659,
Lincoln Mass. 01773

Girls have been experiencing the outdoor life on Laurel Lake since 1929. Stressing friendship and confidence, the camp encourages all girls to pursue individual interests at the same time they learn to explore new activities. Four- and six-week sessions are offered each summer with the possibility of a two-week camp "tryout" for young, first-time campers. Activities include swimming, boating, sailing, canoeing and wind surfing. Girls can also participate in diving, arts and crafts, horseback riding and theater. A ropes course and lifesaving instruction are part of the summer curriculum. Campers range in age from 8 to 15. Four-week sessions cost approximately $1,600 and eight-week sessions are about $2,850. The camp season is from the latter part of June until mid-August.

Kingsbury Hill Riding Camp
Dennison Pond Rd., Francestown
• (603) 547-6624

For a girl that loves horses, we can't think of anything more fun than owning a horse for part of a summer. As soon as the camper arrives at camp, she'll be given "her" horse. With staff supervision and training, the girls learn stable management by caring for their own horse throughout the session. Each girl is responsible for daily grooming, care and feeding of her horse. She'll also receive riding instruction at the appropriate level (from beginner to advanced) and participate in overnight trail rides. And just in case she doesn't want to spend every hour in the barn, the camp offers art and swimming. The camp is for ages 8 to 16. Sessions are one, two or four weeks long, and the cost is $550 per week.

Cooks are frequently part of the scene at our annual events, so be prepared to eat your share of pies — apple in the fall and blueberry in late summer.

Annual Events

We think annual events offer both newcomers and visitors a great opportunity to learn about New Hampshire. Many of our festivals take place on "Main Street," which is a great way to see small-town New England at its best. Local artists, craftspeople and entertainers are usually on hand, providing local color. And cooks are frequently part of the scene, so be prepared to eat your share of pies — apple in the fall and blueberry in late summer. Strawberries are the highlights of June festivals, and starting in late March, just about every food item is covered with maple syrup or made with maple sugar.

If you have little ones, or if you just love a parade, watch the local papers and bulletin boards. New Hampshire boasts a growing number of community parades, not just for the Fourth of July (festive) and Memorial Day (solemn), but now for Christmas, Labor Day and Halloween, too. Some are exclusively kids, school bands and fire trucks, but many have floats, acrobats, antique cars and as many local politicians as you can line up behind a banner.

In this chapter, we've highlighted some of our favorite annual events. We've given approximate times of the month for each event. Always call ahead for exact dates as well as details on tickets (if necessary). Ask about accommodations when you call. It's not unusual for local motels, country inns and bed and breakfast inns to have special rates for festival attendees.

Most events are free although you'll pay for food and amusement rides. Depending on the festival, you might pay for musical concerts or other cultural entertainment. We've been as specific as possible, but be aware that pricing policies may change. It's always a good idea to review all costs when you call about dates.

We've organized this chapter in chronological order by month beginning with January. Within each month the festivals are listed in regional order: Merrimack Valley, Seacoast, Lakes, White Mountains and Great North Woods, Dartmouth-Lake Sunapee and Monadnock. Not every region has an event every month. Remember to call ahead, wear comfortable shoes and have fun.

January

Merrimack Valley Region

First Night
Various locations in Concord
• (603) 639-1926

About 20 sites invite celebrants to an alcohol-free, art-centered welcome of the New Year. The purchase of an $8 button entitles the wearer to attend musical and dance performances, puppet theater, movies and video showings, archery demonstrations and laser shows. There are also fireworks, street performers and hot-air balloon launches that everyone can enjoy, with or without buttons.

Martin Luther King Jr. Day
New Hampshire College, 2500 N. River Rd., Manchester
• (603) 645-9608
Notre Dame College, 2321 Elm St., Manchester • (603) 645-1270
St. Anselm College, Abbey Rd., Goffstown • (603) 641-7219

New Hampshire has steadfastly refused to officially observe Martin Luther King Day, settling instead for a more generic "Civil Rights Day" without a holiday. Nevertheless, these local colleges all have special programs on what would be the Monday holiday. Lectures and memorial services honor the slain civil rights leader, and all are open to the public without charge.

Seacoast Region

First Night
Various locations, Portsmouth
• (603) 431-5388, (800) 639-9302

Portsmouth's First Night offers a wealth of activities with an emphasis on music at 43 indoor and outdoor venues. One year's celebration included a Beatles tribute band, an Elvis impersonator, stand-up comedy and a hypnotist. A unique feature of Portsmouth's First Night is a giant puppet parade, and the evening concludes with fireworks. A $9 button admits you to all activities.

Lakes Region

First Night
Various locations, Wolfeboro
• (603) 569-2200

Wolfeboro is a relative newcomer to First Night, but this is a community that knows how to put on a show, and they're rapidly establishing a loyal following. Films and music, a dance contest and jugglers are among the activities that welcome the New Year. Admission, by button, is $7.

February

Merrimack Valley Region

Granite State Camper and RV Show
State Armory, River Rd. at Amoskeag Bridge, Manchester • (207) 865-1196

When winter is at its dreariest, the chance to go indoors and check out all the latest in camping equipment can be irresistible. From pop-up trailers to luxurious 35-foot motorhomes, you'll find inspiration here. Somewhere the sun is shining — maybe it's time to follow it? This show is held the first weekend in February. Admission is $3.50 for adults, $2.50 for children.

Winter Carnival
Wasserman Park, Naticook Rd., Merrimack
• (603) 882-1046

Every year on a weekend in early February the Merrimack Parks and Recreation Department puts on this great local gathering. There are games and contests for kids of all ages, sleigh-rides (or hayrides if there's no snow), ice fishing on Naticook Lake and plenty of hot drinks and snacks for sale. All kinds of community organizations help out, and it's a nice way to meet your neighbors. Some activities have fees.

Farm and Forest Exposition
Center of New Hampshire Holiday Inn, 700 Elm St., Manchester
• (603) 271-3788

The second weekend in February brings farmers, lumberjacks and city slickers together for a celebration of two of New Hampshire's most important industries. Trees and farm animals come indoors, and demonstrations, exhibits and awards invite New Hampshire families to explore the variety of agricultural and forestry products featured. Friday night is 4-H night, with special activities for kids. There is no charge to attend the Exposition.

Interfaith Peace Celebration
Maple St., Henniker
• (603) 428-3366

For two decades the people Henniker have joined in a work of prayer and education known as the Henniker Peace Community. Their annual observance falls on a weekend near Valentine's Day, and is co-sponsored and co-hosted by St. Theresa's Church and the Henniker Congregational Church. Music, readings, and discussion are focused on a

INSIDERS' TIP

Watch for banners and posters announcing upcoming Old Home Days celebrations. These are great local festivals, generally featuring local musicians, games and races for kids, lots of food and a variety of old-fashioned activities.

different theme each year (in 1999 the topic was Ireland's Peace Process). The day concludes with a potluck supper.

Fishing Derby

Pinnacle Mountain Fish and Game Club, Cemetery Rd., Lyndeboro • (603) 654-2590

This kids' event is cosponsored by the Souhegan Valley Boys and Girls Club. The derby is open to youth up to age 18. Members of the Fish and Game club provide instruction and loan their ice-fishing equipment to participants. The Fire Department does ice-safety demonstrations. There are snowmobile rides, games and of course, a bonfire. Families are encouraged to bring hot dogs and marshmallows as well as a picnic lunch. There is no charge to participate in the derby.

New Hampshire Boat Show

State Armory, River Rd. at Amoskeag Bridge, Manchester • (207) 865-1196

Enjoy a great slice of summer in the middle of winter. All kinds of boats are on display, from speedboats to sportfishing boats to cabin cruisers. Great displays of equipment, accessories and safety planning fill out the show. Admission costs $3.50 for adults and $2.50 for children. The show is generally held the last weekend in February.

Seacoast Region

Winterfest

Various locations, Somersworth • (603) 692-7175

Every year in early February, just about when we're beginning to think winter will never end, the festive folks over in Somersworth put on this wonderful family weekend. Ice skating, a bonfire, dogsled races and hayrides, snowball-throwing contests, a ham and bean supper and a talent show are all part of the goings-on, which take place in several locations around town including the schools, Lions Club Skating Rink, and the Sunningdale Country Club. The indoor carnival for children is always a hit, but the slide and glide (cardboard sled) derby may be the highlight of the festival.

Swing Into Spring Arts & Crafts Show

Yoken's Conference Center, Lafayette Rd., Portsmouth • (603) 528-4014

More than 125 crafters, great food, live music and great ideas make this a bright spot on the mud season calendar. Whether you're looking for a nice Easter gift or some new ideas for your own craft projects, you'll find something perfect. Admission to the show is $2.50, and children younger than 12 are admitted free.

Lakes Region

Great Rotary Fishing Derby

Meredith • (603) 279-6121

Each year the Meredith Rotary releases tagged rainbow trout in New Hampshire lakes. Then, in early February, a whole village of ice-fishing huts appears on Meredith Bay, and more than 6,000 fishermen, fisherwomen and fisherkids drop their lines in hopes they'll land the biggest fish and the biggest prize. You must have a valid fishing license and buy a derby ticket to be eligible for the $46,000 in prizes. The entry fee is $20.

World Championship Sled Dog Derby

Laconia • (603) 279-5063

Some people call this the most prestigious annual sled dog race on the planet! Mushers from all over North America converge on the Lakes Region for this open-class race, which is run the third weekend in February. The start/finish line is on Main Street in Laconia, while the 18-mile course winds over the fields and lakes that surround the city. There is no charge to come and cheer on the dogs (and their owners). Pray for snow, because for two straight years Mother Nature has rescheduled this race.

Winter Carnival

Remick Country Doctor Museum, Tamworth • (603) 323-7591

One weekend in mid-to-late February the Tamworth Outing Club, the Recreation Department and the folks at the Museum sponsor an old-fashioned winter carnival. There's sledding, horse-drawn sleigh-rides and cross-country skiing around the grounds. Try your hand at the snowball-throwing contest or your feet at the snowshoe obstacle course. You can join the snow-sculpture contest or just gape at the entries. There is no charge except for food.

White Mountains and Great North Woods Regions

Hannes Schneider Meister Cup Race

Cranmore Mountain, Skimobile Rd., North Conway
• (603) 356-5543, (802) 457-9194

Hannes Schneider revolutionized skiing with his methods of teaching in the Ski School he founded right here at Mt. Cranmore more than 60 years ago. The New England Ski Museum and the New Hampshire Make-A-Wish Foundation co-sponsor this skiing event in his honor the last weekend in February. The weekend includes a snow train, reminiscent of those that brought skiers to the White Mountains from Boston years ago. There's a cardboard box derby, a torchlight parade, a fashion show featuring vintage ski outfits, and a reception with autograph party with stars of the professional ski racing circuit. The highlight of the weekend is the Meister Cup itself, in which teams of skiers compete in numerous events and divisions. Our favorite is the 10th Mountain Division competition. Team members are veterans of the 10th Mountain Division who fought in the Italian Alps during World War II. Many of them are now in their seventies and eighties, but they're still able skiers and eager to win the competition between regiments.

Dartmouth-Lake Sunapee Region

Dartmouth Winter Carnival

Dartmouth College, Hanover
• (603) 646-3399

The first Dartmouth Winter Carnival was in 1911. In 1916 National Geographic called it the Mardi Gras of the North. It remained the premier collegiate winter weekend until 1999. Upset with the college president's recent declaration that the "Greek" social club system would have to be overhauled and made coed in order to exist, the student leaders of Winter Carnival canceled many activities in protest. We don't know what February 2000 will bring; you might want to call ahead. Normally, Winter Carnival is held in early February. The fun begins on Thursday night with opening ceremonies on the Dartmouth Green. Skiing competitions are held on Friday and Saturday at the Dartmouth Skiway. Races include men and women's Giant Slalom, individual cross-country and cross country freestyle relays. Races are intercollegiate and intramural. You might have fun watching Dartmouth students brave the cold at Occum Pond during the Polar Bear Swim. The public is welcome at all sporting events. You'll have a chance to see men's ice hockey, women's basketball and men and women's track and field. For ticket information and a schedule of events call (603) 646-2466.

You're welcome to attend the cultural events too. The Winter Carnival usually features movies on Thursday and Sunday nights and musical performances on Saturday and Sunday nights. The cultural events are in Spaulding Auditorium at the Hopkins Center, and admission is charged. Call the Hopkins Center, (603) 646-2422, for prices and a schedule of the cultural events.

INSIDERS' TIP

A big birthday is always cause for celebration. As the nation prepares for the millennium, many New Hampshire communities are celebrating 200 or 250 years since their incorporation. Parades, reenactments and fireworks are often part of the celebration.

March

Merrimack Valley Region

N.H. Philharmonic Kids' Concert

Palace Theater, Hanover St., Manchester
• (603) 647-6476

Each year on a Sunday in early March the New Hampshire Philharmonic Orchestra puts on this terrific concert to introduce children younger than 12 to classical music. The pieces are selected for their interest to young people and there are explanations and introductions to the works as the concert goes on. Frequently other arts organizations are involved in the presentation as well — in 1999 the New Hampshire School of Ballet performed interpretive dance as the orchestra played. Audience participation with movement and sound is also encouraged. Tickets are free for children 12 and younger, while adult tickets are just $7. Each adult may bring as many as four children. See our Arts and Culture chapter for more about the Philharmonic Orchestra and the Palace Theater.

New Hampshire Fishing and Sportsman Show

Rockingham Park Indoor Pavilion, Rockingham Park Blvd., Salem
• (603) 528-4014

It's a bit early to be dropping a line or setting up a blind, but the first weekend in March is a great time for checking out new equipment, learning new tricks, improving your skills and getting ready for the season to come. Experts offer seminars and workshops on such topics as turkey hunting and fly-tying. In 1999 a falconer spoke on "Hunting with Raptors." A wildlife exhibit and fish tank intrigue kids and adults alike. Outfitters and guide services are on hand to discuss options and help you plan trips. Admission to the show, which runs Friday night and all day Saturday and Sunday, is $6 for adults and teens. Children younger than 12 are admitted free with an adult.

New England Craft and Specialty Food Fair

Rockingham Park Indoor Pavilion, Rockingham Park Blvd., Salem
• (603) 755-2166

An indoor fair to brighten a dreary time of year, this gathering of juried artisans in early March features homemade and handmade crafts, foods and specialty items. Craft demonstrations may inspire you to try your own skills, or you may be content simply to enjoy the music, sample some gourmet goodies and enjoy a break from the slush outside. There is a $2.50 charge for admission.

Made In N.H.-Try It, Buy It Festival

State Armory, River Rd. at Amoskeag Bridge, Manchester
• (603) 626-6354

Here's a trade fair entirely filled with merchandise produced in New Hampshire. You may be surprised at the variety of items on display. It's not just crafts — there are lots of high-tech and manufacturing businesses here too. Although chances are you won't take home an industrial-quality synthetic sapphire, you may well find a gem. This show is generally held the third weekend in March. Admission is $4 for adults and $2 for children younger than 12.

Maple Weekend

Various locations State-wide
• (603) 225-3757

On the last weekend in March the state's maple-sugar producers go all-out to share this sweet season with everyone. In 1999 50 sugarhouses participated. Depending on the location and the weather you may get to eat sugar on snow, watch the boiling process, take a sleighride through the sugarbush or here the sap dripping musically into old-fash-

INSIDERS' TIP

There are very few events scheduled in March, clearing the decks for our most important annual events: Town and School District meetings.

ioned pails. Everywhere you'll enjoy free samples!

White Mountains and Great North Woods Regions

Maple Syrup Festival at The Rocks

off U.S. Rt. 302, Bethlehem
• (603) 444-6228

The Rocks Christmas Tree Farm is owned and operated by the Society for the Protection of New Hampshire Forests. Every year in mid- to late March, they have a Saturday program devoted to maple syrup. You'll learn how to identify sugar maples, tap a tree, gather sap and turn the sap into syrup. You'll have a chance to taste syrup too. Donuts and sour pickles are the traditional foods of sugaring time. The cost is $5 per person, and you'll need to reserve a spot at this popular spring ritual. To get there, take Exit 40 off Interstate 93 and go east on U.S. 302 for a half-mile. Turn right opposite the Exxon station and follow the signs to The Rocks.

Monadnock Region

Breath of Spring Flower Show

Cheshire Fairgrounds Arena, N.H. Rt. 12 S., Keene
• (603) 355-6335 x 159

On the last weekend in March, when you're really itching to get into the garden but the ground is still frozen 6 inches down, 12,000 square feet of plants and flowers is just what the doctor ordered. There are information displays, vendors touting the benefits of their gardening gizmos and workshops led by Master Gardeners from the Extension service. You can learn about compost or roses, dried flowers and healing plants, or combating bugs and weeds. And there are flowers: tens of thousands of flowers, all displayed in designs around a whimsical theme (in 1999 it was *The Wizard of Oz*). Trees and shrubs blossom, waterfalls and streams beckon with their musical call. The show runs from Friday noon to Monday evening, and opens early on Saturday and Monday to accommodate the disabled and senior citizens in a less-crowded atmosphere. Tickets are $4 in advance and $6 at the door, and benefit Hospice Care and Maternal and Child health programs.

April

Merrimack Valley Region

Merrimack Valley Christian Film Festival

Salem Tri-Cinema, N.H. Rt. 28, Salem
• (978) 937-4013

Each year during the week between Palm Sunday and Easter a number of churches in the Salem-Haverhill (Mass.) area sponsor this free film festival. There are movies for children, teens and all ages, as many as 15 movies running on a variety of schedules in the three cinemas. Guest appearances by actors and producers round out the schedule. All the movies have Christian themes (in 1999 there was a definite "end-of-the-world" theme in honor of the millennium). Admission is free.

Amherst Outdoor Antique Auto Swap & Sell Meet

N.H. Rt. 122, Amherst
• (603) 673-2093

This is the opening day for two enormous flea markets on N.H. 122 and for this antique auto show. The flea markets run every Sun-

INSIDERS' TIP

Spring brings strawberry festivals; fall celebrates apples and pumpkins. These local harvest parties, typically on the village green or church lawn, may include art shows, craft fairs, games and music, but the focus is on food. You have never tasted so many different apple desserts, pumpkin breads or strawberry pies!

day, but the cars are only here on the last Sunday of the month. Antique auto buffs from across New England head to Amherst for these sales, and the sight of all those Model Ts and Studebakers on the highway is a welcome sign of spring. Both flea markets and the auto show run through October.

White Mountains and Great North Woods Regions

Ammonoosuc Amble

Profile High School, N.H. Rts. 18 and 116, Bethlehem
• (603) 444-2464

This USA Track and Field-certified 5-mile road race and walk benefits the Ammonoosuc Community Health Services. Runners and walkers love the race — maybe because it's cool in Bethlehem in April — and the event is beginning to attract participants from as far away as Montreal and Rhode Island. The race is held on a Saturday in mid-April and is followed by an awards ceremony, which includes a raffle with great prizes of weekends for two at a local inn and artwork by talented locals. Register by April 1 and be the first on your block to have a T-shirt from this up-and-coming event. Information and registration forms are available from Ammonoosuc Community Health Services, Mt. Eustis Road, Littleton, NH 03561.

May

Merrimack Valley Region

Taste of Nashua

Main Street, Nashua
• (603) 882-3281

This early-May event, sponsored by Destination Downtown, enables guests to sample the delicious cuisine at a number of the great restaurants along Main Street in Nashua (see our Restaurants chapter). The evening begins at the Hunt Building and includes musical entertainment at a number of the participating restaurants. The event concludes with music, a raffle and dessert at 14 Court Street, the theater that's home to the American Stage Festival and Nashua Theater Guild. This event is limited to 600 people, and at $15 each it traditionally sells out. It's not really geared to children.

Wood Day at Shaker Village

288 Shaker Rd., Canterbury
• (603) 783-9511

The Shakers were known for the beauty and durability of their woodworking, and this annual celebration in early May honors that tradition. Develop your woodworking skills and learn about traditional techniques of joinery and carving. See how the Shakers made musical instruments and hear them played. Admission is $8.50 for adults and $4 for children ages 6 to 15. Those younger than 6 get in free, as does anyone who brings an instrument to join in the music.

Doodlebug Pulls

Intervale Rd., Canterbury
• (603) 783-0354, 798-5215

Doodlebugs are tractors that were built on the chassis of old cars during WWII when new farm equipment wasn't being built. The Doodlebugs Homemade Antique Tractor Club is dedicated to the preservation of these pieces of American history. The club hosts tractor pulls on the second Sunday of the month from May through October. The days are a real family affair. People bring lawn chairs and picnics, or enjoy the hearty barbecue lunch. There is no charge to attend.

Kiwanis Spring Trade Fair

Everett Arena, 15 Loudon Rd., Concord
• (603) 226-8016

They call this a trade fair, and it is an opportunity for local businesses to show off their wares. But the emphasis is on the "fair," and the atmosphere is more carnival than trade show. There are rides for the little kids, clowns, games, food and entertainment. A parade on Thursday evening and fireworks on Saturday night complete the fun. The Trade Fair is always the weekend after Mother's Day. There's no charge to attend.

Kidfest

Center of New Hampshire, 700 Elm St., Manchester • (603) 669-5777

This annual event sponsored by WZID radio brings every kind of kids' entertainment together for what feels rather like a slightly-crazed trade show, except that all the business executives are less than 5 feet tall. Live music, comedy and visiting stars (the Rugrats appeared in 1999) provide entertainment. There are carnival activities like a ball pit and an inflated "moonwalk" as well as a petting zoo. The winning robots from the FIRST competition go through their paces, and there are jumprope teams, cheerleading teams and martial arts schools doing demonstrations. Lots of products kids love are on display, too, from computers to clothes. Adults and older children pay $3 to attend, children five and younger are free.

Greater Nashua Flower Show

Hunt Memorial Building, 7 Main St., Nashua • (603) 882-1613

The ongoing restoration of the beautiful Hunt Building gets a double boost from this annual spring event. All funds raised go to the restoration fund, and the show gives everyone a good look at what they're preserving! Local florists contribute intriguing and delightful displays related to a different theme each year (in 1999 it was opera). There are also demonstrations by local artists and a display of children's art in the building. Admission to the show, which is open from 10 AM to 7 PM on Saturday and 10 AM to 5 PM on Sunday costs $5 for adults and $3 for children younger than 10. If you're up for a really special event, dress up and come by for the sneak preview/champagne gala on the Friday evening. Those tickets are $25.

Herb and Garden Day at Shaker Village

288 Shaker Rd., Canterbury • (603) 783-9511

Whether you're interested in herbs for cooking or traditional herbal medicines, you'll learn something interesting at this annual end-of-May event. Guided walks of the nature trails, a Maypole dance and games for the children make this a family event. If you're inspired by what you see, there are plants for sale too. See our Attractions chapter for more about Shaker Village.

Seacoast Region

Children's Day

Downtown Portsmouth • (603) 436-3988

On the first Sunday in May children are the guests of honor at a party that fills downtown Portsmouth. Clowns and costumed characters walk the cobblestones. Balloons and face-paints adorn the kids. There's lots to see and lots to do, all free and courtesy of the Portsmouth Chamber of Commerce.

New Hampshire Tow Association Wrecker Rodeo

Hampton Beach State Park, Hampton Beach • (603) 926-8718

If someone in your house is a truck fan, this is definitely the place to be on the middle weekend in May. Beginning with a tow truck parade on Saturday morning, the "rodeo" includes demonstrations, exhibits, contests and a chance to get up close and personal with some really, really big trucks. There is no admission charged.

Chowder Festival

Prescott Park, Marcy St., Portsmouth • (603) 436-2848

At the end of May each year, more than 20 restaurants contribute their finest chowders for public scrutiny and enjoyment. This Seacoast tradition is hosted by radio station WOKQ and the Prescott Park Arts Festival. "Chowda," as we know it here in New England, is a thick, milky soup with lots of potatoes and — well, here there are 20 different ands. Try them all, then vote for your favorite. A $5 donation is requested.

Lakes Region

Winni Derby

Center Harbor • (603) 253-8689

This fishing contest with $40,000 in prizes is the World Series of angling in the state. The goal is to catch the biggest landlocked salmon

Photo: Hampton Beach Chamber of Commerce

Keep a look out for the free outdoor concerts at Hampton Beach.

or lake trout in the Big Lake, and the truly devoted start planning their strategy long before ice-out. More than 3,000 people participate each year, at a cost of $25 for adults or $15 for a Junior Division entry for ages 15 or younger.

Family-A-Fair

Sandwich Fair Grounds, Center Sandwich • (603) 447-5922, (800) 322-4166

This beginning of May gathering drew 1,500 people its first year, guaranteeing that it would return as an annual event. Each year more local people (and the few early-season visitors) join in the fun. Face-painting, balloons and games attract families with young children, and the refreshments include cotton candy and peanut butter sandwiches! Entertainment is scheduled throughout the day, all of it appropriate for kids. There is no charge to attend the fair, and almost everything for sale during the day is in the 25¢ range.

Farm Festival

Remick Country Doctor Museum, Tamworth • (603) 323-7591

One weekend at the beginning of May the farmhouse and grounds at the Country Doctor Museum spring to life in the old-fashioned style. Come by to milk cows and feed chickens, have a hayride and learn about life on the farm when grandma was a girl. Don't worry, it's not all work and no play! No admission charged, food is for sale.

NASCAR Busch Grand National Race

N.H. International Speedway, Loudon • (603) 783-4744

Depending on your interests this is one of those events you either plan on or plan around. Serious racing fans descend upon Loudon and the surrounding area at least one weekend each month: the NASCAR Busch Grand National race in mid-May is the first big race of the season. See our Spectator Sports chapter for more about the Speedway.

Porky's Cruise Night

Porky's Restaurant, N.H. Rt. 25, Moultonboro • (603) 253-6226

This is one of those little local curiosities that sometimes grow into major events. Every Thursday night from 6 to 8 PM throughout the summer (starting around Memorial Day) you'll find dozens of antique and classic cars gathering at Porky's. Folks come from as far away as central Massachusetts for an evening of ogling engines and caressing fenders. Classic rock 'n' roll plays in the background, the ice cream sales skyrocket, and for two hours people show off their "babies." Raffle tickets provide for snacks and trophies for the end-of-the-season party the Sunday after Labor Day. Hop in the Woody and come-on-down!

Great Smith River Canoe Race
Albee Town Beach, N.H. Rt. 28, Wolfeboro • (603) 569-5454

This Insider favorite takes place every year in mid-May. Paddlers of all abilities, from novices to expert, compete against others of similar skills, with first, second and third prizes awarded in 17 different classes. Registration for racers costs $8, but there is no charge to watch and cheer.

White Mountains and Great North Woods Regions

Lilac Time Festival
Main St., Lisbon • (603) 838-6336

The lilac is our state flower, and every Memorial Day Weekend Lisbon celebrates what is usually the peak of bloom for these sweetly scented flowers. (We say usually because a late spring can have the Lilac Festival preceding the actual bloom of these beautiful white or purple flowered shrubs.) With or without blooms, all the fun takes place on Main Street. Saturday starts with a pancake breakfast at the Main Street church for the Lisbon Shared Ministry. The parade kicks off at 11 AM with floats sponsored by local businesses. A special stamp cancellation can be obtained at the post office on Saturday from 9 AM to noon. Throughout the weekend locals and residents of nearby towns have a flea market on the church lawn, while vendors and amusement rides are set up on Main Street.

Sunday features a morning church service in honor of Memorial Day and an afternoon with lots of live music on Main Street. Everyone enjoys the fireworks show on Sunday night. On Monday, Little Miss Lilac is crowned (she's selected based on raffle ticket sales) and plants a lilac tree with Miss New Hampshire. All events are free, but you will pay for food and amusement rides.

Dartmouth-Lake Sunapee Region

Dartmouth Powwow
The Green, Hanover • (603) 646-2110

The first Dartmouth Powwow was held in 1972. It's organized by the native American students at Dartmouth and is going strong after 25 years. It's held on the Saturday and Sunday of Mother's Day weekend. The Powwow celebrates Native American culture. Everything sold and on display is made by Native Americans. The event encourages those who attend to participate. Dance demonstrations are followed by dance competitions open to all. Craft and food vendors set up stalls on The Green. Here's your chance to sample buffalo burgers, Indian tacos, venison sausage and Shinnecock succotash. The Saturday night community dinner is open to all. Dancers, drummers, singers and elders are served first, followed by festival attendees. The dinner is served as long as the food holds out. The dinner is free, but you will pay for all food from vendors.

Monadnock Region

Arts and Film Festival
Main Street, Wilton • (603) 654-6564

A Saturday near the end of May brings lots of attention to downtown Wilton and the Annual Arts and Film Festival. Not many people realize that the Town Hall Cinema in Wilton hosted the premiere of the movie Star Wars and that it's crucial for those of us who like independent as well as (some) Hollywood films. Building on the belief that movies can be art as well as entertainment resulted in the current festival. Original student films might be featured as well as one or two classics. In addition to movies, local artists and crafts people set up booths along Main Street. Children line up for the local face-painting expert, and everyone enjoys the performances on the Main Street stage. You'll see everything

Agricultural Fairs

Close-up

County fairs are a remnant of a simpler time and a promise for a bright future. New Hampshire has a dozen agricultural fairs every fall, each with its own flavor but with the same familiar features. You'll find midways with rides and amusements, arcade games and food vendors galore, but beyond the carnival atmosphere you'll get to review your neighbors' hard work. Prize pumpkins and glowing jars of jam, prize-winning pies and beautiful dried flowers will be on display. Liquid embroidery and fabric-painted T-shirts share space with handmade quilts, christening gowns and braided rugs.

County 4-H groups put together great displays of their projects, many camping at the fairgrounds to care for their livestock. Horse and oxen pulls are a favorite entertainment, as are the pageants to choose a fair queen and performances by local music groups.

Spend an evening or a weekend at an agricultural fair and connect with our country heritage. Most fairs charge admission, averaging about $5 for an adult ticket, with multi-day discounts.

Merrimack Valley Region

- Hopkinton State Fair (603) 746-4191, Labor Day Weekend
- Hillsborough County Fair (603) 588-6106, Weekend after Labor Day
- Deerfield Fair (603) 463-7421, Last weekend in September

Seacoast Region

- Stratham Fair (603) 772-2990, Last weekend in July

The Lakes Region

- Belknap County Fair (603) 267-8135, Third weekend in August
- Plymouth State Fair (603) 536-1690, Fourth weekend in August
- Rochester Fair (603) 332-6585, Ten days in mid-September
- Sandwich Fair (603) 284-7062, Second weekend in October

Photo: Sally Wilkins

Agricultural fairs highlight New Hampshire's rural heritage and give 4-Hers a chance to shine.

White Mountains and Great North Woods Regions

- North Haverhill Fair (603) 787-6696, Last weekend in July
- Lancaster Fair (603) 788-4531, Last weekend in August

Dartmouth-Lake Sunapee Region

- Cornish Fair (603) 542-4622, Third weekend in August

Monadnock Region

- Cheshire Fair (603) 357-4740, Last week in July

from ballet to contra dancing exhibitions. And, of course, the food vendors help keep cholesterol counts from dipping too low. Call ahead to check on ticket prices for films. They range from free to about $5.

June

Merrimack Valley Region

Hot Air for High Hopes

Balloon Festival
Emerson Rd., Milford
• (603) 673-70051

This event raises funds to grant wishes for children with chronic and terminal illnesses. The balloons are the focus of the event, with launches each morning and evening of the second weekend in June (weather permitting) and a "Glow," each evening, in which the balloons are filled but remain on the ground. All day long the grounds are filled with people enjoying kids' activities, a classic car show, balloon crew competitions and demonstrations of karate, dance and skydiving. Hundreds of vendors offer food, crafts and fun merchandise. Helicopter rides and balloon rides are available by reservation. There is no admission charge, just a $1 donation when you park your car.

Joseph Campbell Festival of Myth, Folklore and Story

Union Square, Milford
• (603) 672-4412

In just a few years this mid-June celebration, organized by the local group Keepers of the Lore, has grown to attract hundreds of listeners to enjoy storytelling, poetry, music, dance and drama reflecting dozens of different ethnic and cultural heritages from around the world. A jester, bagpiper, puppets and drummers were among the artists who shared their stories in 1997. One venue features members of the New Hampshire Storytelling Guild all day free of charge, a pass for the other 30-odd performances at locations around the Oval costs just $8 for adults and $5 for children younger than 13.

Rose Show

Nashua Mall, Broad St., Nashua
• (603) 673-0754, 595-4501

Members of the New Hampshire Rose Society sponsor this annual event in mid-June (just when you're looking at those tired rose bushes in your yard and wondering what's wrong). Come to see new varieties and old favorites, gather tips for growing and enjoying roses, or just to inhale!

Summer Block Party

Downtown Nashua
• (603) 882-3281

One Saturday in mid-June the Downtown Destination people close down Main Street for this great community event. An estimated 3,000 to 4,000 people attend each year, enjoying bands, mimes and street performers, demonstrations of square dancing and martial arts and a variety of activities for children. The hit of the day (so to speak) is the dunking tank. Many local dignitaries, including the mayor, spend the day being dropped into a tank of water by softball-tossing citizens.

Solstice Celebration

America's Stonehenge, Off N.H. Rte 111-E, North Salem • (603) 893-8300

This prehistoric stone circle is believed to be a solar calendar, and these days on the solstices and equinoxes modern Druids and pagans gather to recreate the ancient celebrations (without the human sacrifices!). On the day of the summer solstice, the park is open to the public and there's a traditional midsummer celebration with music, food and games for all. Admission is $7 for adults, $5 for ages 13 to 18 and $3 for ages 6 to 12. Younger children are admitted free of charge.

N.H. Community Theatre Association Drama Festival

Palace Theatre, Hanover St., Manchester
• (603) 880-0243

Every year for more than 25 years the New Hampshire Community Theatre Association has gathered in Manchester for this celebration/competition. Regional theater companies from around the state perform their short plays or skits, one after another. Between performances the judges discuss and score the play just completed, and after two days of marathon theater, the "best production of the year" is named. Tickets to the plays are $10 per day. Please do not bring children younger than 6.

Seacoast Region

Market Square Day
Downtown Portsmouth
• (603) 431-5388, (800) 639-9302

This street festival, sponsored by Pro Portsmouth, has grown over two decades to include a 10K road race, Kids Court games and entertainment, more than 250 vendors from around New England, and, of course, street performers and food! The day, which is always the second Saturday in June, concludes with an evening concert and fireworks over Portsmouth Harbor. All activities are free, and go on rain or shine (well, once they had to close down when it *really* poured).

Civil War Encampment
Strawbery Banke Museum, 64 Marcy St., Portsmouth • (603) 433-1100

The 54th Massachusetts Regiment sets up camp on the grounds of the museum on a weekend in mid-June. Visitors explore the life of ordinary soldiers in the Civil War as well as life on the home front. Authentic artifacts, clothing and games bring the time to life, and special presentations provide more information. Admission to the encampment and the Goodwin House is $5, or $12 to include the whole museum.

Somersworth International Children's Festival
Downtown Somersworth
• (603) 692-5869

Nearly 20 years ago, some people in Somersworth decided the community needed something to bring them together, and the International Children's Festival was born. Last year an estimated 50,000 people attended the mid-June gathering. They come for music and dancing in the streets and fireworks in the sky. They enjoy refreshments from many lands and artistic performances from many cultures. Pony rides, a petting zoo and costumed characters enchant the children, who also enjoy the many hands-on activities available. The whole event raises money for arts in the schools and a scholarship fund.

Localpalooza
Festival Pavilion, Somersworth
• (603) 692-5869

We wondered how Somersworth could afford all the great festivals they put on every year (we've only given you a taste of them here). This is a big part of the how. Local rock groups put on a marathon seven-hour performance toward the end of June each year at this new 8,500-seat pavilion. Tickets are $10 in advance, $12 at the gate.

Lakes Region

Motorcycle Week
All over Laconia
• (603) 366-2000

Nearly a quarter-million motorcycles gather in Laconia every second week in June for this incredible event. Now more than 75 years old, this is one of three major motorcycle rallies around the country. Activities (some of which cost money) range from races (foot and hot rod as well as motorcycle) to fireworks, with pancake breakfasts and a chili cook-off for daring palates. The week includes photography exhibits, guided tours of the countryside and even church services. But the main activity of the week is cruising up and down the strip. You have to see this to believe it.

Classic Motorcycle Races
N.H. International Speedway, Loudon
• (603) 783-4744

Loudon hosts the oldest motorcycle race meet in the country during the second week in June. Since the construction of the speedway, the setting is much more attractive, but the traditional atmosphere of this gathering is, well, rough. (Every year controversy rages over the raunchy behavior of the crowds.) The races include a Grand Prix for classic antique motorcycles, a road racing series, amateur races and, finally, a pro classic. Admission to the racetrack ranges from $10 to $25; attendance at the peripheral activities is free.

Twilight Madness

Downtown Wolfeboro • (603) 569-2200

The last weekend in June brings Wolfeboro's version of the block party, an evening of music and art, food and fun, all easily enjoyed in the compact downtown center. Kayaking in the afternoon is followed (coincidentally) by a demonstration by the fire department's fire and rescue boat squad. Area restaurants offer samples of their specialties under a big tent, while other local businesses feature in-store specials and balloons for kids. There's no charge for the festival, which kicks off the summer season in Wolfeboro.

Hobie Cat Championship Race

Ellacoya State Park, Rt. 11-A, Gilford • (603) 293-8151

Experienced members of the racing circuit and recreational sailors alike enjoy participating in this annual meet at the end of June. The colorful sails of Hobie cats and catamarans make this an attractive spectator event, too, and there are family-oriented activities and even child-care at the park so parents can enjoy the race knowing their kids are having fun. Many spectators take their own boats out to watch the race from the water, while others cheer from the shore.

White Mountains and Great North Woods Regions

Mount Washington Road Race

Great Glen Trails, N.H. Rt. 16, Pinkham Notch • (603) 466-3988

For more than forty years this annual exertion has been known as one of the toughest footraces in the United States if not in the world. More than 1,000 of the world's top runners arrive in New Hampshire the third weekend in June to run *up* the Auto Road. If you want to run, you'll need to contact the organizers, Granite State Race Services in Newport, (603) 863-2537. Otherwise you can position yourself along the route or at the summit to encourage the runners.

Lupine Festival

Sugar Hill • (800) 237-9007

The second and third weeks of June focus on the beautiful fields of blooming wild mountain lupine that abound in the countryside near Franconia Notch. The two- to three-foot-tall spikes of pink, blue and white blossoms cover the open fields. The Presidential mountain range in the background adds a majestic touch to the picture-postcard scene. The two-week festival involves 60 events at 18 different locations. Many of the inns in the area offer free teas, and artists' studios are open to the public. Passbooks to the festival are $8 each or two for $15. Each event has a page giving details including date, time, place and whether the event has an additional fee. For example, a wine tasting might have an additional charge above the $8 passbook. You couldn't pick a more beautiful time to visit the White Mountains Region.

Old Time Fiddler's Contest

Whitcomb Field, Stark • (603) 636-1325

We don't pick favorites, but if we did this would certainly make a run for No. 1. The Fiddler's Contest is more than a quarter-century old and always takes place on the last Sunday in June. It draws about 35 contestants from New England, ranging in age from 4 to 87. These nimble-fingered musicians compete in six age-based divisions for an audience of about 2,500. The festival begins with the flag-raising ceremony at noon. The senior division fiddles first. After each contestant in a particular division has performed, the entire division gets together and has a jam session while the judges confer. Bring a picnic, but don't bother to pack dessert. Homemade cake is sold by the slice. You can get food and cold drinks, too, but the event keeps the outside vendors to a minimum to protect the true New England spirit of the day. Admission is $7 for adults and $3 for kids younger than 13.

Audi-Mt. Washington Hillclimb "Climb to the Clouds"

Great Glen Trails, N.H. Rt. 16, Pinkham Notch • (603) 466-3988

The last weekend in June is the time for this remarkable auto race, billed as the nation's oldest motorsports event (although its current incarnation only dates back to 1990). Drivers from around the U.S. and Canada are joined by some from as far away as Europe in what appears to non-racers as a foolhardy, high-speed ascent of the 7.4 mile Auto Road. The race itself is on Sunday, but there are practice runs Friday and Saturday and a carnival and antique auto show at the base of the mountain on Saturday.

Motorcycle Ride-In and Blessing of the Motorcycles

Shrine of Our Lady of Grace, U.S. Rt. 3, Colebrook • (603) 539-5015

The ritual blessing of the bikes at 1 PM on Sunday is the highlight of an end-of-June weekend of motorcycle cruising between Columbia and Pittsburg. There's a steak cookout on Friday evening in the Kiwanis Park in Colebrook and a Rodeo at Murphy's Dam in Pittsburg on Saturday. Saturday evening, cyclists can choose between a chicken barbecue at the Pittsburg Fire Department and a Biker's Ball at the Colebrook Country Club. Then on Sunday morning everyone gathers for a pancake breakfast at the Shrine. Those so inclined can worship at the regular Sunday Mass, while the blessing is open to everyone — and we're talking a couple of thousand bikes! It's a classic North Country event.

Monadnock Region

International Festival

Downtown Keene • (603) 358-5344

One Saturday early in June Keene's Main Street turns into a mini Epcot. Children are issued passports that they can have stamped as they move from one country to another, trying out unique activities and interesting foods. They may take off their shoes and stamp grapes in Italy, smack a piñata in Mexico or watch sumo wrestlers in Japan. Music and dance and food are the predominant themes of the day, as vendors raising money for a variety of local organizations offer their wares up and down the street.

Monadnock Valley Indian Festival and Powwow

Cheshire County Fairgrounds, Rte.12, Swanzey (Keene) • (603) 647-5374

In less than a decade this mid-June event has become a New England tradition, drawing Native Americans to celebrate their heritage and others to watch, enjoy and learn. Music dominates the weekend, as drumming echoes off the surrounding hills and dancers in full regalia swirl past despite the typically hot and humid conditions. Visitors are welcome to join in. There are demonstrations of traditional crafts, foods, educational and art for sale.

July

We won't attempt to note all the Fourth of July events here. Wherever you find yourself on the Fourth, check out the local paper for a traditional Independence Day celebration. In every area at least one town will have a parade, where you'll see not only the high school marching band but a grand assortment of doll carriages and bicycles, ancient veterans in uniform and earnest scouts trying to stay in step, and fire engines whose sirens wail as the children of firefighters toss candy from the backs of the trucks. Art shows and carnivals, pancake-flipping and pie-eating contests, and local politicians kissing babies are all traditional attractions. You won't find fireworks scheduled everywhere, as the cost is so high, but again the local paper will tell you where they will be. If you find a nice open hill you may be able to watch several displays simultaneously.

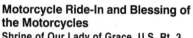

Merrimack Valley Region

Race Fever
Downtown Concord
• (603) 624-2508

The weekend of the Winston Cup NASCAR race in Loudon, Concord goes crazy. In a spirit of "if you can't beat 'em, join 'em," the city turns Main Street into a giant street festival. There's no charge for this. Vendors sell pennants and posters, street musicians perform, and the drivers generally come around to sign autographs and rub shoulders with their fans. The race, and Race Fever, are always in early July.

Antique Fire Apparatus Meet and Muster
Memorial Field, Pembroke
• (603) 632-4998

Every year the New Hampshire chapter of the Society for the Preservation and Appreciation of Antique Motorized Fire Apparatus in America (say that three times fast!) gathers on the third Saturday in July for a fun fireman's muster. All the traditional events are here, with climbing ladders, rolling hoses and, of course, spraying water, but the atmosphere is non-competitive and even kids get to try the hoses. The day begins with breakfast, and then a parade of all the old trucks. There are food vendors, a flea market and fun for the whole family.

Brewed and Baked in the Granite State
Nutfield Brewery and Ale House, 22 Manchester Rd., Derry
• (603) 434-9678

On a Saturday in late July this microbrewery hosts a very tasty gathering which raises money for local charities. There are a variety of beers and ales on tap, and wonderful breads and soups, cakes, cookies and other delicious fare. Run the AmeriBrew 5K first and you can snack without guilt. About 2000 people attend each year. There is no charge to attend, just to eat and run!

Seacoast Region

Revolutionary War Festival
Various locations in Exeter
• (603) 772-2622

It took two weeks for the Declaration of Independence to make the long journey from Philadelphia to Exeter, which was the capital of New Hampshire at the time. So every year Exeter spends the weekend that falls two weeks after the Fourth of July celebrating independence with this charming festival. In recent years the event has attracted between 5,000 and 10,000 people over the three days. A highlight of the weekend is the chance to see an original draft and an original broadside (announcement) of the Declaration of Independence. An encampment of Revolutionary War re-enactors opens a window into a time past. There are British troops at the Garrison who can tell you about their side of the story as well as militias in tents on the grounds of the American Independence Museum. Skirmishes are likely as the two sides meet amid the tables of crafts and baked goods, and a full battle is waged on Saturday afternoon. A canoe rally, live music, dancers and other entertainers provide diversion for the crowds. Particular favorites are the representatives of several local Native American tribes.

Sea to Summit Triathlon
New Castle Beach, N.H. Rt. 1-B, New Castle • (603) 772-3106

Serious athletes and madmen (and madwomen) participate in this annual mid-July race, which begins with a 12-mile kayak from New Castle Island up the Piscataqua and Salmon Falls rivers to South Berwick, Maine.

INSIDER'S TIP

The New Hampshire Humanities Council sponsors dozens of fascinating lectures, discussions, films and workshops every year as well as the annual Chautauqua in July. Call (603) 224-4071 and ask to be put on their mailing list.

Close-up

Summer Music

Many communities stage free outdoor concerts during July and August. Some towns have beautiful old bandstands, a couple have newly constructed shells, and some just set up chairs on a platform. People bring lawn chairs, blankets and baby carriages and sit back for an evening of music that might feature an American Legion band one week and a choral society the next. Most concerts are weather permitting, although some have an indoor option in case of rain.

Merrimack Valley Region

Summer Music Series
Downtown Concord • (603) 225-8690

From the end of June through mid-August, the Concord Recreation Department sponsors free concerts on Thursday evenings at Eagle Square (off Main Street). These concerts feature local talent in every style from brass quintet to classic rock and roll to children's music. On Tuesday nights the Never's Band, a local favorite, plays traditional marching band tunes at Bicentennial Square, the State House Plaza or Eagle Square. All concerts are free, although a $1 donation to defray costs is suggested.

Photo: Sally Wilkins

Music under the stars is a favorite summer activity.

Music for Manchester
2321 Elm St., Manchester • (603) 669-4298

Notre Dame College invites visitors to enjoy an eclectic concert series four Wednesday evenings each summer. Jazz, calypso and Celtic music have been featured in past years, and the series always concludes with the 39th Army Band.

Music at the Heart of It
Hampshire Plaza, 1000 Elm St., Manchester • (603) 668-3800

Free lunchtime concerts in the sunshine, right in the center of town. Bring a bag lunch on Thursdays and enjoy a musical picnic in the middle of the work day. Performers and musical styles vary. The series runs from the week after the Fourth of July through the end of August.

— continued on next page

Manchester Summer Concert Series

Veterans Park, Elm St. (Across from the Center of New Hampshire), Manchester • (603) 645-6285

Thursday evenings from 8 PM to 10 PM Veteran's Park fills with music lovers and city dwellers enjoying the cooling evening. Traditionally this series begins after the Fourth of July with the Shaw Brothers, a New Hampshire duo and Insider favorites, and closes at the end of August with the New Hampshire Philharmonic Orchestra. In between you'll hear local high school bands, community chorus groups and visiting bands from the Armed Forces along with other professionals. These free concerts are held rain or shine, although if the weather is "catastrophic" (their description) they'll postpone until Friday evening.

Sounds on the Souhegan

Emerson Park, Milford • (603) 673-3403

For years the summer concerts took advantage of Milford's classic bandstand, but the traffic in the Oval proved to be too large an obstacle to musical enjoyment. Now each Wednesday evening in summer the sign is on the bandstand, and the show is in Emerson Park, down by the river next to the Post Office. (They move into the Town Hall if it rains.) Concerts are from 7 to 8:30 PM and generally feature local bands or vocal artists. The final concert of the year is always the Temple Town Band. The Temple Town Band was the first town band formed in America. The earliest record of their playing was at a local memorial service for George Washington in February 1800. In 1983 they marched in the Fourth of July parade in the nation's capitol.

Seacoast Region

Prescott Park Arts Festival

Prescott Park, Marcy St., Portsmouth • (603) 436-2848

Thursday afternoons bring out local rock musicians, while Sunday evenings feature a mix of musical styles by local artists. The concerts are just a fraction of the multilayered, summer-long festival.

Lakes Region

Riverside Concert Series

The Mill Plaza, Laconia • (603) 524-8813

A variety of bands play in this pleasant downtown park on the banks of the Winnipesaukee River summer Thursdays at 6:30 PM.

Savina Hartwell Memorial Concerts

Tilton Island Park, Tilton • (603) 286-3232

Locals like to bring a picnic supper to these concerts on Sunday evenings and enjoy the summer breezes before the music starts at 6:30 PM.

Music at the Marketplace

Weirs Beach Marketplace, Weirs Beach • (603) 366-5800

This tourist haven has free concerts four nights a week. The Barbershoppers chorus entertains Wednesday at 7:30 PM. The other evenings' shows are from 7 to 10 PM: Friday the shows feature duos (usually instrumental), Saturday the bands come in with rock, blues, country and oldies shows, and Sunday evenings the Boardwalk Jazz

Quartet takes the stage. There are wooden bleacher seats, kids dance on the lawn, and everyone has a great time. No alcohol is available, but New Hampshire's own JB Scoops ice cream is available in all flavors! (There's no Music at the Marketplace on Thursday because that's the night for Square Dancing down on the Boardwalk.)

Friends of the Bandstand Concerts

Community Bandstand, Wolfeboro • (603) 569-2189

The Cate Park Band is a group of local musicians who gather on summer Wednesday evenings to rehearse from 7 to 7:30 PM and then perform from 8 to 8:45 PM. All musicians, resident or visiting, are invited to join in, regardless of age or ability.

Dartmouth-Lake Sunapee Region

Mary D. Haddad Bandstand Concerts

Sargent Common, New London • (603) 526-6575

These band concerts are held every Friday night from the end of June to the end of August. In case of rain the concerts move next door to the town hall.

There the racers exchange their kayaks for bicycles and begin the 90-mile back-road race to Pinkham Notch. At the Dana Place Inn, bikes are parked, and the final leg of the journey begins — and "leg" is the correct term, as the athletes run up Mount Washington to the finish line at 6,288 feet. And you thought you were tired!

Bow Street Fair

Downtown Portsmouth • (603) 433-4793

The third weekend in July transforms the historic waterfront district into a giant art show, with everything from pottery to jewelry on display. Musicians perform everything from Celtic folk tunes to hot jazz on the stage at Harbor Place throughout the two-day fair, which is free.

Chautauqua

Strawbery Banke, Marcy St., Portsmouth • (603) 224-4071

Every year during the last week in July, the New Hampshire Humanities Council organizes this three-day event under a big tent on the grounds of Strawbery Banke. These are "history comes to life" performances: Scholars on a particular time period or movement in history come to talk about what happened in the character of a key figure of the time. The lectures are supplemented with live entertainment by local artists, workshops for children and adults and a chance to have breakfast with one of the "historical people." There is no charge to participate.

Cochecho River Festival

Henry Law Park, Henry Law Ave., Dover • (603) 742-2218

This community gathering at the end of July includes carnival games, demonstrations of martial arts, in-line skating, jump roping and gymnastics. A 5K road race tours the city and draws more than 300 runners. Pony rides and a trampoline are particular favorites with the kids. There's an ice-cream smorgasbord in the afternoon and a chicken barbecue prepared by the Dover firefighters. There's no charge for the festival, only for food.

Lakes Region

Old Time Farm Day

N.H. Farm Museum, Milton • (603) 652-7840

This Saturday in early July is the most popular event on the museum's calendar. Visitors get a chance to try their hands at the daily activities of a bygone era. Kids learn to milk cows, while parents marvel at the regulation of temperature on a wood cookstove.

Admission, which includes the regular museum tour, is $5 for adults, $1.50 for children ages 3 through 12 and free for kids younger than 3. See our Attractions chapter for more on the N.H. Farm Museum.

Wildlife Festival at Science Center of New Hampshire

N.H. Rt. 113, Holderness
• (603) 968-7194

Come for a variety of activities including wild animal programs, story telling, music and crafts for the whole family. Refreshments are served. The festival is held on a Sunday in mid-July. Regular admission to the museum applies ($8 for adults, $3 for ages 5 to 15, younger than 3 and members free). See our Attractions chapter for more on the Science Center of New Hampshire, which will be renamed the Squam Lakes Natural Science Center on January 1, 2000.

Brewfest

Gunstock, N.H. Rt. 11-A, Gilford
• (603) 293-4341, (800) GUNSTOCK

The annual brewfest at Gunstock brings in more than 50 companies to show off their wares. Both microbrews and major brewing companies from around New England are featured during the two-day party. Demonstrations and brewing tips are of interest to the home-brewing crowd, and plenty of supplies are for sale if you're bitten by the bug while you're there. Live rock 'n' roll music plays throughout the weekend and there's lots of food for sale. Games of volleyball and basketball arise spontaneously and there are some brew-related contests like keg-tossing and keg-rolling, which is rather like log-rolling only without the river. Pony rides and a moonwalk will entice the children. Admission to the brewfest, which runs from noon to 6 PM both Saturday and Sunday, is $9 each day for adults (price includes limited sampling of the beer) and $4 for ages 6 to 20 (who must be accompanied by a parent or guardian). Children 5 and younger are admitted free. The brewfest is always on a weekend in late July or early August — call for details.

NASCAR Winston Cup Jiffy Lube 300

N.H. International Speedway, Loudon
• (603) 783-4744

The second weekend in July is one of the biggest weekends at Loudon, as the big stars of the NASCAR circuit arrive to compete for the Winston Cup. Official attendance typically tops 90,000.

Bluegrass Festival

Smith Meeting House, Gilmanton
• (603) 224-3690

One weekend in mid-to-late July the Smith Meeting House hosts this Bluegrass Festival, complete with a dozen bands, a Sunday gospel hour, down-home cooking and a chicken barbecue. Some folks bring the camper and spend the night, others come just for the day. Tickets are $15 for Saturday and $10 for Sunday. Children younger than 12 pay $5 for either day. Meal tickets cost $7 for adults and $5 for children. All proceeds go to the restoration fund for the Smith Meeting House.

Hebron Fair

Hebron Common
• (603) 744-2824

For almost a half-century the people of Hebron have been coming together at the end of July for an old-fashioned fair. Bands play, kids ride ponies and try their luck at the dunking booth, and parents scout out the offerings at the auction. There are lots of craftspeople and artisans but no midway, as the organizers want to preserve the small-town feel. There is a rummage sale and snacks to buy. Admission is free.

INSIDERS' TIP

The weekends between Thanksgiving and Christmas bring a wealth of holiday craft fairs, some tiny, some enormous. Keep an eye out for posters or signs at schools and churches announcing these great community events.

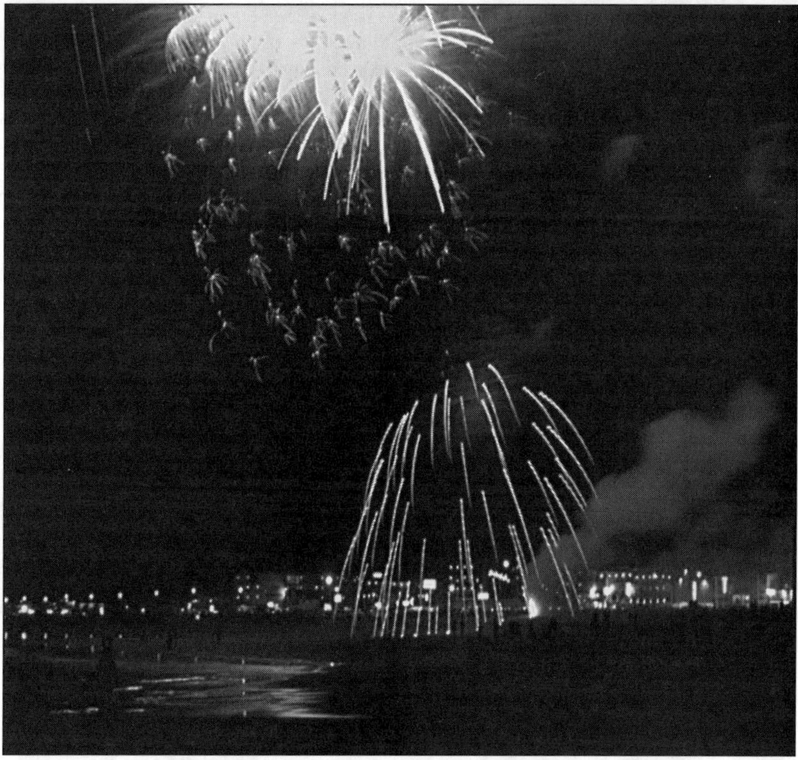

Photo: Hampton Beach Chamber of Commerce

Towns and villages all over the state host Fourth of July celebrations.

Melvin Village

Community Church Fair
Melvin Village
• (603) 544-9661

This is a classic little church fair, with homebaked goodies for sale, a white elephant table, handicrafts and old books for sale. There's even a frog-jumping contest! Lunch is served, and refreshments are available all day long. The fair is always on a Saturday in mid-to-late July.

Canterbury Fair

Crane Park, Canterbury • (603) 783-4349

This end-of-July event is an old-fashioned fair that's been a favorite for more than 40 years. Morris Dancers and a children's theater entertain guests. Farm animals and traditional crafts are on display. There are antiques for sale, a chicken barbecue and plenty of games and music.

Antique & Classic Boat Show

Public Docks, U.S. Rt. 3, Weirs Beach
• (603) 524-0348

This annual gathering of antique boats at the docks in Weirs Beach takes place at the end of July each summer. More than 100 boats, beautifully restored and lovingly cared for, remind guests of a time not so long past when these craft were the main form of transportation for summer people in the Lakes Region. Costumes and period music are all part of the fun. The show is free, and boat owners love to talk about their boats.

Granite Kid Triathlon

Brewster Beach, Wolfeboro
• (603) 569-5639

This is an age-appropriate version of the popular Granite Man race, with kids competing with others in their age groups in a swim-bike-run combo race. The end-of-July event is sponsored by Wolfeboro Parks and Recreation, and there is no charge to participate.

Loon Festival

The Loon Center, Blake Rd., Moultonborough
• (603) 476-LOON

This annual event in late July or early August benefits the Loon Preservation Committee. Artisans display their work, kids enjoy games and activities, and everyone learns about loons and the efforts to protect them and their habitat. There's no charge for this day-long event. See our Parks and Open Spaces chapter for more on the Loon Center.

White Mountains and Great North Woods Regions

New Hampshire Inter-Tribal Powwow

Shrine of Our Lady of Grace, U.S. Rt. 3, Colebrook
• (603) 539-5015

This annual gathering of Native Americans from all over Northern New England and Eastern Canada is a colorful event which can be very educational (and a lot of fun) for non-Indians and those who know they have some Indian ancestry but have never learned about that heritage. You'll see traditional clothing, hear ancient and re-discovered music and languages, enjoy indigenous foods and learn about medicinal plants and other wisdom. There is Mass at the Shrine every day as well as sweat lodges and sacred dance. The Powwow is generally held in late July.

Dartmouth-Lake Sunapee Region

Garden Club Antique Show and Sale

Main St., New London
• (603) 526-4739

You can't beat the charm of this New London outdoor fair in mid-July. Dealers set up their wares — in this case beautiful antiques — on the town green, and you can just stroll through the displays of slant-top desks and pine country furniture. The New London Garden Club sells plants and flowers, and the whole town comes out to enjoy midsummer in New England. In case you love fried dough, you'll be glad to know that food vendors are included in the fun. Build a romantic getaway around this weekend-long event. Be sure and reserve a room early, because we aren't the first Insiders to recommend New London.

Dorchester Old Home and Family Day

On the Common, off N.H. Rt. 13 Dorchester
• (603) 786-9704

The Dorchester Grange has sponsored this festival at the end of July for 75 years. Dorchester is a village of 300 people in a part of the state that's barely been touched by the impacts of development in New Hampshire, and this festive weekend is worth attending just for a peek at the way things used to be. The day begins with a parade of antique cars, homemade floats, kids on bikes, doll carriages and local dignitaries. Children's games and an auction follow. There's no charge for anything except the ham and bean lunch, which is just $5.

Monadnock Region

Hillsborough Balloon Festival

U.S. Rt. 202, Hillsborough
• (603) 464-5858

One of the best country fairs in New Hampshire is this annual balloon event in mid-July. For four days the sky is filled with beautiful hot air balloons with lift-offs morning and evening (weather permitting), tethered rides during the day and the evening "glow" to wow everyone at dusk. On Saturday evening there is also a stunning fireworks display. The weekend also includes an antique car and truck show, a traditional tractor-pull with a twist (the tractors are *lawn* tractors), pancake breakfasts, live music, a parade, a 5K road race, and a carnival midway that will have you reminiscing about your youth. Admission is free and there is a $3 donation for parking. Proceeds for the event support the Hillsborough Fire Department, Chamber of Commerce and Lions Club.

Fitzwilliam Antiques Fair

Town Common, Fitzwilliam
• (603) 585-3134

This charming Monadnock town has a heavy concentration of antiques experts, and for more than 20 years the Fitzwilliam Common has been the place where about 55 antiques dealers gather for a mid- to late-July weekend. (More dealers would come, but the Common can't hold any more.) You don't have to be an expert or have access to a blank check to have fun. The goods include formal furniture, Shaker furniture, linens, ephemera and jewelry. We suggest you write the Fitzwilliam Historical Society, Post Office Box 87, Fitzwilliam, NH 03447. It's a good idea to include a stamped self-addressed postcard for them to relay dates to you.

August

Merrimack Valley Region

Mother Ann Day

288 Shaker Rd., Canterbury
• (603) 783-9511

Mother Ann, the foundress of Shakerism, arrived in America on August 6, 1774. Every year the Museum at Shaker Village commemorates that event with a special day featuring readings from Shaker works and music played on traditional instruments. Mother Ann Day is always the Sunday closest to August 6, the date she actually got off the boat. See our Attractions chapter for more about Shaker Village.

Show 'n' Shine Classic Cars

Anheuser-Busch Brewery, Merrimack
• (603) 595-1202

This fun event on the first Saturday in August has been showcasing classic cars for a quarter-century. Literally hundreds of classic and antique cars line the driveways around the brewery and the Clydesdale Hamlet. There's live music, lots of food, and of course tours of the brewery. The show runs from 10 AM to 3 PM and there is no admission charge.

New Hampshire Antiques Show

The Center of New Hampshire Holiday Inn, 700 Elm St., Manchester
• (603) 286-7506

The New Hampshire Antiques Show is considered by many to be the best summer antiques show in New England. With 63 exhibitors you're sure to find something that whets your acquisitional appetite. Most of the dealers are from New Hampshire, but dealers from Vermont, Massachusetts, New York and Pennsylvania also attend. We were delighted by the range of prices as well as the variety of goods for sale and on display. Botanical prints, corner cupboards, hooked rugs and a hand-carved Noah's Ark complete with animals were just a few of the items coveted by your on-the-scene Insiders. This is a visitor-friendly show with lots of fun trade talk among dealers and more than a little bartering. The show runs for three days in early August, usually around the second weekend of the month. Call for admission information.

Downtown Old Time Fiddling Championship

Eagle Square, Concord
• (603) 225-5512

This end-of-August competition is rapidly becoming an Insider favorite. Between 30 and 50 fiddlers from around New England come to show off their skills and compete for prizes in this musical feast. It's a real family event, with awards for the oldest and youngest fiddlers, those from the farthest distance and even some sibling teams. There is no charge to participate or attend, and no vendors are set up (although all of Main Street is available to meet your needs to shop and snack).

New Hampshire Custom Brewfest

Riverside Park, off Commercial St., Manchester • (603) 622-0000

Fans of New Hampshire's many microbreweries will want to visit this festive gathering alongside the Merrimack. You show your ID to purchase a small glass and then buy as many tickets as you want for a dollar each. Tickets in hand, you wander from one tap to another, sampling everything from White Mountain's Tuckerman's Ale to Woodstock's Pigs Ear Brown to Nutfield's 1847 Stout, with a rich variety in between. There are sausages on the grill and other snacks available, and a modicum of entertainment for the children, although Mom and Dad will have more fun if they leave the kids with Grandma. Bring them home some T-shirts instead. The Brewfest is generally on a Saturday at the end of August.

Seacoast Region

Candlelight Tour of Historic Houses

Downtown Portsmouth • (603) 436-1118

This mid-August stroll has become a tradition. A late-summer evening on the Seacoast is a lovely time for a walk, and touring six of Portsmouth's historic houses by candlelight is a lovely walk to take. Tickets for the stroll are $15 for adults and $7.50 for children.

Lakes Region

Alton Old Home Week

On the Waterfront, Alton Bay • (603) 875-0109

Most towns are content with an Old Home Day — Alton needs a whole week in the middle of August to include all these activities. There's an antique boat show and a water-skiing show, stunt bikes and square dancers. Insiders bring lawn chairs for outdoor music and movies, magic shows and a parade. There's lots of food for sale, of course, and a craft sale, but all activities are free.

Taste of Newfound

Bridgewater Town Hall, N.H. Rt. 3-A Bridgewater • (603) 744-2222

This is one of the biggest events of the year in this small town. The first Monday in August, 16 area restaurants serve samples of their specialties to guests who've paid $15 for the chance to try some of everything. There is musical entertainment, a clown who makes balloon animals and a great chance to meet, nosh and talk. Only 225 tickets are sold each year, and it's always a sellout. The Taste raises funds for Bristol Community Services, an all-volunteer organization that is mostly involved with providing transportation for senior citizens and others without wheels.

New England Antiques and Collectibles Festival

Sandwich Fairgrounds, Center Sandwich • (603) 539-1900

More than 200 exhibitors flock to this antiques show in beautiful Center Sandwich where there's more than just antiques for sale. You'll find hay rides, entertainment and refreshments in abundance. Admission is $2.50 for adults, and children get in free. The show goes on, rain or shine, the first weekend in August.

Pittsfield Rotary Balloon Fest

Drake Field, Carroll St., Pittsfield • (603) 435-6767

This balloon rally and festival takes place every summer at the beginning of August. In addition to morning and evening balloon launches the festival features arts and crafts tables, a road race, a canoe race, theatrical performances and lots of food. There is no charge for admission.

Huggins Hospital Street Fair

Brewster Field, S. Main St., Wolfeboro • (603) 569-2200

For more than 60 years the Huggins Hospital auxiliary has run this wonderful street fair, generally on the first weekend in August. Activities include something for everyone, with animal rides, games and balloons for the kids, an auction, prizes and entertainment. All kinds of goodies are for sale, from baked goods to sports equipment, and there's wonderful food, with refreshments on sale all day, a chicken barbecue one night and a lobster feed the other. No admission is charged.

Barbershop Jamboree

Alton Bay Community Center and Central School, School St., Alton • (603) 875-5777

For nearly half a century the Lakes Region has hosted this delightful day-and-a-half of four-part harmony. Once a family gathering that grew, the event is now sponsored by the Nashua Chapter of SPEBSQSA (the Society for the Preservation and Encouragement of Barbershop Quartet Singing in American) along with members of the Downing family. Performers come from as far away as Florida to participate in the musical day, which includes performances, a competition and a musical "afterglow." Tickets are $5 for adults and $1 for children younger than 12. Proceeds are split between local causes and the Heartspring program for children with speech disorders. The Jamboree is generally a Friday evening and Saturday in early August.

Lakes Region Doll, Bear and Miniature Show

Gilford Middle High School, Belknap Mountain Rd., Gilford • (603) 524-0129

This mid-August show brings dealers and doll-lovers from all over New England together. Table after table displays dolls (and bears) of all kinds, including many miniatures and a themed display put together by club members. Door prizes and lots of enticing additions to your collection add to the fun. Admission costs $2 for adults and $1 for children, and lunch is available at the show, which begins at 9:30 AM and runs until 3 PM.

Squam Lake Canoe Day

Squam Lakes Assoc. Headquarters, U.S. Rt. 3, Holderness • (603) 968-7336

Canoe races and a canoe parade, antique canoes and a floating band are all part of this annual community gathering. The Battle of the Towns is a highlight of the day, which is generally the second Saturday of August. There is no cost to attend, but bring some pocket money for the hot dog roast.

Fine Arts and Crafts Festival

Mill Falls Marketplace, U.S. Rt. 3 and N.H. Rt. 25, Meredith • (603) 279-6121

This annual mid-August event goes beyond the displays of juried artists and crafters with entertainment, music, food and fun. For two days an open-air marketplace overflows with juried art works, crafts and toys. There is no charge to attend this fair.

Victorian Country Fair

New Hampton School, Main St., New Hampton • (603) 744-2765

This fair in mid-August sets the atmosphere with horse-drawn rides, strolling musicians and the New Hampshire Wheelmen with their old-fashioned bicycles. The Fifth New Hampshire Regiment (Civil War) sets up an encampment on the grounds. Even the items on the vendor tables are reminiscent of the 1800s, and many of the fairgoers join the organizers and vendors by arriving in costume. The fair is free, and funds raised by sale of goods and rental of tables goes to the restoration of the Daniel Smith Tavern in New Hampton Village.

Summer Dinner

Loon Center, Lee's Mill Rd., Moultonboro • (603) 476-5666

This popular mid-August event is a fundraiser in support of the work of the Loon Preservation Committee. The evening includes a guest speaker, live music, an auction and raffle and, of course, dinner. The response has been so great that it's outgrown the capacity of Castle in the Clouds, so in 1999 the dinner is being held at the Lakeview Inn in Wolfeboro. Priority is given to members of the committee, but the public is also welcome. Tickets are about $40. Call the Loon Center for information and reservations.

Artists in the Park

Cate Park, Lake St., Wolfeboro • (603) 569-4994

This art show, sponsored by the Governor Wentworth Arts Council, has been held in mid-August for 15 years. The day also includes entertainment and activities for children, and the show goes on rain or shine.

Granite Man Triathlon

Carry Beach, Wolfeboro • (603) 569-5639

This event attracts more than 300 athletes to compete as individuals or relay teams in a race that begins with a three-quarter-mile swim, follows with a 15-mile bike race through Wolfeboro and Tuftonboro and concludes with a 4.2-mile run. Registration monies fund a scholarship in memory of a local boy who died in 1981 on a search-and-rescue mission on Mount Washington. There's no charge to watch the race, which takes place in mid-August.

Old Truck Meet

N.H. Rt. 125, Barrington
• (603) 664-9761

Every summer in the middle of August, the Granite State Chapter of the American Truck Historical Society sponsors this gathering of trucks and truck-lovers. In 1997 more than 500 antique pickups and tractor-trailers, doodlebugs, tractors and dump trucks were on display in the field behind Calef's General Store (see our Shopping chapter). Breakfast and lunch are served under a tent, snacks and ice cream are for sale all day, and tables of antique motoring memorabilia and parts are displayed for sale.

Smorgasbord Supper

Town Hall, Washburn St., Alexandria
• (603) 744-2222

This all-you-can-eat feast has been put on every year for the last 30 years by the Volunteer Fire Department Auxiliary. It's how they pay for fire trucks and turnout gear in this small town. The dinner, which is always the third Saturday in August, features ham, turkey, Swedish meatballs, clam casseroles and other local favorites. The rolls are baked in a wood-burning range. Try some pickled beets or different kinds of salad, but be sure to save room for pie! The cost of this indulgence? $7.

White Mountains and Great North Woods Regions

Pemi Bluegrass Festival

Branch Brook Campground, N.H. Rt. 49, Campton • (603) 726-3471

This annual early August celebration of bluegrass music is a weekend of fun for all ages. A dozen bands provide entertainment over the course of the weekend (a big tent is set up to provide shade or shelter as needed). There are workshops for musicians and aspiring musicians of all ages, and instruments are provided if you don't have your own. Everyone is invited to join a country dance on Saturday evening. The amenities of the campground include swimming, fishing, canoe and tube rentals and a playground, and field camping is free with the purchase of a three-day ticket (water and electric extra). Tickets for the whole weekend are $32 in advance or $38 at the gate. Friday evening, Saturday evening or Sunday tickets are $16 each, and a ticket for all day Saturday is $22. Children younger than 12 attend for free, while teens ages 12 to 16 pay half price.

Double R Rodeo

Attitash Bear Peak, Bartlett
• (603) 374-2368

Attitash Bear Peak has hosted this IPRA (International Professional Rodeo Association) event since 1990. It's the only rodeo in New England and lots of fun for natives and visitors. Classic Rodeo events such as steer wrestling, calf roping, barrel racing and Brahma bull riding are part of the event held in late August. The event is held over a three-day period, but the action is the same each day. The Western theme continues with country music, line dancing and a country barbecue dinner. Admission to the rodeo is $10 for everyone older than 12, $5 for kids ages 5 to 12 and free for children younger than 5. The tickets are good for one day. Dinner is served in an outdoor tent, and prices average about $10 a meal.

Mount Washington Bike Race

Mount Washington Auto Road, Gorham
• (603) 447-6991

This bicycle race is sponsored by the Tin Mountain Conservation Center. The best place for spectators is along the Auto Road itself or at the summit. Parking facilities at the summit are reserved for those involved in the race, so if you want to see the finish you need to climb to the top via the 7.5-mile auto road or one of the many trails up the mountain. The race begins at 7:30 AM. Don't confuse the hillclimb with the bicycle race series here that runs through July and August. Those races, while challenging, remain on the relatively flatter terrain of the Great Glen cross-country trails.

Moose Festival

Colebrook and Pittsburg, New Hampshire, and Canaan, Vermont • (603) 237-8939

The Moose Festival takes place in three towns over three days the weekend before Labor Day weekend. The plans may change slightly from year to year, but the following events are typical of the fun you'll have in very northern New England. The festival kicks off in Colebrook on Friday morning. The sidewalk sales begin at 9 AM, and the street fair starts at 3 PM. You can get a great view of the area by taking a scenic train ride or a tethered balloon ride. The chicken barbecue starts at 5 PM and lasts as long as the chicken holds out. The Colebrook Boot Scooters show off their country line dancing skills on Main Street at 6 PM, followed by the Mock Moose Parade and Moose Festival Kickoff Dance under a big tent.

Pittsburg is the scene for Saturday's fun. At 6 AM take a guided moose tour through "Moose Alley" followed by the Moose Watchers Breakfast. The fun continues with the Moose Country Arts Fair which features a moose calling contest and a mock moose stew cook-off. Take a blast through the past at the Antique, Classic and Street Rod Auto Show. The evening fun moves across the Connecticut River to Canaan, Vermont, for a roast beef dinner and dance. Canaan hosts a moose tour and breakfast on Sunday morning followed by a "Christmoose" crafts fair and moose burger barbecue cookout. The event closes with one last tour by the antique and unique automobiles. You'll pay for food and dances, but the fairs, contests and parades are free.

Dartmouth-Lake Sunapee Region

Annual League of New Hampshire Craftsman's Fair

Lake Sunapee State Park, N.H. Rt. 103, Newport • (603) 224-3375

The New Hampshire Craftsman's Fair is a traditional event in the state and in 1998 celebrated its 65th year. The fair opens on Saturday of the first weekend in August and runs for nine days. You'll find at least 150 separate booths of League members with crafts ranging from toys to jewelry, from woven throws to hand-blown glass. Besides the individual booths, you'll enjoy the large exhibits featuring furniture on one floor and wearable art on the other. Given our cold and long winters, it shouldn't surprise you that our woven wool crafts are both beautiful and practical. Concession stands are on the grounds or you can bring a picnic. Admission to the fair is $6 for adults and $4 for seniors. Children younger than 12 are admitted for free.

Monadnock Region

Festival of Fireworks

Silver Ranch Airpark, N.H. Rt. 124, Jaffrey • (603) 532-4549

More than 35,000 come out on a Saturday in mid-August for this amazing fireworks display. Jaffrey's own Atlas Advanced Pyrotechnics, one of the leading manufacturers of fireworks in the United States, puts on a show for the locals that's a symphony of booms and bursts. Music, lasers and more than 8,500 fireworks are all choreographed by computer and precise electronic firing to celebrate a particular theme. Proceeds from ticket sales go to support the Jaffrey Chamber of Commerce. (Traffic for this event is a strain on little Route 124, and the festival may be moved to a larger venue in the next decade.) You can see some of the show from any clearing in the area, but much of the detail work is near the ground and only visible from inside the park.

Lafayette Artillery

Civil War Re-enactment

Carnival Hill, off Park St., Wilton • (603) 654-9754

No battles were fought in New Hampshire during the War Between the States, but that hasn't stopped the Lafayette Artillery from remembering and honoring their predecessors. The unit was formed in 1804 and has never been inactive. For 10 years they've been the organizing force behind this growing local re-enactment. The event usually takes place the last weekend in August. Soldiers start setting up their camps and positions on Saturday morning and break camp by Sunday afternoon. Visitors are welcome to walk through the camps and observe the authentic details of both the Union and Confederate armies. It's free and a lot of fun. From Main Street in Wilton, head up the hill on Park Street (across from the Post Office) and drive for about .6 miles. Carnival Hill is on your left. You'll see signs pointing the way.

September

Merrimack Valley Region

Riverfest

Arms Park, Commercial St., Manchester • (603) 623-2623

This huge celebration of Manchester's riverfront community is always held the weekend after Labor Day. A regatta, races in canoes and kayaks and a kids' fishing derby keep the focus on the river, despite the presence of arts and crafts by juried artists, food vendors and a whole section of activities just for kids. Musical entertainment in many styles culminates with the New Hampshire Philharmonic playing the 1812 Overture while the fireworks go off. Admission is just $5 for the whole day, and kids younger than 10 get in free, although you'll pay for rides. Parking in the mill section of town is always tight, so Riverfest runs free shuttles from marked parking lots throughout the city.

Kiwanis Antique & Classic Car Show

N.H. Technical Institute, Institute Dr., Concord • (603) 226-8016

This wonderful antique auto show is always held the Saturday after Labor Day. More than 300 old cars and trucks compete for prizes in 25 categories, but for many of the 2,000 guests, the details are not as important as the atmosphere. Kiwanis provides snacks and lunch foods, runs a raffle and organizes games and activities for the whole family.

New Hampshire Antiquarian Book Fair

Everett Arena, Loudon Rd., just off Exit 14 off I-93, Concord • (603) 654-5688

You don't have to be an expert in first editions to have a grand time at this wonderful book fair. For nearly a quarter-century, New England book dealers have assembled in New Hampshire. They arrive with a wide array of books sure to please everyone from the humblest browser to the most sophisticated expert. This fair offers something to both the specialist and the generalist. Whether you're turned on by militaria, Victoria or dementia, you're sure to find something to buy or at least covet. The fair is usually held on the second Sunday in September. It opens at 9:30 AM and closes at 4 PM. Admission is $2.

Twist the Night Away

Downtown Nashua • (603) 882-3281

Destination Downtown salutes the bebop days of the 50s and 60s at this mid-September festival. Main Street is closed to traffic, and vintage vehicles line the street. Tribute groups fill the air with that old-time rock 'n' roll, and there are hula-hoop contests and prizes for costumes.

Beaver Brook Fall Festival

Maple Hill Farm, 117 Ridge Rd., Hollis • (603) 465-7787

For two weekends at the end of September each year, the folks at Beaver Brook celebrate harvest time with this fun festival. An art exhibit fills the old barn, children's activities explore the wonders of fall, local musicians entertain and artisans demonstrate their skills. Meet the resident owl, buy a dried arrangement to take home and wander the grounds as the foliage is just beginning to turn colors. See our Parks and Open Spaces chapter for more about Beaver Brook.

Seacoast Region

Chili Cook-off and Best of the Bean

Prescott Park, Marcy St., Portsmouth • (603) 436-2848

This festival is all about glorious beans —

coffee and chili. More than 500 gallons of chili and a wonderful selection of coffees tempt the tastebuds under a late September sun. A $5 donation is suggested. The feast is sponsored by radio station WHEB and the Prescott Park Arts Festival.

Grand Old Portsmouth

Brewer's Festival
Strawbery Banke, Marcy St., Portsmouth • (603) 433-1100

Portsmouth has a long history of brewing fine ales. This end-of-September fall festival explores and celebrates that tradition. Guests see historic brewing demonstrations and sample the latest microbrews, enjoy live music and check out home-brewing equipment. Children make traditional crafts and play games.

Tickets to the Brewer's Festival are $5 per day or $12 for a two-day pass, which includes admission to the museum. Children younger than 6 get in free.

Lakes Region

Gunstock Country Jamboree

Gunstock, N.H. Rt. 11-A, Gilford • (800) GUNSTOCK

This annual Labor Day weekend tribute to old-fashioned country living brings residents and visitors together for instructions in line-dancing and archery, contests of the pie-eating and sack-race variety, and lots of great music and dance with a country twang. Kids enjoy the bubble-gum blowing contest and the water-balloon toss. Admission in 1998 was $6 for everyone age 13 to 64, $4 for those older or younger and free for children younger than 5. Tickets are discounted a dollar for people camping at Gunstock and anyone who pays taxes in Belknap County (that includes summer people as well as year-round residents). Great food is on sale all day.

NASCAR Winston Cup New Hampshire 300

N.H. International Speedway, Loudon • (603) 783-4961

One of the biggest NASCAR events of the year at the Speedway, this is the last time the big stock car stars appear in New England for the season.

Wool Day at Canterbury Shaker Village

288 Shaker Rd., Canterbury • (603) 783-9511

On the third Saturday in September, Shaker Village celebrates the fiber arts. From the sheep to the closet, you'll get a chance to watch shearing and spinning, tapestry weaving, quilting and lace making. Learn from the demonstrations, buy from the vendors or just enjoy. See our Attractions chapter for more about Shaker Village.

Altrusa International

Antique Show and Sale
Interlakes High School, N.H. Rt. 25, Meredith • (603) 279-6121

In less than 10 years this has become one of the big antique shows, drawing dealers from around New England at a time when the Lakes Region is teeming with foliage-tourists. In addition to furniture and primitives, the show features lots of antique ceramics, jewelry and glass. It's always held the third weekend in September. There's a $3 admission charge.

Mustang Show

Funspot, U.S. Rt. 3, Weirs Beach • (603) 594-0838

Every year in mid- to-late September New Hampshire highways undergo a sudden transformation, as Ford Mustangs of all eras converge on the Lakes Region. This gathering, sponsored by the New Hampshire Mustang Club, is for owners and aficionados alike to look, learn and love these classic sports cars.

White Mountains and Great North Woods Regions

New Hampshire Highland Games

Loon Mountain, Lincoln • (800) 358-SCOT

If you like the sound of bagpipes, be sure and come to Lincoln for The New Hampshire

Highland Games. It's the largest Scottish gathering in the Eastern United States. Over two dozen pipe bands, each with about two dozen members, perform at the opening and closing ceremonies. Besides music and marching, everyone has fun watching a real mix of competitions. You can check out the Sheepdog or Highland Dance Competitions, the Kilted Mile Run or the New England Scottish Heavy Athletics Championship. You can participate in whiskey tasting seminars or learn all about the McAnybody's at a genealogical workshop. The event is always in mid-September. The 1999 dates are September 16-19.

Dartmouth-Lake Sunapee Region

New Hampshire Women's Music Festival

Ragged Mountain Ski Area, Ragged Mountain Rd., Danbury • (603) 225-3501

This celebration of women and music is rapidly becoming an Insider tradition. On a Saturday in mid-September the hills come alive with music of every imaginable tradition. You'll hear jazz and blues, tight four-part harmony and acoustic rock, African and Native drumming, fiddlers and gospel singers. If you're familiar with the Lilith Fair you'll have heard of many of these performers. Many women who come as spectators bring their instruments, too. The day is filled with singing, dancing, drumming and connecting. The event is organized by the New Hampshire Feminist Connection and ticket sales benefit the New Hampshire Breast Cancer Coalition. Ticket prices in 1998 were $15 in advance (by mail or from many independent book, music and natural food stores in northern New England), $20 at the gate. Teens ages 13 to 17 cost $20, children 12 and younger are free.

October

Merrimack Valley Region

Harvest Day at Shaker Village

288 Shaker Rd., Canterbury • (603) 783-9511

Celebrate the harvest with hayrides, bobbing for apples, milking goats and traditional children's games. Get an up-close look at draft horses and mini-horses, sheep and llamas, pigs and goats. This is a great way to introduce children to the Shaker legacy. Harvest Day is always the first weekend in October. A farmer's market offers fresh produce to take home. See our Attractions chapter for more about Shaker Village.

Great Pumpkin Festival

On the Oval, Milford • (603) 672-4567

This festival of the Great Pumpkin (did you know if not for pumpkins the early colonists might have starved?) has grown like a pumpkin in the few years since it began. It fills the entire second weekend in October with harvest festival activities. The Town Hall is haunted, there's scarecrow making, tractor-pulled hayrides, great food and wonderful crafts. Magicians, puppeteers, comics and musicians entertain, and everyone is welcome to join in the country dancing in the evenings. Saturday night is the time for the mass lighting of carved pumpkins.

Nashua River Harvest Festival

Riverfront Park, Front Street, Nashua • (603) 882-3281

Activities at this festival celebrate Nashua's waterfront heritage (and the reclamation of the Nashua River). Canoe and kayak races, street performers (they close Front Street) and bands entertain children and adults. Harvest-

INSIDERS' TIP

Be sure to read the local papers for more information on small-town happenings. In addition to the standard rundown of fairs and festivals, church socials and flea markets are common throughout the summer.

themed activities include a pumpkin-decorating contest and bobbing for apples, and harvest foods and gifts are on sale. There's no charge to attend this festival, which is in the second half of October.

Seacoast Region

Renaissance Festival

Pierce Island Park, Mechanic St., Portsmouth
• (603) 436-2848

Ever wish you'd been a knight in shining armor? Or a traveling minstrel? This festival invites you to journey through time to a fair where jousting and juggling entertain kids of all ages. Admission to the festival, which takes place in mid-October, is $3. Many visitors come in costume, so if you're so inclined, feel free. Traditional foods and crafts (and some modern foods as well) are on sale.

Lakes Region

Moultonboro Lions Club

Craft Fair and Flea Market
Lions Club, Old Rt. 109, Moultonboro
• (603) 323-7346

This is a nice combination event, with high-quality craft items by area crafters, delicious baked goods from the Lions and assorted used items in the flea market section. Lunch and snacks are available. There is no charge for admission to the fair, but you'll pay for food. It's held on the first Saturday in October (when foliage in the Lakes Region is prime).

New Hampshire Marathon

Registration at Newfound Memorial School, Union St., Bristol
• (603) 744-2649

Well, it's not as famous as Boston's or New York's, but our scenery's better! The 26-mile marathon course runs around Newfound Lake. There's a concurrent 10K race and a Health Walk, so everyone can get involved (and justify attending the pasta supper the night before). The marathon is always on a Saturday in early October.

Oktoberfest

Gunstock, N.H. Rt. 11-A, Gilford
• (603) 293-4341, (800) GUNSTOCK

Well, okay, everyone does an Oktoberfest now — but not everyone can feature our great New Hampshire brews! This tribute to the hop takes place in mid-October. Activities include music and dancing, games, food and, of course, beer. Daytime admission is $8 for ages 13 to 64, $6 for kids 6 to 12 and seniors. Teens must be accompanied by a parent or legal guardian. At night there's a show featuring Bavarian music and dance. Tickets are $13 for reserved seating and $10 for general admission.

Plymouth Fall Festival

Downtown Plymouth • (603) 536-1001

One weekend in early October the streets of Plymouth are transformed into a scene of fun and fantasy. Live music sets the stage. An art show and street dancers intrigue adults, while mechanical rides and horse-and-buggy rides attract the children. It's still warm enough to wander outside, but the heat and bugs of summer are gone. What more reason do you need?

White Mountains and Great North Woods Regions

Annual Railfans Day

Conway Scenic Railroad, N.H. Rt. 16 at Norcross Circle, North Conway
• (603) 356-5251

Railroad enthusiasts from around the northeast gather in North Conway on a weekend in mid-October for two full days of riding and talking trains. Demonstrations and a flea market highlight train paraphernalia, and there is plenty of historic and futuristic train lore for young and old railfans alike.

Monadnock Region

Pumpkin Festival

Main St., Keene • (603) 358-5344

The *Guinness Book of World Records* listing for the most lighted jack-o-lanterns in one place is 17,693, a record set during the 1998 Pumpkin Festival in Keene. The event is always held the Saturday before Halloween. The official pumpkin log-in begins at 10 AM and continues until the official cutoff at 6 PM. At approximately 8 PM the year's total is announced. Everyone is invited to bring a carved pumpkin and a 3-inch votive candle. You'll sign the official Guinness log book and then have lots of fun while the jack-o-lanterns are assembled on scaffolding on both sides of Main Street. The lighting of the pumpkins begins at 4 PM. A parade of children in costumes begins at 1:30 PM, and from 2 until 4 PM kids trick or treat along Main Street. All of the businesses participate, and everyone has a great time watching the kids and the growing fields of carved pumpkins.

Entertainment continues with live music from the Main Street stage. If you're hungry, grab a bite at one of the food vendors or eat in a local Main Street restaurant. You'll have to buy your food, but the official Pumpkin Festival events are free. Hotel rooms fill up nearly a year in advance, so book early if you want to join in the fun.

November

Merrimack Valley Region

Gingerbread Showcase

Kimball-Jenkins Estate, 266 N. Main St., Concord • (603) 225-3932

Every Sunday in November and the first Sunday in December the Kimball-Jenkins Estate sprouts an entire continent of gingerbread. Gingerbread houses, churches, railroad stations and people are everywhere. Learn to construct your own confectionery world: there are workshops for all ages. Or you can buy a finished house to take home. Admission is free; cookies and drinks are for sale inside.

Concord Coachmen Show

Concord City Auditorium, Concord • (603) 226-2863

It's been more than 40 years that the Concord Coachmen have hosted this feast of harmony — a barbershop concert featuring, along with the Coachmen, a number of other talented local quartets. It's generally on a Sunday afternoon in early November. Tickets are about $10.

Holiday Magic Parade

Main St., Concord • (603) 228-1803

On the Saturday after Thanksgiving, Concord welcomes the holiday season with this traditional parade. Marching bands and floats, motorcycle clubs and costumed characters all join Santa for the festivities.

League of New Hampshire Craftsmen Winter Craft Fest

Center of New Hampshire, 700 Elm St., Manchester • (603) 224-3375

What better place to start (or finish) your holiday shopping than with this League fair? You know every item will be of the highest-quality workmanship, and with so many artisans in the same place, there's bound to be something for everyone on your list. Admission to the show is $3.

Capitol Tree-lighting

State House Plaza, Concord • (603) 228-1803

The holiday season officially begins when the governor lights the tree in front of the State House. The Concord High School Band usually plays and everyone sings holiday carols before adjourning to warm up with cocoa and snacks. The switch is flipped at 5:30 PM on the Friday after Thanksgiving.

Seacoast Region

New England Craft and Specialty Food Fair

U.N.H. Field House, Main Street, Durham • (603) 755-2166

Rockingham Park Pavilion, Rockingham Park Blvd., Salem • (603) 755-2166

Get a jump on the holiday season with these great crafts fairs in mid-November, organized by the Castleberry Fair folks in Farmington. Handmade crafts by juried artists and wonderful gourmet foods make terrific gifts. Music to put you in a holiday mood sets the tone of the day, and crafters demonstrate their skills in case you want to try and make some of these items yourself. Admission to the Durham fair is $2.50, in Salem it's $3. Both include free food tasting!

Home for Thanksgiving Weekend
Strawbery Banke Museum, 64 Marcy St., Portsmouth • (603) 433-1100

On the weekend after Thanksgiving, tours of the museum invite guests to learn how Thanksgiving has been celebrated through the last three centuries. Tickets are $12 for adults and $8 for children.

Lakes Region

A Canterbury Christmas
288 Shaker Rd., Canterbury • (603) 783-9511

Shaker Village celebrates Christmas early, the first weekend in November. New Hampshire-made crafts and clothing are on sale at this fair, as are works of art and food in the Shaker tradition. Learn about Shaker Christmas traditions and stroll through the decorated grounds. See our Attractions chapter for more about Shaker Village.

December

Merrimack Valley Region

Midnight Merriment
Main St., Concord • (603) 224-9692

From 5 PM to midnight on the first Friday in December the merchants of downtown Concord welcome shoppers and strollers alike. The city is bright with holiday lights, and decorated shop windows. While horse-drawn carriages and wagons take visitors up and down the street, carolers and musicians fill the winter air with song.

Holiday Stroll
Main St., Nashua • (603) 882-3281

This is the largest of the Destination Downtown events, attracting close to 10,000 people. It's held the Saturday after Thanksgiving. People gather at City Hall, where they're given lighted candles. Santa arrives, riding an antique fire truck, and everyone joins in the cortege up Main Street to the Hunt Building. The city's Christmas tree is lit, appropriate choral music is played and then everyone disperses to enjoy the activities along Main Street, which is closed for the occasion. Performing artists are rotated among several indoor venues (beginning in 1997 they piped the music out to the street). Main Street shops have sidewalk sales and giveaways. Horse-drawn carriages ferry people up and down the street and carolers sing in doorways. At the Hunt building the focus is on the kids, with Santa holding court upstairs and activities like ornament-making downstairs. The whole event is free, and a terrific start to the holiday season.

Amherst Lions Club Crafts Fair
Amherst Middle School, Cross Rd., Amherst • (603) 673-3450

This is one of the longest-running and best-attended of the many Holiday crafts fairs on the first weekend in December. More than 120 vendors offer all kinds of homemade and handmade items. There's something for every taste and every price range and a snack bar if you've over-shopped.

Festival of Trees
Maple Hill Farm, 117 Ridge Rd., Hollis • (603) 465-7787

This fund-raiser for the Beaver Brook Association turns the big old barn at this nature center into a winter wonderland for the first weekend in December. Special activities include ornament-making for kids and snacks for everyone. See our Parks and Open Spaces chapter for more about Beaver Brook.

Seacoast Region

Holiday Parade
Downtown Portsmouth • (603) 436-3988

The first Saturday in December heralds the holiday season in Portsmouth. A parade through the historic downtown, decorated for the season, begins a month-long celebration.

Candlelight Stroll
at Strawbery Banke Museum
Marcy St., Portsmouth • (603) 433-1100

This holiday tradition is a delightful beginning to the season. The first and second weekends in December guests walk through the Puddledock neighborhood by the light of more than 1,000 candles. The historic homes are festooned with decorations authentic to their periods, so you can drop in on a Victorian Christmas at the Goodwin Mansion, watch the Hanukkah candle-lighting at the Shapiro's house, and stop for some Colonial music at the William Pitt Tavern. Carolers sing outside, and there's a bonfire on the green. Cost of the evening is $13 for adults, $8 for children, or the whole family can attend for $28.

An American Girls Christmas at Strawbery Banke Museum
Marcy St., Portsmouth
• (603) 433-1100

If you're familiar with the American Girl dolls and books, you know that each doll represents a different historical period. Strawbery Banke, with its houses from several eras, is a perfect location for this official American Girls Christmas. Guests participate in holiday traditions authentic to each period represented, enjoy a holiday meal and make a craft to bring home. Cost of the day is $18 and includes admission to all buildings. An American Girls Christmas runs the weekend before Christmas and the week between Christmas and New Years Day.

Lakes Region

Christmas Parade
Downtown Rochester
• (603) 332-5080

On the second Sunday in December, well before the early fall of darkness, a crowd gathers on the streets of Rochester for the annual Christmas parade. Snacks and coffee warm the hands while families enjoy the twinkling lights and decorations. The parade features floats by local groups, marching bands from area high schools, lots of fire engines and lots of fun.

Ring in the New Year
Belknap Mill, Beacon St. E., Laconia
• (603) 524-8813

In what was once a common New England tradition, hardy townsfolk gather at 11:30 PM in the Belknap mill to take turns pulling the 1823 bell to welcome the New Year. Hot drinks help dispel the chill, and once midnight has officially arrived, the party's over.

White Mountains and Great North Woods Regions

Harvest-Your-Own Christmas Trees
The Rocks Christmas Tree Farm, off U.S. Rt. 302, Bethlehem
• (603) 444-6228

The Society for the Protection of New Hampshire Forests owns and operates The Rocks Christmas Tree Farm. Beginning after Thanksgiving, and peaking by mid-December, is the Harvest-Your-Own fun at The Rocks. Everyday from 10 AM until 4 PM you harvest your tree right from the forest or choose one of the already-cut trees on display. Continuing until 7 PM are horse-drawn sleigh rides, lots of hot chocolate and a craft shop brimming with Christmas goodies. The first two weekends in December include a New Hampshire Crafts Fair. You'll pay for your tree, but sleigh rides and admission are free. Don't miss Bethlehem in December — lots of people come to town just to get a Bethlehem postmark on their Christmas cards. To find the Christmas trees, take Exit 40 off I-93 and go east on U.S. 302 for a half-mile. Turn right opposite the Exxon station and follow the signs to The Rocks.

The Polar Express (c)
Conway Scenic Railroad, N.H. Rt. 16 at Norcross Cir., North Conway
• (603) 447-3100

A tenth anniversary celebration of Chris Van Allsburg's picture book was such a tremendous success that it became an annual event. Every weekend in December the train departs from North Conway at 7 PM, bound for the North Pole and an encounter with Santa and his reindeer. Tickets are $65 in the dining car Chocorua (dinner included), $40 in first class, $20 for Adults and $15 for children 12 and younger in Coach (Believers 90 and older ride for free). Because of the huge demand there is a lottery for tickets (deadline October 1). Call the number above for information.

Dartmouth-Lake Sunapee Region

Christmas Illuminations

La Salette Shrine and Center, Enfield
Center Rd., Enfield • (603) 632-7087

The La Salette Shrine, near Lake Mascoma, was founded in 1951 as a place of prayer and meditation in a natural setting. Every year during December, the 30-acre grounds are illuminated with more than 25,000 lights proclaiming that "Christ is the Light of the World." You can see the lights on weekends in early December and daily from about mid-December through New Year's Day.

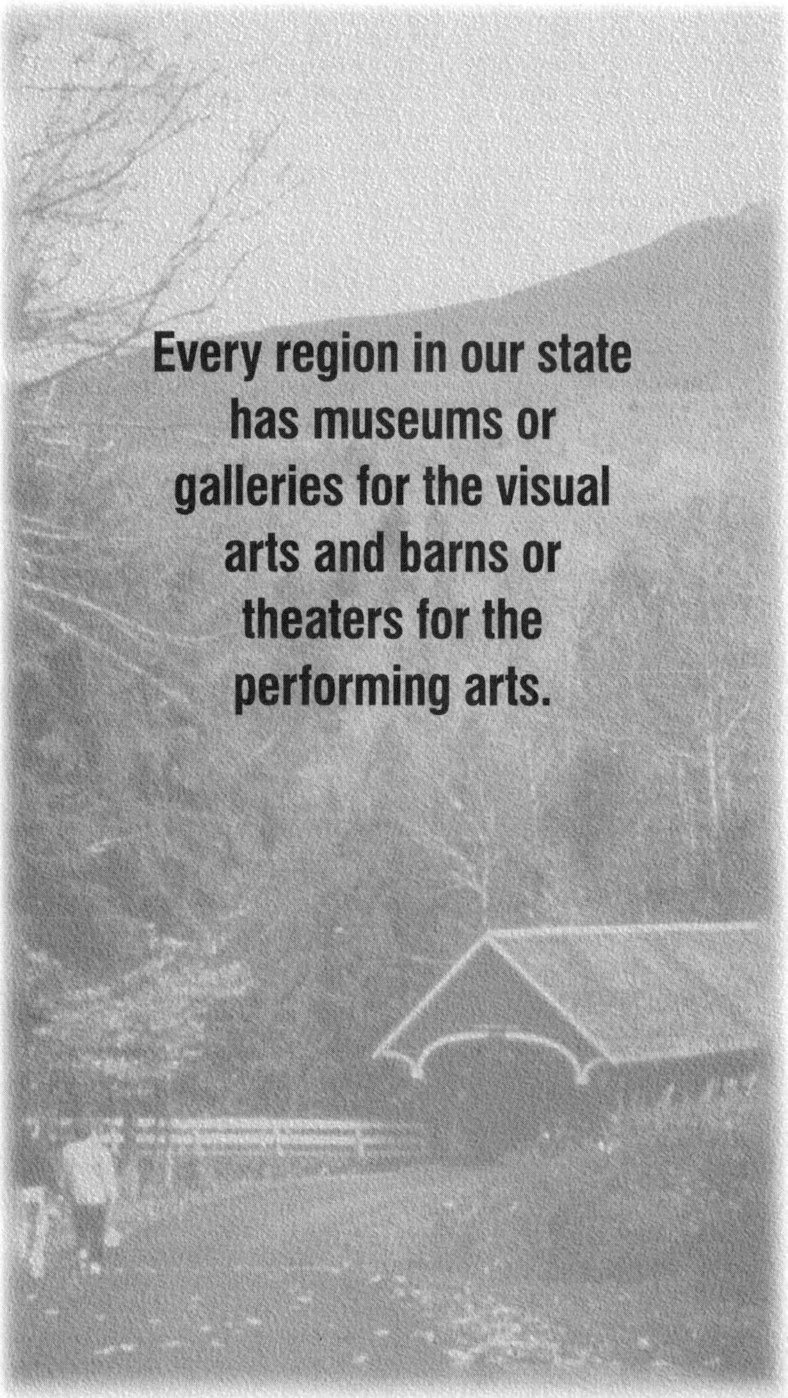

Every region in our state has museums or galleries for the visual arts and barns or theaters for the performing arts.

Arts and Culture

The cultural riches of New Hampshire might surprise those who think art in New England ceases north of Boston. Every region in our state has museums or galleries for the visual arts and barns or theaters for the performing arts. Perhaps New Hampshire respects the power of creativity because as a people we respect the power of the individual voice. The voice is heard at town meetings, where soloists shine. The voice is the poet, writing about Mount Kearsarge. New Hampshire's heritage is one that values individual expression, so it's no surprise that so many artists choose to live (at least part of every year) here.

You're about to have a grand time exploring the work of Frank Lloyd Wright in the Merrimack Valley, listening to chamber music in the White Mountains or attending a marionette opera in the Monadnock Region. The Dartmouth-Lake Sunapee Region features the Hopkins Center and Hood Museum at Dartmouth College. You'll find art ranging from contemporary to classical, murals to movies in this concentrated area of cultural richness. And, no matter what region you're in, you'll have a selection of live theater and musical concerts.

New Hampshire's population of artists swells in the summer. City dwellers who happen to be outstanding musicians, actors, directors or painters are happy to join our less-crowded environs for a sort of artistic R and R in the warm months. The beautiful lakes, mountains and ocean replenish the creative spirit. The performing arts really take off in July as the summer artists arrive for a new season.

Those who prefer studio art likely will find a class or workshop of interest whatever time of year they visit. Perhaps it's the long winter that inspires even the most awkward of us to try our hand at weaving or printmaking.

We've done our best to let you know where to find concerts, exhibits and live theater. Our list of statewide organizations and regional listings of galleries, performing arts groups and venues should help you find all the cultural activities you'll want. Also, to keep you up to date with the most current arts information, we've provide a list of several publications that specialize in arts and cultural events.

Statewide Resources and Organizations

League of New Hampshire Craftsmen

205 N. Main St., Concord
• (603) 224-3375

Don't let the "craftsmen" in the name fool you. All members of the league have been juried by established artists in their field. Their works of blown glass, weaving, pottery, needlework, metalwork and photography are pure art, if not technically fine art. The league traces its origins back to a shop in Center Sandwich, opened under the leadership of Mrs. J. Randolph Coolidge, a longtime summer resident of the Lakes Region. Her vision for training and supporting artists in the state came to fruition with the establishment of the New Hampshire Commission of Arts and Crafts in 1931.

The league sponsors training in both craftwork and marketing, gives scholarships to promising artists and runs a gallery at the headquarters in Concord and eight shops across the state (see our Shopping chapter). It is best known for the annual Craftsmen's Fair, the oldest craft fair in the nation, held the first week in August at Mount Sunapee State Park (see our Annual Events chapter). When you're planning your visit to New Hampshire, call ahead and the league will send you its Crafts and Culture Map of New Hampshire.

New Hampshire Humanities Council

19 Pillsbury St. Concord
• (603) 224-4071

The N.H. Humanities Council funds free public programs in the humanities throughout the state. These range from lecture series and literature discussions to classical language classes and historic re-creations. The N.H. Humanities Council awards grants to nonprofit organizations such as public libraries and local historical societies. Its monthly events calendar, available by mail, details presentations and gives contact information for the local sponsoring organizations.

New Hampshire Writers' Project

PO Box 2693, Concord • (603) 226-6649

Newcomers with an interest in books and writing are advised to investigate the programs offered by the NH Writers' Project. The group sponsors workshops, readings, and conferences. Basic membership is $35 a year. A quarterly newsletter is full of news about awards, contests, and upcoming literary events.

New Hampshire State Council on the Arts

40 N. Main St., Concord
• (603) 271-2789

Believe it or not, this chapter does not list all the arts organizations in New Hampshire! According to the New Hampshire State Council on the Arts, a typical summer season here will see more than 1,000 arts-related events, just from June through August. The council tries to maintain an up-to-date listing of organizations and a running schedule of events as well as supporting and promoting the arts throughout the state. It can suggest specific artists as well as organizations, so if you're looking for an Irish step-dancer or a Native American snowshoe maker, the State Council on the Arts is a good place to start.

Arts Alliance of Northern New Hampshire

Littleton
• (603) 444-1504

For more than 11 years the Arts Alliance of Northern New Hampshire has been an essential link in the flourishing arts activities in the White Mountains and Great North Woods regions. Although savvy to the arts scene throughout the state, the group's specific area of influence spreads northward from Plymouth. The group has just become the operating force behind the annual Music in the Classroom program for local schools. Guest artists perform and share experience with students. The Arts Alliance of Northern New Hampshire publishes a spring newsletter highlighting the summer performance schedule throughout its geographical range. You'll learn about everything from touring stage presentations to local arts and crafts shows. To receive a copy, send a SASE to P. O. Box 892, Littleton, NH 03574.

Statewide Arts Publications

Encore

17 Executive Dr., Hudson
• (603) 882-2741

The Telegraph publishes this weekly entertainment guide on Fridays. *Encore* reviews movies and stage productions, highlights upcoming events and reports on the national entertainment scene. The calendar section (which lists many sites in Massachusetts and New Hampshire) is probably the most accessible and up-to-date listing of arts and cultural events in the state.

Entertainment Times

Keene
• (603) 358-3756

Entertainment Times is published every other Wednesday. It covers all forms of entertainment but is heavily focused on the arts.

You'll find movie and theater reviews, columns on books and music, calendar listings and tips. It's centered on the southwest New Hampshire/southeast Vermont art scene, with some listings from other areas. Pick it up free at local shops or call about receiving a copy through the mail.

Images Magazine New Hampshire

Meredith

• (603) 279-7959

Images New Hampshire, a thick tabloid-size paper, is published bimonthly and covers fine arts across New Hampshire. Reviews of plays and interviews with local artists are interspersed with art reproductions and lots of listings, primarily for art galleries and theater/music events. This is the kind of paper where the advertisements consist of art photos and poetry with a discreet "brought to you by" credit at the bottom, and yet it's distributed free of charge at tourist information centers.

Journal of the Print World

1008 Winona Rd., Meredith

• (603) 279-6479

For 21 years *Journal of the Print World* has been a respected resource to collectors and artists of original prints, both antique and modern. Reviews and notices cover the whole world of art prints. For a year's subscription send $29 to P.O. Box 978, Meredith, NH 03253.

New Hampshire Arts

40 N. Main St., Concord

• (603) 271-2789

Published quarterly by the New Hampshire State Council on the Arts, this newsletter is primarily a resource for artists and art organizations in New Hampshire. In addition to publishing information about grants, contests and other programs, it runs brief features on local artists and their work. You can call for a free subscription.

Portfolio Magazine

One Middle St., Portsmouth

• (603) 431-0114

Portfolio calls itself "the magazine for art, theatre, music and literature on the New Hampshire Seacoast." It's an ambitious self-assignment, one it seems to be fulfilling each month with reviews of local theater productions, performing artists, art exhibitions and events. *Portfolio* has an extensive calendar of events and publishes short fiction and poetry by local writers. The magazine is distributed free across the Seacoast region.

Showcase Magazine

333 Central Ave., Dover

• (603) 742-4455

Published Thursdays by *Foster's Daily Democrat*, this entertainment magazine does the usual listings, events and reviews. Beyond that it has articles and interviews with local people in the arts scene.

Spotlight

111 Maplewood Ave., Portsmouth

• (603) 436-1800

Spotlight is the Seacoast Newspapers' arts and entertainment weekly. It comes out in Thursday's *Portsmouth Herald* and the weekend edition of the *Exeter News-Letter, Hampton Union* and *Rockingham News*. You'll find detailed reviews as well as calendar listings and arts features. It also covers the club scene.

Summer World

1008 Winona Rd., Meredith

• (603) 279-6479

Choosing to turn a liability (winter) into an asset, Sophia and Charles Lane of the Old Print Barn annually publish this celebration of the arts in the Lakes Region and White Mountains. Their goal is "to organize all possible information in the art world for all people in the area." Needless to say, this is one fat newspaper! It's free and available at most local businesses and tourist stops. Pick one up for

INSIDERS' TIP

Don't be shy about showing your own portfolio. Many galleries are happy to schedule an appointment to look at new work.

theater schedules, art shows, concert information and tips on fine dining.

Merrimack Valley Region

Arts Organization

Federated Arts of Manchester
1000 Elm St., Manchester
• (603) 668-6186

Federated Arts of Manchester raises and distributes money to support the arts in the greater Manchester area, publicizes local artists and arts organizations, and encourages businesses and government agencies to support the arts. It organizes a discount-ticket program for member organizations and "On My Own Time," a program for employers to showcase their employees' artistic work.

Museums and Galleries

Lassonde Gallery
150 King St., Boscawen
• (603) 796-6414

This estate, also known as the First Fort site, is on the National Register of Historic Places. This was the first frame house built in Boscawen in 1769 and was made of timbers taken from the dismantled fort. The house now serves as the headquarters of the New Hampshire Art Association and as gallery space for small or specialized exhibitions.

The Open Studio
557 N.H. Rt. 3A, Bow • (603) 225-6119

The Open Studio exhibits works by New Hampshire artists and opens a new show the fourth Saturday of each month. Oils and sculpture, ceramic and watercolor — they've even done an exhibit entirely in chocolate! Serving as a resource and education center for the arts community, the Open Studio also offers workshops and classes in various art forms for all ages. These classes include Creative Kids, an educational program for kids ages 4 through 15, and Media Nights, which give dabblers the opportunity to work with a particular medium along with artists at various skill levels without committing to a whole course. Monday night is pottery, Tuesday is figure drawing, Wednesday is sculpting and Thursday is painting. Media Nights are free for members. Times vary, and there are costs for materials and models. Call for specific details. Gallery exhibits are open year round, whenever anyone is in the building (call ahead). There is no admission price, but donations are gratefully accepted.

Chester Village Cemetery
Rt. 121, Chester

If this seems like an unlikely arts listing, you should know that the stones in this humble country cemetery are regarded as unique examples of American folk art. Reportedly the stonemason modeled the angels on the tops of the headstones after local people, and his opinion of each individual is clearly reflected in the expressions on the stone faces!

The Art Center at Hargate
St. Paul's School, 325 Pleasant St. off Silk Farm Rd., Concord
• (603) 229-4642

In the middle of the beautiful campus of St. Paul's School (see our Education chapter), the Art Center houses the school's art studios as well as an intimate (1,600-square-foot) gallery. It's open to the public from 10 AM to 4:30 PM Tuesday through Saturday, and it's free of charge. Past exhibits have featured artists such as Andrew Wyeth, Winnie Owens-Hart and Zhu Qizhan. Exhibitions are timed to coincide with areas of the curriculum, but you don't need to be studying sculpture or painting to be thrilled at the works displayed here.

The McGowan Fine Arts Gallery
10 Hills Ave., Concord • (603) 225-2515

The McGowan's monthly exhibits of works in many media are enhanced by receptions with the artists and other opportunities to develop an appreciation for the fine arts. The gallery is open 9 AM to 5 PM Monday through Wednesday, 9 AM to 7 PM Thursday and Friday, and 10 AM to 2 PM Saturday. There is no admission charge.

Society for Protection of New Hampshire Forests

54 Portsmouth St., Concord
• (603) 224-9945

The conference room of the society's headquarters (see our Parks and Open Spaces chapter for details) provides a simple backdrop to the works of local artists. All work exhibited is a reflection of the natural world. When you stop to see the art here, you can also take a nature walk or visit the gift shop. The society headquarters are open 8:30 AM to 5 PM daily year round. There's even a playground area for the kids.

The Covered Bridge Gallery

Fountain Sq., Contoocook
• (603) 746-4996

The Covered Bridge Gallery is dedicated to raising awareness of the fine arts in New Hampshire, and to that end it exhibits works of New Hampshire and New England artists in a variety of media. It's open year round from 10 AM to 5 PM every day except Wednesday and Sunday. No admission is charged.

The Ground Floor Exhibition Space

5 Hutchings Dr. off Rt. 130, Hollis
• (603) 465-2011

The airy, sunlit Ground Floor occupies the ground floor of this building, which also houses the Hollis Post Office, a photography shop and several offices. It is also intended as a "ground floor" entry into the world of art exhibition. The space has been set up and is provided as a service and resource to the community. Exhibits, open free to the public, are changed monthly. Past displays have included photography, needlework, watercolors, oils, prints and an annual display by art students at the local high school. The Ground Floor is open 9 AM to 5 PM Monday through Friday and 8:30 AM to 12:30 PM on Saturday. It's closed Saturdays in June, July and August, and like the Post Office, always closed on Sundays.

New Hampshire Antiquarian Society

Main St., Hopkinton • (603) 746-3825

Almost every New Hampshire town has its own Historical Society, with a little museum in a preserved school house or fire station, some treasured pieces of handmade furniture and clothing, and assorted paper records of life in an earlier time. (And a fascinating stop those mini-museums make, if you happen by one on a day it's open!) In Hopkinton, the local preservationists went a good deal further, and the New Hampshire Antiquarian Society is the result. Changing exhibits include portraits by well-known New Hampshire artists, a fashion review of antique clothing, early musical instruments and enough memorabilia of childhood to create a one-room school exhibit. Each June it hosts an art show called Tomorrow's Masterpieces, featuring works by local artists. It also hosts band concerts, lectures and slide shows. An antiques auction is an annual fund-raiser, and to top it off, the Antiquarian Society has published several respected books. The Long Building, a former library, is open from 10 AM to 5 PM on Thursdays and Fridays and from 10 AM to 2 PM on Saturdays. Admission is free.

Chapel Art Center Alumni Hall, Saint Anselm College,

St. Anselm Dr. off N.H. Rt. 114,
Manchester • (603) 641-7470

This center was built around 1920 as the abbey chapel. When the new church was built, the chapel was converted into a spacious (2,800-square-foot) exhibition area. The original ceiling and wall paintings were done by the monks of the abbey, some of whom specialized in religious art. Along with the stained glass, their art legacy enhances the changing displays. The gallery is open free to the public. The school has a small permanent collection, but most of the four or five exhibitions each year are of contemporary art by regional artists. It's open 10 AM to 4 PM Tuesday through Saturday and Thursday nights until 9 PM throughout the academic year (September through April). It's closed during the Christmas break and on school holidays. Programs related to the shows are also offered, and the space is sometimes used for chamber music, as the acoustics are excellent. A taped message at the number above includes current exhibits and directions to the center.

Currier Gallery of Art/ Zimmerman House

201 Myrtle Way, Manchester
• (603) 669-6144

The Currier Gallery is a prestigious museum with a distinguished permanent collection (including paintings by Claude Monet, Georgia O'Keeffe, Edward Hopper and Andrew Wyeth). Having begun with a very small permanent collection, it developed a tradition of loan exhibitions and showcasing outstanding local and regional artists. Gallery tours and occasional musical performances, along with a thriving art school, keep the museum in touch with the community.

Zimmerman House is a unique part of the Currier's permanent collection — a house designed in 1950 by America's great architect, Frank Lloyd Wright. It is the only Wright house in New Hampshire and the only one in New England open to the public. It is furnished in Wright's distinctive Usonian style, and the landscaping and furnishings seem equally organic to the site.

The Currier is open 11 AM to 5 PM Monday, Wednesday, Thursday and Sunday. It's open 11 AM to 8 PM on Friday and 10 AM to 5 PM on Saturday. A special feature is free admission from 10 AM to 1 PM on Saturday. The Currier is closed Tuesdays. Combined tickets for the Zimmerman House and the Currier Gallery can be purchased at the Currier, and the tour for the house leaves from there.

The regular tour of the Zimmerman House is $7 and $5 respectively (free for members). The in-depth tour costs $12 and $9 ($7 for members). Reservations for the tour are recommended. Admission to the Currier alone is $5 for adults and $4 for seniors age 65 and older and college students. Those younger than 18 are admitted free.

Digital Art Gallery

Pioneer Computer School of Visual Art, 324 Commercial St., Manchester
• (603) 623-8293

Here's a gallery in a 100-year-old mill building devoted to an art form that's barely been around for a decade! The art ranges from inspiring to bizarre, and all of it was created using not brushes and canvas but pixels and electrons. The possibilities are, apparently, limitless. Test your own horizons with a Saturday morning class. The gallery is open to the public from 9 AM to 5 PM Monday through Friday.

The Diocesan Museum

140 Laurel St., Manchester
• (603) 624-1729

The Catholic Diocese of Manchester operates this museum in a space designed as a model of a medieval chapel. The exhibits are generally of religious art or work with a religious theme. Best known is the annual display of nativity sets from around the world. The museum is open free of charge from 10 AM to 4 PM Tuesday through Friday. It's also open Monday evenings at 7 PM for guest lectures.

Franco-American Centre

52 Concord St., Manchester
• (603) 669-4045

Adele Boufford Baker, director of the Franco-American Centre, is the calming voice of the French language announcements at the Manchester airport. It's an appropriate introduction, because one of the functions of the Franco-American Centre is to welcome French speakers and lovers of French culture to the state. The art gallery at the center exhibits works of artists with a "French connection," whether they are New Hampshire natives, Canadian cousins or from one of the other French-speaking parts of the world. It has shown the work of Franco-American photographers, Parisian painters and Acadian woodcarvers. The center also hosts receptions for visiting business people and provides interpreters for a number of French dialects, including Creole. It also sponsors concerts in the park and a film series. The gallery is open 9 AM to 4:30 PM Monday through Friday without charge. You don't have to speak French to enjoy it, though they do answer the phone in French. Don't panic, they'll switch to English when they hear you say "hello."

Photo: Andrew Edgar

The Pontine Movement Theatre combines dramatic forms in its original productions. Here, Greg Gathers, co-artistic director, shares a scene from Thornton Wilder's *Our Town*.

Chandler Memorial Library and Ethnic Center

257 Main St. at the corner of Kinsley St., Nashua • (603) 594-3415

The Chandler is a grand old building, worth stopping by just to see the wallpaper, carved woodwork and gas sconces. But since it offers a film series, children's activities, slide shows, folk dance lessons and an ever-changing assortment of craft workshops, you won't need an excuse to get inside. The Chandler is open from 10 AM to 3 PM Monday through Saturday and Thursday nights until 9 PM. It is closed on Saturdays in the summer. Call for a schedule of events.

Hunt Memorial Building

6 Main St., Nashua
• (603) 594-3412

This wonderful old building was an empty derelict when we were growing up. Today it is being painstakingly restored, one room at a time, to its former glory. Dark carved paneling shines, sunlight pours through antique glass and a carillon chimes overhead. The rooms that are finished host community events from art exhibitions and chamber music to flower shows, wine tastings and elegant children's tea parties. Santa is in residence here during Nashua's Holiday Stroll (see our Annual Events chapter). Some events have admission charges but many are free. Call for a schedule or to join the mailing list.

Rivier College Art Gallery

Memorial Hall, Rivier College, 435 Main St., Exit 4 off Rt. 3, Nashua
• (603) 888-1311 Ext. 8276

Don't let the school building look of this place deter you. The art department at Rivier College has a well-deserved reputation for excellence, and the exhibits are well worth the two flights of stairs. The gallery is open Monday through Friday from 11 AM to 3 PM and 6:30 to 8:30 PM (no evening hours on Fridays). There is no admission charge.

Performing Arts

Petit Papillon
Concord
• (603) 224-6463

The Children's Ballet Theatre of New Hampshire was founded in 1985 to provide a performing company for young dancers. Members of the company, ages 10 to 17, are selected by audition and represent a number of area dance schools. The company performs throughout the year, including an appearance at First Night New Hampshire in Concord. Many performances are in hospitals and schools too small to fund enrichment programs. The company depends on contributions to cover costs so the dancers do not have to pay a fee to join.

Granite State Symphony Orchestra
11 Greenwood Ave., Concord
• (603) 226-GSSO, (603) 225-1111 (tickets)

The Granite State Symphony is New Hampshire's newest symphony orchestra, having formed in 1993. Using the Concord City Auditorium as its home venue, this orchestra produces an outstanding classical series each year as well as pops concerts with groups like the New Black Eagle Jazz Band. Artistic director and conductor Robert Babb is also conductor of the Lakes Region Symphony Orchestra in Laconia.

Operafest!
28 S. Main St., Concord
• (603) 229-1842

Promoting opera in New Hampshire by providing quality performances at affordable prices, the Operafest! company is almost entirely made up of New Hampshire residents. In addition to its traditional operatic company, Operafest! has a Children's Chorus that produces two shows each year. The company's home theater is the Concord City Auditorium.

Majestic Theatre Trust
281 Cartier St., Manchester
• (603) 669-SHOW

This nonprofit, volunteer organization supports the performing arts by producing a year-round schedule of shows, hosting guest artists and maintaining a museum detailing the history of Manchester's theaters. The shows are produced at the trust's Msgr. Pierre Hevey Theatre, and each year they include a traditional musical, a children's musical, a concert tribute, at least one drama and several musical revues. The museum's collection is on display at each performance and travels to local events.

Manchester Choral Society
Manchester
• (800) 639-2928

The Manchester Choral Society has been performing for more than 35 years. Members are talented amateurs from around New England, ranging from high school students to senior citizens. With 80 auditioned singers, the Manchester Choral Society is one of the largest performing organizations in the state. The society offers concerts in venues across New Hampshire, has toured in Europe and also cut a critically acclaimed Christmas CD.

New Hampshire Philharmonic Orchestra
83 Hanover St., Manchester
• (603) 647-6476

Established in 1905, the New Hampshire Philharmonic includes professional musicians and talented amateurs from across New Hampshire. They range in age from 12 to 80-plus, and most are volunteers. Under the direction of conductor Patrick Botti (who brings his classical training from the Sorbonne and experience with more than 20 national and international orchestras), the orchestra performs both pops and classical repertoires. A special outreach to the community is its annual children's concert at the Palace Theater, with inexpensive (less than $10) tickets for adults and free admission for kids!

New Hampshire Symphony Orchestra
81 Hanover St., Manchester
• (603) 669-3559, (800) 639-9320

A world-class orchestra directed by conductor James Bolle, the New Hampshire Symphony Orchestra has performed a traditional concert series at the Palace Theater in

Manchester for more than 20 years (including accompanying the Granite State Ballet). The orchestra features the classics of Tchaikovsky, Mahler, Mendelssohn and Bach alongside contemporary pieces, many by New Hampshire composers. It also offers a variety of performances at sites around New Hampshire, including the Music Hall in Portsmouth, the Capitol Center in Concord and spots like the Peterborough Town Hall. It also has been known to offer a family concert accompanied by a petting zoo!

Opera League of New Hampshire

Manchester

• (603) 645-4072, (603) 668-5588 (tickets)

The Opera League of New Hampshire is a nonprofit organization dedicated to bringing the opera experience to the people of New Hampshire, especially children. In addition to regular opera performances, the league goes out into the schools to introduce students to opera or bring children to the Palace Theater for free performances. The regular season is three shows of accessible works, with surtitles if a work is not sung in English.

St. Anselm Abbey Players

Dana Center, 100 College St., Manchester

• (603) 641-7700

For nearly a half-century the Abbey Players have welcomed the people of New Hampshire to their performances. Its season generally includes one serious play, one musical, a family show written by the students, a series of one-act plays directed by students and selected scenes from Shakespeare in honor of his birthday.

Stage One Productions

132 Bridge St., Manchester

• (603) 669-5511

Stage One is a professional theater group that produces more than 30 shows every year. Combining the best local talent with guests from the New York stage, Stage One offers dinner theater during fall and winter at the Chateau Restaurant in Manchester. They also perform at hotels, corporate functions and other special performances, including First Night New Year's Eve celebration. In July and August Stage One performs Broadway-style plays at the Palace Theater.

Merrimack Community Theatre

Merrimack

• (603) 424-5344

The Merrimack Community Theatre is the genuine article: a group of dedicated amateurs who for almost two decades have been producing three shows a year out of their own energy and love for the theater. Performing at Merrimack High School, they have done mysteries, comedies, dramas and even musicals.

American Stage Festival

N.H. Rt. 13 N., Milford

• (603) 673-7515 (summer)

14 Court St., Nashua

• (603) 886-7000 (winter)

The American Stage Festival began as a summer-stock theater in Milford a quarter century ago. Over the years the emphasis shifted away from light entertainment to more serious theater. The stock company was replaced with professional actors brought in just for one production, and a sequence of plays replaced the repertory rotation. In recent years the theater has settled into a routine of offering a summer assortment usually containing a musical, a thriller/suspense piece, a comedy or two and at least one serious drama. Stage Festival audiences have seen a number of world premieres and well-known actors from the stage and television. Most recently, the Stage Festival expanded to a year-round season and purchased the old Nashua Center for the Arts as its headquarters and winter home. A new Board of Directors, focusing on a more mainstream selection of plays and more vigorous support of the Young Company and Peacock Players, raises hopes that the Stage Festival may soon find itself on firm financial ground.

ActorSingers

219 Lake St., Nashua

• (603) 889-9691

Founded in 1955, the ActorSingers is a group made up of talented and energetic amateurs from the greater Nashua area. They perform two major Broadway shows a year, a smaller summer musical and a children's production featuring 3rd- to 10th-graders from area schools.

Granite State Ballet
36 Arlington St., Nashua
• (603) 889-8406

Best known for annual performances of *The Nutcracker,* the Granite State Ballet company produces several shows of particular interest to families and children every year. Many young people who begin with this company have later been tapped to dance *The Nutcracker* in Boston.

Nashua Chamber Orchestra
Nashua
• (603) 673-4100

The Nashua Chamber Orchestra is dedicated to providing the chamber music experience to the greater Nashua community and a performance opportunity to local musicians. It produces annual spring and fall concerts of music by composers such as Bach, Mozart and Handel at the Community Chapel in Nashua and the Congregational Church in Amherst.

Nashua Symphony Association
6 Church St., Nashua
• (603) 595-9156, (800) 639-3101

This association manages both the Nashua Symphony Orchestra and Nashua Choral Society. The 1998-99 season will be its 75th season of enriching the cultural life of southern New Hampshire. Each concert is themed, and most combine classical masterpieces with some lighter works (such as Gershwin). They also do pops productions each winter and spring. Guest soloists often enhance the outstanding performances of these talented amateurs, who have toured in Europe and cut several records during their illustrious history.

Nashua Theatre Guild
Nashua • (603) 888-3630

The Nashua Theatre Guild is a community theater group with a lot of ex-professionals among its ranks. Using the smaller theater at the Nashua Center for the Arts/Court Street Theater as its home theater, the guild performs lots of comedies, mysteries and dramas — everything but musicals, which they leave to the ActorSingers. The Summer of 1998 featured *Twelfth Night* as part of the traditional "Shakespeare in the Park" performances at Greeley Park in Nashua.

Venues

The Capitol Center for the Arts
44 S. Main St., Concord
• (603) 225-1111

Originally opened in 1927 as a vaudeville venue, The Capitol Center houses the Chubb Theatre, New Hampshire's largest theater at more than 1,300 seats, along with the Governors' Hall banquet room. The center also includes Kimball House, a historic home now converted into meeting rooms of various sizes. The center has its own complete video production studio, a catering service and office space for the center staff and a number of other nonprofit arts organizations. The Capitol hosts regional and national touring performers including Broadway musicals, vocal performers, dance companies and orchestras. A special treat at the Capitol is a preshow dinner downstairs at the Governor's. Park once, enjoy an elegant meal (usually themed to match the show), then stroll upstairs to the Chubb for the evening's performance. What luxury! Kids' shows often feature post-performance receptions downstairs.

Kimball-Jenkins Estate
266 N. Main St., Concord
• (603) 225-3932

The Kimball-Jenkins Estate on the North End of Concord is an elegant 19th-century home bequeathed to the people of New Hampshire by the great-granddaughter of the original owner. Formal gardens surround the mansion and add to the time-travel feeling of your visit. (See our Attractions chapter for tours of the house and gardens.) Exhibits of works by local artists are shown every month in the Carolyn Jenkins room, and the Carriage House and Gardens are available for functions and often used as sites for small arts events. We attended a chamber music concert in the Carriage House and were astounded at the quality of the acoustics.

Dana Center at Saint Anselm College

100 St. Anselm Dr., Manchester
• (603) 641-7710, (603) 641-7700

The Dana Center houses the world-class Koonz Theatre on the campus of Saint Anselm College. In addition to being the home theater for the Abbey Players, the Dana Center hosts touring companies and artists from around the country and the world. Ballet and chamber music, one-person plays, Caribbean dancers and Russian choirs have all graced the stage at the Dana. Renowned lecturers and little-known scholars have spoken here. Ticket prices vary with the performance; call for information and reservations. The Dana also offers an international film series, the Dana film series of respected literary films and the occasional just-for-fun films, such as the Halloween Creature 3-D Double Feature, all at no cost.

New Hampshire Institute of Art

148 Concord St., Manchester
• (603) 623-0313

The Manchester Institute of Arts and Sciences was founded in 1898 in the fervor of invention and creativity that marked the turn of the last century. The grand building was constructed for the institute in 1916. It has seen performances by artists from comedian Bennett Cerf to the Trapp Family Singers, and virtually every major presidential candidate of the last three decades has made a stop here. Today the Institute of Art is the only independent college of the fine arts in New Hampshire. (See our Education chapter for details of the program.) The institute sponsors exhibitions by artists from across the country, and its galleries are open to the public free of charge. It also hosts a travelogue lecture/film series called Take Seven that has been going on for a half-century!

Notre Dame College

2321 Elm St., Manchester
• (603) 669-4298

Notre Dame offers a variety of arts experiences to the community. The Art Gallery in Holy Cross Hall is open without charge. The scheduled hours vary to coincide with the school year. The New Thalian Players, a cooperative college and community theater, produce two shows per year (November and April). The music department hosts a holiday concert of songs and hand bells in December and a spring concert in April, and a lecture series and other cultural events are open to the public. Finally, the college offers a free concert series, Music For Manchester, on Wednesday evenings in July. The music ranges from jazz to Celtic and calypso, traditionally concluding with a performance by the 39th Army Band.

Palace Theatre

80 Hanover St., Manchester
• (603) 668-5588

The Palace is one of those old-style theaters with ornately carved woodwork, an intimate stage, gilt chandeliers and balcony seats climbing to the rafters. A profuse variety of performances is held throughout the year. There isn't a bad seat in the house, but the parking situation in downtown Manchester is a nightmare. Experienced theater-goers wear walking shoes with their elegant evening clothes and change in the lobby!

New Hampshire College

2500 N. River Rd., off U.S. Rt. 3, Manchester
• (603) 645-9635

New Hampshire College doesn't have a theater, but that doesn't stop it from offering a wide variety of arts experiences. Using the school's audiovisual studio, small gym and even the athletic center, the Spectrum Cultural Series has presented original plays and touring shows, folk music and show tunes, poetry readings and timely lectures. For the visual arts the Shapiro Gallery, in a quiet corner of the library, offers a new exhibit every month (except August). Recent shows have included oils and watercolors, collages, sculpture and photography. There is no charge for the gallery or any of the presentations, which are open to the public. Call for a schedule and directions.

Seacoast Region

Museums and Galleries

The Art Gallery, University of New Hampshire

30 College Rd., Durham
• (603) 862-3712

The Art Gallery at UNH is housed in the Paul Creative Arts Center on the main campus of the college. The gallery hosts touring exhibitions and pulls together exhibitions of works from private collections around New England. The museum's permanent collection of more than 1,100 works also provides material for display, and, of course, the works of students and faculty are exhibited as well. Of particular interest are occasional major exhibitions built around New Hampshire themes — A Visual History of the Isle of Shoals and New Hampshire Folk Art, for example. The gallery is open to the public without charge from 10 AM to 4 PM Monday through Wednesday, 10 AM to 8 PM on Thursday and 1 to 5 PM on Saturday and Sunday when school is in session. It's closed holidays and in June, July and August.

Lamont Gallery/ Frederick R. Mayer Art Center

Phillips Exeter Academy, Exeter
• (603) 778-3461

This art gallery, in the center of the Phillips Exeter campus, is a truly stunning space. It was built as a memorial by the parents of a young alumnus who died on a Navy submarine in World War II.

The gallery exhibits works of artists from around the world and frequently opens an exhibit with a reception where students and guests can meet the artist. The gallery is open to the public without charge from 9 AM to 5 PM Monday through Saturday, except Wednesday when it closes at 1 PM. Parking on campus is tight, but there is on-street parking on Tan Street, which runs alongside the art center.

Robert Lincoln Levy Gallery

136 State St., Portsmouth
• (603) 431-4230

This N.H. Arts Association gallery offers varied exhibitions of group, theme and juried shows. It also hosts both the Omer T. Lassonde Memorial Exhibition and the Jack Parfitt Memorial Photography Exhibition. Its annual juried exhibitions are open to all regional artists, and it offers art classes for all ages.

Performing Arts

Dover Repertory Theatre Durham Centerstage/ The Mill Pond Center

50 Newmarket Rd., Durham
• (603) 868-2068

Traditional summer-stock theaters were often staged in an old barn at the end of a long driveway. Well, that's exactly what the Mill Pond Center is, but the work of Durham Centerstage is anything but traditional. In this barn you'll find a theater and company that host an intriguing variety of contemporary stage productions, including comedy, drama and even opera.

Hampton Playhouse

357 Winnacunet Rd., Hampton
• (603) 926-3073

The Hampton Playhouse has been doing summer theater for 50 years. Every summer it produces five classic musicals as well as a full schedule of children's productions. Recent hits have included *Carousel, Grease* and

INSIDERS' TIP

Parking at the University of New Hampshire is extremely limited. In most areas it is by permit only, although there are a very few metered spaces by the Arts Center. You'll save time if you park in the visitor lot off Main Street, register your car at the center there and ride the free shuttle bus to the show.

Beauty and the Beast. The theater is air-conditioned and has its own free parking.

North East Youth Symphony Orchestra

151 Stepping Stone Rd., Lee
• (603) 868-3530

This orchestra draws young people from Massachusetts and Maine as well as New Hampshire to perform up to six concerts a season at locations around the state. North East Youth Symphony provides an opportunity for intermediate and advanced students to participate in a symphony orchestra, an experience a private instructor can't often provide. Participants must audition in the spring or fall, and there is a cost to belong to the orchestra. Players are also expected to continue their private lessons and participate in school music programs if they're available.

Ballet New England

135 Daniel St., Portsmouth
• (603) 430-9309

Ballet New England's mission is to bring to New Hampshire the very best and highest forms of dance, and fewer than 20 years it has achieved that pinnacle. The professional company has a repertoire of more than 40 works from classical ballet such as *The Nutcracker* and *Swan Lake* to modern flamenco and exciting original works by its award-winning choreographer and artistic director, Mihailo Djuric. Ballet New England gives more than 30 performances a year, including one for children. The Music Hall is its home theater, but the group also dances in other venues across the region. Members of the company teach at the school and take their show on the road, working as artists in residence at area schools.

New Hampshire Theatre Project

133 Islington St., Portsmouth
• (603) 431-6644

The Theatre Project is an umbrella organization of member artists who reach out to the community. Over the years they have performed for 60,000 area students. More than 100 performances per year in schools and community settings provide the opportunity for children to see and talk with professional actors, puppeteers and other performance artists. For more than 20 years the New Hampshire Theatre Project has also offered professional theater to the public at the McDonough Street Studio and the Music Hall.

Players' Ring

105 Marcy St., Portsmouth
• (603) 436-8123

Over the course of a 10-month season, the Player's Ring, a small (75-seat) theater on the edge of Prescott Park, produces an average of 15 shows, half of them by local playwrights (from within a 60-mile radius of Portsmouth). Most of the actors also hail from within that circle. Beginning in 1996, they extended their season and geography by adding dinner theater in Alton Bay during July and August. The Players' Ring is also available for productions by other theater groups.

Pontine Movement Theatre

135 McDonough St., Portsmouth
• (603) 436-6660

Pontine Movement Theatre bases its art on the premise that "actor" implies "action," and that the natural language of the theater is movement that is supported by text. Using masks, puppets, costumes, sets and narrative, Pontine develops original works that are not quite mime, not quite dance and not quite anything you're expecting. The company is critically acclaimed throughout the Northeast. In addition to regular performances at the McDonough Street Studio, Pontine offers classes and workshops and does special assembly presentations for schools.

Seacoast Repertory Theatre

125 Bow St., Portsmouth
• (603) 433-4472

Seacoast Repertory produces theater year round. After a seven-play season of classic and innovative plays and musicals from September through June, the stage is shared by a three-show summer-stock season of musicals and seven original Youth Theatre productions. The theater also runs a summer camp for the performing arts, PAPA Camp, at Lake Agawam in Maine.

Venues

Paul Creative Arts Center at the University of New Hampshire
30 College Rd., Durham
• Department of Music, (603) 862-2404; Department of Theatre and Dance, (603) 862-3038

The music and theater presentations at the university are a mix of student work and guest performances. Shows are held in Johnson Theater and Bratton Recital Hall. Every genre of theater, dance and music is represented: comedy, opera, ballet, jazz, a capella and chamber music. Call for upcoming events and schedules.

Whittemore Center at the University of New Hampshire
128 Main St., Durham
• (603) 862-4000

With a striking curved glass front that shines brightly in the New Hampshire night, this modern 7,300-seat arena provides a setting for larger events. From rock concerts (Alanis Morrisette holds the record for fastest sell-out performance) to ice shows to dances with Big Bands such as the Dorsey Brothers Orchestra, the Whit offers something for everyone, and a quarter million ticketholders walk through the doors every year. Of course the *most* important show at the Whit is Wildcats hockey. As with any visit to UNH, you are advised to park in an outlying lot and take the shuttle to your destination.

Leddy Center for the Performing Arts
133 Main St., Epping
• (603) 679-2781

The Leddy Center is an anomaly in the arts world: an arts organization that makes enough money to support other charities. This is a tribute to the spirit of its volunteers and the reputation of its shows, which include a mix of traditional and contemporary musicals, an Evening of Jazz at the IOKA theater in Exeter and an annual Gilbert and Sullivan operetta. The Leddy also runs a school of performing arts with classes for all ages (see our Education chapter for more details), using the modern, climate-controlled, 211-seat theater constructed in its 100-year-old building in downtown Epping.

IOKA Theatre
55 Water St., Exeter
• (603) 772-2222

This is another of the old-fashioned theaters from the days when every town had a shiny marquee. IOKA, however, survives — still showing first-run movies and art films, hosting stage performances and renting the marquee for birthday wishes and congratulations to local heroes.

The Music Hall
28 Chestnut St., Portsmouth
• (603) 436-2400, (603) 436-9900, 24-hour film line)

The Music Hall bills itself as the 14th-oldest operating theater in the United States. Whatever the statistic, it is a historic building, reminiscent of the days when next year's Broadway shows were as likely to start out in Portsmouth as in Boston. Originally opened in 1878 with more than 1,200 seats, the theater has been by turns a venue for dance and music, a professional theater, a vaudeville house and a motion-picture palace.

Reopened in 1986 by a dedicated group of community activists (who eventually raised enough money to purchase the building in 1988), the once-majestic theater is being gradually restored to its former grandeur. The theater space now seats 900 people and is acoustically spectacular. It hosts a full calendar of events from October to May, including many of the companies described in this chapter and a number of local and national celebrities. The Music Hall is also known for its special Family Series of performances appealing to younger audiences and an outstanding film series that takes advantage of the largest indoor movie screen north of Boston.

Prescott Park
Marcy St., Portsmouth
• (603) 436-2848

Right in the heart of historic Portsmouth, across the street from Strawbery Banke,

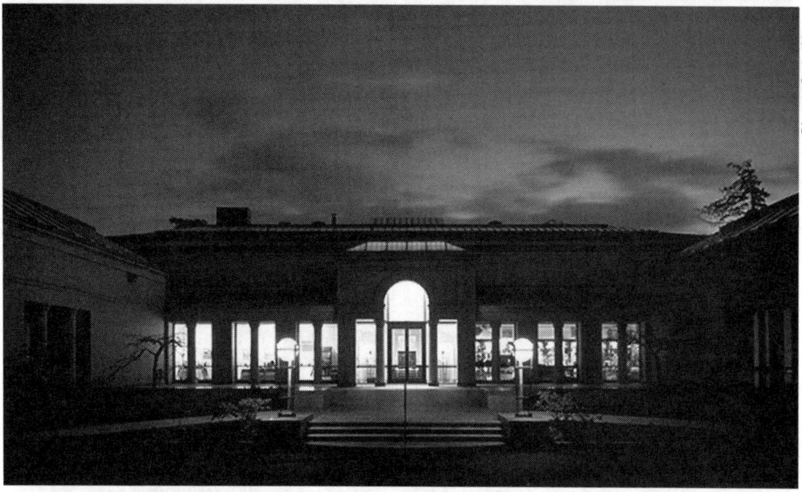
Photo: Craig Alness

Beauty within, beauty without: Evening at the Currier Gallery of Art in Manchester.

Prescott Park hosts the Summer Arts Festival, staging more than 80 art exhibits and events. These include Shakespeare in the Park, an intensive Arts Academy for young people, dancing under the stars and evenings of music and other theater for families.

Lakes Region

Museums and Galleries

Surroundings at Red Gate

123 Holderness Rd., Center Sandwich
• (603) 284-6888

This gallery and shop features the works of many artists primarily but not exclusively from New Hampshire. It has mostly paintings in oil, acrylic and watercolors, carvings and some other media. The gallery is seasonal (warm weather) but also displays works year round at the Corner House restaurant in the village. Call for the date of the annual Meet the Artist day, generally late June or early July, when visitors can chat with the artists and see their new work. The gallery is open 10 AM to 5 PM Monday through Saturday from the Fourth of July weekend through Labor Day.

The Old Print Barn

Exit 23 off I-93, 9 miles east on N.H. Rt. 104 to Winona Rd., Meredith
• (603) 279-6479

The Old Print Barn features six centuries of art on paper. From antique prints to contemporary pieces, all works are originals. Oils and watercolors, etchings and engravings, woodblock prints and lithographs, photographs and drawings are all represented. The collection is international, but of special interest are the many pieces representing New Hampshire's beauty.

The director asks parents to keep children quiet and "in hand" to avoid disturbing others in the gallery. Some families just take the kids to the Science Center at Holderness or Funspot in Weirs Beach while the art lovers indulge at The Old Print Barn.

The barn is open 10 AM to 5 PM daily from Memorial Day to Columbus Day. Its heated winter gallery keeps the same hours from Thanksgiving Day to Memorial Day. No admission is charged.

Riverside Gallery

Elm St., Gilmanton Iron Works
• (603) 364-5578

This gallery, operated by the people from Frates Creative Arts in Laconia, features the works of New Hampshire artists. It also offers some art lessons and has a small theater space where they hope to do children's programs. The gallery is open 10 AM to 9 PM on Monday and Friday from spring to fall and by appointment.

The Tower Gallery
28 Summer St., Northfield
• (603) 286-9999

The Tower Gallery takes its name from the Victorian tower inexplicably added to the front of the historic Jason Foss house, an otherwise classic garrison colonial. It's strange architecture, but it makes a neat gallery space for the display of an eclectic assortment of artwork. Etchings, oils, watercolors and lithographs line the walls, while handcrafted lamps, furniture, pottery and woven goods excite the senses. It's open 10 AM to 6 PM Tuesday to Saturday or "anytime the lamp is lit."

Karl Drerup Fine Arts Gallery
Hyde Hall, Plymouth State College, Plymouth
• (603) 535-2646

This gallery exhibits contemporary works in a variety of styles and media, featuring regional, national and international artists as well as the students and faculty of the college. Graphic design, photography and ceramics are included along with the traditional fine arts forms. The gallery is open 10 AM to 5 PM Monday through Friday (Wednesday it stays open until 8 PM) and noon to 5 PM on Saturdays. Admission is free.

The Art Place
9 Main St., Wolfeboro
• (603) 569-6159

For more than 20 years, The Art Place has featured works of art representing the natural beauty of the New England landscape. Original works of local and regional artists make up most of the selection. All the art is for sale, but visitors are welcome to come in just to feast their eyes. The Art Place is open 9:30 AM to 5 PM Tuesday through Saturday in winter and every day in summer, often until well into the evening.

Performing Arts

New Hampshire Music Festival
88 Belknap Mountain Rd., Gilford
• (603) 524-1000

The New Hampshire Music Festival is a professional orchestra performing chamber music, classical orchestral works and pops. Frequently compared to the Boston Symphony's Tanglewood summer program, the Music Festival's season includes six different shows each summer. On Thursday evenings and alternate Saturday evenings, the orchestra performs in Plymouth at the Silver Cultural Arts Center. On Friday evenings you can hear them at Gilford Middle-High School. After 45 seasons the festival is well-known among the area's summer residents, and reservations are strongly recommended.

Lakes Region Symphony Orchestra
P.O. Box 721, Meridith, NH 03253
• No phone

When the New Hampshire Music Festival shifted its focus to become a professional orchestra, a number of accomplished amateur and retired musicians in the area decided they wanted to continue playing. Thus was born the Lakes Region Symphony Orchestra, a community orchestra performing three concerts a year, just for the love of music. The orchestra includes young students and retired professional musicians, and it is always open to new members. For information on membership or to receive a performance schedule, write the Lakes Region Symphony Orchestra at the address above.

Lakes Region Summer Theatre
N.H. Rt. 25 E., Meredith
• (603) 279-9933, (800) 643-9993

Peter Ramsey grew up next door to the New London Playhouse, so it is not surprising that he has the theater in his blood. It is surprising that after just a decade of producing shows at the high school in Meredith, his old-fashioned summer-stock theater sells enough tickets to be self-supporting. The successful formula is a mix of theater professionals, both actors and technicians, performing famous Broadway musicals in a state-of-the art, 400-seat theater. The actors, who include some of the finest young people on the stage today, stay for the whole season and play a variety of roles in the six different shows. After each performance the actors come into the lobby, still in costume, to meet the audience. Over the course of the summer, the more than 1,000 season-ticket holders really get to know the actors, and that relationship contributes to the energy and family atmosphere at every show. Shows run two weeks each, Tuesday through Sunday, with matinees on Wednesday and Thursday. Tickets frequently sell out, so reserve tickets in advance if you plan to attend on a weekend.

The Barnstormers Summer Theatre

Main St., Tamworth
• (603) 323-8500

New Hampshire's (some say the country's) oldest professional summer theatre company is still stormin' after all these years, having celebrated 50 years of productions back in 1980. Each season they produce eight shows in their delightful old theater, with its comfortable seats, intimate stage and beautiful village setting. In 1998 the theater was extensively renovated, preserving the pleasures of the old theater while bringing in the comforts of both heating and air-conditioning, modern bathrooms and handicapped accessibility. The plays are a mixture of old favorites, modern pieces and an occasional premiere, with the blend weighted toward comedy and light amusement. Eight plays in eight weeks (July and August) equals a year's worth of entertainment.

The Village Players

51 Glendon St., Wolfeboro
• (603) 569-9656

An amateur community theater group with great aspirations, the Village Players have performed in the Lakes Region since the 1930s, producing up to four shows a year including classic dramas and major musicals. In 1995 the group purchased the old Masonic Temple in Wolfeboro, giving them a 200-seat home theater and a huge fund-raising and remodeling project! Volunteers and players are always welcome.

Venues

Alton Bay Pavilion

Alton Bay
• (603) 875-3033

The Pavilion offers a summer full of great entertainment. The schedule mixes dinner theater with the Players' Ring company (see subsequent listing) and evenings of improvisation with live and taped music shows (Big Band and country-western). Ticket prices range from $5 for family theater matinees to $38.50 for evening dinner theater.

Meadowbrook Farm

Musical Arts Center
Meadowbrook Ln., off N.H. Rt. 11-B, Gilford• (888) 5-MEADOW
Ticket Office: 164 Lake St., Laconia
• (603) 528-5550

Meadowbrook hosts big-name acts for outdoor summer concerts. Johnny Cash, Anne Murray and Lyle Lovett were among the recent artists. Shows begin at 7 PM, and ticket prices range from $20 on the lawn to $35 for prime reserved seats. Kids from ages 6 to 12 get a $5 discount on any ticket, and those younger than 6 get in for free.

Frates Creative Arts Center

31 Canal St., Laconia
• (603) 528-7651

The Frates Center is a nonprofit creative arts organization that is very much the brainchild of its director, Larry Frates. His interest in and concern for children shapes the theater company, the touring magic show and the Lollipop Puppet Company, which includes giant parade puppets as well as traditional

INSIDERS' TIP

If you're here for the summer, think about volunteering backstage or in the ticket office of a local playhouse.

theater puppets. For more than 20 years the center has offered lessons in theater, dance, painting and other art media and has sponsored a children's theater troupe. More recently, it has begun a dinner theater, using the Old Town Hall stage in Gilmanton, and has opened the Riverside Gallery in Gilmanton Iron Works. Inspired by the famous briefcase drill teams we've all seen on television, Frates organized the New Hampshire Lawn Chair Brigade, which now marches and performs in parades across New Hampshire.

Silver Cultural Arts Center

15 Holderness Rd., Plymouth State College, Plymouth
• (603) 535-ARTS

This new arts center houses three performance spaces. The 665-seat Hanaway Theater has a traditional proscenium stage and hosts student and professional performances of plays, ballet, opera and symphony. The Smith Recital Hall is an acoustically sensitive facility that seats 174 for smaller vocal and instrumental performances. And the Studio Theatre, seating between 150 and 200 people, is an experimental theater that can be configured in different ways for different kinds of performances.

White Mountains and Great North Woods Regions

Museums and Galleries

State of the Art Gallery

Jackson Falls Marketplace, Jackson
• (603) 383-9441

Artist Barbara Wilson, educated at the Boston Museum of Fine Arts, now runs a gallery in the heart of Jackson, between the post office and the Village School. Works of New Hampshire artists dominate the shows at this gallery, although Wilson is open to all quality work. Many of the works on view are watercolors, oil paintings or etchings, although photography is beginning to be an important component in the gallery. A show of Mount Everest photographs by Rick Wilcox was up during the summer of '97. Barbara is well-known as a source of information regarding the art scene in the area, and her eye for art is much admired and respected. The gallery is open year round, but hours vary. It's best to call ahead.

Mount Washington Valley Art Center and Gallery

N.H. Rt. 16 north of the Scottish Lion Restaurant, North Conway
• (603) 356-2787

This volunteer arts association has become a North Country mainstay since it opened 30 years ago. As a gallery it shows the works of New England artists, including watercolors, oils, pastels and stained glass. The gallery also has photographs and prints on display and available for purchase. The Art Center arm of the association conducts art lessons and workshops including a Friday morning painters' group that visitors are welcome to join. In addition, it sponsors art in the local schools. The gallery is open every day.

Performing Arts

North Country Center For The Arts, Papermill Theatre

The Mill at Loon Mountain, Kancamagus Hwy., Lincoln
• (603) 745-6032,
(603) 745-2141 (box office)

Who says they don't produce musicals anymore? The Papermill Theatre bursts with song from early July to the last days of August. This nonprofit professional theater group produces three musicals each season. Shows

INSIDERS' TIP

High school choral, band and drama club productions are great fun, inexpensive and often surprisingly well done. Keep an eye out for posters in village shops and post offices.

staged in the last few years included *Guys and Dolls* and *Brigadoon*.

The group also produces classic children's fairy tales for the 10-week Children's Theatre Program. In addition to weekly performances at the Papermill, the Children's Theatre performs at several venues throughout the state. Call for information regarding the current season's schedule.

The curtain rises at the 250-seat theater for all programs at 7:30 PM Tuesday through Saturday. All seats are reserved.

This group's newest venture is art shows, held in local storefronts since they have no gallery space of their own. However, initial success indicates that a permanent exhibit space may be found soon. If you're in town during fall, winter or spring, be sure to check on art exhibits.

North Country Chamber Players
Littleton
• (603) 444-0309

This acclaimed 12-member New England chamber ensemble has played together every summer for nearly 20 years. The rest of the year the musicians are principle players in orchestras ranging from The New York City Opera Company to The Minnesota Orchestra. But for six weeks every summer, they return to the White Mountains with the precision of the swallows returning to Capistrano.

The musicians stay with local families. Since there have been so few changes in the group over the years, a strong mutual affection has grown between the people of the region and the musicians and their growing families. The concert festival is called Music in the White Mountains, and performances are held at both the Governor Adams Lodge at Loon Mountain and the Sugar Hill Meeting House in Sugar Hill. The lodge at Loon Mountain is an acoustically ideal setting for the series. In addition to the Music in the White Mountains series, which runs from mid-July to mid-August, various combinations of the North Country Chamber Players perform throughout the summer. Call ahead for reservations and information about all performances. Ticket prices are $19 for a reserved-seat, single-concert ticket, $14 for general admission and $10 for seniors and children younger than 17. Call for information on group and season rates.

Weathervane Theatre Players
Lancaster Rd., Whitefield
• (603) 837-9322

Another classic, this 1860s bright red barn-theater is just a couple of miles outside Whitefield. After more than 30 successful seasons, summer theater here has become a summer tradition. Weathervane players are a combination of professionals, volunteers, interns and apprentices. The theater group is particularly strong in musical theater. A recent season included three musicals: *Grease, Into The Woods* and *Ain't Misbehaving*.

The 233-seat theater fills up quickly, and all seats require advance reservations, so call ahead. Performances begin on the Saturday before the Fourth of July and run nightly, except Sunday, until the Saturday preceding Labor Day. In August the schedule expands to include a 5 PM matinee on Saturdays. The barn-theater is next door to the Whitefield Inn; have a summer supper before or after the evening performance.

Dartmouth-Lake Sunapee Region

Museums and Galleries

Hood Museum of Art
Dartmouth College, E. Wheelock St., Hanover• (603) 646-2808

The Hood Museum of Art at Dartmouth College is one of the oldest and largest college museums in the country. The collection began in 1772 with the gift of a few mastodon fossils and now contains more than 60,000 objects. The museum is proud of its excellent collection as well as its many programs that serve the local community.

The current building opened in 1985. Ten galleries and a 200-seat auditorium highlight the facility, which is adjacent to the Hopkins Center and across Wheelock Street from the Dartmouth Green. The gift shop is between the Hopkins Center and the museum.

Highlights of the collection include art from America, Europe, Africa, Oceania and Native North America. The American art includes works by Gilbert Stuart, Thomas Eakins and Frederic Remington. The 19th- and early-20th-century landscape paintings of the White Mountains Region are a must-see for anyone interested in New Hampshire. The excellent collection of early American silver includes an engraved bowl given by the Royal Governor of New Hampshire in honor of the college's first commencement. You'll find works by Pablo Picasso, Georgia O'Keefe, Henri Matisse and other modern masters. The Harry A. Franklin Family Collection of Oceanic Art is considered the strongest collection of its kind in the United States.

The museum presents approximately 15 shows a year. Each exhibit is accompanied by learning opportunities including lecture series and gallery talks. A recent show, *The Body and Its Image: Art, Technology and Medical Knowledge*, was organized to coincide with the Dartmouth Medical School's 200-year anniversary. Lectures were presented by both medical school and art department professors. A show of paintings from the Indian subcontinent was enriched by a film series featuring the films of Satyajit Ray and a live performance by sitar master Ravi Shankar.

The museum offers special Family Days one Sunday each month from October through April. The day's theme is explored with demonstrations and opportunities for hands-on experimentation. For example, a Family Day topic of Helmets, Hairdos and Headdresses included an exhibit of helmets, crowns and turbans along with a workshop for making your own headdress.

Admission to the museum is free. The hours are 10 AM to 5 PM Tuesday through Saturday and 12 to 5 PM on Sunday. On Wednesdays it stays open until 9 PM. The museum shop opens at 10 AM Tuesday through Friday and noon on weekends and closes every day at 4 PM except Wednesday, when it is open until 9 PM.

AVA Gallery and Art Center

11 Bank St., Lebanon • (603) 448-3117

AVA stands for Alliance for the Visual Arts, a nonprofit group and a vital piece of the New Hampshire arts scene. Most of the works shown are by artists living in New Hampshire and Vermont. The three galleries include the large main gallery, a smaller annex and a members' gallery. Shows usually hang for one month. Annual shows include a Holiday Show in December, a juried show and an exhibit highlighting the work of the artist members.

Shows in the three galleries are often related. For instance, one show featured three exhibits focusing on artful expressions in fabric ranging from textile design to quilt making.

The Art Center runs an extensive Education Program. After-school classes include instruction in drawing, painting and sculpture. Weekend workshops abound in topics such as printmaking, bookmaking and papermaking. If you are going to be in the Lebanon area for an extended stay, check the class schedule. In summer, a two-week watercolor class is held at nearby Saint-Gaudens in Cornish (see our Attractions chapter).

AVA Gallery and Art Center is open Tuesday to Saturday from 11 AM to 5 PM and by appointment. Admission is free.

Marian Graves Mugar Art Gallery

Sawyer Arts Center, Colby-Sawyer College, New London • (603) 526-3759

This college art gallery specializes in contemporary art. While the permanent collection includes old master prints, the seven shows presented each school year concentrate on photography, painting, prints and graphics including computer art. Recent exhibitions have included work by Janet Fish, Peter Milton and award-winning illustrator Tomie de Paola (also a New London resident). Annual shows include a juried show of student work and an exhibition by the art department faculty.

The gallery is open Monday through Friday from 9 AM to 5 PM during the academic year. Prospective students and visitors are encouraged to call the college to arrange visits outside the academic year.

Library Arts Center, Gallery and Studios

58 North Main St., Newport • (603) 863-3040

The carriage house of a Victorian mansion is the home of this multifaceted arts center. Two galleries house monthly changing shows in art, fine crafts, photography and history. The shows are complemented by lectures and performances held in the small theater. Recent shows include a Maxfield Parrish exhibit and works by nationally known artists. The facilities include a studio with pottery facilities and a darkroom. Classes in painting, photography and pottery are available year round. The gallery is open Tuesday through Saturday from 11 AM to 4 PM.

Performing Arts

Opera North

40 College St., Hanover • (603) 643-1946, 603) 448-0400 box office

Opera North's professional musicians and dedicated, mostly volunteer administration work together to bring quality opera to music lovers in New Hampshire. Begun as a grassroots organization in the late 1970s, Opera North attracts musicians from major opera companies including the Metropolitan Opera. Performance seasons are in summer and during the Christmas holidays. As with many other performing artists, these musicians summer in New Hampshire because it's a relaxing and beautiful place to practice and perfect their respective talents.

Opera North is a favorite place for stage-ready singers to train and learn a role and for experienced performers to stretch their skills away from the eye and pen of big-city critics. The company has always maintained high musical standards, insuring a steady supply of excellent singers. Opera North has a home at the Lebanon Opera House but also performs throughout the area. The company is just beginning a series of master classes and young artists workshops.

Venues

Claremont Opera House

Claremont City Hall Claremont
• (603) 542-4433

You'll love this 1897 theater, which dominated the local entertainment scene at the turn of the century. And it's a vital part of the cultural life of the region today. The season runs from late September into the first weekend in May. You might be in town for Gilbert and Sullivan or a concert by the Vienna Boys Choir. You might catch an electronic light show or a Broadway musical. The 10-show season provides a delightfully varied program. The Opera House celebrated its 100th-anniversary season in 1996-97. It had closed in 1963 but was re-opened in 1979 after years of work by dedicated preservationists and strong civic and community support. The Opera House has a capacity of 787. Individual ticket prices range from $10 to $25, with several ticket plans to choose from.

Lebanon Opera House

51 North Park, Lebanon
• (603) 448-0400

Built in 1924 and acclaimed for excellent acoustics, the Lebanon Opera House is a year-round venue for performing arts. The 750-seat theater is in the Lebanon Town Hall on the village green. You can have a pre- or post-performance meal at Sweet Tomatoes (see our Restaurant Chapter), which is a lazy five-minute stroll from the Opera House. Once inside you'll appreciate that every seat has a very good sight line. You might see performances by the Alvin Ailey dance company, the Woody Herman Band or the rock-opera *Tommy*. Opera North productions take over the month of August (see its listing in the Performing Arts section).

Hopkins Center

Dartmouth College, Hanover
• (603) 646-2422

Be sure and check the Hopkins Center calendar as you plan your New Hampshire trip. An amazing array of talent passes through the center's Faulkner Recital hall, Spaulding Auditorium, Lowe Auditorium and Moore Theater. A typical week's events might include more than 10 movies (Hollywood releases as well as foreign and independent films), three recitals and two discovery programs such as "Discover Indian Music."

The award-winning building was the prototype for the design of the Metropolitan Opera House in New York City. Box office hours are 10 AM to 6 PM on Monday through Friday and 1 to 6 PM on weekends. The box-office number will guide you to all events scheduled that week as well as future programs.

Newport Opera House
20 Main St., Newport
• (603) 863-2412

Originally built in 1872, the Opera House burned down in 1885. Luckily it was immediately rebuilt because the town of Newport wouldn't have known how to get all the citizens together without it. Town Meeting is still held here along with school meetings and, until recently, the high school prom.

In addition to civic and social functions, the Newport Opera House is host to year-round arts entertainment. A subscription series runs from September through April and features performances by groups such as the North Country Chamber Players and theatrical productions. If you are lucky you might be in town for a Big Band night of ballroom dancing. The seats are freestanding, so they can be moved to allow for lots of swing. In summer the nonprofit Opera House group presents concerts on the common every Sunday night at 6 PM. Concerts range from country music to chamber orchestras.

Monadnock Region

Museums and Galleries

Church Street Gallery
16 Church St., Keene
• (603) 357-2550

This gallery, just off Main Street, is tough to find but well-worth the effort. Church Street Gallery specializes in emerging art by New England artists. The gallery is on the fourth floor of the Cracker Factory Building. The ceilings are 20 feet high with windows 4 feet by 7 feet. The stunning space has work by more than 40 artists. The Church Street gallery is open from 11:30 AM to 5:30 PM Tuesday through Saturday.

Thorne-Sagendorph Art Gallery
Keene State College, Wyman Way off Main St., Keene • (603) 358-2720

This 4,000-square-foot exhibit space is another reason to visit Keene during your New Hampshire sojourn. In addition to the permanent collection, the gallery has several major shows each year. Recent exhibits included the works of two major contemporary American painters, Fritz Scholder and Jules Olitski. The gallery (which has state-of-the-art security and climate-control) appeals to artists who enjoy the high level of attention as well as the quality of the audience available in southwestern New Hampshire. Every other year the gallery sponsors a juried show of regional artists that includes a people's choice award.

The gallery is open from noon to 4 PM Saturday through Wednesday and noon to 7 PM Thursday and Friday. The gallery is not usually open during college holidays and may be closed on Thursday and Friday during the summer, so call ahead.

Thoreau Gallery and Ravencroft Theatre
Emily Flynn Campus Center, Franklin Pierce College, Rindge
• (603) 899-4150

A revolving series of fine-arts exhibitions is shown at the gallery throughout the academic year. It is open every day from noon to 2 PM and 5 to 7 PM. The academic year is from September through May. The campus

INSIDERS' TIP

Many towns have evening concerts on the green (or square or oval) during the summer. You might hear the town band, high school jazz group or a local quartet. The best way to find out what might be happening when you're in town is to check the local newspaper. It's also a good idea to look for announcements in stores along the main street.

is closed from Christmas break through much of January. It is best to call ahead for schedule and exhibit information.

The Ravencroft Theatre presents a play every fall, a musical every spring and an annual performance of the *Messiah* on the first Saturday in December.

Sharon Arts Center

N.H. Rt. 123, 4 miles south of Peterborough, Sharon
• (603) 924-7256

The Sharon Arts Center was established in 1947 in order "to stimulate, encourage and provide education in the theory and practice of the arts and crafts through instruction, exhibitions and marketing assistance." Tucked away in the middle of the woods is a savvy, yet homey, art gallery and a must-see in the Monadnock Region.

The Sharon Arts Center revamped itself in 1997, and to our eyes the results are stunning. The gift shop — a gallery in itself — has moved into downtown Peterborough's Depot Square. Look for details in our Shopping chapter. The gift shop's departure expands the exhibition space to two spacious galleries. At least six shows are hung every year. A recent exhibit featured nine of North America's foremost wildlife artists. The annual Spring Members Show is a great place to soak up visions of New England life, interpreted by its artists.

Classes for adults and children are held throughout the year. Call or write for a schedule. Past class subjects range from weaving to pysanky, the traditional Ukrainian method of egg-decorating with beeswax. Weekend workshops are just right for temporary residents.

The hours are 10 AM to 5 PM Monday through Saturday and noon to 5 PM on Sunday. Admission is free.

Spheris Gallery

Main St., Walpole
• (603) 756-9617

You might think Boston and New York are the best places for locals to buy fine art. Think again, because this gallery has topnotch contemporary works including paintings, works on paper and photography. By special arrangement with the Vermont Studio Center, the Spheris Gallery features works by the center's visiting artists. Wolf Kahn, Emily Mason, George Tooker and Susan Brearey are just a few of the artists represented here. Feel free to come in and browse — the art is wonderful, and the snob factor is nil. The gallery is open Wednesday through Sunday from 1 to 5:30 PM and by appointment.

Performing Arts

Fitzwilliam Inn Annual Winter Concert Series

N.H. Rt. 199, Fitzwilliam
• (603) 585-9000

Sunday afternoon in the Front Parlor of the Fitzwilliam Inn is a longstanding tradition for local and nearby music buffs. Begun in 1976, the Winter Concert Series is an informal series of free concerts. Musicians from Boston and the region sing (or play) for their supper. You might luck into a piano recital or an afternoon of German song. The series is held every Sunday from January through March. Call ahead to check the time (and make a reservation at the inn's popular restaurant, if you want to stay for supper).

Monadnock Music

Peterborough
• (603) 924-7610

An international group of musicians presents a series of 12 concerts in July and August at the Peterborough Town House. The concerts range from piano recitals to opera concerts. The group also gives 18 free chamber music concerts throughout the summer in towns of the Monadnock Region. Call or write P.O. Box 255, Peterborough, NH 03458 for a schedule.

Peterborough Players

Middle Hancock Rd., Peterborough
• (603) 924-7585

If you want to experience classic New England, head for Peterborough and a performance by the Peterborough Players. The group has entertained summer residents since 1933 and is one of the strongest theater groups in the region. Everyone in the main theater company, The Players, is a professional. Additionally, there is The Players' Second Company, made up of interns and apprentices. The Players have five productions every season, which runs from mid-June to early September. The program choices offer an expert blend of comedy, drama, contemporary and classic plays. There is usually a musical each year as well as a topnotch Shakespearean production. In addition to these main-stage performances, the Players' Second Stage Company usually produces two shows each summer. One, such as *Charlotte's Web*, is geared for children and families, while the other might be a Shakespearean comedy.

The plays are performed in a barn that seats 200. Productions are held nightly except Monday, although the stage is dark for a couple of days between productions. The performances specifically for kids are usually in the morning. Season tickets as well as individual performance tickets are available.

Apple Hill Center for Chamber Music
off N.H. Rt. 9, Nelson
• (603) 847-3371

Reserve Tuesday nights at 8 PM from late June through mid-August for evening concerts at the Apple Hill Concert Barn in Nelson, just 8 miles east of Keene. Donations are requested for concerts, which feature the Apple Hill Chamber Players and festival artists. Bring a picnic supper and eat on the lawn before the concert.

A nonprofit group devoted to communicating through the language of music, the Apple Hill Center for Chamber Music is both a school and performing arts center. Each summer the center holds five 10-day instructional sessions. The faculty and students come from throughout the United States and all over the world. Students are intergenerational and consist of high school students, college and conservatory students, and preprofessional adults.

Andy's Summer Playhouse
582 Isaac Frye Hwy., Wilton
• (603) 654-2613

This is a nonprofit theater by children for audiences of all ages. The summer schedule typically includes five plays as well as comprehensive writing and directing programs for kids. Look for details in our Kidstuff chapter.

Venues

Colonial Theater
95 Main St., Keene
• (603) 352-2033

Great acoustics along with Main Street charm keep the Colonial Theater at the top of the list for the Monadnock Region's performing arts. Built in 1924, the theater alone is a show-stopper for those of us accustomed to charmless 10-screen multiplexes. You might run into a folk concert, a performance by the New Hampshire Symphony, a first-run movie, a silent movie with live orchestra or a Broadway show. Recent live productions included *Fiddler On the Roof, Cinderella* and the Mozart opera *Cosi fan Tutte*.

The box office is open from noon until 6 PM Monday through Saturday and on Sunday prior to performances. A recording of scheduled events is available by phone when the box office is closed.

Redfern Arts Center on Brickyard Pond

Keene State College, Keene
• (603) 358-2168

This two-theater performance center runs a 12-event season from September through April. The main theater seats 570, and the Alumnae Recital Hall seats 360. Programs include all performing arts disciplines. Recent shows included performances by the Trinity Irish Dance Company of Chicago, The Atlantic Brass Quintet, Maria Benitez Teatro Flamenco Dance Company and Cherish The Ladies, a traditional Irish music and dance company.

Towering pines and shining maples cover our hillsides and turn every interstate into an art gallery.

Natural Wonders

John Greenleaf Whittier once wrote: "I spent last summer among the New Hampshire hills, as I have done for several years. Nature never disappoints me." We think you'll agree.

The Great Outdoors is a critical part of how we in New Hampshire define ourselves. Our state is more wooded now than it was a hundred years ago, thanks to the westward migration of farmers in search of soil that produced more corn than rocks. Our two major industries are timber and tourism, a combination that might appear mutually exclusive but in New Hampshire have traditionally worked together. The land-management practices of the paper and lumber interests have maintained the natural beauty that draws the tourist to our lakes and mountains.

In recent years the paper industry has worked hard to clean up its act, and ironically many environmentalists now see the demands on forests from the tourist trade (especially snowmaking and second-home building) as threats to the ecological balance.

When is the best time to visit New Hampshire? Thousands come here every winter, to revel in the pristine snow and crystal air of our mountains or watch the winter surf pound the shoreline. But summer's the season for discovering our 1,300 sparkling lakes, hiking and camping in our forests and paddling or fishing in our rushing rivers. Autumn throws a blanket of blazing color across the hills that attracts leaf-peepers by the busload. About the only time you won't hear recommended is spring — mainly because it's too short and too unpredictable to schedule a visit! But if you manage to catch it, our springtime is a fabulous explosion of birdsong and blossom, thawing the grimmest stone faces into smiles of welcome.

Weather

New Hampshire natives love to grouse about the weather, but deep down we delight in our ability to cope. Old-timers will complain about meteorologists' reports of "wind chill" and "dewpoint." Weather is weather, they believe, and you're just supposed to dress for it. Summer or winter, dressing for it generally means layers — layers that can trap air and insulate you when it's cold; layers you can put on and peel off as a day warms up and cools down. Then there are those perfect days in spring and fall, when the breeze is soft, the air is crystalline and the temperature just right. More than one grumbler has been heard to say that a few days like that are worth suffering through the worst that winter and summer can bring.

Mother Nature's mood swings are fully evident in New Hampshire, resulting in a something-for-everyone crazy quilt that both enchants and infuriates the natives. It was in New England that Mark Twain said, "If you don't like the weather, wait a minute." Barry Keim, New Hampshire's state climatologist, told us, "New Hampshire has such extreme variability that it is impossible to generalize or predict with confidence." A native of New Orleans and no stranger to hot weather, he added, "on a hot day in July, it can be just like Orlando here. Of course, the next day it can be just like Winnipeg."

The "worst weather on earth," according the National Weather Service, has been recorded at the top of Mount Washington, where the average wind is 35 mph and year-round winds of more than 100 mph are not uncommon. The whole state is far enough north to have serious snow any time between Thanksgiving and April, although not always in time for Christmas. Almost every winter we'll have four or five weeks (more in the northern part of the state) when the temperature never gets above freezing and falls well below zero at night. At the other end of the year, our summers are hot and can be sticky, with a week or two of temperatures around 100 degrees (in the inland sections) during an average July and August. (Just enough to make you glad of air-conditioning if you have it, but not enough to justify installing it if you don't!)

Our terrain makes for even more variety of weather. Along the Seacoast, the ocean effect moderates the temperature. It's always a little warmer on the coast in winter and a little cooler in summer. Before the new highway upgrades, on HHH days (hazy, hot and humid) the line of cars heading toward ocean breezes could stretch a quarter of the way across the state! Up north the mountains make their own weather (literally). Take those signs at the bottom of our mountain trails seriously — it really can be 80 in the parking lot and snowing halfway to the summit.

Even smaller hills create microclimates, so that within a given region some folks get more snow on colder nights or some gardeners grow eggplant and melons while others never can. If you're a gardener and familiar with the Agriculture Department's zones, you'll find that most of southern New Hampshire is in zone 5, with the mountains and north of the notches designated as zone 4 and most of the Great North Woods as zone 3. But many people in the south have cool enough summer nights or early and late frosts to be classed as zone 4, and a few have shelter and sun enough to grow plants recommended for zone 6. Call the county extension service for their suggestion, but ask your neighbors what to expect around your place.

Being on the north side of the ridge or in a sheltered hollow can give you your own personal weather! A former road agent recalls a phone call on the night of the first snow after he was elected: "Hi, this is Howard. Are we going to plow?" came the voice of one of his crew. "Soon as it gets to 3 inches," the agent answered, citing the town policy. "I've got 10 outside my door," Howard said. They were only 3 miles apart.

Snow and Winter Storms

In winter we distinguish between snow, snowstorms and blizzards. When it's cold enough, any cloud can produce a bit of snow, which may or may not collect on the ground. Frequently such scattered snow squalls can result in accumulation of 2 to 4 inches in higher locations. That's just plain snow. In a snowstorm, snow accumulates everywhere, first on the grassy areas, eventually on gravel and pavement as well. The severity of a storm can be measured in "inches per hour" of accumulation. When a storm approaches an inch per hour, it's snowing pretty hard. If significant snowfall is expected, the National Weather Service issues "winter storm watches" (indicating that conditions are favorable for a hazardous storm) or "winter storm warnings" (meaning that the hazard is imminent or already reported). They may also issue a "blizzard warning." A blizzard adds high winds to the snow, so that drifting snow and falling branches become part of the impact. Take those storm warnings seriously — sliding off a snow-covered road is no fun, even if you manage to avoid a smash-up.

You may hear a storm referred to as a Nor'easter. These storms occur when a low pressure center pulls water out of the Atlantic ocean and dumps it across New England. A big Nor'easter can pour 2 or 3 inches of rain on the region in 24 hours. Precipitation that would fall as an inch of rain will produce about 10 inches of snow, so a midwinter Nor'easter can shut down even snow-ready New Hampshire for a day or two.

Big snowstorms make for better story-telling, but our more dangerous winter storms are those that come when the temperature is a bit warmer and the precipitation comes as ice. We have several variations of falling ice, but whether the forecast is for freezing rain, sleet or hail, driving conditions will be terrible and power lines will come down. Insiders lay on supplies of water (when the power goes out, your water pump doesn't run) and make sure the wood stove is ready to fire. Only the foolhardy venture forth into the ice: Whatever

INSIDERS' TIP

A hazardous summer road condition occurs when we get heavy rain after a dry spell. Water loosens the oil accumulated on the pavement, making a greasy surface that's surprisingly slippery.

Granite

Close-up

It didn't take long for the early colonists to realize that much of New Hampshire's hilly terrain consists of a thin layer of topsoil over ribs and ridges of bedrock. The rocks that came up with every shovelful of soil, the ledge that poked out of fields and appeared when cellar holes were dug, the gleaming white summits of the mountains and the enormous boulders and cliffs that marked the countryside all revealed the stony character of the region. It's not all granite, but enough of it is to have provided material for buildings and monuments across the state and indeed, the country.

Our state's symbol, a great stone face carved by the hand of nature on the side of Cannon Mountain, and our nickname, The Granite State, both highlight this reality. Granite is more than just common rock. Its distinctive pattern and ability to be polished to a shine are the result of millennia of compression deep in the Earth's crust. Crystals of feldspar, potash and quartz, sprinkled with grains of various darker minerals, reflect light and produce the mottled pattern and variety of colors.

Most New Hampshire granite is gray, white or pink and sparkles with mica. Although earthquakes, volcanoes and glaciers pushed much New Hampshire granite to the surface, commercially valuable granite must be quarried or cut from solid deposits underground where the effects of wind and ice have not damaged the stone. At one time small quarries were common in southern New Hampshire, but today only larger sites produce enough stone to be worth the cost of operation. Quarrying granite is difficult and dangerous, even today.

One hundred years ago, most of the granite workers in New Hampshire were Italian immigrants, descendants of stonecutting families going back to the time of ancient Rome. They brought to the hills of New Hampshire not only their skills with wedges and saws but also their religion, their food and wine, and their tradition of celebrating life. They were not always regarded kindly by their stolid Yankee neighbors, but hard work earns respect here, and over time their sons and daughters became integral parts of the communities. By the time granite memorials were being carved to honor local heroes of World War II, Ciardelli and Infanti were just as much New Hampshire names as Wentworth or Stark.

Today, 10-ton blocks of granite cut from New Hampshire hillsides are shipped to manufacturers around New England and the globe (including Italy). Sliced or cut with diamond blades or high-pressure water knives, our granite is polished for headstones, rough split

Photo: Sally Wilkins

This granite obelisk never made it to its intended buyer. Now it stands in Milford, a silent reminder of the town's quarry workers.

— continued on next page

for paving stone, beveled for curbing and made into counter tops and floor tiles to outfit stylish kitchens and baths. Granite benches and birdbaths, war memorials and mailbox posts all pay lasting tribute to the rugged terrain we call New Hampshire.

it is that you need to do, it will still be there tomorrow, and by then the road will be clear. An ice storm in January of 1998 devastated huge swaths of forest in Northern New England and Quebec. Damage estimates range from $8 million to $20 million, and nine of the 10 counties in New Hampshire were declared Federal Disaster Areas. The maple industry may take 30 to 40 years to recover, and many timberland owners will not live long enough to see their wood lots recuperate. Hiking and skiing trails across the state are blocked with downed trees. (Many ski areas told us they weren't even going to try and reopen some trails until 2000). Everyone who works or plays in the woods should exercise caution: over the next few years the debris on the ground poses a serious forest fire threat, and in the short term lots of dead wood caught in the canopy could fall on loggers or unsuspecting hunters and campers. Look up! On a (literally) brighter note, experts predict stunning foliage seasons in 1998 and 1999. Stressed trees produce more brilliant oranges, reds and yellows.

Mud Season and Frost Heaves

As that snow melts in the spring, New Hampshire braces for its fifth season: Mud Season, or Mud Time, as Robert Frost called it in his poem, "Two Tramps in Mud Time." Warm sun melts the snow and the top few inches of soil, but the next few feet down are frozen, so the water can't sink in. The result is an amazingly sticky, soupy mess that can pull the boots off your feet or hold your car prisoner, with its wheels spinning helplessly in mud up to the axles. Mud season only lasts a few weeks, until the frost is out of the ground, but it's an exciting time of year. When you see the "Road Closed — Mud" sign at the top of a country road, turn around. You'll feel like a fool hiking out to ask some farmer for a tow.

Another sign to watch for in late winter and early spring is the orange-and-black notice "Frost Heaves." Frost heaves happen when water frozen in the ground beneath the road begins to thaw. Heaves can come up overnight, creating unmarked speed-bumps where the road lay smooth just a day before. Those warning signs, if heeded, will save the bottom of your car from brutal scraping and banging.

Summer Storms

We have some exciting weather in summer too — hurricanes and thunderstorms, even an occasional twister. But the combination of uneven terrain and cold ocean water slows summer storms down and breaks them up before they build to the size and destructive power seen in the South or on the plains. Thunderstorms are welcome interruptions during the heat waves of summer, as cool breezes and refreshment mark the end of several days of steamy conditions.

Lightning must be taken seriously, however. Swimmers and boaters should get out

INSIDERS' TIP

Wind chill and heat index are measurements of weather that describe the way it actually feels. Wind chill is a combination of air temperature and wind speed and is more accurate than temperature alone for avoiding hypothermia and frostbite. In summer, the heat index combines humidity with temperature. Since the body is less able to cool itself in high humidity, those who work or play outside in summer should take the heat index seriously.

of the water, and golfers and hikers should avoid exposure at the first sign of an electrical storm. (But never take shelter under a tree on a golf course or other flat area — lightning is most likely to strike the highest point around, which could be your head if you're out on the green or the tree you're sheltering under.)

Animals

The spread of forest lands has contributed to a resurgence of wildlife in New Hampshire, as have antipollution regulations and the efforts of wildlife management experts. Deer populations have actually grown so large (in the near-absence of natural predators) that the New Hampshire Fish and Game Department has adjusted the hunting season to prevent starvation in the herds (see our Fishing and Hunting chapter for details).

Moose, those impressive cousins of the deer whose flat antlers can span 6 feet, are often seen along roadsides throughout the state and present a driving hazard in the North Country. A moose is heavy enough to total your car and so tall that its eyes don't reflect your headlights.

Bears are a growing problem in the mountains and as far south as the Pemigiwasset Valley (northern Lakes region) and eastern Monadnock region as they have learned to look for food from human sources: hikers' backpacks and condominium dumpsters. Our black bears are not as menacing as their Western cousins the grizzlies — in fact, none of these large animals is directly threatening to humans, although a frightened bear can be extremely dangerous. Never feed bears or other wild animals. Once they learn to think of humans as cafeteria workers, they become nuisances.

Believe it or not, the bounties (rewards for killing) on some of New Hampshire's larger predators were only eliminated in the last 20 years — in some cases after the animals were placed on the federal endangered species lists. Officially, the eastern gray wolf, lynx and cougar (or mountain lion) have all been extirpated from New Hampshire, which means they're not completely extinct, but the population is too small to support breeding. Fish and Game officials are no longer so vigorous in their denials of the return of the catamount (what we call the cougar), so the tiny number of Insiders who've reported spotting them hold out hope that cougars, like the moose, may come back from the brink. Still, the numbers are too small for anyone to worry about encountering one.

Our smaller predators include red and gray foxes, coydogs (a hybrid of coyotes and domestic dogs that are particularly threatening because they tend not to fear humans) and the eastern coyote, which has made a big comeback in recent years. Lynx and fishers (a type of large weasel) are other native predators that you may hear but not see. Fishers take the blame for many vanished house cats, although Fish and Game biologists say owls and bobcats are more often the ones dining on pets.

You may see raccoons, although a new strain of rabies that reached New Hampshire several years ago drastically reduced their population. Possums, squirrels (red and gray), chipmunks, rabbits, beaver and skunks are other common wild creatures.

Remember that wild animals are wild. If one appears not to be afraid of you it may well be sick. Raccoons and foxes in particular can pose a rabies threat to humans — never feed or touch these animals, and if you see one in daylight, assume it is unwell. Bats, on the other hand, have an undeserved reputation as major carriers of rabies.

Rabies-prevention treatments are effective when started immediately after exposure, but they are expensive and unpleasant. Unfortunately, once symptoms appear it is too late to treat this fatal disease, so when the possibility of exposure exists, treatment is required. And you don't need to be bitten to be exposed — some farmers have needed treatment after attempting to help an unfortunate, drooling cow.

In Colonial times, rattlesnakes were fairly common in New Hampshire, but they have been nearly eradicated. Two dens are known of in the state, in the isolated, rocky areas favored by the cold-blooded predators. The only reptile you need to watch out for in New Hampshire is the snapping turtle. You'll know if you see one — its shell has a distinctive zigzag shape above the tail. Don't pick it up!

Even a tiny snapper can give you a nasty bite, and a big one can really do damage. Snappers are about the size of a half-dollar when they hatch and over their long lives can grow to nearly 2 feet long, beak to tail. They can stretch their long necks back over their shells to snap, so there is no good way to pick one up. Other turtles in New Hampshire are harmless, but they'd rather go back into the wild than live in your fish tank, thank you.

Bird watchers flock to New Hampshire, binoculars and field guides in hand, to enjoy our rich variety of birds. The brilliant colors of cardinals, tanagers and buntings flash through the woods. The songs of robins and chickadees brighten our fields. We have ruby-throated hummingbirds and bald eagles, wild turkeys and wood ducks. The osprey, or sea eagle, nests along our shores, and the loon's cry marks our lakes. Bluebird populations are beginning to rebound, encouraged by bird boxes and human fans, who keep tabs on their foreign-born competitors, house sparrows and starlings. With more than 100 species of birds breeding in New Hampshire and many more migrating through, this is a wonderful place to expand your life-list.

Along the seashore you'll see cormorants, ibises and a variety of shorebirds, including an occasional rarity if you're experienced enough to pick them out of the crowd. During the spring and fall migrations, the whole Seacoast Region is a veritable Heathrow for birds, with the mixture of sea, shore, brackish marsh, open freshwater and wetlands combining to offer something for everyone. Herons and larks, owls and petrels abound. You'll want a good bird book and your binoculars. You'll find other wildlife at the ocean, too: Harbor seals have become quite common, and if you take one of the many boat trips out into the Gulf of Maine, your chances of spotting dolphins and several types of whales are excellent. Other fun living things to watch for are the sea creatures in the tidal pools and flats. Crabs you'll recognize, but will you know the mussels, clams, sea urchins and sea stars that join periwinkles and barnacles at the water's edge? If this fascinates you, a trip to the Seacoast Science Center will help you sort them out (see in our Attractions chapter).

Along with bluebirds, loons, bald eagles and peregrine falcons have all been making tentative comebacks from the brink of extinction here. Eagles and falcons are still very rare, however. That enormous wingspan overhead probably belongs to a turkey vulture or black vulture or one of our many hawks.

You can see some of those rarer birds up close at the Science Center in Holderness, along with many other wild citizens who've been taken in for care. It's a chance for a good look at the animals in their natural habitat, without danger to them — or to you! (See our Attractions chapter.)

Loons are another concern for environmentalists and tourists. Since the first loon census was conducted in 1976, the population of these fascinating birds has doubled, to just more than 500 breeding pairs. Still the birds are not out of danger. Because they build their nests on floating mats of vegetation, they are at great risk from boats and personal watercraft. As you observe loons diving and cruising, please also observe the restrictions posted around loon nesting areas. Help us keep the haunting call of the loon from becoming a haunting memory.

In contrast to the loons, the great blue heron has thrived in the wake of human development. Beaver ponds abound as the farmers who used to fight the dams have sold to home builders likely to leave the damp areas wild, and road crossings of wetlands sometimes create new ponds where beavers never bothered. The dead trees in the middle of such ponds are prime heron nesting areas, with a feast of frogs and salamanders right on hand for feeding the ravenous hatchlings. If the kids yell "Look, a stork!," it's probably a great blue, standing on one leg atop a ragged stub of an old pine. In a minute sharp young eyes will probably find the huge stick-and-straw nest high in a nearby tree.

INSIDERS' TIP

Use of sweet-smelling shampoos, soaps and perfumes makes you more attractive to insects as well as to members of the opposite sex!

Insects

One reason we have so many birds here is because we have so many insects! Beginning with the infamous black flies of late spring, outdoor activities in New Hampshire are frequently built around the bugs. Transplants from the South often compare those black flies to gnats for the annoying way they swarm around your head. Unfortunately they also pack a nasty bite, to which many people react with painful swelling. Outdoor supply stores offer a wide variety of bug repellents, some of which will repel your human companions as well!

Some gardeners and fishermen venture forth dressed in "bug suits" designed by a New Hampshire local. The suits cover you head to waist or ankle in heavy-duty netting, with elastic at wrist and ankle and no opening around the head at all. Others simply wait a while — the black-fly season is only about three weeks long. It follows the snowmelt, as the flies hatch in the quick-running streams. The black-fly season is generally late April in the south of the state and mid-June in the far north.

Once the black flies are gone, the mosquitos of summer put in their appearance. Mosquitos are a dusk and dawn menace, but during most of the day they are only a problem in thickly shaded areas. Other biting insects to be aware of are deer flies and horse flies around fresh water and greenhead flies at the seashore. We do have hornets, wasps and bees, but except for thieving yellow jackets at picnics, you aren't likely to be troubled by them. You're not likely to encounter any poisonous spiders either.

In recent years New Hampshire has joined the rest of the country as tick territory. Dog ticks are plentiful and are not restricted to dogs — they're just as happy to latch on to you or your kids. Less than a quarter-inch across and flat as paper, they can swell to resemble a soaked raisin after several days of ingesting blood. Check for them at the end of a day outdoors, especially in the folds of skin and in the hair.

On pets or on kids, ticks are disgusting but not particularly dangerous. Legends and tips for removing them abound, but it's really not as complex as some people make it. Trouble is, when you pull them out they may leave their heads behind (more often a tiny chunk of skin comes off with the tick.) Coating the tick with petroleum jelly or touching it with a hot match-head are both designed to get the tick to back out on its own. Traditionally people drop ticks into a can of gasoline to kill them, but a jar of liquid dish detergent will do the trick just as well and is much less dangerous.

More troubling than dog ticks are their tinier relatives, the deer tick. These ticks are too small to see — as small as the period at the end of this sentence. Their bite isn't painful, but they carry the hard-to-diagnose Lyme disease. The first symptom, a "bulls-eye" rash at the site of the bite, often goes unnoticed. Weeks later flu-like symptoms progress to aching joints and fatigue. Fortunately, a blood test for Lyme disease has been developed, and early treatment with antibiotics is effective. Prevention is better, though. Anyone heading into the woods in the summer should carefully check socks and body for tiny ticks upon returning. Experts recommend that people who work in the woods wear long pants tucked into boots to keep the ticks off, but unfortunately most of us prefer shorts in the hot sticky weather. Good news on the

INSIDERS' TIP

Mount Washington's claim to the world's worst weather was briefly threatened in December of 1997 by reports of typhoon winds reaching 236 mph on Guam. The National Weather Service's National Climate Extremes Committee investigated the claim and concluded that the wind damage to the anemometer on the island probably caused an "unrealistically high reading." So New Hampshire's 231 mph wind (in April, 1934) retains the record for another year!

Lyme disease front is the development of a vaccine, newly available in 1998. Ask your health-care provider if you should be vaccinated.

Plants and Flowers

In addition to preventing tick-bites, long pants are the best protection against poison ivy, which some people have suggested should be recognized as our state plant. Commonly described in the rhyme "Leaves of three, let them be," poison ivy comes in both a low-growing variety and a vine that climbs trees and fence posts. The leaves are shiny and green, only turning red in the fall. One way to recognize it is that its leaves are not symmetrical: If you were to fold one in half, the edges wouldn't match. But don't try it! Almost everyone is allergic to poison ivy, and the itching, blistering rash that appears several hours to several days after contact can spoil anyone's vacation. Topical ointments and oral antihistamines will help control the itching if you have a run-in with poison ivy or its less-common cousins, poison sumac and poison oak.

You're equally likely to have a pleasant encounter with wild plants in New Hampshire. Native plants and transplants run wild in our woods, fields and wetlands, with color from early spring to the first snow. Early European settlers brought so many plants with them that nearly 30 percent of our wild plants are introduced species. Our state flower, the lilac, came from England with the earliest settlers. Now it's often found in the woods, where a depression in the ground from an old cellar hole may be the only other sign of an old farm.

Rhododendrons and azaleas are common in yards and gardens (and of course, in Rhododendron State Park), while their wild cousin, the mountain laurel, turns hillsides and forests white months after the snow has melted. Vetches and mayflowers, violets and mallows are plants whose native and foreign varieties live happily together in our soils. Floribunda roses and purple loosestrife, on the other hand, are transplants that have gone too far and are crowding out native plants. Today we are much more careful about not introducing foreign species, although few would want to give up the rich variety we now enjoy.

If you're very lucky, you may come upon our native orchid, the lady slipper, in the woods in late spring. These delicate flowers, a single blossom atop a slender stem, are protected by law — take a photo, but don't pick any!

Even the non-flowering plants in New Hampshire are beautiful. The varied terrain provides us with many different habitats: Hardwood forests yield to grassy intervales, boggy marshlands turn to meadows. Of particular interest are the rare ecological communities we prize. We have the most diverse alpine areas east of the Rocky Mountains. Coastal plain pond shores and basin marshes, which locals call kettle holes for their steep sides, are rare and threatened not only in the United States but also in the world. Bogs and fens, seeps and swamps are all types of wetlands that scientists and environmentalists are struggling to preserve in New Hampshire.

You don't have to be a scientist to appreciate New Hampshire's great outdoors. Even if you don't know a marsh from a pine barren, you'll find vistas you'll want to preserve. Towering pines and shining maples cover our hillsides and turn every interstate into an art gallery. Snow-covered or bare, granite peaks gleam against the sky. Bring your camera and lots of film. From the seacoast to the mountains, we live in a place of spectacular beauty.

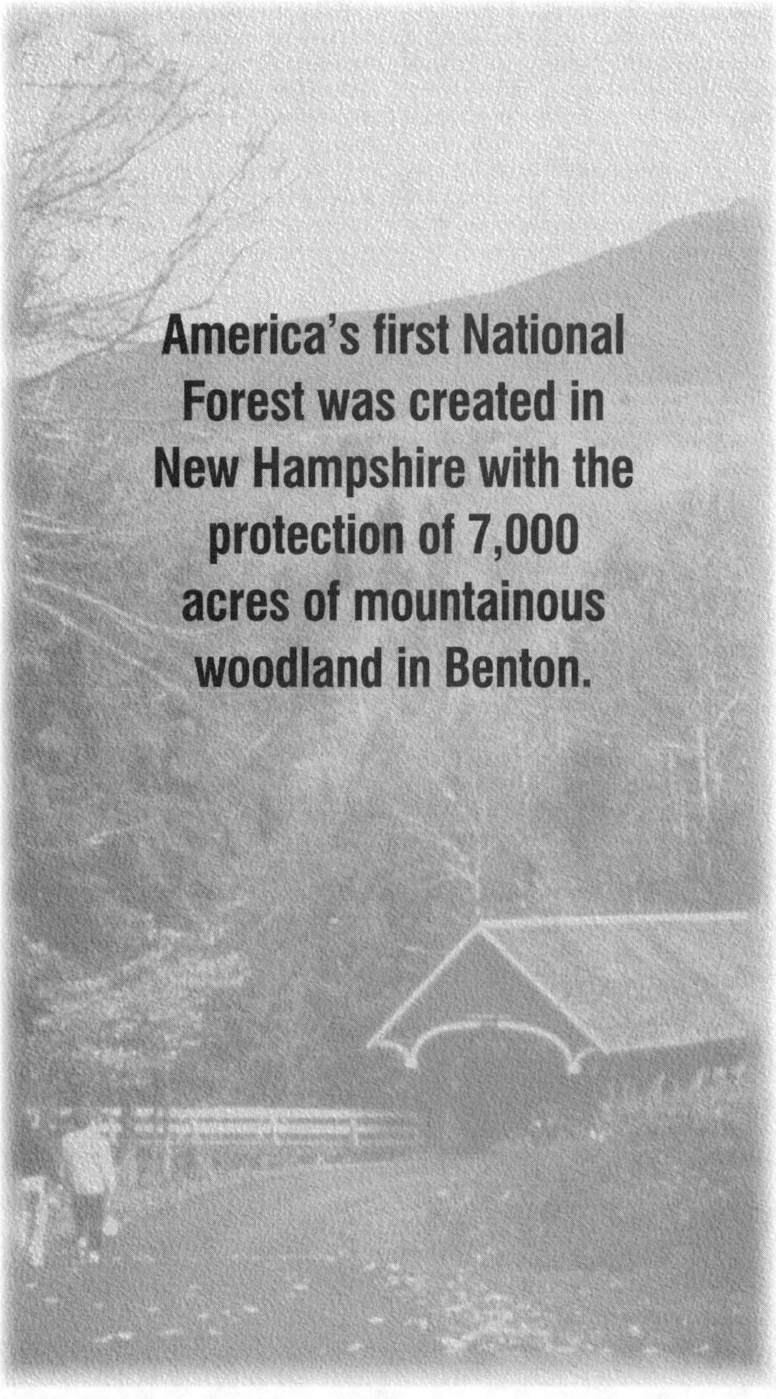

America's first National Forest was created in New Hampshire with the protection of 7,000 acres of mountainous woodland in Benton.

Parks and Open Spaces: Beyond the Village

The Abenaki phrase is Awasiwi Odanack: Beyond the Village. Here in New Hampshire, the natural world around us begs us to leave the creations of humanity behind and spend sometime exploring creation itself. New Hampshire has been twice-blessed, first with a diverse and beautiful landscape and also by the work of several generations of conservationists who have preserved open spaces through private endowment and public protection.

In 1911, in response to a public outcry over the untrammeled destruction of the forest by unwise timber practices, and resultant fires, The United States Congress passed The Weeks Act, establishing the National Forest system. John Wingate Weeks, who introduced the act and was instrumental in its passage, was a Lancaster, New Hampshire, native, Massachusetts congressman and subsequent Secretary of War under Presidents Harding and Coolidge. America's first National Forest was created in New Hampshire with the protection of 7,000 acres of mountainous woodland in Benton. Today that first parcel is a fraction of the nearly 800,000 acres of the White Mountain National Forest. More than half of that acreage is closed to logging, and more than 112,000 acres carry the added protection of being designated wilderness. Wilderness areas are closed not only to logging and mining, but also to the use of any mechanized or motorized equipment. Even trail maintenance is done with hand tools in wilderness areas, and supplies are carried in by backpackers.

Today our open spaces are protected by a combination of private and public efforts. Organizations working to preserve our natural world include national groups like the Audubon Society (ASNH), the National Forest Service (NFS) and the Appalachian Trail Conference (ATC). Statewide we have the Society for the Protection of New Hampshire Forests (SPNHF, sometimes pronounced "spinneff" by Insiders), the New Hampshire Timberland Owners Association (NHTOA) and the Lakes Region Conservation Trust (LRCT), just to name a few. The work is also carried on by New Hampshire chapters of the National Wildlife Federation (NHWF) and Nature Conservancy (NHNC) and our own state Divisions of Forests and Lands (F&L), Parks and Recreation (P&R) and Fish and Game (F&G). You'll find these abbreviations in many of our headers, when the phone number we've given you is not at the location but at the office of the managing organization. Many of these open spaces are not staffed. Trail maps are usually posted or are available in a mailbox at the trailhead/parking area. Returning the map to the box when you leave saves on the cost of printing.

Many of our towns have parks, town forests and other conservation lands preserved by the generosity of individuals and taxpayers. Some of these local open spaces are great stretches of undeveloped forest. Others have nature trails and even educational centers. A few are city parks with playgrounds and ballfields. Most fun to discover are the little green jewels, tucked in between buildings or just steps away from a busy street. Check at your town hall for descriptions and maps of lands managed by the local parks department or conservation commission.

Many of these wonderful open spaces are open to the public at no charge. (A donation sent to the managing organization is a nice way to say thanks!) Day-use state parks charge minimal fees; $2.50 for adults is average. In 1997 the Federal Government established a user fee for the White Mountain National Forest: $5 per day per vehicle parked in designated parking areas or $20 for a season pass. For the most part, maintenance of these open spaces is carried on by small staffs and legions of volunteers. Continued enjoyment depends on the common sense and courtesy of all visitors.

More and more parks are eliminating trash barrels, which attract wasps, skunks and bears. Except in urban areas, you should expect to operate on a carry-in, carry-out basis, which means exactly what it says: Everything you bring in, you bring out again. Many of us learned growing up that it was OK to toss an apple core or other leftover food into the woods, since it would either decay or be eaten by animals. Today, unless you're really in the deep woods, conservationists would rather you didn't leave food out for wild creatures to find. It can create an unhealthy dependence for the animals and contribute to the increasing number of wildlife/human confrontations.

We'd like to recommend The Federation Pledge (from the New Hampshire Wildlife Federation) for all who venture Beyond the Village:

I pledge myself, as a responsible human, to assume my share of the stewardship of our natural resources.

I will use my share with gratitude, without greed or waste.

I will respect the rights of others and abide by the law.

I will support the sound management of the resources we use, the restoration of the resources we have despoiled and the safekeeping of significant resources for posterity.

I will never forget that life and beauty, wealth and progress, depend on how wisely we use these gifts . . . the soil, the water, the air, the minerals, the plant life and the wildlife.

Or, in the words of an old hiker's saying that's easy to remember and obvious even to children: Take nothing but photographs, leave nothing but footprints.

We can barely scratch the surface of our open spaces in one chapter. We've tried to give you a wide selection, from the landscaped to the wild, from the challenging to the easily accessible. In the interest of saving space, we haven't repeated most of the state parks that are in other chapters. Those that are primarily for camping are in our Camping chapter; those that are mainly swimming beaches are in our In, On and Around the Water chapter. Other wonderful outdoors experiences are described in our Attractions chapter. You'll find a selection of hiking trails in our Other Recreation chapter and wildlife management areas in our Fishing and Hunting chapter. Finally, in our Close-up in this chapter, we've suggested other great books you can use to supplement this list.

Think we couldn't possibly have anything left for this chapter? Read on! And then, go play outside.

Merrimack Valley Region

Ponemah Bog Preserve
Rhodora Dr., Amherst
• (603) 224-9909 (ASNH)

Ponemah Bog is a "quaking bog," with a 3-acre pond at its center and a floating mat of sphagnum moss that covers the rest of what was once a 100-acre lake. (Naturalists estimate that the pond may be completely covered by 2065.) Out of the moss grow an assortment of amazing and bizarre plants, including the carnivorous pitcher plant, sundew and bladderwort. At the same time, small shrubs and trees have taken root in the mat, which enables the visitor the remarkable experience of "bouncing" on the mat and watching the trees bob and sway. A boardwalk has been constructed to protect both bog and walker. Please bounce only where indicated on the map (available at the trailhead).

Bear Brook State Park
157 Deerfield Rd., Allenstown
• (603) 485-9874

Bear Brook State Park encompasses 10,000 acres of land, seven ponds, a large marsh, bogs, summits and open ridges. Many of the trails were built in the 1930s by the Civilian Conservation Corps, as were the two summer camps at the eastern end of the park. (One is still used by New Hampshire 4-H; see the Camps section of our Kidstuff chapter.) Most of Bear Brook's 40 miles of trails are open for mountain bikers and equestrians as well as hikers. Trail maps are available at the park or from New Hampshire Division of Parks and Recreation, (603) 271-3254. In addition, the park boasts a wonderful bathing beach, picnic areas, and museums dedicated to Family Camping, the Civilian Conservation Corps and Snowmobiling. Bear Brook's campground is described in our Camping chapter.

Merrimack River Outdoor Education Area and Conservation Center

54 Portsmouth St., Concord
• (603) 224-9945

This 75-acre site houses the headquarters of the Society for Protection of New Hampshire Forests in a solar-heated facility that's worth stopping for by itself (it includes a snack bar and a small gift shop). Pick up a guidebook at the office and follow the steep wooden stairs down the ravine to the floodplain along the Penacook River for a self-guided tour through tree farms and amid the marshes and channels of the floodplain. You'll have a chance to see a variety of wildlife, from woodpeckers to muskrat, as you move from upland wooded habitat to open plains and wetlands.

Silk Farm Wild Life Sanctuary and Audubon Center

3 Silk Farm Rd., Concord
• (603) 224-9909

The Audubon Center includes a wonderful gift shop and educational displays and can provide you with information about all 30 Audubon sanctuaries in New Hampshire as well as maps for the trails out back. Upstairs they've built a wonderful observation room (they call it the aerie) that lets you feel like a bird yourself. But don't end your visit at the house! The longest of three trails around the site leads through various habitats and eventually down to Great Turkey Pond (which does look remarkably like a turkey from above). A boardwalk observation platform allows a wide view of the pond and surrounding marsh. Or, if you have little ones or little time, just amble through the woods on the short nature walk and stop to visit the two resident owls.

Beaver Brook Association

117 Ridge Rd., Hollis
• (603) 465-7787

Talk about vision! Beaver Brook's 1,730-acre reservation includes a demonstration farm, award-winning tree farm, self-guided trails and an education center that offers everything from art exhibits to camp weeks. All of this is due to the foresight and generosity of a few activists and two major land donors: Hollis Nichols, who with his naturalist friend Jeff Smith started the ball rolling in the 1960s, and Harlan Burns, who added his Milford farm to the reservation in 1997. Stop at the office at Maple Hill Farm for information and maps of the more than 30 miles of trails through woods, fields and wetlands.

Elm Brook Park

N.H. Rt. 127, Hopkinton
• (603) 746-4775

Elm Brook Park is an 8,000-acre parcel that's part of an Army Corps of Engineers flood-control project. The artificial lake, created by the Hopkinton Dam, includes a lovely swimming area with a broad sandy beach. Wooded nature trails looping through the park are well-groomed and easily traversed. A side trail leads to a cleared area where an old cem-

INSIDERS' TIP

A vernal pool is a shallow seasonal pond. They form in spring, a natural side-bar to the mud season, and play host to thousands of honeymooning frogs and salamanders. By July, the pool is dried and gone, and the next generation of amphibians has moved into the surrounding woods. Like salmon, these animals return every year to spawn in the same pool where they hatched. Sadly, every year more and more find their old hatching grounds vanished, bulldozed or filled by humans who don't recognize the value of that "big mud puddle."

etery used to be — it was moved because when the reservoir is full, this field is under water. The combination of wooded, open and wetland habitats makes this a wonderful bird-watching spot.

Derryfield Park
Livingston Park

Bridge St. (Derryfield); Hooksett Rd. (Livingston), Manchester • (603) 624-6565

The state's largest city has more than 50 parks facilities within the city limits. These two, on the city's East Side, cover more than 200 acres (250 including the city-owned McIntyre Ski Area, (603) 624-6571, which abuts Derryfield). Both parks have tennis and basketball courts, ball fields and playgrounds. Livingston surrounds Crystal Lake, which allows for swimming or ice skating, depending on the season.

Piscataquog River Park

Electric St. or Precourt St., Manchester • (603) 624-6565

Straddling the river in the Pinardville section of Manchester, the Piscataquog River Park is 120 acres of open space, ball fields and river frontage in the heart of a densely populated urban area.

Rock Rimmon Park

Youville St., Manchester • (603) 624-6565

A favorite with West Side Insiders, Rock Rimmon is the biggest park in Manchester at almost 140 acres. The "Rock" is a sizable hill, with a terrific view of the city from the top of the ledge, which is easily reached by a gentle climb up the back. Bring a picnic, but keep an eye on intrepid little ones!

Greeley Park

100 Concord St., Nashua • (603) 594-3346

This large urban park stretches on both sides of Concord Street and across to Manchester Street on Nashua's north end. Picnic tables and grills, basketball and tennis courts, playground equipment and lots of green grass make this a favorite spot for Nashuans to relax. The park also has an extensive amount of wooded area where you can walk on the spongy pine needles and feel like you're miles away from the city.

Mine Falls Park

Whipple St., Nashua • (603) 594-3411

In the very heart of this old city, 325 acres of land along the recently rescued Nashua River invite hikers, joggers and families to enjoy the natural world. Several walking trails loop through the park between the river and an old canal, which used to power Nashua's mills. You'll find a surprising array of wildlife, especially birds, and an old mill pond, gatehouse and dam. (There are unprotected edges near the dam — keep an eye, and a hand, on any small children.)

Northwood Meadows Natural Area and Pioneer State Park

U.S. Rt. 4, Northwood • (603) 271-3254

This nearly 700-acre parcel was rescued from the bulldozer just six years ago. Now, with the efforts of 350 volunteers and thousands of hours of labor, it's a park with a 1.5-mile loop trail that is completely wheelchair accessible (this also means it's easy to push a stroller). Part wooded, part open, part shoreline, the park attracts many birds and is home to deer and beaver and at least one moose. Fishing, canoeing and picnicking are all possible now, and there are plans for an educational center in the future.

Pawtuckaway State Park

128 Mountain Rd., Nottingham (or N.H. Rt. 156, Raymond) • (603) 895-3031

The campground here is one of the state's most popular, but there is plenty in this 5,500-

INSIDERS' TIP

The early part of the hunting season coincides exactly with our best hiking weather and foliage season. Don't venture into the woods in fall without bright colored hats and clothing (no white!).

acre park to attract day-visitors too. Most well-known is the boulder field, the largest collection of glacial erratics in the world. We're talking about boulders the size of houses, left behind by the glacier like a child's building blocks. Fishing, hiking, birdwatching and mountain-biking are other attractions of this 5,500 acre park (most of which is actually in Raymond, although the street address is Nottingham). The trails wander through wooded upland and marshy habitats, climb the park's three small mountains (one has a fire tower with great views) and explore the edges of Pawtuckaway Lake and Round Pond.

Seacoast Region

College Woods

N.H. Rt. 155A, Durham
• (603) 862-3951

This land, which is owned and managed by the University of New Hampshire, is criss-crossed with paths, some of which run down to the Durham Reservoir. It is a wonderful place to go for a pleasant walk, and bird-watchers love it, particularly at migratory seasons. You may see Swanson's thrush or a dickcissel along with killdeer, great horned owls and flickers.

Great Bay National Estuarine Research Reserve and the Great Bay National Wildlife Refuge

Adams Point, Durham Point Rd., Durham
• (603) 868-1095
Sandy Point Discovery Center, Tidewater Farm Rd., Greenland

This huge (more than 5,000 acres) preserve is a treasure. In winter it's home to bald eagles, pileated woodpeckers, mergansers and many other more common birds. It hosts a year-round population of the non-native, beautiful mute swan. Several threatened plant species, including lady-slipper, are hanging on to existence here. Adams Point offers several places to park, walk and bird-watch as well as launch a boat. At the end of the point is U.N.H.'s Jackson Estuarine Lab, where you can park and wander through fields or observe the bay from the dock. Sandy Point Discovery Center includes a self-guided nature trail and educational exhibits (including a very popular touch tank). The trails and boardwalk here are handicapped-accessible.

Webster Wildlife and Natural Area

off N.H. Rt. 125, Kingston
• (603) 224-9945 (SPNHF)

This 89-acre property in Kingston encompasses a rare Atlantic white cedar swamp, a pond and a bog. A woods road through the property makes for an easy hike into the center of this pristine habitat. (As with all Forest Society properties, motorized vehicles are not permitted and neither is camping.) You'll probably see a variety of water birds, possibly even osprey or bald eagles, during migration.

Fuller Gardens

10 Willow Ave., North Hampton
• (603) 964-5414

This beautiful estate, just across Ocean Boulevard from the beach, was the summer home of an early 20th-century governor of Massachusetts, Alvan T. Fuller. His name for the estate, Runnymede-By-The-Sea, gives a hint at his desire to create an English-style manor home for himself. The house is gone, but the formal gardens remain, offering visitors the opportunity to cross the footbridge in a Japanese garden, explore a conservatory housing tropical and desert plants, and soak in the sight and fragrance of more than 1,500 rose bushes. Statues and fountains accent the flowering display. The gardens are open 10 AM to 6 PM every day from early May through mid-October. The roses are at their best in June and July, but displays of perennials, flowering shrubs, hosta and other flowers make this a lovely spot all season. Admission to the gardens is $4.50; $4 for seniors. Admission isn't charged for kids under 12.

Urban Forestry Center

45 Elwyn Rd., Portsmouth
• (603) 431-6774

This 180-acre park in the middle of a residential neighborhood is managed by the state Division of Forests and Lands with support

Books for the Great Outdoors

The popularity of New Hampshire among wildlife enthusiasts has led to publication of scores, maybe hundreds, of wonderful books, some dating back to the mid-19th century. Here are a few of our favorites:

Close-up

Natural Wonders of New Hampshire, by Suki Casanave. This delightful book gives detailed descriptions of more than 100 places across New Hampshire, with directions and information about some of the flora and fauna you'll find at each spot. Her selection ranges from the formal gardens around some of our historic houses to the wildest forest around the headwaters of the Connecticut Lakes.

New Hampshire Off the Beaten Path, by Barbara Radcliff Rogers and Stillman Rogers. Although it's not an outdoor guide per se, the authors include many natural treasures along with the shops, historic sites and other curiosities they describe. You'll find descriptions of forests and waterfalls, gardens and scenic views, almost all of them accessible by car.

Country Roads of New Hampshire, by Steve Sherman. This is another great book for people who want to see a lot without walking a lot. It's set up as a series of drives, each one meandering through the less-traveled parts of the countryside. If you love the surprise view or quiet pastoral scene but aren't really comfortable exploring roads that aren't on the map, this book can be your passport.

Photo: Tom Wilkins

Conservation lands welcome visitors to the great outdoors.

A Birder's Guide to New Hampshire, by Alan Delorey. New Hampshire is a bird-watcher's dream, with lakes and seashore, mountains and forests and everything in between. But even if you're not carrying your life-list, this book is fun because it describes many little-known spots where, even if you don't notice unusual birds, you'll enjoy the unspoiled natural scene. (Delorey lists birds you might expect to find in each place, but doesn't describe them. In other words, you'll still need your field guide.)

Best Hikes with Children in Vermont, New Hampshire and Maine, by Cynthia and Thomas Lewis. This is a wonderful book because it takes a kids' eye (and leg) view of each hike. (And sometimes grown-ups like to know if this is going to be an easy hike too.) Our one argument with this book is that most of the New Hampshire hikes are way up north, which means, from the most populated parts of the state, a two to three hour drive.

Fifty Hikes in New Hampshire, by Daniel Doan and Ruth Doan MacDougall. This book, originally written in the early '70s, is practically the granddaddy of the hiking guide family. The descriptions and suggestions are still accurate and encouraging, which is why the new edition was released this year.

Hiking New Hampshire, by Larry Pletcher. This book has detailed descriptions of 80

— continued on next page

hikes around the state, delivered in a conversational tone that makes you feel like you're out with a very patient and personable guide. The book is salted with tips on hiking technique, which would make it worth reading even if you were going hiking somewhere else.

The Appalachian Mountain Club publishes guidebooks of every possible description. Two of our favorites are *Nature Walks in Southern New Hampshire* and *Nature Walks in the New Hampshire Lakes Region,* by Julia Older and Steve Sherman. The focus here is on nature walks (as opposed to hikes — most of the 44 Southern and 50 Lakes excursions described here are quite easy). Our copy of the southern book is tattered from being stuffed in the backpack and glove compartment. If you are interested in more challenging treks, check out the AMC White Mountain Guide instead, for dozens of mountain-climbing possibilities. Detailed descriptions, accurate maps and interesting side comments are the trademarks of the AMC guides. For a complete list, call (800) 262-4455.

from the New Hampshire Timberland Owners. The site includes a series of self-guided trails through fields and woods and along a saltwater marsh on Sagamore Creek. A forest management area demonstrates the value of timber management, and an educational center on site offers special programs and information. A unique feature of the Urban Forestry Center is the Garden For All The Senses, designed to be not only seen but also touched and, in season, smelled, heard and tasted. The arboretum here is a great introduction to New Hampshire's plant life.

Odiorne Point State Park and Seacoast Science Center

570 Ocean Blvd., Rye
• (603) 436-8043

Visitors to Odiorne Point have the opportunity to explore seven different habitats within this 330-acre park. From the ocean and shoreline through the tidal area and up to the meadow and woodland, children and adults alike enjoy the scents and sounds of nature. Insider kids are introduced to Odiorne's tidepools in school environmental programs, so those shallow "puddles" teeming with life are always popular spots. Rabbits hop amid the wildflowers, and birds circle overhead as you picnic, walk or simply sit and listen to the waves. The park also includes the remains of several pieces of American history, from the fishing encampments of the Penacook and Abenaki to the earliest explorations by Giovanni da Verrazano in 1524 to the camouflaged fortifications built here during WWII.

The Seacoast Science Center, an Audubon educational center on the grounds of the park, offers a chance to get indoors and some wonderful hands-on introductions to the sea as well as splendid views of the water. (See our Attractions chapter.)

Star Island

Isles of Shoals, Rye
• (603) 964-7252

The Isles of Shoals are a string of small islands — some of them no more than large boulders, really, 10 miles off Portsmouth Harbor in the Atlantic Ocean. Most of them belong to Maine, and the best-known, Appledore, is home to a marine lab operated by Cornell University. Star Island, at 48 acres, is the largest of the chain in New Hampshire waters. If you take the morning cruise with the Isles of Shoals Steamship Company (see our Attractions chapter), you can disembark at Star Island for a three-hour stopover and return home on the later tour (you must make arrangements to do this in advance). There are no amenities on Star Island except restrooms, but the ocean breezes, wild birds and remote atmosphere make this a favorite with Insider naturalists.

Lakes Region

Knights Pond Conservation Area

Rines Rd., Alton

The Knights Pond area is a wonderful example of private land protection. The Lakes

Region Land Trust owns only a small portion of this 307-acre wildlife refuge. The rest remains in private ownership, protected from development by permanent easements. Snapping turtles and largemouth bass share the pond, and seven native orchids (including the endangered small whorled pogonia) live within the protected land. Loons and eagles frequent the pond, which was created and is maintained by a crew of resident beavers. A 2-mile loop trail around the pond invites visitors to explore the woods and leads to the beaver dam. A trail map, available from LRCT or at local shops and tourist information centers, details restrictions on use of the property, which include no campfires, no motorized vehicles and no use between 10 PM and 4 AM.

Franklin Falls Dam Project

46 Granite Dr., Franklin
• (603) 934-2116
Smith River Rd., Bristol

The Franklin Falls Dam is open most of the time but can be closed by the Army Corps of Engineers when there is a danger of flooding downstream. The 3,900 acres of river valley remain open, available to hold floodwater for controlled release, but it's generally just a long, pleasant parkland along both sides of the Pemigewasset River. Old farm fields, some grown up with wild flowers, some still hayed, occupy about 500 acres, while the rest is a hardwood forest. Horseback and mountain-bike riders and hikers enjoy the views, while others picnic, cast a line or just relax at spectacular Profile Falls (on the Bristol end of the park).

Paradise Point Nature Center Hebron Marsh

N., Shore Rd., Hebron • (603) 744-3516

These two Audubon Society properties on Newfound Lake provide a chance to explore some very unusual habitats, including an old-growth forest area that is very rare in New Hampshire (most of New Hampshire was completely logged in the 18th and 19th centuries). The chance to explore both a marsh (sunlit) and a swamp (wooded) in the same day helps clarify the differences between these two types of wetlands. Watch for loons on the lake. Trails on the Paradise Point site vary in difficulty and in the habitats they explore. The Nature Center is small but interesting, and the gift shop offers a variety of nice gift items. At Hebron Marsh you'll climb to a treehouse observation deck for a wonderful view of the marsh and its inhabitants. The Nature Center is open daily from 10 AM to 5 PM in summer and 10 AM to 4 PM weekends from Memorial Day to mid-June and Labor Day to October 1. The grounds are always open.

Sculptured Rocks Natural Area

off N. Groton Rd., Groton
• (603) 271-3254 (P&R)

This is an amazing spot, very out of the way but well worth the drive. Ice-age potholes, worn and sculpted by the effects of roiling water and whirling stone, make a stunning centerpiece for this pleasant, shady spot. A bridge spans the river and a woods road allows for walking, but most people never get past the water. Take your shoes off and wade, at least, or jump in if you're brave and hardy. There are no services here at all so make a

INSIDERS' TIP

Deer ticks are a problem in most of New Hampshire's woods and fields. These tiny ticks, about the size of the period at the end of this sentence, are carriers of at least two debilitating diseases: Lyme Disease, which causes arthritis if left untreated, and Human babesiosis, which is generally just annoying but can be fatal. Good tick-protocol includes long pants tucked into socks and careful self-inspection at the end of your walk. The tick is generally on the body for several hours before biting, and it takes several more hours for the pathogens to be transferred. Lyme disease can be treated with antibiotics.

bathroom break before you leave civilization behind.

Science Center of New Hampshire at Squam Lakes

N.H. Rt. 113, Holderness • (603) 968-7194

The Science Center combines a user-friendly series of nature trails and demonstrations with some more challenging hiking opportunities and a year-round wildlife conservation program. The center is open to the public in summer. In winter it runs educational camps and workshop days when you can join one of the staff naturalists or experts from local colleges in bird-banding, snow studies and a variety of other outdoor winter explorations. Call for a list of upcoming events and see our Attractions chapter for more about the Science Center.

Loon Preservation Committee/ Markus Sanctuary

Lees Mills Rd., Moultonborough
• (603) 476-LOON

This labor of love has seen success in the return of the loons to Lake Winnipesaukee. In 1976, there were no nesting pairs on the big lake and only 271 pairs in the state. Over the last 20 years, the population has more than doubled. Loons nest at the very edge of the lake, with their nests floating among the grasses. Increasing use of the lakes, especially by motorized boats and Jet Skis, has caused escalating mortality rates among these treasured birds. The 200 acres of the Markus Sanctuary includes 5,000 feet of undeveloped shoreline, prime nesting sites for loons. The Loon Preservation Committee has constructed a cedar raft complete with dirt and vegetation and shielded with snowfence to further protect the birds. This imitation shore is less vulnerable to the impacts of wakes and drought than the real thing. Trails through the site include a view of the floating "Loon Hotel."

Cooper Cedar Woods Jennings Forest

N.H. Rt. 11 (Cooper); Middleton Rd. (Jennings), New Durham
• (603) 224-9945 (SPNHF)

These two very different properties offer an interesting contrast. The 30-acre Cedar Woods features an interpretive trail through a bog with a valuable stand of Atlantic white cedar and another of black spruce. Deer and other wildlife, including numerous waterfowl, call this wild wetland home. Just 2 miles away, the Jennings Forest is a 376-acre tree farm, long managed to produce forest products and provide wildlife habitat and watershed protection. Woods roads lead through the forest to a beaver meadow and a forested wetland along a brook, making for easy and interesting hiking. (Despite the width of the roads, recreational motorized traffic is not allowed on Forest Society lands.)

West Rattlesnake and Five-Finger Point

Pinehurst Rd., Sandwich
• (603) 968-7336
(Squam Lakes Association)
• (603) 968-7900
(Squam Lakes Conservation Society)

There are two routes up West Rattlesnake — the very easy Bridle Path Trail from N.H. Rt. 113 and the much-less-traveled, somewhat steeper Pasture Trail from Pinehurst Road. West Rattlesnake is beloved for the incredible views it offers after comparatively little climbing. Even small children can reach these ledges and enjoy a picnic "on top of the world." (But keep them away from the edge!) You may choose to continue along the Ridge Trail to East Rattlesnake, or take a detour from the Pasture Trail to explore Five-Finger Point, a small peninsula, shaped vaguely like a hand, which allows you to walk close to the water, wade along the secluded beaches and nibble on wild blueberries.

White Lake State Park and Pitch Pine National Landmark

N.H. Rt. 16, West Ossipee
• (603) 323-7350

White Lake State Park is known for the campground and bathing beach that attract locals and visitors alike. But there is also a little-used trail that circles the lake, inviting you to explore both a sandy shoreline and the wooded uplands of the stand of pitch pine, which has been declared a National Landmark because it is rare to find this habitat so far north. Under pitch pines' canopy, birches, scrub oak and wild blueberries flourish. (The Nature Conservancy has purchased 573 acres of pine barrens nearby, which will eventually include trails and educational signs for public use.)

White Mountains Region

Nansen Wayside Park

N.H. Rt. 16, Berlin
• (603) 271-3254 (P&R)

You'll know you're here when you see the 170-foot steel-framed Nansen Ski Jump. Visitors are banned from using the ski jump, but it makes a great backdrop for a photo. You can launch your boat into the nearby Androscoggin River. The 6-acre park is a great place to picnic. The evergreen trees and the sounds of the river make this roadside stop a gem. It's open all year, but it's not cleared of snow in winter so you'll need a snowmobile to get around!

Crawford Notch State Park

U.S. Rt. 302, Hart's Location
• (603) 374-2272

At this state park, you can hike along the 6 miles of trails that connect with the Appalachian Trail. The 5,950-acre park in the middle of the White Mountains National Forest includes a visitors center at the Willey House. It is named for a family killed as a result of a massive avalanche in 1826. Fish in the mountain streams, hike along the self-guided nature trail or just relax and enjoy the cascading waterfalls.

Dixville Notch State Park

N.H. Rt. 26, Dixville
• (603) 788-3155

Dixville Notch is the northernmost and the smallest of the state's notches. Enjoy waterfalls and a scenic gorge on the two mountain brooks within the 137 acres of park land. Hiking trails for Table Rock begin here. Called Table Rock because it's no wider than a table, this rock platform extends out from the north side of Mount Gloriette. It's 2,700 feet high, and on clear days successful hikers will get great views of the Balsams Wilderness Resort and Lake Gloriette. Two excellent roadside picnic sites make this a favorite place to stop the car and take a break.

Echo Lake State Park

River Rd., west of N.H. Rt. 16, Bartlett and Conway
• (603) 356-2672

As you drive the path to Cathedral Ledge, you'll see experienced climbers scaling the mountain to the same destination. The name of the ledge comes from early climbers who claimed to see the shape of a cathedral in the cliffs. Besides the fun of watching the climbers, you can swim in the lake and enjoy the convenience of both a beach and bathhouse. You'll get dramatic valley views of the Saco River. There's also an Echo Lake in Franconia State Park.

Eisenhower Memorial Wayside Park

U.S. Rt. 302, Carroll
• (603) 271-3254 (P&R)

You'll find this small park on the east side of U.S. Route 302 about 2 miles north of Crawford Notch State Park. You can take a short walk and get a grand view of the Presidential Range and Mount Washington. Bring binoculars for a close-up view of the tracks of the Cog Railway that climbs Mount Washington, and, if your timing is right, for a view of the train itself as it makes the difficult ascent.

Franconia Notch State Park

Interstate 93, Franconia • (603) 823-5563

You've got 6,440 acres to play in here. This is the home of the Old Man of the Mountain, Echo Lake, Profile Lake and Lonesome Lake. The Cannon Mountain Ski area is in the

INSIDERS' TIP

A neat forest isn't a healthy forest. Dead trees and downed brush provide important shelter and food for wildlife and return nutrients to the soil as they decay.

Flume Gorge in Franconia Norch has a walkway where you can hike along and enjoy the views.

park, as is the deep glacial pothole known as the Basin. The Appalachian Trail crosses the park just a mile north of the Flume. Eight miles of I-93 wind through the park. Passengers will wish for a swivel neck to catch the views as you turn right, left, up and down. Drivers need to keep their eyes on the road. Follow the signs to the visitors center near the base of the Flume. You can see a short film on the park and pick up information on all the park's attractions. The park is open year round.

Lake Umbagog National Wildlife Refuge

Errol • (603) 482-3415

Right now this refuge consists of 4,000 acres. Another 4,000 acres in the area is controlled by the New Hampshire Fish and Game Department. (The goal is to increase land-protection to 13,000 acres.) It is the richest wildlife habitat in the state, with the most diverse animal population. You'll see loons, bald eagles (we have one bald eagle family in the state and they nest here) and osprey. Birders come for the 25 species of warblers, and it is not unusual to see moose. Insiders and locals know the correct name is Umbagog Lake as opposed to Lake Umbagog. Unfortunately, the National Wildlife Service forgot to check before naming the area.

Milan Hill State Park

east of N.H. Rt. 16, Milan
• No phone

Milan Hill State Park is a great place to stop as you tour the upper reaches of New Hampshire. From the fire tower, you'll get a great view of northern New Hampshire, southern Canada and the White Mountains and the Presidentials. Walking trails are marked, and the picnic area includes a shelter. The 127 acres include cross-country ski trails.

Moose Brook State Park
U.S. Rt. 2, Gorham • (603) 466-3860

This park is about 2 miles west of Gorham, and many people use it as base camp while they hike the Presidential and Crescent ranges. Mountain bike and walking trails, picnic grounds and showers make this a favorite family spot. This is also a popular spot to cross-country ski and snowmobile.

Mount Washington State Park
Mount Washington Summit • (603) 466-3860

This 52-acre park at the top of Mount Washington is the end of the trail whether you hike, drive or ride the rails up 6,288-foot mountain. You can't spend the night, but daytime amenities include a post office, snack bar and gift shop. This state park is surrounded by the White Mountain National Forest. The state park is open from Memorial Day through Columbus Day. See our Attractions chapter for details on the Cog Railway and auto routes to the top and our Other Recreation chapter for basic hiking information.

White Mountain National Forest
Headquarters: 719 North Main St., Laconia • (603) 528-8721

The 773,386-acre forest is New Hampshire's biggest tourist attraction. (The actual New Hampshire acreage is 714,336. The total acreage includes a portion of the national forest that's in Maine.) It covers nearly 80 percent of the entire White Mountains region. More than 6 million people come here each year to enjoy the 45 lakes and ponds, 750 miles of fishing streams and more than 1,200 miles of hiking trails. Forty-nine towns are within the forest's boundaries.

Beginning in May 1997, the White Mountain National Forest began participating in an experimental parking-pass program scheduled to run through 1999. The program requires that all unattended cars parked in the White Mountain National Forest have a pass displayed on the dashboard. A seven-day pass is available for $5, and an annual pass is available for $20. To order your pass, send a check or money order payable to USDA-Forest Service and mail it to, White Mountain National Forest, 719 Main Street, Laconia, NH 03246. Mark your envelope "Attn: Fee Program" and include your name, address, telephone number and license plate numbers. The pass is good for up to two vehicles, so include both license-plate numbers if you plan on parking more than one car. You may also buy a pass at many locations within the region. To obtain a list of locations, call or write The White Mountain National Forest at the address and phone number in the header. The fees collected are to be used for managing and maintaining recreation opportunities within the White Mountain National Forest.

The land is administered by the United States Forest Service. Note that this land is a designated forest, not a park. This means that the land is managed for multiple uses, including timber, water, recreation and wildlife. Approximately 60,000 cords of wood are commercially harvested per year. Over half of the land is closed to timber harvesting, including the 114,932 acres set aside as a designated wilderness area. Wilderness areas do not allow roads, mechanized vehicles (including bicycles), power tools or permanent structures. The White Mountain National Forest is mostly known for its mountains, including the 48 mountains known as the 4,000 Footers. The crown jewel of the mountains is Mount Washington at 6,288 feet. Other presidentially-named mountains are Adams, Eisenhower, Garfield, Jefferson, Lincoln, Madison, Monroe and Pierce. An excellent guide to the mountains and their trails is the *Appalachian Mountain Club White Mountain Guide.* You can get this book in all New Hampshire bookstores (see our Shopping chapter) and most stores that sell hiking equipment (see our Other Recreation chapter).

Dartmouth-Lake Sunapee Region

Mount Cardigan State Park
follow signs from the intersection of U.S. Rt. 4 and N.H. Rt. 118 in Canaan • (603) 271-3254 (P&R)

This 5,000-acre state park includes most of Mount Cardigan, which has an elevation of 3,100 feet. A hike on Mount Cardigan is one of the best in the region (look for details in our Other Recreation chapter). Don't miss the delightful picnic area with beautiful pine trees and great rock formations. It's on the western slope of the mountain. The park is open from mid-May until mid-October.

Gardner Memorial Wayside Area
N.H. Rt. 4-A, Springfield
• (603) 271-3254 (P&R)

Meet a friend here for a private picnic alongside a classic babbling brook. You'll see the remnants of the 18th-century mill, and if the weather is warm, you might want to take a quick swim in the cool water.

Mount Sunapee State Park
N.H. Rt. 103, Newbury
• (603) 763-2356

This 2,893-acre park is at the northern end of Lake Sunapee. It's best known for downhill skiing in winter and fishing in summer. You can hike or ride the chairlift to the 2,743-foot summit for spectacular views of the surrounding mountains, lakes and valleys. Enjoy the beach at Lake Sunapee or take the 1-mile Solitude Trail to the White Ledges over Lake Solitude. Adventurous (and very fit) hikers can attempt the Monadnock-Sunapee Greenway trail connecting Mount Sunapee with Mount Monadnock. See our Other Recreation chapter for details on hiking this 49-mile trail.

Pillsbury State Park
N.H. Rt. 31, Washington
• (603) 863-2860

With more than 8,000 acres, this is a gem of a park with very few visitors. Insiders know that both Pillsbury and Wadleigh state parks in the Dartmouth-Sunapee region do not get the crowds you'll run into in the White Mountains region. We don't want to ruin a good thing by attracting too many visitors, but these parks are delightful wide-open spaces. You can rent canoes and explore May Pond with or without your fishing gear. Wildlife includes bear, moose, deer and otter. Birds you're likely to see include great blue herons, harriers and osprey.

Wadleigh State Park
N.H. Rt. 114, North Sutton
• (603) 927-4724

At this park you're less than five minutes from I-89, but you'd never know it as you enjoy the peace and quiet of Kezar Lake and the 43-acre park. Bring a picnic or pick up a sandwich at Vernondale Store, which is within easy walking distance of the park on N.H. Route 114. We've never seen a traffic jam or heard a horn in this oasis. If the doctor tells you to take a few days off the fast track, we recommend that you come here. Please don't bring your beeper or cellular phone.

Winslow State Park
Off N.H. Rt. 11, south of Wilmot or Exit 10 off I-89
• (603) 271-3254 (P&R)

You might be glad to know that you don't have to climb Mount Kearsarge on foot in order to get the view. Take the auto road part way up the northwest slope of Mount Kearsarge to an elevation of 1,820 feet. It ends at a delightful picnic area with views of both the Green Mountains in Vermont and the White Mountains in New Hampshire. For those who would like a little exercise after lunch, you can continue to the top of 2,937-foot Mount Kearsarge on the mile-long trail from the picnic area.

Monadnock Region

Rhododendron State Park
Just off N.H. Rt. 119, Fitzwilliam
• (603) 271-3254 (P&R)

You'll find this National Natural Landmark 2.5 miles west of downtown Fitzwilliam. Rhododendron State Park has more than 16 acres of wild rhododendron, *Rhododendron*

INSIDERS' TIP

There are 95 designated EPA Superfund sites in New Hampshire, a legacy of our industrial heritage and the presence of military bases here since Colonial times.

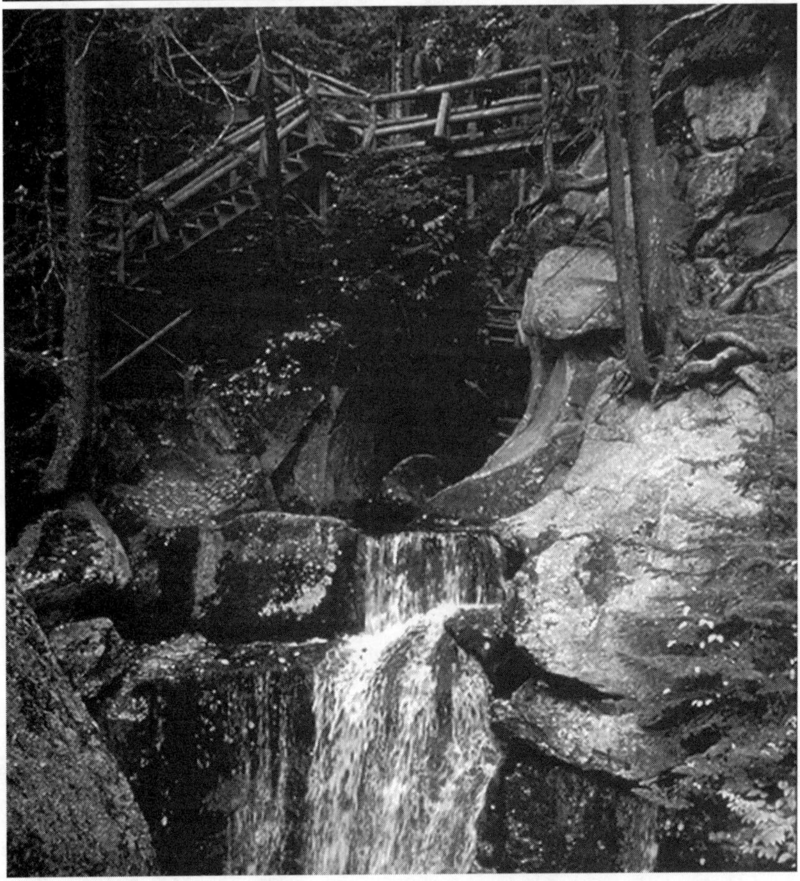

Photo: Dick Hamilton/White Mountain News Bureau

Hiking in the White Mountains will yield beautiful scenery, such as Paradise Falls at Lost River Gorge.

maximum. While most guidebooks suggest that the peak of bloom occurs in mid-July, Insiders know that even late-blooming rhododendron are at their peak here in late June. Visitors arriving in mid-July should expect fewer blossoms than those arriving two or three weeks earlier. In bloom or not, this wonderful natural area with trails, wildflowers and breathtaking views of Mount Monadnock is a treat. This park is a great spot for picnics.

Greenfield State Park
N.H. Rt. 136, Greenfield
• (603) 547-3497

This 401-acre state park is a favorite with campers (see our Camping chapter), but it's also a great spot for a daytrip. Rent a boat or enjoy the beach in summer. Cross-country ski or snowmobile in winter. Greenfield is a favorite of families living in the Monadnock region.

Harris Center for Conservation Education
341 King's Hwy. (N.H. Rt. 123), Hancock
• (603) 525-3394

The 2,000 acres of wildlife habitat at the Harris Center are primarily for conservation and environmental education programs. The center is open to the public, but if you are going to spend any time here, consider becoming a member. Membership is $30 a year and includes a newsletter and calendar of events. You can participate in the annual bird survey, usually held in June on Mount Monadnock. You can also learn about trail work in weekend workshops devoted to keeping the center's trails clear for hikers.

Monadnock State Park

N.H. Rt. 124, Jaffrey
• (603) 532-8862

Some Insiders might say that a visit to the Monadnock region is not complete without a climb up Mount Monadnock. It is the biggest draw in the region and the most-climbed mountain in the United States. (Numbers aren't available, but it is generally reported that Mount Monadnock has more people reach the summit than any mountain in the world except possibly Mount Fuji in Japan.) The park and visitors center are open all year. Pick up a guide to the more than 40 miles of trails within the park — most leading to the 3,165-foot summit. It is a favorite spot for winter camping and a popular fair-weather picnic destination. No pets are allowed in Monadnock State Park.

Miller State Park

N.H. Rt. 101, Peterborough
• (603) 924-3672

This park was established in 1891 and named for James Miller, a hero in the War of 1812. You can drive or hike to the 2,090-foot summit. The auto road up Pack Monadnock ("Pack" comes from the Indian word for little) leads up 2,090 feet to a outstanding view of the region. There are maps to help you know what you are looking at and nearby trails for hiking. In fall this is an excellent spot for watching migrating hawks. Admission to the park is $2.50 per person. Children younger than 12 are not charged.

Sheiling Forest

Old Street Rd., Peterborough
• No phone

Sheiling is Scottish for shelter. The 45 acres were shelter to Elizabeth Yates McGreal as her home before she donated the forest to the state in 1980. McGreal was a Peterborough resident and ardent conservationist. The 2 miles of easy self-guided trails wind through forested land with streams, wildflowers and huge, glacier-deposited boulders. (It is estimated that the boulders are about 18,000 years old.) Pick up a picnic in Peterborough and enjoy this low-key park along with the locals. It's a great place for little kids to hike. Pets on leashes are welcome.

Pisgah State Park

Old Chesterfield Rd., Winchester
• (603) 239-8153

New Hampshire's largest state park is 13,800 acres of mostly undeveloped land. It's in the southwest corner of the Monadnock region. The park overlaps the towns of Winchester, Hinsdale and Chesterfield. The brand-new visitors center (funded by donation and built by volunteers) opened in the fall of 1997. Information about the park is also available at each of the nine trailheads. These trailheads are clearly marked, and all have an information board and map box. The excellent maps show short, medium and long hikes. From the top of Mount Pisgah (1,300 feet) you'll get a great view of the Connecticut River to the west and Mount Monadnock to the east. The park does not allow camping, but you are welcome to bring your pets as long as they are on a leash.

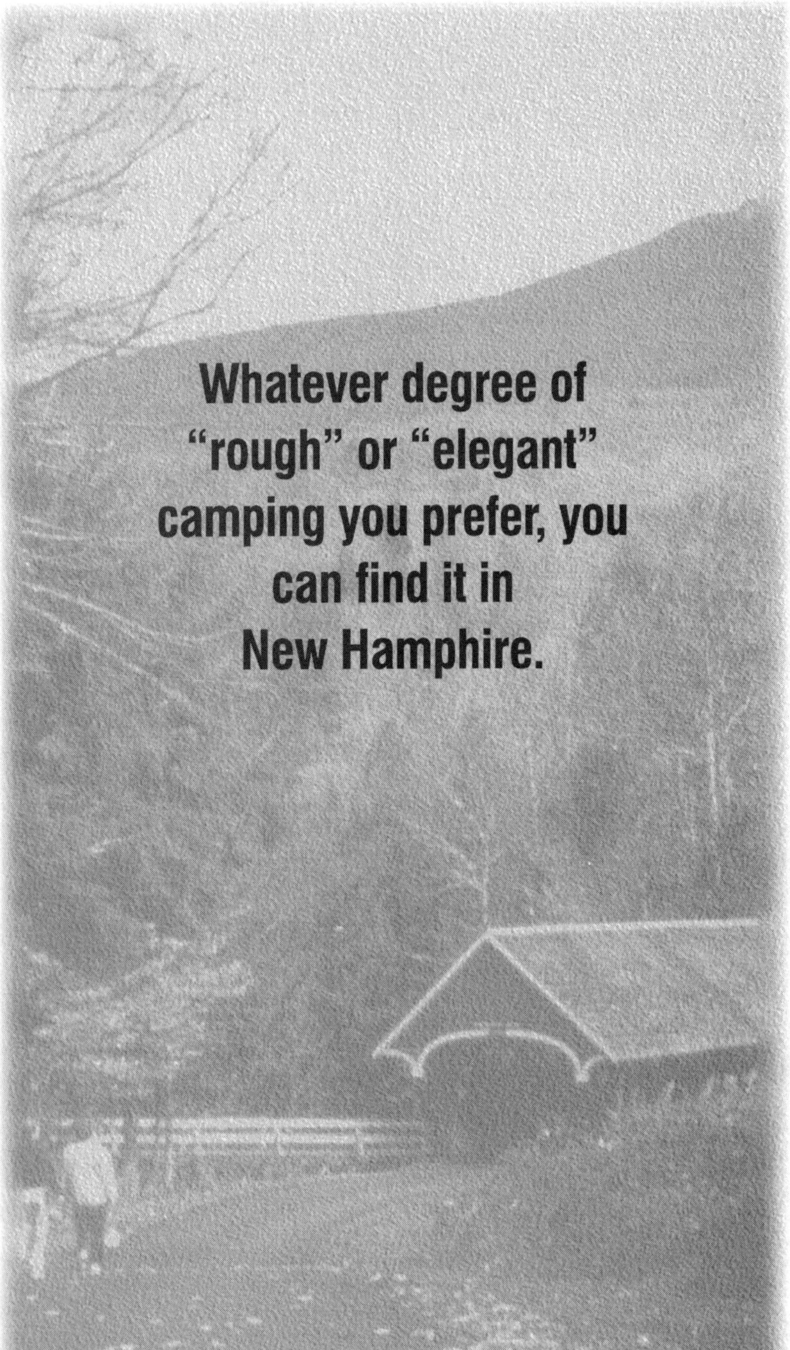

Whatever degree of "rough" or "elegant" camping you prefer, you can find it in New Hamphire.

Camping

Ah, camping! The crisp air, the crackle of the fire, the smell of canvas and citronella. New Hampshire's public and private campgrounds have been welcoming visitors since long before the golden age of motoring began. In all regions of the state, you can find campgrounds run by second and third generations of the same family and campsites reserved for certain summer weeks by second and third generations of other families.

Camping has changed enormously since we were kids. Gone are the heavy canvas tents that leaked if you touched them when they were wet. Gone, too, are the pit toilets, discreetly hidden downwind of the campsites and reached by a bumpy path with a dying flashlight in the middle of the night. Today even tent camping is comparatively luxurious — and with RVs, campers can quite literally enjoy all the comforts of home. In fact, for some RVers, camping *is* home. At some campgrounds, more than half the campsites are "seasonals," where the RV stays year-round and the people return every summer to plant flowers and renew old friendships.

We're assuming, however, that you're camping not in lieu of buying a summer cottage but for more traditional reasons — the freedom to stay where you like, the inexpensive alternative to motel rooms, the fun of cooking and eating outdoors. Whatever degree of "rough" or "elegant" camping you prefer, you can find it in New Hampshire.

The camping season in New Hampshire depends on your comfort level and the licensing of the various campgrounds. There are campgrounds offering year-round camping, but these are mostly for people with big, heated RVs. There are people who will camp out in tents in the snow or even bivy on the mountain with frost forming in their beards. (One of us is married to such a camper.) In general, however, campgrounds open between mid-April and mid-May and close around mid-October to mid-November. Even those that are open in winter often close for a month or so between the end of foliage and the beginning of hunting season and another month in early spring (mud season).

Be warned that on summer weekends, it can be almost as difficult to find a campsite as it is to find a motel room. A couple of years back, because of the incredible demand for sites on summer weekends and complaints that people coming from more than an hour or two away could *never* get sites, New Hampshire's state parks began taking reservations. More than half the tent sites are still let on a first-come, first-served basis. An even smaller percentage of RV sites are kept unreserved. The rest of the state park sites can be reserved by calling (603) 271-3628 from 9 AM to 4 PM from the Monday after New Year's Day to Columbus Day. (From May through August the office is open until 7 PM). You can reserve a site for a minimum of two nights (three on long holiday weekends) and a maximum of 14 nights. You must call at least seven days in advance and have a credit card for payment. Payment must be received one week prior to your arrival.

If you're within a week of your arrival, try calling the park directly. If it still has reservation slots available, the staff can book them during that last week. Most of our private campgrounds also recommend reservations, especially if you want a waterfront site. Both state and private campgrounds generally require a minimum two- or three-night stay for a reservation. On the other hand, midweek or off-season, you should be able to drive around any region until you find something you like.

We've included all of the state park campgrounds here, but only a fraction of the more than 150 private campgrounds in the state. Look for a complete listing in the annual camping guide *New Hampshire Loves Campers*, published by the N.H. Campground Owners'

Association and available at tourist information centers across the state or by calling (603) 846-5511.

Wonderful spots abound, so if you find those we've mentioned are booked, ask the staff to recommend others in their area. More than one campground owner told us that they're happy to recommend their associates, and they know better than anyone how to match visitors with parks that will suit them.

Most campgrounds can accommodate a mix of tents, trailers and RVs — we'll let you know if a campground is exclusively one or another. Several campgrounds have recently added cabins you can rent by the night: these are like camp cabins, the kind with screen windows and no heat, in which you roll out your sleeping bags on bunks. Basically they allow you to camp out without bringing a tent. RV accommodations are generally described in terms of "hookups." A basic two-way hookup provides water and electricity. Add sewer and you have a three-way hookup. Four-way includes either phone service or cable television, and five-way hookups have both.

Most campgrounds will accept a credit card in payment or to hold a reservation; we have noted those that don't. Pets on leashes are allowed in most campgrounds but not allowed at all in others (we'll tell you which ones). Please observe these requirements: Sneaking your pet in doesn't do anybody any favors! Even campgrounds that welcome pets won't love you if you leave your animal unattended while you go off for the day or let your dog bark all night.

The Appalachian Mountain Club maintains a number of campsites for hikers in the White Mountains. Some have tent platforms, and most are within easy walking distance of privies and a water tap. Reservations for AMC campsites are not available, so it pays to arrive early, set up and then hike out and back from your site. (See our Other Recreation chapter for more on the AMC hut system and the close-up in this chapter for information on backcountry camping in the White Mountains.)

We've given you single-night prices for campgrounds. (The range, where there is one, generally reflects differing levels of service on different sites. Sites labeled "tent sites" usually have no hookups available.) There is often a discount for multiple nights. In most cases the base rate covers a family group (often two adults and any number of children, but sometimes only two), with an added charge for additional people. When you make your reservation, your host will want to know how many tents or trailers you'll be using. Some sites are larger than others, and campgrounds have limited capacity. Reserve two sites together if you're anticipating overnight guests.

If the campgrounds indicate you can fish there without a license, it's because they maintain their own pond. Otherwise, check our Fishing and Hunting chapter for details on obtaining a fishing license.

Merrimack Valley Region

Note: The Campground Owners' Association calls this the "South Central Region."

Bear Brook State Park

N.H. Rt. 28, Allenstown
• (603) 485-9869, (603) 271-3628 (State Parks reservation #)

Bear Brook is an Insider favorite for the variety of activities available (see our Parks and Open Spaces chapter). The 97 campsites here have their own swimming area, separate from the day-use beach. The campground can accommodate RVs up to 35 feet long but provides no hookups. Amenities include flush toilets and showers, a laundry and dump station. Ice and firewood are available at the small camp grocery store. Sites cost $14 per night.

Silver Sands Campground

N.H. Rt. 102, Chester • (603) 887-3638

Silver Sands caters to families, with swimming, canoeing, boating and bass fishing (no license required), all available on their beautiful pond. You'll also find horseshoe pits and a playground, volleyball and softball games and other planned activities. The 90 sites are fairly large, with some close together for families or those who like the community feeling, and others more widely separated. Both shady and open sites are available. Sites have three-way hookups. Sani-service and a dump station are available for sites without sewer hookups. Ice, wood and groceries are available at the campground's own store. They advertise night security guards and a security gate, although you certainly don't feel like you're in an urban area when you're there. Sites cost $18 per night.

Hillcrest Family Campground
78 Dover Rd., Chichester
• (603) 798-5124

Hillcrest is a modern campground with a pleasantly old-fashioned feel. Of the 120 sites, 70 have four-way hookups with cable TV and metered electricity, and another 45 have two-way hookups. RVers can choose open or wooded sites (all the no-service and two-way sites are wooded). There are planned activities and games for kids all summer, nature trails and minigolf on site and a recreation room and playground along with volleyball and horseshoes. Take turns swimming at a pond and a large in-ground pool. Hot showers, flush toilets and laundry facilities make tenting easy. Campsites rent from $22 to $28 per night. Hillcrest also has a few log cabins for rent from $42 to $52 per night.

Sandy Beach Family Campground
677 Clement Hill Rd., Contoocook
• (603) 746-3591

Sandy Beach offers 180 sites with two-way hookups and an on-site sani-service and dump station. Most of the sites are seasonal, and many of the guests have been summering there for years, but a few tent and RV sites are available for shorter stays. The beach is indeed sandy and beautiful, and the lake is crystal clear and reportedly full of trout. The campground also provides a boat ramp (no motors) and has a playground and tennis court. The grocery store is comparable to that in some small towns. Price per night is $20.

Hidden Valley R.V. & Golf Park
81 Damren Rd., Derry • (603) 887-3767

This expansive park covers 800 acres, preserving a rural oasis in fast-growing Derry. The golf course, a nine-hole par 3, is open to the public. It has 300 secluded campsites and two open safari areas. About two-thirds of the sites have four-way hookups with cable TV. At the other end of the camping spectrum, you can choose one of 25 designated tent sites. Swim, boat or fish on their private lake (no license required). The modern facilities, playground and special events make this a family-friendly spot. Sunday worship and potluck suppers contribute to the community feeling here. Sites range between $20 and $25.

Circle 9 Ranch Campground
Windymere Rd., Epsom • (603) 736-9656

Circle 9 is a year-round campground with a twang — a country-and-western twang, that is. Live music and dancing in the hall every Friday and Saturday night attracts country-and-western fans from New Hampshire and Maine for some toe-tapping and line dancing. (Lessons are available.) The campground offers 140 sites — some wooded, some open — with three-way hookups (a few also have cable). Amenities here include a store, playground and rec hall, a private pond for fishing, trails for mountain biking, a pool and a whirlpool. There are showers, flush toilets and a laundry. In winter there's a skating rink on site. Sites cost between $21 and $27.

Mile Away Campground
41 Old West Hopkinton Rd., Henniker
• (603) 428-7616, (800) 787-4679

Mile Away is a year-round campground, with 200 sites (94 with full service). Some sites are wooded, some are open, and there is a safari area as well as private sites along the shore of a small lake. Swimming, boating and fishing are available on French Pond, and the recreation on site includes a player piano and organ along with a pool table, big-screen TV/VCR, playground and game room. The large fireplace in the lounge is a gathering spot in winter, and the full kitchen there can be used by guests with prior arrangements. Boat rentals and minigolf are available, as are phone hookups. A full schedule of activities for all ages is planned. There's bingo on Wednesday nights and free minigolf for the children on Saturday mornings. Prices are $23 to $29.50 ($23 in winter).

Friendly Beaver Campground
Old Coach Rd., New Boston
• (603) 487-5570

Friendly Beaver is open year round, keeps up an amazing schedule of activities both summer and winter and runs a full recreation program (including trips to Nova Scotia and Boston). The playground has a castle, the campground has three outdoor pools and an indoor pool with whirlpool, and there are pony rides for the kids. Two rec halls, one for adults and one for kids, provide for a variety of activities. Most sites are open and ringed with trees, but some are wooded. Most sites have three-way hookups. A few are "rustic" tent sites. The campground offers every conceivable service, from showers to dump stations to groceries. Prices range from $26 to $30.

Pawtuckaway State Park
128 Mountain Rd., Nottingham
• (603) 895-3031, (603) 271-3628 (State Parks reservation #)

Possibly the most popular campground in the state, public or private, Pawtuckaway has a loyal following among Insiders. And no wonder, with all that the park has to offer. Hiking and biking through the park's 6,500 acres or canoeing and paddleboating on the placid lake, the Pawtuckaway experience can be like camping "in the good old days," except with flush toilets and showers. RVs up to 35 feet long are permitted, but there are no hookups on site and no dump station. Pets are not permitted at Pawtuckaway. The 193 sites grouped in different areas around the park range from $14 to $20 (waterfront sites on Big Island cost the most).

Pine Acres Recreation Area
74 Freetown Rd., Raymond
• (603) 895-2519

With 350 campsites on 125 acres of level, sandy soil, Pine Acres is one of the biggest campgrounds in the state. It has four swimming areas on its pond, along with a giant water slide and pool. Fishing and boating on (inaptly-named) Dead Pond, biking, hayrides and minigolf augment the recreation hall, three playgrounds and various games. It also has a full activities schedule with everything from Easter egg decorating (in June) to formal dances for teens. About one-third of the sites have two-way hookups, and Pine Acres can rent you a pop-up trailer if you'd like. Choose between wooded or open sites, near the water or back in the woods. Modern bathrooms and laundry facilities make your visit more pleasant. The cost is $29 to $33 per night.

Cold Springs Campground
N.H. Rt. 114, Weare
• (603) 529-2528

Cold Springs is a bit more like a small town than a campground. Guests gather at the pavilion across from the store to sit and talk while their kids swim in the three pools and the sandy-bottomed pond. There's a restaurant, modern restrooms and a full schedule of activities. The playground is designed for little ones, but teens don't lack for activity with the horseshoe tournaments, rec room and snack bar. Of the 310 sites, more than 100 have full hookups, and only 10 are designated tent sites. Could you guess they also sell RVs? Sites cost between $26 and $30.

Cold Brook Campground
539 Battle St., Webster
• (603) 746-3390

For those who prefer it, Cold Brook offers a quiet camping experience, with canoeing and fishing on Blackwater river, shuffleboard and a playground but no big rec hall or video games. The 60 sites are easy and level, with some three-way and some two-way hookups. There are flush toilets, hot showers and laundry facilities. Prices range from $15 to $18.

Seacoast Region

Note: the Campground Owner's Association includes in the Seacoast Region some towns we place in Lakes and Merrimack Valley regions.

Barrington Shores Camping Area
70 Hall Rd., Barrington • (603) 664-9333

Barrington Shores' 142 sites offer a variety of experiences, from secluded woodland sites to lakefront spots to a safari field and rental cabins. The RV sites have three-way hookups. Two sandy beaches for swimming on Swains Lake, bass fishing, a rec hall and game room, hayrides, horseshoes and planned activities all summer guarantee that you'll find something to your liking to do. The campground has modern plumbing, a laundry, a dump station and a store with propane, ice and firewood as well as groceries. Guests can rent boats and canoes for exploring the lake. Sites range from $23 to $30, and the cabins, which have showers, are $50 to $70 per night.

Old Stage Campground

46 Old Stage Rd., Dover • (603) 742-4050

This campground is mostly in Madbury, although the access is from Dover. You'll find plenty to do here. The pond and pool, game room and hayrides attract the kids, while relaxing adults are drawn to the fishing, hiking and quiet wooded sites on the Bellamy River. This modern campground has 130 sites, most able to accommodate RVs with both two-way and three-way hookups. Flush toilets, laundry, a store and planned activities including bonfires round out the picture. Prices range from $22 to $24 per night.

Exeter Elms Family Campground

188 Court St., Exeter • (603) 778-7631

Exeter Elms offers family camping in any style, from rustic to elegant. The 200 wooded sites are divided into three categories: full (three-way) hookups, two-way hookups and water only. There are modern bath facilities and a laundry. The campground enjoys a full mile of frontage on the Exeter River, with great fishing a natural result. There's a pool if you don't want to swim with the fish and a playground for the children. The list of activities seems endless and includes holiday celebrations (Christmas in summer, Halloween in summer, etc.), potluck suppers, dances and live entertainment. If that's not enough, the campground is just a couple of miles from downtown Exeter. Prices are $18 to $28.

Exeter River Camping Area

13 South Rd., Fremont
• (603) 895-3448

This pleasant campground is a bit old-fashioned: two-way hookups, no boat rentals or carnivals. It does have shady sites for tents or RVs (sani-service is available), a rec room and a lovely sandy beach on the river where you can swim, fish or launch your canoe. Modern plumbing is a welcome concession to the demands of camping in the '90s. Sites cost $18.

Hampton Beach State RV Park

N.H. Rt. 1-A, Hampton
• (603) 926-8990, (603) 271-3628 (State Parks reservations #)

This is the only RV park right on the New Hampshire coast. All 28 sites are reserved for RVs (three-way hookups), and pets are not permitted. There is a camp store, ocean swimming and all the activities of Hampton Beach (see our Attractions chapter) right next door. Sites cost $30 per night.

Wakeda Campground

N.H. Rt. 88, Hampton Falls
• (603) 772-5274

This campground has been operated by the same family for three generations. More than 400 sites along a network of roads are the work of many family members, who cut the lumber for the buildings and picnic tables from the trees they cleared from the sites. Don't worry, they left plenty of trees for shady sites. Some have three-way hookups, some are completely rustic, and most are in between. Clean, modern toilets and showers are within easy walking distance of each site. Wakeda has lots of activities, electronic and athletic games, a playground and a pavilion. Special features include pancake breakfasts on Sundays and make-your-own sundaes on Saturday afternoons. Prices range from $17 to $28. Five pull-through sites are available for $35. Credit cards are not accepted.

INSIDERS' TIP

A waterfront site is attractive, but probably not the best choice if you're traveling with small children.

Sanborn Shore Acres

N.H. Rt. 121, Hampstead
• (603) 329-5247

Sanborn Shores is primarily a seasonal campground, with some sites available for shorter stays. Seasonal sites have four-way hookups with cable; short-stay ("transient") sites have three-way hookups. Sites are open, and the area is landscaped. The modern restrooms are heated and handicapped-accessible. Sanborn Shores offers a 180-foot sandy beach on Big Island Pond, so swimming, boating (you can rent dock space for your boat) and fishing are part of the routine. There are many other planned activities for the whole family: pizza parties, theme weekends and arts and crafts, bingo games and professional entertainers. A snack bar means you don't need to cook unless you want to. Summer rates are $22 per night, and winter rates are $15.

Country Shore Camping Area

N.H. Rt. 125, Kingston
• (603) 642-5072

Country Shore has more than 100 sites, carefully laid out so that although they're tightly spaced, the sites feel quite large and private. All the sites are level and easily accessed, and all have three-way hookups. (This is definitely an RV park, although it doesn't call itself one. Most campers are seasonal.) Showers and toilet facilities are available. The modern facility includes boat docks as well as a fishing dock on Country Pond, ball fields and a playground. There is swimming on their sandy beach and lots of fun with ice cream socials, dances and contests. Sites here are $22 per day for a family of as many as five.

Forest Glen Campground

N.H. Rt. 155, Lee • (603) 659-3416

This family campground has 150 wooded sites spread out over 65 acres along a large network of roads. The park runs from the highway to Lake Wheelwright, where a sandy beach, boat launch and docks invite guests to enjoy the water. It has a playground and rec building with some planned activities, but most campers find plenty to amuse themselves with. All the sites have two-way hookups and cable. We asked if they had a noise problem (Lee is home to two speedways), and they said in honesty you can hear the nearer track, but it's not loud enough to be a disturbance and the races are always over by 11 PM. Prices range from $18 to $22.

Great Bay Camping Village

56 N.H.Rt. 108, Newfields • (603) 778-0226

With more than 115 sites along the Squamscott River, Great Bay combines the best of inland and seacoast camping. Their sites are shady but not dark, and no license is required for fishing in the tidal Squamscott (see our Fishing and Hunting chapter). Families are especially welcome, and children are encouraged to bring bicycles, join in the arts and crafts classes and learn to love camping! Great Bay Camping Village offers the amenities modern camping kids expect: video games, basketball, a pool and a calendar of activities. The rustic sites here are all back away from the river, which may indicate a bias in favor of the RVs or may just reflect the times. Bring the boat or rent a canoe — the whole Seacoast is spread before you when you set out from here. Prices range from $17 to $23.

Angle Pond Grove Camping & Recreation Area

N.H. Rt. 121-A, Sandown • (603) 887-4434

This is an RV park with three-way hookups on all 140 sites. (It does have a few cottages to rent if you have no trailer, but no tents are allowed.) The modern facility includes numerous sports fields, bocce courts

INSIDERS' TIP

It is very bad form to collect wood for your fire from around the campsite, and, of course, you would never cut a tree on private property! However, if you keep your eyes open, you're sure to find a downed branch or two along the roadside that you can break up and bring back for the campfire.

Backcountry Camping

Close-up

Backcountry camping is allowed without a permit in the White Mountain National Forest, but some restrictions apply. You should always camp at least 200 feet from any lake or stream and 200 feet from (or at least out of sight of) any trail or roadway. In designated Wilderness Areas a maximum of 10 people can camp together, and this guideline is valuable in other backcountry areas as well. If your group is larger than 10, consider breaking up or camping in designated campsites.

Don't burn or bury food scraps or waste — carry out everything you carry in. If you can't bear the thought of carrying out your own waste, bury it at least six inches deep. (You do have a shovel, right?) Use a camp stove and don't build fires, which scar the landscape even when they don't get out of control. Again, this is required in wilderness areas but recommended everywhere.

Photo: Tom Wilkins

Backcountry campers use stoves for cooking to avoid damaging the forest floor.

Always wash at least 200 feet from any open water (your dishes and yourself). Better yet, leave the soap at home. It's bad for fish and attracts bugs and bears. In bear-trouble areas (which are posted at trailheads), hang your food at least 25 feet from your tent, at least 15 feet off the ground and 10 feet out from the trunk of the tree. Try to blend in with your environment, visually and in scent and sound. You've succeeded if another group hikes past you and never knows you're there.

For a helpful brochure on backcountry camping with detailed restrictions for various areas, contact the Forest Service in Laconia, (603) 528-8721, or any Ranger Station in the White Mountain National Forest.

and a rec room with an arcade. A variety of activities are scheduled, including bonfires and dances for children and adults. The 500-foot sandy beach and picnic area are open for day use, but the security gate and card system discourages troublemakers, and the day users and campers don't seem to conflict. Pets are not allowed. Sites cost $18 per night.

Tuxbury Pond Camping Area
88 Whitehall Rd., South Hampton
• (603) 394-7660

Tuxbury Pond offers a choice of shady and sunny sites, some on the lake, and most with two- or three-way hookups. The huge sandy beach and crystal-clear lake is an invitation to swim or boat, while the playing fields, playground, game room and activities schedule (ceramics classes, bingo, hayrides and candy hunts, just to list a few) promise to keep everyone busy and happy. During the week the restaurant is open from 8 AM to 8 PM. On weekends the hours are extended to 11 PM. Many sites and the modern restrooms, showers and pavilion are handicapped-accessible. The cost is $23 to $25.

Lakes Region

Ames Brook Campground

Winona Rd., Ashland
• (603) 968-7998, (800) 234-7998

With just more than 40 sites on this 27-acre site, this is camping with elbow room. The RV sites have three-way hookups and cable, and the tent sites are large and private. Modern facilities include toilets and free hot showers, a swimming pool, playing courts and a kids' playground. The game room (with pool table), store and laundry room are air-conditioned. (Who would think doing laundry could be so attractive?) Weekends in July and August, guests are invited to enjoy hayrides, ice cream socials and water aerobics. Each month there is one weekend when a minimal stay is required (Memorial Day, Motorcycle Weekend (see Annual Events), Independence Day, Labor Day and Columbus Day). Prices range from $21 to $26 per night.

Yogi Bear's Jellystone Park

N.H. Rt. 132, Ashland • (603) 968-9000

Most campers are familiar with the Yogi chain. This park is consistently rated in the franchise's top 10 on its review for excellence. More than 260 sites, mostly open but some wooded, feature two-way hookups. Tons of supervised activities for children are the trademark of this chain, and the Ashland park offers daily hayrides, arts and crafts, movies at the indoor and outdoor theaters, parties, games and visits with Yogi and Boo-boo. Swimming, fishing and canoeing in the Pemigewasset River are some of the grown-ups' choices. Minigolf, billiards and the arcade satisfy the teens. Yogi has a pool and hot tub, full bathrooms, a laundry and general store to provide for you as well as, of course, picnic areas. Sites cost $36 to $43 (all sites are half-price from mid-May to mid-June and Labor Day to Columbus Day).

Deer Cap Campground

N.H. Rt. 16, Center Ossipee
• (603) 539-6030

Deer Cap is a year-round campground, with a heated pool and ice cream shop in summer and cross-country ski trails in winter (see our Winter Sports chapter). The 70 sites are large and clean. Most are nicely shaded, but there are some open, grassy sites that are better for winter. Sites have two-way hookups. The bathrooms are heated, and there are hot showers. The park has a nice playground, and children stay here free. Sites cost $15, and there is no "extra person" charge for children.

Lake Ivanhoe Campground and Inn

631 Acton Ridge Rd., East Wakefield
• (603) 522-8824

In addition to an old-fashioned inn being operated as a bed and breakfast, there are 74 campsites here at the edge of the lake. Some are wooded, some grassy, and services range from rustic sites with no hookups to three-way hookups. There are a few sites with trailers for rent. Modern restrooms and free showers, a laundry room and camp store make for easy camping whether you're in a pop-up or a 35-foot trailer. The park offers hayrides, minigolf, swimming and fishing along with a playground and game room. Boats are available to rent. Costs range from $23 to $30.

Thousand Acres Family Campground

1079 S. Main St., Franklin • (603) 934-4440

This is a large park (hence the name) with 150 spacious sites, both in open, grassy areas and secluded in the woods. One-third have two-way hookups, a few have three-way. The park has all the modern amenities such as flush toilets and hot showers, which are included in the price per site. It also has canoes available without charge for paddling about their private pond (no fishing license required). Every weekend it offers free hayrides, ice cream socials and free arcade games and movies. Sites cost $22 to $24 per night.

Ellacoya State Park

N.H. Rt. 11, Gilford
• (603) 293-7821, (603) 271-3628
(State Parks reservation #)

This is an RV park (no tents allowed) with 38 three-way hookup sites. It's immediately adjacent to Ellacoya State Beach, 5 miles south of Weirs Beach. A bathhouse and laundry are available, and there is a central fire ring for the guests' use. No pets are allowed at Ellacoya. Reservations should be made through the state reservations number. The rate is $30.

Gunstock Campground

N.H. Rt. 11-A, Gilford
• (603) 293-4341, (800) 486-7862

Many Insiders have mixed feelings about the success of the year-round campground at Gunstock, since it is partly taxpayer-funded (it's owned by Belknap County) and competes with other area campgrounds. For visitors what counts is that the park's efforts to attract non-skiing visitors means horseback riding and mountain biking are available in the park for summer guests (for an additional fee). There's a swimming pool and special events every month. Of the 280 sites, more than half are for tents. The remaining sites have two-way hookups, and the park offers all the modern amenities. Sites range from $20 to $28.

Bethel Woods Campground

U.S. Rt. 3, Holderness • (603) 279-6266

This lovely campground welcomes guests to the Squam Lakes area with 93 shaded sites. About 58 are designed for RVs and have two-way hookups. The park's modern amenities include not only restrooms and a laundry, but also a pool with sauna and sun deck, a club room and arcade and children's play areas. Potluck suppers and hayrides highlight summer weekends. Prices range from $18 to $22.

Paugus Bay Campground

Hilliard Rd., Laconia • (603) 366-4757

Paugus Bay was recommended to us by another Insider when we said we liked the comforts of modern camping but not the temptations. Most of the 170 sites are seasonal and have two- or three-way hookups, and there are restrooms, showers and a laundry. Activities for kids include swimming, Ping Pong, outside games and a playground. Since our kids are drawn to video arcades like moths to the old flaming lantern, we appreciate the fact that the only extra-fee activity here is canoe rental. Prices are $29 to $31 per night.

Harbor Hill Camping Area

189 N.H. Rt. 25 E., Meredith
• (603) 279-6910

Go through Meredith and up the hill out of town, and you'll find this wonderful campground in the woods. The 140 sites are divided between seasonal and overnight guests. Some sites have two-way hookups, some have three-way, and there's a loop of tent sites without service for traditional camping. A pool, play area and sports court are provided for guests. Groceries and propane are available at the store. Prices range from $20 to $26. Harbor Hill also has a few rustic cabins for $45 per night.

Meredith Woods Four Season Camping Area

N.H. Rt. 104, Meredith • (603) 279-5449
Clearwater Campground• (603) 279-7761

"You've got to see Meredith Woods," we were told over and over. "You won't believe Meredith Woods." They were right. This painstakingly leveled and groomed park is an RV paradise, complete with five-way hookups, heated indoor pool, rec room and whirlpool. The 101-site park is owned by the same people who've run Clearwater Campground across the street for years, and the beach and boat dock at Clearwater are available for campers from Meredith Woods.

The big attraction here comes in winter, when snowmobilers appreciate the instant access to the trails network and the warm welcome when they return.

Clearwater, the "parent" campground, has 156 sites, half with two-way hookups. Playgrounds, rec rooms and planned activities are available for campers in addition to the lakefront options. Cost is $33 per night ($22 to $33 in the off-season).

Pine Woods Campground
Moultonborough Neck Rd., Moultonborough • (603) 253-6251

Pine Woods is right on Moultonborough Neck, within walking distance of the Kona Wildlife Management Area, the town beach and the boat slips. The 100 sites here are private and wooded. Almost all have two-way hookups. Modern facilities and conveniences give you more time to enjoy the pool, playground and weekend entertainment or to walk the nature trails and explore the lake. Prices are $18 to $24.

Twin Tamarack Family Camping & RV Resort
N.H. Rt. 104, New Hampton • (603) 279-4387

With 256 sites, some in the woods and some open, Twin Tamarack has something for just about everyone. At least 100 sites have three-way hookups and the rest have two-way hookups. The park caters to families, with a pool and hot tub, sandy beach for swimming, boat rentals and boat launch and a playground. A children's rec program and cable TV hookups are available too. The emphasis here is on quiet enjoyment of nature, with the unusual (for the Lakes Region) stipulation that motorcycles are not allowed. Sites cost from $28 to $32 per night.

Plymouth Sands Campground
Smith Bridge Rd., Plymouth • (603) 536-2605

On the shores of the Baker River, Plymouth Sands offers 80 wooded and partially shaded tent and RV sites, more than half with two-way hookups and about 30 with sewers. The tent sites here are a bit far from the bathrooms and showers, but the trade is that the sites lie very close to the sandy beach. Quiet activities and a playground make this a pleasant spot for a family trip. Sites cost $16 to $21.

Baker River Campground
56 Campground Rd., Rumney • (603) 786-9707

This is a small (50-site), quiet campground in the Baker River Valley. Sites are large and screened with large shade trees. There's plenty of room for a screen house or an extra tent for the kids. Most of the sites have two-way hookups, and a few have sewer. The dump station is free. Rent tubes and canoes for plying the Baker River or just enjoy swimming into it from the sandy beach. A children's play area and a video game room help kids feel at home, and, of course, you'll squeeze in a trip to the neighboring Polar Caves (see our Attractions chapter) while you're here! Sites are $20 per night.

White Lake State Park
N.H. Rt. 16, Tamworth • (603) 323-7350, (603) 271-3628 (State Parks reservation #)

White Lake State Park has about 200 tent sites (no hookups), some right on the water, which are very popular. The campground has showers and a store. It rents canoes for exploring the lake. There is a sandy beach here and wonderful nature trails (see our Parks and Open Spaces chapter). Pets are not allowed in the park. Prices are $14 to $20.

Chocorua Camping Village
N.H. Rt. 25, West Ossipee • (603) 323-8536, (888) 237-8642

This highly rated campground has 130 wooded sites alongside a pristine pond with a stunning view of Mt. Chocorua's bare top. (It also has six very nice waterfront cabins with kitchens and baths for rent at $69 to $98 each.) Some sites have two- or three-way hookups, others are designed for tents or pop-ups. All have access to hot showers, the laundry and a large number of activities including swimming and hiking.

A craft shop and canoe and rowboat rentals suggest other possibilities, and the option of supervised games, crafts, hikes and movies for the children make those possibilities real. Prices are $22 to $32.

Willey Brook Campground
883 Center St., Wolfeboro • (603) 569-9493

Willey Brook is a simple campground, with fewer than 50 wooded sites for RVs (two-way hookups) or tents. The owners stress the "back to nature" theme and encourage their guests to take advantage of the recreational riches of the surrounding area during the day. If this basic approach appeals to you, you'll be glad to know that while they don't have a video arcade, the bathrooms are clean, the showers are hot, and the sites are well-maintained. Prices range from $14 to $16.

White Mountains and Great North Woods Regions

Mollidgewock State Park

N.H. Rt. 16, Errol
• (603) 482-3373, (603) 271-3628 (State Parks reservation #)

You can roll out of your tent and wake up with a refreshing swim in the chilly waters of the Androscoggin River. The 42 tent sites at Mollidgewock are favorites for bird lovers, canoers and kayakers because of the proximity to both Lake Umbagog and the rapids of the Androscoggin. Two miles north of Errol on N.H. Route 16, above the dam, is the public boat launch for Lake Umbagog. For a trip on the rapids, just push off from your riverside campsite. Pit toilets and water spigots as well as firewood and ice are available. The park is carry-in/carry-out, which means you won't find trash containers. The campground is open from mid-May through mid-October. The cost is $14 per site per night.

Moose Brook State Park

U.S. Rt. 2, Gorham
• (603) 466-3860, (603) 271-3628 (State Parks reservation #)

Hike the Presidential Range from your base camp in this 744-acre state park. The facilities were built in the 1930s by the government-sponsored Civilian Conservation Corps (CCC). The buildings have stone fireplaces, and you'll enjoy the sandy-bottomed pond for swimming. If you don't consider swimming to count as washing, you'll be glad to see the bathhouse with showers. The 50 tent sites include 43 in the campground and seven very close to the swimming pond. You can fish for bass and trout in the park. Gorham is just 2 miles away in case you need to do a quick load of laundry or grab a pizza for the campfire. The park operates on a modified carry-in/carry-out system in that the campground has a dumpster. The cost is $14 per site per night.

Dry River Campground

Crawford Notch State Park, U.S. Rt. 302, Hart's Location
• (603)374-2272, (603) 271-3628 (State Parks reservation #)

You can hike along 6 miles of trails throughout nearly 6,000 acres of wilderness in the heart of the White Mountains National Forest. Fish for trout in the mountain streams or just relax and enjoy the cascading waterfalls. The camping is primitive — pit toilets only — but the scenery and hiking, which includes a portion of the Appalachian Trail, can't be beat. Thirty tent sites are available, and it's OK to bring your pets. Be sure you've got all your provisions before setting up, because it's at least 12 miles to stock. The campground is open from mid-May through mid-October. The park operates on a modified carry-in/carry-out system since the campground has a dumpster. The cost is $12 per site per night.

Lafayette Campground

Franconia Notch State Park, 8 miles north of North Woodstock via U.S. Rt. 3, Lincoln • (603) 823-5563, (603) 271-3628 (State Parks reservation #)

You've got 6,440 acres to play in here. This is the home of the Old Man of the Mountain, Echo Lake, Profile Lake and Lonesome Lake. The Cannon Mountain ski area and the

INSIDERS' TIP

Campgrounds that allow pets expect your pet to be leashed at all times and never left alone at the campground. If you leave your campsite be sure to take your pet with you.

deep glacial pothole known as the Basin are in the park.

The Appalachian Trail crosses the park just a mile north of the Flume. Campers will love the 97 tent sites, showers and flush toilets. You'll find a camp store as well as a recreation center. Swimming, boating and fishing are all nearby. No pets are allowed. The campground is open from mid-May through mid-October. The cost is $14 per site per night.

Cove Camping on Conway Lake

Stark Rd., 1 mile east of N.H. Rt. 113, Conway

• (603) 447-6734

Families have enjoyed camping on these 4.5 miles of lakefront for more 40 years. The 90 sites include 43 RV sites with water and electricity hookups. The campground has a sanitary service station. Wooded and lake sites are available, and you can rent a tent. Amenities include boat rentals, a camp store, a recreation hall that shows nightly movies and a playground. Picnic tables and fireplaces are available throughout the campground. Modern facilities include a laundry room, flush toilets and hot water showers. Activities include bass fishing, swimming, Ping-Pong and billiards. The campground is open from late May through mid-October. Prices begin at $20 a day for a tent site and $26 for an RV site. Dogs are allowed after Labor Day.

Lake Francis State Park
River Road, off U.S. Rt. 3, Pittsburg

• (603) 538-6965, (603) 271-3628 (State Parks reservation #)

These 42 tent sites are favorites of anglers. The 2,000-acre man-made Lake Francis is an ideal spot for rainbow trout, salmon and pickerel. Some of the sites have platforms, and you can choose between wooded or open locations. The park doesn't advertise swimming because there are no lifeguards, but the water is clean, so hop right in. Just 2 miles from the camp is a beach area. Flush toilets, sinks and a dump station are all present. You won't find any hookups, but a few RVs can be accommodated. The campground is open from mid-May through mid-October. The cost is $12 to $16 per site per night.

Coleman State Park

Diamond Pond Rd., off N.H. Rt. 26, Stewartstown

• (603) 237-4520, (603) 271-3628 (State Parks reservation #)

This 1,500-acre park is nestled in the deep forest of the Connecticut Lakes area on Little Diamond Pond. Drive 12 miles east of Colebrook on N.H. Route 26 and turn north on Diamond Pond Road. The trout fishing is excellent in the pond and connecting streams. Hunters take advantage of the long camping season, which starts in mid-May and continues through mid-December. Thirty tent sites are available in addition to field sites (no hookups) for RVs. Pit toilets are the extent of the amenities. You can bring your pets. The cost is $12 per site per night.

Ammonoosuc Campground

U.S. Rt. 3, Twin Mountain

• (603) 846-5527

You're just a quarter-mile from the intersection of U.S. routes 3 and 302 and in the midst of the White Mountains at this year-round campground. Bring your skis and snowmobiles for the winter and your bathing suits and hiking boots for summer. The sites are all surrounded by trees. Full RV hookups are available at 75 sites, and an additional 20 sites have water and electricity. Twenty-four sites are primative. You'll find a swimming pool and playground on premises as well as a laundry and dump station. A small store is next door to the campgrounds. Flush toilets, sinks and hot showers are available, and the bathrooms are heated in winter. Nightly rates are $21 for full hookups, $20 for water and electric sites and $18 for plain tent sites.

Dartmouth- Lake Sunapee Region

Mascoma Lake Campground

N.H. Rt. 4A, Enfield

• (603) 448-5076, (800) 769-7861

A total of 90 campsites include 60 with RV hookups and 30 for tents or pop-up trailers. The sandy beach on Lake Mascoma is a great place to swim, fish and boat. Metered and bottled gas is sold, and a small camp store is right on the premises. Seasonal as well as overnight sewer sites are available along with flush toilets, sinks and hot showers. Pets are OK as long as they are leashed. The campground is open from mid-May until mid-October. Take Exit 17 off Interstate 89 and head east on U.S. Route 4. Turn right again onto N.H. Route 4A, and the lake and campground are less than a half-mile on your left. Nightly rates are $25 for a full hookup, $21 for water and electricity and $18 for unadorned tent sites.

Storrs Pond Campground
N.H. Rt. 10, Hanover
• (603) 643-2134

Thirty-five secluded campsites surround the 15-acre Storrs Pond. Seventeen of the sites include water and electric hookups. You can swim in the pond, which has two separate sandy beaches, or choose the swimming pool. Both the pond and pool have lifeguards until at least 5 PM. Amenities include a playground area with a covered pavilion, picnic tables and fireplaces, a snack bar and tennis courts. The toilets flush, and the showers have hot water. Firewood and ice are sold. The park is open from mid-May through mid-October. Take Exit 18 off I-89 and drive through Hanover on N.H. Route 120. Go north on N.H. Route 10 and follow signs to Storrs Pond. Nightly rates for sites with water and electricity are $22 on weekends and $17 during the week. Plain tent sites are $17 on weekends and $12 during the week. This campground allows pets on leashes.

Otter Lake Campground
N.H. Rt. 11, New London
• (603) 763-5600

This small, 28-site campground has graced Otter Lake for more than 40 years. Wooded and water-view campsites are dotted throughout the 14-acre grounds on the 180-acre lake. All sites include water and electricity. You can swim, rent canoes and paddleboats and fish for bass and pickerel in Otter Lake. Flush toilets and hot showers are a few of the amenities. The kids will enjoy the playground, and you can buy firewood and ice at the campground. A general store is down the road at the other end of the lake. Leashed pets are OK. The campground is open from mid-May through mid-October. It's just a mile west of Exit 12 off I-89 on N.H. Route 11 (Otterville Road). Sites are $18 per night.

Loon Lake Campground
Reeds Mill Rd., Croyden
• (603) 863-8176

If you like to camp on a lake, but the sound of motorboats drives you crazy, this is the place for you. Loon Lake doesn't allow boats with motors. And, if you don't have your own boat, you can rent a paddleboat or a canoe. The 118 wooded campsites include 90 sewered RV sites. Flush toilets and hot showers are on-premises, and the camp store stocks basics such as milk and ice. Hiking trails are clearly marked throughout the 750 acres. Two beaches on man-made Loon Lake (on many maps this lake is still called The Overflow) include one for adults only and one with a great kid's playground. You can fish in the lake too. Pickerel, perch and bass are plentiful, and the owners have recently introduced rainbow trout. The campground is open from mid-May until mid-October. Nightly rates are $18 for tent sites, $22 for sites with water and electricity and $24 for RV sites with full hookups.

Northstar Campground
N.H. Rt. 10, Newport
• (603) 863-4001

Camp along the Sugar River in your choice of 55 sites — from pine groves to grassy meadows. The spring-fed pond is perfect for swimming, and trout fishing is great at the river. You can play horseshoes and volley-

INSIDERS' TIP

Keep some matches in an empty film canister and an old newspaper under the seat of the car, and you'll always have a dry start for your fire.

ball, and the group area includes a covered pavilion. The kids will enjoy the playground, and you'll all have fun during the special theme weekends. Some recent themes were "Christmas in July" and a "1950s Weekend." Ask about planned events when you call for reservations. The campground doesn't have full RV hookups, but water and electricity are onsite as well as flush toilets and hot showers. You're just 4 miles south of Newport for laundry and grocery needs. The campground is open from mid-May through mid-October. Rates are $16 a night for two with an additional $2 charged for each child older than 3 and $7 for each additional adult.

The Pastures Campground
N.H. Rt. 10, Orford
• (603) 353-4579

The Pastures is the only campground in New Hampshire that's right on the Connecticut River. It's a popular stop for those traveling the river via canoe. Campers looking for peace and quiet will be happy here. The 60 sites are all in open pasture land — not the usual New Hampshire woods. All have water and electricity, and there's a dump station for RVs. You can get firewood at the campground, but that's about all. The Orfordville General Store is just a quarter-mile up N.H. Route 10 and has everything from deli sandwiches and soft ice cream to ice, milk and cereal. The campground is open from mid-May through mid-October. The cost is $15 a night for tents, $16 for vehicles less than 25 feet long and $17 for those more than 25 feet long.

Pillsbury State Park
N.H. Rt. 31, Washington
• (603) 863-2860, (603) 271-3628 (State Parks reservation #)

Hikers love Pillsbury State Park for the trails along the 52-mile Monadnock-Sunapee Greenway that connects Mount Monadnock to Mount Sunapee. Bring your canoe and fish for largemouth bass and pickerel in the 149-acre May Pond. Some of the 30 primitive campsites offer direct paddle-in access to the pond. A strict carry-in/carry-out policy is the rule here since there's not an on-site Dumpster. Outhouses with pit toilets are the extent of the amenities. The campground is open from mid-May through mid-October. The cost is $14 per night.

Monadnock Region

Field & Stream Travel Trailer Park
5 Dupaw Gould Rd., Brookline
• (603) 673-4677

Field & Stream is a four-season park designed to handle any RV on the road (although tenters are welcome too). All 54 sites have four-way hookups, and some also offer cable-TV. The sites are in a grassy, open area, with partial shade for those around the edge. You can swim at the sandy beach and fish in the stream, or you can take a canoe up Gould Mill Brook to Lake Potanipo. Hot showers and a laundry make "roughing it" less rough for grown-ups, while a game room, badminton/volleyball court and play area amuse the kids. There's a dump station on site, but the honey wagon makes rounds to empty the sewage tanks on RVs. Propane is available at the camp store, as are camping supplies and groceries. Sites cost between $15 and $22.

Oxbow Campground
N.H. Rt. 149, Deering
• (603) 464-5952

Most of the campers here come for a whole season, but the campground welcomes transients. The 80 RV sites have full hookups as well as optional cable television and telephone hookups. The recreation room is more likely to be the scene of a game of cribbage than MTV. Other activities include swimming in the sand-bottom pond and canoeing in the Contoocook River, which is 2 miles north of the campground in Hillsborough. The campground is open from May 1 until mid-October. Daily rates are $18 for unadorned tent sites, $20 for electricity only and $23 for full hookups. Call for seasonal rates.

Greenfield State Park
N.H. Rt. 136, Greenfield
• (603) 547-3497, (603) 271-3628 (State Parks reservation #)

This 401-acre state park is ready for campers with 252 tent sites, flush toilets and showers. Instead of carry-in/carry-out, garbage bags are provided, and trash containers are on-site. You won't find RV hookups, but some sites can accommodate trailers up to 35 feet long. The park is very popular with families. Otter Lake has three beaches, and one is reserved just for campers. The lake has good bass fishing, and you can rent a canoe if you want to try your hand at paddling on calm water. Pets on leashes are allowed, but no pets are allowed on the beach. The campground is open from mid-May through mid-October. The cost is $14 per night.

Monadnock State Park

N.H. Rt. 124, Jaffrey

• (603) 532-8862, (603) 271-3628 (State Parks reservation #)

If you want to get to know the trails of Mount Monadnock as intimately as possible, and you aren't lucky enough to live in the region, we suggest you camp here at one of 21 primitive tent sites. Three-quarters of the 40 miles of trails to the summit are easily joined from the campground area. The park is open year round, making it the only winter state park camping opportunity in the region. Cross-country skiing and winter climbing are the favorite activities of the cold weather camper. The park has pit toilets and a bathhouse with running water. Note that the bathhouse is open only in warm weather. No pets are allowed anywhere in the park. The cost is $12 per night.

Shir-Roy Camping Area

N.H. Rt. 32, Richmond

• (603) 239-4768

You'll find 100 campsites surrounding the 42-acre Cass Pond. Forty-three of the sites are seasonal. All of the sites have water, and many have electricity. No sites have full RV hookups. Besides fishing for largemouth bass, you can enjoy swimming and boating in the pond. The campground rents canoes, paddleboats and rowboats. The small camp store stocks essentials such as ice, firewood and milk. The recreation room does have video games, but the campground stresses that it's a place for families who enjoy the quiet of the Monadnock Region. Washing machines and dryers as well as flush toilets and hot showers are on the premises. The campground opens in late May and closes in the first week of October. Overnight rates are $18 for a plain site and $21 for a site with electricity.

Forest Lake Campground

N.H. Rt. 10, Winchester

• (603) 239-4267

Most of the recreation at Forest Lake Campground is centered around the 87-acre Forest Lake. Besides swimming and boating, you can fish for largemouth bass, pickerel and brown and rainbow trout. You can rent canoes and rowboats. Tennis and basketball courts, shuffleboard and a game room are right at hand. Picnic tables and fireplaces are sure to inspire the cook. The campground is open from May 1 until October 1. Most of the 150 sites are seasonal, but about 30 sites are reserved for overnight campers. Flush toilets and hot showers are on hand. Some of the RV sites are sewered, and there is a dump station. Overnight rates are $18 for a plain tent site. Call for seasonal information.

Our abundant forests, rivers, lakes, ponds and streams have always attracted people to New Hampshire.

Fishing and Hunting

Fishing and hunting are two of New Hampshire's most popular recreational activities. Our abundant forests, rivers, lakes, ponds and streams have long attracted people to New Hampshire.

The ability to hunt and fish — to live off the land — was essential to the lifestyle of the self-sufficient New England settler. Early in the 20th century, many animals — wild turkey and beaver are good examples — had nearly been wiped out by over hunting. The clear-cutting forestry practices begun during the second half of the 19th century also harmed animal populations by destroying their habitat. Appreciating the fact that the state's tourist trade depended upon its natural resources, New Hampshire began to protect its forests and thereby its wild animal population. Species rebounded as the forests were restored and hunting limits were imposed.

The track record on fish is not as good. As a nation we were slow to recognize the effects of pesticides and industrial wastes in our waters. Pollution combined with overfishing to endanger many of our fish. The Atlantic salmon has disappeared from our rivers (see our Close-up in this chapter on the demise of the Atlantic salmon). Today, environmental education and law enforcement are cleaning up our rivers. New Hampshire waters are cleaner than in the past 40 years and should continue to improve with the cooperation of anglers.

To help make your fishing or hunting trip rewarding and safe, we suggest hiring a guide. New Hampshire has a rigorous licensing procedure for guides for both fishing and hunting, and these people can save you a lot of wasted time. Not only will guides be able to take you to the best places to achieve your sporting goals, they will also make sure you have the proper provisions for any expedition. A lot of our land is rugged, and it makes sense to learn the territory from an expert. You can get a current list of guides from the New Hampshire Fish and Game Department, (603) 271-3421.

You may want to pick up a copy of the *New Hampshire Atlas and Gazetteer,* published by DeLorme of Freeport, Maine, (207) 865-4171. It includes a 35-grid map of the state as well as exhaustive information on hunting preserves and fishing spots. The New Hampshire Atlas and Gazetteer is available at all bookstores and many stores specializing in hunting and fishing. A great source for trout fishing is *The Atlas of New Hampshire Trout Ponds,* published by Northern Cartographic of South Burlington, Vermont, (802) 860-2886. The book includes a chapter on fishing strat-

INSIDERS' TIP

Even nonhunters wear lots of bright red and orange clothing during hunting season in October and November. Bright hats, scarves and jackets are wardrobe necessities so that hunters won't mistake you for wildlife. And don't forget to outfit your dog. A bright neck-kerchief is a good idea for outdoor pets.

egies as well as detailed maps of ponds and lakes in the state.

New Hampshire hunters and anglers have two great newspapers available to them. *Hawkeye Hunting and Fishing News* is a monthly newspaper, available by subscription at P.O. Box 371, Milford, NH 03055, or free at many local shops. *New Hampshire Sportsman* is another monthly that can be purchased at most grocery and convenient stores or by subscription from 111 Maplewood Avenue, Peterborough, NH 03801.

New Hampshire Fish and Game Department
2 Hazen Dr., Concord
Licensing and Guide Information: (603) 271-3421, (603) 271-3422
Law Enforcement: (603) 271-3127
Wildlife Programs: (603) 271-2461
Fisheries Programs: (603) 271-2501
Marine Fisheries: (603) 868-1095
Animal Damage Control: (603) 225-1416
Engineering and Environmental Services: (603) 271-2224

The New Hampshire Fish and Game Department has four regional offices. Regional offices have conservation officers who can answer questions about a particular geographic area. We have indicated which regional office has jurisdiction over the tourism regions defined by our maps.

Region 1, 629-B Main St., Lancaster, (603) 788-3164, covers the Great North Woods region and the White Mountains region north of the White Mountain National Forest.

Region 2, P.O. Box 417, New Hampton, 03256, (no street address, write or call for information) (603) 744-5470, covers the southern portion of the White Mountains region, the Lakes region and the Dartmouth-Sunapee region.

Region 3, 225 Main Street, Durham, (603) 868-1095, covers the Seacoast region and the eastern portion of the Merrimack Valley region.

Region 4, 25 N.H. Rt. 9, Keene, (603) 352-9669, covers the Monadnock region and western portion of the Merrimack Valley region.

Fishing

Regulations

Whether you fly-fish or use more conventional tackle, be sure to read the *New Hampshire Freshwater Fishing Digest* published by the New Hampshire Fish and Game Department. The digest is essential reading for all anglers, whether you're planning a summer lake outing, a week of fall salmon fishing or a winter stint in an ice-fishing shack. Call (603) 271-3421 or (603) 271-3422 to order the digest, or pick one up when you buy your license. See our gray box in this chapter for information on the New Hampshire Fish and Game Department.

Fishing licenses are required for freshwater fishing, but you do not need a license for saltwater fishing. Freshwater licenses are required of all residents older than 15 and all nonresidents older than 11. Licenses must be carried on your person while fishing. Fishing licenses can be purchased from licensing agents, the Fish and Game main office in Concord and some town and city clerks. Licensing agents are usually found in local general stores and fishing and hunting supply stores (see the end of this chapter for information on fishing and hunting outfitters). The state has more than 450 licensing agents. Call the licensing information number, (603) 271-3421, for the names and addresses of local licensing agents.

Current annual license prices range from no cost for residents age 68 and older to $96 for a nonresident combination fishing and hunting license. An all-species fishing license is available for $23.25 for residents and $35.50 for nonresidents. Warm-water fishing licenses, which exclude trout, salmon and American shad, cost $17.75 for residents and $29.50 for nonresidents. A one-day family license is available for both residents and nonresidents for $25. Additionally, nonresidents can purchase three-day, seven-day and 15-day licenses at costs ranging from $18.50 to $27.50.

Now that the license is out of the way, it's time to discuss rules. Most lakes, ponds and rivers have specific restrictions about where to fish, what you can fish for and the kind of fishing allowed. Many ponds, for example, are fly-fishing only. The New Hampshire Freshwater Fishing Digest discusses all exceptions to the general rules under the listings for specific lakes, ponds and rivers. Rules also include appropriate seasons for species. Seasons rules apply to both open-water and ice fishing. Ice fishing isn't allowed on every pond and lake. Rules apply to the number of fish that can be caught each day as well as minimum weight and/or length for each species.

What You're Likely to Catch

The first New Hampshire settlers were fishermen who set up shop on the coastal islands. You can still find lots of saltwater recreational fishing in the Seacoast region, even though the commercial catches have shrunk due to overfishing the offshore waters. From Portsmouth and Rye, you can join a deep-sea charter boat adventure. Bluefish are found offshore, and in summer you might have a go at tuna. Inshore at the Seacoast, you'll be fishing for striped bass.

The salmon found in New Hampshire are landlocked salmon. Landlocked salmon season begins April 1. Early salmon fishing is best in lakes — Lake Francis, Winnipesaukee, Sunapee and Newfound to name a few — and on the Upper Connecticut River during the summer and fall. Salmon fishing in other rivers is possible in fall as the fish travel up the rivers that feed into lakes.

We've got lots of trout in New Hampshire. Lake trout are the frequent quest of ice fishers. You'll also find brook, rainbow and brown trout in most lakes, rivers and ponds. Trout like cold water so as the summer progresses and the water warms up, you'll need to stick with the cold-water habitats. The *New Hampshire Atlas and Gazetteer* has excellent charts regarding cold- and warm-water locations. Bass, both largemouth and smallmouth, are also abundant in the state. Smallmouth bass are more likely in the cold water of the northern part of the state (or southern locations with cold water), while largemouth bass are more likely in the warm-water lakes and ponds. Other warm-water species include pickerel, perch, horned pout and occasionally northern pike.

Where To Fish

Once you've read the *New Hampshire Freshwater Fishing Digest* and bought your license, you're ready to enjoy our beautiful lakes, ponds and streams. Below you'll find just a sampling of specific fishing areas in each region.

Merrimack Valley Region

The many rivers of this central valley are alive with fish, now that the pollution of two centuries of industrialization has begun to clear. The Merrimack River itself, 50 miles long and almost a half-mile wide where it passes through Manchester, tempts anglers with large- and smallmouth bass, crappies and perch, pickerel and bluegill as well as the ubiquitous horned pout and walleye. Fishing is not allowed from just above the dam at Amoskeag and for 500 feet below the dam. Please help with the restoration of Atlantic salmon by releasing any young salmon you catch as quickly and gently as possible. Fish and Game has pictures to help you distinguish between young salmon and brown trout, which are strikingly similar in appearance. Almost all the major rivers in the Merrimack watershed have been stocked with these once-common fish. With a special permit you can catch and keep brood salmon, which have been released into the Merrimack (these are the stock that provided the eggs for the young salmon in the restoration project).

INSIDERS' TIP

Please don't use lead sinkers when you fish. They get lost and fall to the bottom of lakes and ponds where they are likely to be swallowed by loons and ducks. Lead poisoning ensues, killing the waterfowl.

East of the Merrimack you'll find trout (and stocked Atlantic salmon) in the Suncook and the Soucook rivers. There is excellent fishing at Bear Brook State Park — both on Bear Brook and in Archery Pond. (Archery Pond is restricted to fly-fishing, with a two-per-day limit on brook trout.) West of Concord, the Contoocook River is great for smallmouth bass, but also offers largemouth bass, horned pout and pickerel. The Contoocook is part of the Hopkinton/Everett Flood Control Project and is surrounded by plenty of open space as it bends and winds along from Henniker toward the dam in Weare. West of Henniker restrictions apply in the mile up- and downstream of the paper mill dam. These details are all in the digest provided by Fish and Game and available wherever you get your fishing license.

You'll want to try the Souhegan River in Milford and Amherst, where you can find trout racing through rocky riverbeds and making lazy turns around sandbanks. The Piscataquog River winds down through Goffstown and is quite broad by the time it reaches Manchester; you'll find lots of trout and an occasional salmon along its branches. You'll find trout in the Nissitissit River and even the Nashua River, but be aware that no fishing is permitted for 200 feet below the Jackson Falls and Mine Falls dams as well as for 200 feet above Jackson Falls.

The Merrimack Valley's lakes and ponds offer good fishing too: A record largemouth bass was caught and released at Horseshoe Pond in Merrimack, and another impressive largemouth was pulled from Lake Potanipo in Brookline last summer. Baboosic Lake in Amherst is home to some sizable bass, but you have to fish from a boat to try for them. Pennichuck Pond in Hollis and Nashua is popular with anglers from the greater Nashua area, as is Witches Brook in Hollis. Massabesic Lake in Manchester and Auburn is a favorite spot with Insiders. You can fish from the shore or take a boat out on the 2,500-acre lake and try your luck with bass, perch, pickerel and horned pout as well as brown and rainbow trout. Out in Barnstead, Suncook Lake offers a variety of warm-water fish including bass and perch.

Seacoast Region

The Lamprey and Exeter rivers are popular with seacoast fishing fans. They're both great trout streams, and the Lamprey also boasts some keeper-size Atlantic salmon. Another great trout stream in this region is the Winnicut River in Greenland. Because the whole coastal plain is laced with streams, you can drop a line off a bridge on almost any back road in the region with at least a decent chance of catching something. Many seacoast campgrounds offer fishing as an activity for their guests (see our Camping chapter).

The Piscataqua River, Hampton River and Little Bay are all tidal, as are the Oyster River in Durham and Bellamy south of Dover. These waters offer a challenge for sportfishers along with some mighty stripers. (The striped bass is a conservation success story. Once feared on the road to extinction, these beautiful fish are thriving in New Hampshire's tidal waters.) Prime time for fishing, especially from bridges, is just when the tide is turning. Boat fishing on the rivers around Great Bay is another kettle of fish (you should excuse the expression), and Insiders recommend you get some lessons from an expert — probably the owner of the boat!

Freshwater ponds in the Seacoast region boast some great fishing too. Insiders tell us Lucas Pond in Northwood is one of the best right now, while Pawtuckaway Lake in Raymond and Powwow Pond in Kingston are perennial favorites. Expect to find bass, crappie, perch and pickerel along with horned pout in warmer waters and rainbows and brownies (trout) in cold water.

Deep-sea fishing is popular on the Seacoast. Several charter boats operate out of Rye and Hampton. (We've included some in the Outfitters section of this chapter.) Trips can be as short as two hours or as long as 12 hours, with cod and haddock, mackerel, bluefish and sometimes tuna on the line and whales, dolphins and sharks for entertainment. Closer to shore the take is likely to include striped bass, flounder and cusk.

In winter eel fishing is regaining popularity on the Lamprey and Swampscott rivers. One Insider speculates that chlorine in sew-

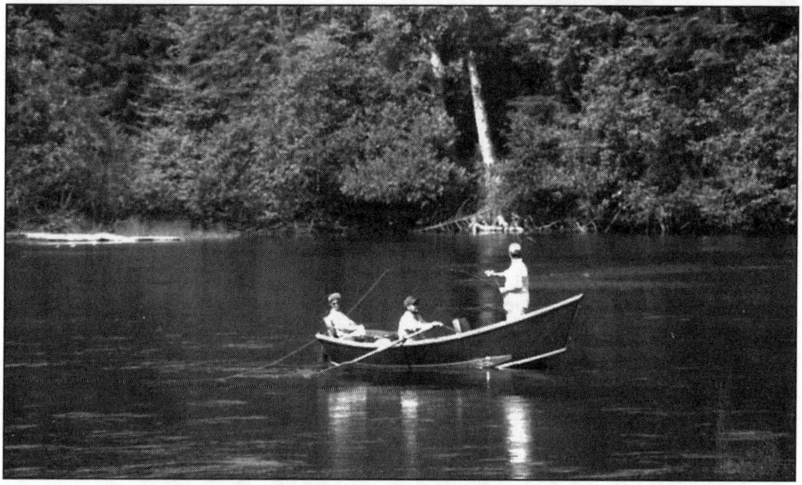
Photo: David A. Leach Photography

Spend a day searching for the "big one" on the Saco River.

age outflow may have been the cause of their decline in the '70s, and that now the new sewage treatment and stricter regulations are finally bearing fruit (or fish). Most eel fishing is done through the ice with a long (12- to 15-foot) spear.

Lakes Region

Not surprisingly, the Lakes Region is a terrific fishing mecca. With ice-fishing growing in popularity, fishing is now a year-round sport. But it's not all on the lakes. The Bearcamp River in Tamworth and Ossipee is popular for trout fishing and smelt. The Pemigiwasset River starts in the White Mountains but still has plenty of good fishing spots left between Plymouth and the Franklin Falls Dam. (See our Parks and Open Spaces chapter for the wonderful park created by the Dam Project area.) This southern part of the Pemi is one of the few places you can keep the Atlantic salmon you catch (but observe the restrictions on size and methods of catching them).

One of the richest watersheds for fishing in the state feeds the Merrymeeting River in Alton and Merrymeeting Lake in New Durham. Between them they shelter large- and smallmouth bass, pickerel and horned pout, landlocked salmon, and lake and rainbow trout. There are restrictions on fishing from the river right in the center of Alton but not farther downstream toward the marsh.

Both warm-water and cold-water fish can be found in our bigger lakes. Newfound and Big and Little Squam lakes to the west, Ossipee and Ayers in the east and Winnisquam and Winnipesaukee in the center of the region are all rich in trout, bass, pickerel and landlocked salmon. Trophy fish for both bluegill and chain pickerel are taken from Lake Winnipesaukee, and Insiders expect to find trophy-size landlocked salmon there in summer. Trout stocking on Newfound and Squam lakes over the last 10 years is paying off with fish in the 18- to 20-inch range. You might catch whitefish in these big lakes too. Insiders insist you'll catch bigger fish with bait than with flies. Several Lakes Region guides and boat captains are listed in the Outfitters section of this chapter.

White Mountains and Great North Woods Regions

The mountains provide lots of clean cold water, which is an ideal environment for trout. You'll find brook, rainbow and brown trout throughout the region. Beginning in the Great North Woods region, the fishing centers around the First, Second and Third Connecticut Lakes north of Pittsburg. Fish for salmon and lake trout in the First Connecticut Lake. The same goes for the Second Connecticut Lake with the addition of brook trout. The Third Connecticut Lake is best known for lake and rainbow trout. Lake Francis is good for rainbow trout, salmon and pickerel. Trout ponds are abundant throughout the Pittsburg area. For names and locations, refer to the books mentioned in the introduction of this chapter.

South of Pittsburg, in Columbia, try Fish Pond for brook and rainbow trout as well as largemouth bass. Simm's Stream is also in Columbia and a good place to fish for brook trout. So is Nathan Pond in Dixville.

East of Columbia and southeast of Dixville, the Androscoggin River begins about 30 miles south of the Canadian border at the outlets of the Magalloway River and Umbagog Lake. The best time to fish for landlocked salmon and brook, brown and rainbow trout is from ice-out — usually in April — to about mid-July. By mid-July the fish have retreated to the colder water in Umbagog Lake. Use the public boat launch on N.H. Route 16 above the dam at Errol for access to Umbagog Lake. Warm-water specialists can try their luck for pickerel and horned pout. Follow the Androscoggin River south to Dummer and Little and Big Dummer Ponds. Brook trout are present in both, and Little Dummer Pond also has brown trout. The Pemigewasset and the Saco rivers in the White Mountain National Forest have good brook trout fishing.

Dartmouth-Lake Sunapee Region

The region gets part of its name from Lake Sunapee so it's only appropriate that you try your luck there. You can fish for many New Hampshire species in Lake Sunapee, including smallmouth bass, pickerel, salmon and lake trout. The lake covers more than 4,000 acres. Not far from Lake Sunapee, in New London, you can fish both Little Sunapee Lake and Pleasant Lake. In spring, try Pleasant Lake for salmon and brook trout. You may also find smallmouth bass, pickerel and horned pout. The latter three fish are your most likely catches in Little Sunapee Lake.

For warm-water fishing only, try Goose Pond. It's just west of Hanover in Canaan and has both largemouth and smallmouth bass, white perch and pickerel. South of Goose Pond is Lake Mascoma in Enfield. Cold-water fish include rainbow and brook trout. Warm-water species include largemouth and smallmouth bass, white perch, pickerel and horned pout. The Mascoma River at the western end of the lake is a good spot for brook, brown and rainbow trout. Also in Enfield are Crystal Lake and George Pond for horned pout and pickerel.

Just on the border of the Dartmouth-Lake Sunapee Region and the Lakes Region are the Newfound River and Newfound Lake. You can try your hand at fly-fishing on the river — that's the only fishing allowed — and catch salmon, brook and rainbow trout. The lake also has salmon and rainbow trout as well as lake trout and the usual trio of smallmouth bass, pickerel and horned pout.

Monadnock Region

Beginning in the southwest corner of the region in Hinsdale, you'll want to try your luck on the Connecticut River. Depending on the time of year, you'll find everything from largemouth and smallmouth bass to salmon and brown and rainbow trout.

East of Hinsdale in Pisgah State Park, drop a line in the Pisgah Reservoir. You could catch smallmouth bass, bluegill and black crappie. Pickerel and horned pout could also end up on your hook. The most abundant fishing area in the region is just west of Peterborough

INSIDERS' TIP

Our waters are cold, especially in spring and fall. You'll be glad if you have a special pair of insulated socks under the boots of your waders.

around Hancock, Harrisville and Dublin. Besides being a beautiful spot to study Mount Monadnock, the 239-acre Dublin Lake is a haven for brook trout. Silver Lake in Harrisville is a favorite for rainbow and lake trout.

North of Harrisville in Nelson and Hancock is Nubanusit Lake, home of the state-record lake trout, which weighed in at 15 pounds. North of Nelson in Stoddard are Highland Lake and Island Pond. Highland Lake has smallmouth bass and brook and rainbow trout. Island Pond also has brook trout as well smallmouth bass, white perch and pickerel.

Another great place to fish is Spofford Lake. It's about 7 miles west of Keene in Chesterfield. The lake has more than 700 acres with largemouth and smallmouth bass, white perch, pickerel, northern pike and horned pout.

Hunting

Every year 90,000 hunters enjoy the rich game opportunities in New Hampshire. It is not always easy for nonhunters to understand the joy others find in this recreational sport, but in New Hampshire we do our best to share our land with care. Mutual responsibility is important in keeping open land safe for hunters and nonhunters. In the last decade there have been no nonhunter fatalities in the state. Most accidents involve hunters hurting or killing other hunters or themselves.

One reason we need to share with care is that all land is considered open unless posted or unless the user has been notified that his or her presence is not allowed. You may hunt on private land that is not otherwise posted or restricted according to New Hampshire law. One restriction, regardless of posting, is that it is illegal to shoot a firearm or bow and arrow within 300 feet of a permanently occupied dwelling without permission of the owner or occupant. Neither can a firearm be discharged within 300 feet of any commercial, educational or medical building or outdoor public gathering place. On the other hand, most public lands, including the White Mountain National Forest, are open for hunting. Hunters should stay away from campgrounds and open areas, but the burden of care is on both the hunter and nonhunter. Beginning in early September, anyone enjoying the forests or woods should wear bright orange or red clothing, especially hats and jackets since the top half of you is most visible. Bear season begins the first week of September, and some types of deer may be hunted through late November. Other species such as fox can be hunted through March.

General Information

Those interested in hunting and trapping need to order the New Hampshire Hunting and Trapping Digest published by the New Hampshire Fish and Game Department. The pamphlet gives details on licenses for residents and nonresidents, hunting and trapping seasons, weapons restrictions, educational requirements and geographic restrictions. See our gray box in this chapter for information on contacting the New Hampshire Fish and Game Department.

New Hampshire requires all first-time hunters, bowhunters and trappers to complete an education course before receiving a license. The maximum charge for the course is $2. Contact the Fish and Game main office in Concord to find out the next scheduled class in your area. Experienced hunters, bowhunters and trappers with proof of a previous license are excused from this requirement. The hunter-safety course includes 16 hours of instruction on the safe use of firearms, hunting ethics, compass skills, outdoor safety and wildlife identification. The bowhunting course consists of 10 hours of specific bowhunting instruction including methods, equipment and ethics. First-time trappers receive 12 hours of instruction on responsible trapping techniques including appropriate trap selection and trapping techniques.

Many types of hunting and trapping licenses are available for residents and nonresidents. Be sure to read the *New Hampshire Hunting and Trapping Digest* before planning your expedition. We'll give a few rules and prices here, but the digest is essential reading for any hunter or trapper. Anyone hunting bear and turkey must have a license regardless of age. A bear license is $3, and a turkey license is $6 for residents and nonresidents. A resident hunting license is $15.50 and a nonresident hunting license is $70.50. Additional fees are charged for special weapons such as muzzleloaders and special game such as pheasant. Prices and requirements are subject to change.

Beginning in 1998, anyone hunting migratory game birds must have a Migratory Bird Harvest Information Program (H.I.P.) permit. These permits are free and are attached to your hunting license if you intend to hunt migratory game birds. Migratory game birds include all ducks and geese, snipe, coots and woodcocks. The purpose of the permit is to help Fish and Game staff survey hunters regarding the impact of hunting on these birds.

If you want to hunt for moose, you must enter the lottery for a moose permit. All hunting license agents have lottery applications and information sheets by the end of January. Completed moose applications are mailed to Fish and Game headquarters in Concord and must be postmarked before the last Friday in May. The lottery is held in June, and successful applicants are notified by mail. Moose season is one week in late October.

Where to Hunt

The New Hampshire Fish and Game Department administers nearly 29,000 acres of wildlife management areas and conservation easements, which are also open to the public for hunting. Below you'll find brief descriptions of some of these areas in each region. The term big game refers to black bear, deer, moose and wild turkey. Small game are gray squirrel, hare and rabbit. Game birds are partridge, pheasant, quail, wild ducks, wild geese and woodcock. Furbearing animals are beaver, bobcat, coyote, fox, mink, muskrat, otter, raccoon and skunk. The abbreviation WMA stands for Wildlife Management Area.

Merrimack Valley Region

There's a surprising amount of hunting available even in this most urbanized portion of our state. If you look at a map, you'll notice a lot of open area east of Concord. In the vicinity of Saddleback Mountain in Northwood and Deerfield, the Forest Peters, Woodman Marsh and Lamontagne Wildlife Management Areas are close to each other. Forest Peters is rich in furbearing animals, and you might find bear or moose in these woods as well. Lamontagne is not the biggest area, at less than 350 acres, but it offers one the widest varieties of animals, with everything from bear and moose to skunks and otter. The bird selection is a little limited here, with only turkeys, partridges, ducks and woodcock in any quantity. Waterfowl hunters are better off at Woodman Marsh, less than a mile away.

West of the capital, Perkins Pond in Weare is a favorite with Insider hunters. The mixture of mountains and marshland give this 300-acre area a variety of wildlife worthy of a much bigger site. Bear and moose share the woods with deer, and you may find mink along with foxes and raccoons. Bird hunters will be happy with the geese, ducks and woodcock. Coyotes are everywhere, and farmers will be more than happy to have you wear one home. Because of their rapidly increasing population, there is no closed season on coyotes.

The Milford Fish Hatchery grounds are a rich wildlife area. You won't find moose or bear in this floodplain, but it's a favorite in bird season and one of the few locations recommended for quail and pheasant. All the furbearers are possible finds in this area too, including the elusive bobcat. This land is surrounded by residential neighborhoods and farms, but not thickly wooded, so it shouldn't be hard to be sure where you are.

You might not expect to find any hunting in the Route 3 corridor, but at Dumpling Brook in Merrimack, hunters bring home deer and moose, all kinds of small game and a large selection of furbearers including bobcat, beaver and mink from within sight of the turnpike.

Seacoast Region

There's no hunting right along the ocean, but, as you might expect, the Great Bay area is a bird-hunter's paradise. Hunters can find otters, mink, beaver and raccoons in this marshy landscape. Just upstream of the estuary, the Bellamy River Wildlife Management Area in Dover is a popular destination, with small game including partridge and quail along with waterfowl and furbearers.

The Demise of the Wild Atlantic Salmon

At one time, all of New Hampshire's rivers with an outlet or connection to the Atlantic Ocean — the Merrimack, Androscoggin, Connecticut, Saco and Souhegan, for example—were fertile with wild Atlantic salmon. The fish used to swim from the northern Atlantic Ocean into New Hampshire's rivers to spawn.

The Industrial Revolution was the beginning of the end for the once-abundant wild Atlantic salmon. During the late 18th and early 19th century, dams built to control water flow for energy use blocked the returning salmon from getting to their spawning grounds. In less than 10 years, rivers that were dammed lost their native salmon population.

Valiant restocking efforts in the Merrimack River by U.S. Fish and Wildlife, with the cooperation of New Hampshire Fish and Game and dedicated volunteer organizations such as Trout Unlimited and the Atlantic Salmon Federation, were in full swing by the 1970s.

To understand the difficulty of the task, we must include a too brief discussion of the stages of development for the Atlantic salmon. (While the natural development process is nearly absent from New Hampshire rivers, the full cycle still occurs in undammed rivers in Maine and parts of eastern Canada.) The newly hatched egg is called an alevin. Once the egg sac is gone and the new life begins swimming, it is a fry. Once the fry becomes 2 or 3 inches long, it is called a parr. Parr live in the river for two years, becoming about 10 inches long. After two years in the river, the parr turn silver and are ready to head out into the ocean and are called smolt. A fish that returns to the river after one ocean winter is called a grilse, but those that stay two years at sea are called salmon.

Photo: Tom McMillan

Anglers no longer catch wild Atlantic salmon in New Hampshire's rivers.

Back to restocking. Early efforts involved the 10-inch-long smolt. Eggs were laid and fertilized in the hatchery, and the young were nurtured for two years until they became smolt. These fish were released into the river just in time to head out into the Atlantic Ocean. Unfortunately, these hatchery-raised fish lacked survival smarts and were quickly devoured by predators (bluefish and striped bass, for example). Restocking efforts now concentrate on the very small fry (now you know where "small fry" comes from!). Larger numbers of fry are released into the river, and the subsequent parr have two years in the river to develop into smolt before heading into the ocean.

Despite the restocking efforts, the New Hampshire wild Atlantic salmon population is minimal at best. Anglers wishing to try their luck at catching Atlantic salmon in the Merrimack River will want to plan for the annual April release of hatchery brood stock

— continued on next page

below Sewall's Falls Dam in Concord and Franklin Dam in Franklin. A special salmon stamp is required for your New Hampshire fishing license and can be obtained when you purchase your license. Contact the New Hampshire Fish and Game Department, 2 Hazen Drive, Concord, (603) 271-3421, for more information on the release.

Farther inland, the Sargent Wildlife Management areas in Newton and Webster Wildlife and Natural Area and Bakie Conservation Easements in Kingston are easily reached and offer plenty of deer, virtually all the waterfowl and furbearing animals. (See our Parks and Open Spaces chapter for more on the Webster property.) Hunting is permitted on all Society for Protection of New Hampshire Forest lands. Do observe hunting courtesy in residential areas!

Lakes Region

Hunting in the Lakes region is rich. The Merrymeeting Wildlife Management Area in Alton and New Durham is home to black bear and wild turkey, bobcat and geese. You'll find all the furbearing animals here too. Also in New Durham, the Powder Mill Fish Hatchery grounds are a great place to hunt for waterfowl and otter as well as other small furbearers. You might even find your bear here. Up in the Moose Mountains of Brookfield the Jones Brook Wildlife Management Area is one of the state's largest at almost 1,500 acres. Moose, bear, deer, fox, mink and muskrat are among what you'll find there.

Over in Gilmanton and Gilford, just 6 miles as the crow flies from the arcades of Weirs Beach, is Hidden Valley Conservation Easement, one of the largest tracts of open hunting territory in the state. On more than 3,000 acres in the Belknap mountains, hunters track bear, deer, moose and bobcat and try their luck on all the smaller prey as well.

Two conservation easements in Loudon, Bergeron and Osborne, offer a rich hunting experience in a much smaller area. Here you'll find turkey, pheasant, partridge, geese, ducks, bobcat, bear, beaver and mink. Lots of deer and rabbits mean lots of coyotes too.

After several years of controversy, Fish and Game has begun a controlled hunt to manage the deer on Long Island in Moultonborough. Isolated from predators, the deer population there has ballooned and now suffers from lack of habitat and winter food. Another favorite place to hunt along the big lake is Kona Wildlife Management Area on Moultonborough Neck. This parcel shelters bear and moose as well as the ducks and woodcock you'd expect at a lake. All the small animals are plentiful here too.

White Mountains and Great North Woods Regions

The Great North Woods has miles of wilderness, which makes Pittsburg the unofficial headquarters of the New Hampshire hunting scene. Gray WMA (206 acres) and Brown WMA (803 acres) are both in Pittsburg. Both areas have black bear, deer and moose as well as some species in each of the other categories.

Lime Pond is a 354-acre conservation easement in Columbia with a wide variety of hunting possibilities. All species of big game and furbearing animals are present as well as woodcock, wild duck and partridge. Less than 3 miles from the Maine border on the Androscoggin River east of Gorham is Millbrook Trust, a 279-acre conservation easement. The area has black bear, moose and deer along with partridge and woodcock. Otter, raccoon and coyote are also present.

On the Connecticut River near Stratford is Fort Hill WMA. The 611 acres have moose, deer, black bear, hare, wild turkey, many of the game birds and all the furbearing animals except bobcat. Also on the Connecticut River is the 81-acre Bedell Bridge conservation easement area. Deer, moose and wild turkey are here along with all the small game except rabbit. Wild duck, wild geese and woodcock represent the game birds, and all the furbearing animals with the exception of bobcat are present.

Dartmouth-Lake Sunapee Region

East of Lyme and Hanover in Dorchester, you'll find the adjacent WMA lands of Cummins Pond and Mascoma River for a total of 2,650 acres. The only animals not listed for at least one of these areas are rabbit, pheasant and quail. The Grafton Turnpike running east out of Lime is the best route for getting there.

Farther south and just east of Lebanon is Enfield WMA in Enfield. Here you'll find more than 4,400 acres for hunting everything but rabbit, quail and pheasant. Exit 14 off Interstate 89 is on the southwestern portion of this WMA. Near Exit 11 of I-89 is Chadwick Meadows Marsh WMA. The 100-acre area is just off N.H. Route 114 south of New London in North Sutton. All of the big game except wild turkey are represented along with wild duck, wild geese and woodcock. The only exception in the furbearing animal category is bobcat.

Less than 6 miles east of Chadwick Meadows is the 1,000-acre Kearsarge WMA. All the furbearing animals (including bobcat) are here as well as deer, black bear and wild turkey. And you'll have a chance with all the small game and game birds excepting rabbit, quail and pheasant.

Monadnock Region

In Hancock, you'll find both Carpenters Marsh WMA, with 290 acres, and Evas Marsh, with 106 acres. In the first you'll find all the listed species except rabbit, pheasant, quail and bobcat. The same goes for Evas WMA with the added exceptions of black bear and wild turkey. East of Hancock in Greenfield is Powder Mill Pond WMA. Big-game species are deer and moose. All of the small-game species are included, and all the game birds except pheasant and quail are found in the 127 acres. Furbearing animals in the area include fox, mink and muskrat.

To the southeast, in Lyndeborough just west of Mont Vernon, is the Piscataquog WMA. The 129 acres include the usual suspects and exceptions — that is to say, no black bear, rabbit, pheasant, quail or bobcat.

Hunting and Fishing Outfitters

Merrimack Valley Region

Silver Arrow Archery
106 Fordway Ext., Derry • (603) 434-0569

Silver Arrow specializes in supplies for the traditional and primitive archer. It offers longbows, custom-made bows and a large variety of arrows and can custom-make appropriate accessories to fit your needs. Silver Arrow's selection is sold nationwide through its mail-order catalog.

Riley's Sport Shop Inc.
1575 Hooksett Rd., Hooksett • (603) 485-5000

Riley's claims to have the largest selection of firearms in New England, and we don't doubt it. Whether you're a beginner or an experienced hunter, this shop will have what you need, and the staff will teach you how to use it properly. Won the moose lottery and need a bigger gun? Riley's has lots of used and refurbished firearms in all sizes.

Steve's Sportsmen's Den
1562 Hooksett Rd., Hooksett • (603) 485-5085

There are plenty of gun dealers along the strip in Hooksett. We like Steve's because it's

INSIDERS' TIP

If you hit and kill a deer with your car, it's yours unless you refuse it. One of the rites of spring in New Hampshire is the annual Fish and Game Road Kill Auction, when taxidermists and others bid on the frozen remains of deer, raccoon, moose and bear turned down or left behind by drivers.

a real outfitting operation, with equipment for fly-fishing, angling, archery, hunting and trapping. This includes clothing, boots, snowshoes, topo maps and lots of good advice.

Wildlife Taxidermy & Sports Center

2188 Candia Rd., Manchester
• (603) 625-9958

Talk about a full-service operation! These folks can outfit you, instruct you (there's even an indoor archery range) and then preserve your prize fish or fur for proud display. They sell Nature Bound canoes, which are built right here in New Hampshire.

Hunter's Angling Supplies Inc.

Central Sq., New Boston • (603) 487-3388

Visitors' heads turn as they drive through New Boston Village. Why are those people fishing in the parking lot? Well, actually they're testing their new reels and rods. Insiders drive from all over the southern part of the state to shop and swap tales and advice at Hunter's. The store stocks everything fishing-folk need.

Weare Center Store

1437 Gen. John Stark Hwy. S., Weare
• (603) 529-9997

Need hunting equipment? This store has it — ammo, animal calls, camo clothing, tree steps and stands, you name it. It has supplies for muzzleloaders as well as shotguns and rifles. Oh, you meant archery? Bows and hangers, arrows and arrow pullers, quivers and cables, right this way. Don't forget to buy your license and all the stamps you need. Thinking of fishing instead? Fishing tackle, bait, decoys and packs are over there. Need ice-fishing equipment? Of course it's here. Would you like to buy a snack or maybe pick up some grinders (New Hampshire for submarine sandwiches) and coffee at the deli? Weare Center Store also offers camping supplies and plain old-fashioned advice.

Seacoast Region

Hampton Harbor Tackle

1 Ocean Blvd., Hampton Beach
• (603) 926-1945

For saltwater fishing you need different bait and heavy-duty equipment. Hampton Harbor, on the state pier, has everything you need for an introduction or a marathon trip. It's open from April to September with live bait, fishing tackle, fuel and information.

Fox Ridge Outfitters

400 N. Main St., Rochester
• (603) 335-2999, (800) 243-4570

Fox Ridge supplies everything you could need for fly-fishing or angling (including fly-tying workshops on Thursday nights). It also has a large selection of firearms, hunting accessories, boots and clothing. Let the staff set you up before you set out on your trek in search of game.

Big Al's Gun & Sport Shop

U.S. Rt. 1, Seabrook
• (603) 474-9043

Big Al's sells everything you need for hunting and fishing, including all the variations on licenses. Archery equipment, fishing tackle and hunting accessories are all here. Big Al's buys and sells antique guns as well as a large selection of hunting arms.

Taylor's Trading Post

248 Littleworth Rd., Dover
• (603) 742-5931

Taylor's has bait and fly supplies for saltwater fishing, lures for trout and bass and whatever else you need. Its Hunter's Corner has supplies for archery, riflery and muzzleloading. Taylor's can sell you a license or register your boat too.

INSIDERS' TIP

Public health officials advise eating no more than four freshwater fish meals per month to limit exposure to mercury, a toxic pollutant concentrated in the bodies of fish. Young children and women of childbearing age should eat freshwater fish just once a month.

Deep-Sea Fishing

Al Gauron Fisheries Inc.
State Pier, Hampton Beach
• (603) 926-2469, (800) 905-7820

This is a big operation with four boats, a three-season schedule of two-hour, half-day and full-day cruises, and all the supplies you'll need for a great fishing experience. There's free parking and you can leave your car there if you want to walk to the Hampton Beach attractions after your cruise.

Smith & Gilmore Fishing Pier
3-A Ocean Blvd., Hampton
• (603) 926-3503

With three busy boats, Smith & Gilmore offers day- or night-fishing trips for all tastes. You can go for the whole day for $35 ($12 for children younger than 12 and $25 for those older than 64), or go for the morning or afternoon for $20 (kids pay $12; seniors, $17). If you just want to try it, they also do two-hour trips for $12, $8 for children. If you don't have a deep-sea rod, you can rent them for $2 to $4. Smith & Gilmore also does Wednesday night fireworks cruises and whale watches every afternoon. On shore they have a restaurant and a Lobster Pound as well as a bait and tackle shop. Boats go out from April through October.

Eastman's Fishing and Marine
River Rd., Seabrook • (603) 474-3461

With six boats running daily from April through November, Eastman's offers both charter and walk-on fishing trips as well as whale watches and fireworks cruises. You can choose a morning, an afternoon or a full day of fishing at sea. On land, Eastman's has a tackle and bait shop and restaurant.

Lakes Region

High Point Upland Hunting Preserve and Gun Dog Training Center
N.H. Rt. 28 S., Alton • (603) 875-3552

In the game-rich Merrymeeting Marsh area, this preserve invites hunters to bring their dogs for four- and six-week training programs in the field with real quail, pheasant, chukar and huns. Both dog and hunter will be better prepared for the hunt after working together with these experts.

Skip's Gun Shop
16 Pleasant St., Bristol • (603) 744-3100

Skip's sells and repairs guns and handles both fishing and hunting licenses. Gunsmithing is done right on the premises for quality and quick turnaround.

Capt. Joe Nassar
U.S. Rt. 3, Holderness
• (603) 968-7577

When he's not cruising tourists around on the Squam Lakes Tour (see our Attractions chapter), Captain Joe loves to take fishing fans out for a half- or full-day excursion on the lake. He provides the tackle and the expertise, snaps your picture with your prize trout or landlocked salmon and will even clean your fish for you!

Martel's Bait & Sport Shop
49 Winnisquam Ave., Laconia
• (603) 524-2431

Martel's sells a complete line of new and used equipment for hunting and fishing, from licenses to guns and rods to bait. The staff is always ready to explain and give advice too.

Conway's Bait & Tackle
N.H. Rt. 25, Moultonborough
• (603) 253-6491

In a region full of fishing suppliers, this is the place most Insiders mention first. Conway's sells bait and tackle of all kinds along with supplies. It also sells registration for your boat and licenses for you. No boat? The store will rent you a rowboat, paddleboat or canoe by the hour, day or week, and Conway's sits right on Lake Kanasatka so you can take off from the parking lot. The only thing it doesn't sell is advice — the staff gives away lots of it.

Paugus Bay Sporting Goods
Weirs Blvd., Laconia
• (603) 524-4319

Paugus Bay sells every conceivable fishing lure along with live bait, tackle and licenses. It prides itself on giving up-to-the-minute tips on where the fish are biting. It also sells archery equipment.

Gadabout Golder Guide Service
79 Middleton Rd., Wolfeboro
• (603) 569-6426

This guide service is based at Lake Winnipesaukee but also leads trips throughout New Hampshire. Owner "Gadabout" Golder is a certified fishing instructor and licensed New Hampshire guide. He offers lessons in fly-casting, guides wading trips for anglers and fly-fishers and runs fishing cruises. A half-day on Lake Winnipesaukee costs $175 to $230 (depending on the number in your party), a full-day runs $225 to $300. The addition of ice-fishing makes this a nearly year-round operation.

White Mountains and Great North Woods Regions

Dad's Tackle Box
Main St., Berlin
• (603) 752-4400

Whether you're an ice-fisher, fly-fisher or a worm-and-hook fisher, Dad's can supply whatever you need. The store carries live bait as well as fly-tying materials. During hunting season in October and November, you can get ammunition and camouflage hunting outfits. It's open every day except for Sundays in summer.

Corey's Sports Shop
35 Meadow St., Littleton
• (603) 444-6261, (800) 888-7228

Corey's has a great selection of new canoes. You'll find everything you need for hunting and fishing, including licenses. Besides canoes the shop sells binoculars, fly-fishing gear and conventional tackle. If you see an angler with a secret weapon and need to find one for yourself, give Corey's a call. If the shop doesn't have it, the staff will find it. It also carries a full line of archery equipment. The store is open every day all year.

Hunter's North Country Angler
N. Main St., North Conway
• (603) 356-6000

You'll find everything you need to fly-fish at Hunter's. The store carries a full line of rods, reels, flies and fly-tying supplies. You can pick up a pair of waders or a new vest. It's open every day from 9 AM to 5 PM, but is closed on Mondays in what they describe as the dead of winter and we translate as January, February and early March. Hunter's also has a branch in New Boston (see our Merrimack Valley section).

Dartmouth- Lake Sunapee Region

The Lyme Angler
8 S. Main St., Hanover
• (603) 643-1263

You can get both hunting and fishing supplies and licenses at the Lyme Angler. It's the only full-line Orvis dealer in New Hampshire, and it carries a full line of outdoor clothing for men and women. Last time we were in town, it was advertising a free spey rod class for interested fly-fishers. The Lyme Angler will book fishing guides for individuals and small groups.

Dickie's Outdoor Sports and Power Equipment
94 N.H. Rt. 103, Newbury
• (603) 938-5393

If you're fishing or hunting in the Lake Sunapee area, you'll want to check out Dickie's. It has been in business for 47 years and sells everything you'll need for your outdoor adventure. Hunting and fishing licenses, fly-fishing gear, conventional tackle as well

INSIDERS' TIP

In New Hampshire it is illegal to carry a firearm on an off-highway recreational vehicle.

as hunting supplies, including ammunition and archery equipment, are available. Dickie's is open every day all year.

Monadnock Region

Morse Sporting Goods

85 Contoocook Falls Rd., Hillsboro
• (603) 464-3444

At Morse you can get everything from your hunting or fishing license to the equipment needed to exercise that license. Morse has it all including fly-fishing and archery gear, live bait and outdoor clothing. Whether you're after bears or brookies, this is a place to get started in style. Morse Sporting Goods is open every day all year.

The Family Barber Bait and Tackle Shop

293 E. Main St., Marlborough
• (603) 876-4518

This is small-town living at its best. Get your hair cut at the same time you get your fishing license or register your boat. This shop carries mostly conventional tackle, but it does have a few flies and fly-rods. It does not carry hunting supplies. The shop has a full line of ice-fishing equipment. It's open every day but Wednesday except in winter, when the store is open every day.

With so many lakes and rivers, there's scenery and action to suit everyone in every region.

In, On and Around the Water

Summers here are short, but they're hot and sunny while they last. Fortunately our delightful bit of seashore, our 1,300 lakes and our miles of sparkling rivers are there to offer a cooling splash. Whether you want to catch some surf, go for a swim, spread your sails or shoot the rapids, you'll find a place in New Hampshire to suit your desire.

Boating and paddling are very popular watersports in this state. With so many lakes and rivers, there's scenery and action to suit everyone in every region. You can sail and motor in our lakes, canoe and kayak on our rivers. If you'd rather just ride, check out our Attractions chapter for cruises on the lakes or off the coast.

Although our surf isn't high by California standards, surfers and sea kayakers can be seen all along the shore in spring and fall when the waves are at their best. Rubber suits are recommended for either activity: The ocean off New Hampshire's beaches tends to run between 50 and 60 degrees all summer. We also attract a few sailboarders whose brightly colored wings echo the kites tethered to those who watch from the sand.

Another colorful watersport that's becoming popular here is parasailing. This sport, a sort of combination of water-skiing and hang-gliding, involves being towed behind a boat while attached to a parachute. As you pick up speed, the wind picks you up. Essentially you become a human kite. Obviously it's important that the boat operator knows exactly what he or she is doing and knows the water and the air above it well. Although some outfitters will rent parasailing equipment, we don't recommend you try this on your own. See our Outfitters section at the end of this chapter for a few recommendations on who to try.

In this chapter, we give you information on some great places to swim, boat, canoe and kayak. Because bodies of water typically cross town lines, we've arranged the Lakes and Rivers sections of this chapter alphabetically by the names of the bodies of water within each region.

Swimming

If you're looking for a nice sandy beach for a pleasant day of swimming, New Hampshire has plenty for you to choose from. In this chapter we've described the great beaches at our many state parks. In addition, many towns maintain pools or small beaches on lakes or ponds. Often residents pay a flat fee to use the beaches for the whole summer, but nonresidents can pay to use the beach for a single visit. Nonresident admission usually costs about $2. We haven't included town beaches here because they're generally small and hard to find. You can call the Recreation Department in town to see if there is a local swimming area open to the public.

Many local swimming holes are posted "No swimming" or "Swim at your own risk" only because there are no lifeguards there. But some tempting locations that attract swimmers are definitely too dangerous to attempt. Never swim in the pool below a dam, where eddies may be strong and sudden releases of water may be unpredictable. And never, ever swim in the many granite quarries around our state. Nearly every summer someone dies in our quarries, generally from diving. Quarry waters are crystalline and cold, and thrill-seekers love to jump from the sheer cliffs left by blasting. But the bottoms of quarries are littered with chunks of granite, which can shift position, and rescue efforts are hampered by the very rock-faces that make the dive so appealing. In a word, *don't*.

Most of the ocean shore is open to the public at either state or town parks. (Although the intertidal beach is technically public property, it is courteous to respect the few stretches of privately owned shoreline.) The beach varies from rocky at the north end (Rye) to silky white sand at Hampton and gets coarser again as you continue south. Alcohol and pets are not allowed on the beach (prohibitions you will see violated regularly). Hours vary as you go from towns to state management areas, but all the beaches are open from at least midmorning to dusk. (Hampton Central is open until 2 AM.)

We have mentioned many state parks in the following sections. Admission fees are the same for all New Hampshire state parks: $2.50 for everyone older than 12 and free for those 12. and younger. New Hampshire senior citizens who are 64 or older also get in free.

Beaches

Merrimack Valley Region

Bear Brook State Park

157 Deerfield Rd., Allenstown • (603) 485-9874

This huge state park has visitor facilities including a sandy swimming beach with lifeguards, a bathhouse and restrooms, canoe rentals, a boat launch, a store and a fishing area all on Catamount Pond. There are also large pavilions and picnic areas in a wooded section of the park. Some parts of the park are handicapped-accessible. (The campground at Bear Brook described in our Camping chapter is on Beaver Pond and has a swimming area open only for those camping in the park.)

Silver Lake State Park

N.H. Rt. 122, Hollis • (603) 465-2342

This park offers swimming on a 1,000-foot sandy beach, with lifeguards and a bathhouse with restrooms. Enjoy picnicking, volleyball and plenty of room to spread out, but proximity to Nashua and Massachusetts guarantees that this state park will be full on any summer weekend. Parking is across the street — take advantage of Hollis' special-duty traffic officers, as N.H. 122 is a busy thoroughfare.

Pawtuckaway State Park

N.H. Rt. 156, Nottingham and Raymond • (603) 895-3031

This very popular park offers a 700-foot sandy beach on Pawtuckaway Lake, with a bathhouse, restrooms and lifeguards on duty. There is a picnic area near the beach, and hiking trails wind throughout the park. Canoe rentals and a boat launch are also available. See our Camping chapter for information on the large campground within the park.

Clough State Park

Clough Park Rd., Weare • (603) 529-7112

This park (pronounced "cluff") sits in a hollow at the bottom of the Everett Flood Control Dam project. The pond is generally about 140 acres across, and the beach is 900-feet long, sandy and pleasant. The surrounding area is wooded and offers great picnicking, and you'll never guess you're so close to Manchester and Concord (less than 10 miles from either as the crow flies). There is a bathhouse with restrooms, and lifeguards are on

INSIDERS' TIP

There are two Echo Lakes in the White Mountains, a fact which used to drive us crazy when we were kids. The one in Franconia Notch State Park has a campground and boat launch as well as a beach. Echo Lake State Park, west of North Conway, has only swimming.

duty. Fishing is allowed. (When there is serious flooding in the spring, the park looks awful, as if some insect had munched through the forest, but it recovers fairly quickly and the swimming isn't impacted.)

Seacoast Region

Hampton Beach

Ocean Blvd., Hampton • (603) 926-8717

Arcades and vendors, fireworks and playgrounds, sand and surf — Hampton Beach has it all. (See our Attractions chapter.) It also has crowds — nearly a quarter-million visitors on a hot summer weekend! The state provides lifeguards, restrooms, a first-aid station and a boat launch. The Chamber of Commerce and area businesses provide entertainment and food.

There are actually three beaches in the stretch we all call Hampton Beach: Hampton State Beach, Hampton Central State Beach and North Beach. Hampton State Beach is at Hampton Beach State Park, where the RV campground is. It costs $5 a car to park here on weekdays, $8 on weekends and holidays. Hampton Central is where all the arcades and the Sea Shell amphitheater are. Parking here is metered ($1 per hour with an eight-hour maximum) and limited. There are many parking lots a block back from the beach though, with an average charge of $5 to $10 per day. Continue up to North Beach, and you'll generally find much smaller crowds, open spaces and a quieter beach experience. North Beach is narrow, though. Sometimes at high tide the water comes right to the sea wall. North Beach is divided into North Side Park, Bicentennial Park and North Hampton Beach, which are all town-maintained, and North Beach State Park. All these have metered parking at $1 per hour. North Hampton and North Beach State Park have restrooms and lifeguards.

Kingston State Park

N.H. Rt. 125, Kingston • (603) 642-5471

This 44-acre park on the shore of Great Pond offers freshwater swimming in the Seacoast region. You'll find a sandy beach and a grassy area for sunbathing. The park has lifeguards and two bathhouses with restrooms. There is also a picnic area. The park is open from 9 AM to 7 PM every day in summer.

New Castle Beach

Wentworth Rd., New Castle • (603) 436-1992

This town beach has a playground and picnic area with grills as well as nice sand and a boat launch. The view across the harbor is lovely, and you are miles from the crowds and chaos. There is a charge of $2.50 for adults. Children up to age 16 and seniors older than 64 get in free.

Rye Beach

Ocean Blvd., Rye • (603) 926-8717

North of Little Boars Head and Fox Hill Point, the beach turns pebbly with intermittent stretches of sand. The Rye section includes (from south to north) Bass Beach, Rye Beach and Jenness Beach State Park. The beach is broken by Ragged Neck and Rye Harbor, where there are state parks but not great swimming. North of Rye Harbor the beach begins again, with Foss Beach and Rye North Beach, Wallis Sands and Wallis Sands State Park. Parking is free at the town beaches and metered at the state parks ($1 per hour) except at Wallis Sands State Park, where it costs $5 per car during the week and $8 on weekends and holidays.

Seabrook Beach

Ocean Dr., Seabrook • (603) 926-8717

This is a quiet, pebbly beach separated from the highway and the local houses by a strip of sand dunes. There are no bathrooms or other facilities and no parking except for handicapped spaces. There is parking a short walk away from the beach on N.H. Route 1-A.

Lakes Region

Wellington State Park

off N.H. Rt. 3-A, Bristol • (603) 744-2197

A half-mile of sandy beach on pristine Newfound Lake offers some of the state's nicest swimming. Lifeguards are on duty. Bathhouses, restrooms and a store are all available, and there is a picnic area in a pine grove along with some nice hiking trails. Wellington also provides a boat launch. The park is open 9 AM to 7 PM every day during the summer.

Ellacoya State Park

N.H. Rt. 11, Gilford • (603) 293-7821

This state park offers 600 feet of sandy beach on the state's largest lake, Winnipesaukee. It has a picnicking area and a bathhouse with restrooms, and lifeguards are on duty. The campground is only for RVs (see our Camping chapter). The park is open from 9 AM to 7 PM throughout the summer.

White Lake State Park

N.H. Rt. 16, Tamworth • (603) 323-7350

In addition to camping and hiking, this park offers a nice sandy beach with lifeguards, a bathhouse and restrooms. There is a picnic area, and canoe rentals are available. Standard state park admissions apply.

Wentworth State Park

N.H. Rt. 109, Wolfeboro • (603) 569-3699

This small park offers very nice swimming, with a gradual drop-off that lets even little kids walk "way out." The beach is mostly sandy, with picnic tables on the grass close enough to watch the kids from. Lifeguards and a bathhouse with restrooms are provided.

White Mountains and Great North Woods Regions

Echo Lake

Franconia Notch State Park, I-93, Franconia • (603) 823-5563

You can swim in the 28-acre Echo Lake and enjoy the long, wide beach area seven days a week from 10 AM until 6 PM. You can bring a picnic or grab a bite at the snack bar. The bathhouse is a convenient place to change out of your wet bathing suit. The park opens at 10 AM and closes at 6 PM. The season begins in mid-June and runs through Labor Day.

Echo Lake State Park

River Rd., west of N.H. Rt. 16, Bartlett and Conway • (603) 356-2672

You won't find a prettier place to swim than Echo Lake. Please note that this Echo Lake is separate from the one of the same name in Franconia Notch State Park. The beachfront on the lake is just right whether you have a toddler who loves to dig or a teen who is perfecting a tan. Bring binoculars and watch the hard-working rock climbers on White Horse and Cathedral Ledges while you relax. Bring your own food if you want to picnic. Amenities include a vending machine for soft drinks and a bathhouse for changing clothes. The park is open from 9 AM to 8 PM from mid-June through Labor Day.

Forest Lake State Beach

Forest Lake Rd., off N.H. Rt. 116, Dalton • (603) 837-9150

The cold water in this mountain lake will cool off the hottest hikers. You'll enjoy the 200 feet of swimming beach on Forest Lake along with the shady picnic grove. There's a bathhouse for changing. The swimming season is mid-June through Labor Day from 9:30 AM until 6 PM. You'll find this state park about 10 miles north of Littleton. It's in the White Mountains Region, but it's just south of the Great North Woods and certainly worth of a visit from anywhere in the state.

Dartmouth-Lake Sunapee Region

Lake Sunapee State Beach

Mount Sunapee State Park, N.H. Rt. 103, Newbury • (603) 763-2356

Float on your back and gaze at beautiful Mount Sunapee. Or stake your claim (and towel) to a piece of the 300 yards of beach that are open to the public. You'll enjoy the shady picnic area whether you bring your own food or take advantage of the on-premises snack bar. The bathhouse makes it easy to change before driving home after a day in the sand. The beach season starts in mid-June and runs through Labor Day.

Wadleigh State Beach

Wadleigh State Park, N.H. Rt. 114, North Sutton • (603) 927-4724

We love this quiet spot on Kezar Lake. The sandy beach is sparsely populated, and kids can swim without being crowded. Bring food and enjoy the shady picnic area. If you forget your lunch or decide to stay through the supper hour, the Vernondale Store on N.H. Route 114 is near the park entrance. You'll find sandwiches, cold cuts and cold drinks for an impromptu meal. The beach park opens at 10 AM on weekdays and 9 AM on weekends. It closes at 8 PM.

Monadnock Region

Greenfield State Park

N.H. Rt. 136, Greenfield • (603) 547-3497

This is the only public swimming spot with lifeguards in the Monadnock region. The small camp store has ice, soft drinks, snacks and hot dogs, and you can bring your own picnic for a more elaborate lunch. The park opens at 10 AM during the week and 9 AM on weekends and closes every day at 8 PM. The beach season starts in mid-June and runs through Labor Day.

Boating

Public access to New Hampshire lakes and ponds has often been a controversial issue. Technically, any "Great Pond" (one with more than 10 acres of surface area) is public water. Getting a boat into some of the lakes can be a challenge, however, if all the surrounding land is in private ownership. Obviously landowners who pay premium prices and taxes for waterfront property do not appreciate people traipsing across their lawns or picnicking on their beaches!

In the Lakes Region, many motels and cottages have moorings or launches available for the use of their guests. Moorings can also be rented through the same agencies that rent vacation properties in the Lakes Region. We've given you some public launch descriptions in this chapter, but your best source of information is local marine supply stores, many of which have their own docks and parking areas. They will know about public launches that have been opened recently, which landowners don't mind if you put in at their sites and where you can leave your car and trailer.

New Hampshire requires all powered boats, regardless of size, to be registered. Many local agents (hardware stores, marinas and boat dealers) can issue registrations, as can Department of Motor Vehicles substations. Or you can write to the Department of Safety, 10 Hazen Drive, Concord, NH 03301. Registration fees vary with the length of the boat, horsepower of the engine and make, model and year of manufacture (just like a car). (The range is so broad as to span from $18 to $1,800.) Boats legally registered in other jurisdictions may be used in New Hampshire waters for up to 30 consecutive days. Motorized boats up to 26 feet long must have a whistle and a type B-1 fire extinguisher on board and readily at hand.

Every boat up to 16 feet in length and every canoe or kayak in New Hampshire waters must have at least one Coast Guard-approved type IV personal flotation device (PFD) on board for each person in the craft. Boats longer than 16 feet must have a type III for each person and at least one type IV device you can throw. In other words, be sure you have a life jacket for every passenger and, in a bigger boat, a life preserver besides. The new "vest" type life jackets are comfortable, and even teens generally don't object to wearing them. Although the law only says they must be in the boat, we recommend a policy that everyone wears one all the time. Trying to put on a life jacket after an accident is not a pleasant experience.

Any boat operating at night or in reduced visibility must have a conspicuous white light visible in all directions. This applies even to canoes and rowboats. Motorized boats are also required to display standard red/green running lights.

There are many regulations regarding speed and operation of boats in New Hampshire waters, particularly in the vicinity of divers, swimming areas and bridges. Call the Marine Patrol office at (603) 293-2037 for a booklet, and review the regulations before your trip.

In addition to statewide regulations, some lakes have maximum horsepower limitations, and motorized craft are prohibited on lakes smaller than 75 acres. These restrictions are strictly enforced, as they were enacted for the protection of the lake and shore habitat.

New Hampshire Marine Patrol enforces all boating regulations in the state. They asked us to remind everyone to read notices posted at public launch sites, as many of our lakes and ponds have their own restrictions in addition to (or even superseding) those laid

INSIDERS' TIP

Portsmouth Harbor, at the mouth of the Piscataqua River, is a commercial port teeming with tankers, tugboats and a current that averages 4 knots. It's not for novices. Explore it on one of our many cruises and leave the driving — ah, navigating — to the pros.

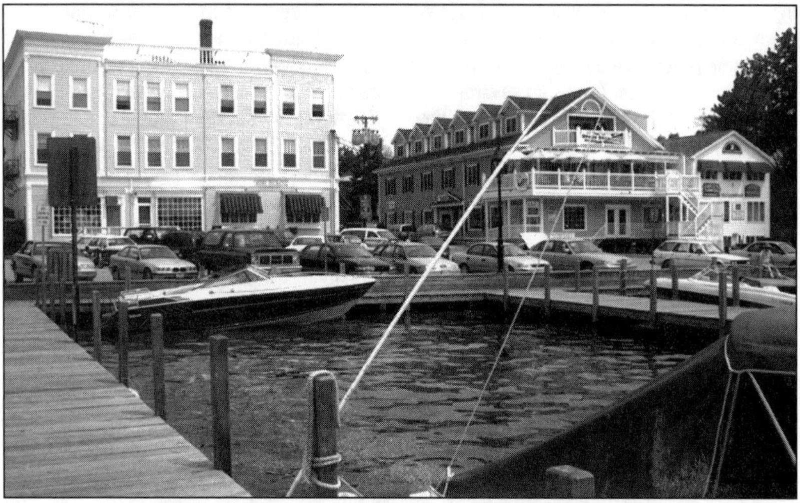

Wolfeboro was one of America's first waterfront resort towns.

down by the state. They also strongly urge anyone using personal watercraft (Jet Skis) to call Marine Patrol at (603) 293-2037 and inquire about specific bodies of water before heading out. Local boat dealers and sailors confirmed that the regulations are too cumbersome for easy recollection or summary!

Want to put a boat in the ocean? You'll find public docks and ramps at Rye Harbor State Park on the northern end of the Seacoast and Hampton Beach State Park at the southern end. There is also a public launch at Odiorne Point State Park in Rye, at the far end of the park road away from the Science Center and the tide pools. You'll actually be putting in to Seavey Creek, which opens into Little Harbor and from there into the Gulf of Maine.

Lakes and Ponds

Merrimack Valley Region

Massabesic Lake
Auburn

At more than 2,500 acres, this is the largest lake in the Merrimack Valley. It has two lobes connected by a tiny narrows where the N.H. Route 28 Bypass crosses it, and the primary launch site for the lake is there. Other launches are on N.H. Route 121. There is no swimming allowed in Massabesic because it's a public water supply. Motorboats are allowed, and a 45 mph speed limit is in effect at Massabesic.

Pawtuckaway Lake
Nottingham/Raymond

There is good access to this 900-acre lake from Pawtuckaway State Park (see our Parks and Open Spaces chapter), with lots of parking at the launch site. It is essential that boaters exercise care in this lake with its popular swimming beach. A 6 mph speed limit is enforced in the Bay of Fundy area.

Seacoast Region

Great Bay
Durham, Dover, Newington, Greenland, Stratham, Newmarket

This inland saltwater bay is a favorite for bird-watching, hunting, fishing and recreational boating. It's not very deep, and large mudflats appear at low tide. The most popular launch spot for Great Bay is Adams Point, on Durham Point Road off N.H. Route 108. The launch will accommodate a canoe or small boat at high tide. At Chapman's Landing, just off N.H. Route 108 in Stratham at the southern tip of the bay, New Hampshire Fish and Game provides a boat launch with lots of parking and facilities. There are several other launches along the southern edge of the bay. Just remember you have to come back when the tide is at or above the level at which you put in!

Lakes Region

Chocorua Lake
Tamworth

This is a windswept 223-acre pond at the base of Mount Chocorua. No motorboats are allowed on this lake. Access for nonmotorized craft is just off N.H. Route 16 north of the village of Chocorua. There is plenty of parking here in addition to a good spot for turning trailers around.

Newfound Lake
Bristol/Hebron

Newfound's 4,100 acres are among New Hampshire's most pristine. It is a favorite with both sailors and motorized boat owners, although it has a reputation for tricky winds. The best public access to the lake is from a launch at Wellington State Park (see the park's description in our Beaches section).

Lake Ossipee
Ossipee

At just more than 3,000 acres, Lake Ossipee is a popular lake at the southern edge of the White Mountains. There are several launches that are available to the public for a fee. At Deer Cove (off N.H. Route 16), there's an excellent ramp available without charge, and you'll find plenty of parking.

Squam Lake
Holderness

Squam Lake is a large lake, almost 7,000 acres, divided into two lobes (most people call them Squam Lake and Little Squam Lake). U.S. Route 3 crosses the narrows between them. There's a launch on N.H. Route 113 just beyond this point (but we do mean "on Route 113" — you'll be backing around in the road). There is good parking across the street. A better spot is further along U.S. 3 at the Colonial Motel, but you have to pay to use it. Access to Little Squam Lake is by two ramps on River Street, which runs off U.S. 3 between Ashland and Holderness. There is very limited parking for either of these. Squam Lake is beautiful, popular and rather treacherous, with its many coves, inlets, islands and sumberged rocks. The speed limit on the lake is 40 mph, and it drops to 20 mph after dark.

White Oak Pond
Holderness

White Oak was probably once attached to Squam Lake. It's only divided now by a bit more than the width of U.S. 3. There's a launch spot, which is just less than 2 miles east of the place where the road crosses Squam Lake. Motors on the lake are limited to no more than 7.5 horsepower.

Wentworth Lake
Wolfeboro

Wentworth Lake is connected to Winnipesaukee's Back Bay by a series of narrows, one of which is large enough to have its own name, Crescent Lake. There is a ramp into Crescent Lake at the point where N.H. routes 104 and 109 cross the narrows. You'll find a good amount of parking. There is also a launch at Wentworth State Park (see our Beaches section).

Lake Winnipesaukee
Alton Bay, Gilford, Weirs Beach, Meredith, Center Harbor, Melvin Village, Tuftonboro, Wolfeboro

To Insiders this is simply "The Big Lake" — all 45,000 acres of it. Numerous public launch facilities dot the shoreline, although several of them suffer from a lack of adequate parking. Two of the best access points are at the north end of the lake. One is across from the Chamber of Commerce in Center Harbor,

INSIDERS' TIP

No pets are allowed on state park beaches.

right on N.H. Route 25. The other is in Moultonborough, on Blake Road, where there are two ramps and (hooray!) excellent parking. On the east side of the lake there is good access at Melvin Village across from the Libby Museum on N.H. 109. One of the most popular launches is in Wolfeboro, just off N.H. 109 behind the town hall. And finally, there is public access with a ramp at Ellacoya State Park in Gilford (see the park's description in our Beaches section or in our Camping chapter).

Lake Winnisquam
Laconia, Belmont, Gilford, Meredith, Sanbornton, Tilton

Winnisquam is long and skinny, with just more than 4,200 acres of surface. It's one of two lakes in Laconia, and there's a launch right downtown at the end of Whipple Avenue. On the opposite side of N.H. Route 107 there's another launch, from Laconia's Opechee Park, into Winnipesaukee's Opechee Bay (which is separated from the big lake by a dam).

White Mountains and Great North Woods Regions

Conway Lake
Conway, Eaton

This is a large lake that doesn't get too much traffic. The launch is at the north end of the lake where a small inlet runs up toward U.S. Route 302 as it heads for Maine. Mill Street leads to the launch, where there's parking for several vehicles. The turnaround is in the roadway, but it's not a busy street.

Lake Francis and the Connecticut Lakes
Pittsburg

Way up at the Canadian border in the Great North Woods Region, you'll find the headwaters of the Connecticut River. This territory is home to bald eagles and osprey, moose and bear and very, very few people. U.S. Route 3 runs along the river and skirts the lakes, and there are numerous boat launches where the road and water are close together. Lake Francis State Park offers primitive facilities and a ramp on one of the inlets of that dammed lake, which you can reach by River Road off U.S. 3. There are chemical toilets at the launches in the Connecticut Lakes State Forest, a narrow strip of protected corridor along U.S. 3. If you're starved for human contact or real plumbing, you may need to continue on up to the Customs Station at the border north of the Fourth Connecticut Lake. But if you're seeking a placid day "away from it all," these lakes may be just what you need.

Umbagog Lake
Errol

Umbagog straddles the New Hampshire/Maine state line, and its nearly 8,000 acres are spread and twisted into dozens of little coves and inlets. Most of the land on the New Hampshire side is under conservation easements to protect the marshy habitat. There is a launch at Sargent Cove, just west of the state line at the south end of the lake off N.H. Route 26, and another just east of Errol off N.H. Route 16, upstream of the Errol Dam. The lake is far enough from everything to be quite unspoiled and lightly used.

Dartmouth-Lake Sunapee Region

Grafton Pond
Grafton

This is a popular pond, with swimmers and anglers sharing the water with boats. Motorized craft are restricted to no more than 6 horsepower to protect the habitat and the

INSIDERS' TIP

Milfoil and fanwort, both "fuzzy" green pond weeds, are non-native aquatic plants that are beginning to threaten native species. One of the best ways to prevent transfer of these weeds to other lakes and ponds is to take your boat and trailer through an automatic car wash.

users. The launch is on Potato Road next to a dam, as is the swimming area.

Mascoma Lake
Enfield, Lebanon

More than 1,000 acres of water surface attract many boaters to this lake every summer. Its location, close to Interstate 89 and Lower Shaker Village, bring it to the attention of passing tourists and residents alike. There are two good public launches on the lake, one at Shaker Bridge on N.H. Route 4-A and the other closer to the Enfield Shaker Museum at Shaker Lower Village.

Lake Sunapee
Newbury, Sunapee, George's Mills, New London

This has long been one of New Hampshire's most popular lakes, and at more than 4,000 acres, it's by far the largest in the region to which it gives its name. There are public launches at both ends of the lake, one at the north end in New London, (take a right at Exit 12 off I-89) and the other in Newbury at Mount Sunapee State Park.

Monadnock Region

Dublin Lake
Dublin

Dublin Lake is actually a pond, one of dozens scattered across the Monadnock region. The lake is perhaps best known for the treacherous stretch of N.H. Route 101 that curves along its bank, which has been the focus of more than two decades of community vs. state battles (no one likes the dangerous road, but no one wants it moved to their backyard, either). It would be too bad to stop with controversy, however, as the sight of sailboats skimming across the waves should remind us that this beautiful lake is much more than a traffic hazard.

Constant winds make Dublin Lake tricky for canoeing but perfect for sailing. The launch site is at Lake Road, about 4 miles from N.H. Route 101 (across the lake from the infamous curve). Parking is rather limited, given the popularity of the lake.

Otter Lake
Greenfield, Bennington

This 60-acre lake is heavily used, as it is the site of a very popular swimming beach and a campground (see Greenfield State Park in the Beaches section and our Camping chapter). Boaters are therefore restricted to a "no wake" speed limit. It's still a beautiful place to get out on the water. The launch is a half-mile beyond the park entrance on Forest Road.

Nubanusit Lake
Hancock, Nelson

Nubanusit and its sister, Spoonwood Lake, form an odd-shaped donut, curling around a large peninsula that's almost an island. Unfortunately — or perhaps fortunately for those Insiders who like the isolation and privacy of this lovely spot — the launch, at the northeast shore of the lake on Kings Highway, is rather rough.

Contoocook Lake
Jaffrey, Rindge

Contoocook's 200-plus acres remain popular with boaters and fishermen, although the milfoil here is a textbook example of why environmentalists fear the invasive plant. The public launch is off U.S. Route 202 in Jaffrey. *Please* clean your boat and trailer and flush your motor before you leave this parking lot to avoid spreading milfoil to other lakes.

Paddling

Most of what we've said with regard to boating also applies to canoes and kayaks. They do not need to be registered, but you must have one life-jacket or buoyancy device for each person in the craft. There are many more canoe/kayak launches than full-size boat launches. Many of these launches are on private property and are open through the generosity of landowners, and most are built and maintained by volunteers from local conservation commissions and outdoors clubs. Visitors are welcome to use them but are asked to respect the work they represent. If no trash barrels are present, take your rubbish with

Photo: Hampton Beach Chamber of Commerce

Sunbathers bask in the New Hampshire summer at Hampton Beach.

you. Stay within the marked areas, and park only in designated spots.

Any outdoor activity involves risk, and paddling is a prime example. When choosing a place to canoe, take your own ability and experience into account. A large lake may have stiff winds that can make navigation difficult. Rivers and streams offer a variety of experiences, from the quiet, winding stretch amid fields and woodlands to the roar of whitewater or the expanse and current of a great river. The Appalachian Mountain Club's *River Guide — New Hampshire/Vermont* is an excellent handbook, with good descriptions of individual sections of rivers that include classification, seasonal navigability and a general description of the territory. The book also includes safety tips and warnings.

In general, our rivers are highest in early spring, when snowmelt combines with still-frozen ground to create extensive flooding. Many Insiders look forward to an annual spring ritual of paddling across corn fields and golf courses. Four months later in the dog-days of August, the same river may be so low as to be unnavigable. Most rapids are fastest in high water, but some don't appear until the level drops.

Narrow stream beds and high boulders create rapids in many rivers. Some are miniature — short enough or shallow enough that a worst-case scenario would leave you feeling soaked and silly. Others can be very tricky and dangerous, even for experienced paddlers. Never paddle alone, and never venture into unknown waters without information on what to expect. We've listed some local guides in this chapter. Others may be available: Ask at outfitters and marinas.

Along the Seacoast, tides and undertows are an additional source of concern. The larger rivers are tidal well inland, with resultant current changes and varying depths. Channels are marked, and charts of the area are detailed. Boaters of all kinds are strongly urged to take advantage of them. Be aware that tide charts report the times of high and low tide at the ocean. Times upstream in the tidal rivers

INSIDERS' TIP

It's a good idea to have an extra paddle in the bottom of your canoe. Inexperienced paddlers may lose one overboard, and it can take a long time to return to shore if your paddle power is lost or reduced.

will be considerably later. Maps and river descriptions generally give the tide differential at spots along the river, for example, "+1 hr" means one hour later than the time at the mouth of the river.

New Hampshire rivers are cold! Even in summer, the water coming down out of the mountains stays bracingly chilly. In early spring hypothermia is a serious threat. A wet suit is a necessity for kayakers during much of the year.

Rivers

Merrimack Valley Region

Merrimack River

Franklin to Concord to Manchester to Nashua

New Hampshire's great river begins where the Pemigewasset and the Winnipesaukee join in Franklin and runs into the Atlantic in Newburyport, Massachusetts. In between it traverses rural countryside and our most congested urban areas. Traveling the Merrimack is like paddling through our state's history.

There are many accesses and ramps along the banks of the Merrimack. Some sections are relatively easy to navigate. There are several large dams on the river, however, and releases or electric power demand can alter the current significantly. The river should be avoided in high water because landings and the approaches to the dams can be very difficult. Save it for those times when the smaller rivers are too shallow to float even a canoe.

Put in behind Franklin High School (this is actually the Winnipesaukee) for about 17 miles of quick current with some Class I rapids. About 2 miles below Hannah Dustin Island you can take out if you'd rather avoid the Class III rapids through the next couple of miles around what used to be Sewall Falls Dam. There is another put-in just upstream of Exit 16 off Interstate 93. The following 24-mile section is an easy paddle to Concord, where the launch ramp is near the Interstate 393 cloverleaf, north of Bridge Street.

The next 18-mile section of the river is fairly easy paddling, although it is broken up by several dams, which you will have to portage around. In Manchester you take out at the bridge to portage around the Amoskeag Dam and fish ladder.

The next 5 miles of the Merrimack include some of the river's trickiest rapids, several sets of Class III falls and a nasty sewage outfall. Conditions here are entirely dependent on the actions of the Public Service Company dam, which can be reached at (603) 225-6182 for information about the water level at the dam.

Unless you're here for the rapids, you can skip the city section and put in below the railroad bridge at River Park, then enjoy almost 12 miles of gentle travel with just a couple of Class II rapids, down through Merrimack into Nashua, where you can take out at N.H. Route 111, just south of the Nashua River and a mile north of the Massachusetts state line.

Souhegan River

Greenville to Wilton to Milford, Milford to Merrimack

The upper portion of the Souhegan offers lots of challenging Class III and IV rapids over 12 miles, from the put-in below the old hydroelectric plant off N.H. Route 31 in Greenville all the way to the dam in Wilton. Below Wilton the river's rocky bottom provides a Class II ride until the river widens and spreads as it reaches Milford. Take out at the ball field behind the school. Some people choose to portage by car here, as it's about a mile across the Milford Oval to the next put in, off either Souhegan Street or Nashua Street below the two Milford dams. The next 10 miles offer a pleasant trip through open fields (and golf courses) with just a couple of Class II rapids and one short Class III. Most people take out at the Turkey Hill Bridge in Merrimack. The last 3 miles wind through a residential area and require a short portage around Wildcat Falls, but there is a certain satisfaction in following the river all the way to where it joins the mighty Merrimack.

Seacoast Region

Five major rivers and numerous smaller streams converge in Great Bay, funnel through

Little Bay into the Piscataqua and flow out to the Atlantic. As the rivers and Great Bay are tidal, it is possible — by taking advantage of the tide — to run them in both directions. Put in at Dover Point, where Hilton Park off U.S. Route 4 offers parking, restrooms and a boat launch. From there you can go south to explore Great Bay itself or turn into the Lamprey or Squamscott rivers, head west to the Oyster River or work your way north on the Bellamy River. You can also head down the Piscataqua toward Portsmouth if you're an accomplished paddler and don't mind lots of traffic.

If you prefer to start upriver, you can put into the Bellamy at Sawyer's Mill, on Mill Street in Dover, about 4 miles north of Little Bay. The put-in for the Oyster River is about 3 miles inland, in Durham at Jackson's Landing, which you'll find off Old Piscataqua Road. The state maintains a boat launch off Main Street in Newmarket on the Lamprey River, a short 1.5 miles from Great Bay. The Squamscott, in contrast, begins at the Exeter River in Exeter, and you can put in about half-mile downstream from the center of town from the Swasey Parkway and enjoy a 6 mile run down to Great Bay.

Lakes Region

Baker River

Wentworth to Plymouth

This is a pleasant stretch of river that winds through sandy bankings and steep wooded hillsides. Put in just below the bridge on N.H. Route 25 in Wentworth for a series of Class I and II rapids in the first 10 miles, followed by gradually decreasing current and eventually flat water at the point where the Baker joins the Pemigewasset. Take-out is at a dirt road that leads to a municipal parking lot right in downtown Plymouth.

Bearcamp River

Bearcamp Pond to Bennet Corners to West Ossipee

The river begins in meadowland, winding along lazily for about 3 miles until you reach the beginning of a very challenging 4-mile whitewater section at Bennet Corners. You can put in off Bearcamp Pond Road at the pond and take out at the N.H. Route 113 bridge to avoid the rapids, or if you're up to Class III and IV rapids, run on through to the dam at South Tamworth. The rapids continue below the dam all the way to Whittier, where there is a put in off Old N.H. Route 25. From there the river winds on gently for another 10 miles to a take-out on N.H. Route 16 just before Ossipee Lake.

Pemigewasset River

Plymouth to Bristol to Franklin

The first 15 miles of this stretch are easy, scenic and navigable through most of the year. Put in from the municipal parking lot off Main Street in Plymouth, and you can ride the current almost all the way to Bristol. (There are put-ins on River Road in Bridgewater and at N.H. Route 104 in New Hampton if you don't want to go the whole length.) Below the Ayers Island Dam in Bristol, the rapids can be quite challenging, Class II or III. If you'd rather, you can skip the rapids and put in again off Flood Plain Road. The river passes through what used to be the town of Hill, before it was moved to provide floodway for the Franklin Falls flood-control project. Take out at that dam, which is accessible from N.H. Route 127, or you can portage and continue another 14 miles to the Public Service Company dam in Franklin. This last stretch is very calm (deadwater).

White Mountains and Great North Woods Regions

Saco River

Crawford Notch to Bartlett to Center Conway

The Upper Saco (pronounced Sock-O) offers challenging Class III and IV rapids over a 6-mile stretch that also boasts some of the most stunning scenery in New Hampshire. Put in is at the Davis Path footbridge, which necessitates a difficult portage around a narrow gorge, or at Notchland off U.S. Route 302, which requires permission from the landowners at Inn Unique. Or put in at the Sawyer Rock Picnic Area on U.S. 302 and avoid the Class IV rapids. There is still plenty of challenge in the last 3 miles before the river arrives in Bartlett.

In Bartlett there is a put in on River Street with a parking area. Over the 20 miles from Bartlett to Conway, the river gradually smooths out, although the current is swift and the river tends to be something of an obstacle course, with downed trees, large boulders and rapids and eddies caused by bridge supports. Several take-outs are possible as the river passes through farmland west of North Conway or at a covered bridge in Conway just below where the Swift River joins the Saco. Stay in the river for 2 miles featuring mostly Class II rapids — and one very tricky Class III section — right through Conway and Center Conway, where you'll take out at the U.S. 302 bridge or continue on in to Maine.

Connecticut River

Pittsburg to West Stewartstown to North Stratford to Hanover

Here in the Great North Woods you are at the very beginning of New England's longest river. Put in at the covered bridge off U.S. 3 just south of Pittsburg and run the Class I and II rapids 9 miles until you come to Canaan Dam. There's a Class III rapid below the dam, which can be avoided by putting in at West Stewartstown where N.H. Route 114 becomes Vt. Route 114. The next 20 miles are fairly shallow and gentle, with a few Class II rapids through Colebrook. Look to the Vermont side of the river for a great view of the other Monadnock! A disintegrating dam provides some more challenging rapids about 6 miles southwest of the Columbia covered bridge, and then the river gradually settles down as it approaches North Stratford. The next stretch, from North Stratford to Hanover, offers almost 125 miles of placid, meandering river with numerous access points.

Androscoggin River

Umbagog Lake to Errol to Berlin

Another river in the Great North Woods is the Androscoggin. N.H. Rt. 16 runs parallel to this river, making for easy access. The 3 miles north of the launch off Errol Dam Road are slow moving and marshy — you can row upstream to the lake. There are some rapids below Errol Dam that are very popular, and other Class I and II rapids lead up to the Seven Islands bridge. The river winds through wooded hills for 30 miles, with numerous places where you can put in or take out (including several dams where you have to). At Pontook Dam in Dummer, you'll find a parking area and restrooms. Ask here about scheduled releases from the dam if you want to ride the whitewater below.

Mad River

Waterville Valley to Campton to the Pemigewasset

The Mad River drains a steep watershed, and during high water in spring it can provide almost 15 miles of whitewater, including some Class III and IV rapids. On the other hand, in summer there are stretches where you are likely to have to portage in the riverbed. Put ins are at N.H. Route 49 in Waterville Valley, at Six-Mile Bridge and at the Campton Campground, all on N.H. 49. The river slows down as it approaches Campton Pond, and you must portage around the Campton Dam. The rapids below the dam and through Campton are tricky, so you may want to stop here and put in again in the Pemigewasset where it runs beside U.S. 3 in West Campton.

Pemigewasset River

Woodstock to Blair Bridge

This 20-mile stretch of river includes some rapids (mostly Class I and II) and a good deal of quick water in the springtime. Later in the season there is still usually enough water for a pleasant trip. Put in is at N.H. Route 112 in North Woodstock. The first 4 miles are quite challenging. Less-experienced paddlers should put in at the bridge on N.H. Route 175 in West Thornton. The river is winding and has many shifting channels and numerous places where you can take out or put in.

Dartmouth-Lake Sunapee Region

Blackwater River

Cilleyville (in Andover) to West Salisbury

West Salisbury to the Contoocook

The Blackwater River runs through a rural

area that very few people bother to visit. The scenery is lovely, and the river offers both gentle paddling above the flood control dam in West Salisbury and wild whitewater below. Put in just below the intersection of N.H. routes 4-A and 11 in Andover. The first 3 miles include a short Class III rapid followed by some Class I and IIs. You can put in at the covered bridge on U.S. Route 4 in Andover if you prefer to skip the whitewater. The river flattens out here and twists through a series of ponds and marshes, eventually widening into a broad section known as the Bay. A broken dam at the bottom of the bay requires you to take out — you can stop here or put in again below the dam and continue downstream for about 12 miles of beautiful countryside. The current is fairly quick with only a couple of rapids. A much greater hazard here is downed trees. There is a take-out at a dirt road about a mile upstream of the flood-control dam in Webster.

Below that dam the Blackwater River is one of the most challenging rivers in the state. Class III and IV rapids here include boulders, notches, holes and turbulence the AMC guide compares to a washing machine. Survive it, and you'll pass into a gentle 6-mile section that joins the Contoocook at Broad Cove in Hopkinton.

Mascoma River

Canaan Center to Mascoma Lake to Lebanon

Remainders of old dams and some railroad bridges contribute to the rapids in Canaan, which are considered Class II. It slows as it reaches U.S. Route 4 and runs smoothly and quickly through West Canaan and Enfield, where there are several road crossings and easy accesses. Cross the north end of Mascoma Lake and take out at the dam. You can stop here if you're not a whitewater fan, or put in below the dam for about 5 miles of very popular whitewater, mostly Class II with some Class III/IV sections. Take-out in Lebanon is at a parking lot just before the N.H. Route 120 bridge.

Monadnock Region

Ashuelot River

Lower Stillwater (in Marlow) to West Swanzey

Choose whether you want to begin with a Class III rapid and put in either above or below "Surprise Rapids," which you can examine from the bridge on N.H. Route 10. After a mile of relatively easy paddling, there's a 2-mile stretch of very challenging whitewater, with Class III and IV rapids galore. The river calms down a bit as it approaches Gilsum, but you'll still need to keep your wits about you. There's a picnic area in Gilsum just below N.H. Route 10, where you must take out because the Gilsum gorge is just ahead. Below the gorge the road is close to the river, and you can put in again. This next section, about 4 miles long, is predominately Class II rapids, followed by 5 miles of quick current leading up to the Surry Mountain flood control dam, where you have to take out. Below the dam the river is mostly smooth, winding 7 miles through open land and into Keene. You'll have to take out to get around the Keene flood control dam, but there's a nice park here. Smooth paddling continues for another 9 miles into West Swanzey, where yet another dam interrupts the river. Theoretically you could continue on the Ashuelot all the way to the Connecticut, but Insiders suggest waiting until pollution-control measures improve the water, which has been severely impacted by nearly two centuries of industrial waste.

Contoocook River

Jaffrey to Bennington to Hillsboro to West Henniker

The first section of the Contoocook is almost 7 miles of Class II rapids in early spring,

INSIDERS' TIP

Beach sandals or waterproof shoes keep kids and grown-ups from complaining about the "icky" moss-like growth on some lake bottoms. The shoes are also handy for the hiking trails that surround many of our public lakes.

interrupted by a narrow gorge that can sometimes provide a Class IV but more often requires a portage. Put in at the bridge on U.S. Route 202 just below the Cheshire Pond. You have to take out at the dam in Peterborough, where you may decide to quit or put in again to enjoy the calmer 12-mile paddle from Peterborough to Bennington. This is considered one of the nicest canoe trips in the southern part of the state.

Several dams and a paper mill in Bennington require a long portage here or make it a good place to begin a trip north. You can put in at the bridge near the paper company. From Bennington the river winds along through wooded countryside to Hillsboro, where two dams and treacherous rapids require you to take out. For a challenging whitewater workout, put in again below the village by the railroad bridge. After about 4 miles of smooth current, 2 miles of Class III and IV rapids begin, including one rapid known as the Freight Train. The river runs quickly into West Henniker, where a dangerous dam necessitates a quick take-out at N.H. Route 202.

Outfitters and Guides

Merrimack Valley Region

Hannah's Paddles Canoe Livery

15 Hannah Dustin Dr., Concord
• (603) 753-6695

These folks will rent you a canoe or kayak with all the necessary equipment and take you to the start of your Merrimack River trip in their van. You can choose to put in at Franklin, Boscawen or in between for a 5-, 10- or 15-mile trip through one of the most pleasant sections of the Merrimack. Bring a picnic, stop and swim at one of the many beaches you'll pass, take a couple of hours or the whole day. All the trips end at the Hannah Dustin Memorial, where your hosts will take you out and transport you back to your car. Cost of an all-day rental ranges from $25 to $40 per boat. Hannah's Paddles will also transport you and your own canoe if you'd like to make this trip without spotting cars. Reservations are strongly encouraged.

All Outdoors

321 Elm St., Manchester
• (603) 624-1468

Right downtown in our largest city is this great outfitting shop. It has canoes and kayaks for sale (and kayaks to rent, at $20 to $30 per day), along with all the peripheral equipment and advice you'll need to get started. As you might have guessed from its name, All Outdoors also supplies hikers, climbers and skiers.

Seacoast Region

New England Fishing Gear

200 Spaulding Tnpk., Portsmouth
• (603) 436-2836

This store has marine hardware, supplies, equipment and clothing for professionals and hobbyists alike. It has harbor charts, mooring equipment, saltwater fishing tackle and fiberglass repair kits. The store is closed Sunday.

Great Bay Marine

Off Spaulding Turnpike on the Piscataqua River, Newington
• (603) 436-5299

You might suspect that a marine supply house that gives its address according to a river map (Nav. Chart No. 13285) rather than a street map would be a sailor's favorite. This is a big marina, offering repowering, refinishing and repairs; a ship's store with a full line

INSIDERS' TIP

If you're planning a day at a lakeside beach during August, there's a good chance you'll see lots of ripe blueberries on bushes bordering the beach between the woods and the water. Help yourself, but be sure and rinse them thoroughly before eating.

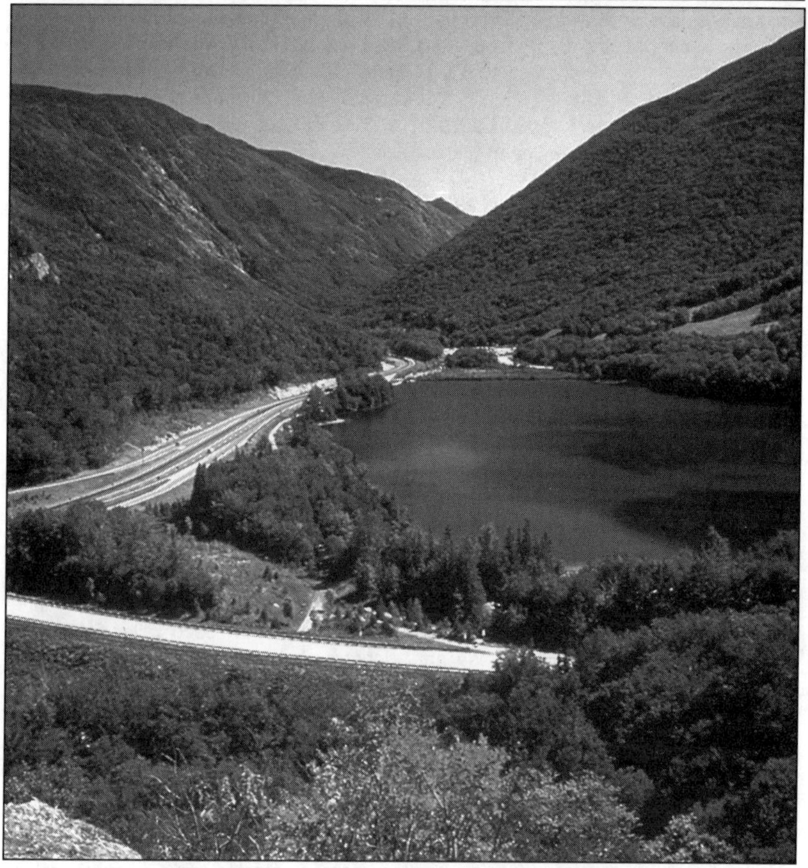

Echo Lake, nestled in Franconia Notch, offers opportunities for all kinds of water recreation.

of equipment; and lifts and trailers and dockage for pleasure craft and commercial boats. It offers showers and a restaurant, a welcome touch after days on the waves, as well as sewage-pumping and boat transport. Oh, you can get here by car too.

Lakes Region

Wild Meadow Canoes
N.H. Rt. 25, Center Harbor
• (603) 253-7536, (800) 427-7536

Although the name says canoes, Wild Meadow also rents and sells kayaks and other small boats by the day or week. Rentals range from $25 to $40 per day, depending on the type of craft, and include all the necessary equipment for safe use. Motorized fishing boats are available for rent by the week. Wild Meadow also offers lots of information and advice and does boat repair and service.

Irwin Marine
958 Union Ave., Laconia
• (603) 524-6661

The folks at Irwin Marine have been supplying and servicing Lakes Region boaters for almost 80 years, so they really know the area and the business. You'll find a complete ship's store with equipment, maps and knowledgeable advice on the side. Irwin also sells and services boats of all kinds, including pontoon boats, canoes and in- and outboard motorboats.

Weirs Beach Marine & Boat Tours

Winnipesaukee Pier, Weirs Beach
• (603) 366-4311, (800) 366-8119

This outfit will rent you an 18- or 23-foot boat with a 120-horsepower motor for two, four or eight hours. Corresponding prices are $90, $145 and $190. For an additional charge of $25, you can also rent water-skiing equipment. You must be at least 21 and provide a credit card and photo ID to rent a boat. Weirs Beach Marine provides a "crash" training course (their term!) and charts of the lake before you head out across the waves.

Winnipesaukee Kayak Company

N.H. Rt. 109, Wolfeboro
• (603) 569-9926

These experienced kayakers offer individual and group lessons and guided excursions on the Saco and Merrymeeting rivers and on Wentworth, Winnipesaukee and Squam lakes. They'll also take you sea kayaking. The company rents and sells kayaks and canoes of all kinds as well as all the peripheral equipment you could need. Rental costs $30 to $50 per day, depending on the style and size of the boat, and includes all the equipment. You can leave your car in their lot and get directly into the water, or tie the boat on the roof of your car and head out.

White Mountains and Great North Woods Regions

Downeast Whitewater

U.S. Rt. 302, Center Conway
• (603) 447-3002

If you've always wanted to try whitewater kayaking, this is a great place to learn. Downeast Whitewater runs two, three and four-day classes in whitewater kayaking on the Androscoggin River near Errol. A two-day class costs $170 per person including equipment and a campsite but no meals. If you prefer a quiet canoe trip to the Lake Umbagog Wildlife Refuge, you can get a guided tour including a luncheon cookout for $49 per person. Without the guide and the lunch, you can rent a canoe with all necessary equipment for a total of $37 including transportation to and from the lake. The company also runs river raft trips. The outfitter rents and sells canoes, flat-water kayaks, whitewater kayaks and all necessary equipment. The season runs from mid-April to mid-October.

Saco Valley Canoe

Junction of U.S. Rt. 302 and N.H. Rt. 113, Center Conway
• (603) 447-2444, (800) 447-2460

If you've never taken a canoe trip, you might want to start with one of the three daytrips offered by Saco Valley Canoe. The longest trip is 11 miles and takes about five hours, and the shortest is nearly 4 miles and takes about two hours. The cost is $27 per canoe during the week and $35 on weekends. The price includes equipment and transportation.

The outfitter also organizes overnight trips. Saco Valley Canoe supplies the canoes and paddling necessities, you supply everything else including camping equipment and tents. And if you fall in love with the river life, you can buy everything you need for a lasting relationship.

Canoe King of New England

1618 White Mountain Hwy., North Conway • (603) 356-5280

You can buy and rent everything you need for canoeing and kayaking at Canoe King of New England. Canoes rent for $20 a day, and kayak rentals begin at $15 a day. Rentals in-

INSIDERS' TIP

The best rapids occur when flood control or power company dams release large volumes of water into a river — generally in mid-spring. You can call the dam's office to find out when these releases will occur.

clude life jackets, paddles and a roof-top carrier for transporting the boat of your choice to your destination. Shuttle service to and from river put ins is extra. Ask about the price when you call to reserve your watercraft. You can buy both new and used canoes, kayaks and equipment here. The store is open every day, with reduced weekend hours during winter.

Dartmouth-Lake Sunapee Region

North Star Canoe Rentals

Balloch's Crossing, N.H. Route 12A, Cornish • (603) 542-5802

Balloch's Crossing is about 2.5 miles south of the Windsor-Cornish covered bridge over the Connecticut River (see our History chapter for a photo of the bridge), and it's where you'll find North Star Canoe Rentals. Leave your car and get a ride to a launching point upriver. Enjoy the outstanding views of Mount Ascutney in Vermont while you have an easy paddle on flat water. Take out back at Balloch's Crossing. A 12-mile journey costs $20 per person and a 4-mile trip is $12.50 per person. Balloch's Crossing was historically a busy Connecticut River landing. What is now the Hammond family farmhouse and headquarters of North Star Canoe Rentals was variously a hotel and boarding house providing lodging for those traveling or doing business on the river.

Eastern Mountain Sports

Powerhouse Mall, N.H. Rt. 12A, West Lebanon • (603) 298-7716

You can buy canoes here and buy and rent touring and sea kayaks. All kayaks cost $20 for the first day and $5 each additional day. Paddles and life jackets are included as well as cords for securing the kayak to your car. The store suggests that the touring kayaks (also called flat-water kayaks) are OK for up to Class II whitewater. The store is open every day. Call ahead to reserve your rental. EMS sells everything you could want to go with your new canoe.

Monadnock Region

Eastern Mountain Sports

1 Vose Farm Rd., Peterborough • (603) 924-7231

Read about Eastern Mountain Sports in our Dartmouth-Lake Sunapee section on outfitters in this chapter. The rentals prices and equipment are the same. You'll find equipment for winter sports and for staying warm. During boating season, you can inspect many different types of kayaks and canoes and receive lots of great information from the knowledgeable sales team.

Whether you favor a wild ride down the mountain or a quiet trek through open fields, bundle up and enjoy the crisp, cold air.

Winter Sports

In most Americans' eyes, winter sports and politics put New Hampshire on the national map (and given the scheduling of our first-in-the-nation primary, maybe politics should be considered a winter sport). Whether you favor a wild ride down the mountain or a quiet trek through open fields, bundle up and enjoy the crisp, cold air.

Historically New Hampshire locals preferred sledding on their hills and sleigh rides on snow-covered roads. The Dartmouth Outing Club, founded in 1909, started the Winter Carnival shortly thereafter, a tradition they continue to this day (see our Annual Events chapter). The idea caught on, and by the mid-1930s two dozen communities had organized Winter Carnivals. Intrepid folk could sled, skate and flirt in a different town each weekend from Christmas to Town Meeting. The Boston and Maine Railroad began running "snow trains" from Boston on winter weekends, and New Hampshire's reputation as a winter holiday destination grew.

Skiing

People have been skiing for thousands of years, but until this century they skied for transportation, not for fun. Recreational skiing moved from Scandinavia to Europe at the turn of the century and came home with our troops after the Great War. In New Hampshire, Winter Carnival organizers introduced skiing along with the traditional coasting events in the '20s, and in 1936 the State Planning Commission began the process of developing trails specifically for skiing. In those days skiing was mostly cross-country, as any downhill skiing necessitated serious climbing! The Tramway on Cannon Mountain opened in 1938, just a year before Hans Schneider opened a ski school at Mount Cranmore and introduced New Englanders to the European art of skiing. Ever since then people have come to New Hampshire to enjoy the thrill of high-speed Alpine descent and the peace of slipping through the woods on silent wooden wings. Today the mountains are busier than ever. Fast-paced, multi-passenger lifts whisk skiers to the tops of mountains before they have time to get chilled. Snowboarders make even the most daring skier look sedate, while tubing is fun and easy for anyone.

Modern snowmaking equipment ensures that the slopes stay covered with or without cooperation from Mother Nature, and many mountains have added night skiing to extend the opportunities. Some ski areas provide for cross-country skiers too, with groomed trails and rustic bridges over frozen streams. Kids' programs, snack bars, equipment rentals and even day-care facilities make it possible for the whole family to enjoy a day, or a week, at the slopes.

The ski season still depends on the weather, not necessarily for snow, but for cold (even machines can't make snow at temperatures much above freezing). Typically skiing starts around Thanksgiving in the north, and by Christmas vacation all the ski areas are offering at least some skiing, if only on machine-made snow. (Incidentally, the constant grooming means the surface is very consistent these days — not light and fluffy but never horribly icy either. The "granular" nature of machine-made snow is therefore less obvious.) Depending on the season, skiing may peter out at the southern areas by the end of February. Up north they enjoy spring skiing in April, and on Mount Washington the ski season begins at the end of the avalanche season in March and some years runs into early summer.

If you've never skied before, plan to rent all your equipment at the slopes. The staff will be able to help you find the right sizes and types of equipment for your height, weight and experience, and you'll be able to make adjustments once you've tried them out. Recently all the excitement has been over parabolic, or shaped skis. The shaping enables the skier to "carve" the snow with much less effort than a straight ski requires. The result is a much faster learning-curve, and the faster you learn, the more time you have to enjoy the sport.

Whatever you'd wear in the snow at home will be fine for skiing. If you don't have snow at home, plan on layers for warmth (silk or polypropylene long underwear is the best base), at least two pairs of socks and a waterproof outer layer made of one of the new synthetic fabrics that "breathe." You definitely need a hat and good gloves or mittens. You don't need goggles or high-tech accessories unless you really want them, although with the thinning ozone layer experts warn that some form eye-protection is more important now than it was when we learned to ski. Good, unbreakable sunglasses will do.

Lift ticket prices vary tremendously from one area to another and even at a single mountain, depending on which lifts are included. Weekend and holiday prices are highest, and in 1998-99 ranged from $27 to $48 for a full-day, all-lift adult ticket, with an average of $37. Ticket prices are lower on weekdays, and most areas offer a discount for juniors (typically ages 6 to 14) and seniors (older than 65 or 70). Most places have free skiing for children younger than 5 or 6. Other savings options include half-day tickets, after 3 or 4 PM tickets and, at some areas, pay-by-the-run tickets. Areas that open early in the season or stay open in spring with a small number of trails may charge lower prices during those times. Keep an eye out for package deals that combine rentals or lodging with tickets and discount coupons at fast-food restaurants and gas stations.

If you stay in commercially maintained and groomed ski areas, you will not have to think about hazards like avalanches, falling ice, getting lost or being injured and alone. Grooming crews keep the snow packed down, and slopes or trails that are dangerous will be closed (don't ski past those CLOSED signs! There's a reason they're closed, and they're not being patrolled.) Ski patrol teams monitor open slopes and trails regularly and will be there within minutes if you are injured. They are also responsible for "policing" the slopes and enforcing safe skiing techniques.

If you're new to skiing, you'll benefit greatly from a few lessons. You'll also be glad to know that ski trails are labeled according to difficulty. In alpine areas, green circles are easiest (novice) and black diamonds are the most challenging (signs explaining the distinctions are posted prominently). Cross-country trails may also be marked Easier, More Difficult and Most Difficult, but the Nordic areas we talked with all emphasized the variation among ski areas. One place's Easy trail might be labeled More Difficult elsewhere. Your best bet is to ask specifically about how steep or rough the terrain is when you check in. At state parks and other recreation areas that allow skiing but are not operated as ski areas, use good judgment as you choose your route.

If you ski or hike in the backcountry, you need to be aware of winter's dangers. Avalanches are not a Rocky Mountain exclusive. The White Mountains have hundreds of avalanches every winter, and eight people have died in New Hampshire avalanches in the last 25 years. Avalanches occur when there is unstable snow (not packed or somehow attached to the underlying snow) on open slopes. The official avalanche season is December through April, but a late or heavy winter may extend the danger into June. Although avalanches can happen at any time, they are most common during or immediately after a storm. Avoid steep, open terrain covered with new snow, and check the avalanche hazards posted at base huts and ski information centers. Never, ever travel alone in avalanche-prone areas, and always carry shovels and probes (along with your ski equipment if you're skiing) in the backcountry.

Falling ice can happen anywhere there are steep slopes or overhangs, and the chunks can be as big as cars. This is most likely in spring when rising temperatures cause the accumulated ice to shift and crack. Be aware of what's uphill of you and of large trees or boulders that might provide shelter. If you hear a crack or boom, or if someone yells "ice," take shelter first and then look.

Skiing, especially downhill (or Alpine), is

the specialty of the North Country, and there are only a few ski areas in the southern regions of the state. Cross-country (or Nordic) skiing can be practiced anywhere. All the state parks are available for winter hiking and cross-country skiing without charge, although only Odiorne on the seacoast and Monadnock in the Monadnock region are staffed in winter.

Snowmobiling

Another winter sport not limited to mountain slopes is snowmobiling. Once regarded as a menace, these high-powered vehicles have attained a measure of respectability as the users have joined together to insure that riders drive safely and respect private property. Ridden irresponsibly, snowmobiles can do serious damage to farmers' fields, sensitive terrain and some kinds of wildlife. New Hampshire riders demonstrate that they don't have to cause damage by staying on marked trails or in areas designated for snowmobiles. Snowmobile operation falls under the jurisdiction of the New Hampshire Department of Fish and Game. Violations of snowmobile regulations can effect your driving record and driver's license.

New Hampshire has 6,000 miles of snowmobile trails and 45,000 registered snowmobiles. Registration is required and costs $35 for New Hampshire residents and $45 for out-of-state owners. We have 200 registration centers throughout the state including most snowmobile dealers. New Hampshire has reciprocal registration agreements with Maine and Quebec. Therefore, a snowmobile registered in New Hampshire does not need additional registration for operation in Maine or Quebec and vice versa.

There is a wonderful network of snowmobile trails in the North Country (Great North Woods Region) called the NH/VT Commerce Zone. Under a reciprocal agreement between New Hampshire and Vermont, machines can travel on all 228 miles of trails without having to register in both states. These trails are in turn linked to the New Hampshire corridor system, more than 6,060 miles of trails through private and public lands that are maintained by the local snowmobile clubs with assistance from the state. Maps of the corridor system are available from the New Hampshire Bureau of Trails, P.O. Box 1856, Concord, CT 03302, (603) 271-3254. (The trail corridor map is also printed on the back of the New Hampshire Highway map that goes out with the tourism packet.)

Snowmobile rental is common in the White Mountains but virtually unheard of in other regions. If you've never driven one before, do ask for training before you start out! Snowmobile safety falls under the responsibility of the N.H. Fish and Game Department, (603) 271-3129. In addition to training programs, Fish and Game officers also enforce the laws governing snowmobiling in the state.

Snowmobiling fatalities are on the rise, and most are speed- or alcohol-related. Serious snowmobilers look with trepidation on the influx of joyriders. Private landowners may close their property, and the state may step in with increased regulation if the snowmobilers can't reverse the trend themselves. Training, publicity and a willingness to "interfere" when a fellow rider is out of line are the only hope of saving lives and restoring the sport's image in the public mind.

In addition to the state trail maps, dealers and snowmobile clubs can supply maps (there may be a small charge) of local trails. The NH Snowmobile Association, 722 Route 3A, Suite 14, Bow, NH 03304, (603) 224-8906, is an association of local snowmobiler clubs. It teaches safe riding, promotes good relationships with landowners and organizes events throughout the season. In 1998 the NHSA received an Outstanding Achievement Award from the American Council of Snowmobile Associations for their efforts in promoting safety awareness. It also publishes the *Sno-Traveler*, New Hampshire's official snowmobiling newspaper and the best source of contacts with local people who can tell you where snowmobiling is allowed in their communities.

Ice-skating

Many communities have ponds they keep scraped or fields they flood for skating. Many resorts provide skating areas for their guests. A few towns and cities have rinks open to the public. Hours and prices are both minimal;

call your local parks or recreation department for details.

Use caution if you skate on our lakes, ponds and streams. The ice should be at least 3- to 4-inches thick to be considered safe for skating. If you're not sure, you can call the local police department's non-emergency number to ask if the ice is safe. Stay away from open areas or places where the water is likely to be running beneath the ice (near dams, waterfalls and other outlets).

Other Winter Sports

For downhill skiing, you need a mountain, and you pay someone to run those lifts and tractors. Cross-country skiing benefits from grooming and trail maintenance, and it's really nice to ice skate where you don't have to shovel first. Other winter sports depend less on commercial support: snowshoeing, ice-fishing, ice-climbing and winter hiking. Some resorts and commercial operations arrange planned activities in these sports, but most enthusiasts make their own fun.

There is no doubt that one of the most stunning experiences a New Hampshire winter has to offer is a trek into the woods, away from the shops, the cars and the crowds. Whether you're climbing with crampons and ice axe, waddling across deep powder on snowshoes or schussing through the woods on skis, the silence of the snow-covered forest is unforgettable. You'll see evidence of the winter lives of animals, cross lakes and waterfalls frozen in time and maybe stand at the top of a ledge with a breathtaking view across miles and miles of valley. It's a wonderful way to spend a day — but please be wise and plan well. Dress in layers. Always carry food, water (insulated so it won't freeze), sleeping bags and bivouac sacks (a bivy sack is a waterproof miniature tent) and spare socks and mittens. If you'll be above treeline you must have a balaclava or face mask too.

The biggest killer in the White Mountains isn't ice or snow, it's cold. Hypothermia weakens your judgment so that you can make unwise decisions or dangerous choices. Even experienced climbers have been trapped, and killed, by unexpected weather changes or pushing to hike just a bit too far. The Insiders who work with AVSAR (Androscoggin Valley Search and Rescue) are expert volunteers, but there is a limit to how quickly a team of 10 or 20 people can search a wilderness bigger than the state of Rhode Island. If you're new to winter hiking, you'll be safer and probably have more fun on one of the wonderful hiking and climbing trips led by experienced guides

Important Numbers

Statewide: **Ski New Hampshire**, (800)88-SKI-NH, is a 24-hour hotline that will connect you to any one of 35 Ski New Hampshire Alpine and cross-country resorts. Call for details about ski passes and vouchers. Ski New Hampshire offers four pass options, and all include money-saving vouchers. Ski New Hampshire can help you plan your vacation and give you up-to-date lodging information. To plan your visit, call for a **Winter Vacation Kit**, (800) FUN-IN-NH, ext 100. For information about **New Hampshire State Parks**, call (603) 271-3254.

The White Mountains Region: **Country Inns in The White Mountains**, (800) 562-1300, can help you with package plans as well as details on skiing from inn-to-inn. The **Franconia Notch Chamber of Commerce**, (800) 237-9007, is a great help in planning your winter skiing getaway. The **Lincoln-Woodstock Lodging Bureau**, (800) 227-4191, has details on accommodations and ski packages in every price range. Call for details about the **Mount Washington Valley**, (603) 356-3171 or (800) 367-3364, for lodging and activities. For information on the **Northern White Mountains**, call (800) 992-7480. Details on Bed and Breakfast inns as well as motels is available to help you plan your winter package.

Dartmouth-Lake Sunapee Region: The **Lake Sunapee Business Association**, (800) 258-3530, can help you plan your winter vacation.

The Lakes Region: To plan winter activities in the Lakes Region, call (603) 253-8555 or (800) 60-LAKES.

Important numbers for snowmobile information: **New Hampshire Fish and Game**, (603) 271-3127; **New Hampshire Trails Bureau**, (603) 271-3254; **Snowphone** (800) 258-3609.

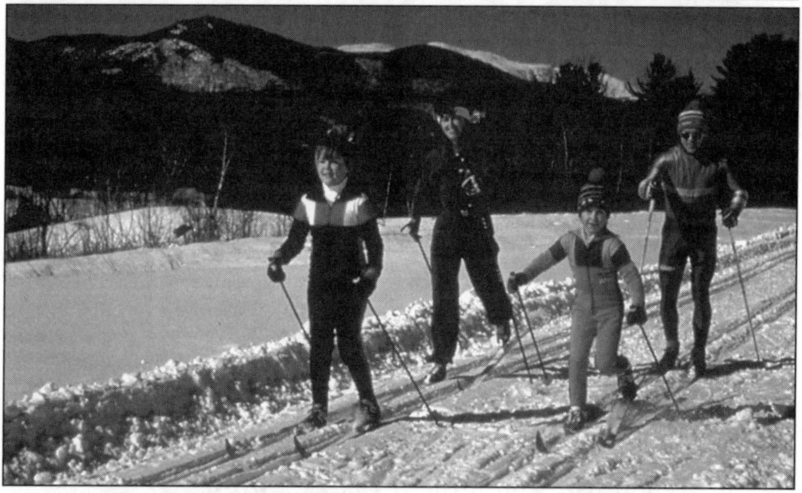

Photo: Bob Grant

Cross-country skiing is a fun winter sport the whole family can enjoy.

from the Appalachian Mountain Club, Eastern Mountain Sports or the Adventure program at the Greater Manchester YMCA.

For winter hiking, the Appalachian Mountain Club's hiking programs and workshops go on all winter. Call (603) 466-2727 for more details about the AMC, and see our Natural Wonders chapter. In the White Mountains Region, Eastern Mountain Sports, Main Street, North Conway, (603) 356-5433, (800) 310-4504, offers ice-climbing and winter-mountaineering lessons for all ability levels. They also lead winter ascents of Mount Washington. Call for details and schedules.

Ice diving is another surprising winter sport. You must be an experienced diver with advanced open-water certification and drysuit training to ice dive. Those who already love diving find that the challenge, the teamwork and the stunning water clarity make diving beneath a thick layer of ice a thrilling experience. Many who are trained and certified at the Lake Winnipesaukee program go on to dive on Arctic and Antarctic expeditions. If you want to try ice diving, Dive Winnipesaukee, Main Street, Wolfeboro, (603) 569-2120, offers classes.

For More Information

For more about winter sports, local publications can be very helpful in providing up-to-date information. *Winter in New Hampshire* is a monthly newspaper full of facts and listings of all kinds. Inside are more special events, contests and carnivals than any one family can exhaust. Look for this free paper in the tourist information centers and in local shops. While you're in the tourist information centers, look for the weekly *Ski Week* that has detailed listings of ski areas and special events. It also includes calendar listings and short articles, tips for beginners and experienced skiers alike and the occasional nostalgia piece.

Merrimack Valley Region

Downhill Skiing

Pat's Peak Ski Area

Flanders Rd. off N.H. Rt. 114, Henniker • (603) 428-3245, (888) PATS PEAK

Despite a vertical drop of only 710 feet, Pat's Peak offers a complete ski experience, from beginner slopes to some of the steepest trails in New Hampshire. A special snowboarding area provides for those wild riders, while the NASTAR race trail lets skiers test their skills. Snowmaking covers 90 percent of the mountain, and night skiing (in January and February only) is available for all ability levels. A total of seven lifts service the 19 trails, which are evenly divided among novice, intermediate and expert difficulty. Special events are scheduled throughout the season, some to raise money for good causes and some just for fun. Pat's Peak is open 9 AM to 4 PM Monday through Friday and 8:30 AM to 4 PM Saturday and Sunday. Night skiing is available from 3 to 8 PM Monday through Thursday and until 9 PM on Friday. Pat's Peak provides child care for little ones 6 months to 6 years old. There are ski and snowboard lessons for all abilities and regionally renowned cookies too.

Cross-country Skiing

Bear Brook State Park

N.H. Rt. 28, Hooksett

• (603) 485-9874

This 9,600-acre park is laced with trails, and trail maps are available at the parking lot or from the state parks number, (603) 271-3254. All trails are open to skiers for free, and many also allow snowmobiling. Be aware that some of the trails are very steep. (The park map shows elevations — the closer together the lines are, the steeper the slope.) If you come on a Saturday morning, don't miss the snowmobile museum on your way in!

Beaver Brook Association

Brown Ln., Hollis

• (603) 465-7787

The trails on Maple Hill Farm are accessible at no charge all winter long for snowshoeing, cross-country skiing, winter hiking and nature walking. Thursday afternoon guided walks will teach you to read the signs of wildlife in the woods. Some snowshoes are available to borrow and should be reserved in advance. See our Parks and Open Spaces chapter for more details about Beaver Brook.

Robert Frost Farm Historic Site

N.H. Rt. 28, Derry

• (603) 432-3091

The farm where America's great poet observed and wrote about New Hampshire's snows is closed in winter, but visitors are welcome to enjoy the cross-country ski trails through the farm. Some cross open fields, others wind through the woods. You can almost hear Mr. Frost's gravely voice reciting "Looking for a Sunset Bird in Winter:" "When shoeing home across the white/I thought I saw a bird alight." (See our Attractions chapter for details about the farm.)

Adventure YMCA

116 Goffstown Back Rd., Goffstown

• (603) 497-4663

The Goffstown Y offers instruction in telemark skiing (a cross-country/downhill combination) and year-round rock-climbing lessons. Lessons range from $50 to $85 (lower for members) at sites throughout the state. Call for the season's detailed plans.

Hampshire Hills Ski Touring Center

Emerson Rd., Milford

• (603) 673-7123

Nine gently sloping wooded trails totaling 4 groomed kilometers invite a quick lunch-hour ski break, as this health club is conveniently located just off N.H. Route 13 in Milford. Rentals and lessons are available, and there is a nominal charge for nonmembers to ski.

Pawtuckaway State Park

Off N.H. Rts. 101 and 156, Nottingham and Raymond

• (603) 895-3031

This 5,500-acre park is a favorite summer camping destination. In winter the park is closed, but there are trails open for

INSIDERS' TIP

Take a companion along if you ski, skate or hike in unfrequented or backcountry areas. A simple injury can quickly turn fatal if you can't get out of the cold.

snowmobiling, cross-country skiing, snowshoeing and hiking. Trails are fairly level around Lake Pawtuckaway, others climb into the Pawtuckaway Mountains. Maps are available at the parking lot, or you can call the New Hampshire State Parks information number, (603) 271-3254, to request trail maps.

Clough State Park
Off N.H. Rt. 114, Weare
• (603) 529-7112

Trails are open to skiing and snowmobiling, although no maps are available for this park. The fifty-acre park is entirely within the flood zone, so the trails are fairly level. (The trees may look awful. If so, be assured they're not all dead, they were just under water sometime last spring.) The park is closed during the winter, but you can ski for no charge.

Seacoast Region

Cross-country Skiing

Urban Forestry Center
Elwyn Rd., Portsmouth
• (603) 431-6774

This educational center, run by the Society for Protection of New Hampshire Forests, has trails through 180 acres of woods that are available for snowshoeing and cross-country skiing in winter. See our Parks and Open Spaces chapter for more information.

Odiorne Point State Park
N.H. Rt. 1A, Rye
• (603) 436-7406

Seaside cross-country skiing is allowed in about half of this 370-acre park. Trails wind through the woods and up and down over the low hills, or you can stay close to the Seacoast Science Center (see our Attractions chapter) and within sight of the water, where it is fairly flat — but windy! The park is staffed only on weekends, and there is no charge in winter. The Science Center is open all year too — if you get chilled, step inside and check out the tidepools!

Lakes Region

Downhill Skiing

Gunstock
N.H. Rt. 11A, Gilford
• (603) 293-4341, (800) GUNSTOCK

Gunstock is a full-service winter resort, offering downhill and cross-country skiing, snowshoeing and snowboarding, lessons, night skiing and an active apres-ski atmosphere for young and old. With a vertical drop of 1,400 feet, Gunstock offers 45 trails ranging from easy to expert, with the largest number in the intermediate level. There are seven lifts, including two surface lifts and a quad chair. Snowmaking on 98 percent of the mountain and lessons for all ability levels and ages make this an attractive destination for winter fun. A special feature here is the noon groom — actually three-times-a-day grooming that guarantees top-condition trails all day long. Gunstock is so sure you'll be satisfied, it offers a money-back guarantee. The area opens at 9 AM Monday through Friday and 8:30 AM Saturday and Sunday. It stays open until 10 PM every night except Sunday and Monday, when it closes at 4 PM. Day care is offered for ages 6 months and up, and ski-school options start at age 3.

Tenney Mountain Ski Area
N.H. Rt. 3A S., Plymouth
• (603) 536-4125, (888) TENNEY-2

With a 1,400-foot vertical drop and four lifts servicing 33 trails, Tenney Mountain offers a variety of skiing for all abilities. More than half the trails are intermediate level, 12 percent are novice and 30 percent are expert level. Snowboarding is allowed on all trails, and there is a half-pipe as well. Snowmaking covers 90 percent of the mountain, but Insiders who are good skiers particularly like the fact that some trails on the mountain are left natural and ungroomed. This is a family-oriented ski area, built around the needs of the condominium owners in the development (although not restricted to them). The day-care center takes children age 6 weeks and older, and ski lessons are offered to children as soon as they can stand. The rental shop offers all the latest equipment for both skiers and boarders. Tenney is open seven days a week from 9 AM to 4 PM.

Cross-country Skiing

Deer Cap Ski Touring

N.H. Rt. 16, Center Ossipee
• (603) 539-6030

Year-round camping makes this an unusual spot for a winter vacation. The 10 cross-country trails (totaling 15 kilometers of groomed trails) are open to the public for $3. The trails wind through the woods over mostly gentle, riverside terrain and offer something for every skier from novice to expert. Rentals are available on site. There are warming huts for chilled skiers, and it's just a quick skip up to North Conway for shopping if the weather turns sour.

Red Hill Inn and Ski Touring Center

N.H. Rt. 25B, Centre Harbor
• (603) 279-7001

Red Hill Inn has an informal 5-kilometer trail network through the woods and down to Squam Lake. There is no charge to use the trails, but visitors are asked to sign in at the inn's desk. (See our Bed and Breakfasts and Country Inns chapter for more details about the Red Hill Inn.)

Gunstock Cross-Country Center

N.H. Rt. 11A, Gilford
• (603) 293-4341

In addition to Alpine trails, Gunstock offers 52 kilometers of cross-country trails, 37 kilometers groomed and 15 backcountry. The terrain is a mixture of level and hilly terrain, some open but mostly in the woods. Cross-country tickets range from $5 to $10 a day.

Perry Hollow Cross-Country

King's Hwy., Wolfeboro
• (603) 569-3055

The country club no longer grooms specific trails on the golf course but the scenic countryside still invites cross-country skiers of all abilities to explore and enjoy, and the country club owners don't object. There is no charge for skiing. Most of the terrain is level and open.

White Lake State Park

N.H. Rt. 16, Tamworth • (603) 323-2087

This park offers trails for snowmobiling, snowshoeing and cross-country skiing at no cost. Most are fairly level. No maps are available for this park. (See our Parks and Open Spaces chapter for details.)

Nordic Skier

N.H. Rts. 28 and 109, Wolfeboro
• (603) 569-3151

In the heart of the Lakes Region, Nordic Skier offers 20 kilometers of groomed, tracked trails and more than 20 kilometers of backcountry skiing for $5 a day. Trails vary in difficulty, with an even mix of easy/beginner and intermediate/advanced trails. Lessons, rentals and maps are available.

Snowmobiling

Meredith Woods 4 Season Camping Area

Off I-93 at Exit 23, Meredith
• (603) 279-5449, (800) 848-0328

RV and trailer campers are welcome here year round. They can enjoy the indoor pool, hot tub and game rooms as well as groomed snowmobile trails that connect directly to the state trail corridor system.

White Mountains and Great North Woods Regions

Downhill Skiing

Attitash Bear Peak

U.S. Rt. 302, Bartlett
• (603) 374-2368

Part of The Presidentials Resort along with Cranmore, Attitash is undergoing a major building phase. It is a growing resort as opposed to a mom-and-pop ski area. Management knows what makes for good skiing, and they are proud of the snowmaking capacity that covers 97 percent of the 45 trails. The vertical drop is 1,750 feet, and 11 lifts serve the area including one high-speed detachable quad, one fixed quad, three triples, four doubles and two surface lifts. Attitash Bear Peak is the only ski area in the state that offers Smart Ticket, a pay-by-the-run lift-ticket system. The new novice trail from the top of Bear Peak gives less-experienced skiers a great extended run.

Child care covers kids 6 months to 5 years old. The ski school has Perfect Kids for 4- to 6-year-olds and Adventure Kids for ages 7 through 12. Private and group lessons are available as well as Learn to Ski and Learn to Snowboard packages. Snowboarders will enjoy both a park and a half-pipe. Alpine and snowboard equipment is available for rent.

The slopes are open Monday through Friday from 9 AM to 4 PM and Saturdays, Sundays and holidays from 8 AM to 4 PM. Lodging options include the new Grand Summit Hotel, Attitash Mountain Village (condominiums) and nearby motels (see our Hotels and Motels chapter). Ski packages are available.

Bretton Woods

U.S. Rt. 302, Bretton Woods
• (603) 278-5000, (800) 232-2972,
Snowphone: (603) 278-5051

It's hard to keep your eyes on the trail when you're skiing in the thick of the White Mountains and looking at Mount Washington and the surrounding Presidential Range. Bretton Woods is another picturesque standout in a state that excels in mind-expanding scenery. The terrain favors intermediate skiers. Two hundred trail-acres with 32 trails are open for skiing and snowboarding. Forty-four percent of the trails are intermediate with the remaining 56 percent evenly split between novice and expert. The trails are wide and offer lots of space for families with differing abilities to ski together.

The vertical drop is 1,500 feet. The expert skiing has gotten a boost recently with the addition of 25 more acres devoted to glade skiing. Snowboarders enjoy the full use of trails as well as a half-pipe. All trails filter to the lodge, so it's easy for groups to meet up at the end of the day.

The five ski lifts include one T-Bar, two doubles, one triple and one detachable quad. Three trails and two lifts are open for weekend night skiing. Rental equipment includes shaped skis. The ski school offers Skiing with Shape, a learning package for beginners and intermediates. The package includes parabolic ski rentals, a parabolic ski lesson and a novice lift ticket.

Child-care facilities are on-site for kids 2 months to 5 years old. Private and group lessons and Learn to Ski and Learn to Snowboard packages are offered. Kids have the option of a full-day ski school program. Bretton Woods also has excellent cross-country facilities (look for details in our cross-country ski section).

Operating hours are from 9 AM to 4 PM Monday through Thursday, 9 AM to 10 PM on Friday, 8:30 AM to 10 PM on Saturday and 8:30 AM to 4 PM on Sunday.

All Bretton Woods lodging is under the Mount Washington Hotel and Resort umbrella. The Mount Washington Hotel is closed November through April (although there are rumors that it may soon be open year round). Skiers can choose from the upscale Bretton Arms, an elegant inn built in 1896; the Bretton Woods Motor Inn, with a more casual family-style atmosphere (and indoor pool); and the slopeside condominium units available for rent through the Mount Washington Hotel and Resort. A regular shuttle service travels between the Alpine and cross-country centers and all three lodging areas.

For great food, be sure to try Top O'Quad Restaurant at the top of the quad chair lift. There's also Fabien's at the base, serving solid ski food. Darby's at the Bretton Woods Motor Inn has family-style dining and, as you might

INSIDERS' TIP

Mittens are warmer than gloves because there's more air circulating around your fingers.

expect, the Bretton Woods Inn is a more formal dining choice (see our Restaurants chapter.)

Bretton Woods is independently owned as opposed to being a member of a multi-resort partnership. The resort is proud that one of the owners is the general manager and believes that personal involvement and hands-on snow shoveling is the key to guest satisfaction. It's just across the valley from Mount Washington, so there is always lots of snow.

The Balsams Wilderness
N.H. Rt. 26, Dixville Notch
• (603) 255-3400

If you want to learn to ski in the lap of luxury, this is the place. This 15,000-acre resort in the Great North Woods is a gem any time of year, but the winter packages are hard to beat. Prices range from about $95 to $154 per person per night including a full breakfast and dinner along with dancing and movies every night. In addition to skiing, the resort offers ice-skating, snowshoeing and sleigh rides. Look for details on this resort in our Accommodations chapter.

The Alpine skiing ranges from moderately easy to moderately difficult trails. The trails include runs from the top of the mountain for novices. The vertical drop is 1,000 feet with three lifts (two are T-bars). The cross-country facilities are among the best in the U.S. (details follow in our cross-country section).

Guests at the resort ski for free with a moderate charge for equipment rental. But you don't have to be a guest to ski here. Day skiers pay between $15 and $25 for lift tickets. Snowboarders will enjoy both the park and half-pipe.

Child care is provided at no cost for guests. The Learning Center offers lots of lesson plans including kids' ski programs for ages 3 to 12. The ski hours are 9 AM to 4 PM every day.

King Pine Ski Area at Purity Spring Resort
N.H. Rt. 153, East Madison
• (800) 373-3754, Snowphone: (800) 367-8897

We've always said the quality of mom-and-pop operations depends on just whose mom and pop we're talking about. Well here you know you're talking about the Hoyt family because they've been behind Purity Spring Resort since it opened in the late 1800s, with the ski area added in 1962. Dedicated to providing families with an affordable place to ski, King Pine offers 17 trails (50 percent for novices) on 60 acres with a vertical drop of 350 feet. This may be the smallest mountain in New England with Alpine skiing facilities, but don't discount the quality here — the runs may be short, but they can be challenging. There are also groomed cross-country trails, snowboarding facilities and a pond for ice-skating.

You can rent cross-country and Alpine skis along with snowboards, ice skates and snowshoes. Sign up for a Learn to Ski or Learn to Snowboard package as well as group and private lessons. Lift tickets are reasonable with rates as low as $5 for a beginner triple chair with access to 4 trails. As an added family feature, children 5 and younger and adults 70 and older ski for free. There is a snack bar in the Pine Mountain Base Lodge.

The skiing begins every day at 9 AM and goes to 4 PM on Monday, Wednesday, Thursday and Sunday. Seven trails are open for night skiing until 9:30 PM on Tuesday, Friday and Saturday.

The lodging varies, with 74 rooms available in winter. Deluxe accommodations are available in a newer building that also has an indoor pool. Two big, old inns offer rooms with both private and shared-bath options. Three all-you-can-eat meals are included in the weekend rates, and breakfast and dinner are included during midweek. In lieu of lunch, midweek skiers get free lift tickets. The average daily price per adult with double occupancy and including meals is $70, $24 a day for juniors ages 4 through 12 and $5 a day for children younger than 4.

Cannon Mountain
Franconia Notch
• (603) 823-5563, Snowphone: (800) 552-1234

Very challenging, brutally cold, an amazing drop, wonderful skiing — that's Cannon. With a 2,146-foot vertical drop, this is an Alpine skiing locale sure to please the best skiers. Cannon was the site of the first World Cup Race held in the United States. You'll find 38 trails totaling 163 acres. Ninety-seven percent of the trails are covered by snowmaking. Just more than 50 percent of the trails are rated intermediate with the remaining trails split between expert and novice. Try gladed skiing on two new trails: Turnpike, a 500-foot intermediate, and Banshee, a 2,000-foot upper intermediate. The first aerial tramway in the country was at Cannon. The six current lifts include an 80-passenger tramway along with one quad, one triple, two doubles and one surface.

There is something for everyone at Cannon. Snowboarders are more than welcome and will enjoy both the Terrain Park as well as the half-pipe. Seniors (65 and older) who are New Hampshire residents get free weekday lift tickets, and kids 5 and younger ski for free.

All guest services are centered in Peabody Lodge. You can buy lift tickets and rent equipment here. The Ski School has group clinics, private lessons and Learn to Ski and Learn to Snowboard classes. Child care is available for kids ages 1 to 6. The SKIwee instructional programs are for 4- to 9-year-olds.

When hunger strikes, look for one of three cafeterias — at Peabody Lodge, the tram stop at the bottom and at the top — as well as a deli and a snack bar. The hours are from 9 AM to 4 PM every day. You won't find lodging at state-owned Cannon.

Black Mountain
N.H. Rt. 16B, Jackson
• (603) 383-4490

A fun family resort with 30 trails, Black Mountain is where lots of New Hampshire kids have learned to ski. The family pricing can't be beat (kids 5 and younger ski free), and lots of two- and three-day packages are available.

The vertical drop is 1,100 feet. The four lifts include one triple, a double, a J-bar and a platter pull. A half-pipe, snowboard park and the Snow Tubing Park guarantee fun for all the kids. The Snow Tubing Park is open on weekends and holidays.

Child care is for kids 6 months to 5 years old, and the ski school has programs for kids 3 to 12. The school also offers a full range of instruction for adults.

If you aren't a skier, snowboarder or tube lover, you can spend time on a sleigh ride. And if you've never seen a one-horse open sleigh, you will here. Family sleigh rides and dog-sled rides — just for kids — can be arranged. Food and lodging are at the base in Whitney's Inn.

Wildcat Mountain Ski Area
Pinkham Notch, N.H. Rt. 16, Jackson
• (603) 466-3326

The highest ski area in New Hampshire at 4,062 feet, Wildcat Mountain is completely within the White Mountain National Forest. While snow bragging is common, the 40 trails here get as much snow as anywhere in the state. The mountain is right across from Mount Washington. The views are spectacular, and the wind is cold.

An old-fashioned, classic New England ski area, Wildcat does not have condominiums or other slopeside lodging. It does have a brand-new high-speed detachable quad lift that travels from the base to the summit in 7+ minutes. The total number of lifts is seven. The vertical drop is 2,100 feet. Thirty-five percent of the trails are expert, 45 percent are intermediate and 20 percent are novice. Insiders love Wildcat.

Wildcat opens at 9 AM Monday through Friday and at 8:30 AM on weekends. It closes every day at 4 PM. Child care for children ages 6 months to 6 years is available, and the ski school offers lessons beginning with 4 year olds.

Loon Mountain
Kancamagus Hwy., (N.H. Rt. 112), Lincoln • (603) 745-8111, Snowphone: (603) 745-8100

More people ski at Loon Mountain than any other New Hampshire ski resort. Constantly in the news with expansion plans, the resort works hard to maintain its popularity. The modern facilities appeal to families with young skiers as well as snowboarding teenagers. Almost two-thirds of the 43 trails are intermediate. Beginners have a 20 percent share, while experts share a 16 percent portion. The vertical drop is 2,100 feet. Recently added Alpine garden facilities under the gondola on the Picaroon trail have bumps and jumps. The eight lifts include one high-speed detachable quad, a four-person high-speed gondola, two triples, three doubles and a free pony tow. The snowboarders have both a park and a half-pipe. You can cross-country ski on 25 kilometers of groomed and tracked trails.

The ski school offers a variety of instruction with both group clinics and private lessons. Special Learn to Ski and Learn to Snowboard packages are also available. Loon Mountain is the only location in the eastern United States to serve as an Atomic CarvX Learning Site. Skiers who take part will be using the latest in parabolic ski equipment. The programs are called 1-2-3 Learn to Ski and Intermediate Express. For the rest of us, equipment at the two rental shops includes Alpine, snowboards, snowshoes and ice skates.

The Governor Adams Lodge and the Octagon Lodge are the centers of activity at the base. There's Wanigan's Deli for sandwiches and Java Junction to make sure you don't miss your hometown coffee bar. Each lodge has a lounge — The Paul Bunyon Room in Governor's Lodge and Babe's in the Octagon Lodge. The Summit Cafe is at the top of the gondola, and Camp 3 is a ski-to cafeteria that you can get to by both beginner and intermediate trails.

You can ski out the door of your condominium at the Mountains Club Resort on Loon. An indoor pool, the Granite Grill Restaurant and ice-skating are some of the basic amenities available. The schedule of activities is always changing.

The Children's Center, an 8,600-square-foot space, is devoted to everything concerning kids including child care, ski school and rentals. The child-care facilities are for kids 6 months to 8 years old. The ski school options begin with the P.K. Boo Bear program for 3- and 4-year-olds and range up to the Teen Mountain Adventure Program for skiers ages 13 through 16. In between is Kinder Bear for ages 5 and 6 and Adventure Camp for 7- to 12-year-olds. Keeping kids in mind, Loon has a Wildlife Theater as well as a Children's Theater for non-slope entertainment. Just in case your kids want more slope action, send them out to the 2,600-foot Snubber beginners trail for Night Tubing. Since lift service is available, you might as well join them.

The many packages available make it easy to find the right plan for your group. It's best to make plans and reservations in advance.

Cranmore

Skimobile Rd., North Conway • (603) 356-5544, Snowphone: (800) 356-8516

Now part of the Presidentials ski area, Cranmore considers itself the home of American skiing. The 36 trails are on 190 acres just a mile from town. Of the trails, 45 percent are rated intermediate, 35 percent novice and 20 percent expert. The vertical drop is 1,200 feet. Use any of the six lifts including three doubles, one surface, one triple and one high-speed detached quad. Our skiing friends love Cranmore for the wide range of trail difficulty.

Cranmore is proud of its reputation as having great skiing for the entire family. The Tiny Turns program is one-on-one hourly instruction for kids ages 3 to 6. SKIwee is a daily program for kids ages 4 to 6. Snowboarding facilities include a half-pipe and a park as well as Learn to Snowboard programs and snowboard rentals. The ski school offers group, private and learn-to-ski lessons. Child care is available for children 6 months through 8 years old.

You'll find a wide range of ticket prices including multi-day, twilight, senior (older than 70) and junior (younger than 15) plans. Night skiing is available Thursdays through Saturdays and on holidays. Cranmore opens at 9 AM Monday through Friday and at 8 AM on weekends and holidays. It closes at 4 PM Sunday through Wednesday and at 9 PM Thursday through Saturday and on holidays.

You can get soup and sandwiches at the top in the Meister Hut. The Pub is at the bottom, and a cafeteria is in the main base lodge. All close by late afternoon, but North Conway is just a mile away. Look for details in our Restaurants chapter.

Lodging is available in two and three-bedroom condominiums. All have washers and dryers, full kitchens and sleeping lofts. Prices range from $175 a night for a group of four, midweek, to more than $300 a night for a group of eight on a holiday weekend. Lodging prices include full use of the Cranmore Sports Center, which has an indoor pool,

Jacuzzi, climbing wall and complete Nautilus system.

Tuckerman Ravine

off N.H. Rt. 16, Pinkham Notch
• (603) 466-2725
(Appalachian Mountain Club)

Our expert Insider is adamant that Tuckerman Ravine is only for very experienced skiers, preferably those with lots of mountaineering experience. Tuckerman Ravine, on the east side of Mount Washington, is 600 feet of vertical relief cut by glaciers.

There are no lifts, and the hike in is at least 2.5 miles from the AMC camp at Pinkham Notch. And that hike just gets you to the ice steps. Then you hike up until you're ready to ski down. Once you start down, there's no stopping until the bottom. Be prepared for lots of falling objects including people, ice and rock.

Tuckerman Ravine is famous for spring skiing. Snow blows into the bowl all year, and by spring the snowpack has settled. Warm spring weather bonds the snow layers, and you'll find snow here into the summer. Be sure and check avalanche conditions and talk with skiers familiar with the area before you attempt it.

Waterville Valley

1 Ski Area Rd., Waterville Valley
• (603) 236-8311,
Snowphone: (603) 236-4144

Former United States Olympic skier Tom Corcoran developed this longtime family vacation destination into a one-stop, self-contained, year-round recreational village. The town is about 450 acres with the rest of the land belonging to the White Mountain National Forest. The beautiful Town Square is nestled in the valley and looks more like the 18th century than the 20th, but the construction is modern and the conveniences are up to date.

The skiing on Mount Tecumseh is plentiful with 49 trails totaling 255 acres. The vertical drop is more than 2,000 feet, and 60 percent of the runs are intermediate with the remaining trails evenly divided between novice and expert. The trails are wide, making for lots of room to ski with friends and family. Twelve lifts keep traffic from building up. Lifts include one high-speed detachable quad, three triples, four doubles and four surface lifts. Lift service now goes to the half-pipe park. Snowboarders also have a park and mogul fields for serious fun.

And don't worry if your teen is a snowboarder and you're an avid cross-country or snowshoe type. There are rentals and trails for all. See our section later in the chapter for more on the cross-country facilities. Ice-skaters will love the new indoor ice arena in Town Square with an Olympic-size hockey rink. Lessons and rentals are available.

Child care covers kids ages 6 weeks to 4 years old. Ski programs for kids are divided into SKIwee for 3- to 5-year-olds, Mountain Cadets for ages 6 to 8 and Mountain Scouts for 9- to 12-year-olds. The ski school also has group and private lessons along with Learn to Ski and Learn to Snowboard packages. The trails are open from 9 AM to 4 PM Monday through Friday and 8 AM to 4 PM on Saturday and Sunday.

The Central Reservations Center does an excellent job of matching skiers and lodgings. The packages and prices are too numerous to detail, but we'll give a general rundown. Be sure and ask whether your lodging package includes use of the Athletic Center. The center is not managed by Waterville Valley, but use of the facilities is often available. The options include indoor swimming pools, tennis, racquetball and squash. Lodging choices range from the 52-room Valley Inn with its first-rate restaurant to the Golden Eagle condominium units with full kitchens. There are 80 rooms in the Snowy Owl and 32 at the Silver Fox Country Inn. Both of these locations serve a continental breakfast (see our Accommodations chapter).

INSIDERS' TIP

Just because there is bare ground outside your window doesn't mean your ski weekend is off. There may be plenty of snow, machine-made and natural, on the slopes. Call ahead!

Town Square in the Valley includes the Common Man restaurant with classic American food. Alpine Pizza and Chile Peppers are also in the center of things. On the mountaintop you can stop in at The Schwendi Hutt for solid fuel or try Sunny Side Up at mid-mountain. The base lodge has a cafeteria as well as a restaurant and lounge on the top floor.

Once you arrive at Waterville Valley, you can park the car and forget about it until it's time to leave. There is shuttle service throughout the village connecting inns, lodges, condo units and facilities for cross-country, Alpine, snowboarding and ice-skating.

Cross-country Skiing

Many cross-country ski facilities are also Alpine ski areas. Read both sections as well as the introduction to this chapter for help planning the right vacation for your family.

Bear Notch Ski Touring Center

U.S. Rt. 302, Bartlett
• (603) 374-2277

Sixty kilometers of skate-groomed and tracked trails along with unlimited backcountry skiing make up the beautiful terrain here. Ski past fields, rivers and streams — even a waterfall along the aptly named 5K Waterfall Trail. Beginners will love the easy access to trails along the Saco River. You don't have to be an expert to get great views. Intermediates will want to try the 8K Yates Farm Trail. Fees are $6 to $8 for the day. Kids 7 and younger and adults older than 70 ski for free. The center is open every day from 8 AM to 5 PM.

Bretton Woods

U.S. Rt. 302, Bretton Woods
• (603) 278-3322

One hundred kilometers of trails for traditional and skate skiers make Bretton Woods a favorite for cross-country buffs. Trails include 5 kilometers of backcountry, 90 kilometers of skate-groomed and 95 kilometers of groomed and tracked. The full-service cross-country center includes a cafeteria, rental shop and retail store with all the latest equipment. You can ski every day from 8:30 AM to 4 PM for $9 to $13.

The Balsams Wilderness

Dixville Notch
• (603) 255-3400

The 76 kilometers of trails include 10 kilometers of backcountry and 65 kilometers of both skate-groomed and tracked trails. A remote ski area open through March, The Balsams is well worth the drive north. *Snow Country* magazine rates the premier cross-country facility in the Great North Woods as one of the best in the United States. Skiing is free for guests and $15 for others. The trails are open from 9 AM to 4 PM every day.

Franconia Village XC Ski Center at the Franconia Inn

N.H. Rt. 116, Franconia
• (603) 823-5542, (800) 473-5299

Beginners to experts will enjoy the beautiful terrain in Franconia. Sixty-five kilometers of groomed and tracked trails, 5 kilometers of skate-groomed and 20 kilometers of backcountry trails are divided into 20 percent expert trails and 40 percent for both beginners and intermediates. The snow covered White Mountains surround you as you ski both wooded and open trails. Once you've mastered the basics and consider yourself an intermediate, try the Inn-to-Inn loop. You'll visit four classic inns as you ski the 19K trail. Snowshoes and ice skates as well as the required environment for such equipment are part of this full service XC ski center. It's open every day from 8 AM to 4:30 PM. The cost is $8 for adults and $7 for juniors.

Great Glen Trails at Mount Washington

N.H. Rt. 16, Gorham
• (603) 466-2333

It's all here — from cross-country to kicksledding to snowshoeing. The 40 kilometers of trails include 20 kilometers of backcountry, 20 kilometers of groomed and 14 kilometers of tracked skiing. Twenty kilometers of trail are skate-groomed, and the facility has snowmaking capacity. Beginners and those who like to take it easy like the fact that 80 percent of the trails are suitable for beginners. You'll also enjoy the organized guided skiing tours led by naturalists. Learn to identify animal tracks and other evidence

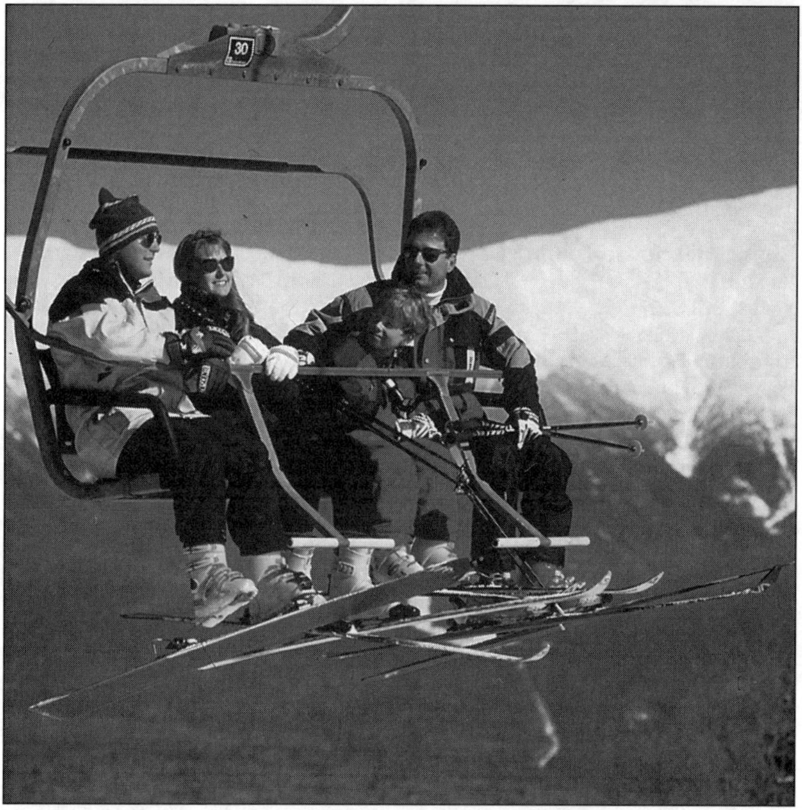

Photo: Bob Grant

Mount Washington looms as skiers ride the Quad Chairlift at Wildcat.

of the nocturnal activities of the neighborhood coyotes and bears. The timber-frame base lodge is open from 8:30 AM to 4 PM every day. Cross-country fees are $9 to $14.

Mount Washington Valley Ski Touring

N.H. Rt. 16, Intervale
• (603) 356-9920

You'll find 60 kilometers of tracked trails here with 20 kilometers skate-groomed trails. The backcountry has 5 kilometers of trails. You're skiing in the Saco River Valley with breathtaking mountain scenery along the river. The Mount Washington Valley is also a great place for inn-to-inn touring. The hours are 8 AM to dusk every day, and prices range from $5 to $8.

Jackson X•C

Main St., Jackson
• (603) 383-9355

Enjoy the beauty of Jackson along with the charming inns and restaurants by skiing the "out-the-door" trails. Pick up your maps here and choose from beginner, in-

INSIDERS' TIP

Save the easy cross-country trails on golf courses for a day when the air is still. On windy days their lack of shelter can make them brutally cold and no fun for children.

termediate and expert trails. There are 158 kilometers of trails including 63 kilometers of backcountry skiing and 96 kilometers of groomed and tracked trails. If you're really good, try skiing the 18 miles from the backside of Wildcat into the heart of Jackson. The center is open every day from 8 AM to 4:30 PM. Prices are from $7 to $12.

Sunset Hill House Touring Center
Sugar Hill
• (603) 823-5522

Adjacent to the Sunset Hill House, a beautiful country inn, this Nordic center offers tobogganing, snowshoeing and ice-skating in addition to cross-country skiing. Set on 680 acres, the 60 kilometers of trails include 20 to 30 kilometers of groomed trails and one backcountry trail. No trails are skate-groomed. Beginners to experts will find terrain ranging from open fields to forests.

Bring your own skis or rent from the Sports Shop in Franconia. The center does rent snowshoes, but they do not have cross-country equipment or ice-skates. A warming hut is open on weekends. Skiing is free for guests at the inn and $5 for visitors. Although families are welcome, it is a couples kind of place.

Waterville Valley Nordic Center
Town Square
• (603) 236-4666

Another piece of the extensive resort at Waterville Valley, the Nordic Center offers more than 105 kilometers of cross-country trails. Backcountry trails total about 35 kilometers with the remaining 70 kilometers skate groomed and tracked. If you've ever had Olympic daydreams, live out your fantasies on the expert trail called White Mountain Criteria. This popular trail is 5.5K of classic New England grueling uphills and fast downhills. The staff has mapped out loops for rank beginner through experienced expert. You can ski on weekends from 8 AM to 5 PM and from 8:30 AM to 4:30 PM Monday through Friday. The cost is between $7 and $11.

Snowmobile Rentals

Bartlett Rental Center
U.S. Rt. 302, Bartlett Village
• (603) 374-6039

The snowmobiles for rent here are Ski-Doo Safaris. Rates range from about $40 an hour to $250 for 24 hours. Helmets are included, but you need your own boots and gloves. Trail maps are provided. Reservations are accepted for groups renting three or more machines.

Northern Snowmobile Rentals
190 W. Main St., Conway
• (603) 447-4337

Here you'll find brand-new Polaris snowmobiles for rent. Most have two-up seating. You can rent by the hour, half-day or full day. Maps, helmets and appropriate clothing are available for sale or rent. You must be a licensed driver, and a $500 deposit on a major credit card is required.

Prices range from about $40 an hour or $250 a day on weekends to $100 for a half-day during the week. Bud Stellati offers nighttime guided tours during the winter. Call ahead for schedule information.

Profile Motors
N.H. Rt. 16, just south of Conway Village
• (603) 447-3845

New Ski-Doo snowmobiles are the vehicle of choice here. Helmets are included in the rental. Prices range from about $45 an hour to $150 for half-days and $225 for a full day. Major credit cards are accepted for the necessary $500 security deposit. It is recommended that you reserve at least two to three days in advance.

INSIDERS' TIP

Spring is a great time to buy winter sports equipment. Many specialty sports stores that rent the newest equipment have spring sales to make room for next season's new designs.

One Wheel Drive Inc.
U.S. Rt. 302, North Conway
• (603) 356-3522

You can rent new snowmobiles here. Drivers should be 18 unless traveling with a parent, but all renters must have a driver's license. All major credit cards are accepted for deposit. Weekday prices range from $35 an hour to $200 for a full day. On weekends the rate is always $40 an hour. Call at least a week in advance to reserve for weekends, school vacation periods and holidays.

Town and Country
Main St., East Conway
• (603) 939-2698

Brand-new one- and two-person Polaris snowmobiles are available for rent here. Five hundred miles of groomed trails in Maine and New Hampshire are right out the back door. Prices range from $32 an hour to $150 for the day. Helmets are included, but riders must supply their own gloves and boots. All major credit cards are accepted. Maps are provided, and specific trails are suggested to coincide with your time expectations. It is best to reserve in advance, especially on weekends and during school holidays.

Northern Enterprises Snowmobiles of Pittsburg
Main St., Pittsburg (603)
• 538-6352

You must have a driver's license to rent here. Rentals begin at $80 for a half-day and $130 for a full day. Trails and helmets are available. Snowmobiling is a new favorite pastime in the Great North Woods, so it's a good idea to reserve a couple of weeks in advance if you are planning on renting during a busy holiday time.

Dartmouth-Lake Sunapee Region

Downhill Skiing

Dartmouth Skiway
Canaan Tpk., Lyme Center
• (603) 795-2143

Dartmouth College is proud of the 81 U.S. Olympic Ski Team members among its many distinguished alumni. The champs may have trained here, but the Skiway is quick to point out that you don't have to be a contender in order to enjoy the 104 acres of trails. The vertical drop is 968 feet, and half of the 16 trails are for intermediates. The remaining eight trails are divided between novice and expert. The snowboard facilities include a park and rentals. The facility has three lifts including one quad that keeps lines to a minimum.

Mount Sunapee
N.H. Rt. 103, Mount Sunapee
• (603) 763-2356

This year-round resort is proud of the diverse skiing options it offers families. The 37 trails are geared to the intermediate skier, but the 1,510-foot vertical drop guarantees some excitement for the expert. The eight lifts include three triples, two doubles and two surface. Insiders like Sunapee for the good skiing as well as the great views of Lake Sunapee. It's not huge, but it's a lot of fun.

A cafeteria at the summit and two lodges at the bottom offer places to get warm and nourished. The no-frills friendly atmosphere makes this a family favorite. Child care begins with 1-year-olds and includes kids as old as 6. The Little Indians Kids Ski School program is for kids ages 3 and 4. You can ski from 9 AM to 4 PM every day.

Whaleback
I-89, Exit 16, Lebanon
• (603) 448-1489

This family ski area is reasonably priced and a great place to bring the kids for an introduction to skiing. The 26 trails on 65 trail-acres share one base area, making it easy for groups to meet up at a designated spot. The majority of the trails are rated intermediate, and the vertical drop is 700 feet. Snowboarders are welcome, and facilities include a half-pipe.

Night skiing is available every night except Sunday. Monday through Thursday the hours are 10 AM to 9 PM. On Fridays you can ski from 10 AM to 10 PM. Skiing on Saturday and Sunday begins at 9 AM with skiing until 10 PM on Saturday and 4 PM on Sunday. Note that child care is only available on weekends and holidays. Look for lodging details in our Hotels and Motels chapter as there are no slopeside accommodations.

Ragged Mountain Ski Area
Ragged Mountain Rd., Danbury
• (603) 768-3475, Snowphone: (603) 768-3971

Another great family ski area, Ragged Mountain is a spot where generations of skiers have learned their skills. The vertical drop is 1,250 feet with 31 trails divided among novice, intermediate and expert. The new Spear Mountain expansion has a triple chair for five new trails and 10 acres of glade skiing. Additional lifts include three doubles and two surface lifts.

The rates are modest — especially if you are older than 70 or younger than 6, in which case you ski for free. The child-care facilities have hourly as well as full-day rates and are for kids as young as 6 weeks old. The ski school has great packages for kids with lifts, lessons and rentals included in the price.

The weekday hours are 9 AM to 4 PM. On weekends and special holidays, the ski area opens at 8:30 AM. Look for lodging details in our Hotels and Motels chapter as there are no slopeside accommodations.

Cross-country Skiing

Eastman
Exit 13 off I-89, Grantham
• (603) 863-4500

Thirty kilometers of groomed trails along with 15 kilometers of skate-groomed trails are just part of the winter scene at this small modern facility. In addition to skiing, you can enjoy sledding, snowshoeing and ice-skating. Lessons and rentals are available. Fees are between $6 and $9.

Norsk Cross-country
N.H. Rt. 11, New London
• (800) 426-6775

Twenty-six trails cover 75 kilometers to make this one of the top cross-country centers in the region. Sixty-five kilometers are tracked, and 20 kilometers are skate-groomed. There are also 6 kilometers of backcountry available. About half the terrain is intermediate, about a third is easy and the rest is challenging; one trail is so steep it's called the Freefall! Wednesdays have special "Soup and Ski" rates that include lunch. The center is open every day from 9 AM to 5 PM. Daily rates are between $8 and $12.

Monadnock Region

Downhill Skiing

Temple Mountain
N.H. Rt. 101, Peterborough
• (603) 924-6949

Temple Mountain is the only Alpine-skiing facility in the Monadnock region. A small, independently owned operation, it works hard to provide big-mountain equipment at small-mountain prices. After a year of financial woes kept Temple closed during the 1997-1998 ski season, the mountain re-opened in 1998 and locals have enjoyed great skiing throughout the winter.

The six lifts include one quad, two doubles, two rope-tows and one T-bar. The vertical drop is 600 feet, and 16 trails are divided among 40 trail-acres.

Lots of kids come here, and the snowboard facilities include a half-pipe. Kids love the night skiing too, and the mountain is open every day until 10 PM. It opens at 10 AM during the week and at 8:30 AM on weekends.

The 50 kilometers of cross-country trails include 30 kilometers of tracked and 15 kilometers of skate-groomed trails. You can cross-country ski at night Wednesday through Friday. Call for details about telemark clinics as well as local lodging packages.

Cross-country Skiing

Sargent Camp
Windy Row, Peterborough/Hancock
• (603) 525-3311

Boston University owns and maintains this 850-acre woods. With 12 miles of cross-country trails open to the public, it is a local favorite.

The trails range in difficulty from novice to expert and cover a variety of open and wooded terrain. Prices are modest, and rentals are available. Call ahead to check on hours.

Windblown Cross-country Skiing

N.H. Rt. 124, New Ipswich
• (603) 878-2869

This topnotch, family-run cross-country ski center is a great place to enjoy the beauty of the Monadnock Region. The trails are well-marked for the beginner, intermediate and advanced skier. Twenty-five kilometers are tracked and 20 kilometers are skate-groomed. Five kilometers of trails are backcountry. The terrain is an even mix of hills and fields, with something for every ability.

Windblown is open every day from 9 AM to 5 PM. Prices range from $9 to $11 a day with discounts on morning (9 AM to 12 PM) and afternoon (2 to 5 PM) tickets.

Woodbound Inn

62 Woodbound Rd., Rindge
• (800) 688-7770

You don't have to stay at the inn to ski, but guests ski free. The rest of us pay just $6 to $8 to enjoy 18 kilometers of tracked cross-country trails. The terrain is both wooded and open meadow and is equally divided between beginner, intermediate and advanced trails. A part of the 9-hole, par three golf course becomes a practice area for those new to the sport of cross-country skiing. You can warm up in the lounge and refuel in the restaurant. Look for details in our Country Inns chapter.

We have lots of wonderful trails through the woods and along streams that can be enjoyed by preschoolers and grandparents and everyone in between.

Other Recreation

We've given you chapters on winter sports, watersports, fishing and hunting and camping. We've talked about our wonderful places to get outdoors and told you about people who specialize in entertaining kids. There's a calendar full of things to do in our Annual Events chapter and more fun beyond our borders in Daytrips. If you still can't think of anything to do, you can take a hike! Or take a ride. Or take a swing, or just take a chance. Surely you'll take something to heart.

League sports, for both children and adults, are definitely an element of the active New Hampshire lifestyle. Just about every town has a recreation department that organizes teams. For children, soccer, baseball, basketball and lacrosse are the most popular league sports. In summer just about every town has a youth swim team. Adults play softball and baseball, basketball and soccer in recreation leagues—some more competitive than others! Check at town hall to see what recreation options your town offers.

A great source of inspiration and information for these activities is *New Hampshire Outdoor Companion*, a free newspaper available at tourist information centers. It's published bimonthly year round. This paper provides dozens of listings of events, hikes, races, workshops and other activities; contact information for guides, climbing schools and outfitters; and helpful articles on subjects from bugs to boots to boat trips.

Take A Walk: Hiking

Hiking in New Hampshire is not just for the rugged outdoors types. We have lots of wonderful trails through the woods and along streams that can be enjoyed by preschoolers and grandparents and everyone in between. There are even a couple of trails under construction that are designed to accommodate wheelchairs. Many of these gentler trails are included in our Parks and Open Spaces chapter. But, of course, our mountains are what really get people's attention. From Mount Monadnock, historically the second-most-climbed mountain on the planet (after Japan's Fuji), to the peaks of our 4,000-foot mountains and on up to the summit of Mount Washington, New Hampshire's mountain hiking attracts people from around the world. And with good reason: The views from many peaks are unbeatable.

Many mountains along the East Coast are higher, but, being farther south, they are covered with trees. For example, climb to the top of Clingman's Dome in North Carolina, at 6,643 feet the highest point on the Appalachian Trail, and you have to scale a tower before you can appreciate your efforts. In contrast, at our latitude the treeline is between 4,500 and 5,000 feet. New Hampshire has more than a dozen mountains in that range and even lower mountains with bare summits because of the preponderance of ledge. On a clear day it feels like you really can see forever.

Hiking above treeline has certain risks. The same winds and weather that prevent trees from growing at these locations will buffet hikers who find themselves on the summit in a storm. Even without a storm, winds on some of the higher summits average 20 mph or stronger all the time. Hikers in the mountains should always be cognizant of the weather, both the forecast before setting out (listen for the "higher elevations" portion of the forecast) and the signs in the sky while hiking. At minimum, even day-hikers in summer should carry warm clothing, high-energy food and a sleeping bag. Be sure you have adequate water for your trip: A quart every four hours is recommended. Hike with a small group, and be sure that someone knows where you are going and when you expect to return. Stay on marked trails, and use common sense. Don't push yourself beyond your strength or keep climbing when instinct says to turn back.

Remember that it will take you at least as long to hike back down as it does to climb up (often down is slower, as you have to pick your footing). Find out what time sunset will occur. It gets dark earlier in the mountains and earlier still in the woods. And snow and ice can remain in shaded parts of the high summits right into August. We've had the experience of climbing into Tuckerman's Ravine (on Mount Washington) when it was 85 degrees Fahrenheit and humid at Pinkham Notch and below freezing and snowing like crazy before we reached the ravine. We were glad we had snowpants, hats and mittens in our backpacks, even if we did look pretty silly when we hiked back down into summer. Common sense is better than foolish pride and a lot safer too.

New Hampshire Insiders who travel out-of-state to climb in higher mountains have told us that New Hampshire's White Mountains are much more challenging than their elevations would indicate. One pair of hiking buddies reported that the 13 14,000-foot peaks they scaled during an 11-day trip to Colorado were a "piece of cake" compared with New Hampshire's Presidential Range. Trails in the White Mountains (and elsewhere in New England) are steeper and more rugged than typical trails in other parts of the United States, where hiking trails are likely to be graded and use switchbacks to prevent erosion in steep terrain. Experienced hikers from other parts of the country frequently make the mistake of starting up Mount Washington at 10 AM, which doesn't leave enough time to reach the summit and get back to base before dark.

We mentioned some great hiking guides in our Parks and Open Spaces chapter. For hiking in the White Mountains, the bible is the *AMC White Mountain Guide* (from the Appalachian Mountain Club). It is available in local bookstores, or you can order it direct from the AMC, 5 Joy Street, Boston, MA 02108, (617) 523-0655. This guide describes individual trails, tells you what hazards to watch for and gives average times for each segment of the trail. It covers mountains all over New Hampshire, not just those in the White Mountain National Forest.

Merrimack Valley Region

Uncanoonuc Mountains

Off N.H. Rt. 114, Goffstown

The Uncanoonuc Range divides Bedford and Goffstown and overlooks the city of Manchester. Although the trailheads are less than 10 miles from Manchester, the mountains give you the feeling that you're out in the middle of the woods. The trail to North Peak begins on Mountain Road and is blazed with white circles. It climbs steeply in a few places (the climb gains about 730 feet over three-quarters of a mile), eventually bringing hikers to a ledge outcropping with spectacular views across Goffstown and past Mount Kearsarge. The Uncanoonuc Nature Trail to South Peak is easier but less pristine, gaining only 600 feet in elevation over a mile-long trail. The old trestle is left from a cable car that used to run up the mountain (don't try to descend this way, it's a mess). There is an amazing view of Manchester from the summit, but it includes a virtual forest of cell-phone and radio towers. This trail begins on Mountain Base Road. Either hike averages about 40 minutes each way.

Seacoast Region

Blue Job Mountain

First Crown Point Rd., Strafford

There aren't many mountains in the Seacoast; in fact, this is the only one. At 1,356 feet it doesn't sound very impressive, but wait until you see the views! On a clear day (and if it's not clear, don't bother with this one), you can see skyscrapers in Boston and the snow on mounts Washington, Monadnock, Sunapee and Kearsarge out in the western part of the state. The half-mile climb is easy, even for children, but the summit tends to be windy, so bring sweaters. Don't forget a picnic. The trail is blazed in red. Plan at least a half-hour hike each way.

Lakes Region

Mount Major

N.H. Rt. 114, Alton

This mountain offers terrific views of the Lakes Region. The trail leaves from a well-marked parking lot 2 miles north of Alton Bay. It starts out as a logging road, then climbs steeply through woods and crosses some ledges before reaching the summit. This trail is marked with dark blue blazes. It's about 1.5 miles each way and should take just less than three hours round trip.

Mount Morgan and Mount Percival

N.H. Rt. 113, Holderness

These are the two highest peaks in the Squam Range. As the trailheads are less than a half-mile apart, it is possible to climb up the Mount Morgan trail, take a spur trail to the summit for views of the cliffs and then cross the ridge to the summit of Mount Percival via the Crawford-Ridgepole Trail. From the summit you then descend on the Mount Percival Trail and walk back to your car. Each of the main trails is about 1.5 miles long. The ridge crossing is almost a mile, and you'll do about a half-mile road walk on N.H. Route 113. Plan for between three and four hours for the loop, depending on how many pictures you take.

White Mountains and Great North Woods Region

Hiking is one of the most popular activities in the White Mountains region. We'll give you a quick overview but suggest that you review the books that have been written on the subject if you're planning an exclusively hiking vacation. Start your research with *Fifty Hikes In the White Mountains* by Daniel Doan and the *AMC White Mountain Guide*, published by the Appalachian Mountain Club. Both books are available at the bookstores mentioned in our Shopping chapter as well as most stores specializing in outdoor clothing and equipment. Also check out *Hiking New Hampshire* by Larry B. Pletcher, a Falcon Guide.

Please remember that weather in the White Mountains changes rapidly. Mount Washington is infamous for high winds and sudden snow and ice storms.

Appalachian Mountain Club Huts

AMC, Pinkham Notch Visitors Center, N.H. Rt. 16, Pinkham
• (603) 466-2721

Hikers in the White Mountains can take advantage of the eight huts owned and managed by the Appalachian Mountain Club (AMC). The huts are about a day's hike from each other along New Hampshire's 56 miles of the Appalachian Trail. Services vary from hut to hut, but all offer hikers a place to spend the night (reservations are required), eat and take shelter. The huts, from east to west, are Carter Notch, Madison Spring, Lakes-of-the-Clouds, Mizpah Spring, Zealand Falls, Galehead, Greenleaf and Lonesome Lake. The huts do not have electricity or showers, but they offer clean drinking water, bunks, pillows and blankets (campers should bring their own linens). The price varies depending on services. Carter Notch is self-service, and overnight charges are $14 for AMC members and $18 for nonmembers. Full-service huts with two all-you-can-eat meals range in price from $40 to $60 per night depending upon day of the week, time of year and AMC membership status. Zealand Hut is the smallest with accommodations for 36. Lakes-of-the-Clouds Hut is the largest with space for 90 people.

Day hikers are welcome to use the huts as rest areas. All huts have toilets and drinking water. You can fill up your water bottles and take a minute to evaluate your route. Access to the huts is by foot. The huts are all near major trailheads, so you can park your car and hike in. For more information on which trails go to which huts, accommodation features of individual huts and reservations, contact the Appalachian Mountain Club at the phone number above.

Kancamagus Highway

N.H. Rt. 112 between Conway and Lincoln

Kancamagus Highway (N.H. Route 112) is an excellent access to several hikes suitable for the nonexpert. The Boulder Loop Trail is a self-guided 3.5-mile walk. To get there from Conway, travel west on the Kancamagus Highway for about 7 miles. Turn right (north) onto Dugway Road and cross over the Swift River. You'll see signs for parking and can pick up the informational pamphlet at the trailhead. You should allow about three hours for this hike. Wear sturdy shoes or boots, and be sure and take along enough water for your group. Midway between Conway and Lincoln on the Kancamagus Highway, you'll see signs for Sabbaday Falls. The 1-mile round-trip walk from the roadside picnic area to the falls is graded and suitable for casual hikers. If you approach the Kancamagus Highway from Lincoln, 9.5 miles out of town, you'll find parking for the hike to Greeley Ponds on the south side of the road. The round-trip hike to the ponds is 4 miles, and a suggested hiking time is 2.5 hours. You might want to take a picnic with you (please bring out all that you take in). These beautiful ponds are between Mount Osceola and Mount Kancamagus. The walk is gentle, and the views are spectacular.

Franconia Notch State Park

I-93, Franconia
• (603) 823-5563

This state park is another great starting point for hiking. Artists Bluff and Bald Mountain are two destinations from the same trail that are recommended for intermediate hikers. (Artists Bluff is a rock clearing exposing the full beauty of Franconia Notch.) You can park at Echo Lake State Beach and enjoy a round-trip hike of 1.5 miles in less than 1.5 hours. You'll get great views of Echo Lake and Cannon Mountain.

You can climb Cannon too, although most people choose the tramway as the easy way up. Pick up maps for the Kinsman Ridge, Hi-Cannon and Profile Lakes trails at the state park's visitors center. These trails join to make a 7-mile loop that transverses Cannon. Don't try this trek unless you are an experienced hiker with good boots, as parts of the trail are steep and rocky.

Mount Washington

Western access: Cog Railway Hikers Parking Lot, Base Rd. off U.S. Rt. 302, Bretton Woods
Eastern access: AMC Pinkham Notch Visitor Center, N.H. Rt. 16, Pinkham
• (603) 466-2721

The toughest hike in the White Mountains region is Mount Washington. At 6,288 feet, it is the tallest mountain east of the Rockies and north of the Mason-Dixon Line. You can reach the summit by car and rail (see our Attractions chapter) as well as by foot. The first known climb to the summit was in 1642 by Darby Field and two Indian guides.

If you want to climb Mount Washington, do your homework. Not only should you be an experienced hiker, but you should also read and study the many materials about the mountain. Even knowledgeable hikers are surprised by the ferocious winds and quickly changing weather on the mountain, especially above treeline. From the west, the Ammonoosuc Ravine Trail starts at the Cog Railway's base station and continues up to the AMC Lakes-of-the-Clouds hut. Assess the weather here before continuing to the summit via Crawford Path. The other main trail that starts near the Cog Railway parking lot is the Jewell Trail. Start your climb early — the

INSIDERS' TIP

For those who like to hike with competition and "certifiable" accomplishment as added factors, there's the Four Thousand Footers Club. The club was formed in 1957 by the Appalachian Mountain Club (AMC). To become a member you must climb the 46 "official" mountains in The White Mountains that are higher than 4,000 feet. (The official list is important — some mountains higher than 4,000 feet don't "count" because of the proximity of one 4,000-plus-foot summit to another.) Contact the AMC Boston office, (617) 523-0655, for the list of 4,000-foot peaks and qualification information.

round trip is at least eight hours for the 8- to 10-mile loop and you don't want to start your descent past noon.

Other areas of Mount Washington you may want to explore are Tuckerman Ravine and the Alpine Garden. Tuckerman Ravine, on the southeast slope of Mount Washington, is the basin formed by glacier action thousands of years ago. Above the ravine is the Alpine Garden, best approached from the eastern access point. Botanists have long explored this arctic zone for rare plants found nowhere else in the United States except for Alaska. Both hikes start from the AMC Pinkham Notch camp. You can park here, pick up maps and double-check your provisions and equipment based on current weather information.

Dartmouth-Lake Sunapee Region

Mount Sunapee

Andrews Brook Trail, Mountain Rd., Newbury

Hikers in the region shouldn't miss climbing the Andrews Brook Trail up Mount Sunapee, which has an elevation of 2,743 feet. Drive south from Newbury on N.H. 103, turn right on Mountain Road and drive for 1.2 miles until you see the marked trailhead on your right. Park on the shoulder (you'll probably see other cars) and follow an old logging road into the woods. Follow the orange blazes. About 2 miles from the trailhead, you'll arrive at the shore of Lake Solitude. Continue around the lake and join up with the Lake Solitude Trail marked by white blazes. This trail takes you to the summit of Mount Sunapee. Those who prefer a shorter hike can take the tram from the State Park (see our Parks and Open Spaces chapter) to the summit and climb down to Lake Solitude.

Monadnock-Sunapee Greenway

Mount Sunapee Summit, Mount Sunapee State Park, N.H. Rt. 103, Newbury
• (603) 763-2356
Mount Monadnock Summit, Mount Monadnock State Park, N.H. Rt. 124, Jaffrey
• (603) 532-8862

You can travel from Mount Monadnock to Mount Sunapee along the 49-mile Monadnock-Sunapee Greenway. For a trail map and description of the hike, contact the Society for the Protection of New Hampshire Forests, 54 Portsmouth Street, Concord, (603) 224-9945.

Mount Kearsarge

Kearsarge Valley Rd., off N.H. Rt. 11, Wilmot

One approach to Mount Kearsarge is from the auto road in Winslow State Park (see our Parks and Open Spaces chapter). Park in the lot near the picnic area. Hike along the rocky 1.1-mile trail to the 2,937-foot summit. Follow the red trail blazes. You'll start out in the woods, where you'll see white birches, spruce and fir trees. You'll notice the ground becoming smooth rock, and soon you come into the open where the blazes are painted on rocks. The summit is wide open with views of Pleasant Lake in New London and Lake Sunapee and Mount Sunapee in Newport. The hike up takes about an hour, while the trip down can

INSIDERS' TIP

If you meet a bear (very possible) or mountain lion (extremely unlikely), experts recommend that you do the following things: 1) Look big — spread your jacket out with your arms and hoist your pack up over your head; 2) Make noise — bang pots and pans, blow a whistle or shout; and 3) Stand still, then back slowly away. Your goal here is not to threaten but to convince the wild animal that you are a fellow member of the top of the food chain, not a new kind of prey. Above all, do not run away, as flight triggers the predator instinct even in an animal that wasn't hungry when it met you.

be completed in about 30 minutes. The smooth rocks might make the hike difficult for walkers with weak ankles, but beginners with proper footwear should enjoy this short excursion. As always, be aware of the weather, and remember how quickly rain and wind can make a mountain top dangerous.

Cardigan Mountain
West Ridge Trail, off N.H. Rt. 118, Canaan

Another fairly easy hike in the region is the West Ridge Trail up Cardigan Mountain. The trail is 1.3 miles long (one way). Park in Mount Cardigan State Park and follow signs to the trail. The descriptive term "bald" is sometimes used to describe this mountain. Fires burned most of the trees in 1855, and the mountaintop has never recovered. You'll hike across slabs of granite as you approach the 3,121-foot summit. More challenging hikes up Cardigan begin at the Appalachian Mountain Club (AMC) Cardigan Lodge on the eastern side of the mountain. For information, contact AMC in Bristol at (603) 271-3254.

Monadnock Region

An excellent new book, published in 1997 by New England Cartographics, is *Hiking the Monadnock Region* by local writer and hiker Joe Adamowicz. You'll find the book in Monadnock region bookstores as well as many stores specializing in outdoor equipment. The book details 26 day hikes and nature walks in the region.

Mount Monadnock
N.H. Rt. 124, Jaffrey
Lake Rd., Dublin

Mount Monadnock, with an elevation of 3,165 feet, is the most popular hike in New Hampshire and commonly proclaimed the second-most climbed mountain in the world after Mount Fuji. Trail maps are available at Mount Monadnock State Park in Jaffrey (see our Parks and Open Spaces chapter). The hike up Mount Monadnock can vary depending on which trail you pick. There are six main trails and 24 connecting trails cutting through the mountain. The White Dot Trail is a 4-mile round-trip hike that begins near park headquarters. It is the most direct and most traveled trail. If you start from here, you might want to branch off on a connecting loop or take a different route down. The longest route and one favored by many longtime hikers of Monadnock is the Pumpelly Trail, which begins just off Lake Road in Dublin. The trail is 9 miles round trip. If you're driving west on N.H. Route 101, Lake Road is a left turn after you've passed through the town of Dublin. If you can, plan to hike Mount Monadnock during the week to minimize the chance of crowds.

Pitcher Mountain
N.H. Rt. 123, Stoddard

One of our favorite hikes is the low-key hike up Pitcher Mountain in Stoddard. Look for signs to Pitcher Mountain Farm as you drive into Stoddard on N.H. Route 123 from Hancock. The parking area is a half-mile north of the farm. The white trail is not as steep as the blue, but either can be climbed in about 15 minutes. Forest fires destroyed the trees in the area in 1941, so you have a clear view of the region including Mount Monadnock to the south and Mount Ascutney in Vermont to the northwest.

Crotched Mountain
N.H. Rt. 31, Greenfield

Crotched Mountain in Greenfield is another favorite hike in the region. Travel to Greenfield on N.H. Route 31 and follow signs to the Crotched Mountain Rehabilitation Center. Pass by the center's entrance, and look for a gate blocking vehicles on your left. The Greenfield Trail is 4 miles round trip, about 2 hours at a comfortable pace. The beginning of the trail is thick with blueberry bushes, which will be loaded with fruit in August. Parts of the trail are very wooded, but the 2,055-foot summit is clear and rocky.

Take a Ride: Mountain Biking

In recent years the popularity of mountain biking has exploded in New Hampshire, as it has in many places. Most notably, many of our ski areas are now open all summer, providing trails for mountain bikers and even lift rides to the tops of trails for bikers and bicycles.

Mountain biking brings with it its own set of rules and responsibilities. With the proliferation of bikers, there have been some unfortunate abuses of trails, and many private landowners and local conservation commissions have begun to prohibit bikes because of the damage to plants and to trails themselves. In addition, many hikers have developed an intense dislike for mountain bikes, which seem to have turned their quiet woodland walks into risky ventures through territory dominated by zooming wheels.

To avoid further restrictions on mountain bikes, trail riders need to remember to slow down, ride soft and pitch in. Slow down: Never ride faster than you can see. You never know when you're going to turn a corner and find a family walking with small children or a group of llama trekkers. Ride soft: Carry bikes through wet or muddy areas and streams, and always stay on the trail. Don't leave ruts, which channel water and destroy trails. And pitch in: Never leave litter in the woods, and take advantage of your pack to bring out the litter of those who are less considerate.

The New England Mountain Bike Association has a helpful newsletter and organizes rides and races around New England. You can contact them at (800) 57-NEMBA. You might also want to look for a great book called *Cycling the Backroads of Southern New Hampshire* by Linda Chestney, or contact the Granite State Wheelmen (c/o Dave Topham, 2 Townsend Drive, Salem, NH 03079), a group that organizes on- and off-road bike rides for riders of all ages and abilities (and genders, despite its name). Falcon Publishing also offers *Mountain Biking Northern New England* by Paul Angiolillo and *Mountain Biking the White Mountains (West)* by J. Richard Durnan.

Merrimack Valley Region

Bear Brook State Park

N.H. Rt. 28, Allenstown • (603) 485-9874

There are about 40 miles of trail available for bikers in this large park (see our Parks and Open Spaces and Camping chapters for more about Bear Brook). In addition, the No. 15 snowmobile trail runs through the park and connects it to other good riding territory around Lake Massabesic. Trails traverse a variety of habitats, including woods, meadows and marshes, with a lot of climbing and fairly rugged terrain.

Seacoast Region

Pawtuckaway State Park

N.H. Rt. 156, Raymond
· (603) 895-3031

All the trails in this big park are open for mountain biking, although "some are better than others," according to the staff. A map is available at the visitors center when you enter the park. Ask there about trail conditions, which vary with the weather.

Lakes Region

Gunstock Recreation Area

N.H. Rt. 11-A, Gilford
• (603) 293-4341, (800) GUNSTOCK

This ski area is working to become a year-round resort, with mountain biking and horseback riding as big parts of that plan. It has more than 50 kilometers of trails and rents bikes and helmets at $10 to $16 for two hours or $20 to $30 for a whole day. The horseback trail rides are guided and cost from $25 for a

INSIDERS' TIP

Don't Drink the Water! Our mountain streams look crystal clean, but giardia, a nasty intestinal parasite, is endemic in New Hampshire waters. Long-distance hikers should carry a 10-micron filtration device, and day hikers and trail riders should carry enough drinking water for their party.

one-hour midweek ride to $42 for two hours on a weekend.

Old Hill Village

N.H. Rt. 3-A, Bristol

When the Franklin Falls Flood Control Project was built, the entire village of Hill was moved to higher ground. The roads were left behind and now provide some intriguing riding inside the flood control area (see our Parks and Open Spaces chapter). Mountain bikers (and equestrians) enjoy flat stretches through flowering meadows, steep bits that climb away from the river, wooded paths and streambeds.

Nordic Skier

47 N. Main St., Wolfeboro

• (603) 569-3151

This cross-country ski facility has expanded its operation to include biking. Bike rentals, at $20 to $35 per day, include helmets, maps and water bottles. Nordic Skier organizes weekly rides and also coordinates a fun trip called "Biking By Boat," which involves a 30-mile ride with the return trip on the M/S *Mt. Washington*. Cost of the combination varies (see our Attractions chapter for more on the M/S *Mt. Washington*). In addition to rentals, Nordic Skier does repairs, a nice thing to know when your derailleur's been derailed by a rock.

White Mountains and Great North Woods Regions

Attitash Bear Peak

U.S. Rt. 302, Bartlett

• (603) 374-2368

You've got three choices for biking adventures at Attitash Bear Peak. Advanced riders will want to hop on the triple chair lift for a quick trip up the mountain. The 3-mile downhill ride of thrilling trails should please the daredevil in every group. The round-trip cost is $8 per adult and $6 for kids younger than 12. An all-day pass is $19. A less-challenging biking choice is the Thorne Pond Interpretive Trail. The trail winds along the Saco River. There are picnic tables as well as stops detailing information about animals in the region. You can also get a shuttle ride to the White Mountain National Forest, which has more than a hundred miles of trails ranging in difficulty from beginner to advanced. The round-trip shuttle cost is $5. Bike rentals at Attitash range from $15 for two hours to $50 a day.

The Balsams Wilderness Resort Mountain Bike and Nature Center

N.H. Rt. 26, Dixville Notch

• (603) 255-3921

We can't say enough about the beautiful Great North Woods terrain at the Balsams Wilderness Resort. You will enjoy the 50 kilometers of trails whether you're a guest of the resort or just visiting for the day. The trails range from a gentle rolling hill terrain to more advanced mountainous descents. Guided trail rides are offered throughout the summer and fall. Biking is free for guests at the resort and $5 for visitors. Two-hour bike and helmet rentals are $15 for adults and $10 for kids younger than 16. Bikes with front suspension are an additional $5 per rental.

Cannon Mountain

Franconia Notch State Park, I-93, Franconia

• (603) 823-5563

You can enjoy free access to the paved 8-mile Franconia Notch Recreation Path. The path is a great way to enjoy the many sights in this park, including the Old Man of the Mountain and the Flume, which is where the path ends. Those who prefer their paths wild and unpaved will have a great time riding on Cannon Mountain. There's no lift service available for bikers, so be sure your quads are in top shape. Bikes and helmets can be rented at Peabody Base Lodge for $10 an hour.

Base Camp Adventure Center

Town Square, Waterville Valley

• (603) 236-4666

The Base Camp Adventure Center in Waterville Valley is a great spot for groups with various levels of thrill seekers. You'll enjoy more than 30 miles of trails. Some are graded logging roads where families can bike side by side, and others are single-track trails. Trail passes are $6 for adults and $5 for kids younger than 12. Riders who love downhill biking will be glad to know they can ride the lift to the summit of Snow's Mountain (2,090 feet). The all-day lift ticket/bike rental package is $40 for adults and $32 for kids younger than 12. You can rent bikes and helmets for $20 for a half-day rental or $30 for the entire day. Full-suspension bike rentals are slightly more expensive.

Dartmouth-Lake Sunapee Region

Mount Sunapee State Park

N.H. Rt. 103, Newbury
• (603) 763-2356

You can ride for free around Lake Sunapee. Intermediate and expert mountain bikers may want to take the chairlift to the top of Mount Sunapee to enjoy several trails down the mountain. A new chair lift was installed in the summer of 1998. Bike rentals are not available. Check the Specialty Stores section at the end of this chapter for rental outlets in the region.

Monadnock Region

Pisgah State Park

Old Chesterfield Rd., Winchester
• (603) 239-8153

Pisgah's 13,500 acres make it New Hampshire's largest state park and one of the best parks for mountain biking. Trail maps are available at each of the nine trailheads in the park and at the new visitor center. You can also order trail maps for the park from the New Hampshire Division of Parks, Bureau of Trails, P.O. Box 1856, Concord, NH 03302 or call (603) 271-3254.

INSIDERS' TIP

Whether riding or hiking, keeping to the trails will prevent degradation of the surrounding wildlife. This is especially important in high elevations. Many fragile plants live in the alpine terrain above treeline, some surviving only in a few spots in New Hampshire and nowhere else.

Take a Swing: Golf

Merrimack Valley Region

Amherst Country Club

76 Ponemah, N.H. Rt. 122, Amherst
• (603) 673-9908

This 18-hole, 6000-yard course is a par 72 layout. Greens fees are $28 during the week and $38 on weekends. Powered carts are $12 per person, and pull carts are $3. Tee-time reservations are accepted five days in advance by telephone and seven days in advance in person. After your round you'll enjoy relaxing in the lounge. Hot lunches, sandwiches and your favorite beverages are all on tap. Please note that metal spikes are not allowed.

Candia Woods Golf Links

313 South Rd., Candia
• (603) 483-2307

This 18-hole, 6307-yard par 71 course is well-conditioned and not so difficult that duffers can't have a good time. Greens fees are $27 during the week and $37 on weekends. Carts are $12 per person. Metal spikes are not permitted on the course. Amenities include a driving range if you want to practice or warm up before your round and a lounge in case you need a little sustenance after play. You can make reservations up to five days in advance.

Windham Golf and Country Club

1 Country Club Rd. (off Londonderry Rd.), Windham
• (603) 434-2093

Open since 1994, Windham Golf and Country Club is proud to have already made the top 10 in *Golf Digest*'s annual state-by-state course rankings. The 6033-yard, par 72 course is open to the public. Reservations for tee times are accepted five days ahead. Greens fees on weekends are $49 with a cart and $37 if you walk. You can play nine holes after 4 PM on weekends for $26 with a cart and $20 if you walk. During the week, you'll pay $42 to ride for 18 holes and $30 to walk the distance. The fees are halved for nine holes. The on-site restaurant doesn't have a name, but it serves sandwiches and drinks.

Seacoast Region

Exeter Country Club

Jady Hill Rd., Exeter
• (603) 778-8080

This nine-hole course is a 3200-yard par 36 layout. After noon on weekends and throughout the week, the course is open to the public.

Reservations are not accepted. Greens fees are $16 for nine holes and $24 for 18 holes during the week and $17 and $27 respectively on weekends. Powered carts are $10 for nine holes and $20 for 18. Pull carts are $3. The lounge serves sandwiches along with beverages.

Portsmouth Country Club

1 Country Club Ln., Greenland
• (603) 436-9719

Golf Digest consistently rates this 6609-yard, par 72 course as one of New Hampshire's top five. Visitors will be glad to know the semiprivate status means it is open to the public with a few restrictions. Nonmembers can't reserve a tee time more than a day in advance.

On weekends no tee times are available to visitors before 1 PM. Greens fees are always $50 for nonmembers. Carts are $22, and pull carts are $3. The 19th hole is open to all players, and sandwiches are served along with beverages.

INSIDERS' TIP

Abandoned firetowers are tempting to climb but dangerous. Resist. If you want to climb a firetower, the N.H. History Museum in Concord has a restored one you can climb for a great view of the city.

The Old Man of the Mountains watches over the state.

Lakes Region

Indian Mound
Old (N.H.) Rt. 16, Center Ossipee
• (603) 539-7733

The 18-hole layout here has something for everyone. The front nine on this 5700-yard, par 70 course is relatively flat, while the back nine is mostly rolling hills. The greens fees are $32 for tee times before 3 PM and $18 after 3 PM. Powered carts are $22 per cart for 18 holes and $12 for nine. Reduced greens fees are not available for nine holes. Reservations are accepted on Wednesdays for the following seven days. Captain Lovewell's Tavern serves sandwiches and beverages.

Laconia Country Club
674 Elm St., Laconia
• (603) 524-1274

This championship course is open to the public during the week. The 6483-yard, par 72 layout was built in 1922 and has hosted both ladies' and men's state tournaments. Greens fees are $85 including carts. There is no strict reservation policy, but it is suggested that you call at least two days in advance for a tee time. The restaurant is always open to the public and serves lunch every day. Beverages and sandwiches are available throughout the afternoon.

Lake View Golf Club
Ladd Hill Rd., Belmont
• (603) 524-2220

You'll get spectacular views of Lake Winnisquam from this nine hole, 3110-yard, par 35 course. Greens fees are $14 for nine holes and $20 for 18 holes. This is a great walking course, but carts are available for $12 for nine holes and $20 for 18 holes. As with other nine-hole courses, you'll find two sets of tees for each green, allowing for an 18-

hole round. Tee-time reservations are not accepted. The lounge and snack bar will help in keeping your energy levels, if not your swing, steady.

White Mountains and Great North Woods Regions

Colebrook Country Club
N.H. Rt. 26, Colebrook
• (603) 237-5566

Golf is popular in all of New Hampshire, including the Great North Woods. The course at the Colebrook Country Club has nine greens and 18 tees. The distance going out is 2891 yards. Coming back is 3002 yards (one hole is a par 6 each way). Both nines are par 36. You can rent golf clubs for $5, hand carts for $3 and powered carts for $15 (nine holes) and $20 (18 holes). Greens fees are $18 for adults and $12 for players younger than 18. Children younger than 5 play free. Ladies play for $10 on Wednesday, seniors get the same break on Monday, and everyone plays for $10 after 5 PM. The office at the Colebrook Country Club Motel opens at 7 AM.

The Balsams Grand Resort
N.H. Rt. 26, Dixville Notch
• (603) 255-3400

The Panorama course was rated the No. 1 golf course in the state in *Golf Digest*'s 1997 ranking. The course was designed by legendary golf architect Donald Ross and built in 1912. It is a 6804-yard par 72 mountain beauty with wide but rarely level fairways and small, difficult greens. Beginners and those with high handicaps are encouraged to play the nine-hole Coashaukee course. The golf facilities are primarily for guests at this resort, and greens fees are included in the room rate. (Read about the luxury of the Balsams Grand Resort in our Hotels and Motels chapter.) Players who are not guests need to inquire about play, as availability depends upon guest requirements.

Androscoggin Valley Country Club
U.S. Rt. 2, Gorham
• (603) 466-9468

This 18-hole, par 70 course measures 5764 yards. The Androscoggin River runs parallel to much of the course, and if Mount Washington isn't hiding in a cloud, you'll get a great view of its 6,288-foot peak. The course opens at 7:30 AM during the week and 7 AM on weekends. You can reserve a tee time the day before you plan to play, and if you want to warm up, there's a practice range. On weekends greens fees are $24 for 18 holes and $15 for nine. During the week you'll pay $20 for 18 and $15 for nine. Riding carts cost $25 for 18 holes and $15 for nine holes. Hand carts are $3 and $2, for 18 and nine holes respectively. The 19th hole is supplemented by a snack bar and beverage cart.

Dartmouth-Lake Sunapee Region

Eastman Golf Links
Exit 13 off I-89, Grantham
• (603) 863-4500

This 6338-yard, par 71 course is not for the golfer with a slice or a hook off the tee. The course is cut right through the woods — you won't have the luxury of adjacent fairways. The course was built in the early 1970s, and while members get the first stab at tee times, the public is welcome to play here. Nonmembers can reserve a spot two days in advance (members can reserve tee times a

INSIDERS' TIP

Do not begin your hiking career trying to conquer Mount Washington. Work up to this difficult challenge with shorter hikes. Not only will you learn from the basic hikes, but you will also break in your boots and find out what clothing works best for you. Also remember that when hiking, discretion is the better part of valor. If you are getting exhausted or cold, turn around.

week ahead). Greens fees are $38 at all times. Powered carts are $15.50 per person. The Grill Room serves lunch and dinner throughout the golf season.

John H. Cain Golf Club

Unity Rd. (off N.H. Rt. 11), Newport
• (603) 863-7787

This 6005-yard, par 72 course is a regional favorite. Originally a nine-hole course, the layout was expanded in the last decade to its current 18-hole design. Tee-time reservations are accepted seven days in advance. Greens fees are $27 on weekdays and $31 on weekends. Carts are $22. A discount rate of $26 per round including cart is available Monday through Thursday after 3 PM. The discount rate is $30 including cart after 3 PM on Friday, Saturday and Sunday. Pull carts are available for $4 per round. A snack bar and air-conditioned lounge should satisfy all food and beverage needs.

The Country Club of New Hampshire

Kearsarge Valley Rd., North Sutton
• (603) 927-4246

This 6600-yard course is consistently rated by *Golf Digest* to be one of the top 75 public courses in the country. The par 72 layout was designed by William Mitchell and hosts the New England Senior Championship every June. Tee times can be reserved seven days in advance. Greens fees are $27 during the week and $34 on weekends. Powered carts are $24 for 18 holes and $14 for nine. The bar serves sandwiches as well as beverages.

Monadnock Region

Tory Pines Resort

N.H. Rt. 47, Francestown
• (603) 588-2000

Donald Ross designed the original nine-hole course here in 1929. That layout is now the front nine of the par 71, 18-hole course. The course is 5500 yards long and is open to the public. Per-person greens fees are $45 with a motorized cart on weekends and $32 without a cart. On weekdays you'll pay $38 with a cart and $25 if you want to walk. Tee times may be reserved five days in advance. You can get lunch and drinks in the tavern at the resort.

Shattuck Golf Course

28 Dublin Rd., Jaffrey
• (603) 532-4300

This challenging 6077-yard, par 71 course is not for the beginner, at least not if you want to make it home before dark. The course, designed by Brian Silva, opened in 1991. It has consistently made the top five in *Golf Digest*'s New Hampshire rankings. Weekend tee times can be reserved beginning the preceding Tuesday, and weekday starts can be reserved two weeks in advance. Greens fees are $45 Monday through Thursday, including powered carts. The rates are lower for starts after 2 PM, check when you make reservations. Weekend and holiday fees are $43 plus $13 per person for powered carts. (Unless you're very fit, you'll want a cart — remember, Mount Monadnock is in Jaffrey too.) The 19th hole serves sandwiches and well as beverages.

Bretwood Golf Course

E. Surry Rd., Keene
• (603) 352-7626

The two 18- hole courses here are gaining respect throughout New England. The North Course is a 6345-yard, par 72 layout. Rated in the New Hampshire top five by *Golf Digest*, the course hosts the New Hampshire Open every year in late July. The South Course is also a 6345-yard par 72. During the week both courses operate on a first-come, first-served basis with greens fees of $25. Reservations for weekend tee times are accepted beginning on Wednesday. Weekend greens fees are $32. Powered carts are $20 per cart, and pull carts are $2.

Pine Grove Springs

N.H. Rt. 9A, Spofford
• (603) 363-4433

This is a nine-hole course with two sets of tees giving you the opportunity to play 18 holes. Each nine is a 3000-yard par 36. Weekday greens fees are $12 for nine holes, $15 for 18 holes and $20 for all-day play. Weekends are $15 for nine, $20 for 18 and $25 for all-day. Tee times are always on a first-come, first-served basis. The lounge serves sandwiches and beverages.

Take a Chance!

Whether you're fulfilling a life-long dream or having a mid-life crisis, sometimes you just want to do something different. Something a little silly, maybe just a little daring, something that will challenge you to stretch your wings if not the credulity of your friends or spouse. We've found you a few.

Granite State Over-30 Baseball

(Mostly Merrimack Valley)

This is not your father's slo-pitch league. The seventeen teams of the Granite-State Over-30 Baseball League include a few former major-leaguers and a significant number who have played minor league or Division 1 college ball. Everyone is here for both the fun and the competition. The season runs from April to August. Each team plays 18 games before the playoffs. Most games are on Sunday mornings, and the annual all-star game is played at Holman Stadium in Nashua. Although they've been playing organized ball for nearly a decade, this league has no office or mailing address. Watch local bulletin boards for information, or e-mail MLReed371@aol.com for more information.

boulder morty's

25 Otterson St., Nashua

• 603 88-MORTY

boulder morty's is an indoor rock climbing gym located just off South Main Street in downtown Nashua. Here you can keep in shape for your next expedition, or learn the ropes (literally) if you've never climbed anything steeper than a staircase. With more than 8,000 square feet of climbing space and 75 different stations, you won't get bored despite the lack of views. The fully-trained staff members are prepared to explain technique and guide beginners through each step of the climb, and the changing routes, overhangs and rolling boulder area offer challenges even for expert climbers. For safety, beginners are required to pass a basic class on climbing and belaying. All necessary equipment is available for rent at the gym. Some of the folks from boulder morty's also lead outdoor climbing expeditions, so you can take your skills from the gym to the mountains.

Manchester Indoor Paintball

250 Commercial St., Waumbec Mill, Suite 4003, Manchester

• (603) 623-8222

Inside this old mill building you'll find 13,000 square feet of paintball territory. Obstacles large and small provide for a challenging battlefield, yet the whole facility is handicapped-accessible. Games are refereed and there is an observation deck so non-combatants can watch the fun. A strategy room is available for planning. You can come in on your own and join a battle or gather a group for a day of fun. Games begin at 4 PM and 7 PM Monday through Friday, Saturday and Sunday at 8:30 AM, noon, and 3:30 PM. There's also a game at 7PM on Saturday. Reservations aren't required, but call ahead to be sure there isn't a private session scheduled. Cost to play as a walk-on is $15 and includes a face shield (required). You can bring your own paintball gun or rent one from them for $5 including 12 oz of CO2. You must use their field paint balls at $6 for 100 or $70 for a half-case. Anyone age 12 or older can play. Wear long pants and long sleeves. You can rent a poncho for $3, although the paint washes out of your clothes.

Adventure Games Paintball Park

158 Deering Center Rd., Weare

• (603) 529-FLAG, (603) 529-PARK

This outdoor paintball park was featured in a number of television specials about paintball, having opened in 1987 when the sport was just in its infancy. The park is open to the public every weekend during a season that runs from early March until Thanksgiving (but the office is open daily to book parties). Games are played from 8 AM to 4 PM. Up to 200 players can battle at one time in this park, and they will place walk-ons on teams according to ability. Experienced staff and judges are on the field at all times. The Walk-on fee is $10, although there are many special days each month when fees are reduced

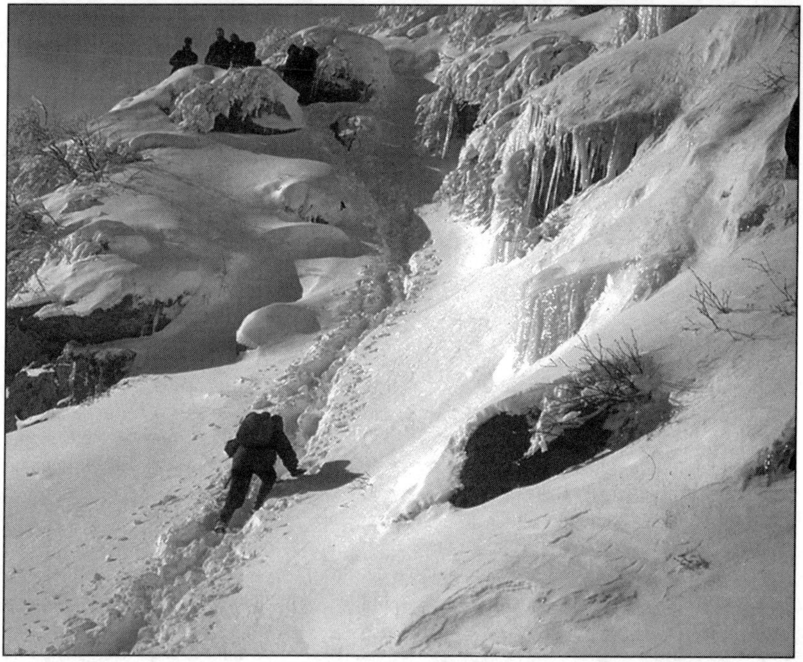

A Thanksgiving weekend climb in Tuckerman Ravine offers a winter hiking experience.

or even waived. You must also buy paintballs (you cannot bring your own) and you may rent equipment if you don't own it. They estimate a full day of paintball costs $30 to $50. You must be 12 years old to play and anyone younger than 18 must have a waiver signed by a parent. The park offers the use of their picnic area with barbecue pit after the game, but no alcohol is allowed while the game is in progress.

Canobie Paintball
Roulston Rd., Windham
• (603) 893-1863

Canobie Paintball has a fun variety of settings on its 10-acre site: 12 different fields including a village, a wilderness and a castle. They are set up to run simultaneous games on the various fields, so they can accommodate a lot of players. All games are refereed, and safety goggles with facemasks are required (and provided). Walk-ins are welcome: arrive between 8:00 and 8:30 AM to receive training and briefing, and you'll be placed on a team. A photo ID is required, and you must be 18 to play (13 to 18 with parent's written permission). For a group of 20 or more they will assign refs and you can run a private game. There's a nice covered patio with a grill where you can have a cookout. They sell cookies and drinks. Cost to play is $15 if you bring your own gun, $25 with one of theirs. Either way you must buy their paintballs. Canobie Paintball is open Saturdays and Sun-

INSIDERS' TIP

Never done this before? The Greater Manchester YMCA probably has a workshop just for you. Rock-climbing, mountaineering, guided hikes and mountain bike excursions (throughout the state) are all on their schedule. Call (603) 497-4663 and ask about Adventure Education.

days year round, and every day but Monday in summer (Memorial Day to Columbus Day).

Specialty Stores, Guides and Schools

Merrimack Valley Region

All Outdoors

321 Elm St., Manchester
• (603) 624-1468
210 Daniel Webster Hwy., Nashua
• (603) 888-6573

This outfitter is a favorite with outdoorsy Insiders. It has a great selection of topnotch equipment for climbing and hiking, skiing, biking and paddling and helpful staff who actually hike, bike and climb in their spare time. The Nashua store isn't quite as large but the selection is still excellent.

Benson's Ski & Sport

401 Daniel Webster Hwy., Merrimack
• (603) 424-7641

Benson's occupies an old barn with a good assortment of high-quality equipment for outdoor activities. Depending on the season, it may be displaying mountain bikes and backpacks or cross-country skis and snowshoes. The staff can help you find the right fit for your size and skill.

Eastern Mountain Sports

Mall of New Hampshire, 1500 S. Willow St., Manchester • (603) 647-0815
Pheasant Lane Mall, 310 Daniel Webster Hwy., Nashua • (603) 891-1180
Mall at Rockingham Park, 99 Rockingham Park Blvd., Salem
· (603) 894-5331

The big boys in the outdoors outfitting business, this local company offers everything you could need for any outdoor activity. Clothes and food, climbing gear and tents, backpacks and boots are just a few of the items in stock. The staff at EMS stores are generally knowledgeable and can help you determine which equipment best suits your needs.

Goodale's Bike & Ski

46 Main St., Nashua
• (603) 882-2111, (800) 291-2111
1197 Hooksett Rd., Hooksett
• (603) 644-2111

This full-service bicycle dealer has been serving the Greater Nashua area for almost 80 years. The big shop on the Manchester-Hooksett Road opened to be more accessible to that population center. Both stores offer two floors of high-end bikes, cycling clothes and accessories, including everything from tire pumps to carrying racks for your car. Each also has a service department that can do minor repairs or major overhauls on virtually any make and model bike (whether purchased there or not). In winter the main section of each store is filled with Alpine and Nordic skis, skewers, snowboards and snowshoes, and the technicians mount bindings and do ski tune-ups and repairs. The stores sell and service bicycles year round.

Seacoast Region

Philbrick's Sports

181 Lafayette Rd., N. Hampton
• (603) 964-5581

An Insider favorite, Philbrick's carries equipment for every kind of sport. The staff are knowledgeable and able to help you select the right mountain bike, skis or other equipment for your size and ability. They can do repairs and routine maintenance as well. And they're known for a wonderful mud-season special: credit for whatever you spend in February which you can redeem in March! It's a great way to get set

INSIDERS' TIP

In professional golf, the "senior" designation begins at age 50. If a course has special rates for seniors, you may be able to qualify even though you're not yet eligible for the AARP.

up for summer sports or take advantage of end-of-season specials on the winter gear.

Exeter Cycles
4 Portsmouth Ave., Exeter
• (603) 778-2331

Here's a bike shop where the proprietor is a cyclist with thousands of miles of experience. The shop sells and services all brands of bikes. It even carries tandems. It also offers a full line of accessories including baby-joggers and trailers, car racks and all kinds of cycling clothing, gloves and helmets.

Eastern Mountain Sports
Fox Run Mall, Fox Run Rd., Newington
• (603) 433-4764

Like all the EMS stores (see Merrimack Valley, Monadnock and White Mountains listings), this shop offers a wide selection of outdoors equipment and good advice from a knowledgeable staff.

Lakes Region

Nordic Skier Sports
N.H. Rt. 28 and N.H. Rt. 109, Wolfeboro
• (603) 569-3151

This store began with cross-country skis, but even in New Hampshire the trails aren't snow-covered all year long, so off-road bikes were a natural complement. The staff here rents and sells bikes, but employees also repair, tune and ride them and can help you decide what you'll need and where to go. The store also stocks accessories and clothes. Rentals cost $15 for a half-day or $20 for a whole day, which includes a helmet, a lock and a map of area trails.

White Mountain and Great North Woods Regions

Moriah Sports
101 Main St., Gorham
• (603) 466-5050

This store is a complete outfitter for outdoor enthusiasts. It focuses on bikes — road and mountain — and has a full-time mechanic on staff. In addition to bikes, it carries all backpacking equipment, helmets, shoes and any equipment that you might have left at home or discovered as a new essential. Moriah's also organizes group rides every week for mountain and road bikers of all abilities. The store is open every day all year.

Ragged Mountain Equipment
N.H. Rt. 16 and U.S. Rt. 302, Intervale
• (603) 356-3042

This full-service outdoor equipment store concentrates on all-season backpacking and technical climbing. It manufactures its own outdoor clothing and equipment and stocks lines made by other manufacturers. It has a repair department as well as book and map departments. Free maps are available for local hikes and mountain-bike trails. The store is open every day all year.

Appalachian Mountain Club
Pinkham Notch Visitors Center, N.H. Rt. 16, Pinkham
• (603) 466-2721

The Appalachian Mountain Club is the oldest conservation and recreation organization in the United States. The information center is the place to call for hut reservations (see our Take a Hike section for the White Mountains), trail maps and info on the many programs offered by the club. You'll find year-round activities in topics such as adventures in backpacking, animal tracking and canoeing.

Eastern Mountain Sports Climbing School
Main St., North Conway
• (603) 356-5433

This school is fully accredited by the American Mountain Guides Association. The school offers instruction for all levels of rock climbing and ice climbing. The programs include guided winter ascents of Mount Washington. In addition to the school, you'll find an EMS retail store that carries all outdoor equipment from skis and snowshoes to tents, sleeping bags and camping gear. A full line of clothing, including boots, is another feature of this great outfitter. EMS does not carry bikes or specialized bike clothing or equipment. The store is open seven days a week throughout the year.

www.insiders.com
See this and many other Insiders' Guide® destinations online.
Visit us today!

Dartmouth-Lake Sunapee Region

Claremont Cyclesport

4 Middle St., Claremont
• (603) 542-2453, (800) 831-2453

This shop specializes in bikes and bike accessories. You'll find road bikes, mountain bikes, hybrid bikes and bikes for children. Equipment includes helmets, racks, water bottles and all clothing. The shop rents a few bikes, including a tandem. Call ahead to make sure it has what you want. The store is open every day but Sunday.

Omer and Bob's Sport Shop

7 Allen St., Hanover
• (603) 643-3525

This sports shop specializes in bikes during the summer and skis during the winter. It also carries a solid line of sporting equipment including in-line skates and tennis racquets. Besides equipment you'll find all the requisite clothing as well as a full bike and ski repair department. They'll send you next door to The Dartmouth Bookstore for maps and specialty books (see our Shopping chapter for more on this great bookstore). The store is open seven days a week throughout the year.

Tom Mowatt Cycles

213 Mechanic St., Lebanon
• (603) 448-5556

You'll find 10,000 square feet of bikes here. About 80 percent of sales are mountain bikes, with the rest divided between road bikes and hybrid bikes. Besides bike sales, the store has a full fleet of bikes for rent. The cost is $20 per day and $14 per half-day. For rental periods of three days or longer, the daily rate drops to $14. You'll find clothes, helmets, racks and other bike equipment as well as a full repair department. In winter the store carries a full line of snowshoes. The store is open seven days a week throughout the year.

Eastern Mountain Sports

Powerhouse Mall, N.H. Rt. 12A, West Lebanon
• (603) 298-7716

This full-service sports equipment and outdoor outfitter is a premier source for clothes and equipment for almost all outdoor activities. It doesn't have bikes, but you can find all your hiking and camping supplies under one roof. It carries a wide selection of boots as well as an excellent supply of maps and books specializing in outdoor activities and field guides. The store is open every day throughout the year.

Outspokin'

889 N.H. Rt. 103, Newbury

• (603) 763-9500

This bike shop is full of new beautiful bikes. It specializes in mountain bikes and offers a variety of rentals, ranging in price from $20 for a basic bike up to $35 for one with full suspension. Group and multi-day discounts are also available. You'll find Greg Lemond bicycles and road frames as well as bikes by Schwinn and Gary Fisher. A full-service repair shop is on-premises. When snow arrives to end the biking season, this is a great spot for snowshoes and snowboards. The store is closed on Mondays.

Monadnock Region

Eastern Mountain Sports

1 Vose Farm Rd., Peterborough

• (603) 924-7231

This is a great place to look for just about anything needed for hiking and camping. It doesn't have bikes, but the tents, sleeping bags and complete line of clothing for adults and children more than make up for this omission. Look for the complete EMS write-up in the Shopping chapter. The store is open every day all year long.

Spokes and Slopes

7 School St., Peterborough

• (603) 924-9961

This full-service bike and ski shop can fulfill your equipment and clothing needs for both activities. They also rent bikes for $15 a day. Look for details in our Shopping chapter.

Banagan's Cycling Co.

41 Central Square, Keene

• (603) 357-2331

You can find everything you need for all kinds of biking here. Road bikes, mountain bikes and hybrid bikes are all sold, and you can rent Cannondale mountain bikes. The non-suspension bikes are $20 a day, and front-suspension bikes are $25 a day. Banagan's has a full line of specialty clothing and equipment for bikers. Anything you need to look or feel like a bike pro is here. The store is open seven days during spring, summer and fall, but hours vary during the winter so it's best to call ahead.

If you love baseball, make the pilgrimage to Fenway Park.

Spectator Sports

Our immediate reaction to the idea of a spectator sports chapter was, "People in New Hampshire are too active to be spectators — we do sports instead of watching them." Obviously we were wrong, as the information in this chapter will show. Relax, sit back and eat a few French fries.

We are grateful that Boston takes on the regional responsibility of providing people throughout this area access to live professional sports. Ice hockey's Bruins and basketball's Celtics play at the Fleet Center in downtown Boston. The Red Sox play at Fenway Park, which is also right in the city. If you love baseball, make the pilgrimage to Fenway. Even if you hate the American League's designated hitter rule, you'll love this classic baseball park. We hear talk of new stadiums and preserving the Green Monster (the notoriously high and shallow left field boundary), so don't put that pilgrimage off too much longer. The New England Revolution play professional soccer and the New England Patriots pro football at Foxboro Stadium 30 miles southwest of Boston.

Every region except the White Mountains and Great North Woods offers college sports. You might get a chance to see the Franklin-Pierce women's soccer team play. They are two-time NCAA Division II National Champions. The popularity of soccer in New Hampshire has made this a likely spot for semiprofessional soccer league teams: the Phantoms call both Keene and Manchester home. Professional baseball returned to Nashua when the Atlantic League's Nashua Pride kicked off their season in 1998.

And if you thought auto racing only happened in North Carolina, you'll be pleased to learn that in New Hampshire you can watch everything from go-cart to NASCAR racing. New Hampshire also has greyhound raceways that double as sites for parimutuel betting and simulcast racing. Legislators are contemplating allowing video gambling at a few locations.

And you should know that high school sports are a big part of our local scenes. You don't have to have kids on the team in order to enjoy the local games. Football and soccer games might be held any autumn day, including Saturday. And basketball — girls and boys — keeps us cheering through winter. Read about upcoming games in the local newspaper.

Professional Sports

Baseball

Boston Red Sox
Fenway Park, Yawkey Way, Boston, Mass.
• (617) 267-1700 ticket information/box office

Along with the rest of New England, New Hampshire Insiders follow this American League team to heights of expectation and depths of despair. Traditionally the Sox field strong teams with big hitters, classic pitching and a left-on-base average that reduces grown fans to tears of frustration. They almost always make a run for the pennant, holding our attention until the weather turns chilly in the fall, and about once a decade they flirt with the World Series. But as every fan knows, since the fateful day in 1920 when then-owner Harry Frazee sold Babe Ruth to the New York Yankees, the Sox have never won the Series (they had won it in 1915, 1916 and 1918). Insiders call this The Curse of the Bambino. We also refer knowingly to The Wall, or Green

Monster, which makes left field short (tough for pitchers) but high (tough for hitters), and off which balls bounce erratically (tough for fielders).

Fenway is the oldest park in Major League Baseball, and its downtown location turns ballgame parking into a free-enterprise bonanza for area businesses. Many New Hampshire Insiders leave their cars at the Alewife MBTA (Boston subway system, commonly called the "T") station (Red Line), which is at the junction of U.S. Route 3 and Mass. Route 2 north of the city. Take any train to Park Street, change to the Green Line (D branch) and ride the T to Yawkey Station. They run extra trains before and after games. If you really want to drive, take Interstate 93 S. from the Lakes Region or Merrimack Valley. Stay on I-93 all the way into Boston. The traffic gets quite heavy as you approach the city — stay to the right on the Lower Deck (of the elevated highway). Take the Storrow Drive exit and stay on Storrow Drive W. to the Fenway/Kenmore exit (it's a left exit). Stay left on the overpass. Go right at the light onto Boylston Street. Avoid the pedestrians (everyone in Boston walks wherever they please). You'll be able to see the ballpark on your right as you negotiate Boylston Street. The third set of lights is Yawkey Way, but you'll be busy checking out parking lots before you get there.

From the Seacoast, take Interstate 95 S. to U.S. Highway 1 S., cross the Tobin bridge in Boston, merge onto I-93 and immediately get off on Storrow Drive and follow the directions above. From the Monadnock Region you can take either N.H. Route 13 or N.H. Route 12 south to Mass. 2. Mass. 2 runs east all the way to Cambridge. From there you can follow the signs to Storrow Drive and follow the same directions. Note that the connection from the end of Mass. 2 to Storrow Drive involves five sets of lights, one bridge and two rotaries (traffic circles). It's not for the fainthearted. Notice that the Alewife MBTA station, with its lovely parking garage, is right at the end of Mass. 2. (See our Daytrips chapter for more about driving in Boston and information about Boston's public transportation system, the T.)

Red Sox tickets may be ordered in advance or purchased at the gate. Prices range from $12 in the bleachers to $21 for an upper-box seat. Early in the season you can usually buy bleacher seats on the day of the game, unless the Yankees are in town. As pennant fever builds you'll find tickets harder to find.

Nashua Pride

Holman Stadium, Amherst St., Nashua • (603) 883-2255

Nashua has seen several professional baseball teams come and go in recent years, but Insiders are very excited about this latest entry from the independent Atlantic League. Unlike some earlier franchises, the Pride appear to bring real money and familiar players to the equation (former Red Sox star Mike Easler was the manager in their opening season, then moved up to a job in the bigs, as did several players.) We hope they will enjoy many seasons in historic Holman Stadium, which is being treated to a $750,000 upgrade but still looks very much as it did when Roy Campanella and Don Newcombe played here with the Brooklyn Dodgers affiliate in 1946. The Pride played 59 home games between mid-May and Labor Day. They had to sell 1,600 tickets per game to break even, but the stadium seats 4,700, so there are always good seats available. The mascots, Shag the Lion and the crowd-favorite prankster Monkey Boy, keep everyone smiling, and a couple of nationally known mascots, Sport and the San Diego Chicken, are booked to visit Holman through the summer. Pride caps, T-shirts and other apparel are selling at the Lion's Den Gift Shop on Main Street, the sun is shining and the natives are humming "Take me out to the ball game."

Basketball

Boston Celtics

Fleet Center, One Fleet Center, on Causeway St., Boston, Mass. • (617) 523-6050 ticket information

For NBA play, Celtics magic runs deep, from Bill Russell, Bob Cousy and John Havlicek to Larry Bird and Reggie Lewis. Red Auerbach's cigar is an Insider icon. But recent years have been bleak, and the move to the shiny new Fleet Center (directions below) has increased ticket prices without improving the score. Hopes ran high when fabled coach Rick Pitino came on board, but even he has proved unable to work a miracle. Still, some wise trades and abysmal seasons have earned the Celtics several top draft picks. The trouble is after the Larry Bird era, Celtics fans came to believe a playoff berth was our divine right. Tickets range from $10 to $200.

The new Fleet Center has all the modern conveniences: air conditioning, a video scoreboard, escalators and adequate restrooms. The Fleet's new parking garage is probably the best thing about the new complex, as it can now accommodate more than 1,000 cars in legal spaces! Take the North Station/Causeway Street exit off I-93 directly to the Fleet Center garage. Enter from Nashua Street, and the garage elevators will bring you up into the North Station section of the Fleet Center. You can also come to the game by train (North Station is at the Fleet Center), or leave your car at an outlying MBTA station (Alewife in Cambridge, or Riverside in Newton) and take the Green Line or Orange Line to North Station.

Football

The New England Patriots
Foxboro Stadium, 60 Washington St., Foxboro, Mass.
• (508) 543-1776

The New England Patriots began the 1997 season with their 13th coach since their birth as the Boston Patriots in 1959 as part of the American Football League. Thirteen wasn't a lucky number for Pete Carroll, who succeeded the brilliant and mercurial Bill Parcells. The Patriots were knocked out of the playoffs early. (You may remember that the '96 season ended when the Patriots lost to the Green Bay Packers in Super Bowl XXXI.) The Patriots have traded shrewdly though and have several years with excellent draft picks coming up. The Patriots have decided to move to Hartford, Connecticut beginning in the 2000 season. All plans are subject to change: mayors, voters and taxes may cause team owners to think twice when the costs for all parties are added up. But for now, the 1999 season will be the last one in Foxboro. Whether New Hampshire Insiders will make the trek to Hartford to watch the Patriots remains to be seen. Some say that the added distance still won't equal the time it takes to negotiate the parking nightmare in Foxboro. Directions to the stadium are in our soccer write-up.

You'll need to tune in on the tube or befriend a season-ticket holder if you'd like to see any of the current season's home games. Individual game tickets go on sale in mid-June and are sold out in a couple of hours.

Hockey

Boston Bruins
Fleet Center, One Fleet Center, Boston
• (617) 624-1900 ticket information

These have been dark days for the once-mighty Bruins of the National Hockey League, but the hiring of coach Pat Burns has a light flickering at the end of the Callahan Tunnel. They made the playoffs in his first two seasons, and everyone agrees that the next few years will be a rebuilding time. Insiders remember the glory days of Bobby Orr and Phil Esposito, Cam Neely and Ray Bourque, and hope for a return to greatness. With the climate controls at the new Fleet center, however, the unpredictable weather that helped win a few Bruins games is a thing of the past.

The Bruins play at the Fleet Center. We miss the historic old Boston Garden (but not the rats or the obstructed-view seats). The Fleet Center tour (every hour from 10 AM to 4

INSIDERS' TIP

Since greyhounds run for only a few years but potentially live for many more, it's nice to know that the Greyhound Placement Service is there to match these intelligent and graceful dogs with loving owners when they retire from racing. Call (603) 497-2148 to find out more.

PM, seven days a week) includes a visit to the Boston Garden History Center as well as a peek at the famous parquet floor. For directions to the Fleet Center, see our write-up for the Celtics. The NHL season runs from October to April. Ticket prices ranged from $20 to $75 in 1999.

Soccer

The New England Revolution

Foxboro Stadium, 60 Washington St., Foxboro, Mass.
• (508) 543-0350, (800) 946-7287 for schedule and tickets

The New England Revolution are one of 10 U.S. teams in Major League Soccer. Sixteen home games are played at Foxboro Stadium (directions below). The 1999 season began in mid-March and the team is very happy to have Walter Zenga returning as goalkeeper. Playoff games can keep the season alive until the end of October. The Revolution's first season was 1996, and attendance and enthusiasm for the team exceeded expectations. Sports fans in the United States are fast discovering the thrills of soccer, and nowhere is it more exciting than in New England. Ticket prices range from $10 to $25. The MLS championship game is slated to be held in Foxboro in the fall of '99.

Directions to Foxboro Stadium from New Hampshire: From the Seacoast Region take I-95 S. to Exit 9 in Massachusetts. Exit 9 is also the Wrentham exit. You will exit onto U.S. Route 1 S. Go 4 miles on U.S. 1 (Washington Street). Foxboro Stadium will be on your left. From all other regions your best bet is to take I-93. Travel south on I-93 from anywhere in the state. You'll drive through Boston on I-93. You will exit off I-93 S. onto I-95 S. at Exit 1. Traveling on I-95, go south to Exit 9 at Wrentham. Exit onto U.S. 1 S. and go 4 miles on U.S. 1 (Washington Street). Foxboro Stadium will be on your left.

The Phantoms

One Park Avenue, Hudson
• (603) 882-3198, Tickets (603) 578-5588

The New Hampshire Phantoms play in the D-3 League of the United System of Independent Soccer Leagues, and the Lady Phantoms play in the Women's League of the same organization. Both teams split their home games between Singer Family Park in Manchester and Owl Field in Keene. In 1997 a brand-new English-style brick stadium was constructed in Manchester as the Phantoms' home field. From the home stands you have not only a great view of the pitch but also the Merrimack River beyond. In 1998 the men's team came *this* close to winning the National Championship, losing the final game in overtime. They have hopes of becoming a farm team for the Revolution. The women's team has also done well, although the women's league itself is a bit more tenuous than the men's. Call the Phantoms' office in Hudson for schedules. To reach Singer Park, take the Granite Street exit (Exit 5) off I-293. Follow the signs for Singer Park (yes, you will feel as if you are driving through a parking lot. It's okay.) To get to Owl Field, take N.H. Route 101, or N.H. Route 9, 10 or 12 to where all those roads intersect outside Keene (yes, this is a crazy intersection; hang in there). At the lights find Route 10 South. At the next set of lights take a left onto Winchester Street, another left onto Krif Road and follow it to the field. Phantoms tickets are $8 for adults and $4 for children but a youth pass for $10 gets children into all the home games all season!

INSIDERS' TIP

Cy Young, for whom Major League Baseball's annual award to the top pitcher in each league is named, played for the Red Sox from 1901-08. He pitched a perfect game against the Philadelphia Athletics on May 5, 1904.

Racetracks

Greyhound Racing

Seacoast Region

Seabrook Greyhound Park
New Zealand Rd. (N.H. Rt. 107), Seabrook • (603) 474-3065

You can see live greyhound racing all year, but it's best to call ahead since racing action varies from season to season. Even if live racing isn't scheduled the day you're in town, you can place bets and watch simulcast racing on television. The dining room seats 900, and the Granite Room is available for private functions. The doors open at 11 AM and close at 11 PM every day. The admission charge for live racing is $1. There is no charge for simulcast viewing.

Lakes Region

Greyhound Park
N.H. Rt. 106, Belmont • (603) 267-7778

You can watch live races here every day from early June until the end of September. The rest of the year you can keep up with racing via the 200-plus televisions bringing in the action from more than 40 tracks. The doors open at 11 AM and close at 11 PM. Simulcast viewing is free, and the admission charge for live racing is $1.

Monadnock Region

Hinsdale Greyhound Park
N.H. Rt. 119, Hinsdale • (603) 336-5382

Place your bets folks. Live greyhound racing is held every day except Tuesday, and evening races are held on Friday and Saturday nights. When the dogs aren't running, you can wager and watch races around the country. Besides greyhounds, you can keep up with horse races and pay-per-view boxing. The dining room is open for lunch every day and for dinner on Thursday, Friday and Saturday. There is no charge for admission.

Horse Racing

Merrimack Valley Region

Rockingham Park
Rockingham Park Blvd., Salem • (603) 898-2311

The live racing season runs from early June to late September. Racing is held on Saturday, Sunday, Monday and Wednesday, but it's always smart to call ahead. Simulcast racing can be seen every day. The park opens at noon and closes at 11:30 PM. The dining room, clubhouse and sports bar are open every day. The admission is $1 for simulcast and $2.50 for live racing. Children younger than 12 are admitted for free.

Auto Racing

Merrimack Valley Region

New Hampshire International Speedway
N.H. Rt. 106, Louden • (603) 783-4931

This is the largest sports facility in New England. The speedway seats 78,000, and the parking is free. You can see car and motorcycle racing events here from April 1 to November 1. NASCAR Winston Cup and Indy Racing League as well as amateur events are on the schedule. Call ahead to check the schedule for specific dates. Food options include a 160-seat restaurant in addition to 14 permanent concession stands. Ticket prices vary depending on the event, but the average admission ticket is $10. (Winston Cup races will cost much more.)

Sugar Hill Speedway
197 Sugar Hill Rd., Weare • (603) 529-2479

Sugar Hill features go-cart racing for everyone ages 8 to 80. You can see it here every Sunday afternoon from the first weekend in May until the first weekend in November. You can watch racing on Saturday night too, as drivers tear it up around the one-fifth mile oval asphalt track. The admission for adults is $8 on Saturday night with the first race at 6:30 PM and $5 on Sunday afternoons with the first race at 1 PM. Children 12 and younger are admitted for no charge.

Monadnock Speedway
N.H. Rt. 10, Hinsdale
• (603) 239-8800

The action is on Friday nights from late April through late September. The track features NASCAR and Winston Racing Series with pro-stocks, light-models, strictly stocks and mini-stocks. The gates open at 5:30 PM, and qualifying starts at 7 PM. Admission is between $10 and $12 for everyone older than 12 and $2 for kids 12 and younger.

Seacoast Region

Star Speedway
Exeter Rd., Epping
• (603) 679-5306

The Saturday night racing season begins in early April and runs until late October. The quarter-mile circular track is asphalt. The gates open at 4 PM, with the first race at 6 PM. Seven divisions can race here, and the evening is usually over around 11 PM. Concession stands are the food supply. Tickets are $12 for the stands and $20 for the stands and pits. Children 12 and younger get in free with an adult.

White Mountains and Great North Woods Regions

Riverside Speedway
Brown Rd. Groveton
• (603) 636-2005

Five divisions compete here on a quarter-mile, high-bank asphalt track. The season opens in early May and runs through early September. The fast food is varied with a larger-than-usual menu that includes burgers, fried dough, fried onion rings and baked potatoes. Grandstand admission is $8 for adults and $2 for children younger than 12. Admission to the pit areas is $15 for adults.

White Mountain Motorsports Park
463 Daniel Webster Hwy., Woodstock
• (603) 745-6727

This 5,000 seat stock car raceway opens in early May and has races once a week through late September. From May to mid-June, enjoy the fun on Sunday afternoons at 2 PM. In mid-June the racing switches to Saturday nights. Admission is $9 for adults and $2 for kids younger than 12. If you've got a self-contained camper, you can park overnight.

Dartmouth-Lake Sunapee Region

Claremont Speedway

110 Thrasher Rd., Claremont
• (603) 543-3160

The one-third mile asphalt oval track is open for stock car racing on Saturday nights from the end of April until early September. Five divisions race here, and the action usually runs from 6:30 to 10:30 PM. Snack-bar food is available. Admission is $8 for adults and $2 for kids ages 7 to 12. Kids 6 and younger get in for free.

College Sports

Merrimack Valley Region

New Hampshire College

2500 N. River Rd., Manchester
• (603) 668-2211

The New Hampshire Penmen's nationally ranked men's basketball team plays home games in the college's gymnasium, which seats 2,500. To get to the campus, take Exit 9 N. off I-93 on to N.H. 3 headed north (away from Manchester). Go left at the first intersection, follow the road to its end. Turn right on Bicentennial Drive and then right again onto North River Road. New Hampshire College is a quarter-mile farther on the left. New Hampshire College also fields men's and women's soccer teams, men's baseball and women's cross-country. Anyone is welcome to attend home games on the campus.

St. Anselm College

100 St. Anselm Dr., Manchester
• (603) 641-7000

The St. Anselm Hawks men's and women's basketball teams have been at the top of their Division II leagues for several years now, and the ice hockey team continues to set records. Women's softball is a new force to be reckoned with, as they won their first Division II ECAC championship in 1997. Other varsity sports, including soccer, tennis and lacrosse, round out the program and attract a loyal following. And in 1999 the Hawks football program returns for its first full season since the program was suspended for World War II. The Hawks were always local favorites and many old-timers have been seen dusting off their pennants and reminiscing about the glory days! With a 5-1 record in exhibition in 1998, there is hope that the Hawks will amply fill the gap the fickle Patriots may leave behind. The Stoutenburgh Gymnasium is across Rundlett Hill Road from the Dana Center, and the fields are behind the Dana Center, so there is adequate parking on-site unless there's a game and a production at the theater simultaneously. Take N.H. Route 114 N from the junction of N.H. Route 101 and N.H. Route 114 in Bedford. Continue until you come to St. Anselm's Drive on your left at the second set of lights. The campus is about 1 mile up the road on the right. Drive past the main entrance and most of the college to turn right on Rundlett Hill Road or you will have to drive all the way around the campus to get there.

Seacoast Region

University of New Hampshire

Main St., Durham
• (603) 862-1234

The U.N.H. Wildcats fields Division I teams in 23 varsity sports since the budget-cutting

INSIDERS' TIP

At this writing the going rate for parking spaces around Fenway Park is $12 to $15. If that seems outrageous, consider McDonald's parking lot on Boylston Street. The price is the same, but the restaurant donates the proceeds of ball-game parking to the Ronald McDonald House for families of children with cancer.

elimination of the baseball, men's lacrosse and men's and women's golf teams (golf will continue as a club) in 1997. The Wildcats Football program is Division I-AA. Of all Wildcat sports, only ice hockey makes money — and you'll be hard-pressed to find an available ticket among the 7,000 seats at the Whittemore Center Arena for hockey. The women's ice hockey team is the reigning U.S. champs, and the men made it to the "Frozen Four" of the 1998 national tournament and came within one overtime goal of winning the National Championship in 1999. There is some hope that the basketball teams might be able to move into the black if their success continues. Despite pleas to sacrifice the program in order to save the four eliminated sports, the football team is making progress, and football tickets can be scarce too. All teams play on the campus, at the Whittemore Center Arena, Memorial Field, Cowell Stadium or the Field House. From N.H. 4 take N.H. 155A past the agricultural school and directly to the visitor's parking lot. It's a short walk to the athletic facilities, or you can hop on one of the frequent shuttle buses. Don't bother trying to park near the fields or stadiums — there is no parking, and tyou will get towed!

Lakes Region

Plymouth State College
15 Holderness Rd., Plymouth
• (603) 842-6900

Competing in Division III, the Plymouth State Panthers have developed something of a powerhouse reputation, having gone to the postseason in football, ice and field hockey, men's and women's soccer, and women's tennis and volleyball as well as men's and women's basketball and men's wrestling — not to mention all the great Panther teams that didn't make the playoffs! The Physical Education Center on the campus houses a 2,000-seat gymnasium, pool and field house and encompasses 33 acres of playing fields.

Dartmouth-Lake Sunapee Region

Dartmouth College
Main St., Hanover
• (603) 646-2466 (tickets)

Dartmouth Teams compete in NCAA Division I (I-AA in football), the Ivy League and the ECAC (Eastern Collegiate Athletic Conference). More than 1,000 students compete in nearly 500 intercollegiate contests annually. Men and women each have 16 varsity teams. You'll pay to see basketball (men and women), football and ice hockey, but the other sports are free to watch. Call the Athletic Ticket Office at the number above for information. Besides advising you on ticket availability and cost, the staff can fill you in on what events are taking place during your visit. You might catch field hockey or soccer on Chase Field or watch a crew race on the Connecticut River.

Colby-Sawyer College
100 Main St., New London
• (603) 526-3000

The equestrian team at Colby-Sawyer is one of the country's strongest. They were the Intercollegiate Horse Shows Association winners (translation: National Champions in riding) in 1989 and 1994. The 15 intercollegiate teams compete at the NCAA Division III level. Exceptions are the women's and men's alpine ski racing teams, which compete in NCAA Division I. The school is a member of the Eastern Collegiate Athletic Conference and the Commonwealth Coast Conference.

INSIDERS' TIP

No team has won as many pro basketball championships as the 16 won by the Boston Celtics. But the team has struggled in recent years, making tickets to Celtics' games at the Fleet Center easier to come by.

Monadnock Region

Franklin Pierce College

College Rd., Rindge

• (603) 899-4000, (603) 899-4222 (sports information)

The 10 intercollegiate teams at Franklin Pierce compete at the NCAA Division II level and are members of the New England Collegiate Conference. The excellent women's soccer team (NCAA Division II National Champs in 1994 and 1995) plays in the fall. In winter, check out the men's ice hockey team, which plays as a member of the American Collegiate Hockey Association (not NCAA for this sport). Lacrosse — both men's and women's — is the featured spring sport along with baseball and softball. Franklin-Pierce teams are very good small college teams with frequent appearances during national championships. The men's basketball team made four NCAA tournament appearances during the '90s.

One of the nice things about living in New Hampshire is being close to Boston, but not too close.

Daytrips

Those of us who live here don't feel the need to leave that often (OK, maybe in February), but if we want to take a quick trip outside our borders, we're lucky to have three wonderful states for neighbors. Here, we'll fill you in on our favorite nearby getaways.

We share our entire southern border with Massachusetts, and we've written about two trips here — both very different. Boston, the dominant New England city, is a treat even for confirmed Granite Staters. And for those who prefer to see more of rural New England, we've suggested a way to get a quick look at western Massachusetts and an introduction to Pioneer Valley, the Mohawk Trail and the Berkshires region.

Maine is our Seacoast (as well as eastern) neighbor. We've managed to find a few places that aren't the usual tourist spots. And you really shouldn't come to New Hampshire without getting at least a glimpse of the charm of Vermont. It's to the west just across the Connecticut River, and it has better farmland, fewer rocks and more taxes than New Hampshire. Any of these trips will add to your knowledge and appreciation of New England. We call these daytrips because you can get there and back in one day. The trips are arranged by region with starting points in each geographic area except The White Mountains region. The distances vary, and driving times can depend on traffic. Have fun and drive carefully.

Daytrip from the Seacoast and Lakes Regions: Maine's South Coast

Just across the Piscataqua River from Portsmouth is the delightful southern coastal region of Maine. Now we'll confess that for many Insiders, this daytrip is a regular event with one purpose only: shopping. But there's more to the south coast than factory outlets, and we're going to show you some of it.

Beginning from Portsmouth, take Interstate 95 over the bridge into Maine. Drive past Exit 3 to stop at the Tourist Information Center for brochures and maps. From the rest area parking lot, take a right where it says "To 95 South," then follow the signs for U.S. Route 1 (don't actually get on I-95). Take a right on U.S. 1 toward Kittery. The 2-mile stretch of road in front of you is the outlet shopping capital of the New England coast.

There are 14 shopping centers along this strip, plus many individual stores, including the **Kittery Trading Post**, an outdoor equipment emporium that has been here since the 1930s. Among the 120 factory outlets you'll find Dansk, Eddie Bauer, Corning and Bose. The **Tanger Outlet I** alone has something for everyone: American Tourister, Liz Claiborne, OshKosh, Van Heusen and Black & Decker. There's Polo/Ralph Lauren at the **Outlet Village** and Oneida at **The Maine Outlet**. Royal Doulton China and Levi's are at the **Kittery Outlet Center**, Brooks Brothers is at **Tanger Outlet II**, and Benetton, Pfaltzgraff and Reebok are at the **Tidewater Outlet Mall**. This just scratches the surface! If you're a dedicated shopper you'll want to pick up the *Factory Outlet and Off-Price Handbook* at any tourist information center in New Hampshire or Maine (it covers both states), and come back to finish another day.

Meanwhile, there is more to Kittery. Go under the sign for I-95, then take the immediate left exit to stay on U.S. 1. (Don't take the bypass.) The road winds around a bit, but if you follow the signs you'll be fine. Go left at the junction with Maine Route 103, and stay on it through the village and past the Portsmouth Naval Shipyard, the center of a longtime border dispute between Maine and New Hampshire. The big white building you'll see across the harbor was the U.S. Navy Prison for many years. The road winds through a lovely village, and you won't believe you're just a couple of miles from the frenzy of the outlets.

As you approach Kittery Point, **Fort McClary**, (207) 439-2845, comes up on your right. This little-known spot, fortified since the earliest Colonial days, was the site in 1721 where the town of Kittery erected six cannon to defend their sovereignty over the Piscataqua against "the unjust actions of the Government of New Hampshire." (New Hampshire was charging a tariff on goods shipped through the port, which Kittery claimed as its territory.) The blockhouse contains a self-guided history of the fort, and the views across the harbor from the grassy plain are delightful. The great granite blocks are not the ruin of some other fort but the remnants of a Civil War project that was never completed. The park is open daily from 9 AM to dusk. Admission is $1. A picnic area, just up the road on the left, is also part of the park. Follow Maine 103 along Kittery Point to where a small sign directs you toward Fort Foster. **Fort Foster Park**, (207) 439-3800, offers beaches and playgrounds in addition to picnicking and is a popular spot for windsurfing and scuba diving. Admission is $2 for adults, $1 for children ages 12 to 18, and $2.50 per vehicle to park (children younger than 12 are free).

Get back on Maine 103 and continue north and east. You'll come into York, where the **Old York Historical Society**, (207) 363-4974, complex is on your right. Park on Lindsey Road (marked with a blue hospital sign). Six buildings from the early 1700s, including a tavern, jail (or gaol) and schoolhouse, have been restored and are open to the public Tuesday through Sunday from mid-June to September 30. Admission to all six buildings is $6.50 for adults and $2.50 for children ages 6 to 16, with no charge for children younger than 6. You can buy a family pass for $16.

When you leave Old York, go right on U.S. Route 1-A toward York Harbor and York Beach. If it's summer, sit back and enjoy the scenery, as this can be a slow drive. Notice the mix of old and new houses. You can tell the oldest houses by the many-paned windows. Old glass panes were small, and the glass, if it's original, is wavy and bubbly and possibly a bit purple. At high tide the surf pounds just a few feet to your right as you head out toward the point. As the tide goes out, a lovely white beach is revealed. This is a great place to walk and wade, if you can find a place to park along this road.

Just beyond the seawall, take a right toward **Nubble Light** (there is a very discreet sign). It's about a mile out to the lighthouse, where there is some public parking. The visitors center, with a gift shop and restrooms, is open from mid-May to Columbus Day (weekends only in spring and fall). The surf and views from this point are incredible. Notice the open chair on a cable that carries supplies and workers out to Nubble Light. Until the light was automated in 1987, the keeper's children crossed via cable every day to get to school! This area is a great place to stop for lunch. You have a choice of terrific restaurants, such as Fox's Lobster House, (207) 363-2643, or Lighthouse Restaurant, (207) 363-4054. We like Fox's because we could sit on the porch overlooking the waves, but at either place, the seafood is exquisite.

After lunch, retrace your way off the point and follow U.S. 1-A back up to rejoin U.S. 1. Now it's time to make a choice. If this is a kids-oriented trip, go left. Just a quarter-mile back is **Yorks Wild Kingdom**, (207) 363-4911 or (800) 456-4911, a zoo and amusement park. Elephants, kangaroos and tigers await you, and there's even a roller coaster. Admission to both sections of the park is $12.75 for adults, $9.50 for children ages 4 to 10 and

INSIDERS' TIP

Keep an eye out for posters advertising fund-raising lobster and clam bakes. They're an inexpensive way to enjoy local seafood delicacies.

Even on a clear day, the White Mountains create their own weather.

$3.50 for kids up to age 3. The park is open daily 10 AM to 5 PM all summer (until 6 PM from July to Labor Day).

If this is a grown-up trip, take a right on U.S. 1 toward Ogunquit and Wells. Ogunquit is a famous artist's colony and home to **The Ogunquit Playhouse**, (207) 646-5511, the oldest summer theater in Maine. You might want to visit the **Museum of American Art**, (207) 646-4909, on Shore Road. Admission to see this collection of 20th-century art is $3 for adults or free for children younger than 12. The **Marginal Way**, a mile-long footpath along an impressive bluff where pounding surf and ocean spray paint an ever-changing picture, is a great place for a stroll. The path, and the road, lead to **Perkins Cove**, where you'll find cute shops and restaurants and fishing boats.

Return to U.S. 1 and continue north and east about 4 miles to Wells. Stay on the main road for assorted shops, and the **Wells Auto Museum**, (207) 646-9064, an interesting collection of cars from the early 1900s to the 1960s. Admission to the museum is $4, $2 for children ages 6 to 12, and free for those younger than 6. As you drive along U.S. 1 you'll find antiques shops and used bookstores on every corner, or take any right and drive down to the ocean, where 7 miles of white sand may entice you out of your car.

Be sure to stop at **Lighthouse Depot**, (207) 646-0608, at the north end of town. This truly amazing shop carries every conceivable lighthouse book, knickknack and trinket imaginable and publishes *Lighthouse Digest Magazine*. You can also stock up on Maine souvenirs — from plastic flying disks and lobster refrigerator magnets to stuffed moose and hand-carved models and ships.

Continue north on U.S. 1 to The Kennebunks. Kennebunk, Kennebunk Beach and Kennebunkport were among Maine's premier vacation communities long before the son of one summer family was elected president. The George Bush clan still summers in Maine, but without the huge retinue of press and security that once turned the whole point into one gigantic traffic jam. If you take Parson's Walk out to Cape Arundel to see the waterspout, where waves crashing into a narrow opening in the rocks shoot up in a spectacular spray, you'll walk past Walker's Point and the Bush compound. Back toward the mainland, Kennebunk is a town of Victorian and Edwardian mansions, the most famous of which is the bright yellow and white "Wedding Cake House," that has graced countless calendars and postcards. Local legend reports that the builder of this house had it decorated like a wedding cake for his bride, whose wedding festivities had been disrupted when the sea-captain groom was called away by an emergency on board his ship. Whether it's true or not, the house is stunningly decked-out with ornate carved white wood trim that does indeed look like icing. The house is privately owned and not open to the public. Stop at the **Brick Store Museum**, (207) 985-4802, in Kennebunk for information about the walking tour of the historic district. If you decide to go through the museum, admission for those older than 12 is $5, and children younger than 12 are free.

Follow U.S. 1 north to Log Cabin Road (marked "To Kennebunkport") and go right. The **Seashore Trolley Museum**, (207) 967-2800, is on U.S. 1-A. Established in 1939 and still expanding, this place is a train-lover's delight. There are more than 200 cars in the collection, and from May to October for $8 ($4.50 for children 6 to 16, younger than 6, free) you can enjoy unlimited rides on restored trolleys. Or if shopping is more your style, follow your nose down into Kennebunkport. It's a picture-postcard village where countless little shops and snack places line tiny lanes that wander out to the water's edge.

Cross the bridge on Maine Route 9, and you'll come to an intersection with Beach Street. Take a left if you want to go down to the water or to visit the shrine at **St. Anthony's Monastery**, (207) 967-2011. This Franciscan monastery is open daily from 6 AM to 6 PM in winter and 6 AM to 8:30 PM in summer, and it's a quiet spot in a hectic season.

Continue west on Maine 9 through the **Rachel Carson National Wildlife Refuge**, (207) 646-9226. The entrance is less than a half-mile past the Wells town line on the left. The 1-mile, self-guided trail is an easy walk. This 4,800-acre refuge in a huge marshy area is wonderful for bird watchers and a tribute to the naturalist who raised the alarm about pesticides in the food chain nearly 40 years ago with her best-selling book, *Silent Spring*.

Maine 9 rejoins U.S. 1 in Wells. Follow it south past the Lighthouse Depot (second chance!) and shops. At the junction of U.S. 1 and Maine 9, take a right and follow Maine 9 west (more antique shops and used books) to the Berwicks. Stop in North Berwick at the **Old Corner Convenience Store and Country Kitchen**, (207) 676-9585, for an enormous piece of perfect homemade pie with a big mug of coffee. If it's time for dinner, there's a different homemade specialty each night. Then continue on Maine 9 into South Berwick. This is the birthplace of Sarah Orne Jewett, author of many Maine novels, including *The Country of the Pointed Firs*. The family home is preserved as the **Sara Orne Jewett House Museum**, (207) 384-5269, operated by the Society for the Protection of New England Antiquities. Admission costs $4 for adults and $2 for children ages 6 through 12, with no charge for those younger than 6.

Take a left where Maine 9 joins Maine Route 4 W. In less than a mile you'll cross the river and be back in New Hampshire. Take N.H. Route 4 west to N.H. Route 16 a few miles north of U.S. Route 4 and I-95. At any point along this trip you can hop back up on the interstate and head back to New Hamp-

INSIDERS' TIP

Down East is a nautical term from the sailing era, when sailors followed the prevailing winds ("downwind") along the coast from New York and Massachusetts toward Maine.

The Village of Shelburne Falls, Massachusetts

Just in case Williamstown is a little farther than you want to drive (say you're starting in Wilton instead of Keene), we thought you'd like to know about the charming Victorian village of Shelburne Falls. It's about halfway to Williamstown from Keene, just off Mass. Route 2. Turn off Mass. 2 onto Mass. 2-A when you see the signs for Shelburne Falls. Follow the signs to the Visitors Center and park right on Bridge Street. Walk about one and a half blocks and make a left on Deerfield Avenue just short of the Iron Bridge over the Deerfield River. You'll immediately see the **North River Glass** on your right. Stop and watch artists blow and shape the hot glass, then head to the shop where you can buy hand-blown glass pieces. The vases are particularly tempting. From the glassworks, continue down the hill and you'll see **Mole Hole Candles**. You can watch as different candles are made by hand. Then take a minute to enjoy the gift shop, which has a section for candle seconds. You'll see everything from dripless tapers in varying lengths to delightfully scented candles in apothecary jars and snifters. You can check off lots of Christmas gifts in just a few minutes.

Photo: Nancy Elcock

The Village of Shelburne Falls turned an obsolete trolley bridge into a horticultural wonder dripping with vines and flowers.

If you do decide to shop around, your traveling companions can explore outside. Just below the waterfall are several glacial potholes. Geologists say they were formed over several million years. The scenic overlook provides a great view and a safety fence. The waterfall itself was a rich salmon fishing grounds until 20th-century pollution ruined the spawning grounds. Once you've explored Deerfield Avenue, retrace your steps, cross Bridge Street and walk a block and a half following the signs to the **Bridge of Flowers**. It was a trolley bridge across the Deerfield River joining the town of Shelburne Falls and Buckland until the trolley became obsolete in 1928. Town citizens converted the old bridge into a horticultural wonder beginning in 1929 by planting the abandoned eyesore with vines, shrubs and flowers. The bridge was refurbished in 1983, with local gardeners in charge of orphaned plants until the new bridge was complete. Now the bridge has a paid, full-time gardener along with lots of help from the local garden club. You'll see more than 500 plant varieties beginning with tulips in May and continuing through October with chrysanthemums.

shire. Be aware, however, that on summer Sunday evenings the backup from the York toll booth is frequently as much as 15 miles long. That's why we're bringing you back through Dover.

Want to explore more of Maine? Pick up a copy of *The Insiders' Guide® to Maine's Southern Coast*.

Daytrip from the Merrimack Valley Region: Boston

Insiders will tell you that one of the nice things about living in New Hampshire is being close to Boston, but not too close. The Hub of the Universe offers something for everyone, of which we're giving you just a sampling. Even so, there is too much here for a single trip. Pick and choose according to your interests, and plan to visit more than once.

You can drive to Boston on I-95 from the Seacoast area, Interstate 93 from the Merrimack Valley or Interstate 90 (the Massachusetts Turnpike) from the west (N.H. routes 12 and 13 both run south to join Mass. Route 2 just west of where it connects to Interstate 190. Take I-190 south to I-90, and then head for the city).

Driving in Boston is a legendary nightmare. The famous "cow path" roads are confusing and poorly marked, and the infamous Boston drivers are most often compared to those in Rome. In addition, parking in the downtown area is very limited and very expensive. In other words, you really *don't* want to drive around the city. Fortunately, Boston is small enough to walk across or around comfortably (the major tourist sites are grouped in a 3-square-mile section), and the mass transit MBTA (known to Insiders as the T) is convenient and safe. As an added incentive, the T offers a one-day "Passport" for just $5 (seven days for $18). The pass allows unlimited use of all subway lines, buses and commuter rail lines within the city. It also entitles you to discounts on tickets at more than two dozen area attractions. You can leave your car at an outlying MBTA station (the Red Line's Alewife at the intersection of U.S. 3 and Mass. 2 and the Green Line's Riverside on Mass. Route 128 and I-95 are Insider favorites) or downtown at one of the big parking garages and hop on and off the subway all day. Passes are available at many hotels and newsstands as well as the major MBTA stations.

If you're not up for walking, you can enjoy a narrated tour of all the major historic sites from an old-fashioned trolley car. Three companies offer trolley tours: **Beantown Trolley**, from Brush Hill Tours, (617) 236-2148; **Boston Trolley**, from Minuteman Tours, (617) 876-5539; and **Old Town Trolley**, (617) 269-7010. Or you can opt for a tour on a World War II amphibious vehicle with **Boston Duck Tours**, (617) 723-3825, and see Boston both by land and by sea (or more precisely, river).

MBTA maps in every station will help point you in the direction you want to go, but for the confidence of a map in your pocket or for brochures and information, check out the visitor centers at City Hall Plaza or State Street (Government Center or Haymarket stations) or the information booth on the Tremont Street side of Boston Common (Downtown Crossing or Park Street stations).

We think everyone should see **The Freedom Trail.** Begin from the National Park Service Visitor Center at 15 State Street (Government Center, State Street or Haymarket sta-

INSIDERS' TIP

The Boston CityPass is a new deal for visitors: it includes admission to the Museum of Science and the Aquarium, the Museum of Fine Arts and the Isabella Stewart Gardner Museum, the John Hancock Tower and the John F. Kennedy Museum over at Columbia Point. Passes, available at all these sites, cost $26.50 for adults and $13.50 for children ages 13 through 17 (there is no children's CityPass), and are good for nine days.

tions; Blue, Orange or Green line). Watch the slide show, then join a park ranger on the 90-minute walking tour or pick up a map to guide yourself. Follow the red brick road (actually a line on the sidewalk) and travel back in time to the American War for Independence. Over a route just more than 2.5 miles long, you'll visit the site of the Boston Massacre in front of the **Old State House,** (617) 720-3290, (admission $3), and wander through burial grounds where famous patriots rest. You'll duck to enter **Paul Revere's House**, (617) 523-2338, which costs $2.50 to enter, and look up at the spire of the **Old North Church**, (617) 523-6676, ("One if by land, two if by sea"). The trail ends on the **U.S.S. *Constitution***, (617) 242-4339, still officially in service and manned by a crew of modern sailors in 17th-century uniforms. Do step next door to watch *The Whites of Their Eyes*, a video about the Battle of Bunker Hill, at the **Bunker Hill Pavilion**, (617) 242-5601. You'll also want to board the **Tea Party ship,** (617) 338-1773, even though it's not technically on the Freedom Trail. A pass to get on the ship costs $7; $3.50 for children ages 4 to 12 and $5.50 for teens ages 13 to 18. Children younger than 4 can get in for free, but hang on to them, as this boat is on the water! Many of the 16 sites on the Freedom Trail are free, and those with admission charges offer T-Passport discounts.

Boston boasts a wealth of world-class museums. While you're here, we suggest you take time for the **Museum of Science**, (617) 723-2500, on the Green Line at Science Park Station. This is one of the premier science museums in the country, with 450 interactive exhibits exploring every aspect of science from astronomy and biology to math and physics. Kids love to climb into the Apollo module, peek at the black widow spider (safely behind glass) and climb the musical stairs. If you can drag them away from the central hall, you'll find intriguing displays about habitats and wildlife, an interactive exhibit where you explore your own senses, the world's largest lightning bolt generator, demonstrations of machines and Mobius strips and probability and way more than you can absorb in one trip, not to mention shows in the Charles Hayden Planetarium and the Omni Theater. Admission is $9 for adults and $7 for ages 3 to 14 (younger than 3 admitted free) with an additional charge for the shows at the Planetarium or the Omni ($1 off with T-Passport).

If you prefer your science alive and swimming, try the **New England Aquarium**, (617) 973-5200, on the Blue Line at Aquarium Station. From the harbor seals who greet you outside the door to the colonies of penguins and the sharks and sea turtles swimming around the artificial coral reef in the central tank, you won't forget this up-close encounter with more than 12,000 creatures of the sea. Admission is $11 and $5.50 for children ages 3 to 11, while little ones younger than 3 get in free.

If you're traveling with kids, take them to the **Children's Museum**, (617) 426-8855, or the **Computer Museum**, (617) 423-6758. Both are on Museum Wharf at 300 Congress Street (South Station on the Red Line). These outstanding museums are highly interactive, encouraging children to not only touch but also to climb on, in and around and operate the exhibits. If your kids have seen the children playing on the giant keyboard on Sesame Street, they'll recognize it here (and be disappointed, as ours were, to learn that not everyone gets to jump on the keys). Admission to the Children's Museum is $7 for adults and $6 for children ages 2 to 15, with a $2 charge for 1-year-olds. The Computer Museum is also $7 for adults but only $5 for ages 5 to 18 and free for those 4 and younger.

The **Public Gardens**, on the Green Line

INSIDERS' TIP

Boston's Back Bay is so named because it is built on an area created in the 1800s by filling in a shallow portion of the bay (a project that would never be approved today!). As a result of its recent and planned development, Back Bay's streets are straight and named in alphabetical order, from Arlington to Hereford.

at Arlington Station, is a favorite of the young and the young at heart and not just because of Robert McCloskey's *Make Way for Ducklings*, set in Boston, c. 1940. The landscaping and flowers are outstanding. And yes, the **Swan Boats**, (617) 522-1966, still paddle around the pond in warm weather. A ride costs $1.75 or 95¢ for children 12 and younger. Bring some bread crumbs for Mr. and Mrs. Mallard and all the quacklings. **Boston Common**, across Charles Street from the Public Gardens and above Park Street Station on the Red and Green lines, is a public gathering-spot likely to be filled with office workers having picnics, jugglers and musicians entertaining children and persons of indeterminate sanity proclaiming the end of the world. At the far corner of the Common is the **Robert Gould Shaw Memorial**, honoring the men of the 54th Massachusetts Regiment, the black Civil War regiment made famous by the movie *Glory*. The sculpture was designed by New Hampshire's own Augustus Saint Gaudens (see our Attractions chapter).

Indulge in the **Museum of Fine Arts**, (617) 267-9300, on the Green Line E branch at Museum Station. The collection of American paintings and furnishings is outstanding, as are the paintings by European masters, the Asian art and textiles and the I.M. Pei-designed west wing. Take time for a cup of tea in the Japanese garden. Admission to the museum is $10 for adults and free for children up to age 17.

Once you've seen the MFA, you'll want to check out the **Isabella Stewart Gardner Museum**, (617) 566-1401, at 280 the Fenway, between the Green Line E branch's Museum Station and the Orange Line's Ruggles Station. This was the home to "Mrs. Jack" Gardner, a Boston society woman who died in 1924. In her will she decreed that her home would become an art museum, and that nothing in it could ever be changed. This is why, eight years after art thieves removed almost $200 million worth of paintings from the walls, the 13 empty spaces are still visible and labeled. There's a nice cafe here if you're hungry. Take the time to read the newspaper clippings, they're fascinating. Admission is $10, with no charge for those younger than 18.

Many museums have one afternoon or evening a week when admission is half-price or free. It doesn't hurt to call and ask!

More art awaits the aficionado at the Harvard University in Cambridge, at Harvard Square Station on the Red Line. (Harvard and MIT aren't actually in Boston, they're across the Charles River, in Cambridge.) The **Fogg Art Museum** offers a history of Western art, while the **Arthur Sackler Museum** is dedicated to an Asian and Islamic collection, and the **Busch-Reisinger Museum** collection is primarily of Central and Northern European origin. All three museums, (617) 495-9400, are included in one ticket price of $5, and there is no charge for children younger than 18. Even better, the Harvard museums are free for everyone on Wednesdays and Saturdays from 10 AM to 2 PM.

You can get a spectacular view of Boston from the top of two buildings. The **John Hancock Tower**, (617) 572-6429, takes you to the 60th floor and includes a topographical light show delineating changes in the city since the 1700s. It costs $4.25 to go to the top. The **Prudential Center**, (617) 236-3318, costs $4 ($3 for those younger than 18) for a ride to the 50th floor where the Skywalk provides a 360-degree view across both Boston and Cambridge.

Other Boston sites worth visiting include the birthplaces of several Presidents and other notables, historic and architecturally significant churches, house museums and a wonderful "emerald necklace" of parks and open spaces. You may want dine in elegance at **L'Espalier**, 30 Gloucester Street, (617) 262-3023, where a four-course nouvelle cuisine dinner costs between $60 and $80 per per-

INSIDERS' TIP

Vermont, Massachusetts and Maine have sales tax. New Hampshire doesn't. If you see something you want to buy outside the state, make sure you can't get it for less within our borders.

son. Or eat in historically accurate chaos at **Durgin Park**, (617) 227-2038, in Faneuil Hall Marketplace, where traditional New England meat and potatoes and seafood are served family style at long trestle tables on the second floor of this historic building. The price range here is from $6 to $20. We like to try the microbrews at the **Boston Beer Works**, on Brookline Avenue at Yawkey Way across from Fenway Park. A terrific meal to accompany your beer will be $6 to $12. Or belly up to the bar at the **Bull & Finch Pub** on Beacon Street, (617) 227-9605, recognized by television viewers as *Cheers*. Or you may be happy, as we are, to graze on the varied offerings of dozens of pushcart vendors before heading back to the car and leaving the big city behind.

Daytrip from the Dartmouth-Lake Sunapee Region: Woodstock, Vermont

Start your trip in Lebanon and drive west on Interstate 89. Cross the Connecticut River into Vermont, stay on I-89 past the intersection with I-91 and get off the highway at Exit 1. At the end of the exit ramp, make a left turn onto U.S. Route 4 W. toward Quechee, Vermont. (This takes no more than 10 minutes.) One of the first turnoffs in Quechee is for the **Fat Hat Factory**, Clubhouse Road and U.S. 4, Quechee, (802) 296-6646. It's just off U.S. 4 on your right and well worth a quick stop. Hats, such as hand-knit woolen hats and jester-style felt toppers, are what put the factory on the map (they're sold in more than 28 states), but in addition to hats the store is full of casual clothes and accessories from across the nation. The costume jewelry is particularly playful.

Back on U.S. 4 going west, you'll see an abundance of shops and restaurants on the right side of the road. Stop if you're a shopaholic, but we don't have anything here to rave about unless you happen to be a candle fan. In that case we recommend **New England Candles**, Quechee Gorge Village, (802) 295-5775. You'll see intricately carved candles as well as lots of fun everyday wax designs. Call ahead for the schedule if you'd like to see a carving demonstration. By the way, Quechee gets its name from the Ottauquechee River that runs throughout the area.

From U.S. 4 W., you'll see lots of signs for Simon Pearce. If you make only one stop on your way to Woodstock, this should be it. **Simon Pearce**, in The Mill at Quechee, (802) 295-2711, is both an individual and an enterprise. The man Simon Pearce is from Ireland. Originally a potter, he began working in glass and now runs a business specializing in his original glass and clay designs. In 1981 Pearce moved to the United States and converted this old wool mill into a studio and gallery for his work. You'll find glass blowing, pottery making and rug weaving on the premises as well as a shop specializing in Simon Pearce designs. If that's not enough, you can also eat lunch or dinner here in the casually elegant Simon Pearce Restaurant overlooking the Ottauquechee River. Lunch entrees cost about $10 and feature lamb and rosemary pie, cold and hot pasta dishes with fresh vegetables and Maine crab cakes. Dinner entrees cost about $18 and include filet of sole with almonds, roast duckling and grilled filet mignon. Reservations are not accepted for lunch, but can be made for dinner by calling (802) 295-1470.

If your daytrip concluded at Simon Pearce, you wouldn't be disappointed; but you'll have a lot of fun in Woodstock, so get back in your car and continue west on U.S. 4. You'll be in Woodstock in about 15 minutes.

Woodstock is a quaint yet modern historic village. More than half of the town is included in the National Register of Historic Places. Woodstock was settled in 1765 and became the county seat of Windsor County. It was a thriving 19th-century town. The water from the river powered small businesses, and the fertile land made farming productive. Woodstock might have faded into quaintness during the 20th century except for an important invention over in Farmer Gilbert's hilly pasture. In 1934, the first tow rope was used for helping a human get up a snow covered hill. Thus, winter skiing became a tourist attraction, bringing visitors from all over the world. Farmer Gilbert's pasture is now part of the Suicide Six ski area owned by Laurance Rockefeller.

A parking space right in town might be hard to find, depending on when you are traveling. Summer months and the Christmas holidays are the most crowded. Free all-day parking has been added not far from the center of the town, so follow the parking signs. The main streets in town are Central (U.S. 4) and Elm. Walk to their intersection near The Green, you'll have fun reading the daily town crier — a large blackboard with handwritten announcements of all the day's activities. Continue down Elm Street on the left past about three old houses that are now stores and offices, and you'll arrive at **The Woodstock Historical Society**, 26 Elm Street, (802) 457-1822. If you're an architecture or history buff, be sure and buy their pamphlet called "Woodstock, A Walking Guide" ($2.95). It's a great self-guided tour of 55 structures in the immediate town.

If you continue on Elm Street, you'll see the Ottauquechee River and the wonderful Iron Bridge built in 1869. Cross the bridge, turn right and walk about five minutes on River Road to find the **Billings Farm and Museum**, (802) 457-2355. The farm dates back to 1871 and is still a working dairy. You'll learn about modern agriculture in an authentic 19th-century setting. The museum is open daily from May 1 to October 31. In fall and during Christmas, the farm has special weekend and holiday hours. You can return to town over the Iron Bridge or continue on River Road until you come to Middle Bridge, a new but authentic covered bridge built in 1967. If you cross the river here, you'll be right on The Green, which dates back to 1793. At the western end of The Green is the **Woodstock Town Hall Theater**, (802) 457-3981.

Run by the Pentangle Council on the Arts, you might find a Maybe Mozart chamber music performance during the Down By the River concert series or an indoor Coffee House Concert in the Little Theater of the Town Hall. First-run movies are shown here also. In July a summer festival and crafts fair raises money for the council's school programs. The most fun is had just by walking and looking at the beautiful houses and buildings.

If you're not interested in history or architecture, then you're bound to have lots of fun looking at the modern shops. The Central (Street) business district is less than a mile long, but both sides of the street are full of places to window-shop, browse or spend your children's college tuition. We love **Whippletree Yarn Shop**, 7 Central Street, (802) 457-1325, which has art supplies as well as knitting yarns, patterns and instruction. Embroidery enthusiasts will appreciate **The Stitchworks**, 15 Central Street, (802) 457-2881. The store specializes in custom embroidery and will help you add a personal touch to everything from golf shirts to baseball caps. In case the work can't be completed during your stay in Woodstock, the store will ship the finished design. Antiques experts will have a great time at **American Classics** in Woodstock, 71 Central Street, Upper Level, (802) 457-4337. The gallery features quality Americana from the 18th, 19th and 20th centuries. The gallery is closed on Wednesday. Elm Street has a few gems also. If you like to cook or even just like kitchen equipment, you'll have a great time browsing through **Aubergine**, 1 Elm Street, (802) 457-1340. Besides a superb selection of pots and pans, the store features beautiful bottles of vinegar flavored with lemons and herbs. The owner of the shop is Swiss, so it wasn't a surprise to note the excellent selection of kitchen gadgets that are actually practical. Look for the bottle stoppers from Germany: These inexpensive plastic domes are the best we've found for keeping our sodas from losing their fizz.

Stop by the **Village Butcher**, 18 Elm Street, (802) 457-2756. Next time we make this trip we're taking a cooler large enough to hold a few of the gourmet sausages and roasts we saw. Just across the street is **Shire Apothecary**, 13 Elm Street, (802) 457-2707. You can buy film for your camera and any toiletries you may need, but we like it for the casual, friendly atmosphere. Back where we started, just across from The Woodstock Historical Society, is **Morgan-Ballou**, (802) 457-1321. Sportswear for women is for sale here with beautiful handloomed sweaters.

Take a quick drive outside of town to the **Vermont Raptor Center**, Church Hill Road,

(802) 457-2779. Church Hill Road branches off from Church Street at The Green, and the Raptor Center is less than 2 miles away. The Vermont Raptor Center is an educational center and clinic devoted to birds of prey. You'll see bald eagles, peregrine falcons and snowy owls on the 78-acre grounds. The nature preserve has self-guided trails as well as a shop specializing in field guides and raptor T-shirts.

For food, we like **Bentley's Restaurant and Cafe**, 3 Elm Street, (802) 457-3232. It's like eating in a artsy friend's zany living room. You might be seated at a table with a Victorian couch or armchair, and you'll have fun checking out the Oriental rugs and Tiffany-style lamps. The burgers are great, and beer connoisseurs like the wide variety of microbrews. Bentley's serves lunch and dinner daily. The **Mountain Creamery**, 33 Central Street, (802) 457-1715, specializes in homemade soups and sandwiches upstairs and pastries and coffees downstairs. Soup choices might include a chowder in winter and a cold vegetable choice in summer. The restaurant serves breakfast, lunch and an early supper. Prices in both restaurants are moderate with lunch for two (without beers or dessert) less than $15.

Daytrip from the Monadnock Region: Williamstown, Massachusetts

Begin your trip in Keene and drive south toward Winchester on N.H. Route 10. You'll cross the border into Massachusetts in less than 30 minutes near the beautiful town of Northfield, the northern end of Pioneer Valley. Pioneer Valley stretches down along the Connecticut River to Springfield. The area was one of the first settled because the rich soil in the valley and the transportation opportunities offered by the proximity to the river. Still on Mass. Route 10, cross the Connecticut River near Mount Herman and continue until the Interstate 91 intersection. Take I-91 S. to Exit 26 and get on Mass. Route 2 going west. Within a quarter-mile you'll see the sign for **Three State Viewing** (New Hampshire, Massachusetts and Vermont). A tourist shop and fire tower viewing post mark the beginning of the Mohawk Trail. The **Mohawk Trail**, or Highway of History, is one of the prettiest drives in the Northeast and traces one of the earliest trade routes in America. It joined the English settlements in Boston and Deerfield with the Dutch in New York. The trail was called the Indian path until the English and the Dutch combined forces to disrupt the long peace between the two tribes in the area, the Mohawks and the Pocumtucks. Subsequent to the interference, the Mohawks attacked and slaughtered most of the Pocumtucks in the 1730s. The trail was named The Mohawk Trail in honor of the victors.

Just west of **Shelburne Falls** (see our close-up in this chapter), Mass. 2 begins to run parallel with the Deerfield River. In April it's hard to keep your eye on the road as you see canoes and kayaks battle the spring runoff. You'll notice several Indian trading posts along the winding river valley road. You can pick up a pair of moccasins or a beaded belt as well as a cold soft drink and candy bar. You'll be climbing to an elevation of 2,800 feet as you pass through the town of Florida. Be sure and pull off the road at **Whitcomb Summit**, the eastern summit of the Berkshire Mountains. As the song says, "on a clear day, you can see forever." The road descends with more twists and turns until the final hairpin as you enter North Adams, then it's just 8 miles

INSIDERS' TIP

Boston's Back Bay is so named because it is built on an area created in the 1800s by filling in a shallow portion of the bay (a project which would never be approved today!) As a result of its recent and planned development, Back Bay's streets are straight and named in alphabetical order, from Arlington to Hereford.

to Williamstown. Depending on how often you stop, the drive from Keene to Williamstown is about two hours. Traffic can be heavy during summer and holiday weekends, so if you've got tickets for the Williamstown Theatre Festival, we suggest you allow at least three hours for the trip.

You'll drive into town on Mass. 2 W. There are signs pointing to Mass. Route 43 on your left. Don't turn, but note the intersection since it's where you'll rejoin Mass. 2 to turn eastward and head back to New Hampshire. Mass. 2 is now Main Street, and **Williams College** is all around you. You can tell you're in a college town because you're surrounded by green lawns, red brick buildings and lots of young people. The population of Williamstown is 8,500, and the enrollment at Williams is 2,000. The Williams College Art Museum is on your left. To park, drive past the museum and take the next right at Spring Street. Free municipal parking is at the end of this block-and-a-half-long street. Our suggestions for Williamstown are a stroll on Spring Street and a visit to the **Williams College Art Museum**, Main Street, (413) 597-2429. The original museum structure was built in 1846. Major building additions in 1983 and 1986 include a stunning three-story atrium. The permanent collection and current exhibits are displayed in a series of 14 galleries. Works by American modernists Charles and Maurice Prendergast are among the highlights of the collection. Other major American artists in the collection include Grant Wood, whose painting *Death On Ridge Road* was given to the museum by American composer and lyricist Cole Porter, and works by Georgia O'Keeffe and Edward Hopper. Although the museum has works from many periods, the emphasis is on modern and contemporary art as well as American art. An exhibit each spring highlights the works of graduating art majors. The museum is open from 10 AM to 5 PM Tuesday through Saturday and from 1 to 5 PM on Sundays. The museum is also open on Memorial Day, Labor Day and Columbus Day. Admission is free.

Stroll down Spring Street. This charming street is just a block and a half long. Both sides of the street are full of interesting stores and restaurants. Take a stroll before or after your visit to the Williams College Art Museum. If you're hungry, try the **Cobble Cafe**, 27 Spring Street, (413) 458-5930. It's cozy, with small wooden tables and chairs. The atmosphere is casual and friendly. If you pull out your guidebook, you might get a few suggestions from nearby diners or the easygoing staff. The Thai duck salad with chili peppers, ginger and coconut-lime dressing is just one of several delicious salads on the lunch menu. You can also choose from several original sandwich combinations ranging from grilled eggplant with pesto on toasted sourdough bread to barbecue pork tenderloin served with mango salsa on French bread. If you're staying late, the Cobble Cafe also serves dinner with entrees such as grilled tuna steak and cumin-rubbed lamb shanks.

If you don't have time to sit down or prefer to put together a picnic, you must go to the **Clarksburg Bread Company**, 37 Spring Street, (413) 458-2251. It's open Tuesday through Saturday. There's a weekly baking schedule instead of a menu. The daily offerings include breads, biscuits, scones, muffins and sweets. Trust us when we tell you the double fudge brownies are great. Everything here is wonderful. Some unusual options include spinach and mozzarella biscuits and oatmeal sunflower bread. Plan your day carefully. The bakery closes at 5 PM. Once you've picked out your bread and brownies, cross Spring Street and head into the **Berkshire Hills Market** for some sandwich fillers. The deli counter features pasta salads as well as sliced meats and cheeses. You can pick up soft drinks and chips to round out your meal. Take a few minutes and read the bulletin board near the door — it's fun to pretend you're part of a college town, and who knows, you might find an apartment or a dog.

In case you prefer a dining spot with cloth napkins, walk away from Williams College to Latham Street at the end of Spring Street and try lunch at **Robin's**, 117 Latham Street, (413) 458-4489. The lovely restaurant features lunch dishes such as wild mushroom ravioli, Greek salad with roasted chicken or white bean and roasted garlic pate. Dinner specials go from fancy, such as the smoked mozzerella and sweet red pepper ravioli, to the straightforward and always welcome roast garlic chicken. Robin's has a special cheese or pepperoni pizza for kids at lunch and dinner. Robin's is open Tuesday through Saturday, and if you drive over early in the day, you can stop in for breakfast.

If you can move after all this great food, get yourself to the **Adventure Goat**, 46 Spring Street, (413) 458-2228. You'll find great travel clothes as well as travel books and general gear. Check out the newest in Polartec jackets and pullovers. We found a women's hiking shirt with a beautiful purple wildflower print, proving that trailwear can be lively. You should also head into **The Library**, 70 Spring Street, (413) 458-3436. It's an antiques and gift shop with four to five rooms of furniture, Tiffany lamps, carpet pillows, botanical prints and jewelry. Many parts of the world are represented in the eclectic collection. It's open every day.

We mentioned picnicking above because your next stop has luxurious parklike lawns with picnic tables. Hop back in the car and you're on your way to **The Sterling and Francine Clark Art Institute**, 225 South Street, (413) 458-9545. From Spring Street, head out to Main Street and take a left on Mass. 2 W. You'll enter the traffic circle at the end of Main Street. You'll drive in a horseshoe shape — coming back almost where you began. Take a right turn at the stop sign onto South Street and follow the Clark Institute signs. The museum is a quarter-mile down the road. The **Clark Institute** is a gem of a museum. The marble mansion was built to house the collection of Robert Sterling Clark, an heir to the Singer Sewing Machine fortune. He and his French-born wife, Francine, assembled the collection throughout the 20th century, much of it while living in Paris from 1911-21. The collection opened to the public in 1955. A subsequent 82,000-square-foot addition was built in 1973. Your eyes glide from paintings by Pierre-Auguste Renoir to sculptures by Edgar Degas. Paintings by Winslow Homer are just around a corner. A 1997-98 exhibit highlighted the early works of John Singer Sargent. The museum is open from 10 AM to 5 PM Tuesday through Sunday. It is also open on Memorial Day, Labor Day and Columbus Day. Admission is free.

From the Clark Institute head over to Mass. 43 and take a left. This is Water Street, another "main drag" of Williamstown. In a half-mile you'll see **The Water Grill**, 123 Water Street, (413) 458-2175 on your left. It's open for lunch and dinner every day. Daily blackboard specials complement an already complete menu. Choose Texas-style chili or a seafood club sandwich. If lunch puts a strain on your belt, help is just across the street at **The Mountain Goat**, 130 Water Street, (413) 458-8445. The store specializes in mountain bikes and backcountry equipment. You can buy or rent bikes and outfit yourself completely. Ask about local trails, and pick up maps and tips from the knowledgeable staff.

When you're ready, Mass. 43 will take you right back to Mass. 2. Remember to head east as you leave Williamstown and retrace your path back to New Hampshire.

We can't write about Williamstown without telling you a little about the **Williamstown Theatre Festival**, Adams Memorial Theatre, 1000 Main Street, (413) 597-3400. Begun in 1954, the festival runs from mid-June to the end of August. It is one of the premier summer stage festivals in the United States, with topnotch actors returning every summer to perform in classic and contemporary plays and musicals. Blythe Danner and her daughter, Gwynneth Paltrow, have both acted here for years. The 1997 Tony-award winning actor James Naughton is also a regular performer. Christopher Reeve is a longtime supporter and performer and is currently on the board of directors. The theater is on the Williams College campus just at the intersection of Mass. routes 2 and 7. Performances run from mid-June to the end of August. Afternoon performances are usually scheduled on Thursdays, Saturdays and Sundays. Times and ticket prices vary, so check when you call for reservations.

Real Estate

The real estate picture in New Hampshire is varied and changeable. As in all markets, location is everything, but in New Hampshire, prime location is defined by three things: access, education and zoning. A distance of a couple of miles can mean doubling — or halving — the value of residential property.

Access can be a new highway, a new company moving in or simply a shift in attitude (yesterday's impossibly long commute becomes today's median). Property values in the White Mountains and Lakes regions are driven by second-home sales more than commuting, and proximity to slopes or shore is the measure of access.

New Hampshire school districts are autonomous, and schools vary greatly from town to town. In one community there may be kindergarten, enrichment activities and well-stocked libraries. In the next, the high school may not be accredited. (See our Education and Child Care chapter.) Towns with sizable tax bases (especially those with large amounts of industrial and commercial property) are better able to absorb the costs of education. Those in rural areas may send students to regional schools over which they have little or no control. It was these huge variations and inequities which the State Supreme Court found unconstitutional in December of 1997, and it may be that with a resolution to the school funding crisis, some of these variations between communities will begin to fade. In the meantime, however, newcomers to New Hampshire must investigate these issues when selecting a home.

New Hampshire's zoning laws are local, too. Each community writes and votes on its own code, and amendments are on the ballot almost every spring. In some towns the laws are so restrictive as to invite lawsuits. In others, the code is casually or irregularly enforced. In a few towns, mostly in the rural north, there still is no zoning. Obviously, if the minimum legal lot size in town is 2 or 5 acres, housing costs will be higher than in the next town over where the minimum is a half-acre.

Most New Hampshire homes are served by private wells and septic systems. Typically a bank will want to see both tested before financing a home, and obviously this is in your interest too. If the house you're looking at has town water or sewer, be sure to include those fees or taxes in your calculations.

You will find that some towns encourage subdivisions on private roads. The advantage to the builder is that the cost of construction may be considerably lower. The advantage to the town is that the landowners are responsible for snow removal and general maintenance of the road. (Typically a homeowners association collects fees and administers private roads along with any other commonly held assets.) If you're looking at a home on a private road, recognize that the town still provides police and fire protection to homes on private drives, but the school bus stop will be on the nearest town road. In most cases mailboxes must also be placed on the publicly maintained road.

As a result of all these variables, average prices for the whole state are difficult to define. In the northern part of the state, unimproved land can still be purchased for less than $1,000 an acre. In the southern tier, a single-house lot can cost more than 50 times that amount. New construction is generally more expensive than existing stock, but established homes in prestigious neighborhoods command high prices, and home restoration contractors ask top dollar for antique beauties in almost all regions. The average price of a new two-bedroom home in the state last year was $116,000, but the Seacoast area is much higher and the North Country lower.

Property taxes are a big part of housing costs here and can be difficult to compare because of complex formulas. Tax rate is not a comparable number from town to town. We recommend that you pick a value, say $150,000, and then ask in every town, "What would the taxes be on a house priced at this amount?" Comparing those numbers will give you a much more accurate picture. (This too may change in the post-Claremont era, since in most communities more than 80% of the property tax bill funds local education.)

There are hundreds of real estate agencies in the state. Some are small, independent brokers who sell one or two properties a year. Many are affiliated with large national chains. Clearly we can not review all, or even half, of them here. We have tried to recommend a sampling from each region, with a variety of sizes and specialties, independents and those affiliated with national chains. Not being listed here does not mean there is anything wrong with an agency.

Resources

New Hampshire Association of Realtors
P.O. Box 550, Concord 03302
• 225-4033

This professional association represents Realtors from throughout the state. Call them for local names and contact information in the towns you are investigating.

Home Builders Association of New Hampshire
P.O. Box 2283, Concord 03302
• (603) 228-0351

This chapter of the national association can give referrals of home construction professionals from across the state.

Independent Real Estate Network
c/o Murphy & Murphy Real Estate
23 a Portsmouth Ave., Exeter
• (800) 627-2824 ext. 112

A terrific resource for anyone considering relocating to the Granite State, this cooperative association of agencies throughout New Hampshire offers a unique service: answer a few questions about your interests and needs, and they'll help you figure out which towns and regions best suit you. Let these Insiders share their knowledge of commuting times, school systems, community and recreational resources and real estate trends and your search for the perfect New Hampshire home will be a much simpler process. Learn more, and fill out an online request for their service, at www.irenet.com.

Merrimack Valley Region

The Merrimack Valley includes three of the state's four major cities — Nashua, Manchester and the capital, Concord. Most of the region is within a 90-minute drive of Boston, and the Nashua/Merrimack corridor is home to a number of high-tech firms, including Digital Equipment and Lockheed-Sanders.

The towns of the Merrimack Valley may be divided into three categories: the cities and larger towns (such as Merrimack, Hooksett and Hudson, which are right along the Merrimack); the small towns surrounding them that have become primarily bedroom communities (Hopkinton, Amherst and Londonderry); and even smaller towns further out which have remained mostly rural. Along the river the towns are likely to have some services (town water and sewer, trash pickup), which the smaller communities do not have. And remember, the more restrictive the zoning, the higher the cost of property.

A recurring picture: Property values in a former farming community with a moderately restrictive zoning ordinance escalate wildly when a road upgrade brings it within commuting distance of the Mass. Route 128 corporate corridor. Farms are subdivided, beautiful houses are built, and the town is "hot." After a few years the schools become crowded, so a bond is proposed for new school construction (see our Education chapter for more on school funding). A two-thirds majority is required for the bill to pass. If it does, growth continues, albeit a bit more slowly because of increased property taxes. If it doesn't, property values begin to stagnate. Housing sales in town slow to a crawl. Families move across town lines to places where the schools have better reputations. And the cycle begins again.

Through most of the 1990s Realtors in the

Merrimack Valley Region talked about market strength. Average prices in the southern tier have been escalating at a rate of more than 6 percent annually since 1995. Just as financial experts look to the booming national economy and wonder how long it will hold, local real estate and building industry professionals have been expecting the "bubble to burst" for several years. Still the southern part of the region continues to absorb growth from the spreading Boston work force, and the traditional strongholds of Amherst, Bedford and newly chic Hollis are all seeing new developments. New construction is selling well with some very nice opportunities in the older house market. Condominiums have rebounded and are very popular once again.

Derry is a fast-growing community in the southern end of the Merrimack Valley. A key factor in the town's growth is its proximity to I-93, thereby making it a Boston bedroom community. A realistic rush-hour commute estimate is 90 minutes. A starter home in Derry might be a split-level three-bedroom priced just over $100,000. Push that up to $160,000 if you want to add a bedroom and another bathroom. Most of the new houses are on lots of about 1 acre. There are lots of newcomers in this quickly growing area.

Nashua is another top "work in Boston/ live in New Hampshire" location. In the Nashua area, the location is spoken of in exit numbers off U.S. Route 3 (See Getting Here, Getting Around for details.) A house right off Exit 1 will sell faster than the same house off Exit 8, which is 20 minutes farther away from Boston. And chances are, the selling price is in the near neighborhood of the asking price. The new construction market is active here with demand exceeding supply. New houses with 2,000 square feet are selling in the over-$200,000 range, and a new upscale condominium development at Exit 1 is moving fast at close to $300,000 per unit.

The most popular new house feature is called a farmer's porch — an unscreened front porch where you can watch the kids as they ride their bikes. The rest of the house is open, light and airy. Skylights and gables bring in the sunshine. Late 90s construction favors the "hip roof" and catheral-ceilinged entry, making these homes appear even more spacious.

The condominium market is strong in Nashua after absorbing the leftovers from a decade of a slow market. A two-bedroom, one-and-a-half bath unit in a well-maintained newer building is asking and getting $95,000. Busy professionals who don't want to spend time on upkeep drive the condominium market. Many newer condo communities are "no-lot line" developments: As with any condominium, residents own only "from the walls in," but the units are traditional single-family homes, each with a yard and driveway.

The communities with the strongest reputations are Amherst, Bedford and Hollis. These are well-established older communities with as many charming farmhouses as new neighborhoods. But new is what's selling. In Bedford and Amherst you'll pay $350,000 or more for a 3,000-square-foot newly constructed house (high land costs mean very few smaller homes are being built). To pay less, try Milford to the west or Merrimack to the east. Here, new construction prices are more commonly around $200,000, and 10- or 15-year old homes are in the $120,000 range.

There are a lot of older homes in and around Henniker and Weare. Depending upon the condition of the house, you can still get a five-bedroom fixer-upper for less than $150,000 or spend anywhere from $250,000 to $500,000 on a very well maintained c. 1760 Colonial.

Other attractions in this area are what are known as view properties. As one agent put it, "there isn't much view land left, but we've got a good selection of view properties." So, it's easier to find a house with a view than a scenic building lot. (New Hampshire is much more forested than it was 25 years ago. Keep in mind that many homes that once had splendid views now look out at the woods. If those trees go with the house, you might be able to open up the view with some selective tree cutting.)

If your work situation allows you to live further out, delightful bargains hide in towns like Contoocook and Loudon. How about a four-bedroom "New Englander" (OK, we found out — this term is used to describe a house that doesn't fit any of the classic forms) on 1.5 acres in the $90,000 to $110,000 range?

A popular style of newer home is the traditional-looking open-concept house. The exterior is designed to blend in with the Colonial-style houses in the area while the interior offers open family living space with lots of glass and usually a deck off the back.

Concord is the state capital and a delightful small city with lots of countryside. An older Colonial on 1.5 acres is in the $175,000 range while an older (12 years) two-bedroom condominium can still be yours for about $50,000. The realistic starter price is at least $80,000 in Concord, although prices may drop a bit as you get farther from town. Because Concord is centrally located, residents can get to Boston, the Seacoast Region and the White Mountains in just around an hour.

Real Estate Companies

Buyers View AFB Realty
176 N.H. Rt. 101, Bedford
• (603) 472-5600

First-time buyers and newcomers are likely customers of Buyers View, which exclusively represents buyers. This small but growing firm covers a large part of the Merrimack Valley Region including for-sale-by-owner transactions.

DeWolfe
166 N.H. Rt. 101 W., Bedford
• (603) 471-0777

The DeWolfe real estate enterprise was begun in 1947 by the current president's mother. It is now publicly traded on the American Stock Exchange. Personal attention is the key to their decades of success. The company handles corporate relocations as well as single-family residential sales, and they consider "distinctive properties" their specialty.

Carlson/Norwood Real Estate/ Better Homes and Gardens
197 N. Main St., Concord
• (603) 226-2100

This multi-office agency can help you with your real estate business within a 25-mile radius of Concord and by contacts with Norwood's 10 branch offices across the state. After more than 20 years as a locally owned powerhouse agency in southern New Hampshire, Norwood recently forces with the Better Homes and Gardens network. With agents who both work and live in the communities they serve, and specializing in both commercial and residential properties, Norwood is truly a full-service agency.

Sandy Heino and Associates
185 Main St., Hopkinton
• (603) 746-4645

This company sells a variety of properties, but prides itself on knowing old homes. The company was formed in 1989 with several agents bringing solid experience with them. Sales make them one of the top companies in the area.

Prudential Verani
80 Perkins Rd., Londonderry
• (603) 434-2377

More than 30 years in business has given this busy agency a front-row seat as the Manchester-Derry area has mushroomed. Still operated by the son and daughter of the founder, the agency has grown and diversified as the real estate picture in the state has changed. They joined forces with the Prudential group to add additional strength, and they handle commercial, industrial and rental properties as well as residential listings. More than 50 agents work hard and utilize the latest technology to reduce the stress of relocation, matching buyer's needs with their knowledge of the towns and neighborhoods to find the perfect home.

Century 21 Dick Cardinal Associates
358 Main St., Nashua
• (603) 889-3233, (800) 222-4461

This independent broker brings the power of the Century 21 name and the personal knowledge of a local company together under one roof. The agency has fifteen agents handling properties across southern New Hampshire, but especially in the greater Nashua area. They offer relocation services for people moving from out-of-state or outside the country. They also offer free market analysis for people buying or selling houses for investment or residence in this ever-changing market.

ERA Masiello Group

436 Amherst St., Nashua
• (603) 889-7600

A large (28-agent) office in Nashua is one of this New Hampshire-based realty company's busiest locations. Once again the story is location, and here that usually means, "How close is Boston?" or "Which exit is this near?" ERA is a full-service office, selling both residential and commercial properties with plenty of new construction as well as established neighborhoods. They also handle rentals and offer relocation services.

Joyce McCaffery Realty Inc.

33 Trafalgar Sq., Nashua
• (603) 883-9685

Eight agents in this busy office handle sales and rentals of a wide selection of properties in and around Nashua. They also do property management, so they are very familiar with the rental picture in the city. Once you find the property you love, the sales staff here can assist with the intricacies of Veterans' Administration and Federal Housing Assistance mortgages.

Kopka Real Estate

129 E. Dunstable Rd., Nashua
• (603) 888-4141

Owner Angie Kopka has been bringing her personal touch to the real estate business in Nashua since 1953. She was the first woman and the first New England Realtor to win the Distinguished Service Award from the National Association of Realtors, and at one time hers was the largest real estate office in the state. She has chosen to remain independent in this era of chains and mergers, relying on her many contacts on state boards and agencies, her ongoing study in the field and the resources of the MLS service to enable her to effectively serve all her clients. Personal, confidential attention and local knowledge remain the hallmark of this small agency.

Prudential Crain Real Estate

216 Daniel Webster Hwy., Nashua
• (603) 888-3990
163 Amherst St., Nashua
• 889-3296
4 Derry Rd., Hudson
• 882-1455

This agency, with more than 50 agents in offices in Hudson and at both ends of Nashua, is a major player and highly visible presence in the local real estate scene. They cover a territory from Salem in the east to Mason in the west and as far north as Manchester. A full-service agency, they provide buyer representation, property management, rentals and commercial sales, but residential sales are their strength. Several of the agents specialize in relocation, but the whole team works together, lending expertise in land, financing or investment property as needed. Most of the agents are experienced, and the whole firm has an explicit commitment to a high level of integrity and service to the customer, whether buyer or seller. The success of their efforts is clear in the results of a recent survey: more than 98 percent of customers said they would use them again or recommend them to friends.

Re/Max Properties

230 Amherst St., Nashua
• (603) 886-8800

In its first ten years in operation this independent agency became known as one of the most productive real estate offices in the entire state of New Hampshire. It uses great staff and technology to enable its more than 30 Realtors to serve clients in the most effective possible ways. Advanced communications technology and the Internet are at the service of those buying and selling homes through this office, which handles sales and rentals of land, homes and condos (as well as commercial real estate) throughout the rapidly-growing southern Merrimack Valley.

INSIDERS' TIP

Boathouses can no longer be built over many lakes, including Lake Sunapee. If you have property that has a boathouse, be sure to maintain it. You won't be able to replace it, and it's a very valuable resale item.

Seacoast Region

The Seacoast region extends inland from the narrow strip of coastline, up the Piscataqua River and its tributaries to Somersworth, Epping and Hampstead. The modern, revitalized city of Portsmouth and beachfront communities of Hampton and Rye give way to rolling fields and suburban subdivisions. Note: The New Hampshire Association of Realtors divides the state into 10 regions and defines the edge of the Seacoast region as Newmarket/Newfields/Exeter. While agents in Rye and Exeter handle property further west, the market picture there is more like the description of the Merrimack Valley.

An easy 45-minute drive to either Manchester or Greater Boston, this area is a commuter's paradise and demand is extremely high. Telecommuting is also on the rise in the Seacoast. At the same time, the population of beach towns in summer is 10 times greater than September to May! Appropriately priced property stays on the market only a couple of weeks before selling. There is very little undeveloped land in the Seacoast region, so new construction is quite costly. It's not unusual to pay $130,000 or more for a buildable lot with no improvements.

Portsmouth is a recently revitalized city with a lively historic waterfront and healthy industrial base. In the closing years of the century the average price for a home in Portsmouth passed the $200,000 mark, while the average cost of a home on the island of New Castle was more than $500,000! Further inland, the region is a mix of farm communities and suburbs, and the further you get from the water the lower the housing costs, although there are no bargain communities and very

Photo: Bob Grant

New Castle Harbor is a picturesque New England village.

few fixer-uppers. One broker explained, "Our buyers are almost all two-income families, and they don't have time to work on the house."

There are condominiums in just about every Seacoast community, although Stratham may have the most. The larger condos are in about the same price range as single-family homes. A one-bedroom townhouse in Stratham might be $78,000, but you could spend more than $350,000 for units in Newcastle or Portsmouth. For this price you could expect swimming pools, tennis courts and health clubs along with the usual condominium services of snow shoveling and maintenance.

Demand for rentals in the Seacoast region is very high, driven by the large number of single professionals and the college crowd from the University of New Hampshire. Downtown Portsmouth's vacancy rate is almost nonexistent, but there are rentals available for those willing to move a few miles inland. In Portsmouth landlords don't even have to advertise to fill vacancies! Not all Realtors deal with rental properties. Portsmouth's Chamber of Commerce, (603) 436-1118, has put together a list of member agencies that do.

Exeter is an old-fashioned town, with imposing Federalist homes overlooking a copper-roofed gazebo and a block of stores little changed since most of it was constructed in the 18th and 19th century. The town is dominated by the brick and ivy of Phillips Exeter Academy, one of the country's premier prep schools. Beyond the historic center is a comfortable suburb, where Victorian mansions share a street with tiny Colonial capes, early 20th-century bungalows and every imaginable style in between. There are still some fixer-uppers available in Exeter, but they're going fast!

Rye, Seabrook and Newington all have relatively low tax rates, which make them popular. Come inland as far as Epping or Plaistow and three-bedroom homes can be found in the $140,000 range. A similar home in Exeter or Hampton would be $190,000, and one within walking distance of the Atlantic Ocean or Great Bay would be $275,000. A home on the ocean, if you could find one, would be a half-million or more.

Real Estate Companies

Century 21 Gundalow
1 Madbury Rd., Durham
• (603) 868-1113

This is a medium-size office (nine agents) with the resources of an international franchise at their service. It receives referrals from all over the world. This office covers towns across the Seacoast, focusing especially on the northern end of the region: Dover/Durham/Lee/Madbury and their surroundings. The agents are able to offer newcomers the knowledge gained from many years of living and doing business in the area — not only familiarity with the real estate but also information about child care, public and private schools and the many sports opportunities provided by the university, the towns and the school districts. The company handles rentals as well as sales and works with residential development properties and individual lots.

Russell & Crothers
20 Drakeside Rd., Hampton
• (603) 926-1555

This small, independent agency has been matching people and homes in the Seacoast for 40 years. We spoke with Anne Russell, who counts her husband, daughters and son among the six Realtors in her firm. Their range of interests and contacts enables them to serve any homebuyer. She's a former teacher

INSIDERS' TIP

Realtors warn that many people coming from more urban areas are excited about moving to the country — until the first snowy winter. Is your house rural or is it isolated? If you really want to be out in the country, be sure you're ready to pay the snowplow and drive your kids everywhere. Also remember that the quaint farm on the corner may smell like a farm in the summer!

whose commitment to education continues in her real estate work. The company participates in the School-to-Work program at Winnacunnet High School, and their youngest associate started with them as a high school intern! Russell also encourages buyers to become knowledgeable about the schools in their chosen communities and takes families on tours of the local schools, arranging meetings with teachers, administrators and guidance counselors.

Hunneman Caulfield Coldwell Banker

Fern Crossing, U.S. Rt. 1, North Hampton
• (603) 964-5835
254 State St., Portsmouth
• (603) 436-7501
1247 Washington Rd., Rye
• (603) 964-8565

Recent buyouts have combined these successful agencies into one firm with three offices. Joycelyn Caulfield has been in business on the Seacoast for 35 years and has won numerous awards. Her associates are excited about adding Hunneman's strengths to their own as they continue to serve buyers and sellers across the Seacoast region.

Hall-McGee Realtors Buyer-Brokers of the Seacoast

33 Deer St., Portsmouth
• (603) 436-6636

Beverly Hall and Carolyn McGee are co-owners of this independent agency, which is the oldest and largest exclusively buyer-agency in the Seacoast. They specialize in residential properties, acting as buyer representatives for people moving to the Seacoast area of New Hampshire and Southern Maine.

Preston Real Estate

186 Ocean Blvd., Seabrook
• (603) 474-3453, (800) 424-3453
63 Ocean Blvd., Hampton
• (603) 926-2604

This is a family business with more than 25 years of experience selling and renting homes on the Seacoast. Preston is one of the largest brokers of residential property in this region, where demand far outstrips supply, and has many connections to help you find the right place for your vacation or your new home. Whether you need a long- or short-term rental, during summer vacation or winter's quiet, Preston's is a good place to start your search.

The Lakes Region

In the Lakes Region the real estate boom is dominated by second-home buyers — 60 to 75 percent of the buyers are purchasing second homes. Waterfront properties can bring prices of well more than $1 million, according to Bill Delashmit, past president of the Lakes Region Board of Realtors and a consultant to many buyers of lakefront property. In addition to the attractions of the Lakes Region, homes in this area are convenient to the White Mountains so there's plenty to do in any season.

Access to the lakes drives values from town to town and even within given communities. Wolfeboro has mostly high-end properties, with lots at $350,000 and up, although the highest demand and lowest supply is for land on Squam Lake. A 7-acre vacant lot there sold recently for $780,000, while just outside of town (and away from the lake) the same agency sold a three-bedroom house on 27 acres for $55,000.

Squam Lake was prime territory even before the movie *On Golden Pond* was made there, because development has been very restricted for years, and most properties are passed down in families. Other towns, like Laconia on Paugus Bay and Meredith on Winnipesaukee, saw summer cottages converted to homes and motels to condominiums all along their waterfronts before restrictive laws protecting the waterfront went into effect.

Moultonborough is very popular right now, with excellent frontage on both Winnipesaukee and Squam Lakes and one of the lowest tax rates in the area, thanks to the high percentage of high-end vacation homes in the tax base. Taxes vary greatly from town to town, and buyers should definitely compare property tax bills on lots they're considering. Hebron and Bridgewater, on Newfound Lake, are in the highest demand because their tax rate is quite low. They are also convenient to

Plymouth, which, with a large percentage of tax-exempt properties (college, hospital), has one of the highest tax rates in the state. Taxes on a house in Plymouth would be twice the taxes on the same property in Holderness, and six times what they would be in Bridgewater. The average home in Plymouth sells for between $85,000 and $139,000, but in four years you could easily recover in lower taxes what you paid for property in one of the outlying communities. On the other hand, Plymouth is known for an excellent school system that takes advantage of the college for advanced courses, theater, library and athletic facilities. And with the resolution of the "Claremont" dilemma (see our Education and Child Care chapter) the tax differential should begin to equalize.

Sandwich, known for its lovely historic center, Center Harbor and Tuftonborough look little changed by the years. Laconia and Franklin offer the convenience of the small city but are close to recreational activities. In the Laconia/Weirs area, huge numbers of tourists can be a mixed blessing for full-time residents.

Most people in the Lakes Region commute to Concord or one of the cities — even a few to Massachusetts. The precision tool and die industry in the area remains strong, and machinists are in great demand.

Insiders agree there aren't as many bargains as there were just a few years ago, when bank-owned properties and a difficult economy drove prices down. A very basic but livable home without waterfront today will be about $70,000. Interest rates are still low, prices are recovering but not spiraling, and high taxes are pushing a number of older homes on to the market. For retirees the condominium market can be a real bargain — $60,000 to $100,000 for two or three bedrooms, and for $180 a month in fees you can ignore snow-shoveling, lawn mowing and worrying about the place if you go to Florida from Thanksgiving to Easter.

There is not a lot of vacant land left on the market, and there's very little new construction outside of the resort developments. Most of what's undeveloped will be expensive to subdivide because access roads will need to be built or slopes and wetlands prohibit building on large portions. The open lots that do come on the market range from $15,000 to $150,000, depending on the town and whether they have waterfront. Agents recommend buyers ask for a new survey before purchasing. Years ago surveys tended to be a little loose, and with the value of lakefront property a couple of feet can make a big difference.

Many properties that do not have frontage on a lake have beach access, and almost every town has a public beach and boat dock. These nonwaterfront properties are much more available and affordable, so don't despair if you can't afford to be right on the water!

Real Estate Companies

Century 21 Country Lakes Realty

459 Lake St., Bristol
• (603) 744-5411

Nancy Hand, one of a dozen agents in this office, says that while all the agents do residential listings, several of them specialize in different types of property. They have a timberland specialist, several agents who are particularly experienced with waterfront properties and some who do commercial real estate. Specialists can stay up to date with all the various regulations on different kinds of property. Nancy notes that the building boom continues but the land up here is running out!

Coldwell Banker Old Mill Properties

1 Holderness Rd., Plymouth
• (603) 536-3333

Durward (Woody) Miller, owner of Old Mill Properties, is upbeat about the market in his

INSIDERS' TIP

Covenants are private agreements, not town ordinances. If a resident violates a subdivision's covenant, neighbors must take civil action to enforce the restrictions.

area. His agency is the exclusive agent for the recently revitalized Tenney Mountain Ski Area resort, and in the last three years they have sold every property available despite being in high-tax Plymouth. Six of his agents are certified as buyer representatives. In addition, his agency does not do sub-agency work, as he believes it exposes sellers to undue liability.

Preferred Properties

Rt. 25, P.O. Box 161, Center Harbor
• (603) 253-4345, (800) 639-4022

This independent firm with 16 agents specializes in second homes and vacation properties up and down the Lakes Region, including on the islands, and also handles vacation rentals. In addition Preferred Properties lists boat-related properties such as dock rights, dry racks and other accommodations that are currently in great demand.

New Hampshire Colonials

Squam Lake at Curry Place, Holderness
• (603) 968-7615

What makes this company stand out is the experience of the Realtors, especially owner Dana Armstrong, who grew up on Squam Lake and knows the land and its people well. The six-person agency has been in business since 1932 (Armstrong's mother started the business), so people in town are familiar with them and think of them if they decide to sell. Another distinctive feature is that they have a boat for showing waterfront properties.

McLane Realty

79 Highland St., Plymouth
• (603) 536-8181

This small local agency is the sole survivor of the six agencies that were operating in Plymouth in 1989. (Several newer firms have opened since.) With only three active brokers, they have more than 100 listings in 11 area communities, ranging from vacant land and mobile homes to three- and four-bedroom contemporaries. Because they are a small office, the agents share all the listings so buyers don't have to work with lots of different people to see different properties. About half of the sales they've been involved with this year included a buyer broker; the company offers that service as well as traditional seller listings.

White Mountains and Great North Woods Regions

There is a lot of land in the White Mountains Region — about 1.5 million acres including 722,000 acres in the White Mountains National Forest. Where you are looking is the difference between reasonable and inexpensive. Come to the White Mountains Region for a visit. If you decide to make it an annual vacation spot or year-round retreat, you'll find a myriad of choices.

In the Great North Woods almost all real estate transactions are for vacation property. There are few jobs in the area so most buyers are looking for a second home to enhance their skiing, snowmobiling and fishing interests, which are the main activities here. Anyone needing a mall will travel about 90 minutes to Tilton or Burlington, Vermont.

You might find some real estate bargains in Berlin. Always subject to the boom-and-bust cycles of the logging industries, Berlin was hit hard when state-wide real estate values dropped in the late 1980s. As developers didn't develop, logging and construction jobs were lost. The banks repossessed a lot of houses as jobs disappeared. Berlin is the only

INSIDERS' TIP

Don't underestimate the joys of an attached garage. All areas of the state get lots of snow and clearing off the car can add a lot of time to your morning routine. It is also nice to walk into the house from the car. You'll be glad to reduce your chances of slipping on the ice or disappearing in the mud.

town to volunteer to accept the possible new state prison. You might find a duplex fixer-upper for as little as $10,000. It's important to remember this is a city with a paper mill, and there are days when that industry is noticeable in the air.

The market for land has changed quite a bit since the boom times of the mid- to late 1980s when people were buying land throughout the region as fast as possible. Many of the 1980s buyers were interested in lumber and by now the land has been cut over. But if you are interested in lots of inexpensive land, not too worried about road access and not expecting an old growth forest in your back yard, northern New Hampshire is the place to look.

The real estate market changes as you go south into the White Mountains Region and nearer to the very busy recreation areas of Jackson, North Conway and Waterville Valley. Vacation housing including timeshares and condominiums are popular in Waterville Valley. Prices have stabilized since the boom of the 1980s and the crash of the early 1990s. For the first time since the late 1980s, inventory is down and there is the sense that prices are just beginning to move up. A 3-bedroom cape on a full acre in Bartlett might cost $135,000 while a 2-bedroom condominium with tile floors and super views in the same town is on the market for $90,000. Bartlett is popular both for the great skiing at nearby Attitash as well as the low property taxes compared to nearby areas.

For skiing at Cannon Mountain, Mittersill is the geographic password for prime location. You could buy a four-bedroom chalet in Mittersill for less than $150,000. Another sought-after area is Sugar Hill near Franconia. You can expect to pay about $137,000 for a three-bedroom cape (a one- or one-and-a-half story house) on 2 acres in Sugar Hill. The same house in Lisbon might cost less than $75,000. Interestingly, Sugar Hill was part of Lisbon until 1962.

Just north of Sugar Hill is Littleton. There is less tourism north of Franconia, and Littleton is an important economic hub in the area. Littleton is also only two and a half hours from Boston (add at least an hour if driving in rush hour around Boston) and right on I-93, which is an important factor in pricing. Property within 10 minutes (about 8 miles) of I-93 is more costly than property farther away. Look for a charming log cabin for less than $100,000. A three-bedroom, split-entry could be anywhere from $65,000 to $85,000.

If you are self-employed, not worried about finding work where you live and not looking in the prime ski areas, the prices come down a bit. A place north of the notches and not convenient to I-93 with 1 to 2 acres, three bedrooms and one and one-half baths is not hard to find in the $85,000 to $90,000 range.

It's important to remember that throughout both the great North Woods and White Mountains Region you don't have to spend a lot of money to have a great vacation condominium. For example, in the Conway area an older (15 years) condo with two bedrooms, two bathrooms and a sleeping loft can be found in the $55,000 to $70,000 range. This would include an on-premises indoor swimming pool and great access to skiing. For a three-bedroom, three-bathroom condo in excellent condition that has access to tennis courts and both an indoor and outdoor swimming pool, expect to look in the $80,000 to $120,000 range.

The newest hot spot is Hales Location. All 1,215 acres are in the southeast corner of the White Mountains National Forest. As one agent told us, this is the area that is "becoming something." As you drive across U.S. Route 302, you'll see signs pointing towards new developments not visible from the road. Access to a brand-new golf course and new 2,500-square-foot house on the links can be yours for about $300,000. This would include an attached garage, but no basement.

Hot spots aside, the town with a lot of cachet is Jackson. Some might say it has snob appeal, but we say it has charm. The covered bridge over the Ellis River is right in town, and you can walk less than a half-mile to Jackson Falls on Wildcat River. This quiet town with country inns and cross-country skiing is not for night owls. Strict zoning may be one reason Jackson has survived the 20th century without losing the essence of small-town life. There are more homes than condos and very little new development. It has the highest prices in the Mount Washington Valley area and the fewest available properties.

Real Estate Companies

Wright Realty

N.H. Rt. 16, Box 2510, Conway
• (603) 447-2117

Ten agents work in this busy full-service office. Co-owner Debbie Oldakowski is a past-president of the White Mountain Board of Realtors. The company has been in business for more than 20 years and specializes in vacation homes as well as full-time residences. A survey of more than 500 customers rated the company well because of the care and attention to detail they give every client.

Sally Pratt Realtor

59-63 Water St., Lancaster
• (603) 788-2131

Sally Pratt has been in the real estate business since 1973. She does extensive business in New Hampshire and Vermont and is a past president of the North Country Board of Realtors. She is well-versed in the vacation-home market as well as large parcels of land. She's happy to walk a 100-acre piece of property discussing road access, septic realities and all other considerations of undeveloped property.

Reinhold Associates

55 Cottage St., Littleton
• (603) 444-1177

A Massachusetts native, Richard Reinhold came to the North Country after getting an engineering degree at Northwestern near Chicago. He first owned a small motel in Bethlehem and, during the process of selling it, decided there was room for him in the real estate business. In the business for 20 years, he is experienced in commercial, residential and land sales. He's an expert on the confusing issues of taxes and assessed values.

Dartmouth-Lake Sunapee Region

Locals are of two minds when it comes to real estate in the Dartmouth-Lake Sunapee Region. They might say, "Yes, we have some of the most beautiful land in New Hampshire at the most reasonable prices," but then they will say, "please don't tell everybody, because we don't want to grow too fast."

The abundance of year-round recreation facilities is a major factor in the quality of life in the area. Four downhill ski centers and two cross-country facilities are in the region and Sunapee, Kezar, Pleasant and Little Sunapee lakes provide for summer fun (see our Other Recreation chapter). Positive family lifestyle is the No.1 reason people choose to live here. It seems that transplants from Massachusetts and Connecticut don't mind giving up high-paying jobs in New York City or Boston for the delightful family-oriented environment found here.

Depending on what part of the region newcomers choose, they may have a great time buying their new home. Many Insiders know that the area from Charlestown to Cornish, including Claremont and west to include Newport and Unity, contains some of the best real estate buys in the state. For example, in Claremont a modern construction three-bedroom, two-bath house with a garage and a full acre can be bought for $80,000. If older and larger is your desire, what about a horse farm on 44 acres with a fully restored center-

INSIDERS' TIP

Just as not every real estate sales person is a Realtor, not every agency is a member of the Multiple Listing Service. Those who are can show properties from across the state via computer, saving you lots of time and mileage.

chimney cape, built c.1834, for $225,000? With $150,000 in Cornish you might look for a three-bedroom, one-and-a-half bath, well-maintained house on a 2-acre lot.

In both Hanover and New London, these prices might easily double for the same property. Without question these two towns are the most expensive in the region and probably, block for block, the most expensive in the state. In New London, the least expensive house — if you can find one for sale — might be a tiny two-bedroom ranch on 1 acre for $75,000. There are three condominium areas in New London catering mostly to retired people. In an in-town building the prices range from $75,000 to $260,000. In the very high range, there are the condos at the Lake Sunapee Country Club that can cost up to $600,000 for a fully loaded unit.

Houses on Sunapee, Little Sunapee and Pleasant Lakes are also in the highest range of the region. For example, a three-season (unheated) cabin can cost as much as $200,000, while a contemporary four-bedroom, two-and-a-half bath, 3,000-square-foot home with 115 feet of lakefront can cost up to $650,000. The lakefront property is in such demand that many people are buying cabins, tearing them down and replacing them with custom houses.

The Hanover real estate market is not one for starter homes unless you can start at a minimum of $180,000. The average house costs about $225,000. These are well-maintained homes in a very desirable college-town environment. Spend between $400,000 and $700,000 and you would be part of the high-brow real estate market in Hanover.

If you prefer to build and stay within 10 miles of Hanover, a five-star lot of 10 acres with a bit of a hill, great views and a good septic site might go for $25,000. There are no subdivisions in the area. A typical lot size is 5 to 10 acres. In Unity, the minimum lot size is 3 acres. There are very few lots in Hanover, one of the reasons people on the lakes are tearing down old in order to build new. Of course, as the owners of the large estates with lots of land die, large parcels are broken up with lots from 5 to 15 acres coming on the market.

Remember, this is a great place to live — but please keep it quiet!

Real Estate Companies

Century 21 Highview
130 Pleasant St., Claremont
• (603) 542-7766, (800) 269-2414

The 17 agents in this office can handle any real estate transaction. They work with residential and commercial customers and are knowledgeable about houses, buildings, businesses and land throughout Sullivan County. Roz Caplan is the owner of this office and has been in the business for more than 20 years.

Coldwell Banker Homes Unlimited
112 Washington St., Claremont
• (603) 542-2503

Owner-broker Rick Howard is a native of Cornish and lives in Claremont. The company started as a one-man shop in 1985 and today has nine agents handling residential, commercial and land sales. Rick is also very interested in helping light industrial companies locate in Claremont and the surrounding area. This has been a Coldwell Banker franchise for 10 years.

Coldwell Banker Redpath & Co.
P.O. Box 167, 8 W. Wheelock St.,
Hanover • (603) 643-6406

There are 14 agents in this Hanover office. It has been a Coldwell Banker franchise for 10 years, but owner Ned Redpath has been in the business here since 1978. This is a low-profile, highly skilled group of professionals.

INSIDERS' TIP

Historic districts are overlay zones, separate from and in addition to the town zoning. Most are administered by an appointed commission that reviews proposed changes to buildings within the district and enforces local restrictions.

Colby Realty Inc.

P.O. Box 409, New London
• (603) 526-2471

There are six agents in this office. One agent, Marty Benz, is past president of the Sunapee Region Board of Realtors and knows the area and the market and works hard to find exactly the right property for her clients. She has been a New Hampshire Broker for 10 years.

Magnell, McNamara & Associates

9 S. Main St., P.O. Box 648, Hanover
• (603) 643-6085

This company has been in business in Hanover for more than 12 years. Six agents handle a strong residential business. The office is right in middle size-wise — larger than a mom and pop office but smaller than many multiagent operations.

Monadnock Region

The real estate scene in the Monadnock Region follows the pattern for the state. It all depends on the town. However, one is beginning to hear the term "bedroom community" more and more when talking to Realtors in the area. For example, Rindge, Fitzwilliam and Troy are attracting people who work in Boston, while Peterborough, Hancock and Hillsboro are becoming home to those who work in Nashua or even Concord.

The average lot size in the Monadnock Region is 40 acres, and 1,000 acres is not uncommon. Don't let that scare you. A lot of old estates, apple orchards and farms can quickly up the average for the area. The Monadnock Region has a lot of older housing stock with the average house being more than 100 years old with three bedrooms, one bath and an attached barn or garage

You can easily find a starter home in the region for $80,000 to $100,000. That might mean a house with 1,200 to 1,500 square feet. If you want to build your own, a 1.5-acre building lot is in the $8,000 to $10,000 range. In Rindge, a 2,000-square-foot dwelling with three bedrooms and two baths on 1.5 acres could easily be yours for $125,000.

The entry level in Peterborough is a little higher. Expect to see starter homes in the

INSIDERS' TIP

When talking about towns, don't generalize. People who live in Sugar Hill have been known to take offense when outsiders call it Franconia.

$110,000 to $170,000 price range. Peterborough is one of the most desirable towns in the region. It is very well-established, and there is a bit of sophistication here that sets it apart. Being home to the first free public library and the oldest arts colony (The MacDowell Colony) in the country are two reasons for Peterborough's deserved reputation as a center for culture in New Hampshire. The average price for a home ranges from about $180,000 to $225,000. Land-only lots can cost as much as $20,000 for 2 acres to about $70,000 for 10 acres.

One secret in the Monadnock region is how many wealthy people live here. Secret because for the most part it isn't a flashy, nouveau riche kind of place. You certainly don't have to be rich to live here, but if you want to spend $500,000 to $1,000,000 there are several spots we could show you in Dublin, Walpole, Peterborough and Wilton Center, Fitzwilliam or Troy. "Miniature palaces" might describe these estates. There might be anywhere from 40 to 150 acres, a 3,000- to 6,000-square-foot main house, probably a pool, maybe an indoor pool — a nice touch for winter — along with a riding ring and a barn. These houses are around 200 years old and underwent complete renovations about 25 years ago.

Keene, the only city in the Monadnock Region, has several distinct options for house hunters. A c.1880 one-and-a-half to two-story wood frame house will cost around $85,000. You would have three to four bedrooms, one and a half baths, a living room and a dining room. The same space in a more modern ranch-style would be about the same price. The more expensive houses are the new constructions with more than 1,800 square feet. You might pay up to $150,000 for three bedrooms, two baths and an attached two-car garage.

Real Estate Companies

Prudential Brown & Tent, Realtors

428 Main St., Keene
• (603) 357-5525

This multi-agent office handles commercial and residential real estate throughout the Monadnock region. Whether you're looking for a permanent residence or a seasonal rental, these experts can help you find what you want. Founded in 1983, the company has a fine homes division as well as commercial and investment property specialists.

R.H. Thackston Co. Inc.

800 Park St., Keene
• (603) 352-2223

In business since 1982, Richard Thackston is well-versed in the local scene. He is particularly engaging when explaining the virtues of the region and the high end of the market.

ERA The Masiello Group Real Estate

N.H. Rt. 101 W., Peterborough
• (603) 924-9686
1 Mountain Rd., Rindge
• (603) 899-6505

ERA is the largest New Hampshire-based real estate company. The Peterborough office and the Rindge office are both managed by Maybelle Grolljahn, a vice president with the company as well as a top agent. There are five agents in Peterborough and four agents in Rindge. This is a very versatile company with the abilities to meet the need of almost any newcomer and provide excellent service at the same time.

Leger Realty Inc.

256 Main St., Rindge
• (603) 899-5444

This company is a self-described mom-and-pop operation. Paulette Leger owns the company and her right-hand agent is her husband, Jim. Jim is also the past president of the Contoocook Valley Board of Realtors. They have been in business for three years, and can help with your residential needs.

The low crime levels and the convenience of small-town living are two of the main reasons people choose to retire to New Hampshire.

Retirement

OK, let's be honest. New Hampshire is not the first place you think of when you think retirement. Winter runs from Thanksgiving to April. It brings plenty of snow shoveling, ice-covered branches and power outages. For many years the New Hampshire retirement picture was one of leaving: New Hampshire natives moved to Florida in droves in the '60s and '70s.

The picture has changed in recent years. For one thing, many of the Florida transplants got homesick for seasons — at least summer and fall. They joined a growing number of two-residence retirees — people who sold the big house when the kids were grown and bought two smaller homes, one in New Hampshire and one somewhere warmer such as the Carolinas, Arizona or Florida. Very often the New Hampshire home is a condominium unit, townhouse or single-family house, with an extra bedroom for the grandkids in summer and a homeowners association to make sure the driveway gets plowed in winter. These snowbirds arrive in New Hampshire during April and stay through Thanksgiving or even Christmas.

While we can't say that New Hampshire is a year-round retirement destination, we can tell you that the market is more active than we first thought, particularly in the Seacoast, Merrimack Valley and Monadnock Regions. The low crime levels and the convenience of small-town living are two of the main reasons people choose to retire to New Hampshire. The lack of sales and income taxes also appeals to people on a fixed income. And there are many longtime residents who want to stay in The Granite State, taking very literally the motto "Live Free Or Die."

Many towns have enacted zoning regulations that create special categories of senior housing called adult communities. Generally one member of the purchasing or renting household must be 55 or older (hardly seems like "senior," does it?). The homes may be duplex or detached, manufactured, prefab or stick-built, with garages or garden-apartment style. Get to know the area. Once you've decided what town or region interests you, call real estate agents in the area and ask about senior (or older persons) communities.

In this chapter we will give an overview of senior services as well as details on individual retirement communities.

Senior Services and Agencies

Because New Hampshire is made up of more than 250 communities, a resource center in one town may serve the populations of several others nearby. Sometimes the services are organized by county, sometimes by region and occasionally by state. Since it is impossible to give up-to-date information for every town, we have provided an overview of typical senior services. We also included telephone numbers for important state and national organizations serving seniors.

The best resource for agencies and services in New Hampshire is the local telephone book. All New Hampshire telephone books have a white-pages section called Community Service Numbers before local listings. Within this listing is a special senior citizens' section detailing specific organizations serving that particular area.

INSIDERS' TIP

Keep a small bag of sand inside the front door in winter. Sprinkle the sand on icy spots outside to help prevent slips and falls.

In addition to the Community Service listings in the telephone book, check local newspapers for announcements regarding activities and programs for seniors. Here you will find information regarding medical services (such as blood pressure clinics and flu shots), fitness programs, income tax filing assistance and other programs designed for seniors.

The Retired Senior Volunteer Program (RSVP), (603) 225-1450, is active in many New Hampshire communities. (Note that the state telephone number is listed in our gray box under Corporation for National Service.) Many towns have Meals On Wheels or senior meal programs. Local churches and community centers are often the location for senior meal services. Transportation help is available through the Senior Wheels program, and there are Senior Companion and Foster Grandparents programs in many communities.

Whether your interest is in volunteering your time or requesting aid for yourself or a companion, you will find community support throughout the state.

The *Senior Beacon* is a free newspaper available in shops and libraries around the state. It offers articles of interest to retirees, information about services and a wealth of advertising.

Elder Decisions Retirement Housing Consultants

• (603) 735-6463

In 1995 Bodie Morey established Elder Decisions to assist people exploring their retirement living options. She is familiar with the spectrum of retirement communities and facilities in the state and works to match the retirees with the communities where they will feel most at home. Bodie will help you evaluate your needs and assess your lifestyle and interests with an eye to finding the right match for you. Her fee (about $150) includes a 90 minute interview and assessment, phone calls and a follow-up. (Check with your employer to see if these costs are covered under an employee assistance program.) She makes recommendations, not placements — you control the process and make the decisions. Bodie also works long distance with families in other areas and people relocating from other parts of the country.

Important Statewide Phone Numbers and Services

Alzheimer's Association of Greater New Hampshire, (800) 752-7445

American Association of Retired Persons, (617) 305-0430 (At this time, there is no New Hampshire office of AARP. This Massachusetts number will connect you to the New Hampshire representative in the Northeast office. The nationwide telephone number is (800) 424-3410.)

Adult and Elderly Services, (603) 271-4680, (800) 351-1888

Arthritis Foundation, (603) 224-9322

Community Action, (603) 225-3295 (This umbrella agency can give local information for Meals On Wheels and the Senior Companion Program.)

Corporation for National Service, (603) 225-1450 (Call this group for RSVP information and opportunities in individual communities.)

Medicare Review Organization, (800) 772-0151

New Hampshire Association for the Elderly, (603) 228-1054

State Council on Aging, (603) 448-1680

Retirement Living

New Hampshire is just beginning to see the creation of full-service lifetime retirement communities. It may be that the old house is now too big, the heating bills too high or the upkeep too much work, but New Hampshire seniors — like their counterparts nationwide — are discovering the convenience and practicality of planned retirement communities. Longer life expectancy and better health than previous generations, along with the desire to control as much of one's destiny as possible, have contributed to this rise in planned communities. And with more and more families spreading out across the country, it is harder for parents and children to count on each other as hands-on support systems.

Retirement communities have flexible services and housing options that appeal to many seniors. The lifestyle options range from independent-living tenant to assisted-living resident to full nursing-care patient. For our purposes we have included only those communities that include independent-living facilities. The White Mountains, Great North Woods and the Lakes Region do not have any retirement communities that meet our specific definition.

There are two types of independent-living facilities in New Hampshire. One is a community of homes or apartments designed specifically for older adults. These communities usually have common areas such as pools, tennis courts, libraries and function rooms. Outside maintenance and sometimes heavy indoor cleaning are provided by the community. Meal service varies in these communities. In some complexes, residents have the option of taking meals in a restaurant-like setting, and some plans include one meal per day with rental. Some communities operate on a pay-as-you-go meal basis; others require an up-front purchase. Still others have both options or allow you to move in on a month-to-month rental and then convert to another plan after you've had time to experience the community firsthand.

The second type of independent-living facility in New Hampshire is licensed by the state as assisted living. Many of these small homes, which tend to have about a dozen residents, have opened in historic buildings across the state. The Governor Prescott House in Epping is one such example, providing a beautiful and historic home to residents while the family continues to operate a working farm on the property. The staff at these family-style facilities generally does all the cooking, cleaning and laundry for residents and provides minimal supervision (such as reminding a resident to take medications). Residents come and go as they please, often keep their own cars and, in general, enjoy the advantages of living at home without the burdens of living alone. The staff does not provide nursing care, although visiting nurses or home healthcare staff may come in as they do in private homes. If you ask, these facilities will tell you residents must be independent, which can be confusing since the definition of "independent" varies.

We have not listed these assisted-living facilities in this chapter, as they are numerous and vary greatly. Word-of-mouth recommendations and personal visits are the best way to discover these homes. The Yellow Pages include these listings under Retirement and Life Care Communities and Homes. You can also contact the New Hampshire Association of Residential Care Homes at (800) 533-0906. They have more than 85 members providing assisted-living services.

Merrimack Valley Region

Briston Manor West
37 Ridgewood Rd., Bedford
• (603) 622-8844

On a wooded site in Bedford, just outside Manchester and convenient to the highways, Briston Manor offers one- and two-bedroom units with full kitchens, central air conditioning and private yards. Residents are encouraged to plant flowers or vegetable gardens. Rent includes a daily full-course meal, transportation, housekeeping and a full schedule of community activities.

Havenwood-Heritage Heights
19 East Side Dr., Concord
• (603) 224-5580, (800) 457-6833

On two wooded sites (totaling 19 acres) conveniently close to both the services of downtown Concord and the interstate, this community has been home to hundreds of New Hampshire residents since Havenwood was first built in 1967. It is affiliated with the United Church of Christ but open to people of all backgrounds. It is primarily an independent-living community, although some assisted-living and skilled-care units are available. Types of housing in the community include attached studio "alcove" units, one-bedroom cottages and one- and two-bedroom apartments in the Lodge. Rent for the lodge includes three meals a day in the dining room. Activities on site include exercise classes (aerobics or aquatics in the pool), walking trails and gardening. The community has a well-stocked library and a woodworking shop. Concerts, movies and lectures are offered on-site, as are religious services for various faiths.

Most residents have their own cars and take advantage of the wide range of opportunities available to those living in the capital city. Trips are organized to attractions throughout New Hampshire and Boston for those who don't drive or prefer the camaraderie of a group trip. Residents are welcome to have overnight guests in their homes, and guest cottages are also available for a nominal fee.

Havenwood operates on a pay-as-you-go basis. Heritage Heights, which sits on a bluff with a truly stunning view of the Merrimack River Valley, is a continuing-care facility requiring an entrance fee ($12,000 to $15,000) in return for guaranteed healthcare. Rentals on both campuses are very reasonable (costs are subsidized by the church and donations). Rent includes housekeeping and all utilities except phone and cable television as well as maintenance. Residents are also welcome to use transportation and family services. Meal plans are available for an additional fee. To rent in either campus, at least one resident must be 62 or older. If a couple moves in, the second person must be older than 55.

Pleasant View Retirement Community

227 Pleasant St., Concord
• (603) 225-3970, (800) 340-0311 (in N.H.)

Aptly named, this beautiful building stands on a wooded hillside just outside downtown Concord. Mary Baker Eddy originally left this site to the Christian Science Church for a retirement home, and when operated by the church, it housed more than 300 elderly residents. Today those tiny rooms have been opened up and remodeled (retaining the elegant wood paneling and pink granite) into 70 lovely studio, one- and two-bedroom apartments. Each room has a full kitchen and plenty of room for entertaining or keeping treasured belongings. There are even a few deluxe suites, for which there is a waiting list. Occasional overnight guests are welcome. Residents also have full use of the library, formal living room, on-site theater and hobby studio (we met one resident who continues to paint and sketch professionally), exercise room, game room and heated outdoor swimming pool. Daily transportation is scheduled to activities and appointments in Concord.

There is no entrance fee at Pleasant View (which is no longer affiliated with the Christian Science Church), although a small security deposit is required. Weekly housekeeping, flat linen service, utilities and one meal a day in the formal dining room (dress for dinner) are included in the rent. Meal plans can be purchased for an additional fee, as can additional housekeeping services or home-health visits. There is a skilled-care facility next door, and residents at Pleasant View have priority access there.

New Hampshire Oddfellows Home

200 Pleasant St., Concord
• (603) 225-6644, (800) 678-1333

The New Hampshire Oddfellows Home has provided a rewarding lifestyle to older New Hampshire residents for more than 100 years. Five different floor plans, ranging from apartments with full kitchens to single rooms with shared baths, provide for independent living. Kitchenettes on each floor serve residents in single rooms. The home also has some assisted-living and skilled-care units. The emphasis at the Oddfellows Home is on fellowship, so rental rates, even of apartments with full kitchens, include three meals daily in the community dining room. Rental also includes use of the exercise room, library, daily housekeeping and laundry, an activity program, carport parking and transportation to medical appointments. The Oddfellows Home even has its own radio stations (available only on the grounds of the home), broadcasting music from the '20s to the '50s, old-time radio shows as well as up-to-date news and information. Residents need not be members of the Oddfellows or Rebekahs, but there is a discount for those who are. Daily and monthly rentals vary with the size of the rooms and apartments. There is no entrance fee.

Hillcrest Terrace

200 Alliance Way, Manchester
• (603) 645-6500, (800) 862-9490 (in N.H.)

Hillcrest Terrace, a retirement community built in north Manchester in the early 1990s, offers a variety of one- and two-bedroom floorplans for fully independent apartment living. Some have balconies, some offer a bath and a half, and all have walk-in closets. There is a private dining room available should you want to entertain more guests than your apart-

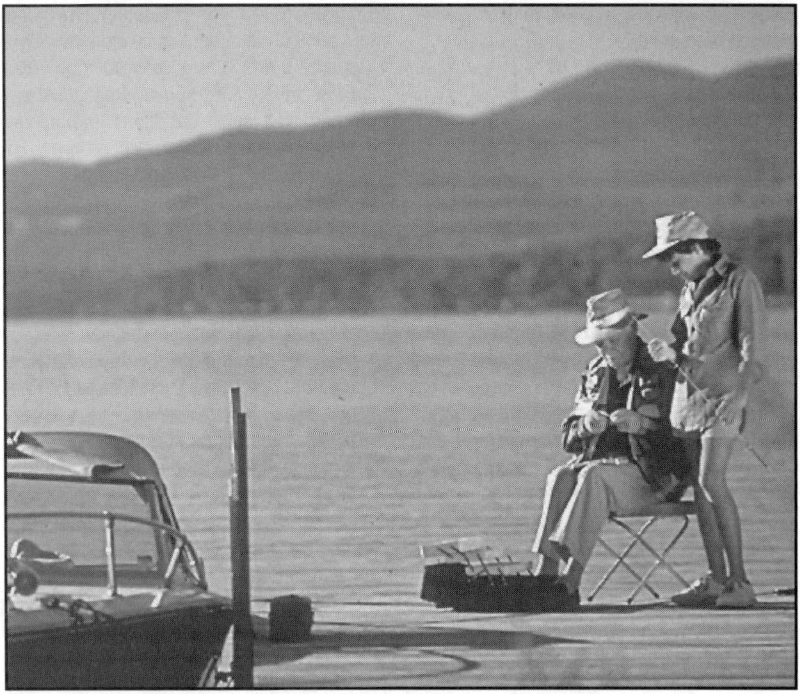

The beauty of summer in New Hampshire is a lure for many retirees.

ment will accommodate. Rent includes 25 meals per month in the dining room, use of the exercise facilities and the health club, library, crafts room, local transportation and many planned activities. Routine maintenance and twice-a-month housekeeping service are also included, as are utilities and air conditioning. Covered parking is available for an extra charge. Hillcrest also offers "Catered Living," a plan that allows residents to pay for such services as errand running and grocery shopping, extra housekeeping and maintenance, and even some daily-living assistance.

Hillcrest has an assisted-living facility on site as well as an infirmary for residents. A rather unique feature of Hillcrest Terrace is that all residents are automatically enrolled in a long-term care insurance plan, the cost of which is included in the monthly fee.

Hunt Community
10 Allds St., Nashua
• (603) 882-6511

The Hunt Community has its own library, woodworking shop, exercise room and craft areas, and it provides transportation to many area activities. Biweekly housekeeping services and cable television are also included. There are clinics on site. Home healthcare, laundry and other services are available at an additional fee. The Hunt offers three plans: a pay-as-you-go monthly rental and two entry-fee plans. Residents who move in on the monthly plan can choose to convert to an

INSIDERS' TIP

Senior discounts at restaurants, movies and concerts are becoming more common. Since the age requirements vary, be sure to ask. You may be a senior in someone else's eyes, even if you aren't in your own.

entry-fee plan at any time within their first two years of residence.

Langdon Place of Nashua
319 E. Dunstable Rd., Nashua
• (603) 888-7878, (800) 241-5852

Each of the Langdon Place facilities offers elegant retirement living in a community setting with a variety of services available as needed. Also look for Langdon Place communities on the Seacoast and in the Monadnock Region. The Nashua Langdon Place is convenient to the city and the highway but far enough out of town to feel country-like. Rental of independent-living apartments (one or two bedroom) include one meal per day (additional meals are available) and heat (and electricity in Nashua only). Residents can also use the facility's library, formal living room, private dining room for functions, movies, transportation and many activities. The Nashua Langdon Place has an indoor pool and air-conditioned units. Assisted-living apartments and rooms on the same site enable residents to continue to live in the community even if their health needs increase. The apartments are particularly helpful when only one spouse needs assisted care. Langdon Place also offers respite care.

No entrance fee is required for any Langdon Place community. They offer a waiting-list registration for people who are ready to make a decision but not ready to move in. Waiting-list membership entitles the member to occasional meals on site as well as participation in activities. It's a good way to get to know the neighbors in advance.

Seacoast Region

Langdon Place of Dover
60 Middle Rd., Dover
• (603) 743-4110, (800) 241-5851

This Langdon Place community is similar to the one described in Nashua. Dover's is more centrally located, just outside the downtown area but in a suburban setting. Dover also has the option of overnight guest accommodations as well as an indoor pool and air conditioning. In addition to independent living, assisted living and respite care, Langdon Place of Dover has a special care unit for seniors with Alzheimer's.

Langdon Place of Exeter
17 Hampton Rd., Exeter
• (603) 772-5251, (800) 241-5837

Convenient to the historic and cultural resources of Exeter, Langdon Place of Exeter offers the complete Langdon Place experience (see our description under Nashua). Exeter has an indoor pool, air conditioning in every apartment and transportation to take advantage of the riches of the area. Overnight guests are welcome to reserve the guest room at the Exeter Langdon Place. An Alzheimer's unit is a new addition in 1998.

Riverwoods at Exeter
7 Riverwoods Dr., Exeter
• (603) 772-4700, (800) 688-9663

With construction just completed in 1997, the Riverwoods community offers flowers, walking and skiing on the wooded, riverside grounds and fresh breezes in the screened porches or solariums built into every apartment. The day we visited it was pouring rain, but several hardy gentlemen were headed out for their pre-dinner walk just the same. A shuttle bus was available for the ladies who preferred a drier outing. Two hundred studio and one- and two-bedroom apartments at Riverwoods include either one or two baths, gracious living rooms, fully equipped kitchens and the already-mentioned porches. The Commons, at the center of the complex, offers a convenience store and gift shop, banking facility, library, woodworking shop, greenhouse, exercise and music rooms, an audito-

INSIDERS' TIP

When investigating retirement communities, ask about covered parking or whether shoveling off your car is included along with plowing.

Welcome home! The wooded lots and country-cottage style homes at Havenwood ensure a New Hampshire feel for retirees.

rium and several lounges. Maybe it's the rarefied air of Exeter, but the residents here are remarkably creative people. Not one but two art exhibits were being shown during our visit. Music and dance lessons are on the activities program, and the garden club keeps fresh flowers on the multitude of dining room tables throughout the summer. One meal per day is included in the rent as are biweekly housekeeping, scheduled transportation, use of the health club and other amenities.

Riverwoods is a continuing-care community. The Lodge, on the same site as the apartments, offers 20 assisted-living apartments, 20 supported-care suites and 20 skilled-nursing rooms. The 90 percent refundable entrance fee guarantees lifetime residency at this beautiful facility.

Langdon Place of Portsmouth

188 Jones Rd., Portsmouth

• (603) 431-2530

Twenty-four independent living apartments in the Portsmouth Langdon Place enjoy all the amenities common to Langdon Place living (see our description of the Nashua location) along with proximity to the ocean! Pools and air conditioning are not included or needed on this campus, which is just 2 miles from the beautiful beaches of Portsmouth and Rye. Langdon Place of Portsmouth also offers assisted living and respite care, and the Clipper Home of Portsmouth, one of Langdon's skilled nursing facilities, is on the same campus.

Webster at Rye

795 Washington Rd., Rye

• (603) 964-8144

On a beautifully landscaped 50-acre site in Rye, just a few miles from the ocean, this community includes 29 one- and two-bedroom apartments for independent living. Along with utilities, the monthly rent includes transportation, maintenance and either two or three meals, depending on the style of the apartment. Housekeeping and laundry are also available. The 24-hour staff at the nursing

INSIDERS' TIP

Local public libraries stock large-print and audio books.

home on the grounds adds security to the lifestyle at Webster. A library, patios for visiting and a nature trail winding through the woods all contribute to the pleasant lifestyle here, and there are lots of organized activities throughout the year. There is no entrance fee at Webster, just a one-month security deposit.

Dartmouth-Lake Sunapee Region

The Greens at Hanover

53+ Lyme Rd., Hanover
• (603) 643-5512

This 28-unit independent-living facility opened in 1981. The apartments are one- and two-bedroom units with full kitchens. Residents can be as independent as they wish, choosing from many activity and care options. The Greens serves a five-course lunch and tea at 4 PM every day and holds a cocktail hour on Fridays. Housekeeping and maintenance service is provided, and there is a full-time assistant to aid with grocery shopping, laundry chores or other daily needs. Cats and small dogs are permitted.

An entrance fee is required and 90 percent is refunded at the time of a resident's departure. The Greens at Hanover is adjacent to the Hanover Terrace Nursing Home, which guarantees cohesive attention should a resident require assisted-living help or nursing assistance.

Kendal at Hanover

80 Lyme Rd., Hanover
• (603) 643-8900

Open since 1991, Kendal has 248 independent apartments ranging from studios to two-bedroom units. Kendal is a full-service lifecare retirement community. In addition to the apartments, there are assisted-living and skilled-nursing facilities for residents.

Closely affiliated with Dartmouth College, Kendal participates in The Institute for Lifelong Education at Dartmouth (ILEAD). More than a third of the residents take part in this continuing education as students and teachers. Professionals from the Dartmouth-Hitchcock Hospital provide medical care.

In addition to maintenance, laundry and full meal services, Kendal offers an array of programs and facilities including fine arts, a computer science lab, swimming pool and fitness center. An entrance fee is required and is not refundable.

Harvest Hill

121 Mascoma St., Lebanon
• (603) 448-7458

Opened in November 1996, Harvest Hill is the lifecare facility of Alice Peck Day Memorial Hospital. Harvest Hill is on 23 acres adjacent to the hospital. The building contains 53 independent-living apartments ranging from one-bedroom, one-bath units to two-bedroom, two-bath deluxe units. All units have full kitchens, although the monthly fee includes three meals a day in the community dining room.

The maintenance service includes housekeeping and laundry, and all units are equipped with a 24-hour lifeline button. The growing number of activities offered at Harvest Hill includes weekly art classes taught by Lebanon College faculty, weekly movies and an exercise room. The Carter Community Center, with a swimming pool and a full program of activities, is just 2 miles away in Lebanon. (Membership is not included in the admissions fee, but twice-weekly van service is provided.)

Admission fees vary depending on the apartment, and 90 percent is refundable to the tenant or estate at the time of departure. There is a monthly fee that includes all utilities except telephone. The monthly fee may change should a resident's care needs increase. The facility gives at least 30 days notice on these changes. Should a resident require assisted care, it is provided in the same apartment unit. Full nursing care requires a move to Alice Peck Day Memorial Hospital.

Monadnock Region

Langdon Place of Keene

136A Arch St., Keene
• (603) 357-3902, (800) 241-5877

An upscale retirement community with lots of choices is the best way to describe Langdon

Place of Keene. Independent and assisted-living apartments and suites are available with an array of services and programs. There is no entry fee; residents pay monthly rent and are responsible for utilities other than heat and hot water. The services offered include transportation, housekeeping, a formal dining room that can be reserved for private functions and a social calendar resembling that of a cruise ship. The cribbage, bridge and walking clubs are just a part of a full social scene. The indoor pool is the scene for "aquacise" classes, and a branch bank and postal center are on the premises.

All levels of care are available including a 25-bed skilled-nursing center. Langdon Place of Keene is dedicated to helping residents remain independent while offering topnotch care and support when needed.

RiverMead Retirement Community

150 RiverMead Rd., Peterborough
• (603) 924-0062, (800) 200-LIFE

A town within a town, RiverMead is set on 56 acres just five minutes from the heart of Peterborough. This nonprofit, full-service lifecare retirement community has independent-living units as well as assisted-living and nursing-care options. The 10 housing styles range from a one-bedroom apartment to a three-bedroom cottage with two-car garage and screened porch.

The entrance fees vary depending on the size of the housing unit. The fee guarantees future needs including assisted living and nursing care at no additional cost. Ninety percent of the entrance fee is refunded (to either the individual or the individual's estate) at the time of the resident's departure.

The community center includes a pool, fitness center, library, cafe and dining room. A hair salon, art studio, woodworking shop and auditorium are also in the center. Services include housekeeping and full property maintenance. Residents enjoy weekly planned activities (such as an outing to Boston) and regularly scheduled shuttle service into Peterborough.

Our state hosts some of the most traditional and prestigious prep schools in the country along with some of the most inventive.

Education and Child Care

In this chapter, we focus on the educational opportunities in the state, giving an overview of public education and recommending some of the bigger and more popular private boarding and day schools. At the end of the chapter, you'll find helpful information about finding child care in New Hampshire. And in the following Higher Education chapter we detail our state's wonderful assortment of higher education opportunities.

In both chapters, we have strayed from our usual organization in that we've divided the chapter into sections, here grouping the Boarding Schools first and then Private Day Schools. Within each section we've kept our usual geographic regions.

Public Schools

We have some of the most highly rated public schools in the country and some very weak districts too. New Hampshire students routinely rank high in national testing scores — fourth in the nation in reading and third in math according to the most recent data. This despite ranking last — by a large margin — in state government support of education (the 49th state on the list funds 27.5 percent, New Hampshire funds 10 percent).

Although we are the last state in the union not to offer public kindergarten to every student, we have nevertheless pioneered a developmental entry program called Readiness that has won acclaim from educational professionals. Readiness is based on the observation that just as children begin to walk or lose teeth at different ages, they develop "readiness" for school at different ages too. School districts with Readiness programs give developmental screening to incoming 6-year-olds and place those students who are "young for their age" in smaller classes with a more active, less pencil-and-paper curriculum than 1st-grade classes.

Publicly funded kindergarten is a perennial discussion in the New Hampshire Legislature. Governor Shaheen ran on a pro-kindergarten platform, and has worked vigorously to support the existing public kindergarten programs and provide fiscal incentives for more districts to offer kindergarten. It may be that this unique New Hampshire feature is finally fading. (On a sad note, many people think public kindergarten will be the death knell for Readiness, although they do not serve the same purpose.)

New Hampshire schools are local and autonomous, with 167 districts around the state operating a total of 310 elementary schools and 72 high schools. In a few cases, the boundaries of a town or city and those of the school district are identical, although they hold separate elections for independent governing boards. More often, a school district is made up of several towns. Some towns are part of more than one school district (typically one for the elementary schools and another for the high school). Further complicating this picture are the state's 67 Supervisory Unions. Some districts have their own superintendent of schools, but most districts share that office. In general, individuals do not deal directly with the school superintendent, so that many people don't even know which SAU (Supervisory Administrative Union) administers their schools.

High schools in New Hampshire are accredited by the New England Association of Secondary Schools and Colleges, which sends teams of educators to inspect schools and examine programs at least every 10 years. Some regional high schools are "cooperatives," meaning they are governed by a school board elected by people from all of the towns sending students to the school.

Other regionals are AREA (Authorized Regional Enrollment Area) schools, governed by one district but accepting students from other districts under a tuition agreement.

School funding in New Hampshire is almost entirely provided at the local level. In a state with no broad-based taxes, this means that property-rich districts have much better equipped schools than those in districts with little or no commercial/industrial tax base or with large amounts of tax-exempt property. The contrast is crystal clear: Property-rich Bridgewater schools spend $4,750 per student each year on a tax rate of $4.92 per thousand, while next door Plymouth spends $4,723 with a tax rate of $22.12 per thousand. The district with the highest per-pupil expenditure, Newington, averages $9,455 per student, with homes assessed at $1.76 per thousand. At the opposite end of the scale, Farmington residents pay $10.68 per thousand in order to support their students at a rate of $1,302 each. You can see how important it is for parents to investigate a school system before buying a home here. (See our Real Estate chapter.)

In December of 1997 the New Hampshire Supreme Court issued a decision in the lawsuit known as "Claremont II" that will have repercussions throughout the public schools in the state. In short, the court ruled that the traditional mode of funding is inherently inequitable and therefore unconstitutional. The decision hinges on a phrase in the State Constitution that commits the State to providing an adequate education and another that requires taxation to be reasonable and proportionate. The court gave the State Legislature until April 1, 1999 to create a method of school funding that would fulfill both requirements.

The result of the ruling was instant political furor. Generations of governors and state legislators have built their careers on a "no statewide tax" platform, and powerful local and business lobbies were quick to take sides in the fray. Several politicians immediately began agitating not to correct the funding inequities but to amend the Constitution to remove the "cherish education" phrasing. Dark comments were made about judges trying to wrest control from the hands of local school boards. (The vast majority of local school board members welcomed the decision as a beacon of reason in a dark night of archaic funding.) The frenzy hasn't solved the educational dilemma yet, but it has led to legislation outlawing "push polling," the practice of spreading propaganda disguised as a telephone poll.

The funding plans proposed at this writing include everything from a statewide uniform property tax to increased cigarette taxes and video-gambling. School districts faced with overcrowded and aging buildings have found themselves virtually unable to plan, since no one can tell what future funding will look like or how it will impact an individual district. District Meetings have become increasingly unwilling to commit taxpayers to any large, long-term expenditures. You can call the Department of Education at (603) 271-6646 for more information about specific districts or schools.

Private Schools

In the private realm, our state hosts some of the most traditional and prestigious prep schools in the country along with some of the most inventive. We have highlighted some of the best and biggest for you.

Our Catholic school system is not as extensive as those in more urban states, but its 25 elementary schools and four high schools are well-respected and serve children from a variety of backgrounds. Many families, even non-Catholics, drive significant distances each day so their children can attend regional parish schools. Contact the Diocesan Schools Office, (603) 669-3100, for a list of Catholic schools.

Protestant Christian schools constitute our largest block of nonpublic schools. Many are tiny, with fewer than two dozen children in kindergarten through grade 12. Often these schools began as a preschool, adding a grade a year as their students progressed. Although there is no central source of information about these schools in the state, parents can check with the Association of Christian Schools International, (717) 285-3022, to request their directory of schools in New Hampshire or ask for information about a particular school. Nineteen New Hampshire schools are members of their organization, and it has information about some nonmember schools as well.

Catholic or Protestant, private or parochial, principals of nonpublic schools we spoke with emphasized that there is no substitute for visiting the school and reading the student handbook and school philosophy.

The New Hampshire Department of Education has a directory of approved nonpublic schools available: Call (603) 271-3495 to request it. The directory will indicate that some schools are "approved for attendance," and some have an "approved program." We spoke with Educational Consultant Dr. Franklin Dye at the DOE, who observed that these different approvals are not particularly useful for parents choosing a school, as some excellent schools are not "approved for program" because they have chosen not to apply for it. (Almost all of those with approved programs were approved on the basis of membership in the New England Association of Schools and Colleges, which has an accreditation process and a membership fee.) Do watch out for those schools that are not approved for attendance, however; either they failed to comply with health and safety inspectors or they refused to submit their curriculum and faculty credentials for review (often on religious grounds). Sending children to an unapproved school means they are legally truant. One such school is in the court system right now, fighting a shutdown injunction on the grounds that schooling children is a parent's God-given right and the state should not have oversight of schools.

Two other useful state phone numbers for parents are the Nonpublic School Advisory Council, (603) 271-3856, and the Home Education Advisory Council, (603) 271-3739. Home schooling is very popular in New Hampshire, at least in part because our state department of education is very supportive of parents who choose to home school. The regulations are straightforward and not onerous, and most school districts are helpful and willing to work with parents and home-school students.

Boarding Schools

All the boarding schools listed below also accept day students unless otherwise noted.

Merrimack Valley Region

St. Paul's School
325 Pleasant St., Concord
• (603) 225-3341

If you've ever been to England, you could be forgiven for thinking you'd been dropped off at Cambridge or Eton when you walk this campus. Earnest young people walk the rolling lawns and wooded paths between gracious brick buildings, and although a mile in either direction will put you on the interstate or in the city, the 1,700-acre site will have you longing to be back at school. St. Paul's is a coed college prep high school, with just more than 500 students in grades 9 through 12. A healthy endowment backs the faculty of nearly 100 instructors, 10 percent with doctoral de-

INSIDERS' TIP

Visit a potential school when it is in session. You and your child will get a more accurate sense of the school's personality. Eat a meal in the dining hall and encourage your child to spend a night in a dorm if that is an option. If you have a student who is particularly interested in one subject, try and schedule the appropriate classroom visit. Read the school newspaper to see what students are doing. Visit art and music studios to get a better understanding of the level of the student work.

grees, more than half with masters degrees. All faculty members live on campus, contributing to the family atmosphere and structure. The school is affiliated with the Episcopal Church, and attendance at religious services is required. The school, though, is open to students of all backgrounds. The curriculum is rigorous and varied, offering six modern languages and two classical choices, dance and ceramics as well as art and music, ethics, architecture and statistics along with English and computers. The athletic department's activities include 17 interscholastic programs and 19 intramural/recreational programs. Crew or riflery, anyone?

Seacoast Region

Phillips Exeter Academy
20 Main St., Exeter
• (603) 772-4311

Phillips Exeter is a prestigious boarding school for grades 9 through 12 that has been educating the sons of the Northeast's upper class for more than 200 years. In the last quarter century, the student body has expanded to include girls, foreign students and students with excellent academic skills who aren't necessarily wealthy. Nearly a third of the 1,000 students enrolled receive some form of financial aid. Virtually all graduates go on to college, including a large percentage who attend Ivy League schools. The campus was extensively renovated in the 1960s, resulting in a facility that's at once traditional in appearance and up-to-date in function. Most students live in the 29 dormitories as do about a third of the faculty, who serve as mentors and advisors.

The curriculum combines traditional academic instruction with the Harkness Plan, a form of Socratic method in which a teacher and a small group of students explore a subject through discussion and discourse. Independent study is also encouraged, especially for upper-division students. Off-campus terms in Washington, D.C., Vermont and abroad offer expanded horizons to students. The school also has an excellent music program and athletic programs in 21 interscholastic sports and 27 intramural sports. Where else can you play men's or women's water polo? Phillips Exeter also offers advanced summer courses for public and private school students and a summer athletics program for sports camps.

Lakes Region

The New Hampton School
Main St., New Hampton
• (603) 744-5401

New Hampton's 280 students are a diverse group of young men and women in grades 9 through 12 representing 30 states and 15 foreign countries. The school specializes in bringing gifted students up to their potential, and approximately half the student body is made up of able students who have been hindered in their academic efforts by differences in learning styles or life issues. They achieve great success through a flexible program of studies combined with high expectations and rigorous study. Classes meet six days a week (Wednesday and Saturday afternoons are for athletics), and there are mandatory proctored study hours from 7:30 to 9:30 every night. In an average year, all graduates go on to college. Student activities include operating a campus radio station and producing several publications as well as interscholastic and noncompetitive athletics from football to snowboarding.

Holderness School
N.H. Rt. 175, Plymouth
• (603) 536-1257

Since its founding in 1879, Holderness has offered a traditional Episcopalian prep school experience to students from a variety of backgrounds. Most of the 270 students are from the Northeast, although a total of 25 states and eight other countries were represented in a typical recent year. The school, which offers grade 9 through a postgraduate year, has high expectations of students in both academics and behavior. It requires students to do community service, and there is a dress code and mandatory chapel attendance. Two-thirds of faculty live on campus and help to mentor and develop a community spirit. The athletic program fields teams in all the usual interscholastic sports and a few less-common ones: bicycling, for example, and ice hockey. Most students participate in a wilderness survival experience during their junior year.

Tilton School
30 School St., Tilton
• (603) 286-4342

In an unusual twist, Tilton, founded in 1845 as a coeducational institution by the Methodist church, became a boys school in 1929, then admitted girls again in the late 1960s. On a hill in the center of the town of Tilton, the 28 school buildings look traditional on the outside, but the program is an innovative, student-directed learning experience. Just more than 200 students in grades 9 to postgraduate concentrate on developing writing ability, computer skills and interdisciplinary learning. Almost all of the faculty live on campus. Special support for students with learning disabilities or academic deficiencies has long been a hallmark of Tilton's program, and almost all of the school's graduates go on to college. The school offers a surprising assortment of athletic choices for its relatively small size, including an indoor hockey rink and four indoor tennis courts.

Brewster Academy
52 S. Main St., Wolfeboro
• (603) 569-7200

Brewster Academy is a beautiful school in a beautiful location. We wonder how anyone can concentrate on studying, but the achievements of Brewster's scholars speak for themselves. Begun as a public regional school, Brewster became a private coed secondary school (grades 9 to postgraduate) in 1965 when the Kingswood Regional High School opened. Today it serves students from 30 states and 18 foreign countries as well as local scholars. Computer technology enables the 340 students at Brewster to experience a 21st-century education in a traditional setting and won Brewster Macintosh's 1997 School of the Year award. Every student and faculty member has a laptop computer, and all the classrooms, libraries and dormitories are networked through Brewsternet, the campus-wide fiber-optic network.

Small (10 to 12 students) classes and supervised study hall during the day as well as study hours in the evening contribute to the school's stated goal of accelerating students' mastery and academic skills. Each student has a personal academic advisor from among the 54 faculty members, who are required to attend a six-week training institute each summer to assure the best practices in teaching and learning. Many of the faculty live on campus with their families, which helps to build the community experience for the student body. A semester abroad in Switzerland or Spain is an added incentive for students in the upper grades to achieve. Students are required to participate in the athletic program, which offers 33 individual and team sports, a state-of-the-art fitness center and a climbing barn. The sailing and crew teams take advantage of Brewster's half-mile of shoreline on Lake Winnipesaukee, while the skiing and horseback riding offer choices for landlubbers. Fine and performing arts and a variety of extracurricular activities round out the Brewster experience.

White Mountains and Great North Woods Regions

The White Mountain School
West Farm Rd., Littleton
• (603) 444-2928

College-bound students in grades 9 through 12 study here in the heart of New Hampshire's White Mountains. The school was originally in Concord and until 1970 was an all-girls facility. In 1935 an intrepid headmistress moved the school to the remote town

INSIDERS' TIP

Phillips Exeter was founded by John Phillips in 1781, in part because he was so impressed by the students at the school founded three years earlier in Andover, Massachusetts by his nephew, Samuel.

of Littleton. The purpose of the move was to give students "a chance to live in and with things that are bigger than they are." The school became coed in 1970 and currently enrolls about 85 students. In keeping with the natural surroundings, the school offers a wilderness skills program, which is accredited by the American Mountain Guides Association. Every year students participate in three academic expeditions that stress interdisciplinary skills. For example, a geology expedition might go hand in hand with rock-climbing. Making students aware of and comfortable in their surrounding environment is fundamental to the education here.

Dartmouth-Lake Sunapee Region

Proctor Academy
Main St., Andover
• (603) 735-6000

The student body here is coed with about 300 students in grades 9 through 12. The school places great importance on informality, trust and accountability. Aptitude and positive attitude are keys to admission. The environment is progressive with lots of support for a rigorous schedule. Students may participate in the Ocean Classroom program, which sails from New Bedford, Massachusetts, to St. Thomas, Virgin Islands, on a 130-foot schooner. It's one example of what students could choose for their annual trimester. The 10-week program gives students the experience of being immersed in one subject. The 2,000-acre campus spreads through Andover. Much of the town's history lives on in contemporary school life. The renovated village livery station, c.1810, is now the school's visual arts studio.

Cardigan Mountain School
Back Bay Rd., U.S. Rt. 2, Canaan
• (603) 523-4321

Cardigan is a boarding school for boys in grades 6 through 9, and enrollment is less than 200. The school prepares boys for competitive secondary schools. The school combines a strong academic program with an environment meant to nourish character development in the areas of self-confidence and discipline. The goal is to educate the whole person and to provide each student with a broad range of ways to experience success and the joy of learning both in the classroom and on the athletic field. The Science and Art facility opened in 1996 and has extensive laboratory and studio space. Computer and language labs are modern and allow for both remedial and advanced work. Complementing the academic program is an extensive outdoor athletic and education curriculum. The wilderness program takes advantage of the natural environment and teaches outdoor skills such as tracking, canoeing and rock climbing. The school was founded in 1945, and the first graduate to walk across the stage in 1948 grew up to be noted criminal defense lawyer F. Lee Bailey.

Kimball Union Academy
Main St., Meriden
• (603) 469-3211

Kimball Union Academy was founded in 1813. It is a traditional college-preparatory school for grades 9 through 12. The school is coed with an enrollment of 275. Boarding students outnumber day students about three to one. About eight to 10 students take advantage of a postgraduate program each year. An endowed program in Environmental Science is integrated throughout the curriculum. In addition to a strong academic program, the school has excellent athletic facilities, including an ice hockey arena. The 1996-97 girls' ice hockey team won the New England championships. Most students participate in at least two competitive sports, with drama and art options available as alternatives. An arts center with a theater is part of the 1,000-acre campus.

Monadnock Region

Dublin Christian Academy
Page Rd., Dublin
• (603) 563-8505

The school handbook states that Dublin Christian Academy is dedicated to the purpose of developing Christian leadership. The school was founded in 1964 and offers a coed education for grades kindergarten through 12 with boarding facilities for grades 7 through 12. Students are encouraged to explore the performing arts including music and speech to complement their academic courses. The school philosophy is that the Bible is God's truth and it should guide daily life.

Dublin School

New Harrisville Rd., Dublin
• (603) 563-8584

This coed school for grades 9 through 12 is in the heart of the Monadnock region. Dublin Lake and Mount Monadnock are in walking distance of the 345-acre campus. The school was founded in 1935 with the goal of providing a college-preparatory education tempered by a high degree of personal attention and a strong sense of community. The enrollment is limited to 100 boarding and day students, and the faculty-student ratio is 1 to 8. The school endeavors to "awaken a curiosity for knowledge and a passion for learning." The school view book contains the following quote by a sophomore, "At Dublin, you always have a voice, and because the community is so small, that voice is always heard." In addition to the excellent academic curriculum, the school is proud of the humanities program, which explores an annual theme with invited guests. Recent themes have included environmental awareness and local history. The weekly guest speakers might be artists, craftspeople and other professionals. The school has an excellent college placement record with 90 percent of students being accepted by their first choice.

Crotched Mountain Preparatory School and Rehabilitation Center

1 Verney Dr., Greenfield
• (603) 547-3311

This school is an integral part of the Crotched Mountain Rehabilitation Center. The 1,400-acre mountaintop campus shows off the mountains of the Monadnock Region. The setting is pastoral, but this state-of-the-art rehabilitation center is very modern. The boarding and day school provide a New Hampshire special education approved academic program for multihandicapped students ages 6 through 21. The residential program consists of two certified skilled-nursing units, nine group homes and a transitional-living apartment complex. The goal for each student is "optimum independence, maximum self-realization and a guided return to the community." Each student is different, but a typical student here has neurologic or orthopedic challenges or both. Students might be autistic or recovering from the effects of traumatic brain injury.

Hampshire Country School

Hampshire Rd., Rindge
• (603) 899-3325

This small boarding school limits enrollment to between 25 and 30 boys and girls. All students board, and most students are between the ages of 10 and 15. The school is open for grades 3 through 12. The school describes their students as having high abilities with a need for extra personal attention, structure and direction in and out of class. Prospective students might be overactive and impulsive or unusually shy and withdrawn. Academic classes have between five and eight students, allowing for excellent teacher-student interaction. The goal of the academic program is to provide elementary and secondary students with a strong foundation in English, mathematics, history and science. The teaching and houseparenting faculty consists of about 12 full-time and four part-time individuals. Students live in one of four family-style dormitories. Each dorm houses about eight students and a houseparent.

In addition to academics, students are encouraged, although not required, to participate in recreational sports. The campus is 1,700 acres with lots of hills for cross-country skiing and hiking. The school offers a full range of athletic activities that involve both students and faculty including soccer, softball, basketball, horseback riding and skiing. In addition to three 12-week trimesters, Hampshire Country School offers a six-week summer school/

camp with two hours of academic classes each day along with traditional camp activities such as archery, canoeing and field trips.

The Meeting School
Thomas Rd., Rindge
• (603) 899-3366

The Meeting School provides an alternative educational environment for high school students in grades 9 through 12. Students live, work and study in a farm atmosphere. The 25 to 30 students and 10 teachers and administrators live together in five 18th-century farm buildings. All members of the community participate in daily maintenance of the facilities including farm chores, cooking and upkeep of the property. The educational philosophy is based on Quaker principles. Students are taught that individual actions always affect the group as a whole. The school encourages nonviolent conflict resolution. Many students continue their education in traditional colleges. The school provides a great deal of attention and focus for students who might not thrive in traditional environments.

High Mowing School
Abbot Hill Rd., Wilton
• (603) 654-2391

High Mowing School is a coed Waldorf high school. Boarding and day students are accepted with a total enrollment of about 110. The Main Building was built in 1787. The grounds are beautiful, with rolling meadows, streams and rock walls. Facilities include a woodworking shop, kiln shed and recycling center. Three art studios and a darkroom are also on campus. High Mowing School is the only Waldorf high school in North America with a boarding program. Students with language proficiency can participate in the international exchange program with European Waldorf schools. The school offers a rigorous academic program that challenges a student's intellect, imagination and social responsibility. Faculty and students live and work together in a friendly and nurturing environment. Each individual is recognized as unique, while at the same time seen in relation to others as part of a global community.

Courses in literature, history, mathematics and science are taught in "blocks" of concentrated study. Block meetings are 1+ hours each day for three to four weeks. Students have 10 blocks each year. The goal is to build a balance between the objective and the subjective aspects of experience. Students write and illustrate their own books for each block class. Yearlong academic courses, art classes and athletics round out the schedule. For one week each year, students set off on independently chosen adventures such as being a farm apprentice or trekking the Grand Canyon. Beginning in the junior year, the college counselor helps students in their search for the right college (or other option) to continue their education and learning.

Private Day Schools

Merrimack Valley Region

Hampstead Academy
51 Maple Ave., Atkinson
• (603) 329-4406

This independent school has 70 preschoolers and 180 students in grades 1 through 8 on two campuses, one in Atkinson and one in Hampstead. The school is committed to offering individualized instruction by maintaining low student-teacher ratios (lots of parental involvement helps!) and the latest in educational equipment and technology. The holistic approach and liberal arts curriculum are designed to enable a diverse assortment of students. The school also provides a varied physical-education experience (from skiing and racquetball to dance and aerobics) in its new gymnasium.

Hopkinton Independent School
1137 Hopkinton Rd., Hopkinton
• (603) 226-4662

Hopkinton is a small town just a few miles from Concord, so this independent school offers both convenience and a wonderful rural setting to 70 students in preschool through grade 8. The focus is on educating the whole child, nurturing the natural love of learning while developing a solid foundation of fundamental skills. Classes are kept small and parents are expected to participate actively in their child's learning. The school also offers a day-care for younger children, an after-school extended day and a whole series of summer programs, including a White Mountains trek and a coastal exploration, a theater camp and a farming experience.

The Derryfield School
2108 N. River Rd., Manchester
• (603) 669-4524

The Derryfield School serves more than 300 students in grades 7 through 12 from the greater Manchester area (the school runs buses from communities with concentrations of Derryfield students). The coed program emphasizes academics, with Latin and Greek in the curriculum as well as computer science and physics. There are programs for students gifted in art and music and an athletic program with interscholastic or intramural teams in all the major sports except football.

Small World Country Day School and Child Development Center
138 Spit Brook Rd., Nashua
• (603) 888-1982

This school has 500 students and nearly 70 faculty members in a new facility that provides a nice environment for learning for grades preschool through 6. The director is committed to building enrichment into every area of the curriculum as they grow. The school offers computer instruction, foreign languages, physical education, art and science projects and music programs as well as the standard elementary school curriculum. Developmentally appropriate small classes, indoor and outdoor play and enrichment, and a hands-on learning environment all contribute to a rich and exciting educational experience. The wooded campus includes swimming pools and walking trails, and a city park across the street provides access to fields, ice skating and sledding. "Wrap-around" care from 6:30 AM to 6 PM addresses the needs of parents and children for stability and comfort.

A special (and representative) feature of Small World's approach to education is the monthly Parents' Night Out, a Saturday evening when the kids can hang out on campus with their friends and give parents an opportunity to enjoy a grown-up evening without guilt.

Monadnock Region

Monadnock Waldorf School
98 S. Lincoln St., Keene
• (603) 357-4442

Students in grades kindergarten through 8 from Massachusetts, Vermont and New Hampshire come here for a Waldorf education. Enrollment is 145 with an average of 15 students per class. The school year begins with an all-student hike to the summit of Mount Monadnock. The school community has natives and newcomers and describes itself as friendly to new families in the school community. Several teachers received their Waldorf training at Antioch New England Graduate School in Keene. You'll find more about Antioch in the Higher Education chapter.

The Well School
360 Middle Hancock Rd., Peterborough
• (603) 924-6908

The Well School was founded in 1967 and educates students in kindergarten through 8th grade. Enrollment is 100, and the average class size is 10. The school believes children should be encouraged to find their own genius. The curriculum includes studio art, band and singing in addition to advanced academics. Drama is incorporated in grades 5 through 8, with every student taking part in at least one play each year. Most teachers are parents (though not necessarily of current students), and many had previous careers other than teaching. For example, a lawyer might teach civics. The school feels it is important to understand the value of work: In addition to the hard work required to succeed academically, each student works at cleaning

INSIDERS' TIP

For a quick assessment of a school district's financial situation, ask what computers students are using.

classrooms or helping maintain the school grounds. Students take turns supervising each other while learning how to work together. Kids who respond favorably to a challenging, competitive environment will do best here.

Pine Hill Waldorf School
Abbot Hill Rd., Wilton
• (603) 654-6003

Pine Hill opened in 1972 with 19 children. It now has 225 students in grades kindergarten through 8 and 15 full-time and five part-time teachers. The campus is on 47 acres with playing fields, woods and an orchard. Although new students enter at every grade, the eight-year program (not including kindergarten) is conceived as a continuous whole. The continuing-class teacher stays with each class throughout the eight years and develops a deep understanding of each child's learning style, interests and abilities. A core belief at the school is that everyone — barring obvious disabilities — has the ability to do everything well. All students learn to play the recorder. Visual arts, manual arts, performing arts and practical activities are fully integrated into the program, often corresponding to academic subjects. Beginning in grade 5, the school day begins with a handshake between student and teacher. After grade 8, students attend a variety of private and public schools. They can continue their Waldorf education just across Abbot Hill Road at High Mowing School (look for our write-up in the Boarding Schools section).

Preschools and Child Care

In the absence of universal public kindergarten in New Hampshire, private preschools and kindergartens have flourished. Montessori schools are popular, as are very traditional church-based programs. To take one representative community, in Merrimack there are seven kindergartens: one commercial program, one nonprofit cooperative and five church-sponsored programs. Kindergarten licensing in New Hampshire is handled by the Child Care Licensing Bureau — it inspects for health and safety criteria but does not review programs or curriculums. The bureau can be reached at (603) 271-4624 or (800) 852-3345 for details of its process or to check on a specific school. A private referral service, American Nanny and Family Care Services, (603) 673-9382, can help with day-care placements and related care arrangements.

Helen Schotanus is the Department of Education's Early Learning Consultant. She can be reached at (603) 271-3841 and is a great guide through the complex maze of preschool and kindergarten issues in New Hampshire.

Most child day care in the state is provided by Family Home Day Care Providers, who are licensed by the state to care for up to six children in their own homes, (if they have kids of their own at home, they can take five others — all the providers' kids count as one), or in unlicensed, informal babysitting arrangements.

There are only a few commercial day-care establishments not associated with preschools, and they are concentrated in our more urban areas. Lists of both licensed Family Home providers and commercial day-care centers are available from the state's Child Care Licensing Bureau, (603) 271- 4624 or (800) 852-3345. *Parenting New England*, a monthly tabloid-sized newspaper published in Hudson, carries advertisements for many preschools and often dedicates issues to topics such as child care, education, school enrichment and after-school care. The paper is

INSIDERS' TIP

The best source of information about preschools is still the grapevine. Ask people at church where their children went to preschool. Stop parents at the post office or the dump and tell them you're looking for suggestions. Summer programs at the library or park are great places to meet other involved parents you can tap for ideas—and make friends!

available in most toy stores and kids' clothing shops in New Hampshire and northern Massachusetts.

In response to changing lifestyles, many school districts now provide some form of extended-day option for their elementary school students. Most often a private provider is given a contract to come in and administer before- and after-school activities and supervision right on the school grounds. Inquire at the school or SAU office to find out if your district has an extended-day program.

Finding the right day care for your child is often a long and difficult process. The best source is a trusted friend with a child a couple of years older than yours, but if you're new to the area, you can't count on that. Plan to call a dozen places, visit those with openings and interview providers. The first couple of visits will help you develop your list of questions and things to look for. Look at the play areas, inside and outdoors. Are there plenty of things for children to do, and are the children free to choose their activities? Are the adults actively involved with the children? (But remember this is day care, not school. You probably don't play with your kids every minute at home, either.) Are there hazards in the environment (busy streets, open water), and if so, how are children kept safe? 477 Know in advance how you feel about television (especially in a home-care setting), snacks and your child riding in the provider's vehicle. Discuss discipline with every provider: What is the policy? How do they handle crises? Are you comfortable with them?

Keep in mind that different settings may be best for different children or even the same child at different ages. Your infant may thrive in the loving arms of a grandmother-type who rocks her, plays with her and stays home all day. Two or three years later the same setting may be too restrictive or understimulating for an active preschooler.

Once you've placed your child, listen to the little one's responses. Stop in unexpectedly once in a while to check on things. (With younger children it's best if you plan to pick them up when you do this, as they can become very upset if you leave again without them.) It is possible, in spite of your efforts, to choose a placement that just doesn't fit. Don't be afraid to keep looking. If your child isn't happy, chances are the provider isn't either. On the other hand, if you think your child is just trying to make you stay home, and that's not an option, you may need to just be firm. Most day-care providers are in this work because they love children. Most children settle in well after a couple of weeks. Family day-care providers often become family friends, with relationships that live long past the day when the kids can start babysitting for others!

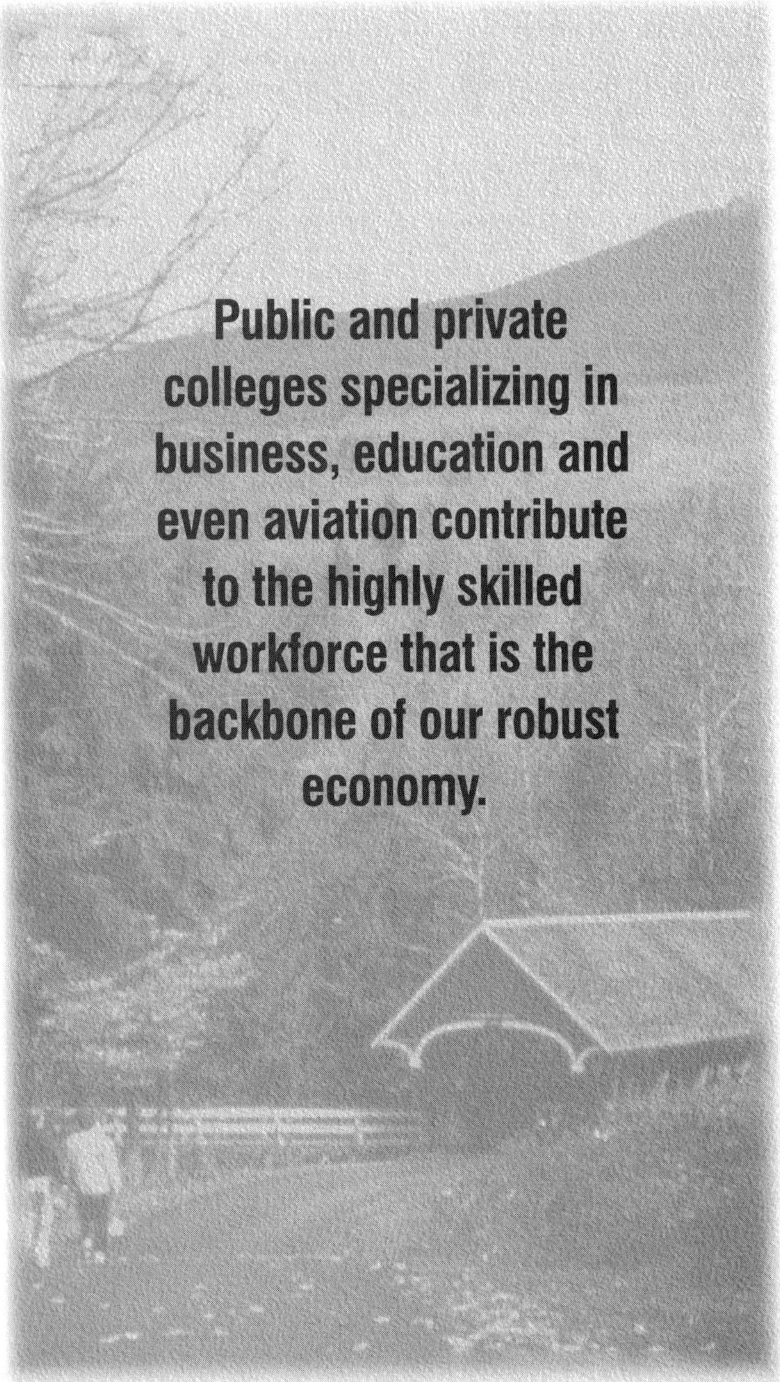
Public and private colleges specializing in business, education and even aviation contribute to the highly skilled workforce that is the backbone of our robust economy.

Higher Education

The first and best-known university in New Hampshire, Dartmouth College, was founded in 1769 as an outreach to the Native Americans of the region. Since then it has maintained a tradition of rigorous academics, a diverse student body and an athletic program that has sent numerous student athletes to the Olympics, especially as skiers. But New Hampshire has a variety of programs to offer for those not looking for an Ivy League education, too!

The state university system developed from the Agricultural Colleges and Normal Schools (teacher's colleges) of the 19th century into the respected University System of New Hampshire. This system incorporates the University of New Hampshire, with its main campus at Durham and satellite campus in Manchester, along with Plymouth and Keene state colleges, the New Hampshire technical colleges and the School for Lifelong Learning. New Hampshire Public Television, which broadcasts from the campus of UNH in Durham, also offers for-credit courses via the electronic classroom.

Public and private colleges specializing in business, education and even aviation contribute to the highly skilled workforce that is the backbone of our robust economy. We also have an impressive assortment of schools specializing in music, art, technology and a variety of service careers. Chances are, whatever you want to study, you can find it here. In this chapter on higher education we have listed the state's colleges, universities and community colleges and presented a sampling of continuing-education opportunities. As we did in our Education chapter, we've grouped types of schools together and then broken the sections down by our usual regional headings.

Colleges and Universities

Merrimack Valley Region

White Pines College
N.H. Rt. 121, Chester
• (603) 887-4401, (800) 974-6372

White Pines opened in 1967, and remains a two-year college with fewer than 100 students. The program is primarily centered on communications and fine arts, and the college is best known for photography and photojournalism. Two-thirds of the men and women enrolled live on campus (freshmen are required to live in dorms). Virtually all the graduates move on to four-year colleges for further study. There is no interscholastic athletic program, but several intramural sports clubs take advantage of the school's rural campus. In 1998 they added an exciting new Artist in Residence program, and in 1999 began enrolling students in a new liberal studies major. Nikki Tilroe advises the Palm of the Hand Stories Puppet Theater company, incorporating dance and mime along with puppetry. (Until Shari Lewis's death in 1998 Nikki spent her summers working with Shari and Lamb Chop!)

Franklin Pierce Law Center
2 White St., Concord
• (603) 228-1541

The Franklin Pierce Law Center is an ABA-accredited law school. In addition to the juris doctor degree, they confer master's degrees in the fast-growing area of intellectual property law. The student body is kept small by choice, and the faculty is made up of lawyers still in active practice. The nurturing and feedback between academia and practice is a major part of what makes Franklin Pierce different. Students choose to concentrate in areas of interest that include health law, business and commercial law, criminal law as well as intellectual property law. Franklin Pierce is committed to encouraging "community lawyering," where legal professionals work for the best interests of the public.

New England College

7 Main St., Henniker
• (603) 428-2223

New England College is one of 30 schools affiliated with Regent's College in London, which offers students the opportunity for an American-style university education in the United Kingdom. The college also has an option of summer study at its sister schools in Japan and Canada. As you can tell, there is an international dimension to the learning that takes place here. With majors in a variety of liberal arts and social sciences, the school concentrates on providing its 700 students with a fundamental liberal arts background that can become the backbone of many different careers. The college also offers a program leading to teacher certification in any of 45 states. The rural location encourages outdoor activities such as skiing, whitewater canoeing and horseback riding. Underclass students (except those commuting from home) are required to live on campus. The college's men's and women's teams, The Pilgrims, play baseball and softball, basketball, hockey (field and ice), men's and women's lacrosse and soccer in the NCAA Division III. The ski teams compete in Division II.

New Hampshire College

2500 N. River Rd., Manchester
• (603) 668-2211

With its main campus in Manchester and continuing education and graduate centers as far afield as Brunswick, Maine, and Puerto Rico, New Hampshire College is a far cry from the small business school founded in 1932. The school's 1,300 full-time and 4,000 part-time graduate and undergraduate students work toward associate's degrees in business, liberal arts and the culinary arts, bachelor's degrees in business, liberal arts and hospitality administration, or graduate degrees in business and community economic development. Recently the school has introduced a three-year bachelor's degree program in business administration. Satellite facilities in Nashua, Salem, Concord, Laconia and Portsmouth offer non-traditional students the opportunity to work toward a degree, and the college also offers distance education courses over the

Internet. Intercollegiate and intramural teams for both men and women range from broom hockey to lacrosse. In recent years the Penmen men's basketball and soccer teams have been nationally ranked in Division III. (See our Spectator Sports chapter.)

Hesser College

3 Sundial Ave., Manchester
• (603) 668-6660

Hesser is a two-year college with an enrollment of 3,000 men and women, most pursuing associate's degrees in business management or early childhood education. It's also the only school in New Hampshire with an approved "Plus 2" bachelor's degree program, which makes it possible for students to receive their associate's degree and then continue on to complete a bachelor's in criminal justice or business administration in two more years. Most students are commuters and nearly 20 percent are part-time. The school fields varsity teams in basketball, men's and women's soccer and volleyball and women's softball that compete in the NJCAA. Hesser also offers courses in Nashua, Portsmouth and Salem.

New Hampshire Institute of Art

148 Concord St., Manchester
• (603) 623-0313

The only fine-arts institution in the state that grants a four-year degree, the Institute of Art serves a diverse body of students from its Beaux Arts facility in downtown Manchester. (See our Arts and Culture chapter.) One of the attractions of the program is that people from the community taking an art course just for personal enrichment work side by side with professionals and students working toward their degrees. The dynamic give-and-take of working artists and aspiring learners informs and enhances the process. Degree students work in one of three concentrations: ceramics and sculpture; painting and drawing; or photography. Other coursework also encompasses fiber, jewelry and a range of humanities courses.

Notre Dame College

2321 Elm St., Manchester
• (603) 669-4298

More than 900 undergraduate women and men and 400 graduate students attend this Catholic liberal arts college in Manchester's residential north end. Several of the campus housing buildings are gracious Victorian homes. The school welcomes students of all faiths and is dedicated to the ideal of education for the whole person, spiritual and emotional as well as intellectual and physical. Undergraduates major in a variety of the arts and sciences, including pre-physical-therapy and pre-physician's assistant programs, while graduate students work toward degrees in education, theology, counseling psychology and physical therapy. The athletic department fields men's and women's teams in basketball, crew, soccer and women's softball that play in the NHIA.

Saint Anselm College

100 Saint Anselm Dr., Manchester
• (603) 641-7000

This highly regarded Benedictine (Catholic) college on the outskirts of Manchester combines the centuries-old Benedictine tradition with the latest technological and scientific advances to bring out the best in the 1,900 undergraduate students enrolled here. About half the students major in the sciences (including an excellent nursing program), and the rest pursue liberal arts, social science or business programs. The Abbey Players the-

INSIDERS' TIP

In addition to the New Hampshire Technical Colleges and the School for Lifelong Learning, several private colleges also offer satellite campuses: Franklin Pierce, Hesser and New Hampshire College all offer classes in Nashua, for example. The local Yellow Pages will help you locate these programs, or you can call a school with a course you're interested in and ask if they have off-site classes.

ater group takes advantage of the state-of-the-art Dana Center for terrific stage productions (see our Arts and Culture chapter). An active campus ministry and volunteer center encourage students to look beyond themselves and give something to the community and the world. The Saint Anselm Hawks compete in the NCAA Division II and the ECAC in baseball and softball, ice hockey, and men's and women's basketball, skiing, tennis and lacrosse. Everyone is very excited because football will be returning to Saint Anselm in 1999 (see our Spectator Sports chapter).

University of New Hampshire at Manchester

400 Commercial St., Manchester
• (603) 668-0700

UNH at Manchester is the commuter college satellite of the main university (below). Classes are held in a converted mill building at 400 Commercial Street in the downtown area. Many students at UNH-Manchester are working full time while completing their undergraduate studies. Others are working toward a master's degree, and others enroll for continuing education or specialized seminars.

Thomas More College of Liberal Arts

6 Manchester St., Merrimack
• (603) 880-8308

This tiny (85 students) coed Catholic college was founded in 1978 on the premise that the purpose of college is not to prepare people for careers but to prepare them for life. To that end the curriculum is unapologetically classical, with majors in literature, philosophy or political science. They have recently added a major in biology. All students spend most of their time in the core curriculum, which is built around a humanities course that studies Western civilization from ancient times up to the post-modern era. All students complete their fine arts requirement during the spring semester in Rome in their sophomore year. The campus is a historic farm, with renovated 200-year-old buildings alongside the newly built dorms and library. Thomas More also offers a summer program for high-school sophomores and juniors interested in experiencing the school's classic approach to education. Students live on campus for 2 or 4 weeks, participate in a variety of on and off-campus activities, and complete an in-depth study of one aspect of Literature, Philosophy, Political Science or Theology.

Daniel Webster College 20 University Dr., Nashua

• (603) 577-6000

Students at Daniel Webster College major in business, computer science, engineering and the nationally recognized flight curriculum. The school's fleet of 23 planes is housed next door in the college's Aviation Center at the Nashua Municipal Airport. The school boasts a state-of-the-art flight simulator and an equally distinctive air-traffic control simulator, used by students in the flight operations and aviation management programs. Seventy percent of the nearly 450 day-division undergraduates live on the 50-acre wooded campus. (The school's flexible program attracts another 800 evening students.) Daniel Webster's Eagles compete in the NCAA Division III/ECAC in men's and women's soccer and cross-country, golf and women's volleyball. There are also a number of intramural sports and athletic clubs for all interests. (Note that the chance to develop computer skills here is not limited to undergraduates: Daniel Webster hosts a Microsoft Certified Technical Education Center.)

Rivier College

420 Main St., Nashua
• (603) 888-1311, (800) 44-RIVIER

Rivier College is an independent coed Catholic college with 1,700 undergraduate and 1,000 graduate students. The emphasis is on liberal arts education with a practical application, and degree programs range from graphics design to exercise physiology. All students do internships senior year in their field of study (although this is fairly obvious for paralegals and nursing students, we found it interesting that art majors intern in graphic design, and English majors intern in public relations and broadcasting). The fall semester of 1998 saw the opening of a large addition to the science building, built to accommodate the school's expanding health science program. The school has also introduced a bachelor's degree in Law and Government, an expansion of the very successful Paralegal program. Most undergraduates live on the suburban campus and take advantage of the wide variety of social and cultural activities. Rivier competes in NCAA Division III in men's and women's basketball, cross-country, baseball/softball, soccer, volleyball and golf.

Seacoast Region

McIntosh College
23 Cataract Ave., Dover
• (603) 742-3518

More than 1,000 students attend this two-year college to prepare for careers in business management, information sciences and computers or as health and legal paraprofessionals. A converted motel serves as dormitory space for freshmen, but most students live off-campus. The school fields both men's and women's softball teams for intercollegiate play. (By the way, this school was founded in 1896 and is not connected with the computer company!)

University of New Hampshire
105 Main St., Durham • (603) 862-1234

UNH at Durham is our biggest state college, with almost 14,000 (11,000 undergraduates) enrolled. As a comprehensive university, the school offers graduate and undergraduate programs in a wide variety of disciplines, from geology and microbiology to theater and French literature. The Thompson School of Applied Science and the Whittemore School of Business are also part of the Durham campus community, further rounding out the academic picture. UNH is a competitive school, and admission, even for in-state students, is considered difficult. The campus is an attractive "town" of more than 100 buildings, including classroom and lab buildings, libraries, arts and athletic centers, and student housing. The UNH Wildcats compete in NCAA Division I (I-AA in football) and have traditionally fielded strong teams in hockey, basketball and skiing. (See our Spectator Sports chapter.) The football program has improved in recent years as well.

Lakes Region

Plymouth State College
17 High St., Plymouth
• (603) 535-5000, (800) 842-6900

Plymouth State College's campus covers 170 acres on both sides of the Pemigiwasset River in Plymouth. Almost 4,000 undergraduates and 400 graduate students pursue 80 majors in the liberal and fine arts, business and physical education. Founded in 1871, the school has really taken off in the last 10 years, building a reputation for solid education in a supportive community and beautiful setting. *Barron's* has noted Plymouth as one of its college Best Buys. About 70 percent of the men and women undergraduates, many of whom are transfers from the New Hampshire technical colleges, live on campus. The prime location between the Lakes Region and the White Mountains and the school's wonderful athletic, art and theater facilities make this a great place to live as well as to study. (See our Arts and Culture chapter.) Competing in Division III, the Plymouth State Panthers have developed something of a powerhouse reputation, having gone to the post-season in nine different sports during the last five years. (See our Spectator Sports chapter.)

Dartmouth-Lake Sunapee Region

Dartmouth College
Main St., Hanover
• (603) 646-1110

A member of the Ivy League, Dartmouth College is a four-year coeducational undergraduate college. More than 11,000 students apply for the 1,080 freshman-class openings. Besides a solid academic record, the admissions committee looks for academic curiosity. Dartmouth students describe the academics as incredibly difficult but are quick to add that the mental challenges are delightfully balanced by the many intramural sports opportunities. The topnotch linguistics student may also be a demon Frisbee player. Dartmouth students are jocks, but put away any image you may have of football players who can't read. These students are challenged in the classroom and challenging on the playing fields.

Relaxation from classroom vigor is also found through sorority and fraternity activities. Traditionally half of the undergraduate student body belongs to of Greek social clubs. These clubs plus student activity clubs are central to the social life of students.

The three graduate schools are The Amos Tuck School of Business, Dartmouth Medical School and the Thayer School of Engineering. Dartmouth offers 18 graduate programs in the arts and sciences. It is the ninth-oldest college in the country. The undergraduate enrollment is 4,275 with students from every state and 54 nations. Besides being a superb school, it is unquestionably one of New Hampshire's most valuable resources. It's impossible to fit everything about Dartmouth into our book, but we'll do our best to give you an overview with resources for finding out more.

The college is in the town of Hanover, on the Connecticut River just north of Lebanon. It's about an hour's drive from Keene (Monadnock Region) and Concord (Merrimack Valley) and only 30 miles from the southwestern corner of the White Mountains National Forest. The most direct route to Hanover is Interstate 89, but you'll see that all signs near Hanover point to Dartmouth. The Dartmouth Green is bordered by North Main Street and East Wheelock Street. Parking is restricted right in town, so it's best to follow the signs to one of several community parking lots. (The parking is by meter so be sure you have some quarters.)

Free tours of the campus are available every day with varying time schedules depending on the time of year. For information call (603) 646-2875. If you can't make a tour, pick up a map at the campus information booth on the Green. Be sure to see Baker Library (you'll find a total of nine libraries on campus with more than 2 million volumes) with the mural The Epic of Civilization by Jose Orozco. He painted the mural while teaching at Dartmouth in the early 1930s. Baker Library has a treasure in the copies of John Audubon's Birds of America originally owned by famed New Hampshire native and national orator Daniel Webster. Most of the college's art treasures are in the Hood Museum across from the Green on Wheelock Street. The Hood is next door to the Hopkins Center. These two buildings are a hub of the arts and culture scene in the region, the state, New England and the United States. Look for more information in our Arts and Culture chapter.

Colby-Sawyer College
100 Main St., New London
• (603) 526-3000

This independent, coed four-year college was founded in 1837. The 180-acre campus is in the center of New London, a picturesque New England town. Enrollment is 750 students, and the average class has about 18 students. Senior faculty members teach first-year students as well as students in upper classes. A favorite area of study, and an unusual one for a small college, is the sports science department. You can earn a Bachelor of Science degree with specialization in athletic training, exercise science or sports management. Complementing this course of study is the 63,000-square-foot Hogan Sports Center. The sports center has a large array of indoor facilities (a good idea with our snowy winters) including a competition-size swim-

INSIDERS' TIP

Ask colleges about their career counseling centers. Are they just for seniors? Do they help alumni? Can they help with summer jobs or are they just for full-time employment? A strong career center will benefit students for many years.

ming pool, lacrosse and soccer areas, and a fitness center with state-of-the-art equipment. Most of the team sports participate at NCAA Division III level. The exception is the ski team, which competes in Division I.

Academic strengths include child development, education, graphic design and nursing. Nursing students are affiliated with local hospitals, including Dartmouth-Hitchcock Medical Center and Alice Peck Day Hospital, both in nearby Lebanon. Colby-Sawyer also offers a program that allows students to design their own major. The college has an active career development program, which offers counseling to help students succeed in their career plans. The school matches students with specific internships and has an active program of alumni mentors to help students get hands-on experience in their field of interest. Colby-Sawyer is a small college that thinks big for its students.

Monadnock Region

Keene State College
229 Main St., Keene
• (603) 352-1909

Keene State College is a four-year liberal arts and sciences public college. The school is coed with 3,900 undergraduate students and 1,000 graduate and continuing-education students. About 2,000 of these students live in campus residence halls. The 160-acre campus is on Main Street in the middle of Keene, population 22,000 and the only city in the Monadnock Region. Students are important to life in Keene, with the college and the town working together for economic growth. The Arts Center on Brickyard Pond has three theaters and eight art studios along with an electronic music studio. The Thorne-Sagendorph Art Gallery attracts great exhibits due in part to excellent facilities. Just a block up Main Street is the Colonial Theater, a busy venue for live concerts, musical theater and first-run movies. (See our Arts and Culture chapter for details.) Unless it's blizzard conditions, students hang out along Appian Way, the pedestrian walkway through campus. The Student Center is new, and just in case students want to get off campus, CityExpress, the Keene public transportation system, serves the campus.

Franklin Pierce College
College Rd., Rindge
• (603) 899-4000

Franklin Pierce College is a combination of educational institutions. The main campus in Rindge is home to a traditional four-year liberal arts college. The college also operates five continuing-education centers in the state, which we discuss in the Continuing Education section of this chapter. Enrollment in Rindge is 1,300. The continuing-education division enrolls 2,400 students. The school was founded in 1962. The Rindge campus has more than 1,000 wooded acres near Mount Monadnock. The college has a unique core curriculum. Using the theme "The Individual and Community," the required 42-credit sequence of courses "explores the concentric circles of self, family, neighborhood, city, state, nation and world in which we all exist." Students combine core-curriculum courses with elective and required courses in their field of study. Franklin Pierce ranks among top teams competing on the NCAA Division II level (see details in the college section of our Spectator Sports chapter). The school has 10 intercollegiate teams and expects to grow during the next few years. The North Fields Activity Center is a 72,000-square-foot recreational facility. Inside are seven stories of practice fields, tracks and aerobics and fitness training rooms. The building is constructed of translucent, high-strength material and supported by a constant source of pressurized air. It looks like a balloon-covered airplane hangar.

Community Colleges and Continuing Education

The core of continuing education at the community college level is The New Hampshire Department of Regional Community Technical Colleges. The schools are dedicated to serving both the businesses and residents of the state. The goal is to prepare students to get a job in their chosen field. The technical colleges emphasize that graduates are competitive in the job market and have the skills to advance on the job. The colleges integrate general education along with specific professional skills development. The schools work with employers to develop a curriculum and practical course of study that addresses the needs of particular area industries. Each school offers several levels of study including (in descending order) associate's degrees, diplomas, certificates and training programs. Seven technical colleges operate in the state, each with different areas of concentration. One school offers most of the medical profession training while another has a strong program in auto mechanics. At the same time, each school has a wide variety of subjects with some overlap. Associate's degrees in accounting and early childhood education are available at several locations, while an associate's degree in culinary arts is only offered through the Berlin location. The schools are Stratham-Pease (Seacoast Region), Concord, Nashua, Manchester-Derry (all in the Merrimack Valley Region), Laconia (Lakes Region), Claremont (Dartmouth-Sunapee Region) and Berlin (Great North Woods Region). The schools also offer classes off campus. For example, the Community Technical College in Claremont will offer classes in Keene. Each school has its own catalog with details on off-campus offerings. Look for individual write-ups detailing the course concentrations in the corresponding region.

Merrimack Valley Region

New Hampshire Technical Institute

11 Institute Dr., Concord
• (603) 271-NHTI

This 225-acre campus just off Interstate 93 is the home to the Christa McAuliffe Planetarium (see our Attractions chapter). The 1,400 students enrolled here have a variety of course options, though most are pursuing degrees in health and human services, engineering technologies, early childhood education, business management and criminal justice. The 400 housing spaces available on campus are generally filled, and students enjoy intercollegiate competition in men's and women's basketball, soccer, volleyball and softball/baseball.

Manchester Community Music School

83 Hanover St., Manchester
• (603) 644-4548

Whether you've always wanted to dust off your old instrument or you're looking for Suzuki violin instruction for your preschooler, there's a class or a program here for you. Serious students can add music theory and chamber music and play in the Greater Manchester Youth Orchestra as they work toward certificates of achievement.

Pioneer Computer School of Visual Art

324 Commercial St., Manchester • (603) 623-8293

A full-time, 200-hour course leading to an Advanced Certificate in Computer Graphics and Desktop Publishing is this school's most popular program. It also offers a certificate in Web-page design and a variety of part-time programs and individual courses. A low student-to-teacher ratio and in-depth instruction attract serious students, who find the latest hardware and software at their fingertips. Encouraging creativity through hands-on computer experience is the key to their graduates' successes. Top corporations regularly recruit Pioneer graduates.

New Hampshire Community Technical College

505 Amherst St., Nashua • (603) 882-6923

Like the Manchester branch, this was formerly known as a vocational-technical school, and the courses offered run the gamut of practical skills-building subjects. Electronics and drafting are specialties here, as are optometric technologies and computer science. The school offers courses in programming languages and a certificate in Web design and Web development. NHCTC Nashua also teaches machine-tool technology, perhaps the hottest job skill in New Hampshire today. If all that sounds awfully mechanical, the massage-therapy certificate program is in Nashua too. Without on-campus student housing, the 500 students enrolled here still find enough time to play intercollegiate baseball and softball, and men's and women's basketball, soccer, tennis and ice hockey.

New Hampshire Community Technical College

1066 Front St., Manchester • (603) 668-6706
Pinkerton Dr., Derry • (603) 432-3962

Students at the Manchester branch of the New Hampshire Technical College study a wide variety of courses, from physical fitness and exercise science to secretarial studies to automotive technologies and welding. Almost all the programs are directly career-related, and with no campus housing this is very much a working-person's school. Despite being an all-commuter school with an enrollment of fewer than 700, they field intercollegiate teams in men's basketball and golf, women's softball, and men's and women's soccer, golf, skiing, volleyball and ice hockey. Recently, the school began offering some classes at Pinkerton Academy's voc-ed building in Derry.

St. Joseph School of Practical Nursing

5 Woodward Ave., Nashua • (603) 594-2567

There was a time when almost every hospital had a nursing school, but most of them are gone. St. Joseph is one of the few left and one of the best. More than 100 students, men and women, combine classwork with supervised patient care to earn the Practical Nursing Diploma. Graduates take a state licensing exam to become Licensed Practical Nurses. St. Joseph now offers both a part-time course, which takes 17 months, or a full-time 48-week course. They also have a satellite program in Keene, where students do their practical work at Cheshire Hospital. Students with St. Joseph diplomas who wish to continue their education can receive advanced placement in Rivier College's associate's degree program.

Seacoast Region

New Hampshire Community Technical College

277 Portsmouth Ave., Stratham • (603) 772-1194
67 New Hampshire Ave., Portsmouth • (603) 334-6306

With a satellite facility at the Pease International Tradeport, the Seacoast Technical College is positioning itself to prepare students for the changing needs of business and industry. To that end they offer not only popular majors in nursing, accounting and automotive mechanics but also degrees in machine-tool technologies, one of the most in-demand skill areas today, and biotechnology and computer sciences for the jobs of the future. There is no campus housing for students, although more than half the 500 students are full-time. Some local residents rent rooms to students.

Lakes Region

New Hampshire Community Technical College

Prescott Hill, Laconia

• (603) 524-3207

This is a small facility on a hill outside of town. The 900 students major in a variety of vocational and business concentrations. Firefighting and graphic arts are the campus specialties. Lack of campus housing doesn't keep the students from participating in campus activities or athletics. Men's and women's teams compete in baseball and softball, basketball and volleyball.

White Mountains and Great North Woods Regions

New Hampshire Community Technical College

2020 Riverside Dr., Berlin

• (603) 752-1113

An aspiring chef with dreams of cooking at one of New Hampshire's year-round resorts might start a career at the New Hampshire Community Technical College in Berlin. You'll take classes in everything from classical desserts to regional American cuisine. The school and the Balsams Grand Resort Hotel work together to offer a three-year culinary apprentice program. Not surprisingly, considering its location in the heart of the timber industry, the Berlin campus also offers courses of study in environmental science and forest information technology. You'll find classes and degrees in surveying technology and water treatment. Associate's degrees in automotive service management and automotive technology are also offered at this location along with general education courses (such as English composition). The Berlin location opened in 1966 and currently has more than 70,000 square feet of modern classrooms, laboratories and shops.

Dartmouth-Lake Sunapee Region

New Hampshire Community Technical College

One College Dr., Claremont

• (603) 542-7744

The areas of concentration for the Claremont location of N.H. Community Technical College are nursing, allied health, human services, business, computer science and industrial technologies. The Allied Health Department includes programs for training medical laboratory and physical therapy assistants. A diploma is offered in practical nursing, and you can earn an Emergency Medical Technician certificate. The school opened in 1968 and currently operates two 16-week semesters in fall and winter.

Lebanon College

1 Court St., Lebanon

• (603) 448-2445

This community college enrollment is 500 to 700 students per semester. Three semes-

INSIDERS' TIP

When recent state budget cuts sounded the death knell of UNH's baseball team, the sports community lost one of its senior members. Although baseball doesn't fit the New Hampshire weather pattern and academic schedule very well, UNH's baseball program actually predated the foundation of the university (going back to the days of the Agricultural School).

ters are offered each year. Students range from ages 8 to 95. The school offers certificate and associate's degree programs. Certificates usually require a year of coursework, and popular programs include computer competency, French, Spanish and creative writing. Associate's degrees require more class credits, and coursework usually takes two years. Associate's degrees are offered in accounting, office technology and business science. Each semester includes special classes for kids. Recent offerings include French, Spanish and computers. The children's programs are popular with students who are home-schooled.

Monadnock Region

Antioch New England Graduate School

40 Avon St., Keene
• (603) 357-3122

Antioch New England is a learning center of Antioch University in Yellow Springs, Ohio. Master's programs are offered in applied psychology, education, environmental studies, and resource management and administration. Doctoral programs include clinical psychology and environmental studies. The school is dedicated to meeting the needs of the adult learner. The average student is 36 and has three to six years of professional experience. Most degree schedules are designed to require only one full day per week on campus. Full weekend courses are sometimes required. Faculty members are seasoned academics and practicing professionals. The school is committed to the cohesive integration of work and study, and all Antioch students are required to learn in the workplace. The 5-acre campus includes a 65,000-square-foot former furniture factory. The building was rebuilt and retrofitted to be environmentally sound and energy efficient and now houses the library, classrooms, labs, studios and offices. No student housing is provided, although housing information is available through the Office of Admissions.

Healthcare

The healthcare scene in New Hampshire is changing, as it is everywhere. Bottom-line pressures and the shift to managed care have impacted almost all of our community hospitals. Some have merged to form larger medical centers. (And some big mergers have later dissolved, unable to reconcile conflicting philosophies or approaches.) Some hospitals have been purchased by big for-profit healthcare corporations. Others have remained independent, branching out to provide specialized care. Many of our community hospitals offer walk-in clinics, rehabilitation units, psychiatric care, respite care and a variety of other services.

Distance from healthcare has always been an issue in our rural areas. Most of our smaller communities are served by volunteer rescue squads and ambulance services. Even with a very quick response time by the rescue squad, however, a long ambulance ride can be a concern. Several of the state's trauma centers have put in helipads so seriously injured patients can be rapidly transported even from remote locations.

A recent improvement in our medical coverage has been the implementation of statewide enhanced 911. Before E-911, not all communities had 911 coverage, and even in those that did there was the possibility of confusion if you called in a fire on, say, Georgetown Drive, to a dispatcher covering five towns, three of them with roads called Georgetown. Now a call to 911 from anywhere in the state is received in Concord, and a computer tells the dispatcher exactly where the call is coming from.

New Hampshire has enjoyed excellent medical care for many years, in part because so many doctors from New York and Boston vacationed here and opened part-time offices. State-of-the-art equipment and training of professionals and paraprofessionals has continued that tradition. The Dartmouth-Hitchcock Medical Center is nationally recognized as a topnotch teaching hospital. And of course, Boston, the medical capital of the nation, is just a couple of hours south of us.

Home births are popular in New Hampshire, although doctors caution against them if your home is more than 15 to 30 minutes from the hospital. A wonderful alternative is the birthing-center option offered at many of our hospitals. Birthing centers are homey, low-key places where husbands and family are welcome, a variety of birth options are encouraged and hospital admission is not required. Midwives are generally welcome (many of our obstetricians have midwives on staff), but the doctor and hospital are available as backups in case of emergency. Many hospitals offer a home visit from an obstetric nurse as part of the delivery package or at a small additional charge.

Home-health and hospice care are available throughout the state from the Visiting Nurses Association and various private care providers, both nonprofit and commercial. In most cases these organizations are affiliated with the local hospital and coordinate care with the physician when a patient is discharged, but you can call them directly too. If you're not sure who to call, the hospital can give you contact information, or you can call the licensing coordinator Theresa Jarvis at (603) 271-4607 to inquire about a specific provider. Many of our hospitals also offer physician referral services. Look for these numbers in our individual hospital write-ups.

As one professional in the state observed, walk-in clinics have not been a great success in New Hampshire. Many opened in the 1980s but have since closed. Maybe its because we're still small enough for people to have their own doctors, or maybe it's a function of complex health insurance requirements. Not all of our regions have walk-in clinics, but we have recommended some in the regions that do have them.

Holistic and alternative approaches to healthcare, on the other hand, have taken off in New Hampshire. Choosing a holistic practitioner can be even more delicate than finding a doctor you're comfortable with. At the end of this chapter you'll find some helpful information for finding a massage therapist, naturopath or other specialist who is just (you should excuse the expression) what the doctor ordered.

Important Numbers

Emergency: 911

ACCESS: Crisis intervention and counseling, 24 hours a day, (800) 987-6562 (from Southern New Hampshire Regional Medical Center)

Ask-a-Nurse, 24-hour service of Optima Healthcare, (800) 437-9666

Alcoholics Anonymous, (800) 593-3330

HELPLINE: (800) 639-5401 (This 24-hour number will refer callers to local crisis-responding agencies.)

Poison Control Center: (800) 562-8236

Child Abuse or Neglect reports: (800) 894-5533 in New Hampshire; (603) 271-6556 outside New Hampshire; (800) 852-3388 after hours

Samaritans Suicide Hotline: (800) 639-5401

Resources and Support Groups: (800) 368-HELP

Merrimack Valley Region

Hospitals

Concord Hospital

250 Pleasant St., Concord
• (603) 228-4677, (800) 327-0464, (603) 224-7879 (physician referral service), (800) 322-2711

Concord Hospital provides medical care for people from 50 communities across the middle of the state, primarily the northern Merrimack Valley. Its 24-hour emergency department is designated as a Level II Trauma Center. Traditional acute-care services in 29 medical specialty areas are enhanced and supported by such options of ambulatory care and a day-surgery center, a sleep center, pain-management program and the New Hampshire Center for Back Care. The hospital has 295 beds for in-patient care. In 1998 the hospital opened the Center for Cardiac Care, offering specialized cardiac surgical procedures. Concord's Family Place was one of the pioneers of family-centered, single-room birthing in the state. Concord hospital sponsors fitness and nutrition classes, health screenings and support groups in the community. Concord Hospital is an affiliate of the Capital Region Health Care group.

Parkland Medical Center

One Parkland Dr., Derry
• (603) 432-1500, (603) 421-2099 (physician referral service)

Parkland Medical Center recently became part of the Columbia Healthcare network, bringing the strength of the largest national healthcare company in the country to the community-size (86 bed) hospital. In 1995 Parkland was named one of the nation's top-100 hospitals in an independent study. The hospital has a 24-hour emergency room and a full spectrum of outpatient services, including an oncology clinic, rehabilitation services and senior care. ElderCare has been a Parkland specialty for years, and the Memory

INSIDERS' TIP

In some towns ambulance service is provided by volunteers. Other communities contract with private ambulance services. Whether or not patients are charged for ambulance transport varies from town to town.

Diagnostic Center at their geriatric unit is recognized throughout the state.

Optima Healthcare Catholic Medical Center

100 McGregor St., Manchester
• (603) 668-3545

Elliot Hospital

One Elliot Way, Manchester
• (603) 669-5300, Ask-a-Nurse
• (603) 626-2626

These two Manchester hospitals merged with great fanfare in the mid-1990s, promising improved medical care at contained costs for the city of Manchester. Optima Healthcare network brought together the two Manchester hospitals and affiliated with St. Joseph's in Nashua, along with a variety of outpatient and community-care providers, in the largest healthcare network in the state. At one time about 900 area physicians were affiliated with Optima.

In 1998 the merger erupted in a firestorm of controversy. Was the Catholic hospital being made an accomplice to abortion, or was it attempting to impose its values on Elliot doctors to restrict access to abortion? (CMC's maternity unit had been closed with all obstetrical care at the Elliot facility.) Was the plan to specialize different services in the different buildings going to reduce access to services for people in Manchester's neighborhoods? Why was the amount of charity care being provided by the combined hospitals dropping? The final straw came when the State Attorney General's office issued a report that Optima had violated a number of the obligations to which both non-profit hospitals were committed. The AG's office recommended that Optima be dissolved. This "unmerger" process is very complex and will take several years to accomplish.

When the dissolution is complete, and if both hospitals manage to survive, the city will once again have two fine hospitals. Catholic Medical Center, on the west side of the river, is known for one of the top cardiac surgery programs in the United States, the New England Heart Institute. Elliot, on the east side, has an excellent trauma center and the Elliot 1-Day Surgery Center on Cypress Street, (603) 627-4889, a freestanding center for surgeries that do not require overnight hospitalization. It's not clear, at this time, how large each hospital will be when the dust settles.

St. Joseph Hospital & Trauma Center

172 Kinsley St., Nashua
• (603) 882-3000, (800) 210-9000 (physician referral service)

St. Joseph's was originally built by the Grey Nuns (Sisters of Charity) and this 218-bed facility is still a Catholic healthcare provider. The state-of-the art medical facility's 24-hour emergency department is the area's designated Trauma Center, supported by a satellite emergency room at the Milford Medical Center (see the Walk-In Clinics section). They offer day surgery through the SurgiCenter and a complete acute-care facility.

Southern New Hampshire Medical Center

8 Prospect St., Nashua
• (603) 577-2000, (800) 628-8070 (physician referral service)

More than 400 primary care physicians and specialists are providers at SNHMC. The 188-bed hospital offers a full range of the most up-to-date inpatient and outpatient services, including a regional Level II trauma center, a dialysis unit and a newborn Intensive Care Nursery. The Birthplace, the medical center's recently renovated family-oriented birthing center, is the second-busiest maternity unit in the state. Beginning in 1998 it became the site of an Obstetrical Residency program affiliated with the Medical School at Dartmouth.

Veterans Administration Medical Center

Smyth Rd. (Exit 8 off I-93), Manchester
• (603) 624-4366, (800) 892-8384

This older facility is undergoing a massive remodeling (much of it done by former patients), and the patient-care methods are being updated too. Emergency Room renovations were completed in 1997, and work on the Ambulatory Care area is underway. More and more treatments are being handled on an outpatient basis, and outpatient clinics in Tilton and Portsmouth provide better access to care for vets in the Seacoast and Lakes regions. (Contact the medical center's 800 number to arrange visits at the off-site clinics.) A 37-bed inpatient-care department provides state-of-the-art treatment for medical and surgical patients. For specialized needs patients are referred to other hospitals in the VA New England system (there are hospitals in White River Junction, Vermont, and in Boston) or elsewhere in the country. The medical center offers annual health-screening clinics for all honorably discharged veterans. Other special services include a Women's Clinic, substance abuse treatment and preventive medicine/patient education.

Walk-in Clinics

Planned Parenthood of Northern New England

82 Palomino Rd., Bedford
• (603) 669-7321

Planned Parenthood offers not only birth-control information and pregnancy testing but also a whole range of reproductive health services for both men and women, including HIV testing and counseling. It has offices in Manchester and Derry as well as this central office and a "Facts of Life" hot line at (800) 359-3359. Call for hours and directions to the clinics.

Triangle Medical Clinic

2075 South Willow St., Manchester
• (603) 645-1102

The Triangle Clinic isn't actually a walk-in clinic, since an appointment is required. The staff is prepared to deal with the unexpected, however, whether that's a sports or work injury, the flu, the mumps or a pregnancy test. Physicals are a specialty here — for work, camp, school, state licensing or the Department of Transportation — and the staff can handle all the immunizations you need for travel abroad. The clinic also offers free blood-pressure monitoring, and it's conveniently located just south of the Mall of New Hampshire. (Is your blood pressure higher before or after you shop 'til you drop?)

Milford Medical Center

442 Nashua St., Milford
• (603) 673-5623

The Milford Medical Center provides topnotch emergency care to the Souhegan Valley, and its intervention has meant the difference between life and death for a trauma victims on the hour-long trip from Wilton or Greenville to the hospital in Nashua. The medical center also handles less-critical care on a walk-in basis and by appointment. Sometimes follow-up visits for surgery in Nashua can be handled here for patients' convenience. The center is open from 7 AM to 11 PM seven days a week.

Health Stop

228 Daniel Webster Hwy. S., Nashua
• (603) 888-9200

This clinic in the middle of Nashua's busiest commercial area is a convenient option for treatment of minor emergencies and routine medical needs. It's open for walk-in examinations from 8 AM to 8 PM, or you can call to make a same-day appointment. Health Stop does physicals for school or camp, lab work, X-rays, flu shots and EKGs along with a number of other procedures.

Salem Family Practice and Walk-In Center

7 Stiles Rd., Salem
• (603) 898-4000

This walk-in clinic is an outpatient service of the Holy Family Hospital in Methuen, Massachusetts. It is open Monday through Friday

INSIDERS' TIP

Some homeopathic and naturopathic practitioners have Yellow Pages listings. You can find other alternative therapists by checking bulletin boards in health-food stores and health clubs, or check your insurance company's list of Participating Providers.

from 8 AM to 7:30 PM and Saturday and Sunday from 9 AM to 3:30 PM.

Mental Health Hospitals

Hampstead Hospital
East Rd., Hampstead
• (603) 329-5311

Hampstead offers resident and outpatient treatment for chemical dependency and other emotional/psychological problems of adults, adolescents and seniors. The Brief Treatment Adult Psychiatric Program is designed to stabilize patients in crisis and mobilize family and community supports for ongoing care. The Eating Disorders Program works with patients and family to address both the physical and psychological/emotional issues associated with these difficult conditions. The Young People's Unit works with both psychological and chemical-dependency illnesses. Hampstead also has a strong Geriatric Psychiatry Program and a Sleep-Disorders Center. In 1998 Hampstead Hospital merged with Seaborne Hospital in Dover and their chemical dependency and detoxification programs operate there.

The Cypress Center/Mental Health Center of Greater Manchester
401 Cypress St., Manchester
• (603) 668-4111

This mental health clinic offers outpatient and 24-hour treatment, intensive therapy and counseling for psychiatric and mental health issues including substance abuse.

Charter Brookside Behavior Health System of New England
29 Northwest Blvd., Nashua
• (603) 886-5000, (800) 866-9006

Charter Brookside provides outpatient treatment for mental and emotional health needs at sites in Nashua, Manchester and Keene. The company also operates this 100-bed inpatient facility in Nashua. The care offered begins with free initial assessments and includes crisis intervention, acute-care and intensive outpatient treatment for problems related to addiction, trauma and psychiatric disease. Family support is an important part of the process, and respite care is available when necessary.

Seacoast Region

Hospitals

Wentworth-Douglass Hospital
789 Central Ave., Dover
• (603) 742-5252, (603) 740-2377 (physician referral service)

With 178 beds, Wentworth-Douglass is the largest acute-care hospital in the Seacoast region. One hundred physicians offer services in more than two dozen medical specialties. The Emergency Department/Trauma Center is open 24 hours a day. The hospital is especially proud of its Birth Center, where the home-style, single-room maternity design is complemented by a Level II Neonatal Nursery. The Seacoast Cancer Center offers advanced medical treatment options and a state-of-the-art Radiation Therapy facility. Wentworth-Douglass has same-day and laser surgery, cardiac services and an extensive outpatient health program covering education, rehabilitation, nutrition and many other treatments. The Sleep Disorders Center and Diabetes Institute offer other innovative approaches to medical care. Call the Health and Fitness Center at (603) 742-2163 to get started on that fitness regimen you've been thinking about!

Exeter Hospitals Inc.
10 Buzzell Ave., Exeter
• (603) 778-7311, (800) 4-EXETER (physician referral service)

The Exeter Cottage Hospital opened its doors 100 years ago, but the visionaries who founded the hospital wouldn't recognize the place today! More than 110 physicians provide care to residents of 15 Seacoast communities at the integrated campus, where the hospital, a long-term care facility and a medical services building are conveniently grouped to provide continuity of care and easy access to services for patients and families. The Family Center incorporates both a single-room concept birthing center that welcomes 900 babies each year and a Pediatric Unit built to accommodate overnight visits from parents. The surgical team has kept up with the latest innovations and developments, including short-term-stay surgeries and laser surgery for some skin and eye conditions. The Cardiac Center has been selected to participate in an international study being done on angioplasty as an early response to heart attacks. Prevention is a focus of the Cardiac Center too, as it is with the Mammography Center and the community outreach programs operated by the rehabilitation and sports medicine teams. The Synergy Wellness and Fitness Center and Health Club invites area residents to design the health routine best suited to their needs.

Portsmouth Regional Hospital

333-343 Borthwick Ave., Portsmouth
• (603) 436-5110, (800) COLUMBIA (physician referral service)

With more than 200 physicians, Portsmouth Regional serves communities up and down the Seacoast, from southern Maine to the Massachusetts North Shore. The 100-year-old local hospital is now part of the national HCA (Columbia) group, operating out of a state-of-the-art facility that's just 10 years old. The 24-hour emergency department includes a trauma team and an advanced cardiac group known as the Chest Pain Center. The Heart & Lung center offers preventative care in support of state-of-the-art acute care including cardiac catheterization, echo-cardiograms, pulmonary testing and rehabilitation services. Nonemergency walk-in care is also available at the hospital 24 hours a day. Other specialized care centers include a short-stay surgical unit, wound care, rehabilitation and a women's care program with family-centered birthing, breast health, cosmetic surgery and emotional/mental healthcare. The Wellness Center offers support and education to the community in a variety of health-related areas such as diabetes management, smoking cessation and yoga, while the Senior Friends Program and the Parent Center provide information and encouragement to families at both ends of life.

Frisbie Memorial Hospital

11 Whitehall Rd., Rochester
• (603) 332-5211

Frisbie Memorial is a 100-bed nonprofit community hospital. The 162 physicians provide a full range of traditional acute-care services, including a 24-hour emergency department and more than 30 medical specialties. Surgical services include both inpatient suites and a same-day surgery unit. Frisbie's BirthCare is built on the single-room labor/delivery/postpartum care concept, providing the opportunity for a homelike birth setting with the hospital backup. Frisbie also offers specialized programs for cancer therapies and geriatric psychiatric needs.

Mental Health Hospitals

Seaborne Hospital

Seaborne Dr., Dover
• (603) 742-9300, (800) 652-4200

Seaborne is a 102-bed hospital dedicated to the treatment of alcohol and chemical dependency. (In 1998 the hospital merged with Hampstead Hospital and now serves as the chemical dependency and detoxification unit of that facility.) Patients may be referred by physicians or they may request admission themselves. Both intensive residential programs and outpatient therapies are available. The hospital also offers specialized treatment for a variety of emotional and psychiatric issues, including abuse trauma and stress re-

INSIDERS' TIP

Calls to 911 made on cellular phones do not connect to the E-911 system. They are relayed to the nearest dispatch center. If you call to report an accident, it will be helpful if you can give location information to the dispatcher.

duction. Continuing care is an important part of the hospital's approach, and it will arrange for coverage in the patient's community if the person doesn't live near the hospital.

Portsmouth Pavilion
333-343 Borthwick Ave., Portsmouth
• (603) 436-0600, (800) 924-1086

The Portsmouth Pavilion offers support and treatment for a variety of psychological and emotional needs. This includes addiction recovery and geriatric, adult and adolescent treatment (both residential and outpatient). The approach includes crisis intervention and management, acute and chronic treatment and aftercare support through community services. Of particular interest is Alternatives, a teens-at-risk community outreach program, Camp Quest, a summer camp program designed to boost self-esteem and coping, and a Challenge Ropes course which is available to organizations and groups interested in this highly successful program for community-building.

Lakes Region

Hospitals

Franklin Regional Hospital
15 Aiken Ave., Franklin
• (603) 934-2060

Serving the towns of the southern Lakes Region from Tilton to Alexandria, this nonprofit, 49-bed facility provides acute care, emergency and critical care and an extensive range of community-outreach programs. A unique approach to healthcare at Franklin Regional is its system of specialty clinics in a dozen medical specialties, providing patients with high-quality care and the comfort and individual attention of the small hospital setting. The Family Birthing Center allows for labor, delivery and postpartum care in a single, homelike room and offers a calm setting for mothers and babies. Franklin even prepares a candlelight dinner for the new parents! At the other end of life, the Hospice Suite was designed to accommodate family members in a room adjacent to the patient's room in the skilled-nursing unit to encourage and support families of terminally ill patients. Community outreach programs include workshops and courses in cooking and CPR, line dancing and weight-loss support, parenting skills and Medicare terms. They've even offered a course on clutter control for stress-reduction (unfortunately, we missed it!).

Lakes Region General Hospital
80 Highland Ave., Laconia
• (603) 524-3211, (603) 527-2819 (emergency)

Lakes Region General is a nonprofit 143-bed hospital offering more than 30 medical specialties. The emergency department is staffed 24 hours a day and is the designated Trauma Center (Level III) for the Lakes Region. The hospital's maternity department is built around The Family Birthplace, with homelike rooms designed for labor, delivery and postpartum care without moving or separating mother and baby. The Community Wellness Center, (603) 524-8475, incorporates a cardiopulmonary gym (stop by for a form to be filled out by your physician, and you can join in the fitness fun). The hospital sponsors support groups and special programs for elders, diabetics, new mothers, asthmatics and more than two dozen other groups with special needs or interests. Of particular interest are the Chronic Pain Management program and the Sleep Lab. The hospital's walk-in clinic is open 365 days a year to treat residents' and visitors' nonemergency medical problems. Lakes Region is also affiliated with the Holistic Health Center in Gilford, (603) 524-9261, which offers naturopathy, acupuncture, aromatherapy and massage therapy. Doctors at the hospital are very comfortable coordinating complementary care with their traditional treatment methods.

Speare Memorial Hospital
16 Hospital Rd., Plymouth
• (603) 536-1120, (603) 536-1120 (physician referral service)

With 47 beds, and a focus on individualized care, Speare Memorial is a friendly community hospital. Extensive and ongoing renovations have kept the hospital's acute-care and intensive-care facilities up to date. Speare has a 24-hour emergency department and physicians in specialties that include obstetrics, pediatrics, surgery, psychiatry, oncology and rehabilitation. At the newly renovated Rooke Family Pavilion, the hospital provides outpatient services to the people of the western Lakes Region from Groton and Warren to Wentworth and as far north as Waterville Valley.

Huggins Hospital
S. Main St., Wolfeboro
• (603) 569-7500

Huggins is an acute-care, nonprofit community hospital with 82 beds and about 50 physicians on staff. For a small hospital, Huggins plays a big part in the healthcare of this community, whose population balloons every summer. In addition to its 24-hour emergency department, Huggins works closely with the nurses at the many area camps, providing emergency care if necessary and support for the camps' own medical services. Huggins is also an important link in the Good Beginnings program, a collaborative effort that provides intervention, assistance and prenatal care to young women, especially those in high-risk pregnancies. The Adult Day Respite Care program is a tremendous service to families of patients with Alzheimer's disease and other chronic illnesses. A single-room-design labor and delivery department, newly expanded day-surgery center and state-of-the-art nuclear medicine equipment are part of Huggins ongoing commitment to the healthcare of the Lakes Region.

Walk-in Clinics

Laconia Clinic
724 N. Main St., Laconia
• (603) 527-2706

This is a multispecialty group practice with more than 20 physicians. The Convenience Care Center is open 8 AM to 8 PM seven days a week, and no appointment is necessary. The on-site lab, X-ray and pharmacy can simplify diagnosis and treatment.

Lakes Region General Hospital Walk-in Care
80 Highland St., Laconia
• (603) 527-2896

Right next door to the emergency department at Lakes Region General Hospital, the

Walk-In Care clinic offers quick, quality care for burns, rashes, sore throats and the host of other ailments that can spoil a vacation. It also does physicals, blood pressure checks and other nonemergency exams. Walk-in Care is open 9 AM to 9 PM every day.

White Mountains and Great North Woods Regions

Hospitals

Androscoggin Valley Hospital

59 Page Hill Rd., Berlin

• (603) 752-2200

Androscoggin Valley Hospital is a 92-bed acute-care hospital that has served the healthcare needs of the Upper Androscoggin Valley since 1905. Modern healthcare services include sophisticated radiology tools such as CT scanning, mobile MRI, nuclear medicine, ultrasound and mammography. Homelike birthing rooms are part of the Valley Birth Place, and the physician-staffed emergency room is open 24 hours a day. The hospital has a psychiatric unit, cardiac rehabilitation program and chemotherapy services. Community services include health fairs, health screenings and a diabetes education program. Additionally, the hospital coordinates Home Health and Hospice Service for the community and an Alzheimer's disease support group.

Upper Connecticut Valley Hospital

Corliss Ln., Colebrook

• (603) 237-4971

This rural 31-bed hospital was built in 1970 and serves an 850-square-mile area that includes 20 towns and 8,500 people in New Hampshire, Vermont and Maine. There is 24-hour emergency care available as well as a walk-in clinic. Inpatient services include obstetrics, medical and surgical care. The hospital is affiliated with the Dartmouth-Hitchcock Medical Center. Community services include disease prevention and screening, health education and school health services.

Weeks Memorial Hospital

Middle St., Lancaster

• (603) 788-4911

Since 1947 Weeks Memorial Hospital has provided a full range of medical, surgical, diagnostic and emergency services for Lancaster and surrounding communities. The 49-bed hospital includes an emergency/outpatient clinic, birthing center and short-stay unit. The outpatient clinic offers specialty clinics by visiting physicians from Dartmouth-Hitchcock Medical Center in rheumatology, allergy, oncology and adult and pediatric cardiology. The Weeks Medical Center was added in 1993. The medical center provides office space for physicians and nurse practitioners and operates satellite facilities in Whitefield and Groveton.

Littleton Regional Hospital

262 Cottage St. (Exit 41 off I-93), Littleton

• (603) 444-7731

This 54-bed community hospital is the primary acute-care facility in the western White Mountains region. The nonprofit hospital opened in 1906 and has constantly expanded its services, facilities and staff to keep pace with growing demand. Current specialties include cardiology, orthopedics, oncology, obstetrics/gynecology and neurology. The hospital has its own CT scanner and the services of a mobile MRI unit. The emergency department offers 24-hour physician-staffed care. The community services include diabetes support groups, health screenings, Alcoholics Anonymous meetings and childbirth education.

Memorial Hospital

3073 Main St., North Conway

• (603) 356-5461

This community hospital, open since 1911, offers walk-in healthcare every day from 8 AM to 8 PM in addition to 24-hour emergency care. The facility has 35 licensed acute-care beds and a wide range of outpatient services ranging from the day surgery center to discharge planning with community health and social services networks. As befits a hospital close to so many of the outdoor adventures in our state, the hospital has a full sports-medicine department including physical therapy services. The radiology department offers everything from X-rays to MRI to nuclear medicine. Within New Hampshire the hospital operates the Carroll County Healthline, (800) 499-4171, which offers confidential health and social service information as well as physician referrals. The Merriman House is a nursing home affiliated with the hospital, and its services include adult day-care programs and respite care for caregivers.

Cottage Hospital
Swiftwater Rd., Woodsville (part of Haverhill) · (603) 747-2761

Founded in 1903, Cottage Hospital was originally housed in the Cobleigh Tavern at the intersection of N.H. routes 10 and 135. The present 48-bed facility was built in 1960 with additional construction in 1970, 1985 and 1996. Modern additions include a birthing center with family-centered maternity care and an intensive-care unit. Special programs in cancer management, cardiac rehabilitation, diabetes management and pain control complement a full range of medical specialties including obstetrics and gynecology, internal medicine, psychiatry, radiology and pediatrics. Facilities include a 24-hour, physician-staffed emergency room and 12-hour, physician-staffed walk-in clinic. Community services offered by the hospital include cardiac and diabetes support groups, free flu clinic for seniors and health screenings.

Walk-in Clinics

The Memorial Hospital
3073 Main St. (N.H. Rt. 16), North Conway • (603) 356-5461

This clinic is open every day, 365 days a year from 8 AM to 8 PM. Trained professionals diagnose and treat minor illnesses that do not require emergency care.

Dartmouth-Lake Sunapee Region

Hospitals

Valley Regional Hospital
243 Elm St., Claremont • (603) 542-7771

Valley Regional is a 71-bed hospital serving nearly 40,000 residents in Claremont and surrounding communities in New Hampshire and Vermont. The hospital offers an integrated healthcare system ranging from intensive care to home-health services. The physician-staffed emergency room is open 24 hours a day. Diagnostic tools include on-site CT scanning, MRI and a full mammography center. As with many hospitals, the focus of the future is on home healthcare and community education. The Good Beginnings Program matches expectant and/or new parents with a trained volunteer to help guide the new family as it adjusts to life changes. The hospital also has a fitness center available to residents of the community for a small charge. Pulmonary and cardiac rehabilitation, home-infusion therapy, discharge planning and home-health services are just a few of the hospital's programs.

Alice Peck Day Memorial Hospital
125 Mascoma, Lebanon • (603) 448-3121

This community hospital opened in 1932 with nine beds and two nurses. Today the 85-bed hospital offers family-focused care to the Upper Valley community. The Immediate Care Center, a walk-in clinic and emergency room, is open every day from 7 AM to midnight. The birthing center includes a full postpartum follow-up as well as an award-winning lactation program. A 50-bed extended-care facility is part of the hospital. The Occupational Health Program offers services to more than 100 area businesses. The program includes injury management, work-site safety services and employee screening (employee physicals as well as drug and alcohol testing). Community programs include nutrition education for Savvy Seniors and a poster contest for local 4th-grade students during National Nutrition Month.

Dartmouth-Hitchcock Medical Center

One Medical Center Dr. (off N.H. Rt. 120), Lebanon • (603) 650-5000

Dartmouth-Hitchcock Medical Center is New Hampshire's only academic medical center. Its components include the Dartmouth Medical School (founded in 1797, the current enrollment is 319), the Hitchcock Clinic (the ninth-largest multispecialty group practice in the United States), the Mary Hitchcock Memorial Hospital (a 429-bed facility) and the Veteran's Affairs Hospital in White River Junction, Vermont. It is one of the finest medical centers in the world. Completed in 1991 after three years of construction, the 1.2-million-square-foot facility is on 225 acres. The building covers 7.8 acres and is one of very few completely new medical centers in the country. One of the center's innovations is the horizontal design system - grouping tests and services for various patient populations next to each other. For example, all cardiac services are together on Level 4. And the neonatal intensive care unit is right next door to the birthing pavilion. The medical complex is joined by a skylit mall. A sort of Main Street, the mall has waiting areas, shops and eateries - even street lamps.

Many of the center's programs are innovative and specialized. For example, the Children's Hospital at Dartmouth (CHaD) was established to provide a regional center for children's healthcare. It is a "hospital within a hospital" staffed by specialists in pediatric medicine, surgery and nursing. CHaD is not a building but rather an extended system of care that offers technically advanced services for infants, children and adolescents. CHaD is fully accredited by the National Association of Children's Hospitals and Related Institutions as one of 124 children's hospitals in the United States and Canada. The Norris Cotton Cancer Center, formerly on the Dartmouth College campus, moved into the new complex in July 1995. More than 1,400 new patients are seen each year, and more than 400 patients are involved in clinical trials testing new therapies and treatments. Researchers here are involved in more than 200 studies with funding of more than $21 million.

Emergency services include the Dartmouth-Hitchcock Air Response Team, DHART. This air transportation service uses a twin-engine helicopter to respond to emergencies. DHART might pick up a patient from another medical facility in the region or respond directly to an accident scene. The service began in July 1994.

The C. Everett Koop Institute is dedicated to the improvement of human health. The former surgeon general (and Dartmouth grad) inspires this leadership group, which designs and implements strategies to enhance the health of individuals, families and communities. The institute links individuals involved in community health with appropriate resources.

New London Hospital

270 County Rd., New London • (603) 526-2911

Founded in 1918 and renovated in 1996, this 91-bed nonprofit community hospital serves the medical needs of the Kearsarge/Lake Sunapee/Newport area. Services include a medical-surgical unit, family birthing center, 24-hour emergency department and a 56-bed extended-care center. The hospital offers physical, occupational and speech therapy; occupational health services; an oncology clinic; and a full range of lab, radiology, nutrition, social work and cardiopulmonary services. Health programs for the community include CPR and first aid training, diabetes self-care and safe-sitter courses.

Monadnock Region

Hospitals

The Cheshire Medical Center

580 Court St., Keene • (603) 352-4111

Established in 1892, this 177-bed acute-care hospital serves as a regional medical referral center. In this capacity the hospital offers a full range of medical and surgical specialties. The Farnum Rehabilitation Center provides both inpatient and outpatient therapy including industrial rehabilitation. The Kingsbury Center for Cancer Care includes radiation and chemotherapies. A modern Birthing Center, special adolescent and adult mental-health units, and cardiac and intensive care units are on premises along with a fully accredited clinical laboratory and radiology department. The Emergency Care and Trauma centers are open 24 hours a day.

Monadnock Community Hospital
452 Old St. Rd., Peterborough
• (603) 924-7191

Founded in 1923, the Monadnock Community Hospital is a 62-bed facility offering a full range of medical services and programs. The physician-staffed emergency room is open 24 hours. Particular strengths include the Senior Mental Health Center, specializing in the mental health needs of people older than 55, and the Maternity Unit, which is one of 49 certified water-birth centers in the United States. The hospital places particular significance on its role in the growing areas of outpatient services and community education. The Partial Hospitalization program offers a break to family caretakers by providing adult day care. The hospital has pulmonary and cardiac rehabilitation programs, nutritional education and counseling and a Women's Health Center. Health Days, cosponsored by a local bank, provide free blood pressure and cholesterol screening throughout the region. The Aquatic Arthritis Program, Diabetes Exercise Program and on-site fitness trail are a few of the newer innovations at the hospital.

Holistic Healthcare

One nice feature of healthcare in New Hampshire is an open and cooperative relationship between traditional and alternative health practitioners. (Practitioners and insurance companies prefer the term "complementary medicine.") More and more doctors are recognizing the value of non-invasive and non-pharmacological treatments. Some have added dietary and other holistic approaches to the tools in their black bags, other routinely refer patients to chiropractors, massage therapists and other practitioners of what used to be called "alternative" medicine. Health insurance companies will even pay for many of these services.

The state licenses practitioners of many forms of healthcare. Naturopathy is a primary healthcare system that relies on education, natural medicine and a variety of therapies to stimulate the body's own self-healing process. Naturopaths are licensed in New Hampshire by the Department of Health and Human Services and must be graduates of accredited naturopathic medical colleges. You can contact Christine Topham at (603) 271-5127 for more information about the licensing program and its requirements. Chiropractors, who manipulate or adjust the spine to relieve a variety of disorders and promote health, are also required to be graduates of an accredited chiropractic college and complete a continuing education requirement to be licensed by the Chiropractic Board of Examiners, (603) 271-4560.

Massage therapy (also called somatic therapy and bodywork) is offered by independent practitioners, at health clubs and even in beauty parlors. Massage practitioners are licensed by the Bureau of Health Facilities after completing 750 hours of training and passing a state exam. You can contact them at (603) 271-4592 to inquire about licensed practitioners. Another form of treatment frequently considered "alternative" is acupuncture, and New Hampshire licenses acupuncturists as well. The Board of Acupuncture Licensing can be reached at (603) 271-4685.

Other forms of holistic healthcare popular in the state include yoga, tai chi and meditation, therapeutic touch and reiki. Add a variety of approaches combining diet and immuno-boosting supplements to improve overall health and combat chronic pain, allergic and asthmatic symptoms, and other resistant, chronic disorders, and you'll see that New Hampshire's reputation for conservative, tradition-bound living doesn't apply to healthcare! Many natural food stores carry herbal remedies and aromatherapy supplies (we've included a couple in our Shopping chapter), but you can find a variety of homeopathic and herbal remedies in ordinary drugstores too. The Natural Health Care Study Group meets twice a month at the Chandler Memorial Ethnic Library in Nashua and hosts speakers to educate consumers about these different modalities. You can call Cynthia Schroer at (603) 886-0114 for more information or to receive a schedule.

Do be aware that some of the alternative healthcare practitioners are also into alternative spiritual experiences. If you're comfortable with that, it's fine, but if not you may want to ask up front what the person's theology is. One Insider was a bit shocked to be told after her son's third visit to a naturopath that his nightmares were the result of his death on a battlefield in a former life! Or you may wish to contact the Board of Examiners of Psychology and Mental Health Practice at (603) 271-6762 to ask about pastoral counselors licensed to offer psychotherapy.

Media

Not so very long ago, the media picture in New Hampshire was dominated by one man. William Loeb, publisher of the *Manchester Union Leader*, built the only statewide newspaper into a powerful political and social force. That his legacy has been ably carried on by his widow, Nackey, is evidenced by the fact that even today, more than 15 years after his death, no one has been elected governor (or even considered a serious candidate) without taking Loeb's "pledge" — an oath never to sign into law a broad-based tax bill.

Today Loeb's influence is waning, not because of any change at the newspaper but because of changes in the state. In 1972, when the *Union Leader* destroyed Edmund Muskie's presidential chances with a single photograph, most residents had reception of only one television station. No newspaper had a circulation even close to the *Union Leader*'s. Loeb attacked Senator Muskie's wife in print, then reported the candidate's reaction with a front page picture of Muskie's angry, snowflake-bedecked face, suggesting that a man who cried over such a trivial thing was too weak to be president. In the absence of any alternative news source, the statement went unchallenged, and Muskie went back to being the Senator from Maine.

Isolated by mountains and valleys, New Hampshire's citizens avoided the homogenizing effects of mainstream media for years. But times change. In the southern tier, people put up enormous antennas to bring in Boston television and radio (especially when the Red Sox were winning). Up north, where the only television available was produced in Portland, Maine, and broadcast from Mount Washington, it became commonplace to see huge satellite dishes alongside tiny homes (which might or might not have had indoor plumbing).

As the population grew and technology changed, other media choices became available. Today the *Union Leader* still has the largest circulation of any paper in the state, but the No. 2 spot belongs to *The Boston Globe*. That paper's weekly New Hampshire section provides a somewhat liberal alternative to the arch-conservative editorial stance of the *Union Leader*, and home delivery of the daily *Globe* allows New Hampshire residents as far north as Concord to read the world and national news without Loeb-ish commentary.

Other daily papers in the state have expanded their coverage beyond their cities as well. But no one does statewide high school sports coverage like the *Union Leader*, and that alone could maintain their dominance well into the next century.

Local news is still the province of the daily and weekly (and sometimes less frequent) local papers. In this day of desktop publishing, even tiny communities often have a tabloid-size paper covering school news, the activities of the selectmen and conservation commission, and whatever political controversy roils the local blood. We can not possibly cover all of them in this guide, but look for them at the community store in the center of town.

Larger, regional weeklies are the main source of news for the average citizen. It's in these that you will meet your candidates for school board and state legislature, find out about the fire department's dispute with the rescue squad and learn what your neighbor's house sold for.

Look for information on specialty publications throughout this guide — the diocesan paper *Tidings* is in our Worship chapter, the *Senior Beacon* is in Retirement, *Parenting Times* is in Kidstuff, etc.

On the television front, our only statewide network affiliate, WMUR in Manchester, continues to grow. Coverage there still runs to "if it bleeds, it leads" journalism — but since that is becoming more and more the norm nationwide, newcomers to the state may not notice.

Upstart WNDS in Derry is giving WMUR a run for its money in the southern tier, and dueling interpretation of Neilsen ratings is becoming a specatator sport. New Hampshire also has an award-winning PBS station, NHPT/Channel 11, that's rebroadcast on translators across the state to reach around the mountains. Several smaller stations have also entered the market, although their broadcast areas tend to be limited. And a few communities have put the local-access possibilities of cable television to good use. Hollis, for example, broadcasts its school district meetings on cable, not only encouraging greater participation but also skirting the issue of not having a hall big enough to seat even a fraction of the town's voters.

Although radio broadcasts are still hampered by the state's uneven terrain, cable television has pulled down many of those three-story antennas, and more recently the mini-satellite dishes have taken the state by storm. Now most New Hampshire citizens can see that the Red Sox don't actually play baseball in the snow, and they can watch *The Today Show* and *Star Trek*.

And today the "information superhighway" runs through the smallest towns and biggest cities alike. Most of our newspapers, television stations and radio outlets now have Websites. Some put whole articles and transcripts up on the web, others offer tantalizing tidbits. Constantly updated traffic reports, school cancellations and breaking news are all advantages to those with Internet capability, along with the chance to compare points of view. Like the rest of the country, residents of New Hampshire are no longer united by a single source of news. Whether that is a change for good or for ill is a judgment for the reader to make.

Daily Newspapers

Merrimack Valley Region

The Concord Monitor

1 Monitor Dr., Concord
• (603) 224-5301

This daily paper (circulation 22,000) covers national news in the front section and state and local (upper Merrimack Valley) news in the rest of the paper. Concord is the state capital, so state politics get good coverage here. The Monitor's mailing address is P.O. Box 1177, Concord, NH 03301.

The Telegraph

17 Executive Dr., Hudson
• (603) 882-2741

This paper, which most Insider's still call "The Nashua Telegraph," has a circulation of 29,000 (35,000 on Sunday). It's the local paper for towns from Derry to Mason, but it provides enough national news from the wire services to be anyone's only newspaper. Special sections cover local news one day each week, and the paper maintains offices in several outlying communities. Mail for the *Telegraph* goes to P.O. Box 1008, Nashua, NH 03061.

The Union Leader

100 William Loeb Dr., Manchester
• (603) 668-4321, (800) 562-8218

The only statewide paper, the *Leader*'s unique style and voice reach a circulation of 70,000 daily, 99,000 on Sundays. National and business news is provided in wire copy, while state and local coverage is staff-written. The

INSIDERS' TIP

The most important section of the local paper is the letters page. Most papers print all the letters they receive, and many people read the letters first. (Sometimes that's all they read!) Here's where you'll hear about the controversies, meet local personalities, see battles waged and gratitude expressed.

Union Leader's staunch conservative editorial writers are very busy these days, with our first-ever woman governor (a Democrat), the school-funding crisis and Supreme Court decision (see our Education chapter) and the early forays of potential presidents. To write to the *Union Leader,* use P.O. Box 9555, Manchester, NH 03103.

Seacoast Region

Foster's Daily Democrat
333 Central Ave., Dover
• (603) 742-4455 , (800) 660-8310

Foster's celebrated 125 years of solid reporting on June 18, 1998. This family-owned newspaper has the largest circulation in the Seacoast region, more than 27,000 each day. *Foster's* does not cover national news but concentrates on local stories. The circulation area is from York, Maine, to Nottingham and as far north as Wolfeboro.

Portsmouth Herald
111 Maplewood Ave., Portsmouth
• (603) 436-1800

The *Herald* has a reputation for even-handed coverage of state and local issues, with a particular eye for business news. Circulation is about 15,000 Monday through Saturday and nearly 17,000 on Sundays. (Careful: The *Portsmouth Herald* is sometimes confused with the *Portland Press Herald*, another great newspaper but one that's published in and for our neighbor state of Maine!)

Lakes Region

The Citizen
171 Fair St., Laconia
• (603) 524-3800, (800) 564-3806

The Citizen calls itself "The Voice of Central New Hampshire" and maintains local bureaus in the Northern Lakes, Greater Plymouth and the Newfound Lake area. It gives a nod to national news, but the focus is on the local happenings. *The Citizen* also has a wonderful column called "Our Yesterdays" culled from its own files and those of its predecessor, the *Laconia Democrat*. It's a fascinating glimpse at everyday life and politics over the last 125 years.

White Mountains Region

Berlin Daily Sun
Conway Daily Sun
64 Seavey St., North Conway
• (603) 356-2999

The sister *Suns*, distributed throughout the Mount Washington Valley and into western Maine, are probably the best of the free papers. They offer in-depth news coverage of local and state issues, along with a brief synopsis of national news. Lots of letters to the editor, moderate and thoughtful editorials, *Peanuts* and *Dilbert* — what more could a reader ask for? Editorial content for each paper is distinct, while the advertising is shared. The *Berlin Sun*'s mailing address is Box 279, Berlin, NH 03570, and their phone is (603) 752-5858. The Conway office receives mail at P.O. Box 1940, North Conway, NH 03860.

Dartmouth-Lake Sunapee Region

Claremont Eagle Times
River Rd., Claremont
• (603) 543-3100

The *Eagle Times*' motto is "Focused on local news," but it offers a wealth of world and national news as well, mostly off the Associated Press wire. The local area it covers includes Claremont, Newport and Sunapee and their surroundings as well as a few towns across the river in Vermont. A centrist editorial stance and frequent special sections make this 83-year-old daily and its weekly sister, the *Argus-Champion*, popular news sources throughout the Dartmouth-Lake Sunapee region. Address mail to the *Eagle Times* to RR 2, Box 301, Claremont, NH 03743.

Valley News
7 Interchange Dr., West Lebanon
• (603) 298-8711

"The Newspaper of the Upper Valley" has good coverage of state and local news, a couple of pages devoted to world and national news, adequate sports coverage and special close-up sections. The *Valley News* has a definite pro-Republican editorial page that features Bob Dole's syndicated column.

Monadnock Region

Keene Sentinel
60 West St., Keene
• (603) 352-1234

The *Sentinel* is a substantial daily focused almost entirely on the news of the Monadnock communities it serves. It offers brief wire-service copy on national news. The op-ed page includes commentary on national issues. An interesting "Living" section rivals those of much larger papers. The *Sentinel* also operates Infoline, a 24-hour news-by-phone service at (603) 352-2424.

Weekly Newspapers

Boston Globe New Hampshire Weekly
1650 Elm St., Manchester
• (603) 644-3900

The New Hampshire section is included with all copies of the *Boston Sunday Globe* sold in New Hampshire, both subscriber and newsstand — about 64,000 papers. The New Hampshire copy runs to coverage of local sports stars, environmental and business news and the occasional political controversy. Since ending the column of local liberal Andrew Merton, the section's tone has been decidedly mellow, but the *Globe* is still the most liberal paper sold in the state.

Merrimack Valley Region

Bedford Bulletin Goffstown News Hooksett Banner
334 N.H. Rt. 101 W., Bedford
• (603) 472-6500 , (800) 977-4432

Neighborhood Publications publishes all three of these papers each Thursday. Advertising is shared, but editorial content is unique and specific to the towns covered by each, and they are great sources of community news. Lots of letters to the editor keep readers up to date on the local controversies.

Derry News
46 W. Broadway, Derry
• (603) 437-7000

This biweekly paper, founded in 1880, now comes out Tuesdays and Fridays. The circulation of 11,500 covers the greater Derry area, including special sections for Chester, Sandown, Windham, Hampstead and Londonderry. Lots of school news and local politics are covered. Mailing address for the Derry News is P.O. Box 307, Derry, NH 03038.

Milford Cabinet Hollis-Brookline Journal
54 School St., Milford
• (603) 673-3100

Local news, local politics, local controversy and local sports — the *Cabinet* has been covering the Souhegan Valley for more than 100 years. Although local tabs have begun to provide alternative news coverage, the *Cabinet* (which comes out on Wednesdays) remains the local paper of record. The *Journal* began as a section of the parent paper a few years back, but now, as Hollis has grown, it has been given a name and publication day (Thursday) of its own.

1590 Broadcaster
502 W. Hollis St., Nashua
• (603) 882-1590

For many years the *Broadcaster* was mailed free to every home rural route box in greater Nashua each Wednesday, but most people only read it for the classifieds. In 1998 the paper undertook a makeover, increasing the news coverage, adding many new columnists and sprucing up the typeface. It's a good source for events listings, local announcements and, still, tons of classifieds,

INSIDERS' TIP

Local zoning codes may regulate the location and appearance of full-size satellite dishes.

and now it's fun to read as well. More than a shopper but not quite a tabloid, the *Broadcaster* is a local institution.

The Salem Observer
373 Main St., Salem
• (603) 893-4356

Published Thursdays, the *Observer* offers community news from Salem, Windham and Pelham, including such traditional small-town paper features as the police blotter, anniversary and birthday announcements and reports from local kids in the military. The *Observer*'s mailing address is P.O. Box 720, Salem, NH 03079.

Village Crier
579 Daniel Webster Hwy., Merrimack
• (603) 424-7610

This local tab has a reputation for fearless coverage of local politics, and Merrimack's politics has landed the city in the national news more than once! (Merrimack has been on the front lines of the New Right battle for control of the schools.) Beyond the editorial and letters pages, the rest of the paper is mostly advertising. Mail for the *Crier* goes to P.O. Box 1000, Merrimack, NH 03054.

Seacoast Region

Exeter News-Letter
Hampton Union
Rockingham News
7 Stratham Ave., Stratham
• (603) 772-6000, (800) 734-7022

The *Union* and *News-Letter* come out on Tuesday and Friday, the *News* is out on Saturday. Combined circulation of these papers is more than 20,000. Advertising is combined, but the news coverage of each paper is distinct, staff-written and local. Rockingham County Newspapers also publishes a monthly for women, *Our Time*, with a surprisingly broad range of subjects, from recipes and book reviews to caring for elderly parents and race relations.

Lakes Region

Carroll County Independent
10 Moultonville Rd., Center Ossipee
• (603) 539-4111

This paper publishes local news and events every Wednesday. The *Independent* covers much the same territory as the *Granite State News*, in a similar format. There is slightly more coverage of towns in the Sandwich range here and a slightly more liberal slant. The mailing address for the Independent is P.O. Box 38, Center Ossipee, NH 03814.

Granite State News
10 Endicott St., Wolfeboro
• (603) 569-3126

The *Granite State News* is published every Wednesday. Since 1859 the *News* has brought its readers local news and accomplishments from throughout the Lakes region. It maintains an interest in local church news and a conservative (even for New Hampshire) editorial stance. The full-size format makes it easier to read than many local tabloid-size weeklies. You can contact them at P.O. Box 879, Wolfeboro, NH 03894.

Meredith News
5 Water St., Meredith
• (603) 279-4516

The *Meredith News*, published Wednesdays, covers Moultonborough, Sandwich, Center Harbor and Meredith and features lots of local news and sports. This is a paper where the local correspondent's phone numbers are still published. It prints the voting records of the local legislators and has a nice looking-back column. There's almost no editorial comment except in letters to the editor. You can write to them, too, at P.O. Box 729, Meredith, NH 03253.

The Record Enterprise
300 Main St., Plymouth
• (603) 536-1311, (800) 491-4612

The *Enterprise* is published on Wednes-

INSIDERS' TIP

Local zoning codes may regulate the location and appearance of full-size satellite dishes.

days, with a circulation of just more than 6,000. This is one of the best of the small weeklies, with detailed events listings and news coverage for the 20 small towns in its greater Plymouth area. All mail for the *Record Enterprise* goes to P.O. Box 148, Plymouth, NH 03264.

The Weirs Times and Tourists' Gazette
U.S. Rt. 3, The Weirs
• (603) 366-8463

This free paper features lively columns, an editorial slant well to the right of Newt Gingrich and plenty of local sports news, but what distinguishes it is the large number of historic pieces. These include fascinating tales from New Hampshire's past, actual reprints of articles from the 1800s and even a history question-and-answer column. In one issue the historian answered whether there are any tornadoes on record in the Upper Valley (answer: yes, two) and what became of the Meredith Diner (someone bought it in the '70s, dismantled it and took it off to parts unknown). Readers are invited to try and "Stump the Historian." You can write to the *Times* at P.O. Box 5458, Laconia, NH 03247.

White Mountains and Great North Woods Regions

Colebrook News & Sentinel
1 Bridge St., Colebrook
• (603) 237-5501

This tabloid-size paper, published Wednesdays, features lots of local tidbits, down-home wisdom, a nature column and news from the schools — some of it reported by kids. To write to them, use P.O. Box 39, Colebrook, NH 03576.

The Courier
365 Union St., Littleton
• (603) 444-3927

Published Wednesdays and reaching more than 6,000 readers from Lincoln north to Jefferson and Whitefield, the *Courier* has been in business since 1889. It's strictly local news, in enough depth to keep voters informed and readers interested. Mail for the *Courier* should go to P.O. Box 230, Littleton, NH 03561.

The Mountain Ear
N.H. Rt. 16, Mountain River Village, Conway
• (603) 447-6336

The *Mountain Ear* is published every Thursday and covers news from Ossipee to Gorham (the Mount Washington Valley). This is local news for residents with advertising aimed at tourists. It includes lots of local sports coverage and a detailed calendar of local programs and events. They'll hear you if you write to P.O. Box 530, Conway, NH 03818.

Dartmouth-Lake Sunapee Region

Argus-Champion
86 Sunapee St., Newport
• (603) 863-1776

The *Argus-Champion* covers the Kearsage/Lake Sunapee region. It provides lots of local news in fair depth, nostalgia, police logs and nice coverage of the local arts scene. Write to the *Champion* at P.O. Box 509, Newport, NH 03773.

Monadnock Region

New Hampshire Week in Review
W. Main St., Hillsboro
• (603) 464-3388

This free weekly comes out Mondays, covering the region from Concord to Keene. It averages half news and columns, half classifieds. The *Review* is liberal only by New Hampshire standards, but the paper takes a pro-Democratic stance, which makes it unusual. Intrigued? Write to the *Week in Review* at P.O. Box 917, Hillsboro, NH 03244.

Monadnock Ledger
20 Grove St., Peterborough
• (603) 924-7172

The *Ledger* says it's "Serving the Heart of the Monadnock Region" with local and school news, politics and advertising for the towns from Wilton and Lyndeborough in the east to Jaffrey and Rindge in the west. The *Ledger*'s special sections distinguish it (very) slightly from its rival paper, the *Transcript*, also published in Peterborough on Thursdays (see later entry). Insiders claim the *Ledger* has a more liberal editorial slant. To find out, write to the *Ledger* at P.O. Box 36, Peterborough, NH 03458.

Peterborough Transcript
43 Grove St., Peterborough
• (603) 924-3333

Published Thursdays just like its cross-town rival the *Ledger*, the *Transcript* covers local politics and events for towns from Greenfield to Dublin (the papers overlap on all but two towns at the edges of the region). The *Transcript* offers an insert, "Monadnock Magazine," a living/arts/events section in tab format, and a looking-back column with tidbits from the paper during the last 100 years. (The newspaper in Thornton Wilder's *Our Town* was modeled on the *Transcript*). The mailing address for the *Transcript* is P.O. Box 419, Peterborough, NH 03458.

Periodicals

With the help of new technologies, New Hampshire has become something of a hotbed of magazine publishing, producing a number of specialty and trade journals for subscribers throughout the region and the country. For the purposes of this guide, we are restricting ourselves to those general interest magazines published for New Hampshire readers (or those who wish they were).

Business NH Magazine
404 Chestnut St., Ste. 201, Manchester
• (603) 626-6354

Business NH is a monthly glossy bringing together items of interest to all types of New Hampshire businesses. Financial trends, legal issues, environmental regulations, healthcare and other topics are all covered with an emphasis on their impacts on business. Of interest to noncorporate readers are the magazine's in-depth presentations on different aspects of life in New Hampshire — education, politics, healthcare, taxes — with charts and statistics galore. You can call them to request their most recent resource guides.

New Hampshire Business Review
150 Dow St., Manchester
• (603) 624-1442

Billing itself as "N.H.'s only other statewide newspaper," the biweekly *Business Review* covers business news from across the state—who's bought new property, opened a new operation or pioneered a new product—with pleasantly readable prose. It takes a light but liberal look at the state's political scene.

New Hampshire Editions
100 Main St., Nashua
• (603) 883-3150

This glossy magazine covers the Merrimack Valley and the Seacoast, with plenty of material of interest to readers in the rest of the state as well. The focus is on business, and the $20 a year magazine is mailed free each month to business addresses. The general interest articles are always interesting and well-done, and profiles of major players in state politics are fascinating. *New Hampshire Editions* also publishes annual special editions on New Hampshire's history and cultural legacy.

Yankee Magazine
Main St., Dublin
• (603) 563-8111, (800) 288-4284

Yankee is the quintessential New Hampshire magazine, which is ironic since most of its circulation is outside the state's borders. Combining a folksy editorial tone, a traditional format and frank fondness for "traditional" New England, *Yankee* offers those who live here (and those who wish they did) a monthly look at New England events, history, myths and traditions. Yankee Publishing also publishes several annuals, ranging from *The Old Farmer's Almanac* to the *Travel Guide to New England*. Mail for *Yankee* should be addressed to P.O. Box 520, Dublin, NH 03444.

Radio

Radio in New Hampshire ranges from country to classical, with just about every format you can think of available somewhere on the dial. Tuning it in is another question. Because of our varied terrain, many stations are only available in their own region. Although this guide covers only the New Hampshire stations, from Manchester south and east you can pick up almost all of the Boston stations as well as local radio. (One exception to the N.H.-only rule: if you're driving into Boston you should know that WBZ AM 1030 has traffic reports every 10 minutes around the clock.)

As you move north or west and particularly as the mountains rise about you, you'll find more and more signals fading — you can pick up Seacoast stations in the Merrimack Valley but most Merrimack Valley stations won't reach the Monadnock Region. It's impossible to drive from the Massachusetts state line to the Canadian border all on one station! We've given you regional designations for the stations below, but the only way to know if you can hear it is to try.

Adult Contemporary

Merrimack Valley — WFEA 1370 AM; WHOB 106.3 FM; WJYY 105.5 FM; WZID 95.7 FM

Lakes — WLNH 1350 FM; WFTN 94.1 FM; WLNH 98.3 FM

White Mountains — WZPK 103.7 FM

Great North — WBRL 1400 AM

Dartmouth-Lake Sunapee — WHDQ 106.1 FM; WASR 1420 AM

Monadnock — WNHQ 92.1 FM, WKNE 103.7 FM

Alternative

Merrimack Valley — WNEC 91.7 FM (New England College)

Seacoast — WPEA 90.5 FM; WERZ 107.1 FM; WUNH 91.3 FM (Univ. of New Hampshire)

Lakes — WSRI 96.7 FM

Dartmouth-Lake Sunapee — WDCR 1340 AM (Dartmouth College)

Monadnock — WKNH 91.3 FM (Keene State College)

Christian

Merrimack Valley — WDER 1320 AM; WLMV 90.7 FM

Country

Seacoast — WOKQ 97.5 FM

Lakes — WFTN 1240 AM

White Mountains — WBNC 104.5 FM and 1050 AM

Great North Woods — WXLQ 107.1 FM

Dartmouth/Lake Sunapee — WXXK 100.5 FM

News/Talk/Sports

Merrimack Valley — WGIR 610 AM; WKXL 1450 AM and 102.3 FM; WMVU 900 AM; WSMN 1590 AM

Seacoast — WTMN 1380 AM (all sports); WTSN 1270 AM, WZNN 930 AM

Lakes — WEMJ 1490 AM

White Mountains — WLTN 1400 AM

Dartmouth-Lake Sunapee — WSTV 1230 AM; WNTK 1020 AM and 99.7 FM

Monadnock — WKBK 1220 AM

Oldies

Merrimack Valley — WNNH 99.1 FM

Seacoast — WMYF 1540 AM

Lakes — WLKZ 104.9 FM; WPNH 1300 AM

White Mountains — WLTN 96.7 FM

Great North Woods — WMOU 1230 AM

Dartmouth-Lake Sunapee — WMXR 93.9 FM

Monadnock — WXOD 98.7 FM

Classic Rock

Merrimack Valley — WRCI 107.7 FM

Seacoast — WBHG 101.5 FM

Lakes — WPCR 91.7 FM (Plymouth College)

White Mountains — WMTK 106.3 FM

INSIDERS' TIP

Satellite systems are popular, but you can't get local programming with one. To get local news — and especially weather — Insiders combine satellite systems with basic cable or a big antenna.

Dartmouth-Lake Sunapee — WFDR 99.3 FM (Dartmouth College)

Monadnock — WKNE 1290 AM

Public Radio

Public radio is rebroadcast on transmitters so the signal is available almost everywhere. There's still no coverage from the White Mountains north, but they're working on it.

Merrimack Valley and southern Lakes regions — WEVO 89.1 FM in the Manchester and Concord areas; and WEVO 90.3 FM in the Nashua area

Seacoast — WEVO 104.3 FM

Dartmouth-Lake Sunapee — WEVH 91.3 FM

Monadnock — WEVN 90.7 FM

Rock

Merrimack Valley — WGIR 101.1 FM

Seacoast — WHEB 100.3 FM

Lakes — WPNH 100.1 FM

White Mountains — WMWV 93.5 FM

Spanish Language

Merrimack Valley — WNNW 1110 AM

Television

In the southern part of the state most people can receive at least some Boston television, and some northern residents watch television from Montreal (in French).

New Hampshire Stations

WMUR TV 9 (ABC affiliate)

WNBU TV 21 (Independent — echoes WABU TV 68 from Boston)

WNDS TV 50 (Independent)

WNNE TV 31 (NBC affiliate)

WPXP TV 60 (Independent)

Channel 11 — New Hampshire Public Television (PBS affiliate)

Boston Stations

WABU TV 68 (Independent)

WBZ TV 4 (CBS)

WCVB TV 5 (ABC)

WFXT TV 25 (FOX)

WGBH TV 2 (PBS)

WHDH TV 7 (NBC)

WLVI TV 56 (WB)

WSBK TV 38 (UPN)

Cable Television

Cable companies contract with individual towns, so coverage and cost vary from place to place. Most communities are served by affiliates of Continental Cablevision or Time Warner Cable, although there are a few independents. The local town office can tell you which company serves its community. Accommodations leave a helpful key to channel numbers beside the television, and most television guides include conversion charts. Economics dictate that a certain density (houses per mile) is necessary to make it worth the company's while to string the cable. This means even in towns served by cable companies, service may not be available to homes in outlying areas.

The religious traditions
of our state
run deep.

Worship

Newcomers to New Hampshire sometimes comment that it seems like a very nonreligious place. Indeed, recent surveys have shown that New Hampshire citizens have a lower than average rate of church attendance. Yet this should not be taken as an indicator that we lack spiritual sensibility. It is more accurate to see this as another manifestation of our intense privacy. What is more personal than one's spirituality? And New Hampshire folk keep their personal lives to themselves.

At the same time, the religious traditions of our state run deep. The oldest artifacts in New Hampshire are the solar calendar stones in Salem, now known as America's Stonehenge. Strikingly similar to Stonehenge in England, the spot appears to have been used for religious rituals at least 3,000 to 4,000 years ago. (See our Attractions chapter.) The Algonkian Indians revered the summits of the White Hills as sacred ground. The earliest white settlers shared a firm conviction that the Almighty had touched this land in a special way. For every person who has ever said, "I feel closer to God in nature than I do in church," New Hampshire is convincing evidence.

Historically, New Hampshire was less rigid in the practice of religion than the other original colonies. In fact, many of our early settlers chose New Hampshire to escape from or avoid the doctrinaire Puritanism of the Massachusetts Bay Colony (which in those days included not only the present-day Commonwealth of Massachusetts but also all of what is now Maine). Still, in order to establish a community as a town in the 1600s, settlers had to call and support a minister. It wasn't until 1968 that the requirement for town support of the Congregational minister was removed from the state constitution (in practice it had long since lost force — not that $100 per annum would support a minister today!).

In more than one community, the church-state connection is memorialized in joint ownership of a building, once the only community hall, now usually called the First Church of whichever town it's in. Puritan in work ethic and dedication to freedom, New Hampshire's early settlers nevertheless put more effort into clearing land and catching fish than scrutinizing the religious sentiments of their neighbors. But they took their own faith seriously. Dartmouth College was founded in 1769 not to compete with Harvard but for the express purpose of preaching to the Native Americans. The school's motto, from the Gospel description of John the Baptist, is "A Voice Crying in the Wilderness." It reflects both the mission and the remote location of the school when it opened.

Most of New England's native people had already been evangelized by French missionaries and were Catholic before the English Colonists arrived. The national conflict between English Protestantism and French Catholicism played out here, often in bloody battles. Our French and Indian War was nothing more than the Western theater of operations of Europe's Seven Years' War. This history no doubt contributed to the antagonism Catholic immigrants from Ireland, Italy and French Canada encountered when they came here later. Widespread acceptance of Catholicism in New Hampshire goes back only to the postwar years. Today Catholics are the single largest religious group in the state, and there are several monastic communities tucked away amid our hills and valleys. The Shrine of La Sallette in Enfield attracts visitors of all denominations with its Christmas display of lights each December, while the Shrine of Our Lady of Grace hosts the Blessing of the Motorcycles and Native American Powwows up in the North Country (see our Annual Events chapter for all these).

Toward the end of the last century, New Hampshire was home to a great movement of "church camps," not camps as we think of them but whole communities of summer cottages, where the land and common buildings were owned by the denomination and members could buy a piece of land and build a summer home. Most of these have since been divided and sold privately, although the Rumney Bible Conference outside of Plymouth is still an evangelical cottage community. Conference centers and retreat houses with various denominational affiliations continue to attract visitors with the opportunity to worship and play in the beauty of the New Hampshire countryside. (See Summer Camps in our Kidstuff chapter for another variation on this theme.)

The Canterbury Shaker Community was one of the largest and longest-lived of that tradition (see our Attractions chapter). Unitarian Universalism has its roots here, fed by the radical notions of graduates of Harvard Divinity School. It was here that Mary Baker Eddy put together the tenets of what became Christian Science, and the Reading Rooms of that tradition can be found in many small towns (see our Attractions chapter for more on Mrs. Eddy's former homes). Here, too, followers of the Maharishi have opened a school of enlightenment, and people interested in exploring the ancient traditions of the native peoples have built sweat lodges and held festivals.

When the Sloane family opened the Cathedral of the Pines in Rindge (see our Attractions chapter), it was not surprising that they designed it to be used for worship by people of all denominations. It still hosts an ecumenical Easter Sunday sunrise service. The controversy over whether local wiccans should be allowed to hold services there as well (the courts said yes) only underscores the diversity of faiths calling New Hampshire home. We have a Baha'i community in the Peterborough area, Eckankar in Nashua and a Hindu ashram in Sanbornton. Neo-pagan sun-worshippers and druids gather at Mystery Hill/America's Stonehenge in Salem to observe the solstices and equinoxes within the stone circle. Jewish synagogues (reformed or conservative) meet in each city and some of the larger towns. There are also Lubbavitcher congregations in Manchester and Bethlehem. (The nearest non-Lubbavitcher orthodox synagogue is in Massachusetts.)

Mormons (Latter Day Saints) have wards throughout the state, and Jehovah's Witnesses have built new Kingdom Halls in some fast-growing suburban areas.

In 1995 our growing Muslim population formed the Islamic Society of New Hampshire. After meeting for several years in a hall on the campus of New Hampshire College, they are now raising funds to open a mosque and school in Manchester.

Christian churches still predominate in New Hampshire. Most of the old white churches-on-the-green are Congregational-United Church of Christ or Unitarian Universalist, although Presbyterian congregations inherited a few. Some of the oldest church buildings in the state have been purchased and refurbished by fast-growing congregations of independent Baptists and fundamentalists. A large number of Protestant denominations are represented here, from the Assemblies of God to Methodists to Seventh Day Adventists.

Nondenominational congregations are probably the fastest-growing category of churches in the state, but you need to know your own particular "faith language" to choose among them. Are you pre-trib or post? Charismatic or fundamentalist? Do you like your worship service music noninstrumental, folk, rock or chorale? There's a church here for you.

As in most parts of the United States the Catholic diocese of Manchester is consolidating, as the many ethnic parishes that once served immigrants in their own languages now struggle to serve an increasingly mobile population with a shrinking supply of priests. (New

INSIDERS' TIP

Hotel bulletin boards often include a list of area church services. At inns and bed and breakfasts, ask your host or check the local weekly newspaper.

The Cathedral of the Pines in Rindge is a magnificent outdoor place of worship.

Hampshire Catholic Charities is the largest service provider in New Hampshire besides the state, with immigrants still a focus of that outreach.) Episcopalians (new or old prayer book), Lutherans (all synods) and Greek Orthodox also have many parishes throughout the state, with the Greek Orthodox and Roman Catholic cathedrals in Manchester and the Episcopal cathedral in Concord.

Many new congregations start out meeting in school cafeterias until they have enough members to afford a building. In some communities several congregations share a church building. You may find Baptists upstairs and Methodists downstairs, or Catholics at 8 AM and Presbyterians at 11. Other congregations have converted vacant warehouses, office parks, stores and old barns into worship spaces. Some churches deliberately choose not to build, meeting primarily in homes and gathering in hotels or conference centers for large-group worship.

In the Lakes Region and White Mountains, some congregations move outside in summer to accommodate crowds of tourists. Others add extra services, or go on-location to provide worship opportunities for tourists right in the resort facilities.

Schools and food kitchens, scout troops and blood drives; the range of activities provided by people of faith in New Hampshire is a vital part of the life of our communities. Often these are joint efforts, with members of many congregations contributing to a food pantry, assistance program or other outreach operated out of one church for the entire community. Perhaps the best-known of these is SHARE in Milford, which is an outreach of St. Patrick Church (Roman Catholic) but receives support, donations and volunteers from al-

INSIDERS' TIP

Just outside of Tamworth village a marble obelisk stands atop an enormous boulder, known to this day as Ordination Rock because the Rev. Samuel Hidden was ordained up there back in 1792. On the other side of the Sandwich Range in North Woodstock, the tiny Rock of Ages chapel perches precariously on a boulder on the side of a steep hill. It's a popular place for *very small* weddings.

most every church and nonprofit group in the area and offers help to anyone in the community regardless of their faith. *Business NH Magazine* named SHARE as 1997 Business of the Year in the nonprofit category, noting that 100 percent of donations the program receives go to the needy. St. Patrick's donates all the operating expenses, including staff and space.

Resources

The Many Faces of God: An Exploration of World Religions The New Hampshire Humanities Council

19 Pillsbury St., P.O. Box 2228, Concord
• (603) 224-4071

This series of workshops, presentations, public programs and seminars has been running for most of a decade, and shows no sign of failing interest. You can join a discussion group, study comparative theology, listen to ancient tales retold by professional storytellers, or follow radio discussions of such topics as "the problem of evil" among representatives of Eastern and Western cultures and faith traditions. Just in 1999 you could study Biblical Hebrew, explore the place of dance in Hindu philosophy, draw a Tibetan-style icon, go on a Buddhist retreat or listen to a veteran of the German resistance discuss the Holocaust. Call for information and schedules, or check your local library for discussion groups.

The Voice

8 Lawrence Rd., Derry
• (603) 437-WDER

The Voice is a monthly newspaper published by the Christian radio station, WDER 1320 AM. It offers a mix of syndicated columns by well-known writers such as James Dobson, columns by local writers and business-people (financial advice, political coverage, music and book reviews). It's a great source of information about events in New Hampshire, and the special issues (on summer camps and schools) are loaded with informative advertising.

Tidings

153 Ash St., Manchester
• (603) 669-3100

Tidings is the official paper of the Roman Catholic Diocese of Manchester. Published every other week, it covers news from Catholic parishes across the state and offers local columns, extensive events listings and wirecopy coverage of national and world news from the Catholic News Service.

Index of Advertisers

Index

C

R